EXCEL

EXPERT SOLUTIONS

EXCEL®

EXPERT SOLUTIONS

Brian Underdahl

Donna Payne

David Maguiness

John Green

Bob Umlas

David Hager

Shane Devenshire

Heidi Sullivan-Liscomb

John Lacher

Conrad Carlberg

Ron Person

Willis E. Howard, III Ph.D.

David Bellamy

Excel Expert Solutions

Copyright© 1996 by Que® Corporation.

All rights reserved. Printed in the United States of America. No part of this book may be used or reproduced in any form or by any means, or stored in a database or retrieval system, without prior written permission of the publisher except in the case of brief quotations embodied in critical articles and reviews. Making copies of any part of this book for any purpose other than your own personal use is a violation of United States copyright laws. For information, address Que Corporation, 201 W. 103rd Street, Indianapolis, IN, 46290. You may reach Que's direct sales line by calling 1-800-428-5331.

Library of Congress Catalog No.: 95-71758

ISBN: 0-7897-0386-6

This book is sold *as is*, without warranty of any kind, either express or implied, respecting the contents of this book, including but not limited to implied warranties for the book's quality, performance, merchantability, or fitness for any particular purpose. Neither Que Corporation nor its dealers or distributors shall be liable to the purchaser or any other person or entity with respect to any liability, loss, or damage caused or alleged to have been caused directly or indirectly by this book.

97 96 96   6 5 4 3 2 1

Interpretation of the printing code: the rightmost double-digit number is the year of the book's printing; the rightmost single-digit number, the number of the book's printing. For example, a printing code of 96-1 shows that the first printing of the book occurred in 1996.

All terms mentioned in this book that are known to be trademarks or service marks have been appropriately capitalized. Que cannot attest to the accuracy of this information. Use of a term in this book should not be regarded as affecting the validity of any trademark or service mark.

Screen reproductions in this book were created using Collage Plus from Inner Media, Inc., Hollis, NH.

Credits

President
Roland Elgey

Vice President and Publisher
Marie Butler-Knight

Publishing Director
Brad R. Koch

Editorial Services Director
Elizabeth Keaffaber

Managing Editor
Michael Cunningham

Director of Marketing
Lynn E. Zingraf

Senior Series Editor
Chris Nelson

Acquisitions Editors
Deborah F. Abshier
Joyce J. Nielsen

Production Editor
Thomas F. Hayes

Copy Editors
Charles K. Bowles II
Linda Seifert

**Assistant Product
Marketing Manager**
Kim Margolius

Technical Editors
Bob Greenblatt
Don Doherty
Forrest Patterson

Technical Specialist
Nadeem Muhammed

Acquisitions Coordinator
Tracey Williams

Operations Coordinator
Patty Brooks

Editorial Assistant
Carmen Krikorian

Book Designer
Barbara Kordesh

Cover Designer
Ruth Harvey

Production Team
Steve Adams
Bryan Flores
Trey Frank
Jason Hand
Daryl Kessler
Clint Lahnen
Glenn Larsen
Stephanie Layton
Michelle Lee
Kaylene Riemen
Laura Robbins
Bobbi Satterfield
Paul Wilson
Jody York

Indexer
Carol Sheehan

Composed in *Helvetica Condensed* and *Stone Serif* by Que Corporation.

As I travel through life's journey, I'm grateful for my fellow traveler, Darlene.

—Brian Underdahl

Acknowledgments

There are many people who play an important role in developing a major book like *Excel Expert Solutions*. I wish I could thank them all personally, but in particular I'd like to thank:

Debbie Abshier, who somehow put together the most talented team of Excel experts available anywhere. We couldn't have done this project if Debbie hadn't been able to convince the experts to join us.

Joyce Nielsen, who has helped me turn quite a few projects into real books. Joyce is the best product developer in the world.

Tom Hayes and his team of editors, the production staff, and everyone else at Que who made certain this book is top quality. I'd like to name all of you, but I don't want some other publisher trying to take you away!

Finally, the Excel experts who agreed to contribute to this project. Some of you shared your expertise in words, and some shared your talents in the form of software. I know this was sometimes a difficult project, but I thank every one of you for rising to the occasion.

About the Authors

Brian Underdahl is an author, independent consultant, and custom application developer based in Reno, Nevada. He's the author or coauthor of over twenty-five computer books, as well as numerous magazine articles. He has also acted as a product developer and as a technical editor on many other Que books.

Donna Payne is a computer consultant based in Seattle, Washington. She is a Microsoft Excel MVP on CompuServe and is a Microsoft Certified Excel and Visual Basic for Applications Trainer. Donna has developed custom applications for international technology-based firms and has performed consulting services for Microsoft and Northern Telecom. She is the originator of a networking group for women programmers. Donna can be reached via CompuServe at **73573.500**.

David Maguiness is a technical writer for Software Artistry, a major developer of client server application software and tools. He has authored or coauthored numerous books about Excel, Quattro Pro, and 123, including Que's *Using 123,* Special Edition, which has sold over 1 million copies. He contributed regularly to *PC World Lotus Edition* and was editor-in-chief of *Absolute Reference: The Journal for 123 and Symphony Users*, Que's monthly technical journal for Lotus spreadsheet users.

John Green lives and works in Sydney, Australia, where he has established himself as a well-respected authority on personal computers. With 30 years of computing experience, a Chemical Engineering degree, and an MBA, he draws from a diverse background. John's main expertise is in financial planning and modeling using spreadsheets.

He wrote his first programs in FORTRAN, took a part in the evolution of specialized planning languages on mainframes such as IFPS and, since 1980, has become interested in spreadsheet systems, including Multiplan, 1-2-3, Symphony, and Excel. He has had extensive experience in ODS, the Macintosh operating system, and Windows.

He was a founding member of the Lotus User's Group in NSW and was on its committee for some years after its inception. John established his company, Execuplan Consulting, in 1980, specializing in developing computer-based planning applications and in training. His clients have included some of Australia's largest companies. He has lectured extensively on spreadsheets and operating systems both in hands-on training and in the seminar environment throughout Australia and has run training courses in China as part of an Australian aid project.

John has written for a number of publications, including *Australian PC World* and *PC Australia* where he had a regular column, "Spreadsheet Clinic." He was involved in editing and publishing a bimonthly newsletter, "The Spreadsheet Advisor," and now has a column in *ROI Magazine*.

John is also an MVP in the Excel Forum on CompuServe.

Bob Umlas is a Microsoft Excel Solutions Channel Partner; the contributing editor to *Excellence, Inside Microsoft Excel* (Including Visual Basic for Applications), and *The Expert* magazines by the Cobb Group; a Heizer/Baarns author; and a freelance consultant using Microsoft Excel to write custom applications. Bob also is a Microsoft-certified trainer for Visual Basic for Applications. He authored several chapters for the book *Excel Professional Techniques* by Que. He was also recently commissioned by Microsoft to write 60 of the questions to be used for the Microsoft Excel 5.0 certification exam.

He has led sessions at several Microsoft conferences, including the most recent "Tech Ed '95" in New Orleans, called "Maximizing Excel Development using Array Formulas." He has had over 200 articles published on tips and tricks and shortcuts using Excel, and co-lead the PC User's Group on Excel, after having lead the New York Macintosh Users' Group on Excel for six years.

Bob currently consults full-time for a Fortune 500 company, doing training, writing Excel macros and VBA procedures, and generally making things easier for the approximately 100 Excel users at the company. He also consults part-time for another Fortune 500 company, which uses a 100,000-line macro-driven system on about 600 desktops worldwide.

David Hager is a frequent contributor to the Microsoft Excel Forum on CompuServe. David has recently shifted his focus from the area of organic chemistry, where he has seven professional publications, to that of designing Excel spreadsheet models. He currently works at a refinery research laboratory in Baton Rouge, Louisiana.

Shane Devenshire is an independent consultant specializing in project management, databases, graphics packages, and the scientific and business application of spreadsheets. He is a founding partner of the MAR&SHA Corporation, a computer consulting company providing application development, programming, and training in both the mainframe and personal computer areas. He has written over 240 computer-related articles for twenty journals here and abroad. He has been a guest editor for *PC World* magazine in 1994 and 1995 and has been on the product review board of INFO World. He has three years experience in the bio-tech arena, five years in business management, and 13 in computer-related industries. He coauthored *Excel Professional Techniques, Using 1-2-3 Release 4 for DOS,* and *Making Microsoft Office Work.*

Heidi Sullivan-Liscomb is a consulting technical writer who got her start working as an intern for MapInfo Corporation in Troy, New York. During her time there, she was fortunate enough to participate in writing the docs for both their Macintosh and Windows products. Heidi graduated Magna Cum Laude with a degree in English Literature and intends to continue writing.

John Lacher, MBA, CPA, is a winner of the Microsoft Excel Most Valuable Professional Award. He is the lead author *of VBA Database Solutions* from Que and is a contributing author to *Office Expert Solutions* and *Building Integrated Office Applications*. John is an independent consultant who provides Excel and Office training and development services to clients around the world via e-mail and Data Conferencing. He has more than 20 years of experience as a developer of computer applications and as a manager in both technical and executive functions. He can be reached on CompuServe at **73447,2431** or over the Internet at **73447.2431@compuserve.com**.

Conrad Carlberg is president of Network Control Systems, Inc., a software development and consulting firm that specializes in the statistical forecasting of data network usage. He holds a PhD in statistics from the University of Colorado, and is a three-time recipient of the Microsoft Excel Most Valuable Professional Award.

Ron Person has written more than 18 books for Que Corporation, including *Special Edition Using Excel for Windows 95*, *Web Publishing with Word for Windows*, and *Special Edition Using Windows 3.11*. He has an MS in physics from Ohio State University and an MBA from Hardin-Simmons University. Ron was one of Microsoft's original 12 Consulting Partners and is a Microsoft Solutions Partner.

Willis E. Howard, III, also known as Bill, was born in Oklahoma City in 1948, although much of his childhood was spent in Huntsville, Alabama. He obtained a BS from Samford University and then a PhD from Northwestern University in 1976. Much of his thesis work in physical chemistry and laser spectroscopy was performed at the Technical University of Munich in Germany. Bill did post-doctoral work at the University of California in Irvine and joined the Bayer Corporation in 1979. At Bayer he has worked in the areas of fluorescence and reflectance spectroscopy, algorithm development, software validation, optical engineering, and system engineering. In his free time, Bill can be found reading, listening to music, eating Chinese food, programming his home computer, investing in real estate, or racing his boat up and down the river. He is a member of the Association of Shareware Professionals (ASP) and has written applications that include relocatable object code processing, cryptography, accounting with Excel, and objectives management in Excel. He is fluent in German, and is starting to learn Chinese with the help of his wife Lena (Liu Chung).

David G. Bellamy is owner of Bellamy Consulting, a project management consulting firm offering services including Project Management system set-up, training, and troubleshooting. He specializes in Microsoft Project scheduling software and Excel spreadsheets. He holds a Professional Degree in Metallurgical Engineering from the Colorado School of Mines. He resides in the Denver, Colorado, area. (303) 425-8942.

We'd Like to Hear from You!

As part of our continuing effort to produce books of the highest possible quality, Que would like to hear your comments. To stay competitive, we *really* want you, as a computer book reader and user, to let us know what you like or dislike most about this book or other Que products.

You can mail comments, ideas, or suggestions for improving future editions to the address below, or send us a fax at (317) 581-4663. For the on-line inclined, Macmillan Computer Publishing has a forum on CompuServe (type **GO MACMILLAN** at any prompt) through which our staff and authors are available for questions and comments. The address of our Internet site, the Macmillan Information SuperLibrary, is **http:// www.mcp.com** (World Wide Web). Our Web site has received critical acclaim from many reviewers—be sure to check it out.

In addition to exploring our forums, please feel free to contact me personally to discuss your opinions of this book:

CompuServe:	**75703,3251**
Internet:	**lgentry@que.mcp.com**

Thanks in advance—your comments will help us to continue publishing the best books available on computer topics in today's market.

Lorna Gentry
Product Director
Que Corporation
201 W. 103rd Street
Indianapolis, Indiana 46290 USA

 Note

Although we cannot provide general technical support, we're happy to help you resolve problems you encounter related to our books, disks, or other products. If you need such assistance, please contact our Tech Support department at 800-545-5914, ext. 3833.

To order other Que or Macmillan Computer Publishing books or products, please call our Customer Service department at 800-835-3202, ext. 666.

Contents at a Glance

Contents

II Successful Application Development   101

4 Creating Effective Documentation   103

5 Protecting Data   119

III Formula Power   139

6 The Power of Formulas   141

14 Mapping Your Data   469

V Designing an Executive Information System   555

VI High-Grade Reporting Techniques   689

VII Programming with VBA   771

23 Managing Dialogs in VBA   773

24   Advanced Dialog Boxes   **799**

25　VBA Arrays　849

A Coding Gems   937

Index

Introduction

Who wouldn't like to have an expert at their side, ready to teach them all the tricks and techniques that make using a powerful program like Excel so much easier? It would be even better if that expert were always immediately available, extremely patient, and gave you a copy of their Excel toolbox, wouldn't it? Well, that's what *Excel Expert Solutions* is all about. We've gathered the top Excel experts and authors from around the world and asked them to share their secrets with you in this book. I'm sure you'll be both surprised and pleased about how much these experts will teach you about using Excel 7 for
Windows 95 to solve real-world problems.

This book is about solutions. You don't use Excel because you want to learn esoteric features of the program, you use Excel to solve problems. In developing this book, we've concentrated on showing you how to do the things you really need to do with Excel. One of the great things about having the experts there to teach you, is that along the way you'll probably find yourself learning that you can do even more with Excel than you ever imagined. Whether you're a seasoned Excel application developer or just an individual Excel user who wants to know more than you'll find in *Special Edition Using Excel for Windows 95,* our experts have something for you!

It takes more than information to solve problems. The right tools will make any task much easier. That's why we've collected the best Excel utilities and included them on the CD-ROM that accompanies this book. The CD-ROM also contains all of the programming examples from the book so you can simply copy them into your Excel workbooks without the hassles of retyping. But our CD-ROM contains even more!

You'll find we've also included a number of tidbits called *Coding Gems*. These gems bring even more expert power to your Excel toolbox. Frankly, you'll be amazed by how much we've included on the CD-ROM. You'll find that the CD-ROM alone is worth many times what you'll pay for the complete book and CD-ROM combination.

What Topics Are Covered in This Book?

You'll see many well-known names as you browse through this book. The authors selected are really the cream of the crop. Let's see what they've done.

We've broken *Excel Expert Solutions* into several sections. Here's what to expect from each of those sections:

Part I: Getting the Most from the Spreadsheet

This part concentrates on showing you how to be more productive with Excel. You'll learn how to save time developing your Excel workbooks, how to use the custom format feature to eliminate problems, how to make AutoFill work for you, and how to get the toolbars that work the way you want.

Part II: Successful Application Development

This section covers the extremely important subjects of documenting Excel applications and protecting your work. Both of these topics directly affect your ongoing investment in your Excel applications, and our experts share their techniques that will reduce your support costs to a minimum.

Part III: Formula Power

This part offers an in-depth study of the many possibilities available to the Excel formula expert. You'll find that Excel can do so much more with advanced formula techniques than you ever thought possible. Not only that, but you'll learn how to create your own functions to extend Excel's power even further. "Formula Power" truly provides the best of the Excel expert tricks and techniques.

Part IV: Effective Data Access and Sharing

This section shows you how to use Excel as an extremely powerful data manipulation tool and how to share that power. You'll find out how to use data from many sources, including the company mainframe, how to share Excel data on your network, and how to use data mapping to present that data most effectively.

Part V: Designing an Executive Information System

This part shows you how to do some pretty amazing things, from selectively choosing which information to use, to designing an application that presents that information so easily even the most computer-phobic executive can access the information without help. In between, you'll learn how to use outlines, filters, and pivot tables to effectively present just the right level of information to suit your needs.

Part VI: High-Grade Reporting Techniques

This section provides advanced forecasting and graphing methods, which allow you to analyze your data more effectively than you thought possible.

Part VII: Programming with VBA

In this section, we cover the Excel programming language, Visual Basic for Applications. Here you'll find the power programming techniques that will enable you to add dialog boxes, arrays, custom menus, and on-line help to your Excel applications.

Finally, Appendix A, "Coding Gems," gives you the opportunity to learn even more special tricks the experts wanted to share. In a series of short pieces, you'll learn special tricks and techniques from the real Excel experts who use Excel everyday.

There you have it. I hope you enjoy learning the secrets of the top Excel experts.

Conventions Used in This Book

There are a number of special elements used throughout the book to help make it easier for you to understand Excel. What follows is a description of these special elements.

Chapter Roadmaps

At the beginning of each chapter is a list of topics to be covered in the chapter. This list serves as a roadmap to the chapter so you can tell at a glance what is covered. It also provides a useful outline of the key topics you'll be reading about.

Notes

Notes present interesting or useful information that isn't necessarily essential to the discussion. This secondary track of information enhances your understanding of Windows, but you can safely skip notes and not be in danger of missing crucial information. Notes look like this:

Note

New custom AutoFill lists cannot be duplicates of existing custom AutoFill lists. Excel ignores empty cells at the end of a list, so it is not possible to create two custom AutoFill lists that differ only by having blank cells at the end of the list.

Tips

Tips present short advice on quick or often overlooked procedures. These include shortcuts that save you time. Tips looks like this:

 Tip

Also consider using the EVEN or ODD function to round up to the nearest even or odd integer.

Cautions

Cautions serve to warn you about potential problems that a procedure may cause, unexpected results, and mistakes to avoid. Cautions look like this:

 Caution

For values greater than 134,217,727, MOD(N,1) returns the error #NUM!. The MOD function returns #NUM! at different values depending on the second argument. To work around the problem discussed in the caution above, you can employ the trick demonstrated in the formula above—that is, taking the MOD of the result of a MOD.

Underlined Hot Keys, or Mnemonics

Hot keys in this book appear underlined, like they appear on-screen. For example, the F in File is a hot key, or shortcut, for opening the File menu. In Windows, many menus, commands, buttons, and other options have these hot keys. To use a hot-key shortcut, press Alt and the key for the underlined character. For instance, to choose the Properties button, press and hold Alt and then press R.

Shortcut Key Combinations

In this book, shortcut key combinations are joined with plus signs (+). For example, Ctrl+V means hold down the Ctrl key, press the V key, and then release both keys (Ctrl+V is a shortcut for the Paste command).

This book also has the following typeface enhancements to indicate special text, as indicated in the following table.

Typeface	Description
Italic	Italics are used to indicate terms and variables in commands or addresses.
Boldface	Bold is used to indicate text you type, and Internet addresses and other locators in the online world.
`Computer type`	This command is used for on-screen messages and commands (such as DOS copy or UNIX commands).
MYFILE.DOC	File names and directories are set in all caps to distinguish them from regular text, as in MYFILE.DOC.

Getting the Most from the Spreadsheet

chapter 1

Creating Applications that Work for You

by Donna Payne

In this chapter

◆ **How to construct powerful, user-friendly worksheets**
Learn some design approaches for creating robust, highly professional worksheets. User-friendliness, among other quality issues, is addressed.

◆ **Sample worksheets**
Sample worksheets based on real-world scenarios are included to illustrate design principles and for possible use in your work.

◆ **Advanced tips from leading Excel developers**
Find advanced user tips from industry experts on everything from automatic links to manipulating worksheet ranges.

Microsoft Excel is the most versatile spreadsheet program ever produced. It can be used to create no-frills, bread-and-butter worksheets or custom applications with sophisticated analytical features. This versatility means that you can spend minutes or weeks creating a single Excel file. However, the amount of time you spend creating a file depends only partly on how simple or complex it is. There are techniques and working habits that allow you to create high-quality, sophisticated Excel applications in surprisingly little time.

The techniques and tips presented in this chapter will help you do this. By investing a little time in learning how to use the many powerful features of Excel efficiently, you will be able to do more with less work.

This chapter introduces basic procedures, concepts, and working habits. It starts with some design considerations that apply to all Excel documents.

Preferred Methods for Constructing Spreadsheets

Spreadsheet applications arguably harness the full power of the computer more than any other application. Some examples of the way Excel harnesses this power are the hundreds of worksheet functions that are ready to be used in your formulas, the multitude of formatting commands and predefined styles, and the possibilities that having 4,194,304 cells to work with present.

Remember to use these capabilities within the restraints of good design. It is important to have a consistent approach to developing spreadsheets using tried and true design principles. Good design can be lacking in even the most experienced developer's work. It is not hard to find examples of spreadsheets that are difficult to read or where the formulas and purposes cannot be deciphered two months down the line. Simple mistakes can kill your killer application in no time.

Planning Ahead

Spend a few minutes visually mapping your spreadsheet, then ask yourself these questions:

▶ Who is going to use the spreadsheet?

▶ What are they going to use it for?

▶ What is the Excel fluency level of the user?

▶ Will the spreadsheet be used across platforms?

The answers to these questions must be factored into many areas of the design of your spreadsheet. This section covers ways to address these design factors.

Formatting

Use formatting wisely, so as not to detract from the clarity of purpose and organization of the data. Follow the universal design principle of "form follows function." Make sure there is a specific purpose for every type and instance of formatting that you use.

This does not mean that you must restrict yourself to bland, utilitarian spreadsheets. Depending on your audience and the impression you want to convey, you may want to use formatting to make the spreadsheet visually appealing or to emphasize some aspect of the content. If you do want to dress up your application, however, remember the other universal design principle that "a picture is worth a thousand words." Use graphic images (this includes charts and graphs, of course) to convey specific messages for an overall look and feel to the spreadsheet, rather than creating an unnecessarily "busy" look with lots of format options.

Character formatting is perhaps the most easily misused area of formatting. Stick to a few carefully chosen fonts, styles, and sizes. Avoid using more than two fonts on the same screen. For on-screen documents, sans serif fonts are generally more readable, especially in smaller sizes. Large blocks of text or worksheets that need to be optimized for printed output are exceptions; use serif in these cases. Some other guidelines in using fonts are

▶ Avoid underline and all caps.

▶ Use bold (not italics) to add emphasis or a feeling of authority.

▶ Avoid italics unless your document will be viewed primarily in printed form, and even then only to emphasize words within lines of text.

▶ Avoid outline, shadow, or other ornamental styles except as part of an integrated design approach that takes into account all of the design elements.

Standard Colors

Use standard colors from the built-in color palette to avoid unexpected and confusing results. You should also specify whether you are using 8-bit or 16-bit color depth. You wouldn't want your dark-colored figures on a financial statement to be mapped to red on another user's color palette! Also be sensitive to how colors can be overused. You may think your rainbow spreadsheet looks pretty neat, but does it obscure and confuse more than it informs?

Column and Row Headers

Format column and/or row headers differently than the rest of your list data (use bold and/or a larger font). This allows you and the Excel software to distinguish between headers and data. Give columns and rows a name. You may know what the data in a list represents now, but will you in six months? And what about your client tomorrow?

User Friendliness

As an intermediate to advanced user of Excel, don't forget that less experienced users may not know how to do things that are second nature to you, like how to save a file, format a number, or hide gridlines. If you're designing a spreadsheet for someone else to use, take into consideration their level of expertise and make the spreadsheet easy *for them* to use and maintain.

The best way to ensure user-friendliness is to pilot your draft spreadsheet with a sample of the target/end-user audience.

 Tip

If you have the opportunity, recruit users who are at various levels of Excel or spreadsheet experience to test your application. Their feedback (ideally recorded on a tape recorder while they are using it) can be invaluable.

Protection

Apply workbook, worksheet, or cell protection to prevent users from inadvertently deleting or changing formulas or data. (See Chapter 8 for in-depth treatment of this topic.)

Buttons and Macros

If you're developing for an inexperienced end-user, consider adding buttons to make it as user-friendly as possible. Think about including buttons for sorting, printing, creating PivotTables, and charting. Attach macros to the buttons that perform these operations.

Screen Resolution

Monitor settings and screen resolution capabilities are important to consider in terms of your end-user. The most common resolutions are 640 x 480 pixels, 800 x 600, and 1024 x 768. The safest bet is to use 640 x 480 (roughly a 15-inch monitor's screen area), but it's best to check with the client.

 Note

The following items are essential to professional-looking and easy-to-use spreadsheets and should always be used in spreadsheets that are created for others to use:

▶ Defined names
▶ Cell notes
▶ Documentation

Microsoft Excel Version

It is important to know which version of Excel the end-user has. If the end-user has version 4 and you develop in versions 5 or 7, many features and all of your Visual Basic for Applications code cannot be used. Choose File, Save As and specify the end-user's file format to avoid problems, but also spend the time to find out what features that you hope to incorporate will be canceled by doing this. Excel 7 users may be consoled by the fact that Excel 7 shares the same basic file format as Excel 5, but some features are not downward-compatible.

Laying Out the Spreadsheet

Many spreadsheets are developed without much thought to the physical arrangement of data or lists on the worksheet. For example, a data list that is placed on a worksheet should be surrounded by blank cells to enable the database features in Excel to correctly execute. Additionally, it is easy to crowd a worksheet with too much information. It is better to make your user scroll than squint.

Whenever possible, use the same page layout principles that apply to other on-line documents:

▶ *Proportion*. The relative size of elements such as headings, text, and graphics should be proportionate to their importance. Disproportion can create mixed messages as to what you really want the user or viewer to focus on.

▶ *Direction*. Optimize the effect of particular areas by respecting the fact that most readers (of Western languages, that is) scan a page from top left to bottom right. Used properly, you can guide the user from important area to important area, eliminating problems from readers passing over what seems difficult, and so on.

▶ *Consistency*. This harks back to the earlier point about not overusing formatting, but also applies to the organization of your document. It is especially important in complex, technical documents such as spreadsheets to use the same formatting (such as type faces and border schemes) as well as data organization schemes throughout all units and subunits. It may help to create a simple style guide document for yourself as a reference for your design decisions. Whether you've recorded them or not, stick to your layout decisions to avoid confusion, create a uniform look and feel, and create a distinctive identity for your work.

Spread the Wealth

There's no need to put all of the information on one worksheet. Consider using several sheets in a workbook to store the data. A good example of this is a monthly budget where each month has its own separate worksheet. A worksheet with consolidated information from all of the worksheets may be used to display summarized data for the aggregate monthly budget.

Calculation

Excel calculates from left to right, and top to bottom. The optimal spreadsheet for calculation performance is tall in height and narrow in width.

Developing for Both the Macintosh and Windows Platforms

With each version upgrade, the difference between Macintosh and Windows versions of Excel becomes less of a factor in development. Excel files created on either platform can be opened and edited on the other. Thoroughly test the application on each platform before releasing it to the user. This section covers some specific areas that you need to take into account for cross-platform development.

Use TrueType Fonts

TrueType fonts are scaleable, like Adobe's Postscript fonts, but are better integrated into both Macintosh and Windows software platforms. Unlike Adobe Postscript, TrueType fonts do not require bitmap versions also to be stored in your system to display font names on font menus. And TrueType fonts do not require a utility like Adobe Type Manager (ATM) to display accurately on-screen.

If you do not have a given TrueType font installed on both platforms, you are asking for problems. A TrueType version of a font on one platform will not render well in off-sizes on the other platform if the other platform has only a bitmap version. Arial, Helvetica, Times, and Times Roman are the most universal TrueType fonts used on both platforms. Sticking to these is your best insurance against end-user font problems.

Conversion

The same font sometimes performs differently on the two platforms—word wrapping and breaking lines in unexpected places. Test this if you think it could be an issue. It's also possible to lose some formatting that has been applied to text when transferring the files between platforms. Again, stick with universal TrueType fonts such as Arial, Helvetica, Times, and Times Roman.

Graphics

Not all pictures will convert well between platforms. You may end up wasting a lot of time trying to correct this, to no avail. Be aware that graphics, especially bitmaps, can increase the size of your application dramatically. This may be a problem for the end-users, depending on their hardware's memory and if they are going to be sending the file through a network.

Dates

Calendar dates are different on the Macintosh and PC. The Macintosh uses the 1904 date system, while Windows uses the 1900 date system. If you plan to develop for dual-platform compatibility, change the Windows version setting by choosing Tools, Options, Calculation tab, Workbook Options setting, 1904 Date System.

Caution

Many times, the date system adjusts between platforms automatically. However, since the date system for the Excel for the Macintosh and Windows are different, you may encounter a four-year difference when transferring Excel files between platforms.

Excel for Windows starts its dates at January 1, 1900; Excel for the Macintosh begins at January 1, 1904. The starting serial numbers are also different. On the Macintosh, the serial number of 0 represents January 1, 1904, while the serial number of 1 in Excel for Windows represents January 1, 1900.

Dialog Boxes

The size of dialog boxes and the system fonts in them may display differently between platforms. There is not much you can do about this problem, however.

Application Window

The Macintosh does not provide an Application window as the Windows environment does. VBA code cannot be used to adjust height and width, top and left, or the caption properties. By inserting the following line of code into your application, you can determine whether your worksheet or application is running on a Macintosh:

```
If Ucase(Left(Application.OperatingSystem, 3)) = "Mac"
```

Save As

Be aware that the Macintosh defaults to saving a new workbook as Workbook1. Windows uses the default of BOOK1.XLS when the Save As command is applied.

Menu Bars

On the Windows platform, if you add more menus than there is space for in a single-line menu bar, the additional menus will wrap to a second line, creating a double menu bar. Doing this on a Macintosh will generate an error message.

DropDown Property

The DropDownlines property is not available on the Macintosh platform. DropDownLines is a unique property to the DropDown object. It takes an integer value that references the number of items displayed in the drop-down list after the user has selected the down arrow accessing the list.

Help

The key for accessing Help in Windows is F1. On the Macintosh, help may be activated by the key combination ⌘-/ or the Help key on Apple Extended keyboards.

Carriage Return

In Windows, Chr(13) is used for a carriage return in VBA. Macintosh uses Chr(10) to insert a carriage return. To control where the text should wrap, insert a carriage return using the CHAR function and the ASCII code for carriage returns.

ODBC Drivers

On Windows, ODBC driver information is stored in the ODBC.INI file in the Windows directory. On the Macintosh, this information is stored in Control Panel in the ODBC Preferences file in the Preferences folder.

Path

The Windows path separator is \. On the Macintosh, the path separator is :. Instead of hardwiring a \ or :, it's best to use the Application.Path separator in VBA.

Solving Real-World Problems with Excel

The power of Excel lies not in its elegant features, but in your ability to apply its capabilities to everyday tasks. With this in mind, this section contains two "real-world" spreadsheets that you can use immediately.

Each spreadsheet is explained in an exercise section. If you're the type of person who enjoys hands-on development, you will find the exercises easy to follow as they take you step-by-step through the development of a usable spreadsheet.

Each file is included on the CD that accompanies this book. You can open a file at any time if you simply want to compare your work with the existing file. These examples are not paragons of sophistication or originality. Their purpose is to offer effective solutions to real-world problems and serve as a springboard for further ideas and development.

Basic Task Manager

The file TODOEXAMP.XLS is a basic task manager. Note that the worksheet is easy to read and there can be no mistaking what the purpose of this spreadsheet is. The column headers are set apart by formatting from the list data. Gridlines on the file have been turned off but a light-gray border has been applied to the list data to allow the user to easily find and separate information. Three basic macros have been attached to three on-screen buttons to apply AutoFilter, to bring up the Sort dialog box, and to Print.

Figure 1.1 is an example of a well-layed-out task manager.

Fig. 1.1

The basic task manager illustrates how a well-planned spreadsheet can be easy to read and understand. It also takes into consideration the automation of simple tasks when designing for less experienced users.

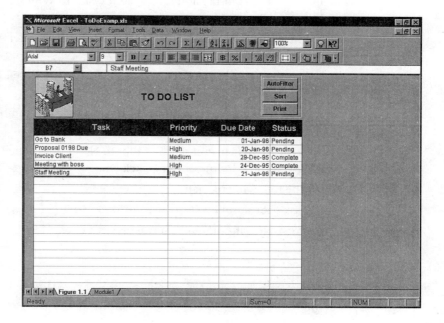

To create this basic task manager for yourself, follow these steps:

1. Open a new Excel workbook.

2. Select All Cells by pressing Ctrl+A or Ctrl+Shift+Spacebar.

3. Choose Format, Cells (or press Ctrl+1).

4. Press Ctrl+Page Up or Ctrl+Page Down to view and select the Patterns tab.

5. Choose the medium-gray shade (if you're counting colors, beginning with the 1st color in the top row and moving right, it's the 14th color) and click OK.

6. Select the entire first row and choose Format, Row, Height. Set the row height to 71. Select the entire second row and set the row height to 25.5.

7. Select each of the following columns individually and either drag the column width to the following width settings or choose Format, Column, Width to display the Column Width dialog box. Set the Column Width of column A to 2, column B to 30, column C to 10, column D to 12, and column E to 8.5.

8. Select cells B1:E1. Press Ctrl+1 and select the Alignment tab.

9. Horizontal options should be set to Center Across Selection. Select Center as the vertical setting. Click OK.

10. Type **To Do List** in Cell B1.

11. Select cell B1 and press Ctrl+1, selecting the Font tab. Select the 11th color of the drop-down list (Navy Blue). Set the Font Size to 14 and the Font Style to Bold.

12. Select cells B2:E2 and press Ctrl+1, selecting the Pattern tab. Select color 14 (Navy Blue). Select the Font tab and set the Font Color to White, the Font Style to Bold, and the Font Size to 11.

13. Select the Alignment tab and choose to horizontally Center Across Selection. Press OK.

14. Type **Task** in cell B2, **Priority** in cell B3, **Date Due** in cell B4, and **Status** in cell B5.

15. Select cells B3:B5. Press the Ctrl+Shift+down-arrow key combination and activate the Format Cells dialog box.

16. Select the Patterns tab and set the Color to None. Select the Border tab then select Outline and the thin line option. Click OK.

17. Apply the following formatting:

   Task data should be formatted to Wrap Text.

   Due Date data should be formatted as a date.

18. Choose Insert, Object. Select a graphic object of your choice.

19. Place the object in the left corner of cell B1. (You can format the object with a dark blue border if you wish.)

20. Insert a module sheet into the workbook. Choose Insert, Macro, Module. It's time to write some simple subroutines. These subroutines will be assigned to button objects on the worksheet to perform simple commands. Copy or type the following subroutines in the module sheet:

```
Sub ApplyAutoFilterToList
Cells(4,1).AutoFilter
End Sub

Sub PerformASort
Application.Dialogs(xlDialogSort).Show
End Sub

Sub PrintHanlder()
Application.Dialogs(xlDialogPrint).Show
End Sub
```

21. Select the worksheet with the ToDo list.

22. Choose View, Toolbars, and select the Forms Toolbar.

23. Click the Create Button tool on the Forms toolbar and draw three buttons on the worksheet named AutoFilter, Sort, and Print. After each button is created, an Assign Macro dialog box will appear. The first button should be assigned to ApplyAutoFilterToList, the second button to Sort, and the third button to Print.

24. Choose Tools, Options, View. Experiment with deselecting options.

It's time to check out your handiwork. You've just completed a quick and attractive worksheet that performs tasks that are assigned to macros.

SiteSurvey

The SITESURVEY.XLS Excel file is a more advanced example of an effective way to gather and store data. In 59 lines of VBA code, you are presented with a fully operational automated data list that can be used by you, your client, or for data entry. This file was created to be used at seminars to gather information from participants and to display promotional information on-line.

This application is easily customizable. Figure 1.2 shows the data entry screen, the only view that is displayed to the user.

Fig. 1.2
The Info button that is associated with the numbered topics is used to call a dialog sheet that displays the desired information.

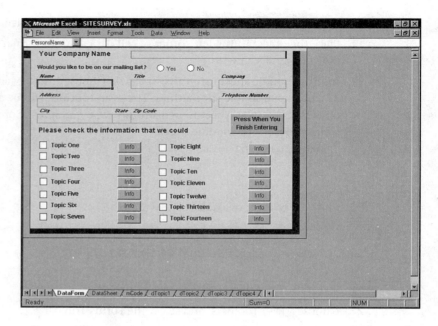

> ## α Note
>
> To make the application more sleek, toolbars have been hidden. To give the application an even more professional appearance, hide the sheet tabs, menu bars, and change the caption.

To see how this custom application was developed, do the following:

1. Open the sample file SITESURVEY.XLS. The application has an Auto_Open macro to activate the DataForm worksheet and to make the active range PersonsName. The AutoOpen macro is as follows:

```
Sub AutoOpen()
    ThisWorkbook.Worksheets("DataForm").Select
    Range("PersonsName").Select
End Sub
```

2. Enter information into the blanks on the dataform. Select various option buttons on the worksheet.

3. Select several information buttons and view the displayed dialog boxes.

4. Click the Press When You Finish Entering button. Your information is entered into the datasheet and the dataform is cleared and ready for the next set of information.

5. Select the worksheet DataSheet.

The DataSheet, as shown in Figure 1.3 is ultimately where all of the data entered by the user will be stored.

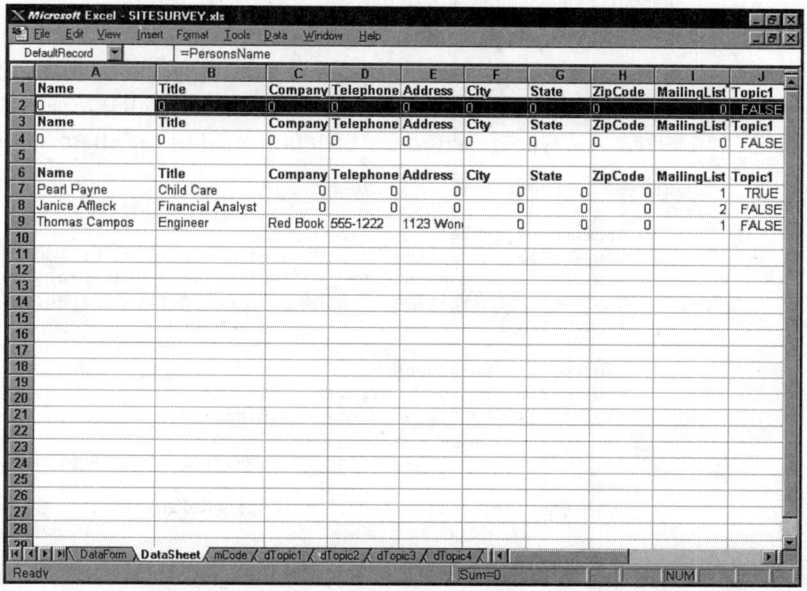

Fig. 1.3

The DataSheet with the named range DefaultRecord selected.

The named range, DefaultRecord in Row 2, contains the default values that reset the worksheet to null values. This clears out the completed dataform and prepares it for the next user.

The named range, TempRecord in Row 4, contains the actual data that was entered into the dataform. As the defined name implies, this is the temporary data that will be transfered to the database.

The named range, DatabaseFieldRange in Row 6, is where the worksheet database is stored.

6. Select various dialog sheets. These sheets begin with a lowercase "d" followed by the sheet name. Each dialog sheet is fully customizable. When you're ready to customize the application and have your information appear when an information button is selected, the textual changes for the dialog boxes are made on these sheets.

7. Activate the module sheet mCode. The VBA code in the module has been fully commented.

Upon opening the workbook, the worksheet DataForm is selected and the active range is PersonsName.

```
Sub AutoOpen()
ThisWorkbook.Worksheets("DataForm").Select
Range("PersonsName").Select
End Sub
```

The buttonhandler subroutine that follows makes code more efficient. Instead of having 16 different subroutines to process, the buttonhandler looks for the name of the button selected, the type of action for each button, and the character definition or button name.

```
Sub ButtonHandler()

''' Declare variables
    Dim sCaller As String    '''Name of the calling button.
    Dim sActionType As String    '''Action code characters 4, 5, 6, 7 of button name.
    Dim sActionDefinition As String '''Definition characters, all characters 8 and
    ➥beyond.

''' Controlling workspace
    Application.ScreenUpdating = False
    Application.EnableCancelKey = xlDisabled

''' Gets the name of the button that was selected (Application.Caller). Make sure it
    ➥starts
''' with btn. Get action code. Get ActionDefinition.

    sCaller = UCase(Application.Caller)
    If Mid(sCaller, 1, 3) <> "BTN" Then Exit Sub
    sActionType = UCase(Mid(sCaller, 4, 4))
    sActionDefinition = UCase(Mid(sCaller, 8, 255))

''' Assigns case by actiontype. One shows dialog, the other calls a subroutine.

    Select Case sActionType

        Case "SHOW"
            ThisWorkbook.DialogSheets(sActionDefinition).Show
        Case "MSUB"
            Select Case sActionDefinition
                Case "SURVEYCOMPLETE"
                    Call SurveyComplete

            End Select
    End Select
End Sub
```

The subroutine SurveyComplete transfers data from the datasheet to the dataform.

```
Sub SurveyComplete()

    Dim iApplicationStatus As Integer
    Dim oDataSheet As Worksheet
    Set oDataSheet = ThisWorkbook.Worksheets("DataSheet")
    Dim oDataForm As Worksheet
    Set oDataForm = ThisWorkbook.Worksheets("Dataform")
```

```
Dim oWholeDataBase As Range
Dim oRowBelowDatabase As Range
Dim oTempRecord As Range
Dim oDefaultRecord As Range
iApplicationStatus = Application.Calculation
Application.Calculation = xlManual
Application.Calculate

With oDataSheet
    Set oDefaultRecord = .Range("DefaultRecord")
    Set oTempRecord = .Range("TempRecord")
    Set oWholeDataBase = .Range("DatabaseFieldRange").CurrentRegion
    Set oRowBelowDatabase = oWholeDataBase.Resize(rowsize:=1).
    ➡Offset(oWholeDataBase.Rows.Count)
    oTempRecord.Copy
    oRowBelowDatabase.PasteSpecial Paste:=xlValues, Operation:=xlNone
    oDefaultRecord.Copy oTempRecord
    .Calculate
End With

'''After selecting the "Press when you finishing entering" button,
'''the ranges are reset to blanks.

With oDataForm
    .Range("PersonsName").Value = ""
    .Range("Title").Value = ""
    .Range("Address").Value = ""
    .Range("City").Value = ""
    .Range("State").Value = ""
    .Range("Zip_Code").Value = ""
    .Range("Company").Value = ""
    .Range("TelephoneNumber").Value = ""
End With
Application.Calculation = iApplicationStatus
End Sub
```

 Tip

After you've finished customizing your application, you'll want to hide and protect the dialog and module sheets and to protect the DataForm.

In a short period of time, you can customize the existing application or use the basic mechanics to create your own application.

Power User Tips

Have you ever wanted to pick the brains of other Excel developers? If so, this section is for you. Some of the top Excel consultants have been asked the question, "What is your favorite advanced Excel tip and would you like to share it?" Many of these tips come from MS Excel MVPs (Most Valued Professionals). These individuals reside on the

MS Excel forum on CompuServe. They are all seasoned professionals who are recognized experts within the Excel community.

Turning Off Display Syntax Errors

*Robert Affleck, MS Excel MVP; Internet: **75450.1754@compuserve.com***

While editing, the VBA Module Editor alerts the programmer to syntax errors in two ways:

▶ A message box is displayed at the time the error is determined.

▶ It highlights the error with a red font.

For experienced developers, the message box is a nuisance, provides little or no help, and requires being closed before moving on to other work.

To turn off the display of syntax errors in a module sheet, choose Tools, Options, Module General, and deselect the Display Syntax Errors option.

Selecting Printers Through VBA

*Rob Bovey, MS Excel MVP; Internet: **76041.2716@compuserve.com***

If you find yourself in a situation where you frequently need to print to different printers, this tip will save you a lot of time. With a short macro and a custom toolbar button, you can create a method to switch to a different printer and print your workbook with one click of your mouse button. The following two macros show you how it's done:

```
Sub BlackWhitePrinter()
    Application.ActivePrinter = "HP LaserJet 4/4M on LPT1:"
    ActiveWindow.SelectedSheets.PrintOut
End Sub

Sub ColorPrinter()
    Application.ActivePrinter = "HP Color LaserJet on LPT2:"
    ActiveWindow.SelectedSheets.PrintOut
End Sub
```

When the BlackWhitePrinter subroutine is run, the default printer is switched to the LaserJet 4 and the selected sheets from the currently active workbook are printed. Likewise, when the ColorPrinter macro is run, the printout goes to the Color LaserJet. You can use either button, regardless of which printer is currently active.

You can find the correct names for your own printers in the Printer Setup dialog box, or you can use the macro recorder. Store these subroutines in your PERSONAL.XLS file and assign them to custom toolbar buttons. You can also assign them hot keys if you would rather activate them from the keyboard.

Using Special Cell Formatting

Conrad Carlberg, MS Excel MVP; Internet: ***71033.2701@compuserve.com***

You can hide and protect worksheet cells to your heart's content, but doing so hides the cell's contents only in the formula bar, not in the cell itself. So, if a cell contains a formula that uses sensitive information—commission percentages, perhaps, or a conditional such as IF(CustName="Jones," "Kites checks," "Checks OK")—then you might want to keep the information from appearing in the cell.

Use the special cell format ";;;" to prevent the cell from displaying its contents. Select the cell, choose Format, Cells, and click the Numbers tab. Choose Custom from the list box, and type ;;; in the Type box.

Now, whether or not the cell is hidden and the sheet protected, or whether the user chooses to display formulas or values in cells, the cell's contents cannot be seen in the cell itself.

Debugging XLM Macros

Bob Greenblatt, MS Excel MVP; Internet: ***71540.3362@compuserve.com***

When debugging XLM macros (I know, few people do this anymore), it is often convenient to activate a worksheet, and then begin stepping through the macro at a certain line of code. To do this, use a very simple macro (beginning in cell A9) assigned to a toolbar button:

```
=REFTEXT(ACTIVE.CELL())=ACTIVATE(INDEX(WINDOWS(3),2))
=FORMULA("=step()+"&A9&"()",a12)
=RETURN
```

Simply select the cell in the macro where you want to start stepping, and press the button. This macro activates the last active worksheet, and begins running the macro in step mode from the selected cell in the macro.

Using Shift+Drag-and-Drop

John Green, MS Excel MVP; Internet: ***100236.1562@compuserve.com***

You can quickly change the order of a list of items by holding down the Shift key as you drag one or more selected cells to a new location in the list. For example, you have a list of city names in a column. The list includes New York, Sydney, London, and Paris, in that order. To place Paris between New York and Sydney, select the cell containing Paris, hold down the Shift key, move the pointer to an edge of the cell until you get the Drag-and-Drop pointer arrow and click and drag up the column. You will find that the mouse pointer takes on a horizontal I-beam shape and highlights the borders between the cells.

Highlight the border between New York and Sydney and release the mouse button. Don't release the Shift key until you are finished. Excel will insert Paris after New York, and move Sydney and London down the list.

This simple technique saves you from having to perform several cut and paste or drag-and-drop operations. It can also be used on rows of data. You can drag more than one cell at a time, so you could have selected both London and Paris and placed them after New York in the example just given. In a table of data, you can drag a whole row or column to a new location. If you write XLM style macros, this is an ideal way of changing the order of macro commands.

Using Automatic Links Between Charts, Pivot Tables, and Worksheet Ranges

*John Lacher, MS Excel MVP; Internet: **73447.2431@compuserve.com***

You can link worksheet data, a pivot table, and a chart so that changes to the data automatically update the pivot table and changes to the pivot table automatically update the chart.

If you name the input range of the pivot table "Database," and use the Data, Form menu option to add new rows, Excel will automatically expand the "Database" range to include the new data. Press the Refresh Data button on your pivot table worksheet, and the new data will be automatically included in the table. If you link a chart to the pivot table, changes in the pivot table automatically update the chart.

You can create a range named "Database" on more than one sheet by including the sheet name in the range name like this: **Sheet1!Database**. You can link a chart to a pivot table by using Ctrl+Shift+*" to select the pivot table for use as the input range to the chart.

Using CurrentRegion with Tables

*Bill Manville, MS Excel MVP; Internet: **73064.405@compuserve.com***

When dealing with a table in a worksheet, you can select the entire table by selecting a cell in the table and then typing Ctrl+*. The equivalent method in VBA is CurrentRegion.

CurrentRegion makes it easier to write VBA procedures which deal with a table whose size is likely to vary from time to time. To convert the formula to values in a table starting at cell A1:

```
Range("A1").CurrentRegion.Copy
Range("A1").PasteSpecial xlValues
```

Plotting Visible Cells Only

*Bill Manville, MS Excel MVP; Internet: **73064.405@compuserve.com***

If you create a chart from a table of data, you may wish to remove some data series from it temporarily, or change the number of data points displayed to make the graph more clearly show the data you are really interested in. To do this, just hide the worksheet rows and/or columns that contain the data you want to hide from the graph.

Jumping to a Called Subroutine from within Another Subroutine

*Donna Payne, MS Excel MVP; Internet: **73573.500@compuserve.com***

Often when writing VBA code, you will call one subroutine from within another subroutine. You may need to review what the subroutine does, or even to edit the existing code. It's fairly easy to find the other subroutine right away if you only have a few subroutines, but what if you have hundreds, and several different module sheets.

To quickly jump to the called subroutine, position your cursor anywhere in the name of that procedure in your VBA code and select Shift+F2. This will find and display the actual subroutine that is being called from the other. This is officially called locating the procedure definition.

Processing Data Using an Array from Range

*Tim Tow, MS Excel MVP; Internet: **72773.1615@compuserve.com***

To quickly process data, you can pull it into a variant array using the syntax similar to the following example:

```
Option Base 1

Sub GetDataIntoArray()
    Dim vArray As Variant
''' get the array
    vArray = Worksheets("Sheet1").Range("A1:C4").Value
''' display an element of the array
    MsgBox vArray(1, 1)
End Sub
```

You can then reference the elements by referencing the two-dimensional array it creates. For example, the array element vArray(1,1) would contain the value in cell A1 (as shown in the MsgBox statement in the example). Use this technique when you want to quickly process data from a worksheet range. It's very fast when compared to doing repeated accesses to worksheet cells.

Note

Note that using Option Base 1 makes the array operations more understandable as an Excel worksheet can be thought of, conceptually, as a large, two-dimensional, one-based array.

The use of variant arrays in this manner is limited to 3276 elements (cells) if you are using Excel 5.0 and 2730 elements if you are using Excel 7.0 (personally, I wish this limitation will go away in future versions).

For further information on these limitations, see the Microsoft KnowledgeBase article number Q137921.

Similarly, you can also write data back to a sheet using a similar syntax. If you're going to place the array, you have to place it in a range that is the exact size of the array. Using the Resize method and the Ubound function makes it easy as in this example:

```
Sub PlaceDataFromArray()
    Dim vArray As Variant
''' get the array
    vArray = Worksheets("Sheet1").Range("A1:C4").Value
''' write part of the array back to another range
    Worksheets("Sheet1").Range("B7") _
        .Resize(UBound(vArray, 1), UBound(vArray, 2)).Value = vArray
End Sub
```

Most commonly, however, if you intend to write data to an array and place it back into the sheet, you will dim the array, fill it (and maybe use the ReDim statement to dynamically resize the array as you fill it). Further, the size of the array that can be placed almost doubles:

```
Option Base 1
Sub DimmedArrayExample()
    Dim vArray(4, 3) As String
    Dim x, y As Integer
''' fill the array
    For x = 1 To 4
        For y = 1 To 3
            vArray(x, y) = "Hello World"
        Next
    Next
''' place the array on the sheet
    Worksheets("Sheet1").Cells(1, 1).Resize(4, 3).Value = vArray
End Sub
```

Navigating Selection Ranges

*Bob Umlas, MS Excel MVP; Internet: **70302.3432@compuserve.com***

To make your active cell within a selection move through the four corners of the selection, highlight the selection, press Ctrl+.(period) twice.

To select everything except the top row of your selection, press Ctrl+.(period) twice, press the Shift + down-arrow key.

To get back to the top-left corner of the selection, press Ctrl+.(period) twice.

Entering Upper Case without a Macro

*Bob Umlas, MS Excel MVP; Internet: **70302.3432@compuserve.com***

Here's a way to enter text into a cell and have it become uppercase *without* a macro.

Assuming the cell in question is A9, then in some distant, unviewable cell, like cell Z9, enter **=UPPER(A9)**. Using the Camera button on the Utility toolbar, take a picture of this cell. Holding down the Alt key, "develop" the picture over cell A9 (position the cursor to the upper-left portion of the cell). Format the picture to have no border, and no fill. Go to cell A9, format the font to be white, and you're done.

Other Miscellaneous Excel Tips

There are a few other tips that might make your Excel developing a bit easier and more productive.

Keyboard Shortcuts

There are some tricky keyboard shortcuts that are useful for selecting special cells. These include the following:

Shortcut Key	Description
Ctrl+Shift+?	Selects all cells containing notes but does not display the cell note dialog box
Ctrl+Shift+*	Selects current range
Ctrl+/	Selects an entire array
Ctrl+[	When a cell containing a formula is selected, cells directly referred to by the selection are selected
Ctrl+Shift+{	Selects all cells referred to by the selected cell's formula
Ctrl+]	Selects cells with a formula that refers directly to the active cell
Ctrl+Shift+}	Selects all cells with a formula that refers to the active cell

Object Browser

Do you believe the statement, "Why remember something when you can look it up"? If so, then you will find the Excel Object Browser invaluable. In a module sheet, press the F2 key to display the Object Browser, select whether you want Libraries from Excel or VBA, or from an open workbook. Highlight the desired Object, and its Property or Method, and click the Paste button. This will paste all of the arguments for the Object.

Custom Lists Shortcomings

The maximum size of a custom list is 2000 characters. This includes the commas that separate the individual items in the list. If you have a custom list in a range and you choose Tools, Options to add a custom list, it will accept the list only up to the point where the 2000th character is reached. Excel does not warn you that the entire range has not been accepted.

If you do the VBA equivalent, you will get an error message, (`AddCustomList Method Failed`).

Conditional Formatting in Pivot Tables

Just as you can set conditional number formatting in a worksheet, you may do the same within a Pivot Table. To do this, select a cell in your pivot table. Choose Data, Pivot Table (in your Pivot Table, you'll need to make sure AutoFormat is selected). Go to Step 3 where you have a layout of your Pivot Table. Double-click a datafield. Choose the Number button and select Custom. Type the custom format in the edit in the dialog box. An example of a custom number format is

    [>=5][Blue];[<5][Red]

This formats any number with a value of 5 or greater with the color blue, and anything under 5 as red.

Placing the Value of a Cell in a Text Box

To assign the contents of a text box to a dynamic value in a cell, create or select the text box. Press the F2 key to activate the formula bar. Select the cell that you want to obtain the value from. Press the Enter key. Now when you change the value in the assigned cell, the text box contents will also change. The same technique can be applied to chart titles.

Restoring Incorrect Number Formats

There is often a conflict between some software packages and Excel that causes the default number formats within Excel to disappear by writing incorrect information to the international settings section of the WIN.INI. To fix the problem, choose Control Panel, International, and then make some change to the currency setting or 100 separator. Close the dialog box and close Windows. Restart and change the settings back, close and then restart. As unlikely as this technique seems, it will correct the problem with number formats.

Set Application.ScreenUpdating to False

To avoid screen updating or flicker each time a change is made to your worksheet, set the ScreenUpdating property of the Application object to False at the beginning of the macro. This is equivalent to the XLM code =ECHO(FALSE).

Summary

In this chapter, you learned how to address some design issues when you are developing a spreadsheet that others will be using. This includes items that are often overlooked by even experienced Excel programmers.

You also were given examples of spreadsheets that you can actually use, either as is or modified. It is hoped that these serve as roadmaps for even more elaborate and advanced spreadsheets, as your needs, time, and, creativity allow and inspire.

Finally, you were given advanced tips and tricks used by other Excel developers as well as helpful user tips for increased productivity for working in Microsoft Excel.

In the next chapter, you learn more about custom formats and AutoFills.

chapter 2

Helping Users with Custom Formats and AutoFills

by Brian Underdahl

In this chapter

◆ **Validate data entry**
You don't need to resort to complex data input validity checking programming to ensure that the user enters proper data.

◆ **Selectively hide or emphasize data**
Use custom formatting when you need to alert users to important data values.

◆ **Use special formats to display data**
Data such as ZIP codes, telephone numbers, and Social Security numbers can be properly displayed using special formats.

◆ **Create custom formats**
Create formats that meet your needs using color, text, and special characters.

◆ **Use AutoFill effectively**
Greatly reduce the effort and errors often associated with entering lists of data.

The best, most sophisticated and effective applications often seem deceptively simple to the user. These applications seem simple because the user never sees all the power, tricks, and fancy techniques hidden in the program. All of these factors combine to make programs easy and intuitive to use, so the user can simply get the job done.

In this chapter we'll look at two powerful Excel features that can solve quite a few problems. Custom formats and AutoFill series may seem like simple tools, but you'll soon see how much these tools can help you.

Let's begin by looking more closely at custom formats, a seldom used but very handy tool in your Excel developer's toolkit. Later you learn how you can use AutoFill effectively.

What Can Custom Formats Do for Me?

You probably already have some ideas about *custom* (or user-defined) *formats*, but you've probably never really thought about all the things you can do with custom formats. In many cases you can even eliminate long formulas or complex programming by simply using a custom format. For example, everyone has probably seen (or created) some variation on the following formula to return the name of the current day of the week:

```
=CHOOSE(WEEKDAY(TODAY(),1),"Sunday","Monday","Tuesday","Wednesday","Thursday","Friday","Saturday")
```

This formula works, but is cumbersome to enter, and is prone to errors—who hasn't forgotten one of the quotation marks or commas when entering this formula?

Another less popular Excel variation on this theme uses the following, somewhat simpler formula:

```
=TEXT(TODAY(),"dddd")
```

At least this formula is easier to enter, but it is still unnecessary. While both formulas accomplish the goal of showing the name of the day of the week, you don't really need either formula. In fact, you can produce the same result by simply using a custom format, *dddd*, on any cell containing a date serial number. Try this:

1. Place the formula **=TODAY( )** in a worksheet cell.
2. Right-click the cell containing the formula.
3. Select Format Cells.
4. Select Custom.
5. In the Type text box, enter **dddd**.
6. Select OK.

Figure 2.1 shows the results of using the different formula and formatting options. Cell A2 shows the result of the TODAY function displayed in General format, cell A3 shows the result of the CHOOSE function, cell A4 shows the result of the TEXT function, and A5 shows the result of the TODAY function displayed in the custom dddd format. You don't have to use the TODAY function to produce the date serial number, of course. The custom format method works with any formula that results in a valid date serial number.

There you have it, by simply applying a custom format you've eliminated a formula, improved the performance of your worksheet a little, and learned how to make Excel do a bit more of your work automatically. Not bad for a feature you probably haven't thought much about, is it? This is one of the secrets of finding expert solutions—use some of the powerful features to accomplish more with less work. Let's examine a few more examples of how custom formats can work for you.

Fig. 2.1

Custom formats can often accomplish tasks you probably thought required formulas or programming.

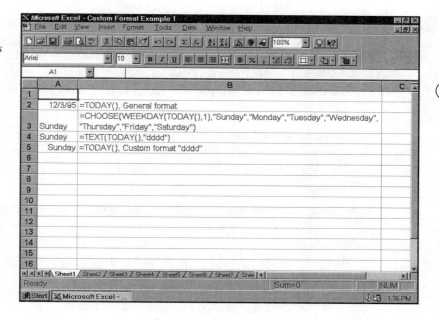

Controlling User Input

One of the most difficult problems most application developers face is controlling users. If only an application's users were as reliable as the program itself, you wouldn't have to worry whether someone might enter improper or invalid data. Unfortunately, that's not often the case. People are only human, after all, and humans make mistakes!

Considering Input Control Options

There are many means of controlling user input in an application, some more effective than others. Excel offers the developer many choices in this area. Choosing the correct method to fit your needs is often a matter of deciding on an appropriate balance between the level of control that is actually required and the amount of effort necessary to provide the solution. Consider these two options:

▶ Program documentation and user training may be all that's necessary if the user input isn't all that critical to the operation of the organization. As an example, an application that displays titles, descriptions, and quantities of movies available for rental at a video store probably won't have too much impact on the bottom line if a customer or clerk enters an incorrect stock number. Because the error would be obvious, you could probably depend on the user to catch and correct their own mistakes.

▶ Total data input validation using advanced VBA programming techniques may be required if even a single error could prove to be a major expense. A real-time stock trading model developed for a major brokerage firm could result in millions of dollars in losses if the application allowed the user to enter invalid data, for example. In such a high-pressure environment, absolute control of user input would be a vital necessity.

Of course, most applications fall somewhere between these two extremes. Usually it's quite important that users enter valid data, but a few simple visual clues are all you'd need to alert the user to errors. Given a little help, most users can actually enter correct information.

In the past, one of the most common methods of validating user input has been to use a formula that tested whether that input fit acceptable parameters. You might use the logical function IF to test user input, accepting the data if it met your test, and rejecting the data if it did not. While this method is certainly effective, it does have its shortcomings. One of the most notable of these is that the results of the logical formula are not displayed in the cell containing the incorrect data. Unless the user happens to look at the result cell, there's a good chance he won't catch his error very quickly, if at all.

Caution

Don't forget that formatting data does not change the data value. If you apply a format that changes the appearance of the data, whether you use one of Excel's built-in formats or a custom format, the value is unchanged. If you must depend on the user to enter valid information, make certain you validate the data using techniques such as those discussed in Chapter 10, "Ensuring Quality Using Advanced Error Checking."

Custom formats offer the developer a unique method of controlling and validating user input without actually changing any data. Using a custom format you can indicate incorrect input directly in the cell where the user entered invalid information. Since this provides immediate feedback when the user makes an error, this method can be quite effective in reducing or eliminating user errors.

Strictly speaking, custom formats don't actually control user input, of course. Absolute control of user input requires much more sophisticated methods, usually involving complex formulas, VBA programming, or a combination of formulas and programming. Still, because custom formats provide instant visual verification of data validity, they can often be employed in place of, or even in cooperation with, additional data verification methods.

Using Custom Formats for Data Verification

The simplest type of data verification you'll probably need in most Excel worksheets is a test to determine whether data fits within an acceptable range. A trivial example of this might be a worksheet that calculates certain employee benefits based on a person's age. Obviously you wouldn't want to allow someone to enter a negative number as their age. Likewise, a worksheet that calculates a sales representative's commissions using product costs as a divisor couldn't allow zero costs, otherwise you'd go broke paying infinite commissions.

Custom number formats provide a simple solution to these types of situations. Let's take a closer look at an example to see how this works.

When you create a custom number format in Excel, you use the following general arrangement:

```
positive number format; negative number format; zero format; text entry format
```

Under this general model, numbers greater than zero use the positive number format, numbers less than zero use the negative number format, numbers exactly equaling zero use the zero format, and text entered into the cell uses the text entry format. As you'll learn later in this chapter, you can greatly expand on the general model by incorporating colors, conditional tests using values other than zero, and descriptive text.

If you're asking yourself how this general model of custom number formats can possibly be used for controlling user input, you've come to the right place. Consider the example of entering someone's age, where you don't want anyone to accidentally enter a negative value, zero, or a text entry. You could use a custom format something like this:

```
##;"Must be positive";"Zero not allowed";"Numbers only"
```

If you apply this custom format to the age entry cell, ages entered as positive numbers will display normally. But if the user enters a negative number, the message Must be positive will be displayed in the cell in place of the number. Likewise, the corresponding message will be displayed if the user enters zero or text. Figure 2.2 shows the results of using this custom format in cells B2:B5.

Adding Text to Ease Data Entry

Computers are great at handling repetitive tasks, but sometimes it seems like they just aren't very smart or flexible about learning those tasks. One such task that seems simple but is often difficult to implement is automatically adding predefined text either before or after data you enter. Custom formats again provide a simple answer.

Fig. 2.2

Custom formats can help you control user input.

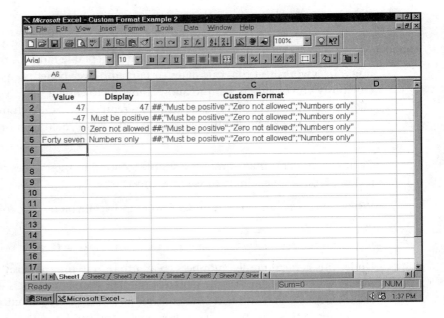

A Text and Number Custom Format Example

Consider the following example. You've been asked to create a worksheet that converts the prices of a line of electronic components from Canadian dollars to U.S. dollars based on both the current market price of each item and the prevailing exchange rate. You want to make certain that everyone understands that the prices being entered by the user are in Canadian dollars, but because both currencies use the same currency symbol ($), you need to add the text "(Canadian $)" to each entry. A custom format provides an easy solution to the problem.

If you want the automatic text to precede the numeric data, use the following custom format:

```
"(Canadian $) "@
```

If you want the automatic text to follow the numeric data, use this custom format:

```
@" (Canadian $)"
```

The position of the @ sign determines where Excel places the numeric value in relation to the added text.

Note the extra space added to each text entry to separate the text from the numbers. In the first case a space is added following the right parenthesis, and in the second a space is added before the left parenthesis. If you forget to add the extra spaces, the text and numbers will be displayed without any spaces, making the value harder to understand.

Advantages and Disadvantages of Custom Formats

Adding text to numeric entries using custom formats offers both advantages and disadvantages compared to other options you might consider, such as converting numbers to text using the TEXT function and then concatenating the text with a string. You may want to consider these advantages and disadvantages and consider how they may affect your worksheets.

One big advantage was mentioned earlier. Custom formats, no matter how they change the appearance of the data, don't change the value of the data. You can still use any custom formatted numeric data without having to convert it back into numbers. Of course, this same characteristic could also be a disadvantage if you've used a custom format that makes it appear as though the cell does not contain a numeric value, as was discussed in the section "Controlling User Input" earlier in the chapter. The value will still be used even if the user doesn't realize it, possibly causing incorrect results.

Possibly the biggest disadvantage to using custom number formats that include text is the extra column width necessary to display values. How much extra column width is needed depends on several factors, including how you added the text:

> ▶ If you add text by including the text as part of one of the numbers formats, such as the positive number format, Excel will display a series of pound signs (#) across the width of the column if the column is too narrow to display the value complete with the text.

> ▶ If you add text by including the @ sign, such as `@" (Canadian $)"` as shown in the previous example, Excel will display the value across adjacent empty cells to the right. You'll once again have to expand the width of the column to accommodate the extra text along with the numeric value if the cell to the right isn't empty and you want to display the entire value.

The normal factors, such as the font you use and the number of digits you want after the decimal point, also affect the column width needed to display numbers in custom formats.

Hiding Data with Custom Formats

You also can use custom formats to hide data you don't want displayed on-screen or in printed reports. I'm sure this fact comes as no surprise—spreadsheet users have long used formatting to hide data. Using custom formats to hide data, however, adds some new dimensions. By using a custom format to hide data, you can be selective in hiding or displaying data based on the value of the data.

In a sales report, for example, you might not want to display any zero values, concentrating instead on results for sales representatives who actually brought in some good orders. You might also create a report that emphasizes those company branches that are losing money by using a custom format that only displays negative numbers.

Hiding data with custom formats is easy. Simply include a blank format specification for the numbers you want to hide. For example, the following custom format displays negative numbers, but not positive numbers or zero:

```
;(#,###.00);;
```

To include a blank format specification, include the semicolon that follows the position of the format specification, but don't include any formatting characters. Remembering the general format of custom formats described earlier, you can see that this example includes a blank positive number format, specifies a negative number format, includes a blank zero format, and skips the text entry format. In this case, the negative number format specified displays negative numbers in parenthesis with two decimal places. The section "Creating Useful Formats" later in the chapter takes a closer look at other custom formatting options.

Emphasizing Important Data

Finally, I'll mention just one more use for custom formats—emphasizing important data. Every business has certain critical information that must be acted on in a timely manner. But important data can be easily lost or overlooked in the overload of data busy executives see daily. By using custom formats, you can make certain that critical information is emphasized, making it stand out from the rest of the more common data.

Suppose, for example, that you have created an Excel worksheet you use to track your stock market investments. You track a broad portfolio of stocks, using a complex set of calculations to project when stocks should be bought and sold. You've determined that if a certain calculation exceeds a specific ratio, it represents a clear warning sign that you should immediately call your broker and sell the stock. Once again, custom formats come to the rescue. Create a conditional custom format that displays results above the specified value in a bright, contrasting color, and you'll immediately recognize the stocks you need to sell. Later in this chapter, "Creating Useful Formats" discusses both conditional custom formats and using colors in custom formats.

Custom Formats Aren't Always Needed

While custom formats are very useful, you'll also find that Excel offers some *special formats* so you don't always have to create your own. These special formats help solve some otherwise difficult data entry issues, making it much easier for users to enter specific types of data. You can use these special formats in your applications rather than trying to create custom formats or educating your users in the proper techniques for entering these types of information.

You also can use the Excel special formats as guides to creating your own custom formats. Because the special formats are simply predefined formats that use the same formatting symbols as custom formats, you can use the special formats as the basis for your own custom formats. Let's have a quick look at Excel's special formats.

Using the ZIP Code Special Format

At first glance, the ZIP code special format might not seem very useful. After all, ZIP codes are simply five-digit numbers displayed without commas, right? Unfortunately, this is not quite true. While most ZIP codes can easily and correctly be displayed in General format, some ZIP codes include leading zeros. Numbers formatted using the ZIP code special format automatically display leading zeros as necessary to display a complete, five-digit number.

The ZIP code special format is the equivalent of the custom format "00000."

One problem you may encounter with the ZIP code special format is that this format does not prevent a user from entering invalid ZIP codes. In fact, this format simply ensures that numbers with less than five digits include enough leading zeros to produce a five-digit number. Numbers with more than five digits appear as entered.

Using the ZIP Code+4 Special Format

The ZIP code+4 special format is an extension of the ZIP code special format, with a dash and four extra character positions to handle nine-digit ZIP codes. The ZIP code+4 special format also properly displays leading zeros as needed.

The ZIP code+4 special format is the equivalent of the custom format "00000-0000."

Unfortunately, the ZIP code+4 special format is not very flexible. If you format a cell with the ZIP code+4 special format, and then enter a five-digit ZIP code, Excel will display a nine-digit ZIP code with four leading zeros. For example, if you enter the five-digit ZIP code 89511 in a cell formatted with the ZIP code+4 special format, Excel will display "00008-9511." The upcoming section "Going Beyond Special Formats" examines a method of dealing with this problem.

Using the Phone Special Format

Telephone numbers can be especially tricky to enter and display in an Excel worksheet. The Phone special format is designed to properly display both seven-digit and ten-digit telephone numbers in the correct format. If you enter 5551212 into a cell formatted using the Phone special format, Excel displays "555-1212" in the cell. If you add an area code, as in 3175551212, Excel displays "(317) 555-1212" in the cell.

The Phone special format is the equivalent of the custom format "[<=9999999]###-####;(###) ###-####". See "Creating Conditional Formats" later in this chapter for more details on using comparison operators to format ranges of numbers based on their values.

The Phone special format really isn't designed to handle special dialing codes, international telephone numbers, or other unusual calling situations. Fortunately, you can use the techniques covered in this chapter to create your own custom telephone number formats to handle nearly any special type of telephone number. As long as you know how the telephone number should appear, you can probably create the custom format you need to properly display the number.

Using the Social Security Number Special Format

Social Security numbers are another type of data users often find difficult to enter, because, to Excel, Social Security numbers look just like a mathematical formula. The Social Security number special format makes entering this type of data quite easy.

The Social Security number special format is the equivalent of the custom format "000-00-0000."

As is the case with Excel's other special formats, the Social Security number special format contains no provision for rejecting invalid entries. Still, you can use this special format as the starting point for your own, more robust version, which does validate the entry. This problem is tackled in the next section.

Going Beyond Special Formats

The special formats are designed to handle special tasks, but, as you've seen, they aren't very flexible. Still, understanding how the special formats relate to custom formats should provide you with some clues to creating your own, more flexible custom formats. Let's look at one very useful example that you can use to replace both the ZIP code and ZIP code+4 special formats.

One shortcoming of both the ZIP code and ZIP code+4 special formats is that they don't do well in handling a combination of five-digit and nine-digit ZIP codes. In this example you'll see how a few simple modifications can make all the difference.

Here are some facts to consider to help determine how to create a universal ZIP code custom format:

▶ ZIP codes must have either five or nine digits.

▶ The first character can be zero.

▶ The largest possible five-digit ZIP code is 99999.

Based on this information alone, you might think that the entire solution to the problem is to format numbers of 99,999 or less as five-digit ZIP codes, and to format larger numbers as nine-digit ZIP codes. As a developer, however, you have to consider the possibility that a user will do something unexpected, such as entering six or seven digits. For example, if the correct ZIP code is 01234-5678, but the user enters 123456, Excel would display "00012-3456" if you used the ZIP code+4 format. To create a bulletproof application, you have to make certain this type of error is not allowed. An additional test must be added to make certain the user has entered a valid ZIP code.

ZIP codes can contain a leading zero, but they never contain two leading zeros. Thus a valid nine-digit ZIP code would always be at least 01000-0000. Removing the leading zero and converting this to a number produces the value of 10,000,000 for the smallest possible valid nine-digit ZIP code.

Because five-digit ZIP codes must be less than or equal to 99,999, and nine-digit ZIP codes must be greater than or equal to 10,000,000, we know that numbers between these two values cannot represent valid ZIP codes. This leads us to the following custom format specification, which should handle nearly all situations:

```
[>=10000000]00000-0000;[<=99999]00000;"Invalid ZIP"
```

In the next section, you'll learn more about creating custom formats and using conditional tests as shown in this example. For now, though, look at the three formats specified in this specification. The first format, `[>=10000000]00000-0000`, tells Excel to display numbers greater than or equal to 10,000,000 in the nine-digit ZIP code format. The second format, `[<=99999]00000`, tells Excel to display numbers less than or equal to 99,999 in the five-digit ZIP code format. The final format, `"Invalid ZIP"`, tells Excel to display the text `Invalid ZIP` for numbers greater than 99,999 but less than 10,000,000.

It's important to note that the custom ZIP code format shown in this example catches most, but not all errors a user might make in entering ZIP codes. It is still possible for a user to enter an invalid ZIP code, but using this custom format greatly reduces the number of errors which go undetected.

Just as the existing ZIP code special formats need a little expert help to make them more robust, the Social Security number special format needs a little help, too. As in the previous example, a good starting point is to consider the range of acceptable values for Social Security numbers:

▶ All Social Security numbers contain nine digits. Thus numbers larger than 999,999,999 must be invalid.

▶ Social Security numbers do not start with a zero, so numbers smaller than 100,000,000 must also be invalid.

Of course these two rules don't totally define the range of acceptable Social Security numbers, but they do provide us with rudimentary validation of acceptable values. Using these two rules, you can create the following improved Social Security number custom format:

```
[>999999999]"Invalid number";[<100000000]"Invalid number";000-00-0000
```

This new custom format rejects values above 999,999,999 or below 100,000,000 by displaying "Invalid number" in the cell. Values within the acceptable range are displayed using the regular Social Security number special format. Once again, a simple modification to one of Excel's special formats provides a much more capable and useful tool.

Now let's have a closer look at the steps you can use to create your own useful custom formats.

Creating Useful Formats

In the first parts of this chapter, you've seen how custom formats can be very useful as you develop Excel applications. This section concentrates on the fine details of actually creating your own custom formats. Even though Excel offers quite a few formatting options for creating your own custom formats, you'll find custom formats aren't all that difficult once you understand how the options are related.

Understanding the Options

At first, custom formats may almost seem impossible to understand. It almost appears as though they work differently every time you use them. In fact, however, there is a method to the seeming madness of custom number formats. Let's break custom number formats down into the basics to make the logic come a little clearer.

You'll recall from earlier in this chapter that custom number formats use the following general model:

```
positive number format; negative number format; zero format; text entry format
```

In fact, custom formats can have any combination of these four sections, but you don't have to specify more than the one section you need to define your custom format. If you don't specify all four sections, Excel uses the following rules to determine how the format specifications apply:

▶ If only a single section is specified, the same format is used for all numbers.

▶ If only two sections are specified, the first section is used to format both positive numbers and zero, and the second section is used to format negative numbers.

▶ If you want to skip a section, include a semicolon to indicate a blank specification. Numbers formatted with a blank specification will not be displayed in the worksheet, but will still be used in formulas.

▶ Text included as part of one of the number formats will display in the worksheet, but will not affect any calculations.

There are special formatting symbols for numbers, dates and times, and text. In some cases the formatting symbols are shared by each of these types of data. Let's have a closer look at the options available for each of these types of data.

Understanding the Number Format Options

The format options for numbers cane a little confusing until you really understand how they work. These options do provide considerable flexibility once you see how they fit together. Let's look at each option in turn.

If you want to display one type of numbers using Excel's default General format, enter the word "General" as the format specification for that type of number. This causes the numbers to be shown as integers, decimals, or in scientific format for numbers that are too wide to fit the column. For example, you might use the following format to display the word "Zip" in place of zero, while displaying all other numbers in General format:

```
General;General;"Zip"
```

You use a decimal point in the number format to indicate where you'd like a decimal point to appear in the number. The number and positioning of digits on either side of the decimal point are controlled by the three formatting symbols #, 0, and ? as follows:

▶ The pound sign (#) works as a wildcard symbol. If the number includes a digit in a position held in the format specification by a pound sign, the digit is displayed. If no digit occupies that position, the pound sign is ignored. This means that fractional values won't display a leading zero if a pound sign appears before the decimal point in the format specification. Trailing zeros to the right of the decimal point also are ignored. Finally, insignificant digits to the right of the decimal point are rounded if too few character positions were reserved by pound signs. For example, if you use ###.### as the format specification, the value .1234567 would appear as .123.

▸ Zero (0) functions as an absolute digit placeholder. If a value does not include a digit in a position where a zero appears in the format specification, a leading or trailing zero is included in the display. As with the pound sign, insignificant digits to the right of the decimal point are rounded if too few character positions were reserved by zeros. Using 000.0000 as the format, the value 12.3 would appear as 012.3000.

▸ The question mark (?) functions as an absolute digit placeholder very much like the zero, but does not display leading or trailing zeros (Excel's on-line documentation is incorrect regarding the display of leading or trailing zeros). The primary use of the question mark is to cause values with different numbers of digits to align based on the position of the decimal point. That is, if you format a column of numbers using the question mark, leading and trailing zeros will not be displayed, but all the decimal points will be aligned.

When combined with the forward slash (/), the formatting symbols display decimal values as fractions. All three formatting symbols work much the same when displaying fractions as they do when displaying decimal numbers. Leading zeros are displayed if you use the zero format symbol. The forward slash division symbols align in a column if you use the question mark formatting symbol.

Include a formatting symbol followed by a space and then the specification for the fractional display to display a value as an integer followed by a fraction. If you do not include the space, Excel will display the value as a fraction. For example, the value 1.25 will appear as 1 1/4 if the format specification is # ##/##, and will appear as 5/4 if the format specification is ##/##.

Use a comma in a format specification as a thousands separator. You also can use commas to scale numbers by thousands by including the comma as the last character in the format specification. Each comma that appears at the end of the format specification scales the display by an extra thousand. So for example, if you want to display a number that represents millions, add two commas to the end of the format specification.

Figure 2.3 shows examples of several of the custom numeric formats mentioned in this section. These examples should provide you with a clearer understanding of how the formatting options work.

Fig. 2.3

Custom number formats provide you with great control over the display of numbers.

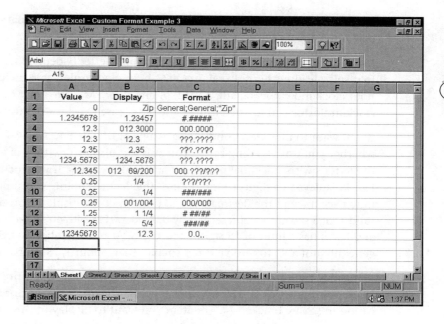

Understanding the Date and Time Format Options

Excel's custom format date and time options are fairly straightforward, although they do hold a few surprises that can cause you problems if you aren't aware of the traps. Let's have a closer look at these options.

The letter *m* is used to indicate both months and minutes. Excel determines whether you want months or minutes displayed by looking at any characters immediately before the m in the format specification. If the m follows the letter *h*, which is the format specification for hours, Excel displays minutes. Otherwise, Excel displays months. This does not mean that the h and the m must be adjacent, however. You can include spaces between the letters as long as no other characters appear between the h and the m.

A single letter *m* displays the number of either the month or the minute without a leading zero. Two m's in the format specification display the number of the month or the minute with a leading zero. Three or four m's display the three letter abbreviation or the complete month name, respectively.

The letter *d* indicates the day. Single and double d's display the number of the day of the month, without or with leading zeros. Three and four d's display the name of the day of the week, either as a three-character abbreviation, or completely spelled out.

You use the letter *y* to indicate the year, either as a two digit or four digit value, depending on whether you include two or four y's. Use a little caution with displaying years—remember that Excel can only correctly use years in the range of the year 1900 to the year 2078. While it is possible to edit a displayed date to show a year value outside this range, Excel no longer recognizes the result as a date. Any calculations you attempt to perform using an out-of-range date will return the #VALUE! error.

Hours are displayed by using a single or double letter *h*, depending on whether you want to display leading zeros. Excel uses a 24-hour clock unless you include one of the 12-hour clock indicators (a, am, A, AM, p, pm, P, or PM). The letter case of the 12-hour clock indicator you use determines the letter case Excel uses in the display.

If you want to include seconds, use a single or double letter *s*, again depending on whether you want leading zeros. You also can display fractions of a second by following the letter s with a decimal point and one to three zeros. If you include the decimal point, Excel displays two digits to the right of the decimal point. You shouldn't expect too much accuracy in the decimal second portion of the display, however, because a thousandth of a second is represented by 0.0000000115740740740741, the date serial number, and Excel has a limit of 15 significant digits. Also, remember that the clock in a PC is generally not able to resolve times smaller than about 1/18th of a second.

To display time as hours, minutes, or seconds, but without limiting the display to a 24-hour, 60-minute, or 60-second clock, enclose the hour, minute, or second format specification in square brackets []. The item you want to display in this format must be the first time format specified in the format specification. That is, if you want to display the total number of minutes, rather than hours and minutes, start the time format specification with [h].

Figure 2.4 shows several custom date and time format options.

Fig. 2.4

You can use date and time format options to display date serial numbers to fit your needs.

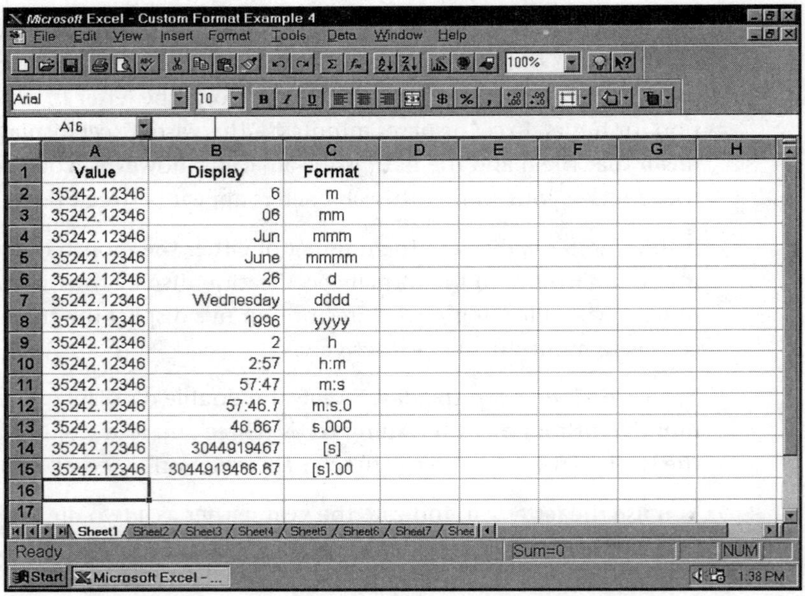

	A	B	C
1	Value	Display	Format
2	35242.12346	6	m
3	35242.12346	06	mm
4	35242.12346	Jun	mmm
5	35242.12346	June	mmmm
6	35242.12346	26	d
7	35242.12346	Wednesday	dddd
8	35242.12346	1996	yyyy
9	35242.12346	2	h
10	35242.12346	2:57	h:m
11	35242.12346	57:47	m:s
12	35242.12346	57:46.7	m:s.0
13	35242.12346	46.667	s.000
14	35242.12346	3044919467	[s]
15	35242.12346	3044919466.67	[s].00

Understanding the Text, Spacing, and Miscellaneous Format Options

Excel offers a real grab bag of various custom format options. These options enable you to include text, special characters, and spacing within a format specification. They also enable you to display numbers as percentages or in scientific format. Note that Excel's on-line documentation incorrectly identifies how many of the special characters are handled by the program. The correct information follows.

2

To include text characters in a format specification, enclose the characters in double quotation marks, as in #.##" Dollars". To include a single special character, you also can precede the character with a backslash (\), for example, #.##\:. Not all special characters require a backslash or quotation marks, however.

The special characters you can include in a format specification include these you can add without enclosing them in quotes or preceding with a backslash:

$ - + ( ) ! ^ & ' ' ~ { } = < > and space

These special characters must be preceded with a backslash (Excel automatically supplies a backslash for the right square bracket ( ])):

\ / : [ ] @ _

Although you can include a blank space in a format specification by simply pressing the spacebar, you may want to consider the slightly more complicated option of including an underscore followed by a character such as the right parenthesis. The reason you might want to use this option is that most Windows fonts are proportional fonts, rather than fixed pitch fonts. In a proportional font, different characters have different widths. By using an underscore followed by a character, you're telling Excel to leave exactly the amount of space required for the specified character rather than the room required for a space character. While the difference in the effect of these two options will be quite small, it may be noticeable, especially in the larger size fonts. If you do use the option of an underscore followed by a character, don't precede the underscore with a backslash, because that would display the underscore itself. For example, to leave a space equal to the width of a uppercase letter M to the right of the digits, you could use #.##_M.

If you include an asterisk in a format specification, the character following the asterisk will be repeated enough times to fill the column width. If the fill character precedes the numeric portion of the format specification, Excel leaves a space between the fill character and the number (unless the fill character is a dollar sign). If the fill character follows the numeric portion of the format specification, the fill character follows the number without adding any extra spaces (unless you include a space manually). You'll probably want to use fill characters in special cases such as check-writing applications to fill out the available space, preventing anyone from modifying the amount of the check. For example, use $**##.## to display a value with a leading dollar sign followed by asterisks, and then the value.

If you include a percent sign (%) in a format specification, the value will be displayed as a percent. That is, the value is multiplied by 100 and displayed with a percent sign. Unfortunately, Excel can become confused if you place the percent sign anywhere except after the 0s. #s. or ?s you use to specify the digits to display. In fact, Excel may place a backslash in front of the percent sign and display the percent sign as a text character if you place the percent sign at the beginning of the format specification. If you include more than one percent sign, Excel multiplies the value by 100 for each percent sign in the format specification, and displays multiple percent signs in the worksheet.

You can display numbers in scientific notation by including e+, e–, E+, or E– in the format specification. This option is most useful in connection with conditional formats, because you can specify that numbers larger (or smaller) than a specified value appear in scientific notation. Conditional formats will be discussed shortly.

Using Colors

One of the surest methods of making certain important values stand out is to display those values in a contrasting color. Of course this technique is most useful for values displayed on-screen rather than in a printed report (unless you can be certain the report will be printed on a color printer, and won't be faxed or photocopied on a monochrome machine).

To specify the color for a section of a format specification, include the name of the color within square brackets in that section. You can place the color specification anywhere within the format specification. Excel automatically moves the color specification to the beginning of the format specification when you close the Format Cells dialog box.

Certain colors serve to effectively hide the value contained in the cell. Specifying the color as white hides the value if the worksheet background is also white. This also prevents the value from appearing in a printed report, but does not prevent someone from viewing the value by selecting the cell.

You can specify colors by typing the name of the color, or by using a color number. Excel recognizes eight color names: black, cyan, magenta, white, blue, green, red, and yellow. Excel also recognizes colors specified as [color x], where x is a number between 1 and 56 (once again, the Excel on-line documentation contains an error in stating the color number can be 0 to 56). To determine the color represented by each number, click the Font tab of the Format Cells dialog box. Then click the down arrow of the drop-down Color list box to display the color palette (see fig. 2.5). The colors are numbered across the rows, starting at the upper-left corner, and dropping down to the left end of the next row as each row ends. Thus the second color in the second row, olive green, is color number 10.

Fig. 2.5

Use the color palette on the Font tab of the Format Cells dialog box to determine color numbers for custom formats.

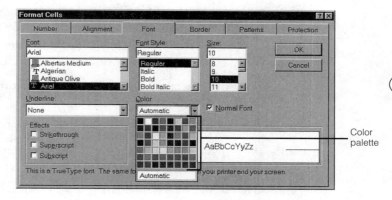

2

If you do not specify a color in a section of the format specification, Excel uses the default color for displaying values in the selected cell. Usually this means black, but can be any color you specify on the Font tab of the Format Cells dialog box.

As an example, suppose you want to display positive values using the default color, negative values in red, zero values as the blue text "ZERO," and text entries in yellow. The following format specification accomplishes this colorful feat:

```
##;[Red]##;[Blue]"ZERO";[Yellow]General
```

Of course, you can use any of the numeric formatting options covered earlier in this chapter to further control how the values are formatted. The color options do not conflict with any of the other formatting options, but rather simply enhance the display to make certain values stand out. Color options work particularly well with conditional formats, which are the subject of the next section.

Creating Conditional Formats

Conditional formats are custom formats that are based on simple formulas, rather than the standard format specification conditions. You can use one of six logical tests in designing a conditional format:

<	(less than)
<=	(less than or equal to)
=	(equal to)
>=	(greater than or equal to)
>	(greater than)
< >	(not equal)

To specify the conditional test for a section of the format specification, include the comparison value and the conditional operator within square brackets in that section. For example, if you want a particular format to apply to values over 5000, include the conditional test as [>5000]. You can only include one conditional test in a section.

You'll recall that the general model for format specifications has three sections for numeric formats and one section for text format:

```
positive number format; negative number format; zero format; text entry format
```

In a sense, the general model could also be specified using conditional tests as follows (although, as you'll soon see, this format specification is not valid):

```
[>0]positive number format;[<0]negative number format;[=0]zero format;
➥text entry format
```

It's important to remember that format specifications can include a maximum of three numeric sections, and these three sections must include formatting instructions for the complete range of numbers. This means you cannot actually include three conditional tests as shown in the previous example. If you were to specify three conditional tests, it would be possible that your format specification might exclude a range of values, leaving Excel with no way to determine how to format the excluded number range. Therefore, you can specify a maximum of two conditional tests, which can appear in the first and second but not in the third section of the format specification. Thus the following format specification is valid, while the earlier example is not:

```
[>0]positive number format; [<0]negative number format; zero format;
➥text entry format
```

When you specify conditional tests, values that meet the first test are formatted according to the first section of the format specification. If you only include one conditional test, Excel then formats negative numbers according to the second section of the format specification, and all remaining numbers according to the third section of the format specification. In the following format specification, numbers greater than 10 will appear in blue, negative numbers will appear in red, and values between 0 and 10 will appear in green:

```
[Blue][>10]##;[Red]##;[Green]##.0
```

If you include two conditional tests, numbers meeting one of those tests use the format specified in the appropriate section of the format specification, while all remaining values use the third section's format.

You can specify two conditional tests while only specifying two sections of the format specification. Although this possibility may seem to violate the rule that the entire range of numbers must have a format available, it does not, because Excel automatically adds a third section that specifies all remaining values will use the General format. Thus you can enter the following format specification:

```
[Blue][>10]##;[Red][<5]##.0
```

If you return to the Format Cells dialog box later, you'll find Excel has changed the format specification to:

```
[Blue][>10]##;[Red][<5]##.0;General
```

Assuming the default text color is black, this format specification displays numbers greater than 10 in blue, numbers less than 5 in red with one digit after the decimal point, and numbers between 5 and 10 in black. You may be slightly surprised to learn that zero appears as .0, displayed in red. This occurs because a zero value meets the second conditional test, which is that it is less than 5. It's important to remember this point, because conditional tests completely modify the normal behavior of format specifications. If you forget this, you may be surprised by the way your custom formats are applied.

You can further emphasize certain values by adding text to a conditional format specification section. One problem with doing so is the necessity of making certain the column width is wide enough to display the complete formatted value including the text. Of course, you can simply display a short text message in a bright, contrasting color rather than the numeric value. For example, suppose you are setting up a worksheet used to calculate the value of orders, and your company has a minimum order of $100. The following format specification would quickly bring sub-minimum orders to the user's attention:

```
[Red][<100]"Under $100";General
```

Once again, Excel will supply the second section of the format specification if you only specify the first section.

If you don't increase the column width, this format specification will display a string of red pound signs stretching across the cell for values under 100. If you do increase the column width, the message "Under $100" is displayed, also in red text, for values under 100. Either way, anyone using the worksheet should certainly see that something is wrong with the order value.

It's important to remember that custom formats simply change the appearance of the displayed data. It's up to you or the user of the worksheet to act on the information which is presented. If you need to make certain that data is valid, you'll have to apply more stringent controls, such as those discussed in Chapter 10, "Ensuring Quality Using Advanced Error Checking."

How Can Custom AutoFill Series Help Me?

No one likes to do extra work, especially if that work is repetitive and boring. Computers, of course, don't mind doing the same job over and over. You might say that doing boring, repetitive work is ideally suited to a computer's capabilities. That's one reason computers make such good tools. You can give them the work you don't want to do, and you'll never hear a complaint.

AutoFill series are lists of values or labels Excel enters automatically based on information you enter to start the list. In this section, you'll see how you can use custom AutoFill lists to increase your productivity while reducing errors—a great combination.

Entering Lists Automatically

Entering the same list of data, the names of months, an incrementing series of numbers, or any such type of list more than once is not only boring and repetitive, but it's also unnecessary and error-prone. It's unnecessary because Excel can automatically enter the values in a list for you, and it's error-prone because anyone can make a typing error, especially when typing in a long list of items.

Excel already knows how to create quite a few different types of AutoFill lists automatically. If you enter a 1 in one cell and a 2 in the next cell and then drag the AutoFill handle, Excel knows enough to fill in the balance of the range with incrementing numbers (3, 4, 5, and so on). If you enter day or month names, Excel fills the range with days or months. Excel can even correctly increment series which contain text and numbers combined, such as 1st Qtr, 2nd Qtr, and so on.

As useful as such incrementing lists may be, they only represent a small portion of the value of AutoFill series. Let's consider other ways you can use AutoFill series to make developing and using Excel applications easier.

Locations Simplified

Do you have a list of locations you must enter often, either while you are building an application or as you use an Excel worksheet? Perhaps you have a list of store locations such as the one shown in figure 2.6.

Retyping such a list each time you need the list is not only tedious, but chances are you'll mistype at least one of the names on the list. Imagine how much more work typing the list would be if it contained twenty, a hundred, or even a few hundred store locations.

Fig. 2.6

You can use an AutoFill series to enter frequently used lists.

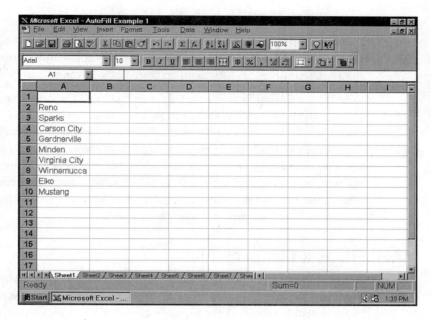

2

Using an AutoFill list isn't the only way to duplicate a long list of location names, of course. You could simply create the list, copy it to the Clipboard, and paste it where you need a new copy. If you only need a few copies of the list, you may even prefer this method, because it is the old familiar route. But lists you need to duplicate more often really do work very well as AutoFill lists. Here are a few reasons you'll want to work with AutoFill lists rather than the copy and paste method:

▶ New objects you copy to the Clipboard immediately replace the existing contents. As you're building or using an Excel worksheet, you'll probably find yourself using the Clipboard for many purposes. Unless you're very careful, you'll probably have to return to the source range to recopy your original list several times during a session.

▶ AutoFill lists remain available no matter how many times you restart your system. After you've created your list, it is immediately available for instant use without going back to the source range to make another Clipboard copy.

▶ Objects copied to the Clipboard use memory, which is only released when the Clipboard is cleared. While it's true a small list won't use too much memory, large AutoFill lists are much more memory efficient than copying large lists to the Clipboard.

▶ You can easily create several different AutoFill lists. To use different lists with the Clipboard copy and paste method, you'll have to continually be copying the currently needed list, rather than just entering the first item and dragging the AutoFill handle.

Names at Your Fingertips

If you only think of using custom AutoFill lists to enter location names, you're ignoring another type of list that is perfectly suited to this application. Lists of names, such as sales representatives or club members, can easily be made into custom AutoFill lists, too.

Consider the following scenario. You're in charge of the organization of a large meeting. Several different functions are planned, including lunches, dinners, seminars, and so on. You must keep track of each individual event, noting not only who will attend, but the amount they've paid, any special seating or meal requirements, and countless other details. You have a master list of all attendees, but you also have several specialized lists of organization officers, speakers, and other VIPs. Why not create custom AutoFill lists in advance for all these different needs? That way you'll be able to instantly and correctly enter those long lists with just a few keystrokes.

AutoFill as a Company Tool

Your uses for AutoFill probably aren't unique. It's likely that many people in your company need to enter the same types of information, and that a lot of time is wasted by different people repeating the same process. You can use custom AutoFill lists as a company productivity tool and make certain everyone has access to those lists. That way no one will have to type the same lists of information, typing errors will be reduced, and your Excel users will think you're a genius.

In most companies, many different people need to use the lists of district offices, store locations, regional warehouses, sales representatives, and so on. Why not create custom AutoFill lists that everyone can share?

Unfortunately, Excel doesn't provide a simple, straightforward method of sharing custom AutoFill lists among different users. In fact, one of the easiest ways of sharing custom AutoFill lists is to re-create those lists on each system. This may sound like an intensely laborious manual process, but fortunately that does not have to be the case. As you'll see in "Sharing AutoFill" later in this chapter, you can easily automate the entire process.

Timesaving Methods You Can Use

AutoFill lists are supposed to save you time, so why not save a bit more time in creating and sharing custom AutoFill lists? This section examines some time-saving methods you can use to reduce the time and effort needed to accomplish these tasks. Let's start by looking at ways you can easily create custom AutoFill lists using existing data. After you've created your lists, you will automate the process of sharing those lists.

Creating AutoFill Series from Lists

The standard method of creating a custom AutoFill list is to select Tools, Options, and enter the individual items in the List Entries box on the Custom Lists tab of the Options dialog box (see fig. 2.7). If you don't mind typing all the items for the list, this method works quite well as long as you don't make any typing errors.

Fig. 2.7

Enter the items for a custom AutoFill list in the List Entries box on the Custom Lists tab of the Options dialog box.

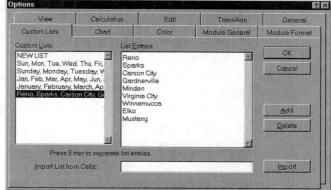

As you type the list items, press Enter after each item to move down the list. You can use any type of label for each item, except that you cannot start an item with a number. The order in which you enter the items determines the order Excel will use in filling in a range with your list. Remember, too, that if you select a fill range that has more or fewer cells than there are items in the list, Excel will use the items starting at the top of the list. If the selected fill range contains more cells than there are items in the list, Excel will use the entire list and then start over from the top of the list. If the selected fill range has fewer cells than the number of items in the list, Excel will use as much of the list as possible.

If you already have a list of items you would like to use as a custom AutoFill list, why bother going through all the work of retyping the list? Why not just use the existing list? Actually, using a list of items already in an Excel worksheet is quite easy. Before you select Tools, Options to display the Options dialog box, select the range of labels in the worksheet. After the Custom Lists tab of the Options dialog box is displayed, select Import to add the labels from the selected range to the Custom Lists box. Select OK to return to the worksheet.

Note

New custom AutoFill lists cannot be duplicates of existing custom AutoFill lists. Excel ignores empty cells at the end of a list, so it is not possible to create two custom AutoFill lists that only differ by having blank cells at the end of the list.

Your worksheet may not contain the nice, neat list of items you want to use to create your custom AutoFill list. Even so, there may still be methods you can use to quickly create just the list you need for this task. For example, suppose you have an Excel database containing sales figures for all of your store locations. Within your database, each store location is listed at least once, but several of the stores are listed numerous times, because they have made many sales. To create a listing of the store names containing one entry for each store so you can create your custom AutoFill list, you can use an *advanced filter*. By using the advanced filter, you can quickly create a list containing a single entry for each location regardless of the number of times a location appears in the database.

For more detailed information on using advanced filters, see Chapter 18, "Drilling Through the Data with Outlines and Filters."

Sharing AutoFill

Custom AutoFill lists can be even more useful when they're shared, but it isn't always clear how you can accomplish this. Because Excel doesn't provide a simple, straightforward method of sharing custom AutoFill lists, one of the easiest ways of sharing them is to re-create those lists on each system. This is not a difficult process, and you can easily automate the whole task with a simple VBA program. Don't worry if you haven't used VBA before; you'll find that this program is very easy to create and use.

Here's what you need to do:

1. In an Excel worksheet, create all the lists you'll want to distribute as custom AutoFill lists. This example uses the single set of nine labels shown in figure 2.6 to create a custom AutoFill list.

2. Choose Insert, Macro, Module to create a macro module page for your VBA program. Unlike some other spreadsheet programs, Excel macros are contained on separate macro module pages instead of on worksheet pages.

3. Enter the following VBA macro:

```
' CreateFill Macro
' Macro for creating custom AutoFill lists
'
Sub CreateFill()
        Application.AddCustomList ListArray:=Range("A2:A10")
End Sub
```

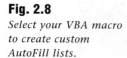

4. Click the worksheet tab to return to the worksheet (probably Sheet1) where you entered the list of labels. If you forget to return to the worksheet before running the macro, you will trigger a run-time error in the macro. This error isn't serious, but it does prevent the macro from executing.

5. Select <u>T</u>ools, <u>M</u>acro to display the Macro dialog box (see fig. 2.8). This dialog box lists all macros in the current workbook and any which are available in other open workbooks.

Fig. 2.8

*Select your VBA macro
to create custom
AutoFill lists.*

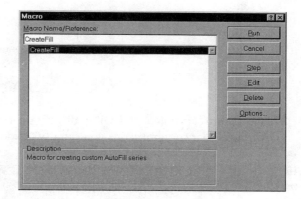

6. Select the CreateFill macro that you just created.

7. Select <u>R</u>un to execute the macro and create the custom AutoFill list.

Now that you have the basic VBA program, it's easy to see how you can expand the module to create an entire series of custom AutoFill lists. Simply duplicate the one command line in the macro,

```
Application.AddCustomList ListArray:=Range("A2:A10")
```

substituting the correct range definition for each of your custom AutoFill lists. For example, if you have a second list in cells B2:B20, add this line to the macro:

```
Application.AddCustomList ListArray:=Range("B2:B20")
```

Make certain you add any additional command lines between the `Sub CreateFill()` and `End Sub` lines.

Because you're creating the CreateFill macro as a tool for the distribution of AutoFill lists to the other Excel users in your company, you'll probably want to make it very easy for anyone to use the macro. One of the best ways to accomplish this is to add a macro button to the worksheet. When a user clicks the button, your custom AutoFill lists are quickly added to their system.

To add a macro button that runs the CreateFill macro, follow these steps:

1. Choose View, Toolbars to display the Toolbars dialog box (see fig. 2.9). You use this dialog box to control which Excel toolbars are displayed.

Fig. 2.9

Use the Toolbars dialog box to display the Forms toolbar.

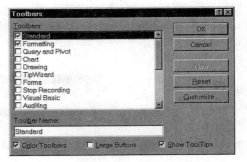

2. Select Forms and then click OK to display the Forms toolbar (see fig. 2.10). The Forms toolbar contains icons you can use to add controls to the worksheet.

Fig. 2.10

The Forms toolbar enables you to add controls to the worksheet.

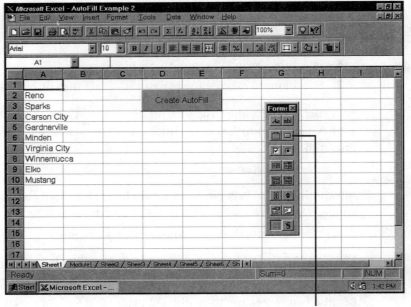

Create Button icon

3. Click the Create Button icon and then drag the mouse pointer across the location on the worksheet where you want to place the macro button. You'll want to make certain the macro button is large enough so you can add some descriptive text, but small enough to keep from covering up too much worksheet space. When you release the mouse button, Excel will display the Assign Macro dialog box.

4. Select the CreateFill macro and then click OK. This assigns your macro to the macro button, so clicking the new macro button will run the macro.

You'll probably want to edit the button label to display something more descriptive than the default Button 1 label. Right-click the button to access any of the button's properties, including the button label text. After you have selected the button label, type in your new label, such as **Create AutoFill**.

For more information on toolbars, see Chapter 3, "Creating Effective Toolbars." For more information on using VBA controls in your Excel applications, see Chapter 23, "Managing Dialogs in VBA" and Chapter 24, "Advanced Dialog Boxes."

Summary

Custom formats and AutoFill lists can save you considerable time and effort if you learn how to add them to your toolkit. Whether you develop Excel applications for yourself or other users, you'll find that these two features can do a lot more than you thought possible. Not only can you make data entry easier and less error-prone, but you can reduce the amount of time required to duplicate frequently entered lists. By using these two tools, you let your computer do the boring, repetitive tasks, giving you and the people who use your workbooks more time to do interesting and creative work.

chapter 3

Creating Effective Toolbars

3

by Brian Underdahl

In this chapter

◆ **Reasons to create toolbars**
Learn why you should consider creating your own toolbars if you want to increase your productivity in Excel.

◆ **Rolling your own**
Learn the methods you need to create effective toolbars.

◆ **Modifying toolbars**
See how you can edit the appearance of toolbars for a more custom look.

◆ **Saving and sharing toolbars**
You'll see how to save and even share your toolbars with other Excel users.

◆ **Using VBA**
For more complete control of your toolbars, learn how to use simple VBA programs.

You may not realize it, but toolbars like those in Excel 7 are major tools for increasing productivity and ease of use. Instead of working your way through a series of menu commands, you simply click a button to perform a task. If you've been using computers for a long enough time, you probably remember when programs were a lot harder to use than they are today. Before graphical user interfaces like Windows became the norm, you had to do everything by entering commands, or at least by selecting items from menus. We've come a long way from those primitive times with programs like Excel 7.

Excel's built-in toolbars are a good example of how far modern application programs have advanced in ease of use. Not only do they give you one-click access to commands, but you can customize them for even more utility. This chapter shows you how much you can do with Excel's toolbars.

Creating toolbars isn't just for application developers, either. Even if you're just an advanced Excel user who wants to make your own personal workbooks easier for you to use, you'll find there are good reasons to build your own toolbars.

Why Create Your Own Toolbars?

Excel's built-in toolbars are really handy, but because they were designed for the average Excel user, they're probably not a perfect fit for either you or the people who use your Excel workbooks. Fortunately, that's an easy problem to solve. You can easily create your own toolbars to work just the way you want. Once you see how handy custom toolbars can be, you'll probably create a whole series of specialized toolbars for different needs. In fact, if you develop applications for other Excel users, you'll soon see that custom toolbars may be some of the most effective elements in your developer toolbox.

Creating your own Excel toolbars is easy. Sure, you can make the task as complex as you want, but when you consider how simple the job can be, there's little reason not to have just the arrangement you want. Let's look at some of the benefits of learning how to create and use your own toolbars.

Automation Made Easy

If you develop Excel applications, you probably use VBA to automate certain tasks. This automation certainly makes your worksheets easier to use, but it can add some complications, too. If users aren't familiar with your program, they may not understand how to run the macros, or even how to perform other simple tasks. This can be especially true if the users are unfamiliar with Excel, because even Excel's menu system can be intimidating to the casual user.

One solution to this is to attach your VBA code to toolbar buttons. With a simple click anyone can run your program. You can even customize the appearance of the toolbar buttons so your users will be able to find the correct buttons easily.

Most applications have multiple processes that may be good candidates for automation. If you design a database application, you may want to have separate program routines for adding new records, finding and editing existing records, printing mailing labels, and generating reports about the people in the database. While you could simply make users employ the standard Excel menus to select and run your macros, your application wouldn't be very easy to use. Nor would it have a very professional appearance.

You could enhance the program by assigning macros to hot keys, but even that isn't the best solution, because your users can easily forget the exact keystrokes necessary to run each macro module. Even if you add your macro to Excel's menus, you'll still probably end up answering more support questions than you would like.

An even better idea is to use a team approach to activating macros. Designate the hot keys your diehard keyboard fans want, but also provide custom toolbar buttons. You may even want to use a three-pronged approach by including a custom menu selection that executes your macro code. That way you'll provide the options that best suit the working style of each of the users. Of course, this is exactly the approach Excel itself uses to provide maximum flexibility. If you do the same, your applications will appear to be a part of Excel rather than simply an Excel workbook.

You'll find much more information on adding your own items to Excel's menus in chapter 26, "Custom Menus."

Even if you aren't creating a fully automated Excel application, you'll find there are still plenty of good reasons for creating your own toolbars. Let's look at another of the advantages of creating your own toolbars.

Tools Ready to Use

One problem you may encounter with Excel's toolbars is that they're simply *too* useful. That is, you can do so much with a single click, that there simply isn't room for every possible toolbar button to appear at the same time. Excel partially works around this embarrassment of riches by dynamically swapping to the appropriate toolbar as the Excel environment changes. Thus, the standard Excel toolbar doesn't have to contain the buttons you use when you're debugging a macro, for example. As you move from task to task within Excel, different toolbars containing new tools replace the normal toolbar.

But even this approach falls short, because Excel has too many tools to fit the toolbars. In fact, each of the normal Excel toolbars really represents a compromise. Microsoft selected the tools they thought would be the most popular for each of the thirteen standard toolbars. While this one-size-fits-all approach represents a good starting point, anyone who's ever tried to wear one-size-fits-all clothing knows that some custom fitting can really improve the final product.

Just as you probably make slightly different food selections in a restaurant than I would, you probably have slightly different preferences when it comes to selecting which of Excel's tools you want to have immediately available at a mouse click. Indeed, the whole concept of having your own set of Excel's tools ready to click and use is one of the best arguments in favor of creating your own toolbars. Imagine how much more useful the toolbars might be if you could simply click one button to insert a new row or add a new worksheet to the workbook. There are well over 200 such useful tool buttons you can add to your toolbars to help you create exactly the mix of tools you want.

In discussing tool button toolkits we've considered the usefulness of creating toolbars for your own use, but you may find custom toolbars even more useful if you are supporting an Excel application designed for other users. Think of how much easier it is to tell a user to click the "insert a blank row" button than to explain the menu selection Insert, Row. Now, imagine how much more useful some of the other toolbar buttons may be to the inexperienced and intimidated user. Not all commands are as easy as Insert, Row! Can you even think of the steps necessary to do a task such as selecting only the visible cells in a selection? Even if you can remember how to do this task, how many times would you have to repeat yourself, or even start over from the beginning, if you were trying to explain the procedure to someone? It really is a lot easier to simply tell someone to click the appropriate toolbar button, isn't it?

You can use custom toolbars to place just the right set of shortcuts at the ready. Whether you are creating toolbars for your own use, or creating toolbars that will make supporting your applications easier, you'll find a great selection of tools ready to use. In fact, even if you only use the toolbar buttons supplied with Excel and never add your own macros to custom toolbar buttons, you'll probably find just the buttons you need. If you don't, that's okay, too. In the section "Adding Custom Buttons" later in this chapter, you'll see how easy it is to program your own toolbar buttons.

Creating Toolbars the Easy Way

Excel's toolbars are fully customizable. You can add buttons to or remove buttons from any of the standard Excel toolbars. You can also create your own completely new toolbars. You can move toolbars around, change their shapes and sizes, and even allow them to float anywhere within your worksheets rather than being docked at the top of the Excel window. For example, in figure 3.1 the Formatting toolbar is no longer docked below the Standard toolbar, but is floating in the worksheet.

 Tip

If you need to see more than the normal number of worksheet rows but don't want to give up your toolbars, undock the toolbars and allow them to float in the worksheet. You can move the toolbars around as necessary to uncover portions of the worksheet.

Fig. 3.1

You can dock toolbars at the top or bottom (and sometimes the sides) of the Excel window, or float them in the worksheet.

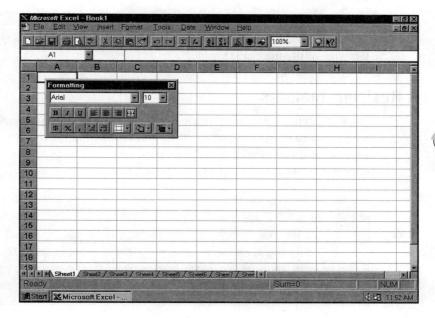

Moving Toolbars

To move toolbars, you simply point to a blank space on the toolbar and drag the toolbar to its new location. As you drag the toolbar, Excel displays a gray outline showing the current shape and location of the toolbar. Notice that the shape of the toolbar changes as the toolbar is undocked from the top of the screen. As you drag the toolbar down over the worksheet, the toolbar becomes more compact as the buttons form multiple rows in the toolbar.

Floating toolbars remain in the same position as you move from sheet to sheet in a workbook. If a floating toolbar appears at the upper-left corner of the worksheet area as shown in figure 3.1, it will stay in the upper-left corner of the worksheet area as you scroll to different columns or rows, or as you move to other sheets in the workbook.

Docked toolbars generally appear in rows starting immediately below the left edge of the menu bar, and just above the input line. Although docked toolbars always appear between the menu bar and the input line, there's no rule that says they must appear in rows starting at the left edge of the Excel window. You can place two or more toolbars on the same row, or even place a toolbar some distance from the left edge of the window. Of course, placing multiple toolbars on the same row often isn't practical, because the second toolbar may disappear off the right edge of the window. Docked toolbars cannot be placed so they disappear off the left edge of the window. If you drag a docked toolbar left of the left edge of the Excel window, Excel will automatically move the toolbar so the left edge of the toolbar is visible.

Resizing Toolbars

Docked toolbars expand to fit the buttons and other controls (such as the font selection box) you add to the toolbar. Docked toolbars use a single row for all controls on the toolbar, so if you attempt to add too many controls to a toolbar, it's quite easy to create a docked toolbar that disappears off the right edge of the window.

 Tip
You can change the width of some toolbar controls, such as the font selection box, by dragging the edge of the control while the Customize toolbar dialog box is displayed. This enables you to change the width of custom toolbars to less than the normal minimum size.

Floating toolbars are more flexible than docked toolbars. The controls on floating toolbars can be arranged in multiple rows, making the toolbar more compact so it covers fewer columns in the worksheet. You can also resize floating toolbars to make them better fit your needs. Simply drag any edge of a floating toolbar to change the shape to a taller and narrower size, or a wider and shorter one. You cannot reduce the width of a floating toolbar beyond the minimum necessary to display the widest control on the toolbar, however. If the floating toolbar contains only buttons, you can reduce the width enough so a single column of buttons is displayed on the toolbar. If the toolbar contains other controls, such as the font selection box on the Formatting toolbar, the width of the widest control determines how narrow the toolbar can be.

Using Standard Buttons and Controls

Excel has nearly 200 standard toolbar buttons you can use on your custom toolbars. These buttons are ready to use; all you need to do is add them to a toolbar and they're ready to perform their preprogrammed tasks. This collection of buttons includes all of the buttons you'll find on the standard toolbars, plus many other useful buttons. Table 3.1 shows all of the standard toolbar buttons, along with their button VBA ID value. You use the VBA ID value to control toolbar buttons with VBA, a topic covered later in this chapter.

Table 3.1   Excel's Standard Toolbar Buttons

Button	Name	VBA ID
	Open	1
	Save	2
	Print	3
	Print Preview	4
	Set Print Area	5
	New Workbook	9
	Insert Worksheet	7
	Insert Chart Sheet	8
	Insert Module	190
	Insert MS Excel 4.0 Macro	6
	Insert Dialog	245
	Find File	177
	Routing Slip	162
	Send Mail	163
	Update File	164
	Toggle Read Only	165
	Undo	10
	Repeat	11

continues

Table 3.1   Continued

Button	Name	VBA ID
	Cut	12
	Copy	13
	Paste	14
	Clear Contents	15
	Clear Formats	16
	Paste Formats	17
	Paste Values	18
	Format Painter	185
	Delete	19
	Delete Row	20
	Delete Column	21
	Insert	22
	Insert Row	23
	Insert Column	24
	Fill Right	25
	Fill Down	26
	Equals Sign	27
	Plus Sign	28
	Minus Sign	29

Button	Name	VBA ID
"*"	Multiplication Sign	30
"/"	Division Sign	31
"^"	Exponentiation Sign	32
"("	Left Parenthesis	33
")"	Right Parenthesis	34
":"	Colon	35
","	Comma	36
"%"	Percent Sign	37
"$"	Dollar Sign	38
Σ	AutoSum	39
f_x	Function Wizard	40
=ab	Paste Names	41
	Constrain Numeric	42
	Outline Border	43
	Left Border	44
	Right Border	45
	Top Border	46
	Bottom Border	47
	Bottom Double Border	48

continues

Table 3.1   Continued

Button	Name	VBA ID
	Dark Shading	49
	Light Shading	50
	AutoFormat	52
	Currency Style	53
	Percent Style	54
	Comma Style	55
	Increase Decimal	56
	Decrease Decimal	57
	Bold	58
	Italic	59
	Underline	60
	Double Underline	176
	Strikethrough	61
	Cycle Font Color	62
	Align Left	63
	Center	64
	Align Right	65
	Justify Align	66
	Center Across Columns	67

Button	Name	VBA ID
	Increase Font Size	71
	Decrease Font Size	72
	Vertical Text	73
	Rotate Text Up	74
	Rotate Text Down	75
	Line	76
	Arrow	77
	Freehand	78
	Text Box	79
	Create Button	80
	Selection	81
	Drawing Selection	184
	Reshape	82
	Rectangle	83
	Ellipse	84
	Arc	85
	Polygon	86
	Freeform	87
	Filled Rectangle	88

continues

Table 3.1   Continued

Button	Name	VBA ID
	Filled Ellipse	89
	Filled Arc	90
	Filled Polygon	91
	Filled Freeform	92
	Group Objects	93
	Ungroup Objects	94
	Bring to Front	95
	Send to Back	96
	Drop Shadow	51
	Drawing	240
	Map	246
	Record Macro	98
	Stop Macro	99
	Run Macro	100
	Step Macro	101
	Resume Macro	102
	Menu Editor	192
	Object Browser	191
	Toggle Breakpoint	193

Button	Name	VBA ID
	Instant Watch	194
	Step Into	195
	Step Over	196
	Area Chart AutoFormat	103
	Bar Chart AutoFormat	104
	Column Chart AutoFormat	105
	Stacked Column Chart AutoFormat	106
	Line Chart AutoFormat	107
	Pie Chart AutoFormat	108
	3-D Area Chart AutoFormat	109
	3-D Bar Chart AutoFormat	110
	3-D Column Chart AutoFormat	111
	3-D Perspective Column Chart AutoFormat	112
	3-D Line Chart AutoFormat	113
	3-D Pie Chart AutoFormat	114
	XY (Scatter) Chart AutoFormat	115
	3-D Surface Chart AutoFormat	116
	Radar Chart AutoFormat	117
	Line/Column Chart AutoFormat	118

continues

Table 3.1 Continued

Button	Name	VBA ID
	Volume/High-Low-Close Chart AutoFormat	119
	Doughnut Chart AutoFormat	145
	Default Chart	120
	ChartWizard	121
	Vertical Gridlines	123
	Horizontal Gridlines	122
	Legend	124
	Camera	125
	Calculate Now	126
	Spelling	127
	Help	128
	Help Topics	248
	Show Outline Symbols	131
	Select Visible Cells	132
	Select Current Region	133
	Sort Ascending	134
	Sort Descending	135
	Lock Cell	136
	Freeze Panes	137

Button	Name	VBA ID
	Zoom In	138
	Zoom Out	139
	Microsoft Word	202
	Microsoft PowerPoint	204
	Microsoft Access	216
	Microsoft FoxPro	160
	Microsoft Project	205
	Microsoft Schedule+	227
	Microsoft Mail	203
	Full Screen	241
	PivotTable Wizard	167
	PivotTable Field	171
	Refresh Data	170
	Ungroup	129
	Group	130
	Show Pages	172
	Show Detail	173
	Hide Detail	175
	AutoFilter	168

continues

Table 3.1 Continued

Button	Name	VBA ID
	TipWizard	179
	Remove Dependent Arrows	147
	Trace Dependents	148
	Remove Precedent Arrows	149
	Trace Precedents	242
	Remove All Arrows	153
	Trace Error	174
	Attach Note	154
	Show Info Window	243
	Check Box	140
	Option Button	141
	Edit Box	142
	Label	199
	Group Box	181
	Scroll Bar	143
	Spinner	183
	List Box	144
	Drop-Down	182
	Combination List-Edit	188

Button	Name	VBA ID
	Combination Drop-Down Edit	197
	Control Properties	238
	Edit Code	244
	Toggle Grid	239
	Tab Order	186
	Run Dialog	187

3

When most people think of Excel's toolbars, they think of the buttons, but they often forget that toolbars can contain several types of controls besides buttons. The twelve items in table 3.2 are not buttons, but they are controls you can use on your custom toolbars. All items you can add to a toolbar, including buttons, are really toolbar controls. You can use either the specific control name or the more generic term *control* when referring to them.

Table 3.2 Additional Toolbar Controls

Control Value	Name	VBA ID
	Color	233
	Pattern	232
	Shape	235
	Borders	198
	Font Color	236
	Chart Type	234
Normal	Style	70

continues

Table 3.2 Continued

Control Value	Name	VBA ID
100% ▾	Zoom Control	189
Arial ▾	Font	68
10 ▾	Font Size	69
▾	Scenarios	166
30) You can delete more than one shee▲ CTRL while you click the sheet tabs, an▾	TipWizard Box	178

As you can see, between the standard buttons and controls you can use on your toolbars, you have quite a range of options. In most cases, you'll probably build your toolbars manually, but as you'll learn later in "Controlling Toolbars Using VBA," you can also create and modify toolbars using VBA. When you use VBA to control toolbars, you must use the correct VBA ID values shown in tables 3.1 and 3.2.

Incidentally, you can determine the names and VBA ID numbers for the buttons and other controls on toolbars using the simple VBA program shown in listing 3.1.

Listing 3.1 A VBA Program to Determine Toolbar Control Names and IDs

```
'Make a table of toolbar button names and VBA ID #s
Sub ShowButtonNames()
'Make Sheet1 the active worksheet
    Worksheets(1).Activate

'Place toolbar name in cell A1
'Replace 14 with the correct toolbar number
        Cells(1, 1) = Toolbars(14).Name

'Start placing button names in cell A2, and VBA ID #s in B2
        For row_num = 2 To Toolbars(14).ToolbarButtons.Count + 1
            Cells(row_num, 1) = Toolbars(14).ToolbarButtons(row_num - 1).Name
            Cells(row_num, 2) = Toolbars(14).ToolbarButtons(row_num - 1).Id
        Next

End Sub
```

To determine the correct toolbar number for the toolbar you want to examine (14 in listing 3.1), select View, Toolbars to display the Toolbars dialog box (see fig. 3.2). The toolbar number is indicated by the toolbar's position in the Toolbars list box, starting with 1 for the toolbar listed at the top of the list box.

Fig. 3.2

Determine the toolbar number by counting down from the top of the Toolbars list box.

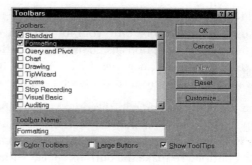

3

Tip

Right-click a toolbar and select Toolbars to quickly display the Toolbars dialog box.

You also use the Toolbars dialog box to create your own custom toolbars. To create a new toolbar, enter the name for your toolbar in the Toolbar Name text box and then select New. Make certain you have entered the correct name before you select New, because Excel does not allow you to rename a toolbar after it has been created. When you select New, Excel will display an empty toolbar and the Customize dialog box as shown in figure 3.3.

Fig. 3.3

After you select New, Excel displays your empty, new toolbar, ready for you to add buttons and other controls.

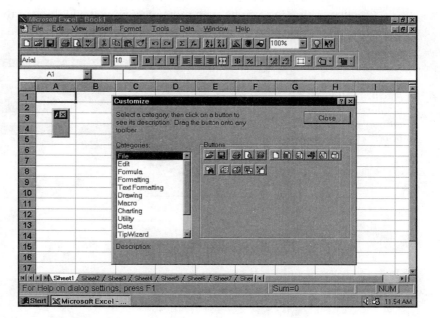

To add buttons or other toolbar controls to your toolbar, drag the button or control from the Customize dialog box onto your toolbar. You can select buttons and controls from any combination of options listed in the Categories list box. If you want to use buttons from several different categories, that's just fine. In fact, you'll probably find the buttons you want to use are spread throughout a number of categories.

As you drag buttons and controls onto your toolbar, consider how you want the toolbar to appear. To leave a gap between buttons, such as the one between the Save and Print buttons on Excel's Standard toolbar, drop the second button when it is not overlapping the first button. To make the buttons appear without any gaps, drop the second button when it is slightly overlapping the first button. Excel automatically aligns the buttons in level rows, so you need not worry whether you're dropping the button a bit too high or too low. Also, Excel automatically expands the toolbar to accommodate as many buttons and controls as you like.

Although it may be tempting to place all buttons on the toolbar without any gaps—because this usually makes the toolbar take up less space—doing so can also cause a problem. If you adjust the size of a toolbar so the toolbar is taller and narrower, Excel breaks the rows at gaps between buttons and controls. If you have a series of buttons arranged in a long row without gaps, Excel tries to keep them together when resizing the toolbar. The effect can be a toolbar such as the one in figure 3.4. All of the buttons on this toolbar except the final button were placed without any gaps. When the toolbar is resized, Excel uses three rows, rather than the two rows you might expect, to display the toolbar. This effect can be even more severe if you add some of the toolbar controls listed in table 3.2, because these controls are all wider than the buttons.

Fig. 3.4

Be careful when placing controls on toolbars to prevent unusual spacing, as in this example.

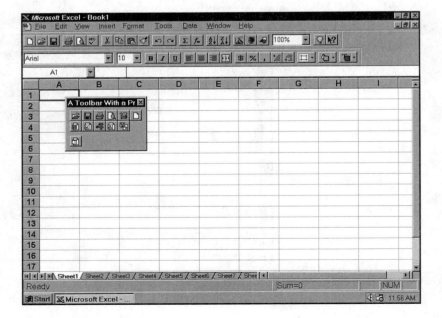

> ⚛ **Tip**
> If you're having problems spacing controls as you would like, add a wide control, such as the Style box to the toolbar. Drag the edge of the toolbar to resize the toolbar, leaving a gap where you can more easily add controls. When you finish adding the controls you want on the toolbar, remove the control you added for spacing.

3

If you encounter a problem such as that shown in figure 3.4 with the appearance of a toolbar, or if you just decide to further modify a toolbar, right-click the toolbar and select Customize. If the toolbar you want to modify isn't currently being displayed, you can select View, Toolbars to display the Toolbars dialog box. Select the toolbar you want to modify and then select Customize. You can then add controls to or remove controls from the toolbar as you like. To remove a control from a toolbar, drag the control off the toolbar. To add a gap between controls, drag the control on the right of the new gap to the right. In some cases this may not produce quite the desired effect, especially if dropping the control causes a different set of controls to stick together. You may find it easier to drop controls off the toolbar and then re-add them. Try resizing the toolbar to a taller and narrower size to give you more room to place the controls as you prefer. You can always resize the toolbar when you're finished to get the size you want. Excel saves the shape and size of toolbars so they have the same shape and size when you later redisplay the toolbar.

Adding Custom Buttons

Even though you have over 200 standard controls you can add to your toolbars, you aren't limited to using those standard controls. The Customize dialog box includes another category of buttons, the custom buttons shown in figure 3.5.

Fig. 3.5

You can add any of the custom buttons to your toolbars to perform tasks not covered by the standard buttons.

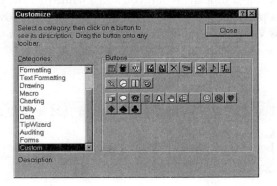

The custom buttons differ from the standard buttons in several ways. Custom buttons do not have any pre-assigned functions; instead they are used to execute macro code you assign to the button. This also means you must add custom buttons to a toolbar using a slightly more complex procedure than is required for a standard button. When you add a custom button, you must specify the macro you want Excel to execute when the button is clicked. After you drag a custom button onto your toolbar, Excel displays the Assign Macro dialog box (see fig. 3.6). Select the macro you want to execute and then select OK to confirm your selection and complete the addition of the button to your toolbar.

Fig. 3.6

When you add any of the custom buttons to your toolbars, you must specify the macro to execute.

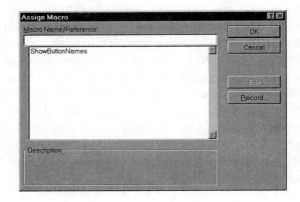

Besides the procedure changes necessary to add custom buttons to a toolbar, you'll find there's another important difference between custom and standard toolbar buttons— custom buttons don't automatically display any useful ToolTip help when you move the mouse pointer over the button. Instead, the ToolTip pop-up box displays the word "Custom" to indicate that the button is a custom button.

Fortunately, there is an easy VBA solution to this problem. Listing 3.2 shows a simple VBA routine that adds the name "Show button names" to a custom button that was added to a toolbar. When you add a name to a custom toolbar button, the name appears as a pop-up ToolTip when the mouse pointer is moved over the button. You could add this VBA macro to the Auto_Open macro, or call it from a VBA macro that displays your custom toolbar. See "Controlling Toolbars Using VBA" later in this chapter for more details on this subject.

Listing 3.2   A Simple VBA Macro that Names a Custom Toolbar Button

```
Sub Nameit()
Toolbars(15).ToolbarButtons(15).Name = "Show button names"
End Sub
```

Tip
You can also refer to a toolbar by name in a VBA macro. Simply replace the toolbar number with the name in quotation marks, such as Toolbars("Standard").

Of course, the simple macro in listing 3.2 is almost too simple to be of much use. For one thing, you must not only know the toolbar number, but you must also know the correct button number for this macro to execute properly. Determining the correct button number may be a little tricky, because Excel includes the gaps between controls in the count of controls on a toolbar. Thus, the thirteenth button on a toolbar may actually be control number fifteen if there are two gaps between buttons before the thirteenth button. If your macro refuses to execute properly, look for a button numbering problem.

Caution
Consider the effects of any macros you assign to custom toolbar buttons. Don't forget that a single click is all it takes to execute the macro. If you have a potentially destructive macro, it probably would be wise to make executing the macro more difficult than clicking a button.

Editing Tool Faces

You may find that the existing buttons just don't have the right appearance to convey the proper function of the macros you attach to those buttons. If so, don't let that stop you from creating custom buttons on your toolbars. If you've always thought you could be the next Picasso, Excel's toolbar buttons can provide you a palette! Before you get carried away, though, realize that you'll be working with a very small and limited palette.

Toolbar buttons come in two sizes. The size you see depends on whether the Large Buttons check box in the Toolbars dialog box is selected (refer to fig. 3.2). If the Large Buttons check box is selected, toolbar buttons are 24 pixels wide by 23 pixels high. If the check box is not selected, toolbar buttons are 16 pixels wide by 15 pixels high. *Pixels* are "picture elements"—the smallest points that can be displayed on your screen. By contrast, a standard VGA screen is 640 pixels wide by 480 pixels high. Super VGA may be 800 by 600, 1024 by 768, or even 1280 by 1024.

You have your choice from a palette of 16 colors for any pixel on a button's face. While this may not seem like much, especially if you have a true color display, remember that the small size buttons have only 240 pixels, and even the large buttons have only a total of 552 pixels. Even if you were allowed to use a larger number of colors, you wouldn't really have much room to display them on the face of your buttons.

Creating and Modifying Toolbar Buttons

You can create toolbar buttons from scratch or start with one of the existing button faces. Either way, you'll find that the process is fairly simple. Let's examine the process of modifying one of the custom button faces to better represent a macro you've attached to the button.

To make any changes to a toolbar or the controls contained on the toolbar, you must first display the toolbar and then place the toolbar into customize mode. Although you can use the keyboard to place a toolbar into customize mode (View, Toolbars, Customize), you must use the mouse to modify the face of a button. To place a toolbar into customize mode with the mouse, right-click the toolbar and select Customize. Next, right-click the button (on your custom toolbar) you want to modify and select Edit Button Image to display the Button Editor dialog box (see fig. 3.7).

Fig. 3.7

Use the Button Editor dialog box to modify or create your own toolbar buttons.

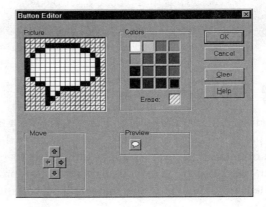

The drawing controls in the Button Editor dialog box are very simple. To change the color of a pixel, select the color you want from the Colors palette, and then click the pixel you want to change. To change a series of pixels to the same color, drag the mouse pointer across the pixels. To start fresh, click the Clear button to remove all color from the picture.

Button faces are drawn on a transparent background. Any pixels that show diagonal stripes are transparent, and will allow the normal background color (usually gray) to show through. If the picture has transparent pixels along an entire row or column at the edge of the picture, you can use the Move arrows to move the entire picture in the direction of the arrow.

When you're editing a button, it's easy to forget how small toolbar buttons really are. The Preview box shows how the button will appear in its actual size, so remember to examine the Preview box as you work. Details that can easily be seen in the Picture box may almost totally disappear when the button is viewed actual size. In particular, it's probably not a good idea to attempt to include text on the face of a toolbar button, because it is unlikely most users would be able to actually read the resulting tiny letters.

When you finish creating your button masterpiece, click OK to save the new button face.

Importing Images

Sometimes it seems like it's just not possible to draw exactly the right face for a custom toolbar button. The Button Editor offers a pretty small and limited palette, and you just may not be able to come up with the effect you desire. One easy solution to this is to import an image and use the imported image as the basis for your new button face.

You can use any graphic image you like as the basis for a new button face. Simply copy the image to the Clipboard, and you'll be able to paste that image onto the button face. Of course, things aren't always as simple as they seem at first glance, and using imported graphics images as toolbar button faces is no exception.

When you import a graphic image, the imported image must fit the limited drawing palette available in the Button Editor. As you'll recall, this means the imported image must fit into either a 16 by 15 or 24 by 23 pixel space, depending on whether you choose to display standard or large toolbar buttons. If you attempt to import a larger image, Excel will shrink the image to fit the available space. Not only that, but Excel also reduces the number of colors to a maximum of 16. These limitations mean that most types of imported graphics images are useless as button faces.

Just because most imported images are useless for button faces, doesn't mean you can't successfully use imported images as the basis for your custom toolbar buttons. There is a ready source of several hundred images in just the right format just waiting for you—the other Excel toolbar buttons. You can borrow the face of any Excel toolbar button and use it as the basis for your custom buttons. You'll want to modify the copied image to prevent confusion, of course, but at least you'll have a good starting point.

To use an existing button face as the starting point for a custom button, you'll need to follow a few simple steps:

1. The toolbars must be in customize mode before you can copy an image from the face of a button. Use <u>V</u>iew, <u>T</u>oolbars, <u>C</u>ustomize, or right-click the toolbar and select Customize to place the toolbars in customize mode.

2. The button whose face you want to copy must appear on a toolbar; you cannot use the face of a button that only appears in the Customize dialog box. If necessary,

drag the button onto your toolbar temporarily to allow you to copy the button's face. You can remove the extra button after you've copied the image.

3. Right-click the button whose face you want to copy, and select Copy Button Image. This places the image of the face of the button on the Clipboard.

4. Right-click your custom button and select Paste Button Image. This replaces the existing image with the image from the Clipboard.

5. Right-click your custom button again and select Edit Button Image to activate the Button Editor dialog box. You can now modify the pasted image to suit your needs.

If you decide you'd rather return to the original button face, use the Reset Button Image selection on the right-click button property menu.

Copying the image from another button only copies the face. None of the source button's function is copied along with the image. Because of this, you'll want to make certain you modify the image enough to prevent confusion. You wouldn't want a user to select a button that deleted all existing data because they thought the button saved the workbook.

Saving and Sharing Toolbars

Customized toolbars wouldn't be very useful if you had to re-create the toolbar every time you or someone else wanted to use the toolbar. Fortunately, that's not the case. In this section we'll look at how Excel saves your custom toolbars, how you can make certain a specially designed toolbar stays with a workbook, and how to have more than one toolbar configuration. We'll also make note of some problems you can inadvertently cause by customizing your toolbars, and see how you can avoid the problems.

Saving Toolbars

Excel automatically saves the current toolbar configuration when you exit from the program, and then restores the same configuration the next time you load Excel. In past versions of Excel, the toolbar configuration was saved in a file named EXCEL.XLB that was stored in the Windows program directory.

Excel 7 for Windows 95 also stores the current configuration in an XLB file in the Windows program directory, but there's a subtle difference in the current program version. Instead of naming the file EXCEL.XLB, Excel 7 for Windows 95 names the file with your user name and adds the XLB extension. There's an important reason for this difference—Windows 95 allows more than one user to log into a single PC, and each user's settings and preferences are automatically restored when the system recognizes the login. Excel 7 for Windows 95 is simply following the Windows 95 standard of allowing users each to have their own set of system preferences without requiring them to manually restore those settings whenever they use the system.

Because Excel 7 for Windows 95 saves your toolbar settings in a file that has your user name, you can easily create and save as many different toolbar configurations as you like. There are two ways to accomplish this, each with its own advantages and drawbacks. You can rename the XLB file in the Windows program directory and create several different copies, each with different configurations, or you can create multiple Windows 95 logons, each with its own configuration. Let's consider some of the advantages and disadvantages of each approach:

▶ Renaming the XLB file is the fastest method of changing Excel's toolbar configuration. Simply restart Excel to use the XLB file that has your user name.

▶ Renaming XLB files may be confusing to users, and is probably not a good choice if you want to minimize the amount of support you'll need to provide.

▶ Multiple Windows 95 logons enable you to change much more than a few Excel settings. You can also change many other Windows 95 settings by simply logging on as a different user.

▶ Multiple logons close all applications prior to logging you on as a different user. This may be inconvenient if all you really want to do is change your Excel toolbar configuration.

Sharing Your Toolbars

You might think that saving your custom toolbars would be enough, but simply saving your toolbars does nothing to allow them to be shared. When you consider how Excel 7 for Windows 95 saves your toolbar settings in a file with your user name, however, this should come as no surprise. If you want to share custom toolbars, you must make a special effort to do so.

You share custom toolbars by attaching them to a workbook. You cannot share toolbars unless you also share the workbook. Custom toolbars can only be attached to a workbook that has a macro module, which isn't a problem if you're working in the workbook you used to create any custom toolbar buttons. If the workbook you're using does not contain a macro module, you'll have to first add one. Use the command Insert, Macro, Module if you need to add a macro module to the workbook.

After you have added a macro module to the workbook, switch to the macro module by selecting the macro module page tab. This won't be necessary if you attach your custom toolbars to the workbook immediately after adding the macro module, because Excel automatically switches to the macro module when you create it. You can only attach toolbars when a macro module is the active workbook page.

Select Tools, Attach Toolbars to display the Attach Toolbars dialog box (see fig. 3.8).

Fig. 3.8

Use the Attach Toolbars dialog box to attach custom toolbars to an Excel workbook.

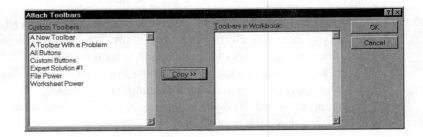

In the Custom Toolbars list box, select the toolbars you want to attach to the workbook and click the Copy button to place the selected toolbars in the Toolbars in Workbook list box. If you accidentally place a toolbar in the Toolbars in Workbook list box, select the misplaced toolbar and click the button that now says Delete. Select OK to confirm your selections. Be sure to save the workbook to preserve the toolbar attachments.

Notice that the Attach Toolbars dialog box only displays the names of custom toolbars. If you modify Excel's standard toolbars, you cannot share those modified toolbars with other users. You can, of course, make a custom toolbar that is a virtual duplicate of a standard toolbar, modify your copy, and then share the modified copy. Other Excel users who receive your workbook with attached custom toolbars can also distribute those custom toolbars using the same methods you used to share your toolbars.

Removing Toolbars

Removing extra toolbars can be simple, or it can be complex, depending on how thorough you want to be in seeing that every trace of the toolbars is deleted. If all you want to do is to remove a floating toolbar from the screen, click the close button in the upper-right corner of the toolbar. To remove docked toolbars, right-click any of the toolbars and remove the selection check mark from the toolbar you want to remove.

To permanently remove a toolbar so it cannot be displayed again, you must first display the Toolbars dialog box by right-clicking a toolbar and selecting Toolbars or by selecting View, Toolbars. Select the custom toolbar you want to remove and click the Delete button. You can only remove custom toolbars. Excel's standard toolbars cannot be removed.

If you've shared custom toolbars by attaching them to Excel workbooks which you then distributed to other users, deleting those custom toolbars on your system has no effect on the other users. This applies even if the other Excel users use the same PC as you do, as long as each user has their own login. The only reliable method of deleting shared toolbars is to delete each user's XLB file in the Windows program directory. Before considering this option, keep in mind that this will also delete any other custom toolbars and toolbar settings from the user's Excel environment—even toolbars you did not share with the user. This would probably not make you the most popular person in the office!

Controlling Toolbars Using VBA

You no doubt have noticed that Excel's toolbars look different at different times. There's a good reason for this appearance change—different toolbars have different purposes, and Excel changes the toolbars to display an appropriate set of tools for the task at hand. For example, the Visual Basic toolbar is primarily useful when a macro module page is the active page. Because of this, Excel generally displays the Visual Basic toolbar only when you switch to a macro module page.

Your custom toolbars are likely even more task specific than Excel's built-in toolbars. Why shouldn't your toolbars work like Excel's standard toolbars, and adjust to suit changing conditions? Not only is this more convenient for the user, but your applications will certainly appear more professional.

Using Custom Toolbars in Your Application

You already know how to create custom toolbars, but have you considered creating custom toolbars specific to certain applications? You might create a toolbar containing buttons that run each of the macros in an application, attach that toolbar to the application workbook, and then automatically display the toolbar when the workbook is opened. You could even hide the standard Excel toolbars while your application is running, and then restore those toolbars when the user exits from your application.

This type of user interface control requires you to use some VBA programming, but that doesn't mean you have to deal with difficult or complex VBA language elements. In fact, controlling custom toolbars using VBA is probably one of the easiest things you can do with VBA. Even if you haven't used VBA before, you'll discover this task is a good introduction into some of the basic concepts of VBA programming.

To understand how you can control toolbars using VBA, you must first understand the idea of *objects* and the process of *object-oriented programming*. Simply stated, objects are things you can examine and control. In Excel, this means almost everything is an object. Toolbars are objects, and so are the toolbar buttons. Object-oriented programming is simply the process of dealing with objects through program commands. You deal with objects by examining and controlling *properties*, or attributes of those objects. For example, a toolbar object has a property called Visible, which is True if the toolbar can be seen, and False if the toolbar cannot be seen.

Each different type of Excel object has its own set of properties. You can use VBA to examine and, in some cases, control those properties. Toolbar objects have twelve different properties, which are discussed in table 3.3.

Table 3.3   Excel Toolbar Object Properties

Property	Description	Type
Application	Shows which application created the toolbar	Read-only
BuiltIn	Shows whether the toolbar is a standard (true) or custom (false) toolbar	Read-only
Creator	Returns a 32-bit integer (5843454C) that represents the string XCEL (included for Microsoft Excel for the Macintosh compatibility)	Read-only
Height	Returns the height of the toolbar in points (one point = 1/72 inch)	Read-only
Left	Returns or sets the number of points from the left edge of the toolbar to the left edge of the docking area or the Excel window	Adjustable
Name	Returns the name of the toolbar	Read-only
Parent	Returns the name of the parent object for the toolbar	Read-only
Position	Returns or sets the position of the toolbar	Adjustable
Protection	Returns or sets how the toolbar is protected from changes by the user (new to Excel 7)	Adjustable
Top	Returns or sets the number of points from the top edge of the toolbar to the top edge of the docking area or to the top edge of the Excel window	Adjustable
Visible	Returns or sets whether the toolbar is visible	Adjustable
Width	Returns or sets the width of the toolbar in points	Adjustable

Properties that are read-only cannot be directly adjusted in VBA. Therefore, you cannot make one of your custom toolbars return the value True for the BuiltIn property. You can both read and write the adjustable properties. For example, to display a toolbar that is attached to a workbook, you can use the following VBA statement (substituting the correct name for *ToolBarName*):

```
Toolbars("ToolBarName").Visible = True
```

You may be surprised by at least one item in table 3.3. Notice that the Height property is listed as read-only, while the Width property is adjustable. This does not mean that you can't adjust the height of a toolbar, but that you can't adjust the height directly. If you think about what happens when you adjust toolbar sizes manually, you'll have a better understanding of this apparent anomaly. Excel does not allow you to control the height and width of toolbars independently. If you make a toolbar narrower, the height increases as necessary to accommodate all the controls in the toolbar. You cannot set both the height and the width—Excel always retains control over one of the two dimensions. That's why the toolbar Height property is read-only. If you could specify exact values for both height and width, you might violate Excel's rules for toolbar sizes by making the toolbar too short or too narrow to hold all the controls.

Let's have a look at how you can use object properties to control the toolbars that are displayed in your Excel application. We'll assume that you attached your custom toolbar to the workbook, and that you named the toolbar "My Toolbar." Further, we'll assume you'll call the two subroutines from the Auto_Open and Auto_Close macros so that the first runs when you open the workbook and the second runs when you close the workbook. This is not the only way you can run these macros, of course; you may choose to display different sets of toolbars at various points in your application. The macro in listing 3.3 hides the standard Excel toolbars and displays your custom toolbar, while the macro in listing 3.4 restores the standard toolbars and hides your custom toolbar.

Listing 3.3   Hides the Standard Excel Toolbars and Displays Your Custom Toolbar

```
Sub ShowMine()
    Toolbars("Standard").Visible = False
    Toolbars("Formatting").Visible = False
    Toolbars("All Buttons").Visible = True
End Sub
```

Listing 3.4   Restores the Standard Excel Toolbars and Hides Your Custom Toolbar

```
Sub HideMine()
    Toolbars("Standard").Visible = True
    Toolbars("Formatting").Visible = True
    Toolbars("All Buttons").Visible = False
End Sub
```

Both listings 3.3 and 3.4 ignore any additional toolbars that the user may have chosen to display. While this probably would not present a problem, you may want to take the user factor into account if you want more complete control over the Excel user interface while your application is running. Don't assume, however, that it's okay to simply hide all toolbars except for your custom toolbar when you start your application. If you do this, you won't know which toolbars the user had selected for display, and you won't be able to restore their settings when your program ends. No one likes arrogant programmers who take the attitude that they know best, and you'll appear to have this attitude if you don't restore the user's selections when your program finishes. Fortunately, there's an easy way around this problem. Before you hide or display any toolbars, examine each toolbar's Visible property using a For...Next loop to see which toolbars the user has selected for display. Save the toolbar status in the workbook, and use this information to determine which toolbars to restore when your application closes. Your users may not realize you've taken these extra steps, but they'll certainly know if you don't!

Programming Toolbars in VBA

Although you can easily display or hide an entire toolbar using simple VBA commands, sometimes you don't really want to act on the entire toolbar. Sometimes what you really want to do is to make certain controls available only when it's appropriate. An example of this might be an accounting application in which you don't want users to print a summary report before they've added all the data. Another example might be a report that consolidates information from several sources, such as from each store location. You wouldn't want someone to produce a report that didn't include all the latest data. Whatever the reason, you probably would like to have some control over when certain program functions are available to the users.

One solution to controlling the availability of certain program functions is to create a number of different toolbars, and then display the appropriate toolbar as needed. This solution was discussed in the previous section, and in many cases would be a good answer. One problem with this solution is that it really isn't very flexible. If you have ten different program functions you want to control in this manner, you'll have to create at least ten different custom toolbars. You may even need to create many more toolbars if the different functions can exist in different combinations. Clearly, this solution is most useful when you don't need a lot of flexibility.

There's another, much more flexible way to control the functions available on your toolbars. Using VBA, you can add and remove individual toolbar buttons on the fly. Not only that, but you can also control the position of buttons you add to a toolbar, the macro that Excel will execute when the button is clicked, and the text displayed in the status bar when the user points to the button.

When you use VBA to control which buttons appear on a toolbar, you can use any of the standard toolbar buttons or any of the custom buttons. You can use either the correct button name or the VBA ID value when referring to standard toolbar buttons, but since all custom toolbar buttons share the name "Custom," your only choice when specifying custom toolbar buttons is to use the VBA ID value. Table 3.4 shows the VBA ID value for each of the custom toolbar buttons. The table also shows the name "Custom" to remind you that you cannot refer to custom buttons by name.

3

Table 3.4   Custom Toolbar Button Names and VBA ID Values

Button	Name	VBA ID Value
	Custom	237
	Custom	201
	Custom	214
	Custom	206
	Custom	207
	Custom	208
	Custom	228
	Custom	209
	Custom	210
	Custom	200
	Custom	215
	Custom	213
	Custom	217
	Custom	97

continues

Table 3.4   Continued

Button	Name	VBA ID Value
	Custom	218
	Custom	219
	Custom	220
	Custom	225
	Custom	226
	Custom	229
	Custom	230
	Custom	231
	Custom	211
	Custom	212
	Custom	221
	Custom	222
	Custom	223
	Custom	224

To add a button to a toolbar, use the Add method. The Add method uses the following syntax:

```
ToolbarName.Add(VBA
ID#,before,onAction,pushed,enabled,statusBar,helpContextID,helpFile)
```

The arguments follow:

▶ VBA ID# is the button's VBA ID number. If you use 0, you insert a blank space between buttons.

- ▶ `Before` specifies the position of the new button on the toolbar, starting at the upper-left corner. The position number includes any spaces on the toolbar.

- ▶ `OnAction` specifies the name of the macro to execute when the button is clicked. If you don't specify a macro, standard buttons will perform their normal actions, but clicking a custom button without an assigned macro will display the Assign Macro dialog box.

- ▶ `Pushed` specifies whether the button looks like it has been pushed.

- ▶ `Enabled` specifies whether the button is enabled or disabled.

- ▶ `StatusBar` specifies text to appear in the status bar when the mouse cursor is positioned over the button.

- ▶ `HelpContextID` specifies the context ID for the custom help topic for the button.

- ▶ `HelpFile` specifies the help file name containing the custom help topic for the button.

 Tip

If you add new buttons to the end of a toolbar, it will be easier for you to delete the correct button when you later want to remove the button.

Listing 3.5 shows how to add the calculator button to the end of a toolbar named Custom Buttons. When the new button is clicked, the macro named My_Macro is executed.

Listing 3.5   Adding a Button to a Toolbar

```
Sub Add_Button()
Set My_Bar = Toolbars("Custom Buttons")
My_Bar.ToolbarButtons.Add Button:=237, OnAction:="My_Macro"
End Sub
```

It's easy to see how you can add buttons to your custom toolbars when you need them. You can also use the Delete method to remove buttons. Unfortunately, removing buttons from a toolbar requires you to know exactly which button you want to delete, which isn't always the easiest task. Each toolbar has an object called the ToolbarButtons collection, and you can use the Count property for this object to determine how many buttons and blank spaces appear on the toolbar. If you added a button at the end of the toolbar by not specifying a position for the button, you can be certain your button is in the position that is equal to the value of the Count property. Listing 3.6 uses the Count property to determine how many objects are on the toolbar, and then deletes the last object.

Listing 3.6   Deleting the Last Button on a Toolbar

```
Sub Delete_Button()
    Set My_Bar = Toolbars("Custom Buttons")
    Last_Button = My_Bar.ToolbarButtons.Count
    My_Bar.ToolbarButtons(Last_Button).Delete
End Sub
```

The macro in listing 3.6 stores the value of the Count property in the Last_Button variable, and then uses the variable to specify which button to delete. Each time you run this macro the last button still remaining on the toolbar is deleted. Eventually all of the buttons would disappear from the toolbar.

You might want to consider some improvements to the macros in listings 3.5 and 3.6. For example, you could test to see if the last button on the toolbar has the proper VBA ID value before you add or delete a button. You might test the value of the Count property to make certain you weren't adding too many buttons to the toolbar. You could combine this test with a test of the width or height of the toolbar, and adjust the shape of the toolbar if it was becoming too wide. You might even add a space before a new toolbar button every time you were about to add button number 11, 21, 31, and so on. This allows your toolbar to adjust more gracefully to being resized.

Power User Toolbar Examples

By now you probably have some good ideas about how to create just the custom toolbars that will suit your needs. But just in case you'd like a little more help, we'll give you two examples of custom toolbars you'll probably find quite useful. Figure 3.9 shows the File Power and Worksheet Power toolbars.

The first example, the File Power toolbar, has the following buttons: Open, Find File, Save, Print, Print Preview, Set Print Area, New Workbook, Insert Worksheet, Insert Module, Insert Chart Sheet, Microsoft Word, and Microsoft FoxPro. This collection of buttons is intended to make working with files much easier, and also makes it easy to switch to Word or FoxPro.

The second example, the Worksheet Power toolbar, has these buttons: Insert Worksheet, Delete, Delete Row, Insert, Insert Row, Delete Column, Insert Column, Trace Error, Clear Contents, Clear Formats, Paste Formats, Paste Values, Format Painter, Camera, Show Outline Symbols, and Freeze Panes. These buttons provide a good combination of tools you can use when you're creating new worksheets.

Fig. 3.9

The File Power and Worksheet Power toolbars help you work with Excel by providing very useful tool combinations.

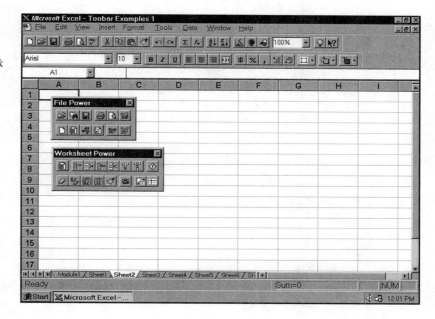

You can probably think of improvements you'd like in these two toolbars. If so, that's great, because Excel enables you to customize your toolbars as much as you see fit. You'll probably also be able to think of even more custom toolbars you want to create. As you do, don't forget that you can attach recorded macros to your custom toolbar buttons, too. Why continue to do the same tasks manually when you can use a single click to make your computer do the work for you?

Summary

Excel's toolbars are remarkable automation tools. I hope this chapter has given you a feel for some of the exciting things you can do with these tools. Whether you're creating custom toolbars for your own use, or making your applications easier to use for other people, Excel's toolbars provide you with a very powerful toolkit.

Successful Application Development

chapter 4

Creating Effective Documentation

4

by Dave Maguiness

In this chapter

◆ **Why should you document your applications?**
In this chapter you'll find benefits for your end-users, other developers, yourself, and your organization.

◆ **When should you document?**
Guidelines for documenting new and existing applications are given here.

◆ **What should you document?**
Essential tasks the end-user will need to know to use your application effectively, and background information the developer will need to know to maintain and enhance your application efficiently are both found here.

◆ **Where should you make your documentation?**
Learn about the tools that are currently available to you for documentation.

All commercial software programs come with documentation. The success or failure of the application depends on the quality of the instructions that are included with the application, because users want clear and thorough instructions on how to use the application with confidence. In this manner, documentation adds value to the application and is tangible evidence of the overall caliber of the application. Therefore, it is essential that you include documentation as part of your complete Excel application package.

Why Document Your Excel Applications?

Documenting your Excel applications can benefit the following people:

▶ The end-user

▶ Other developers

▶ Yourself

▶ Your company

Benefits for the End-User

Because you have a target audience for your application, it is essential that you provide your users with detailed instructions on how to use your application. Because you have probably spent a number of months developing your application, you are familiar with its operation. It is incorrect to assume, however, that your intended audience will know your application as well as you. Applications that contain user-friendly attributes such as shaded areas for data entry and descriptive macro buttons for automated processes still do not contain enough information for proper use of the application (see fig. 4.1).

Fig. 4.1

Users may be baffled as to where to start, no matter how much thought you put into your application.

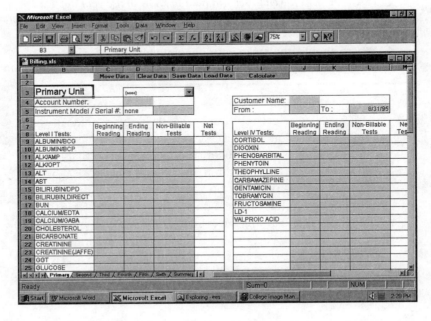

In the case of data entry, for example, the user will not know whether areas designated for data entry need to be completed in a particular order—or on completion of entering data, whether your application needs to be recalculated, printed, saved, and so on.

Providing your users with information about your application enables them to be productive quickly. Rather than having them frustrated because they don't know how to use your application, they can get to work right away. The last thing you want is for users to give up and not use your application due to frustration.

Benefits for Other Developers

When you provide documentation with your application, you provide those who take ownership of your application the means to maintain and enhance it easily. Your application's formula and macro logic may not be readily apparent to another individual who has the responsibility of maintaining the application you developed. Your absence—due to illness, vacation, or promotion—results in a temporary or permanent resource loss which, without proper documentation, can lead to your application becoming inactive or replaced. This harms the company your application was meant to help and is a poor reflection on you. Documenting applications is not only a professional courtesy but a requirement for the long-term success of your application.

Benefits for You

Documentation serves as a reminder so you can effectively support your application. You may, for example, have difficulty remembering the logic of complex formulas, such as the one shown here:

```
=IF(OR($C$3=4,$C$3=5),$N$36+SUM($N$41:$N$43)+$N$45+SUM($E$60:$E$65),0)
```

Proper documentation will remind you that this formula will add the amounts in cell N36 to the sum of the values in range N41:N43 and add this result to N45 along with the sum of E60:E65 if the user enters a 3 or a 5 in cell C3. Otherwise, the cell containing this formula returns zero.

Providing quick and thorough answers to questions about your application ensures the integrity of you and your application. It also reduces the number of telephone calls and visits from users and frees your time for more productive activities.

Benefits for Your Organization

Documentation saves your organization time and expense in training and support. Training time is reduced if documentation is available that explains how-to information adequately. In this manner, your users can spend more time at their tasks than in a training classroom. Documentation is also a resource for you, other developers, help-desk personnel, support analysts, or other individuals assigned to support your application. For example, help-desk personnel and support analysts will likely be familiar with Excel, but documentation provides them with a means to answer questions in a timely and efficient manner. You reduce support expense by providing documentation that helps others understand your application and frees up support resources for other software and hardware support problems.

When Should You Document Your Application?

When to document your application depends on whether the application is new and has never been distributed to end-users, or if it is already in use.

Documenting New Applications

You should begin documenting early in the application's development phase, preferably when the application's feature set has been defined. In this manner, you perform documentation concurrently with each stage of your application's development. Your documentation then reflects the current state of your application and provides you with a tool for monitoring the status of your development progress.

Another benefit of concurrent documentation is that you avoid having to perform documentation after completing application development. Typically, there is very little time between the end of the test phase and the application's release date. The time that is available is usually devoted to corrections to the application's feature set, leaving very little time for documentation. Creating documentation at this point almost always results in incomplete instructions and a "rushed" feel to your documentation.

Rather than performing documentation as an afterthought, create your documentation as you develop your application. Besides more complete and thorough documentation, this gives you the opportunity to include it as part of the application's test process. You gain the advantage of having other user's feedback of your documentation as well as your application. This feedback can help you identify areas in your documentation that you may have overlooked or that need further explanation.

Documenting Existing Applications

The process of documenting previously released applications is similar to documenting new applications. You should begin revising your documentation after you have identified the changes you will be making to your application. For a maintenance release, your documentation should include the corrections you made to your application. For a major release, your documentation should explain the enhancements and new capabilities your application contains. Because you have existing documentation in place, revising and updating your application should require less time and effort than starting documentation from scratch.

What Should You Document?

As mentioned earlier, you may have two distinct audiences for your documentation: the end-user, who needs "how-to" information to use it, and the developer, who requires technical information to maintain and enhance the application. While each group has different documentation requirements, both end-user and developer can benefit from an overview of your application. Explain to your reader what your application is and what results it calculates. For example, you might want to tell your audience that your profit margin application calculates the margin of profit for a particular product, expressed as a percent of net profit divided by total revenues. This background information is a good jumping-off point to the more detailed instructions that comprise your documentation.

4

Documentation for the End-User

The end-user should know how to use your application, and does not, and should not, be bothered with the details of how the application works. To ensure your application is used successfully, your documentation, at a minimum, should discuss:

- Installation and setup
- Navigation
- Data entry
- Calculation
- Printing
- Saving
- Troubleshooting

Installation and Setup

Users need to know what hardware and software requirements the application needs to operate properly (see fig. 4.2). The hardware list should include CPU type and speed, amount of random-access memory, and hard disk space. The software list should include the operating system and version, the version(s) of Excel, and any of the add-ins that are included with Excel that should automatically open when a user starts Excel.

Also, provide installation instructions that are easy to understand, whether your application comes with an installation program you developed or if the user merely needs to copy your application files to a particular directory or disk drive.

Fig. 4.2
Spell out the system requirements and installation steps so your users can get your application up and running.

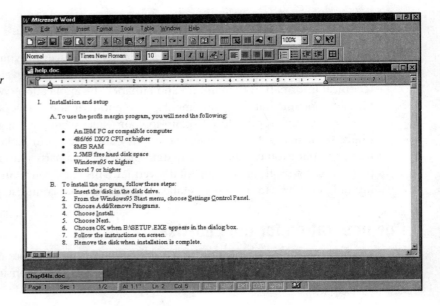

Navigation

You need to tell your reader about the important areas of your application, such as data entry and report areas, as shown in figure 4.3. Explain how to display these areas on-screen, whether they exist on one large worksheet or several worksheets in the file. Explain how to quickly move to these areas, either using Excel's built-in tools, such as the scroll bars and worksheet tabs, or capabilities you have provided, such as clicking macro buttons. Point out what the user should see on-screen after performing one of these techniques.

Data Entry

Data entry is the primary activity of the users of your application and you should provide your users with information to help them enter data efficiently in your application (see fig. 4.4). Thus, you must consider three aspects of data entry so your application will operate properly—where the user should enter data, the type of data the user should enter, and the source. Make it clear to your readers where the active cell should be located before they start entering data, and if a macro makes the first data entry cell the active one. Give your users an idea of how much data they should expect to enter by stating where the data entry ranges are and if they exist on more than one worksheet.

Fig. 4.3
Especially for applications that have multiple areas for data entry, point out any navigation aids or techniques you have provided with your application.

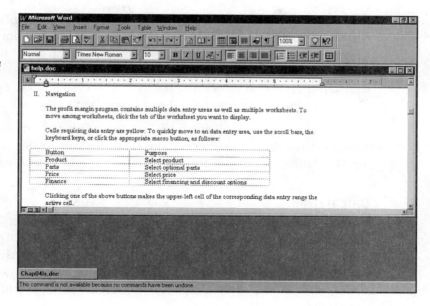

Fig. 4.4
Explain data entry requirements or techniques that are unique to your application.

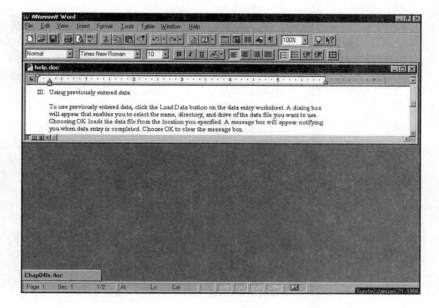

Also, point out what you expect from the data they enter. Describe the type of data they will be entering (numeric, text, or date), and in what cells. Do not assume the user will know, for example, whether your application depends on dates that include the year. You also can do your user a favor and reduce data entry time by including in your instructions only the minimum data the user needs to supply. For example, entering dollar signs and commas are unnecessary because your application will address cell formatting.

If your user will be using an automated process to bring in data to your application, make sure your documentation explains where the data resides. Is the data on a disk, local hard drive, or network drive? Also use the directory and file names.

Calculation

If you've created a large application (one with multiple data entry areas and/or worksheets) you probably have set Excel to manual calculation. Your users need to know when and how to update your application (see fig. 4.5)—by pressing the F9 Calc key or by clicking a macro button that performs a similar function. Omitting this documentation results in your application displaying erroneous results without your users' knowledge.

Fig. 4.5

Remind your users that your application will need to be calculated to display the most current results.

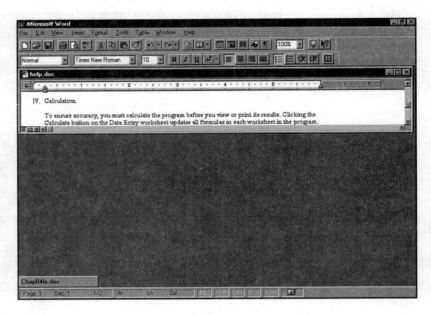

If your application is large, also point out what the user can expect in terms of calculation time. Be sure to base your time estimate on the size of your application and the hardware it is running on. Consider providing several estimates if your application's calculation time is sensitive to the amount of data that is changed.

Printing

Printouts of your application's calculation results provide management with tangible results of your application. Your application should provide accurate reports that are easy to understand. Your documentation, therefore, should instruct end-users on how to generate reports from your application. This includes what to print, when to print, and how to print, as in figure 4.6.

Your documentation should point out what reports your application will generate. Explain to your reader where these reports are. Are they worksheet ranges, and if so, which worksheet in the file is it? Or are they charts, and are they in separate chart sheets, or on one or more worksheets? If so, which worksheets? Don't assume your users will know what comprises a complete set of reports that is appropriate for a current request.

Fig. 4.6

Ensure that your users know your application's proper printing technique.

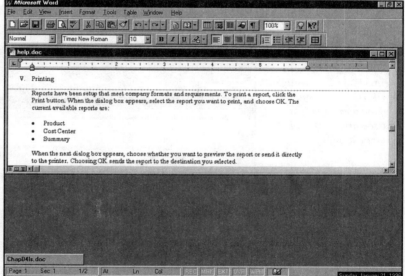

Your documentation should include a discussion of what your application requires before you can print meaningful information. Typically, this includes required data and then calculation. Be sure you point this out with any additional input your application may need, such as changing header or footer information, column headings, and so on.

You will also need to let your user know if your application addresses a specific time frame. Your application may generate end of month, quarter, or annual reports. In this instance, your users should not print or distribute reports until all relevant data has been entered into your application.

After you have specified what and when to print, you need to tell your users how to print reports. Will your users be specifying ranges manually, using print macros, or using Excel's Report Manager? If the user needs to select a worksheet range, make sure you specify the exact range, and then take the next step and tell how to send that range to the printer. In the case of macro-driven reports, point out how to execute the print macro and select the appropriate report. If your application relies on Report Manager, help the user make the appropriate choice from the list of reports in the Report Manager dialog box.

Saving

You should explain to your users when it is appropriate to save and how to go about performing this function, as in figure 4.7. There may be times when it is appropriate to save other than on completion of data entry. For example, your application may require some settings to be saved after a report has been run.

Fig. 4.7

Explaining how to save entered data correctly will reduce the number of support calls associated with your application.

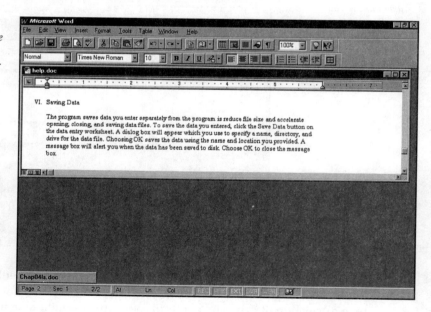

Make sure you explain how to save your application, either through Excel's File menu or a macro button, or by clicking the Save button on the toolbar. In the case of File menu commands, include instructions on whether to use File, Save or File, Save As.

 Tip

For Save As, be sure to specify the naming convention for the file, the directory, and the drive.

Finally, you may have developed an application that utilizes unique file-saving capability. If this is the case, thoroughly explain to the user what is actually being saved, in what file format, and how to do so. For example, your application may mimic a database and one of its features is to load and save data separately from the application. If this is the case, point this out in your documentation. Most users assume the entire file is being saved to disk when they use the File Save button or choose Save from the File menu. To save data separately from your application they will need to execute a macro. You can avoid potential confusion by pointing this out ahead of time in your documentation.

Troubleshooting

Go the extra mile in your documentation and include a section on commonly asked questions. Answers to common questions your users might have will save them time and frustration, and there will be fewer requests for help to you or your company's help desk analysts. For example, you can list possible solutions to printing problems, such as correct Page Setup settings, printer properly turned on with adequate paper and toner, and so on. Going beyond what is expected in documentation by including a troubleshooting-type section shows your users you have their best interests in mind and want them to be successful with your application.

Problem	Solution
Saved files are too large and do not properly load into the application	Choose the Save macro button on the worksheet to save your work. The data is saved separately from the application.
Unable to print what is displayed on-screen	Choose the Print macro button on the worksheet and select the appropriate report from the dialog box.
Error message box appears after selecting product name	Make sure you have the latest release installed with the most current supporting Excel workbook files in your \product subdirectory.

Documentation for the Developer

You should provide enough documentation so that a developer can easily understand the logic behind your formulas and Visual Basic subroutines. If documented properly, another developer should be able to pick up where you left off with minimal help from you.

All formulas except basic SUM formulas should be explained. You should explain the formula's purpose, what it calculates, and the reason you took that approach. Similarly, you should explain the purpose of each of your Visual Basic subroutines, what process it performs, and why you chose that method. For example, you should explain the reason your application might use

```
Sub Select_Range()
    Dim Anchor_Cell
    Anchor_Cell = ActiveCell.Address
    ActiveCell.End(xlDown).Select
    ActiveCell.End(xlToRight).Select
    Range(Anchor_Cell, ActiveCell).Select
End Sub
```

rather than

```
Sub Select_Range()
    Selection.CurrentRegion.Select
End Sub
```

Even though you may remember why you created a particular worksheet formula, or VBA procedure or function, it may not be readily apparent to your colleagues. Provide them with documentation that will get them up and running quickly with your application.

Where Should You Include Documentation?

After you have identified the audience for your documentation, and have decided what you need to talk about to use or maintain your application with confidence, you need to decide what is the best vehicle for your instructions. You can use:

▶ Cell notes

▶ Hidden rows, columns, or worksheets

▶ Separate word processing files

The key is your audience. If you decide to keep your documentation within the application, distribute a version that is appropriate for your audience. For example, if you feel cell notes will adequately document your application, keep an undistributed version for developers in which the cell notes explain formulas and logic rather than data entry instructions.

Documentation for the End-User

> **Tip**
>
> If you and your users' systems are properly configured, you can add sound to your cell notes.

Depending on the complexity of your application, you have a number of appropriate ways to document your application. If your application is relatively simple, and your users are familiar with basic Excel operations (opening files, saving files, printing, and so on), you may decide the information contained in cell notes is sufficient for others to use your application successfully. For example, if your application requires only a few items of data, you can describe that using a cell note like the one in figure 4.8.

> **Tip**
>
> Text boxes, embedded word processing files, and graphic objects in general can be used to document your application, but are better suited to explain your application's results, rather than how to use the application itself.

Fig. 4.8
For simple applica-tions, cell notes provide adequate documentation.

For applications that require more formal explanation, you should document your appli-cation in its own designated area. You can include a separate worksheet in the workbook for this purpose, as shown in figure 4.9.

Alternatively, you can place the document in its own file, such as Windows WordPad or Microsoft Word. Remember, however, you will need to maintain and distribute two documents as part of your application if you choose this method.

Fig. 4.9

Use a separate worksheet for documentation for applications that require more explanation.

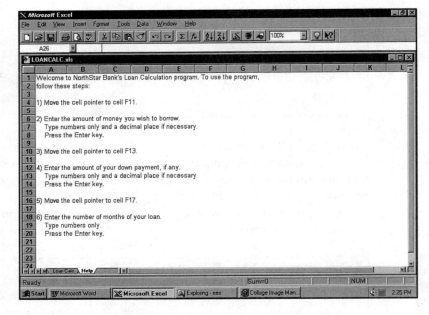

 Tip
There is software that enables you to create your own online help systems. See Chapter 27, "Creating Custom Help for VBA Applications," for more information.

Documentation for the Developer

If developers are your audience, you can use cell notes to explain complex formulas in a cell, as shown in figure 4.10.

This way you are able to provide documentation within the cell and your reader does not have to refer to a separate document to understand your formula's logic.

Or you can place your explanations in the column (or row) adjacent to your formulas. Hiding the column or row prevents unnecessary reading by your users. Similar to user documentation, you can place documentation intended for developers in a separate worksheet which can be hidden, or in a separate word processor file. Distribute a copy to developers only.

One area of documentation you must include with your application is commenting your Visual Basic subroutines. You do this in the VBA module by beginning the comment with an apostrophe ('). Excel Visual Basic ignores this text but these comments provide a valuable resource for you and others who take ownership of your application. The subroutine in figure 4.11 contains comments that explain each step of the subroutine.

Fig. 4.10

Cell notes can be used to explain complex formulas for developers.

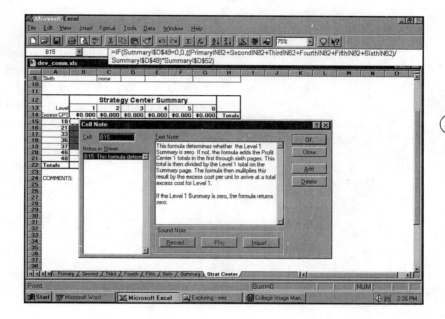

Fig. 4.11

Commenting each line of your subroutines helps others understand your code.

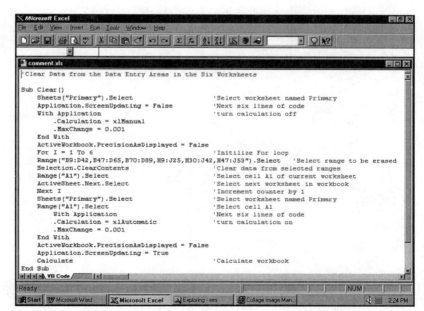

Each statement should be explained so that you or a user will be reminded what the Visual Basic command is doing and the reason why you chose to use that technique.

Summary

In this chapter, you learned the importance of including thorough end-user documentation with your application, as well as documentation which serves as a reference to yourself and other developers. In the next chapter, you'll learn about how to protect your data from unintentional or intentional changes using Excel Visual Basic for Applications.

chapter 5

Protecting Data

5

by Donna Payne

In this Chapter

◆ **How to protect your data without VBA**
Learn how to use built-in features to apply file-level, workbook, worksheet, and cell protection.

◆ **How to protect your data with VBA**
You learn how to apply protection to the workbook, sheet, toolbars, edit box, and objects.

◆ **New protection in Excel 95**
Protection is made easier with Excel 95, especially using UserInterfaceOnly.

◆ **When to create an add-in**
Find out when you want to apply an additional layer of protection to your file and how to create an add-in.

◆ **How secure your file really is**
You learn the pros and cons of applying protecting in Excel.

I f your data is important to you, you need to think about protecting it. Perhaps you've never had any problems with your spreadsheets or applications that would warrant security efforts and you are confident that it would be too unusual for someone to accidentally corrupt your file (if users use it the way it's *supposed* to be used). Maybe you think that no one would have a reason to intentionally alter it. Perhaps you feel what happens to your application after the client has received it in good working order is not your problem.

And did you decline the airbag option on your new car? Presume that Murphy's Law is a certainty. Protect your work, time, and reputation by using protection features at least in documents that will be seen and used by others, and perhaps also in documents that never leave your shop. Ask the following question for each functional area of your spreadsheet: how would it affect my work for someone (including myself) to make changes that are not intended? The answer to this question will help you decide what kinds or levels of protection to consider incorporating in your workbook.

Excel features a full range of protection options, from basic to sophisticated, and from file level to cell level. You can add additional protection by using Visual Basic for Applications.

What Do You Have to Lose?

You know by now how hard it is to develop a professional spreadsheet or custom application, especially one that incorporates VBA code. Why expose yourself to accidental loss of formatting, code, or data? (And don't think that you yourself couldn't possibly end up being the guilty party.) Backup files certainly help, but may be of little help with a complex spreadsheet with many cells referencing each other. One false move in a key cell, and not only is the data that you have input into the spreadsheet hopelessly scrambled, but the formulas are toast too.

Deliberate sabotage and intentional misuse is a possibility that you may not want to think about, but probably should, especially if many users will be accessing and using your file. This concern can be easily addressed by using one of the password options described in this chapter (although there is never an absolute guarantee against determined code stealing crooks).

Which type of protection should you use? Which type of protection offers the most security? How safe is protection, really? These are pertinent questions that are addressed in this chapter. You should familiarize yourself thoroughly with the options before recommending a protection strategy.

As you assess the protection needs of your workbook, you should think about how much a particular kind of protection you are considering could cost you in terms of loss of functionality and ease of use. Not allowing changes to a particular formula might actually cause more problems than it is worth, if there is a possibility that it will need to be altered (while you are on vacation, no doubt). For you as the developer, it's essential that you understand the pros and cons of each type of protection.

Also avoid reaching prematurely for an industrial strength solution, when all you really need is a more modest level of protection, perhaps in only one well-chosen cell or range.

What Can You Provide with Excel's Built-In Protection Features?

There are many ways to protect your file without writing a single line of code. You can shape your design to take advantage of the many built-in options for protection that Excel provides. Protection can be as simple as assigning a password to the file to prevent unauthorized users from opening it, or it can involve different sets of user privileges that can apply to the workbook structure, worksheets, module sheets, rows, columns, or cells.

 Note

Some of the information on accessing built-in protection will be review for the advanced Excel user. If you're already familiar with these options, you may want to skim this section and go to the section, "What Protection Can You Provide with VBA?" later in this chapter.

File-Level Security

File-level security is a built-in option found under the File menu to prevent unauthorized users from accessing the file. Choose File, Save As, Options to access the Save Options dialog box shown in figure 5.1, which presents the choices for applying file-level security.

Fig. 5.1

The Save Options dialog box offers three differing levels of file-level protection.

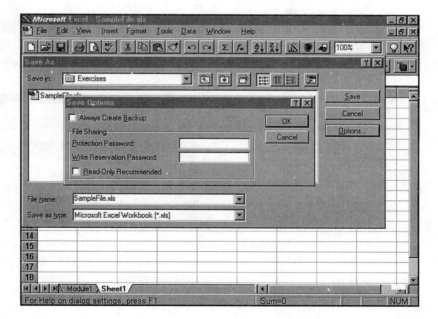

Table 5.1 shows the different types of file-level protection that can be applied to a workbook.

Table 5.1   File-Level Protection

Protection	Result
Password Protection	Password required to open file
Write Reservation	Password required to save changes to the original workbook
Read-Only Recommended	A warning will be displayed that the file should be opened as read-only, but will not require the user to open the file as read-only
Read-Only	Set from Open dialog box; no changes can be made to the original file

 Note

File-level passwords can have as many as 15 characters. Remember that passwords are case-sensitive. If the password won't work, make sure that Caps Lock is not on.

When a read-only recommended workbook is opened, the user sees the dialog box shown in figure 5.2. This is a warning that the file should be opened as read-only, but will not require the user to open the file with read-only protection.

Fig. 5.2

A dialog box appears prompting the user to open the file as read-only.

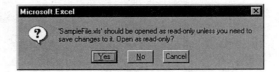

To remove workbook-level protection choose File, Save As, then click the Options button. Clear the password if one has been set and click OK to save the file. Answer Yes to replace the existing file.

After the workbook is open, you can apply several types of protection to limit the user's access to workbooks, worksheets, modules, charts, pivot tables, objects, rows, columns, and cells.

Hiding and Unhiding Workbooks

If you're developing a spreadsheet or application for someone else to use, sometimes hiding the workbook or worksheet will offer enough protection. After all, if the user doesn't know that the worksheet or workbook is available, they most likely won't go looking for it.

When hiding a workbook manually (without VBA), choose Hide or Unhide from the Window menu. If there is no visible workbook, the Unhide command moves to the File menu. Figure 5.3 shows the Unhide dialog box that is displayed when you wish to unhide a workbook that has previously been hidden.

Fig. 5.3
Select the hidden workbook and choose OK.

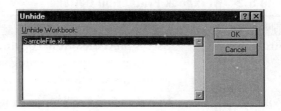

Hiding and Unhiding Sheets in the Workbook

To hide or unhide a worksheet, dialog sheet, chart sheet, or Excel 4 macro sheet manually, choose Format, Sheet, Hide or Unhide.

To hide and unhide a module sheet in the workbook, choose Edit, Sheet, Hide or Unhide.

How Can I Protect the Entire Workbook?

Protecting what the user can do to the workbook is perhaps one of the most powerful methods of security without creating Visual Basic for Applications code or saving the file as an add-in (add-ins are covered later in this chapter).

To apply protection to a workbook, choose Tools, Protection, Protect Workbook. Figure 5.4 shows the dialog box that is used to assign different levels of workbook protection.

> ⚛ **Tip**
> Passwords are optional. To apply minimal workbook protection, you can click OK without assigning a password.

Fig. 5.4

The Protect Workbook dialog box enables you to assign an optional password to protect the workbook structure, windows, or both.

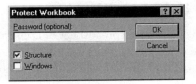

Table 5.2 is a summary of the workbook protection available in the Protect Workbook dialog box.

Table 5.2   Workbook Protection Options

Protection	Result
Structure	User is prevented from copying, deleting, hiding, inserting, moving, renaming, and unhiding sheets within the workbook
Window	User is prevented from resizing the window, and the close, maximize, minimize, and restore window controls are hidden

What About the Worksheet?

To protect and unprotect the worksheet, chart sheet, module sheet, macro sheet, and dialog sheet, choose Tools, Protection, Sheet. Figure 5.5 shows the Protect Sheet dialog box and the options for protecting the worksheet.

Fig. 5.5

The Protect Sheet dialog box sets protection for the parts of the worksheet.

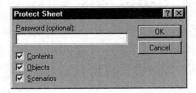

Table 5.3 is a summary of the worksheet protection available in the Protect Sheet dialog box.

Table 5.3   Worksheet Protection Options

Protection	Result
Contents	Protects the worksheet, charts, and cells from alterations
Objects	Protects any object or embedded chart on a worksheet
Scenarios	Prevents changes to the scenarios that you have created

 Note

These options prevent the user from accidentally changing, deleting, or selecting contents, objects, or scenarios on a worksheet.

 Caution

It is possible for the user to override worksheet protection by selecting the worksheet, choosing Edit, Copy, Paste to copy the contents into a new workbook.

Unprotecting a Worksheet

To Unprotect a Worksheet that already has a password, you must know the password. Choose Tools, Protection, Unprotect. Enter the password and click OK.

Hiding Rows and Columns

Often, I'll put formulas and notes that I don't want the user to be able to see inside of a row or column, then hide that row or column. This is useful when you want to keep the row or column close to data to which it refers, but invisible. To hide a column or row, select the entire row or column to be hidden. Choose Format, Row or Column, Hide and click OK. Protect the worksheet so the user is unable to unhide the row or column without a password.

 Tip

When developing a spreadsheet for someone else, turn off the Display Row and Column Headings by choosing Tools, Options, View, Row and Column Headers. This prevents the user from viewing which rows and columns have been hidden.

Protecting Cells and Formulas

By default, all cells on a worksheet are locked when the worksheet is protected. For a user to edit a cell directly on the worksheet, the cell must first be unlocked. To unlock, lock, or hide cell formulas (in the formula bar), select Ctrl+1 to activate the Format Cells dialog box. Choose the Protection tab. The Format Cells dialog box is shown in figure 5.6.

Fig. 5.6

The Format Cells dialog box displays tabs to change the number, alignment, font, border, pattern, and protection settings of the active range.

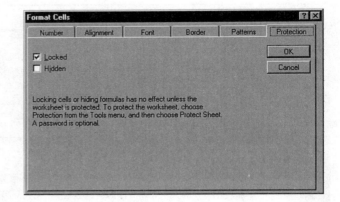

Locked

Locking a cell prevents a user from altering the contents or formula. When the cell is unlocked, and the worksheet is protected, the user is able to edit the cell as if unprotected. If a group of cells is unlocked on a protected worksheet, selecting the tab key will move the active cell between the unlocked cells.

Hidden

By selecting the Hide option, once the worksheet is protected, the user will be able to see the cell value, but not the cell formula. This is useful when confidential formulas make up the value of the cell, for example, sales markups, or raise percentages.

 Tip

Another method of protecting cells is to format the cell format with three semicolons (;;;), locking the cell, and then protecting the worksheet. By formatting the number with three semicolons, you make the cell contents invisible. By locking the cell, you prevent the user from inadvertently deleting or changing the contents, and by protecting the sheet, you put the protection into effect.

Objects

Applying protection to Objects is done in much the same way. Select the Object and choose Format, Object. Figure 5.7 shows the Format Object dialog box.

Fig. 5.7
When the object is protected with the lock option, the object cannot be deleted, reformatted, moved, or resized after the workbook is protected.

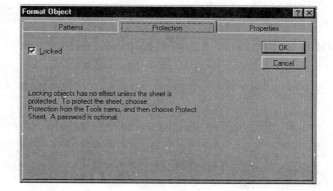

5

 Caution

It's important to remember that the object is not protected until the worksheet is protected.

 Note

Most developers don't realize the value of using the Get Info window. Choose View, Toolbars, Auditing. Click the last button on the right of the Auditing toolbar, the button with the white "i" in a blue background circle.

The Get Info window defaults to showing the cell location, the formula, and any cell notes that may be embedded. When the Get Info window is active, choose Info to view additional information about the cell. This information includes: Cell, Formula, Value, Format, Protection, Names, Precedents, Dependents, and Note.

What Protection Can You Provide with VBA?

Applying protection with VBA code seems like a lot of trouble. It is not, if adequate protection can be implemented by clicking through Excel's built-in features. However, if you have decided you want to set a very robust level of protection, eliminating all but skilled

VBA coders from even beginning to think of cracking your document, then read on. Or, you may find after trying built-in protection options on for size that they don't fit as well as a tailored VBA solution would. In VBA, you can call on specific properties and methods of objects to create a customized profile of what the user is allowed and not allowed to do to your file.

Hiding and Unhiding Workbooks with VBA

To hide a workbook through Visual Basic for Applications code, you must set the Visible property of all windows in the workbook's Window collection to True or False.

A workbook can have many windows, and the names of the windows often change. For this reason, you may want to use a For Next loop to set each Visible property of all of the windows in the Workbook's Windows' collection to True or False.

This subroutine loops through each window in the active workbook and sets the Visible property to False:

```
Sub HideWorkbook()
    Dim oWindow As Window
    For Each oWindow In ActiveWorkbook.Windows
        oWindow.Visible = False
    Next oWindow
End Sub
To unhide each Window in the ActiveWorkbook, set the Visible property to True. An
example of this subroutine is named HideWorkbook.
Sub HideWorkbook()
    Dim oWindow As Window
    For Each oWindow In ActiveWorkbook.Windows
        oWindow.Visible = True
    Next oWindow
End Sub
```

Workbook Protection with VBA

To protect a workbook through VBA, you must call on the Protect method for the Workbook object. The Protect method for the Workbook object takes three arguments:

```
object.Protect(password, structure, windows)
```

Figure 5.8 shows the Protect Workbook dialog box.

Fig. 5.8

*The Protect Workbook
dialog box displays the
three arguments for
the protect method on
the workbook object.*

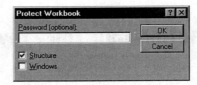

These three arguments are:

- ▶ `password`. A password used to protect the workbook.
- ▶ `structure`. If set to True, the user is prevented from changing the workbook structure. This includes copying, deleting, hiding, inserting, moving, renaming, and unhiding sheets within the workbook. These are the same options that you are presented with when you choose Tools, Protection, Protect Workbook.
- ▶ `windows`. If set to True, the user cannot resize the window. This hides the Close, Maximize, Minimize, and Restore window controls.

 Note

By setting the `windows` argument to True, the user is unable to choose Window, New Window.

5

An example of the VBA syntax used to set the active workbook with a generic password of `mypassword` is:

```
ActiveWorkbook.Protect password := "mypassword"
```

The Unprotect method password, which takes one argument, can be called on the Workbook object to unprotect a workbook.

Protecting Worksheets, Charts, DialogSheets, and Modules

A worksheet can have different levels of protection. Use the VBA Protect method to protect a worksheet, chart, dialogsheet, or module. The Protect method takes five arguments, shown here:

```
object.Protect(password, drawingObjects, contents, scenarios, userInterfaceOnly)
```

The Protect Sheet dialog box and its options are displayed in figure 5.9.

Fig. 5.9

The Protect Sheet dialog box shows four of the arguments for protecting the worksheet. The fifth argument is new to Excel 95, userInterfaceOnly.

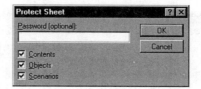

These arguments are:

- ▶ password (Optional). This is a password for the sheet. Because this is an optional argument, you can unprotect the sheet without a password if no password is set. If a password has been set, a password is required to unprotect the worksheet.

- ▶ drawingObjects (Optional). If this is set to True, the drawing objects on the sheet are protected. This argument is not valid for module sheets.

- ▶ contents (Optional). If set to True, the contents of the object are protected. On different sheet objects, this argument protects differently as shown in the following list.

   Module sheet - Source code

   Chart sheet - Entire chart

   Dialog Sheet - Dialog layout and text on controls

   Worksheet - Cells

- ▶ scenarios (Optional - worksheets only). If set to True, or if the argument is omitted, scenarios are protected.

- ▶ userInterfaceOnly (Optional). If set to True or if omitted, the object is protected from the user but not from your macros.

An example of protecting the active sheet with four of the five arguments can be seen in the subroutine ProtectThisWorksheet.

```
Sub ProtectThisWorksheet()
  ActiveSheet.Protect password:="abc123", _
    DrawingObjects:=True, contents:=True, Scenarios:=False, _
        userInterfaceOnly:=True
End Sub
```

DataEntryMode

The DataEntryMode Property can be applied to the Application object to restrict what the user can do in the workspace. When DataEntryMode is turned on, the user is restricted to entering data into unlocked cells of the currently selected range. The DataEntryMode property has three arguments:

- ▶ xlOn. DataEntryMode is on.
- ▶ xlOff. DataEntryMode is off.
- ▶ xlStrict. DataEntryMode is on, and selecting the Esc button does not exit Data Entry mode.

The subroutine `CheckDataEntryMode()` is an example of a macro that checks the type of DataEntryMode protection in place and displays a message box using matching text with the case that is correct.

```
Sub CheckDataEntryMode()
    Select Case Application.DataEntryMode
        Case xlOff
            MsgBox "DataEntryMode is off"
        Case xlOn
            MsgBox "DataEntryMode is on"
        Case xlStrict
            MsgBox "DataEntryMode is set to xlStrict. User cannot use the Esc key to
            ➥escape"
    End Select
End Sub
```

 Tip

Even with a protected chart sheet, the user can still select the chart. To prevent this, place a text box that has been formatted with no border, no fill, and protection in it. Now when you protect the chart sheet by choosing Tools, Protection, Protect Sheet, the user is unable to select the chart.

Making the Worksheet Invisible

A worksheet's visibility can be controlled through VBA with the Visible property. If set to True, the object is visible. When using the Visible property for a chart, dialog sheet, module sheet, or worksheet, you may also set this property to `xlVeryHidden`. This prevents the user from making the object visible.

Here is an example of how to set the Visible property of the Worksheet to False, in effect, hiding Sheet1.

```
Worksheets("Sheet1").Visible = False
```

There are three value settings that the Visible Property can have:

▶ `True`. The worksheet is visible to the user.

▶ `False`. The worksheet is not visible to the user.

▶ `XLVeryHidden`. The worksheet is not visible to the user, and the user is not able to unhide the worksheet by simply choosing Format, Unhide. The only way the Visible property can be reset to True is through another VBA macro.

Note

It is not possible to execute a subroutine to hide a module as xlVeryHidden from the same module sheet that contains the subroutine. To hide the module, you must do so from another module sheet or from the Debug window.

To hide a module using the Debug window, type the following line of code in the top section of the Debug window and press Enter. In this example, the first module of the active workbook is being hidden as xlVeryHidden.

```
ActiveWorkbook.Modules(1).Visible = xlveryhidden
```

The subroutine, HideSheetXLVeryHidden sets the active sheet's Visible property to xlVeryHidden:

```
Sub HideSheetXLVeryHidden()
  ActiveSheet.Visible = xlVeryHidden
End Sub
```

It's often necessary to hide more than one sheet at a time, or to loop through a number of sheets to set the Visible property to xlVeryHidden. Here is an example of how to hide all selected worksheets with one macro:

```
Sub HideSelectedSheetsXLVeryHidden()
    Dim oObject As Object
    For Each oObject In ActiveWindow.SelectedSheets
        oObject.Visible = xlVeryHidden
    Next oObject
End Sub
```

 Note

Notice that, after running this macro, there are no available options to unhide any worksheets manually, nor any indication that there are any hidden sheets.

By changing the Visible property to True, you unhide all sheets that are protected using the xlVeryHidden method:

```
Sub UnhideItAll()
    Dim myObject As Object
    For Each myObject In ActiveWorkbook.Sheets
        myObject.Visible = True
    Next myObject
End Sub
```

User Interface Protection (Boolean)

New to Excel 95, and by far one of the best features of the upgrade, is UserInterfaceOnly protection. By passing a True argument to the Protect method on a worksheet, chart, dialog sheet, or module, the sheet can be protected from user manipulation while allowing macro code to work on the protected sheet itself.

 Note

If you used Outlining, PivotTables, or AutoFilter in previous versions of Excel, you will remember the ordeal of protecting and unprotecting the sheet to carry out the actions with VBA code on a protected sheet. By using UserInterfaceOnly, this is no longer necessary.

5

To see how this works with VBA, assume the subroutine ProtectUserInterfaceExample( ) has been run on a worksheet that contains a list that uses an AutoFilter. Because UserInterfaceOnly is set to be True, applying an AutoFilter without first specifying the argument EnableAutoFilter, the list cannot be filtered on the protected worksheet.

```
Sub ProtectUserInterfaceExample()
    ActiveSheet.Protect Password:="Hello", _
    DrawingObjects:=True, Contents:=True, Scenarios:=True, _
        UserInterfaceOnly:=True
End Sub
```

If userInterfaceOnly is set to True, you can specify three properties to protect worksheet objects from users while the sheet is protected.

- ▶ `EnableAutoFilter`. When this argument is set to True, AutoFilter arrows are enabled. The EnableAutoFilter property applies to each individual worksheet and is not saved with the worksheet.

- ▶ `EnableOutlining`. When set to True, the user can expand and collapse the outline on a protected sheet.

- ▶ `EnablePivotTable`. When set to True, pivot tables on the worksheet are unprotected after the Protect method is called. Users can manipulate the pivot table on the protected sheet.

Using the subroutine ProtectUserInterfaceExample( ), a line of code can be added to set EnableAutoFilter to True, which will allow AutoFilter functionality on a worksheet that has UserInterfaceOnly protection. A line of code can also be used for EnableOutlining and EnablePivotTable.

```
Sub ProtectUserInterfaceExample()
    ActiveSheet.Protect Password:="", _
    DrawingObjects:=True, Contents:=True, Scenarios:=True, _
        UserInterfaceOnly:=True
    ActiveSheet.EnableAutoFilter = True
End Sub
```

You can now manipulate the AutoFilter on the worksheet. Disable the AutoFilter functionality by changing EnableAutoFilter to False, or by omitting it altogether.

 Tip

When you double-click a field in pivot table, a drill-down effect takes place and that data is placed in a new worksheet within your workbook. When you have pivot tables in a workbook that has been structure protected, to avoid returning an error, you'll want to use the OnDoubleClick property to disable double-clicking.

Macros can also be assigned to the OnDoubleClick property. The subroutine OnDoubleClickExample is called and will display a message box when the macro ShowMeDoubleClick is run and the user attempts to double-click on sheet 2 in the workbook.

```
Sub OnDoubleClickExample()
    MsgBox "You Have Double-clicked"
End Sub

Sub ShowMeDoubleClick()
    Worksheets("Sheet2").OnDoubleClick = "OnDoubleClickExample"
End Sub
```

Figure 5.10 shows the results of having run the subroutine ShowMeDoubleClick().

Fig. 5.10

A macro can be assigned to the OnDoubleClick property.

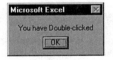

By setting the OnDoubleClick property, you can further control what the user is able to do with your worksheet or application.

Protecting Toolbars

With Excel 95, you can protect what the user is allowed to do to the toolbars. There are varying levels of protection, from the xlNormal (the no restriction constant) to xlNoChanges, which denies changes to the toolbars.

To view these constants, select a module sheet and press F2. This displays the Object Browser dialog box. Select the Excel item from the Library/Workbook drop-down list. From the Objects/Modules list, select Toolbar. Select Protection from the Methods/Properties list. Click the underlined question mark at the bottom of the dialog box.

The following are the levels of toolbar protection that can be applied, and the effect of applying the protection.

▶ xlNormal. No restrictions have been applied to the toolbars.

▶ xlNoButtonChanges. Toolbars can be moved, resized and docked. No toolbar may be added, removed, or repositioned.

▶ xlNoShapeChanges. Toolbars can be moved and docked but cannot be resized.

▶ xlNoDockingChanges. Toolbars can be moved, but cannot be docked or undocked.

▶ xlNoChanges. This is the maximum toolbar protection. No changes permitted.

An example of the maximum protection to a toolbar is demonstrated in the subroutine ProtectToolbarExample:

```
Sub ProtectToolbarExample()
    Toolbars("Standard").Protection = xlNoButtonChanges
End Sub
```

Another method of protecting the toolbar is to hide it. Hide the toolbars by setting the Visible property to False as shown in the subroutine ToolbarVisibleExample().

```
Sub ToolbarVisibleExample()
    Toolbars("Standard").Visible = False
End Sub
```

Also new to Excel 95 is the ProtectionMode property. This property returns a Boolean value. If the userInterfaceOnly argument has been set to True, ProtectionMode property will return a True. If the UserInterfaceOnly argument is False, a False will be returned (see fig. 5.11).

5

Fig. 5.11

The message box displays True if the worksheet has UserInterfaceOnly protection; otherwise, it displays False.

By running the following subroutine, a message box will be displayed indicating if the active sheet has UserInterfaceOnly protection.

```
Sub ProtectionModeExample()
    MsgBox "The protection for this sheet is set to " & _
    ActiveSheet.ProtectionMode
End Sub
```

Designing a Password Edit Box

Excel 95 allows you to quickly encrypt an edit box on a dialog sheet by setting the PasswordEdit property of the edit box to True. When the dialog box is run, the edit box will display only asterisks when data is typed into it.

An example of setting the PasswordEdit property of the edit box to True can be seen in the subroutine, `PasswordEditExample`. In this macro, the sheet `"Dialog1"` contains an edit box. In this case, the edit box selected is the object index 1. When the dialog box is run, anything entered into the edit box will display as asterisks.

```
Sub PasswordEditExample()
DialogSheets("Dialog1").EditBoxes(1).PasswordEdit = True
End Sub
```

Add-Ins

One sure way to increase the security password-protecting edit boxesof your file is to create a protected add-in. An add-in is an XLS application that has been converted to an XLA.

An add-in is a fully compiled version of an XLS file. It cannot be edited, and it is hidden from the user.

Caution
You must have a separate XLS file that serves as your editable file for the add-in. Add-ins cannot be edited; you must edit from the XLS file and resave the XLS file as an add-in.

One thing that an XLA add-in file has going for it is that it handles the Tools, Options, Module, General, Break On All Errors option better than a regular XLS file. An XLS file, even with error handling, breaks when it encounters an error. An XLA file will not.

To create an add-in, first protect the worksheet and workbook. Select a module sheet. Choose Tools, Make Add-In, name the file with the default .XLA name, and save the file to the correct location.

If you choose only to protect the worksheet and not the workbook, the add-in can be broken by running the following subroutine:

```
Option Explicit
Option Compare Text

Sub Breakit()
    Dim oObject As Object
    For Each oObject In Workbooks("Breakexample.xla").Sheets
    If TypeName(oObject) = "worksheet" Then oObject.Copy
    Next oObject
End Sub
```

The subroutine Breakit loops through each worksheet object in the specified XLA file and copies the worksheets to the workbook.

 Note

Option Compare Text is module level and sets the string comparison method to Text. It is required at the top of your module sheet for this subroutine to run without error.

χ Caution

If you don't want your add-in easily broken into, protect *both* the worksheets and the workbook before saving the file as an add-in. Most other ways of protection can easily be gotten around, and some people can even crack add-ins. It's relatively easy to break an add-in that has only sheet-level protection.

How Safe Is Your Data in Excel?

Excel's abundant, carefully designed built-in features and VBA code protection schemes seem to address every conceivable way that a file could be tampered with. But really how safe is it from prying eyes and malicious fingers?

Well, as an indication, you should know that there's a company dedicated to helping people who forget their file-level passwords and can't open their Excel files. The company guarantees a 100 percent success rate at unlocking files and features (and charges a lot of money to do the honors). One wonders who else has hit upon the method this company uses. On the CompuServe MS Excel forum, you'll occasionally hear of a person who boasts that they have written a procedure to crack password codes by using random number generation algorithms. This could be true. The point is that your protection is only as good as the determination and skill (or lack thereof) of code crackers who want to disable it.

This does not mean that you should get carried away with loading every applicable protection feature into your application. Use your judgment, and of course, find out from the client what they think a reasonable level of security would be for the file. In most cases, users for whom you will be creating files will have no idea how to use about 70 percent of the Excel application's features, let alone have a clue about how to begin to break into your password-protected file.

There is one security topic worth mentioning here that may be relevant for those who are developing for or in ultra-high security environments. Up until now this chapter has dealt with how to protect your data; you may want to know how to destroy it. Remember that when you erase data on a disk, it is not actually gone for good until it is overwritten, which may not happen for quite a while, depending on disk space. In the meantime, the files are recoverable through disk utilities. These same disk utilities (such as Norton Utilities) usually offer options to write new, meaningless data over the top of what you have previously "erased," which permanently and irretrievably discards the erased data.

Summary

Protection is a critical element for the Excel developer. As a person who develops applications for others to use, you must be aware of the pros and cons of applying each type of protection to your file.

You have seen examples of how to apply password protection and you've also seen some tricky ways that a code cracker will try to get around the protection that you've implemented. In the "real world" you have to be aware of these issues and try to find the best means possible for protecting your data.

Formula Power

chapter 6

The Power of Formulas

6

by John V. Green

In this chapter

◆ **Using operators**
Knowing the Operators gives you the power to specify your calculations from the simple to the complex.

◆ **Using references**
Using the right References saves you valuable time in spreadsheet development.

◆ **Using functions**
Functions make it easy for you to carry out many often used or difficult calculations.

◆ **Putting it all together**
Through examples, you will see how to combine operators, references, and functions to effectively define advanced calculations.

Formulas are the driving force behind your spreadsheet. Formulas relieve you of the tedious task of having to use a calculator every time you make a simple change to your data. The need for an automatic, computerized recalculation process is the reason that spreadsheets were developed in the first place.

Sometimes just a few additions, subtractions, and sums are sufficient, but if you want to go further than this, Excel has powerhouse calculation capabilities ready for you to tap. Excel has been designed to handle any mathematical process that you can think of and makes it easy to specify and execute those processes.

This chapter introduces you to many examples of how formulas can work for you. Applications that you thought were difficult or impossible might be easier than you thought.

Problems You Can Solve with Formulas

Formulas can solve practically any problem that involves mathematical calculation or text manipulation within cells. What formulas can't do is carry out commands that you would normally execute manually from the menus, such as printing or saving your spreadsheet, or moving or copying data. If you want to automate those processes, you need to set up macros.

Spreadsheets were invented to carry out arithmetic calculations, and that is what they do best. You are provided with all the tools necessary to define the most complex calculations. In addition, there are over 300 worksheet functions built into Excel. Functions simplify some of the more commonly used calculations, such as summing or averaging ranges. They also make accessible many of the more complex calculations used by specialists in statistics, engineering, finance, and many other fields.

As well as numeric data, formulas can manipulate text data. You can combine text and numbers to get meaningful messages for reports or generate information and warning messages in your worksheet. You can search for data embedded in text and extract it. You can format numbers and dates and embed them inside text messages.

Formulas enable you to calculate using dates. Not only can you find out how many days there are between two dates, but also how many months or years, or how many days including or excluding weekends and public holidays. You can calculate, for example, the last day of each month, the last Friday of each month, or the last working day of each month.

Formulas can work with alternatives. The IF function enables you to specify more than one result for a single calculation, dependent on one or more logical tests.

Formulas can search tables. If you can't specify how two variables are related by a formula, you can show how they are related in a tabular format and your formula can match known data and extract related data from the table. It is even possible to interpolate between the table values if you structure the table properly.

The following sections explain these concepts in detail. Through seeing examples of how the various principles can be applied, you will be able to relate these ideas to your own applications and start to realize the full power of Excel formulas.

Using All the Operators

Most Excel users are familiar with the arithmetic operators for addition, subtraction, multiplication, division, and percent. However, this hardly touches the power that is available. There are many additional operators that could be useful to you. The following sections show you how to use the text concatenation operator, the comparison operators, and the reference operators.

Table 6.1 lists the arithmetic operators. The one operator that is not used often by most users is the exponentiation operator. It is more likely to be used by engineers, statisticians, and scientists.

Table 6.1   Arithmetic Operators

Operator	Meaning
+	Addition
−	Subtraction (when placed before a value, as in −1, it is called negation)
/	Division
*	Multiplication
%	Percent, when placed after a value, as in 20%
^ (caret)	Exponentiation (raises a number to a power such as 3^2 = 9)

Usually there is a function to carry out the calculations that would otherwise need exponentiation. An example is the PMT function, which you can use to find the payments per period on an amortized loan.

Figure 6.1 shows some simple examples of exponentiation, raising the number two to powers from zero to three. Raising a number to the power of zero always gives an answer of one. Raising a number to the power of one leaves it unchanged.

Figure 6.1 also shows the more complex calculation required to get the repayments on a loan. It also illustrates the power of functions to free you from having to remember very complex formulas. The PMT function is used in C15. Its arguments are the interest rate, the term of the loan, and the amount borrowed, in that order. Note that the interest rate has been divided by 12 to give the monthly interest rate, and the term in years has been multiplied by 12 to give the term in months. The amount has been negated because Excel normally gives a negative result for payments and a positive result is wanted here.

The same result is achieved in C16 as C15 by using the payments formula. The formula is

```
Payment = Amount * InterestRate / (1-(1/(1+InterestRate)) ^ Term)
```

Fig. 6.1

You can use the expo-nentiation operator to multiply a number by itself a specified number of times.

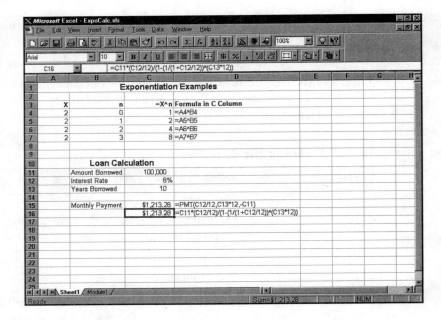

The formula used in C16 adjusts the annual interest rate and term to months as shown here:

```
=C2*(C3/12)/(1-(1/(1+C3/12))^(C4*12))
```

3-D References

Many users take advantage of the 3-D structure of a workbook to hold data for the different divisions of their organization. Each sheet in the workbook has data for a different division. Normally, each sheet has exactly the same structure. The layout of the data in any one sheet is identical to the layout in every other sheet.

If you have this type of structure, you can make use of the functions that can perform calculations over 3-D ranges (see fig. 6.2). Most of Excel's functions do not accept 3-D range references. The functions shown in table 6.2 are exceptions. The most commonly used function in this situation is the SUM function, which can be used to aggregate the cells from the other sheets.

Fig. 6.2

You can use Excel's 3-D formulas to perform calculations across the sheets of a workbook.

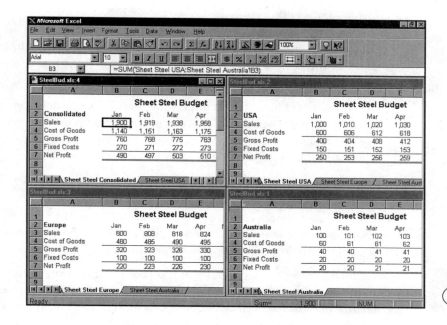

Table 6.2 Functions Used with 3-D Ranges

Function	Purpose
AVERAGE	Averages the values in the range
COUNT	Counts how many numbers are in the range
COUNTA	Counts how many values are in the range
MAX	Returns the maximum value in the range
MIN	Returns the minimum value in the range
PRODUCT	Multiplies all the numbers in the range
STDEV	Estimates the standard deviation of the numbers in the range, based on a sample
STDEVP	Estimates the standard deviation of the numbers in the range, based on the entire population
SUM	Sums the numbers in the range
VAR	Estimates the variance of the numbers in the range, based on a sample
VARP	Estimates the variance of the numbers in the range, based on the entire population

6

Handling Text in Formulas

All spreadsheet users are familiar with formulas that produce numeric results. Not all are aware of the powerful text handling capabilities of Excel that enable you to deal with labels in cells and text strings in formulas.

You can use text functions to display messages in your worksheets that change according to the data in the worksheet. This can be useful for presenting data in a more meaningful context and for producing warning messages. You can also locate text information that is embedded in cells such as a product name or city name.

Concatenation

The concatenation operator, an ampersand (&), joins two pieces of text to form one continuous text value. You can access text in label cells or introduce new text into the formula by enclosing it in double quotation marks.

Figure 6.3 shows some examples of text concatenation. The power of these formulas lies in the fact that, like numeric calculations, they automatically update when there is a change in the referenced cells. One application of these formulas is in a workbook in which you have common headings used at different locations. When you change a single cell containing a product, company or month name, for example, all the other headings change.

Fig. 6.3

You can use the concatenation operator to join text from cells and text in quotation marks.

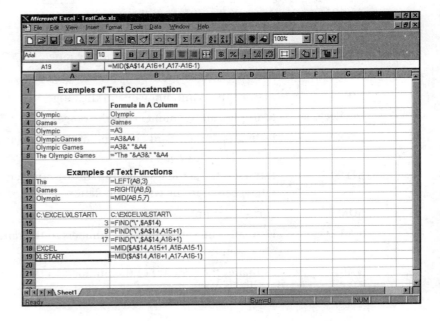

Excel also has many functions for manipulating text data. Table 6.3 shows the text functions. For example, these functions allow you to convert text to numbers and numbers to text, as well as present text in different formats.

Table 6.3   Text Handling Functions

Function	Purpose
CHAR	Returns the character specified by the code number
CLEAN	Removes all nonprintable characters from text
CODE	Returns a numeric code for the first character in a text string
CONCATENATE	Joins several text items into one text item
DOLLAR	Converts a number to text, using currency format
EXACT	Checks to see if two text values are identical
FIND	Finds one text value within another (case-sensitive)
FIXED	Formats a number as text with a fixed number of decimals
LEFT	Returns the leftmost characters from a text value
LEN	Returns the number of characters in a text string
LOWER	Converts text to lowercase
MID	Returns a specific number of characters from a text string starting at the position you specify
PROPER	Capitalizes the first letter in each word of a text value
REPLACE	Replaces characters within text
REPT	Repeats text a given number of times
RIGHT	Returns the rightmost characters from a text value
SEARCH	Finds one text value within another (not case-sensitive)
SUBSTITUTE	Substitutes new text for old text in a text string
T	Converts its arguments to text
TEXT	Formats a number and converts it to text
TRIM	Removes spaces from text
UPPER	Converts text to uppercase
VALUE	Converts a text argument to a number

You can also extract parts of other text strings. Figure 6.3 shows the main ones. LEFT and RIGHT extract the specified number of characters from the ends of strings. MID extracts from any starting character the specified number of characters. The FIND function searches a text string to find another set of characters and tells you the starting character position of the found string. You can designate where it starts searching so that it skips over previous occurrences. The FIND functions used in figure 6.3 show how you can find the first \ in a file path and then find more. The MID function examples show how you can use the FIND results to extract the directory names from the path.

 Note

The SEARCH function is similar to the FIND function. However, SEARCH is not case-sensitive and it allows you to use wild cards. ? matches any character and * matches any sequence of characters. If you need to search for the actual characters ? or *, place a tilde (˜) in front of them.

Including Numbers

Most computer software does not allow you to directly concatenate text and numbers. It is normal to have to convert numbers to a text format before you can join them to a character string. This is not the case with Excel, which can automatically carry out nearly all such conversions for you. Figure 6.4 contains examples of joining text and numbers. In cell A4, the character string "Price = " is concatenated with the cell A3 numeric value of 6.2.

In some cases Excel's conversion efforts are not satisfactory. You can get around this using the TEXT function from table 6.3. (see fig. 6.4). In cell A5, the TEXT function is used to give the cell A3 value a format of "$0.00," just as it might appear in the Format Cells dialog box under the Number tab Custom Category. In A6, the TEXT function has been used in conjunction with concatenation to get the final text required.

Cell A9 shows an example of what happens with dates. The date in cell A8 is displayed using its date serial number rather than the formatted result in cell A8. In cells A10 and A11, the TEXT function displays its power to convert the date into any valid Excel date format.

Fig. 6.4

Excel lets you concatenate text and numbers directly in formulas.

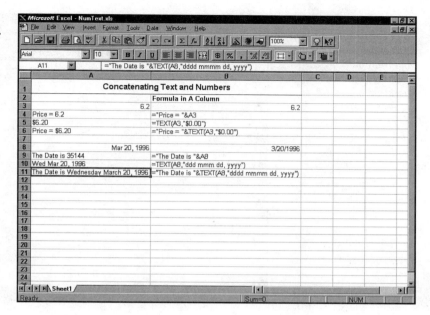

α Note

If you want to use the TEXT function in your VBA macro code, you can do so by preceding the function with the keyword "Application" to specify that it is an Excel worksheet function, not a built-in VBA function. In other words, you have to use the fairly lengthy construction of Application.Text. As a better alternative, you can use the VBA function, FORMAT. It works in exactly the same way as TEXT but has more options, and does not require the Application keyword.

Embedding Quotes

One problem that arises when you manipulate text in formulas is how you specify that the text is to contain one or more double quotation marks. Figure 6.5 shows examples of how this is done. You need to enter two double quotation marks for each single one within the text. When Excel finds two quotes together, it knows that this is not the end of the string, but an embedded quote.

Fig. 6.5

You can specify that your text contains one double quotation mark by inserting two double quotation marks.

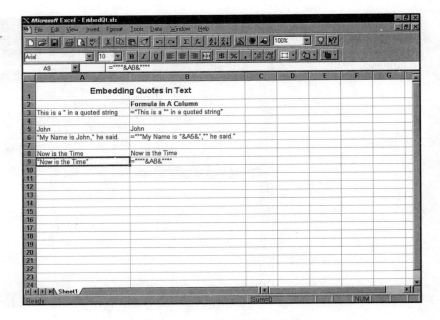

The example in cell A3 is easy to understand. The example in cell A6 is a bit more complex although it follows the same principle. Perhaps the oddest construction is the example in A9, where you want to put quotes around cell referenced text. You have to use four double quotation marks in succession to get one double quotation mark.

Using Names

If you find that you have to refer to the same cells in formulas in different parts of your workbook, you might consider giving those cells names. It is easier to remember a meaningful name than a cell address.

Another advantage of names is that Excel allows you to paste them into formulas from a list. This means that it is easy to recognize your names and you won't misspell the name in this way.

Names also make it easier for you and others to read and understand the formulas. The formula which follows:

    =A5*A6

is not as easy to understand as:

    =AmountBorrowed*InterestRate

You will also find names an advantage when you refer to ranges of cells in which you insert or delete cells. For example, you might have a column of cells containing outstanding invoices. By naming the cells Invoices, you can sum them with the following:

```
=SUM(Invoices)
```

In this case it is a good idea to have the range extend to dummy cells above and below the data as shown in figure 6.6. As long as you insert and delete items between the ends of the range, the name will adjust so that the formula remains valid.

Fig. 6.6

You can use names, such as Invoices, in calculations instead of cell references.

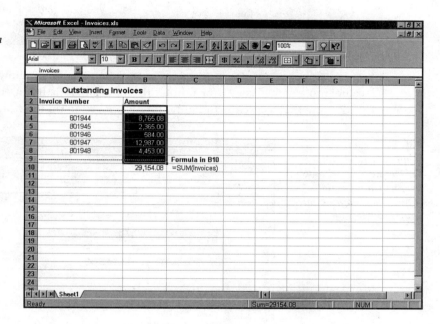

You can define names in two ways, using the Name Box and also by using Insert, Name, Define from the worksheet menu. To define a name using the Name Box, follow these steps:

1. Select the cells on the worksheet that you want to name.
2. Click in the Name Box.
3. Type the name.
4. Press Enter.

To define a name using the worksheet menu, follow these steps:

1. Select the cells on the worksheet that you want to name.
2. Choose Insert, Name, Define, or press Ctrl+F3, to open the Define Name dialog box.

3. In the Names in <u>W</u>orkbook edit box, there might be a suggested name derived from text in the worksheet. You can accept the suggested name or overwrite it by typing the name you prefer.

4. Click OK or press Enter.

 Note

You can't delete names using the Name Box. You have to use <u>I</u>nsert, <u>N</u>ame, <u>D</u>efine to open the Define Name dialog box. Here, you can select a name and click the <u>D</u>elete button.

You can also use names to hold values or formulas. Figure 6.7 shows how you can enter a value into a name. SalesGrowth holds the value of 1.5%. It is used in the formulas in C2:G2. Note that SalesGrowth has no physical location on the worksheet.

Fig. 6.7

You can define names in the Define Name dialog box, which holds data rather than referring to worksheet cells.

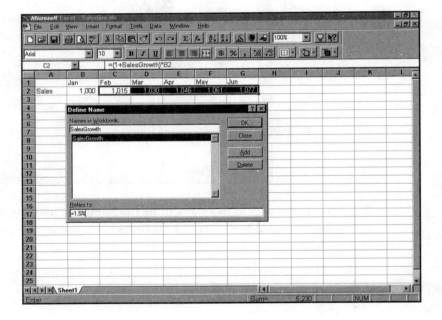

Note

Using the Name Box, you can only define and access names that refer to ranges in the workbook. Names that contain data or formulas must be defined using the Define Name dialog box.

If you want to insert names that refer to ranges into a formula, you can access the list in the Name Box by clicking on the arrow to the right of the Name Box while you are typing the formula. You can also access these names by choosing Insert, Name, Paste while typing the formula. You can't access names holding data from the Name Box. You must either type them yourself or choose Insert, Name, Paste.

Relative, Absolute, and Mixed References

If you want to tap into the most efficient way of copying formulas, you need to be aware of not only relative and absolute references, but mixed references. Table 6.4 shows the alternatives available. The only significance of the dollar signs ($) in cell references is their effect when you copy the formula containing them. They have no effect on the original formula.

Table 6.4   Cell References

Reference	Meaning
$A$1	Absolute reference. When copied, the reference does not change.
A1	Relative reference. When copied to a different column and row, both the column letter and row number change.
$A1	Mixed reference. When copied to a different column and row, the column letter does not change but the row number changes.
A$1	Mixed reference. When copied to a different column and row, the column letter changes but the row number does not change.

6

A reference in a formula which has no $ signs in it is called a *relative reference*. When you copy a formula containing a relative reference to a new cell location, the relative reference changes. When you copy a formula that contains $ signs against both the column letter and the row number, an absolute reference, it remains fixed.

A *mixed reference*, as the name implies, causes either the column or the row reference to remain fixed while the other can change. They are not used as often as relative and absolute references, but they have some interesting applications.

Your aim should be to work as productively as possible. If you can create one formula and copy it to produce others, that is more productive than creating many formulas individually. Knowing how to use all these types of references means you can spend a lot less time setting up your calculations.

Figure 6.8 shows two views of the same spreadsheet, the lower view displays the worksheet formulas. The spreadsheet contains two examples of the use of absolute references. The first is in cell B3, which multiplies $B$7, the cost factor, and cell B2. It is better to think of the B2 cell reference as a reference to the cell above the formula. The copies across row 3 all refer to cell $B$7 and the cell above the formula.

Fig. 6.8

You can use absolute cell references to ensure that when you copy a formula, that reference is fixed on the original cell.

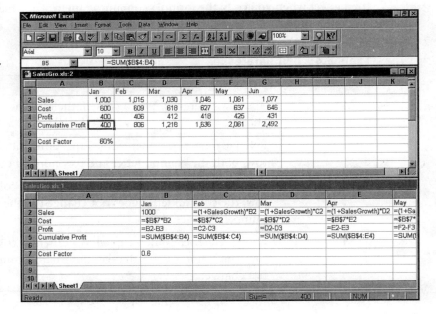

Cumulative Values

Cell B5 in figure 6.8 contains an example of a range reference that has been fixed at one end in cell $B$4 but where the other end has been made relative to the cell above by referring to cell B4. The copies across row 5 also refer to a sum range starting in cell $B$4 and ending in the cell above the formula.

It might seem that the SUM function in B5 is quite unnecessary, but it shows that by thinking ahead, you can save yourself effort and time. Remember that productivity is the aim.

Price Times Units

Figure 6.9 shows how you can use a mixed reference. Cell C10 contains a formula that calculates the January revenue for Apples from the price of Apples in $B4 and the sales in C4. You can copy this formula to create all the other revenue formulas.

When you copy this formula down the C Column, the row numbers change relatively, as required, to refer to the other products. When you copy the formula across the D and E columns, the price reference is fixed in the B column while the sales reference is allowed to change relative to the month.

Fig. 6.9

You can save yourself time by using mixed cell references.

Revenues.xls:1 — C10 = =$B4*C4

	A	B	C	D	E
2				Sales	
3		Price	Jan	Feb	Mar
4	Apples	10.5	1,000	1,015	1,030
5	Oranges	12.4	800	812	824
6	Peaches	15.6	500	508	515
7					
8				Revenues	
9			Jan	Feb	Mar
10	Apples		10,500	10,658	10,817
11	Oranges		9,920	10,069	10,220
12	Peaches		7,800	7,917	8,036
13					

Revenues.xls:2

	A	B	C	D	E	F
2				Sales		
3		Price	Jan		Feb	Mar
4	Apples	10.5	1000	=1.015*C4	=1.015*D4	
5	Oranges	12.4	800	=1.015*C5	=1.015*D5	
6	Peaches	15.6	500	=1.015*C6	=1.015*D6	
7						
8				Revenues		
9			Jan		Feb	Mar
10	Apples		=$B4*C4	=$B4*D4	=$B4*E4	
11	Oranges		=$B5*C5	=$B5*D5	=$B5*E5	
12	Peaches		=$B6*C6	=$B6*D6	=$B6*E6	
13						

Ready — Sum= 10,500 — NUM SCRL

Dealing with Ranges

When specifying ranges in formulas, you can use the three reference operators shown in table 6.5. The first one, the range operator, is the most frequently seen. It is used to include all the cells between the two references and is probably most familiar when used as the argument to a SUM function as in figure 6.8.

Table 6.5   Reference Operators

Reference Operator	Meaning
Range(:)	Produces one reference to all the cells between and including the two references.
Union(,)	Produces one reference that includes the two references.
Intersection(space)	Produces one reference to cells common to the two references.

Noncontiguous Ranges

The union operator can be used to join two or more other cells or range references. It is equivalent to holding down Ctrl as you select a number of different ranges with the mouse. You end up with multiple blocks of cells selected which is called a noncontiguous range.

You should not confuse the union operator with the comma which is used to separate the arguments of a function. Figure 6.10 shows a SUM function that adds up a large number of named cells from row 6 of the spreadsheet. The formula appears to exceed the limit imposed by Excel of a maximum of 30 arguments for a function. There are 35 names in this list.

If you look closely, you will see that there are two sets of parentheses around the names. The outer set is the normal set used by any function. The inner set defines a single argument, which consists of the union of the 35 names. You could add another 29 arguments if you want or put more names into the first argument.

This bit of magic increases the number of ranges that can be referenced by a SUM function and other functions that have a variable number of arguments. The limit now becomes the 1,024 character limit on the length of a formula.

Fig. 6.10

You can overcome the Excel maximum of 30 arguments for a SUM function by using the union operator.

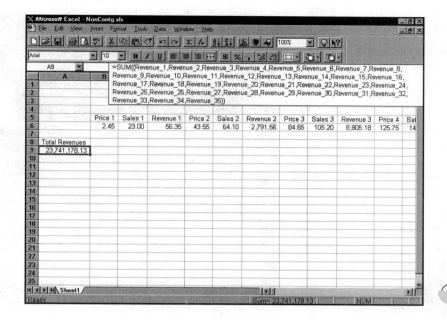

Intersecting Ranges

You can use the blank space character between two range references to generate a reference to the cells that are common to the two, or, in other words, where they overlap. This might seem to be a bit strange, but it leads to some very useful and easily understood formulas. Especially if you use it in conjunction with names that refer to ranges.

Figure 6.11 shows how you can create a set of names from labels in the spreadsheet. You select a block of cells that has labels in the top row and left column, choose Insert, Name, Create from the menu. In the dialog box that appears, make sure that the corresponding check boxes are marked and click OK.

In this example six names are created using the month names and four using the A column headings. The name January, for example, is created referring to the range B2:B5, and the name Sales is created, referring to the range B2:G2.

You can now refer to these names in formulas that use the intersect operator. The formula in cell B10 refers to the intersect of the name June and the name Sales, which is cell G2. The formula in B11 sums a range between the intersect of January and Sales and the intersect of March and Sales. You can see that these formulas are relatively easy to understand.

Fig. 6.11

You can create names from labels in a worksheet by selecting a block of cells and choosing Insert, Name, Create.

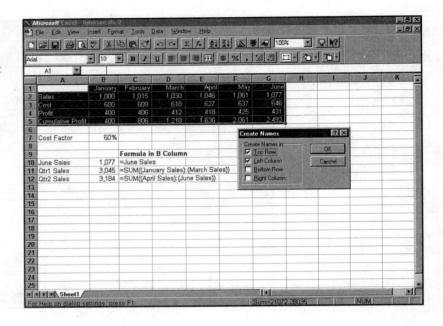

Handling Alternatives with IF

One of the most powerful and useful functions in Excel is the IF function. You can produce alternative calculations or text messages based on a test, comparing two or more numeric values or text strings. The comparison operators that you can use in tests are shown in table 6.6.

Table 6.6   Comparison Operators

Comparison Operator	Meaning
=	Equal to
>	Greater than
<	Less than
>=	Greater than or equal to
<=	Less than or equal to
<>	Not equal to

Numeric Results

Figure 6.12 shows some examples of tax calculations. In row 4 there is a series of profit projections for a new venture. In the first two years, the profits are negative so they are in fact losses. Row 5 calculates the tax payable. Tax is not paid on a loss, only on a profit. The tax rate is in cell B1, which has been given the name of TaxRate.

Fig. 6.12

You can use the IF function to carry out alternative calculations.

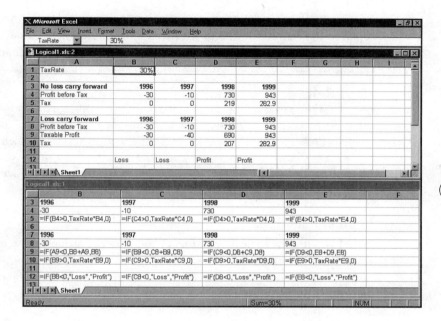

The first example assumes that we cannot carry forward our tax losses. You might be tempted to enter zero values in B5 and C5 and a simple multiplication of profit by the tax rate in D5 and E5. However, this is not a good idea. If new figures are entered or calculated for row 4, and the pattern of losses and profits changes, those calculations would not be correct.

It is much better to use an IF function that allows for the two alternatives. The calculation in B5 says that if the profit in B4 is greater than 0, tax is calculated by multiplying the cell named TaxRate and B4. The alternative calculation covers the case where the profit is zero or less and in this example will simply give a zero result.

Text Results

The calculations in row 12 of figure 6.12 show how you can produce a text string as a result of an IF function. It is done in the same way as a numeric calculation. The text must be enclosed in double quotation marks as covered earlier in this chapter. You could also substitute calculations that give text results.

If you want, you can make one of the results numeric and the other text. For example, in the row 5 calculations in figure 6.12, you could replace the zero result with a text string such as "No Tax Payable."

You might also want to have no result appear as an alternative in some cases. If you replaced the zero result in B5 with two double quotation marks with either nothing or a blank space between them, the cell would appear blank rather than zero.

 Note

Say you calculate a non-numeric result in cell B5, such as a "" or " ". If you then try to use this result in another calculation, such as =B5+B20, Excel will give you a #VALUE! error. To avoid this you can use the N function to convert the non-numeric result to zero. For example, =N(B5)+B20.

Logical Functions

When you use the logical operators to compare two values, they return a True or False result that is mostly used as the first argument of the IF function. When you want to use more complex comparisons involving more than two values, you can use the AND, OR, and NOT functions, which are shown in table 6.7.

Table 6.7   Logical Functions

Function	Purpose
AND	Returns True if all its arguments are True
FALSE	Returns the logical value False
IF	Specifies a logical test to perform
NOT	Reverses the logic of its argument
OR	Returns True if any argument is True
TRUE	Returns the logical value True

Figure 6.13 shows a comparison of three different salary increase policies based on years of service, level, and current salary. The formula in E4 says that if years of service is greater than 5 *and* level is greater than 3, the salary increase is 8%. Otherwise, it is 5%.

Fig. 6.13

You can use the AND and OR functions to evaluate combinations of logical tests. In this spreadsheet, three different policies for granting salary increases are compared.

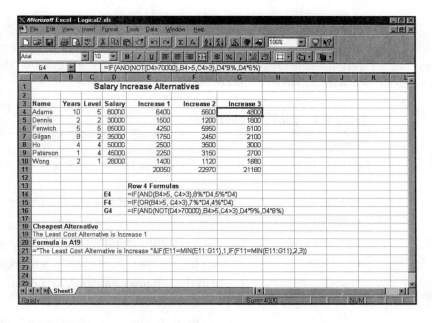

The formula in F4 says that if either the years of service is greater than 5 *or* level is greater than 3, the salary increase is 7%. Otherwise, it is 4%.

The formula in G4 says that if current salary is *not* greater than 70000 *and* years of service is greater than 5 *and* level is greater than 3, the salary increase is 9%. Otherwise, it is 6%.

> **Tip**
>
> If you find the Excel logical functions confusing to use, and you are familiar with the Lotus 1-2-3 logical operators #AND#, #OR# and #NOT#, you can choose Tools, Options, click the Transition tab and check Transition Formula Entry. You can now enter formulas such as =IF(#NOT#D4>70000#AND#B4>5#AND#C4>3,D4*9%, D4*6%), in G4 of figure 6.13. Excel converts this to a form using the logical functions.

The formula in cell A19 of figure 6.13 uses an IF function embedded in another IF function, which lets you generate more than two possible results. This sort of construction can get very difficult to understand if taken to extremes. The calculation appends a 1, 2, or 3 to the preceding text. To decide on the value, it first compares E11 with the minimum value in the range E11:G11. If they are the same, it returns a value of 1. Otherwise, it calculates the second IF, which compares F11 with the minimum of the range. If they are the same, it returns a value of 2. Otherwise, it returns a value of 3.

Getting Data from Tables

When you have data in a table format, you need to know about the lookup functions. A complete list is given in table 6.8. The next sections examine the most useful ones, VLOOKUP, MATCH, and INDEX.

Table 6.8   Lookup Functions

Function	Purpose
ADDRESS	Returns a reference as text to a single cell in a worksheet
AREAS	Returns the number of areas in a reference
CHOOSE	Chooses a value from a list of values
COLUMN	Returns the column number of a reference
COLUMNS	Returns the number of columns in a reference
HLOOKUP	Looks in the top row of an array and returns the value of the indicated cell
INDEX	Uses an index to choose a value from a reference or array
INDIRECT	Returns a reference indicated by a text value
LOOKUP	Looks up values in a vector or array
MATCH	Looks up values in a reference or array
OFFSET	Returns a reference offset from a given reference
ROW	Returns the row number of a reference
ROWS	Returns the number of rows in a reference
TRANSPOSE	Returns the transpose of an array
VLOOKUP	Looks in the first column of an array and moves across the row to return the value of a cell

How you use these functions depends on the table structure. Has the table been sorted into a particular order? Are you looking for both column and row references? Do you need to interpolate between the values shown? The answers to these questions indicate which is the best function, or combination of functions to use to get your result.

VLOOKUP

Figure 6.14 contains a table of bonuses to be paid according to sales achieved. A sales figure is entered in a cell in the D column, and Excel finds the corresponding bonus in the table in A3:B8. VLOOKUP can do this. The first argument in VLOOKUP specifies the value you want to find in the left column of the table. The second argument specifies the table location. The third argument specifies which column of the table will contain the result.

Fig. 6.14

Using the VLOOKUP function, you can have Excel find the row corresponding to a specified value in the left column, and obtain a value from another column on the same row.

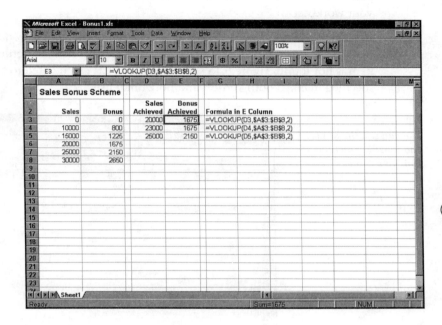

If there is not an exact match for the lookup value, Excel finds the row containing the largest number that is less than the lookup value. VLOOKUP does not interpolate between the table values. It finds the value corresponding to the bottom of the bracket or range that the number falls into. This is illustrated by the example in cell E4, which finds the same bonus for sales of 23000 as it finds for sales of 20000 in cell E3.

 Note

You must make sure that you have sorted the numbers on the left side of the table into an ascending order for this form of VLOOKUP to work properly. You can also have a list of text entries which must be sorted alphabetically in ascending order.

Excel 5 introduced a fourth, optional argument to VLOOKUP. If this argument has a value of True, or is missing, the above requirements apply. If it has a value of False, the list can be in any order and Excel looks for an exact match, returning an error value if the value in the first argument is not found.

MATCH

The MATCH function provides you with a bit more flexibility than VLOOKUP but does not return quite the answer you want in most cases. It returns an index number telling you where the item is in the list. It can be used with a list that is in a column or a row of your worksheet.

In all versions of Excel, MATCH has the capability that was introduced in Excel 5 for VLOOKUP. It can look for an exact match in an unsorted list, returning an error if the item is not found. Figure 6.15 shows how MATCH can be used to find the position of specified items in both vertical and horizontal lists.

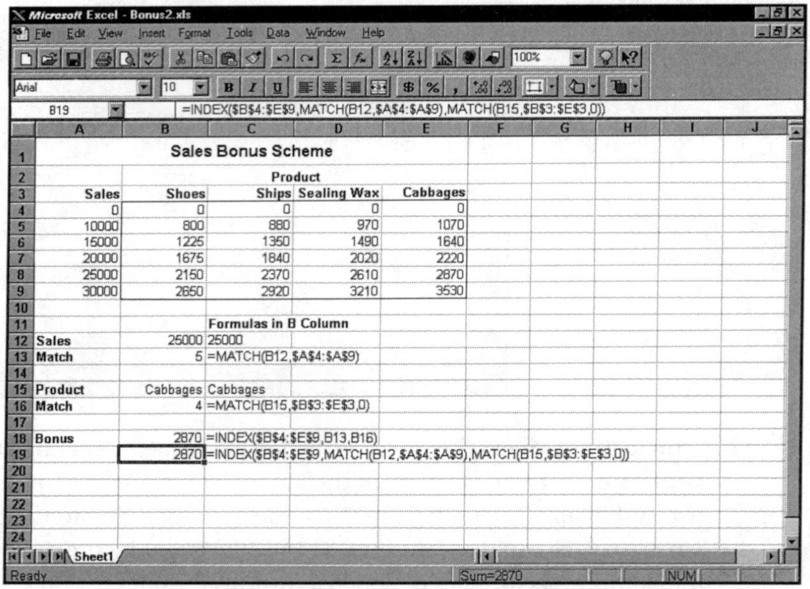

Fig. 6.15

You can use the MATCH and INDEX functions to look up a table.

Cell B13 in figure 6.15 contains a MATCH function that looks for the sales value of 25000 in the range A4:A9. The result indicates that it is the fifth item in the list. When MATCH is used in this way, like the VLOOKUP function, the list has to be in ascending order.

In cell B16, MATCH finds the position of Cabbages in the range B3:E3. Here, the optional third parameter has been given a value of zero. This means that Excel looks for an exact match and the items do not need to be sorted. The result indicates that Cabbages is the fourth item in the list.

Note

The optional third argument of MATCH can be +1, 0, or –1. +1 is the default and finds the largest value in the list that is less than or equal to the search value (the smallest value in the bracket that the value falls into.) The list must be sorted in ascending order.

0 indicates that an exact match must be found. The list can be in any order.

–1 indicates that MATCH must find the smallest value that is greater than or equal to the search value (the highest value in the bracket that the value falls into.) The list must be sorted in descending order.

INDEX

To convert the results of MATCH to something useful, you can use the INDEX function. The first argument of INDEX can be either a list (in a row or column) or a table of data. If it is a list, then the second argument specifies the position in the list and there is no third argument. If the first argument is a table, then the second argument defines the row of the table and the third argument defines the column of the table.

The formula in cell B18 of figure 6.15 shows how you can use the match results from B13 and B16 to find the corresponding bonus in B4:E9. You could also combine the MATCH and INDEX operations into a single calculation as shown in B19.

The combination of MATCH and INDEX is more flexible than VLOOKUP. First, you can locate data that is not immediately adjacent to the search values. Second, although you can look up a table using a combination of HLOOKUP and VLOOKUP, the MATCH/ INDEX combination is easier.

 Note

Don't use VLOOKUP where INDEX is more appropriate. When you want to find an entry in a column, simply by row number, don't put index values in the column to the left of the list and use VLOOKUP to get a result. INDEX gives a result more efficiently and without the need for the extra column.

Table Interpolation

Perhaps you have noted a possible deficiency in the lookups so far. You have not been able to *interpolate*. That is, you have not been able to generate results that lie between the values in the table.

Say that in the bonus scheme you wanted to proportion the bonus according to sales, rather than award the same bonus for all sales between 10000 and 14999. Figure 6.16 illustrates how you can do this.

Fig. 6.16

Using an extra column to hold the marginal rate between each sales category, you can perform interpolation of the table data.

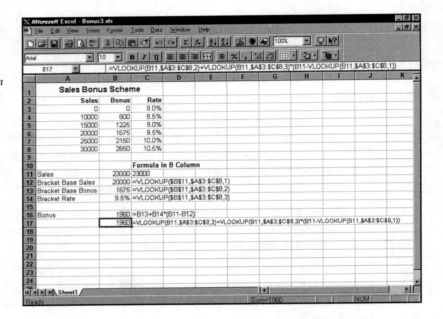

In the table in A3:C8, the B column gives the bonus for the sales indicated in the A column. The C column provides the rate at which sales above the A column value earn bonus, up to the next bracket. If you can find the sales at the beginning of the bracket into which the actual sales fall you can work out the extra bonus earned by multiplying the difference between the actual sales and the base bracket sales by the rate.

The secret is that if you ask VLOOKUP to find a value from column 1 in the table, it gives you the value of sales from the bracket base. Just what you need! In cell B12 of figure 6.16, VLOOKUP looks for the value of 23000 in column 1 and returns the value of 20000.

B13 and B14 find the column 2 and 3 values from the table. B16 combines these figures to calculate the actual bonus. Cell B17 shows how all the calculations can be combined into one.

Handling Dates

If you have to change the dates in a spreadsheet frequently or you want dates such as the last Friday of the month, you can use formulas that automatically recalculate when a new starting date is entered. The key functions you can use are shown in table 6.9.

Table 6.9   Standard Excel Date Functions

Function	Action
DATE(yy,mm,dd)	Calculates a date serial number.
YEAR(date)	Extracts year number of a date serial number.
MONTH(date)	Extracts month number of a date serial number.
DAY(date)	Extracts day number of a date serial number.
WEEKDAY(date,type)	Calculates weekday index of a date serial number. If type is 1 or omitted, the index numbers range from 1 (Sunday) through 7 (Saturday). If type is 2, the index numbers range from 1 (Monday) through 7 (Sunday). If the type is 3, the index numbers range from 0 (Monday) through 6 (Sunday). Type 3 is the same as the Lotus 1-2-3 @WEEKDAY function.
DATEDIF (start_date,end_date,code)	This is an undocumented function introduced in Excel 5. It is identical to the Lotus 1-2-3 @DATEDIF function. It computes the number of time periods between the start and end dates. The time periods computed are determined by the following code values:

d	Days
m	Months
y	Years
md	Days, ignoring months and years
ym	Months, ignoring years
yd	Days, ignoring years

6

Table 6.10 shows some extra functions that only can be used if the Analysis ToolPak add-in has been loaded. Although the ToolPak is provided to all users, not everyone has it installed as it uses extra memory and takes time to load. The EDATE and EOMONTH functions can be easily emulated using the standard functions if you want to avoid loading the ToolPak.

Table 6.10   Date Functions in Excel's Analysis ToolPak

Function	Action
EDATE(date,months)	Calculates the date serial number that is the indicated number of months before or after the date
EOMONTH(date,months)	Calculates the date serial number of the end of the month, which is the indicated number of months before or after the date
NETWORKDAYS (start_date,end_date,holidays)	Calculates the number of days between the start and end dates, excluding Saturdays, Sundays and dates in holidays
WORKDAY(date,days,holidays)	Calculates the date serial number, which is the indicated number of workdays after the date, taking into account Saturdays, Sundays and dates in holidays

Figure 6.17 shows some of the possible calculations. In each case, the first date in row 4 is a manual entry. Row 5 contains formulas that have been copied down.

You can produce some of the series shown in figure 6.17 using the AutoFill feature. However, this is not the most convenient way if you want your cells to automatically update when the first cell changes.

You can easily calculate the same day each month. The formula in B5 is

```
=DATE(YEAR(B4),MONTH(B4)+1,1)
```

You might wonder what happens in the formula after month 12. The month number is calculated as 13, but Excel knows that you really mean month 1 of the next year as shown on row 16 of figure 6.17.

You can also calculate the same day each month using the following formula from cell C5:

```
=DATE(YEAR(C4),MONTH(C4)+1,DAY(C4))
```

Fig. 6.17

You can calculate many useful series of dates using the Excel date functions including the last Friday or working day of the month.

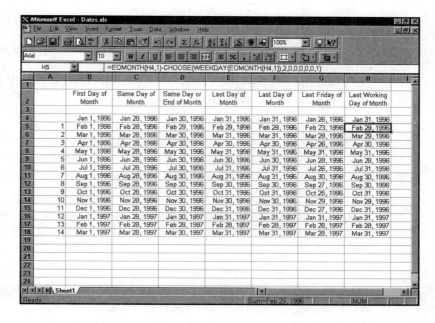

The only problem with this formula is that you can't use days beyond the 28th without eventually causing trouble. If Excel is asked to generate the 29th of February in a non-leap year, it will substitute the 1st of March. In this case, you might prefer to use the ToolPak function, EDATE, as in cell D5:

```
=EDATE($D$4,A5)
```

EDATE calculates a date that is the same day as the date specified in the first argument, but adding the number of months specified in the second argument. However, it ensures that the day does not exceed the last day of the month.

Last Day of the Month

Some people, especially accountants, are anxious to know the last day of each month or some variation such as the last Friday or Thursday in the month. The trick to finding the last day of a month is to find the first day of the following month and subtract 1.

The formula in E5 is

```
=DATE(YEAR(E4),MONTH(E4)+2,1)-1
```

Excel also has a ToolPak function for the last day in a month that is a designated number of months from a start date. To find the last day of the month, which is 1 month after the month in F4, you can enter:

```
=EOMONTH(F4,1)
```

Last Friday of the Month

If you want to know the last Friday (or Thursday or whatever) of the month, you need to determine the day of the week for the last day of the month and adjust accordingly. You can determine the day of the week for any given date using the WEEKDAY function. If you don't specify the type argument, WEEKDAY(date) returns 1, for Sunday, through 7, for Saturday.

Knowing the weekday for the end of the month, you can determine the adjustment to that date to find the previous Friday. If the last day of the month is in fact a Friday, no adjustment is required. If it is Saturday, you have to subtract 1 and so on up to Thursday where you subtract 6.

Here, you can use the CHOOSE function. CHOOSE returns an item from a list. The first argument is the index number in the list and the remaining arguments are the members of the list.

```
CHOOSE(1, "Item1", "Item2","Item3")
```

This formula returns `"Item1"` as it is item number 1 in the list. With an index value of 2 as the first argument, the result would be `"Item2"`.

To calculate the date of the last Friday in the month in G5, you can use the following:

```
=EOMONTH(G4,1)-CHOOSE(WEEKDAY(EOMONTH(G4,1)),2,3,4,5,6,0,1)
```

You can change the pattern of numbers to find any other last day. To find the last Thursday:

```
=EOMONTH(G4,1)-CHOOSE(WEEKDAY(EOFMONTH(G4,1)),3,4,5,6,0,1,2)
```

Last Working Day of the Month

Finding the last working day of the month is a matter of determining if the last day is a Saturday and subtracting 1, or Sunday and subtracting 2. Any other weekday remains unchanged. You can use exactly the same technique as shown previously.

In cell H5, use the following formula:

```
=EOMONTH(H4,1)-CHOOSE(WEEKDAY(EOMONTH(H4,1)),2,0,0,0,0,0,1)
```

Macros Need Not (Always) Apply

There are occasions when it would be nice to access information about the worksheet or the operating environment not normally associated with worksheet functions.

For example, is the worksheet in automatic or manual recalculation mode? Where is the worksheet file stored? Is the worksheet being used on a PC or a Mac? Is a particular cell protected?

You might want to have a text message appear in a cell to warn the user that the spreadsheet is in manual recalculation mode, but have it disappear or change to a confirmation message when the user switches to automatic recalculation. If you have several possible directory sources for files of a certain name, you might want to indicate on the worksheet the exact path and file name so that it appears in printed reports. You might want to display different instructions on a worksheet depending on whether it is being used on a PC or Mac. You might want to display instructions for unprotecting cells and then reprotecting them. Most users would assume that all of these wishes would require a macro solution.

CELL and INFO

Excel has traditionally provided almost every conceivable bit of information about the worksheet, workbook, and operating environment, but through macro functions rather than worksheet functions. Certainly you can write your own custom functions to obtain this information and pass it to a worksheet, using the techniques covered in Chapter 9, "The Power of Custom Functions." However, you can answer the questions posed here, and more, using the CELL function and the INFO function. The information that can be obtained with CELL is described in table 6.11 and you can see examples in figure 6.18. The information obtainable from INFO is described in table 6.13. Examples of INFO are in figure 6.19

6

CELL and INFO were added to Excel for compatibility with Lotus 1-2-3, so much of the information provided has a 1-2-3 flavor. The "prefix" option for CELL returns the label alignment characters from 1-2-3, for example, and the "format" option provides the 1-2-3 format codes, which are covered in table 6.12.

 Note

The "osversion" option of the INFO function might not return exactly what you expect. Under Windows 3.x, it reports the version of DOS in use, not Windows, as DOS is strictly the operating system. Also, under Windows 95, note that if you are running Excel 7.0 this option returns "Windows (32-bit) 4.00." If you are running Excel 5.0 under Windows 95, it reports "DOS Version 7.00."

Fig. 6.18
You can use the CELL function to obtain information about a specific cell including its file path, format, and protection status.

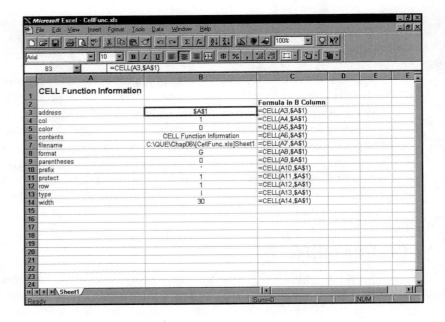

Fig. 6.19
The INFO function gives you information regarding the operating environment. You can determine which version of Excel, what operating system and what platform (PC or Mac) is in use.

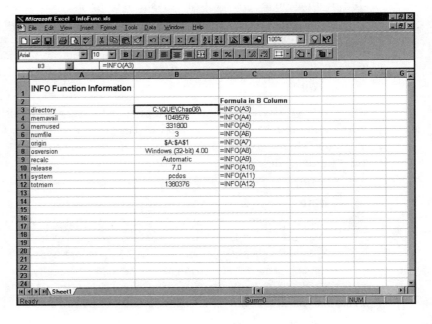

Table 6.11   Information Available from the CELL Function

Info_type	Returns
"address"	Reference of the first cell in reference, as text.
"col"	Column number of the cell in reference.
"color"	1 if the cell is formatted in color for negative values; otherwise, returns 0.
"contents"	Contents of the upper-left cell in reference.
"filename"	File name (including full path) of the file that contains reference, as text. Returns empty text ("") if the worksheet that contains reference has not yet been saved.
"format"	Text value corresponding to the number format of the cell. The text values for the various formats are shown in table 6.13. Returns "–" at the end of the text value if the cell is formatted in color for negative values. Returns "()" at the end of the text value if the cell is formatted with parentheses for positive or all values.
"parentheses"	1 if the cell is formatted with parentheses for positive or all values; otherwise, returns 0.
"prefix"	Text value corresponding to the "label prefix" of the cell. Returns single quotation mark (') if the cell contains left-aligned text, double quotation mark (") if the cell contains right-aligned text, caret (^) if the cell contains centered text, backslash (\) if the cell contains fill-aligned text, and empty text ("") if the cell contains anything else.
"protect"	0 if the cell is not locked, and 1 if the cell is locked.
"row"	Row number of the cell in reference.
"type"	Text value corresponding to the type of data in the cell. Returns "b" for blank if the cell is empty, "l" for label if the cell contains a text constant, and "v" for value if the cell contains anything else.
"width"	Column width of the cell rounded off to an integer. Each unit of column width is equal to the width of one character in the default font size.

6

Table 6.12   Information Returned for "Format"

Excel Cell Format	Code Returned
General	"G"
0	"F0"
#,##0	",0"
0.00	"F2"
#,##0.00	",2"
$#,##0_);($#,##0)	"C0"
$#,##0_);[Red]($#,##0)	"C0-"
$#,##0.00_);($#,##0.00)	"C2"
$#,##0.00_);[Red]($#,##0.00)	"C2-"
0%	"P0"
0.00%	"P2"
0.00E+00	"S2"
# ?/? or # ??/??	"G"
m/d/yy or m/d/yy h:mm or mm/dd/yy	"D4"
d-mmm-yy or dd-mmm-yy	"D1"
d-mmm or dd-mmm	"D2"
mmm-yy	"D3"
mm/dd	"D5"
h:mm AM/PM	"D7"
h:mm:ss AM/PM	"D6"
h:mm	"D9"
h:mm:ss	"D8"

The INFO function is used in the following way:

```
=INFO(Type_text)
```

where Type_text is one of the text strings shown in table 6.13.

Table 6.13   The INFO Function

Type_text	Returns
"directory"	Path of the current directory or folder.
"memavail"	Amount of memory available, in bytes.
"memused"	Amount of memory being used for data.
"numfile"	Number of active worksheets.
"origin"	Absolute A1-style reference, as text, prepended with "$A:" for Lotus 1-2-3 release 3.x compatibility. Returns the cell reference of the top- and leftmost cell visible in the window based on the current scrolling position.
"osversion"	Current operating system version, as text.
"recalc"	Current recalculation mode; returns "Automatic" or "Manual."
"release"	Version of Microsoft Excel, as text.
"system"	Name of the operating environment: Macintosh = "mac." Windows = "pcdos."
"totmem"	Total memory available, including memory already in use, in bytes.

Using the OFFSET Function

Since the first release of Excel, one of the most powerful functions in XLM macros has been the OFFSET function shown in table 6.14. It provides a general way to generate a reference to a range that is a specified number of rows and columns away from a starting point and which has any specified height and width. This might not immediately sound very useful, but turns out to be invaluable when you need to deal with a series of ranges using index numbers, especially in a looping macro procedure.

OFFSET was brought in from the cold in Excel 4.0, where it was made accessible as a worksheet function as well as a macro function. In its simplest applications it resembles the INDEX function, but it is far more powerful. OFFSET has five arguments as shown:

```
=OFFSET(reference, rows, cols, height, width)
```

The arguments are defined in table 6.14.

Table 6.14   The OFFSET Function

Argument	Meaning
Reference	The reference from which you want to base the offset. If reference is a multiple selection, OFFSET returns the #VALUE! error value.
Rows	The number of rows, up or down, that you want the upper-left cell to refer to. Using 5 as the rows argument specifies that the upper-left cell in the reference is five rows below reference. Rows can be positive or negative.
Cols	The number of columns, to the left or right, that you want the upper-left cell of the result to refer to. Using 5 as the cols argument specifies that the upper-left cell in the reference is five columns to the right of reference. Cols can be positive or negative. If rows and cols offset reference over the edge of the worksheet, OFFSET returns the #REF! error value.
Height	The height, in number of rows, that you want the returned reference to be. Height must be a positive number.
Width	The width, in number of columns, that you want the returned reference to be. Width must be a positive number. If height or width is omitted, it is assumed to be the same height or width as reference.

Figure 6.20 shows some applications of OFFSET. Cell B12 references any individual cell in the table by row and column number. You could do this with INDEX, but you would have to specify the entire table range as the first argument, not just the top-left-hand cell. Also note, that OFFSET requires the number of rows and columns away from the start. The second and third arguments of OFFSET would be one unit less than those of INDEX to reference the same cell. Also note that it is possible to have negative arguments with OFFSET, to go above and to the left of the reference cell, which you can't have with INDEX.

Fig. 6.20

Using the OFFSET function, you can generate references to cells and ranges using numeric values. You can reference individual cells in a table, or sum slices of data through a table.

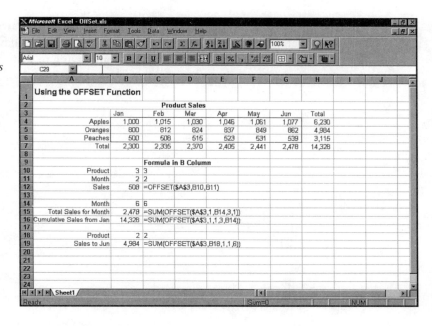

The B15 formula shows how you can combine SUM with OFFSET to total a slice from the table. The range to be summed starts one row down from A3 and the number of columns in B14. The height of the referenced range is three rows and the width is one column. By changing the value in B14 between one and six, you can generate the total any month.

The B16 formula shows how, with a small change, you can get the cumulative sales from January to the month specified in B14. The referenced cells start in B4, offset one row and one column from A3, and extend down 3 rows and across the number of columns in B14.

B19 is a variation on B15. It sums six months for any product specified in B18.

Using formulas like these, you can build up summary reports which extract data and totals from more complex tables, driven by index numbers in a few cells. It is then a simple matter to generate results for a given time period, item or selected items.

Summary

In this chapter you have seen how you can use Excel's operators, references and functions to generate powerful formulas that improve your productivity. Knowing how to apply the tools presented, you can build your applications faster and perform calculations that you might have thought too difficult or impossible.

You have seen how to automate many procedures that others carry out manually such as text manipulation, table lookups and calculation of dates. You have also seen how you can obtain some information and results without having to write macros.

chapter 7

Using Array Formulas

7

by Bob Umlas

In this chapter

◆ **Developing workbooks or applications that run efficiently**
Learn how to readily know where the last cell in a column is and how to directly access the cell where the value differs from the values in the cell above it.

◆ **Solving problems**
See ways you can frequently solve a problem with an array formula where you might think a VBA procedure would be necessary to accomplish the task.

◆ **Matching ranges**
Learn how to determine in one formula if your text matches a particular pattern in an entire range (like First name, space, Last name?) and if not, point to the cell with the error.

The techniques for doing all tasks in this list, and more, are found in this chapter. They all involve using array-formulas. This chapter is a path to mastering the power of formulas in Microsoft Excel. Most people are afraid of using formulas or at least don't really understand how formulas work. This chapter demystifies array formulas, especially in those instances where you are entering them into one cell, as opposed to array-entering a formula over several cells, like the LINEST, MMULT, and FREQUENCY functions usually do.

This chapter is not just a list of cool things you can do, but is also a teaching tool for being able to create array formulas on your own. One key thing to remember is that array formulas are entered by pressing Ctrl+Shift and then pressing Enter. Failing to enter these special formulas this way will produce incorrect results.

Using the OR Function

Using the OR function isn't necessarily using an array function, but it is included here because it deals with array constants in a way you might not be aware. Suppose you have a cell, B1, that you want to test for whether it contained either a 4, 6, or 9. You might be tempted to enter =OR(B1=4,B1=6,B1=9), which would work fine, but there's an easier way (see fig. 7.1).

Fig. 7.1

Using an array formula to simplify an OR condition.

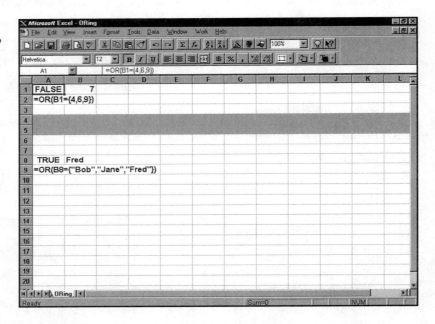

 Note

Microsoft Excel's OR function takes a list of conditions as its argument, like =OR(condition1,condition2,…,condition30), and evaluates each condition as to being TRUE or FALSE. If *any* of the conditions evaluates to TRUE, then the entire expression is TRUE.

Cell A1 contains the formula:

```
=OR(B1={4,6,9})
```

The curly braces were entered to indicate an array constant. When entering an array constant you cannot enter variables, even though their values might be known. That is, if x is defined to be =4, then you still couldn't use

```
=OR(B1={x,6,9})
```

This results in an `error in formula` message.

Also, this formula (and the one in cell A8) is entered normally, *not* as an array function. Cell A8 contains another array constant, shown again in cell A9, this time for text values. Because cell B8 contains "Fred," cell A8 contains TRUE, because it is evaluating B8:

```
={"Bob","Jane","Fred"}
```

which becomes FALSE,FALSE,TRUE. When passed to an OR function, this FALSE,FALSE,TRUE evaluates to TRUE. That is, =OR(FALSE,FALSE,TRUE) is TRUE.

Using Array Formulas and Trend Lines

The formula Excel gives for a trend line is given by the TREND function, and its format is =TREND(y-values, x-values, Const, Stats). This discussion focuses on only the first two parameters in the TREND function (y-values and x-values), but explains in detail how to create more than a simple linear trend. In fact, the discussion goes beyond Excel's built-in limit of a 6th-order polynomial best-fit curve.

As you may know, Excel 7's charting capabilities include charting a power trend line up to the 6th power. This example shows how you can go beyond that. In fact, figure 7.2 shows a set of values with a 7th-degree trend line. This section also shows how you can generate the formula used to project or determine points *not* in the original set of data.

The original y-values are shown in cells A2:A21 of figure 7.2. Cells B2:B21 show the values of the 7th-degree polynomial. Cells D17:K17 show the coefficients a to h in the formula $ax^7+bx^6+cx^5+dx^4+ex^3+fx^2+gx+h$, and cell D18 shows the results of the formula for the 17th value in the series. Cell D19 shows the formula used in D18.

Before you see what to do to get the trend line values in column B, look at figure 7.3.

Fig. 7.2

Worksheet formulas showing a 7th-degree polynomial best-fit curve.

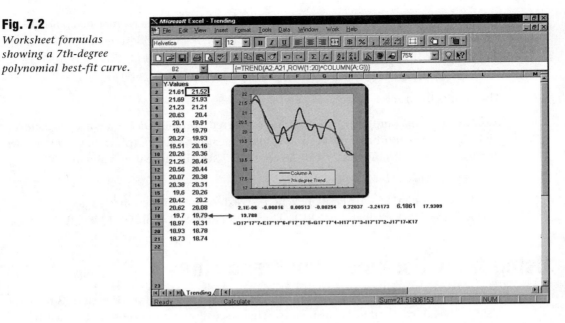

Fig. 7.3

A step in the derivation of an array formula to get a 7th-degree polynomial best-fit curve.

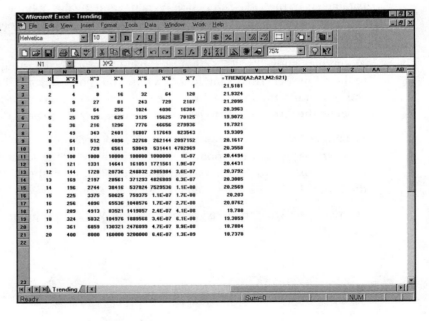

Because the original y-values were independent, the x-values needed are the simple series 1,2,3,...through 20, as shown in column M. To get a second degree trend line fit, you need to square the x-values. That is, column N contains column M squared (the formula in N2 is =M2^2). To get the trend values for this second-degree curve, first select the range U2:U21 and then array-enter

```
=TREND(A2:A21,M2:N21).
```

 Note

Microsoft Excel's TREND function fits a straight line (using the method of fewest squares) to the arrays, and can return the y-values along the line for the array of new x-values you specify. The syntax is TREND(known y's, known x's, new x's, constant). This section shows you how to use the function to fit a curve, rather than a line, to the arrays.

There are a few important things to notice. First, the range U2:U21 must *first* be selected. If you enter the formula into cell U2 and fill down, the results will be erroneous. Second, you must *array-enter* the formula. This is done by pressing Ctrl+Shift+Enter.

Some functions *must* be array-entered, and TREND is one of them (as are LINEST, GROWTH, LOGEST, TRANSPOSE, and others). Other functions are usually *not* entered as array formulas, but can be used to produce special results, as discussed later in this chapter.

To get a third-degree polynomial best-fit line, raise the x-values to the third power. Column O does that, and cell O2 contains the formula =M2^3. Then the TREND formula (array-entered) is:

```
=TREND(A2:A21,M2:O21)
```

This process can be expanded to as many as 16 columns to produce a 16th-order best-fit curve. As mentioned earlier, Excel has up to a 6th-order curve built into its trend lines. So now, as you can see in this example in figure 7.3, column U contains the values for the 7th-order polynomial fit. Notice that the values in column U are the same as the values in column B of figure 7.2.

However, column B was not created using the intermediate results in columns M through S. These values can be created within the formula itself. The actual formula in cell B2 is:

```
=TREND(A2:A21,ROW(1:20)^COLUMN(A:G)).
```

7

Note

The ROW function returns the row number of the reference. In this case, the reference is an array, rather than a single reference, and ROW(1:20) returns {1;2;3;4;5;6;7;8;9;10;11;12;13;14;15;16;17;18;19;20}.

Cells B2:B21 were *first* selected, and the formula was then array-entered. Cells B2:B21 share the single formula. What is ROW(1:20)^COLUMN(A:G)? Let's take a look.

If you were to enter =ROW(1:20) in a cell, click in the text in the formula bar (or double-click the cell with in-cell editing turned on) and press the F9 key, you would see {1;2;3;4;5;6;7;8;9;10;11;12;13;14;15;16;17;18;19;20}. This is, in general, a good technique to generate a list of consecutive numbers. Notice that the numbers are separated by semicolons, Excel's way of indicating that they descend in a column. This is *exactly* what was in cells M2:M21.

Okay, what is COLUMN(A:G)? Once again, let's enter this into a cell and press F9. The result is {1,2,3,4,5,6,7}. Notice that this set of numbers is separated by commas, indicating that they go across a row. It would be easier to look at what gets generated if the formula were COLUMN(A:B), or {1,2}. That is, enter one of the following formulas into a cell:

```
=ROW(1:20)^COLUMN(A:B)
```

or

```
=ROW(1:20)^{1,2}.
```

When you calculate the formula bar you get
=\{1,1;2,4;3,9;4,16;5,25;6,36;7,49;8,64;9,81;10,100;11,121;12,144;13,169;14,196; 15,225;16,256;17,289;18,324;19,361;20,400\}.
Notice that these values are the same as what you see in cells M2:N21 of figure 7.3. These values are each of the values 1:20 raised to the 1st power *and* the 2nd power. Now you can guess what the following formula gives:

```
=ROW(1:20)^COLUMN(A:G)
```

The result is the same as the values you see in cells M2:S21.

What would happen if you tried =ROW(1:20)^ROW(1:2)? Shouldn't that also give the same results? In fact, the results are not at all useful! ROW(1:20)^ROW(1:2) gives the same as ROW(1:20)^{1;2}, which is

```
={1;4;#N/A;#N/A;#N/A;#N/A;#N/A;#N/A;#N/A;#N/A;#N/A;#N/A;#N/A;#N/A;#N/A;#N/A;#N/A;
#N/A;#N/A;#N/A}
```

Why does this happen?

ROW(1:20) is a *vertical* list of numbers; ROW(1:2) is also a *vertical* list. Each value in the numbers 1:20 is being raised to the first power, then the second power, and that's all. Raised to the first power, the first value gives 1. The second number raised to the second power gives 4, and is done. There is no operation on the third number or beyond, so the rest of the values are #N/As. Therefore, you usually want to raise a vertical range to a horizontal power, or vice versa, to get the combinations of numbers you want. Think of it in terms of what was done in figure 7.3—a vertical range of numbers was raised to consecutive powers in *columns*.

See the section "Are There Duplicate Values in Two Ranges?," later in this chapter, for another example of this technique.

Okay, how did you get the coordinates in cells D17:K17 of figure 7.3? Instead of using the TREND function, its sister function, LINEST, was used. Because a 7th-degree polynomial curve was used, you needed eight columns, one for each of the x^7, x^6,...x^n and the constant term. Therefore, select eight columns *first*, then use the same formula and array-enter it:

=LINEST(A2:A21,ROW(1:20)^COLUMN(A:G))

 Note

Microsoft Excel's LINEST function, like the TREND function, uses the least squares method to calculate a straight line that best fits your data and returns an array that describes that line. It can also return statistics about the data, like the R^2 value.

The leftmost term is the coordinate for the x^7 term. Therefore, as you can see in cell D19, in the formula =D17*17^7+E17*17^6+F17*17^5+G17*17^4+H17*17^3+I17*17^2+J17*17+K17, why use the value 17? The 17th value of the series was used as an example. That is, X is 17 where used. If you were to select cell C2, for example, of figure 7.3, and enter:

```
=$D$17*(ROW()-1)^7+$E$17*(ROW()-1)^6+$F$17*(ROW()-1)^5+$G$17*(ROW()-1)^4+$H$17*
(ROW()-1)^3+$I$17*(ROW()-1)^2+$J$17*(ROW()-1)+$K$17
```

and fill down to cell C21, you would duplicate the values of column B. ROW()-1 is used because in row 2, ROW()-1 evaluates to 1; in row 3, ROW()-1 evaluates to 2; and so on down to row 21, where ROW()-1 evaluates to 20. These are the x-values and each is raised successively to the powers of 7,6,...1 because a 7th-degree polynomial equation was used.

It might be interesting to use a 6th degree and compare the coordinates generated to what Excel generates in the chart when you ask for the equation to be displayed.

Here's the same values in the previous example, but this time use:

```
=LINEST(A2:A21,ROW(1:20)^COLUMN(A:F))
```

This formula can be seen in cell D24 of figure 7.4.

Fig. 7.4

Using LINEST to get the coefficients that Microsoft Excel displays in its embedded trend line formula for a 6th-degree polynomial.

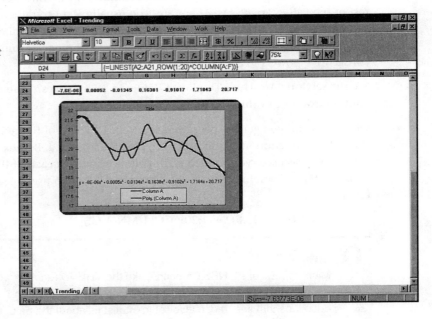

Notice that cells D24:J24 contain the results of the LINEST formula, and the equation on the chart contains the coordinates generated by Excel. You can see that the values are basically the same, but in the chart they are rounded. Therefore, to utilize them more accurately, we need to know how to get the more precise numbers described in this section.

If you want to predict the 21st value, you can use the equation =D17*21^7+E17*21^6 +F17*21^5+G17*21^4+H17*21^3+I17*21^2+J17*21+K17, or just fill down the equation given earlier with the ROW()-1 in it.

Are There Duplicate Values in Two Ranges?

There are times when you have two ranges of values and you need to know if there are any duplicate values within the ranges. Usually, the orientation of the values is the same, but this technique discusses how to make the comparison independent of the orientation (although you will have to take the orientation into consideration to use the correct formulas). Changing the orientation is accomplished by the TRANSPOSE function.

 Note

Microsoft Excel's TRANSPOSE function shifts the horizontal and vertical orientation of an array. For example, if you use TRANSPOSE(A1:A3), you will get a horizontal orientation. If A1:A3 contained 1, 2, and 3, respectively, then the array A1:A3 gives {1;2;3}, and the TRANSPOSE of that array gives {1,2,3} (commas rather than semicolons).

Look at figure 7.5.

Fig. 7.5

Using TRANSPOSE within an OR statement to determine duplicates in ranges.

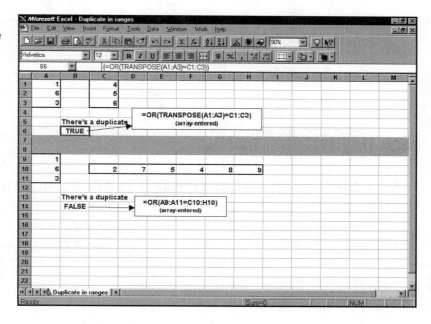

In the top half of figure 7.5, there are two ranges, A1:A3 and C1:C3, and there's a 6 in each range. As you can see in cell B6, the TRUE indicates that there is a duplicate. The text box overlaying cells D4:H5 shows the array-entered formula:

    =OR(TRANSPOSE(A1:A3)=C1:C3) .

The TRANSPOSE function changes the orientation of A1:A3 to horizontal, just so it's the opposite orientation of the second range. By doing this, Excel compares each value in the first array to every value in the second, providing more than a simple one-to-one correspondence. That is, the 4 in cell C1 is compared to {1;6;3}, the 5 in C2 is compared to {1;6;3}, and the 6 in C3 is compared to {1;6;3}, giving nine comparisons in total. In general, the number of comparisons is given by the number of elements of each array multiplied together, in this case 3×3. If you dragged across the formula inside the OR function and pressed the F9 key, you would see

```
{FALSE,FALSE,FALSE;FALSE,FALSE,FALSE;FALSE,TRUE,FALSE}
```

where the eighth value is TRUE because that is the comparison of cell C3 against A2.

Because this array of TRUEs and FALSEs is passed to the OR function, any occurrence of a TRUE results in a TRUE, indicating there's a match, or duplicate. If none of the values match, they will be all FALSE values, which result in a FALSE when ORed together.

In the bottom half of figure 7.5, the comparison is already of differing orientations, so the TRANSPOSE function is not needed, and the range A9:A11 (same values as before) is being compared to C10:H10. There are 3×6, or 18, comparisons. If you press F9 while the formula is selected inside the OR function, you would see, of course,

```
{FALSE,FALSE,FALSE,FALSE,FALSE,FALSE;FALSE,FALSE,FALSE,FALSE,FALSE,FALSE;
FALSE,FALSE,FALSE,FALSE,FALSE,FALSE}.
```

Notice every sixth FALSE is followed by a semicolon, whereas all the others are commas. This indicates the orientation.

A Problem or Limitation Due to a Limit of 256 Columns

There is a problem using this technique. Because one orientation must be row-wise, the maximum number of values that can be compared is 256. How, then, can you find out if there's a duplicate if there are more than 256 values? That is, if the ranges to be compared are A1:A400 versus B1:B400, the TRANSPOSE of either one won't work. The array is "chopped off" after 256 values.

Well, there's another way.

If you compare two ranges by the formula =MATCH(range1,range2,0) and array-enter it, you will see something like

```
{#N/A;#N/A;2;#N/A;#N/A;4;#N/A}
```

where the #N/A's indicate there's no match between the particular element of the first array against all the elements of the second array, and the values indicate there is a match and in what position the match occurs.

Note

The MATCH function returns the position of an element in an array that matches a specified value in a specified way. Its syntax is MATCH(lookup value, lookup array, type). The type used here, 0, indicates *exact* match. For example, MATCH("X",{"F","X","W","Q"},0) returns 2, the position of the "X". These examples, however, use another array as the lookup value, so *each* item in the lookup value is MATCHed against the lookup array and returns an array of values.

You can see in cell A10 (see fig. 7.6) an indication of how many items match between the two ranges, A1:A7 and B1:B4. ("Judy" and "Barry" match.) If you were to drag across the

    MATCH(A1:A7,B1:B4,0)

and press F9, you would, in fact, see the result just indicated. The COUNT function, interestingly, ignores #N/A values and just returns the count of the number of non-#N/A values, in this case, 2.

When this count is 0, there are no matches between the two arrays.

Fig. 7.6

A technique for counting how many items match between two ranges.

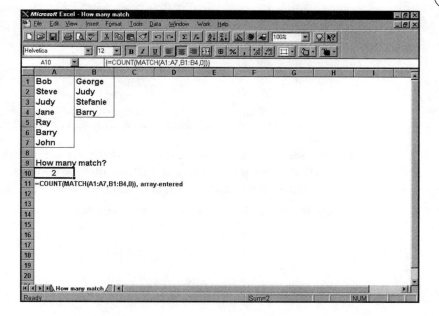

Calculating the Number of Saturdays Between Two Dates

Here is a technique to count the number of times a specific day of the week occurs between any two dates. Of course, it utilizes array-formulas.

Figure 7.7 shows a calendar from June 4 through September 2, 1995. Cells B1:B2 indicate starting and ending dates to be examined. Cell B3 indicates which day you want to count.

Fig. 7.7

Counting the number of times a given day of the week falls between two dates.

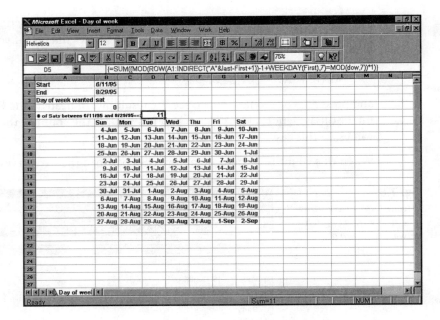

As you can see, there are eleven Saturdays within the given range, as indicated by cells H8:H18 (H7 is before the start date and H19 is after the end date). Cell D5 contains the formula that does the counting. This is the array-entered as

```
=SUM((MOD(ROW(A1:INDIRECT("A"&last-First+1))-1+WEEKDAY(First),7)=MOD(dow,7))*1)
```

Note

The MOD function returns the remainder from a division. MOD(7,4) returns 3, because 3 is the remainder when you divide 7 by 4.

The INDIRECT function changes a text-type reference into an Excel reference. For example, if A1 contains 12.34 and cell B3 contains the text A1 (not "=A1"), then INDIRECT(B3) is 12.34.

The WEEKDAY function returns a number from 1 to 7, corresponding to the day of the week, Sunday to Saturday.

Let's examine this formula in detail—it's not as difficult as it (and many array-formulas) looks at first glance. First notice that range names are used in the formula of cell D5: "last" is cell B2, "First" is cell B1, and "dow" (day of week) is cell B4. B4 contains the formula:

```
=MATCH(B3,{"SAT","SUN","MON","TUE","WED","THU","FRI"},0)-1
```

which takes the text entered into cell B3 and "converts" it into the value needed.

The technique involves first setting up the number of days between the two dates (80, in this case), then making a range of numbers from 1 to this number. To get a range of numbers from 1 to 80, use the ROW function. But the ROW function will not accept something like ROW(1:x) even when x is known.

The INDIRECT function comes to the rescue:

```
INDIRECT("A"&last-first+1)
```

which is INDIRECT("A80"). The fact that cell A80 is empty is irrelevant—it is used to set up a range of values. Therefore,

```
ROW(A1:INDIRECT("A"&last-First+1))
```

becomes ROW(A1:A80), which becomes {1;2;3;4;...;78;79;80}.

This range is adjusted to be 0->79 by subtracting 1, then the weekday of the first date is added back in. In this example, the WEEKDAY of 6/11/95 is 1, so by adding this back in you are left with the same series {1;2;...;80}. This is compared to the day of the week wanted, in this example, Saturday. The WEEKDAY(some-Saturday-date) is 7. Now, there's only one 7 in the range 1 to 80, so that's not very useful.

7

How about taking the MOD of the values 1 through 80—keeping the remainder when divided by 7? This gives the new array {1;2;3;4;5;6;0;1;2;3;4;5;6;0;...;0;1;2;3}. This can be compared to the day of the week except it wouldn't work for Saturdays because that's a 7 and there's no 7 in this new array. So, you need to compare it to the MOD of the day-of-week as well. So far, this accounts for this part of the formula:

```
MOD(ROW(A1:INDIRECT("A"&last-First+1))-1+WEEKDAY(First),7)=MOD(dow,7)
```

This gives you an array of TRUE/FALSE, TRUE whenever the 1 to 80 values equals the MOD(dow,7). Multiplying these logical values by 1 and adding them up gives the answer.

Let's look again, this time with a much smaller range. Suppose the First date were 8/1/95 (Tuesday) and the last were 8/10/95 (Thursday), and you wanted to count the number of Wednesdays. "Dow" becomes 4 (Wednesday is 4),

```
INDIRECT("A"&last-First+1)
```

becomes

```
INDIRECT("A10")
```

because last is 10, first is 1, so last-First+1 is 10-1+1, or 10; and the

```
ROW(A1:INDIRECT("A"&last-First+1))
```

becomes

```
{1;2;3;4;5;6;7;8;9;10}
```

because A1:INDIRECT("A"&last-First+1) has become A1:INDIRECT("A10"), or A1:A10. Now ROW(A1:A10) becomes the array {1;2;3...;10}. Subtracting 1 gives

```
{0;1;2;3;4;5;6;7;8;9}
```

and adding 3 (WEEKDAY(First)) gives the following array:

```
{3;4;5;6;7;8;9;10;11;12}
```

Now taking the MOD of it by 7 gives:

```
{3;4;5;6;0;1;2;3;4;5}
```

Comparing this to MOD(dow,7) is comparing it to 4, which is

```
{FALSE;TRUE;FALSE;FALSE;FALSE;FALSE;FALSE;FALSE;TRUE;FALSE}
```

and multiplying by 1 gives

```
{0;1;0;0;0;0;0;0;1;0}
```

because FALSE * 1 is 0 and TRUE * 1 is 1, and adding these all up gives 2. This means there are 2 Wednesdays between 8/1/95 and 8/10/95.

Finding the Bottommost Cell in a Range

This technique works for both single-column ranges or multiple-column (but contiguous) ranges. Often, the bottommost cell is not necessarily the last cell in a contiguous range of cells. You may have A1:A20, then A30:A35 filled. The bottommost cell is A35. The last cell, found by Edit, Go To, Special, Last Cell is often far beyond the last cell. That's because you may have a reference to a cell that is unused. For example, in cell A1 if you have =J4000, then row 4000 will be the last cell in the worksheet even though there may not actually be anything ever entered beyond row 50. That holds true even if you correct the formula to read =J40. Row 4000 remains the last row because it was once referenced.

 Note

If the last cell indicated by Excel is past what you know is really the last cell, you can find the *real* last used cell by first selecting the last cell, clicking one row down and one column to the right, doing a Find command, entering an asterisk (a wildcard representing any character), and holding the Shift key down, which instructs Excel to search backward. When the "by rows" option is chosen, you will find the real last row. Then reposition the cell to the same starting point, issue the Find command again and choose "by column". This time Excel will find the last used column. The intersection of this row and column found is the real last cell. You can fix the erroneous last cell by selecting all the rows between the real last cell and the indicated last cell and deleting them, then doing the same with the columns, then *you must save and close the worksheet.*

Look at figure 7.8.

Cell G9 is indicating that the bottommost row in range A1:E10 is 9. The formula is as follows, array-entered:

```
=MAX(ROW(1:10)*(A1:E10<>""))
```

 Note

The MAX function returns the largest value in a range.

Fig. 7.8

A formula for finding the bottommost row in a range.

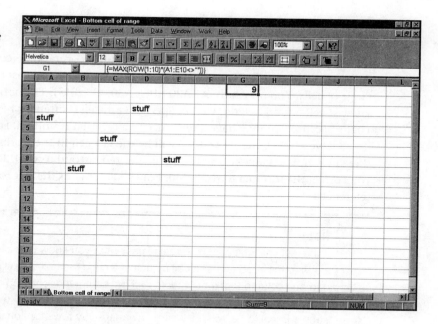

Usually the MAX function would refer to a larger range, something like:

```
=MAX(ROW(1:1000)*(A1:E1000<>""))
```

but the range is kept small here so you can examine the formula more easily. Because you are interested in finding the bottommost row in the range that is *used*, compare the range to blank, or `A1:E10<>""`.

This will return a 10 by 5 array of TRUE/FALSE values. This comparison could also have been done using the ISBLANK function:

```
NOT(ISBLANK(A1:E10)).
```

FALSE means the cell *is* blank; TRUE means the cell has some value.

By multiplying this array by the values

```
{1;2;3;...;9;10},
```

which is done by using

```
ROW(1:10),
```

you get

```
{0,0,0,0,0;0,0,0,0,0;0,0,0,3,0;4,0,0,0,0;0,0,0,0,0;0,0,6,0,0;0,0,0,0,0;0,0,0,0,8;
0,9,0,0,0;0,0,0,0,0}
```

Notice the semicolons after every five values, corresponding to the next row in the evaluation. The zeros are the result of multiplying FALSE by any number. If you visually scan the expansion of the array, you see the first non-zero is a 3. This is in the third row of values, in the set

    {0,0,0,3,0}.

This corresponds to cell D3 in the range A1:E10. The 3 is the result of multiplying TRUE by the corresponding position of the ROW(1:10)—we're in the third "row," and TRUE multiplied by 3 is 3.

If you closely examine the expanded array just given, you'll notice that every non-zero corresponds to the non-blanks in the range. This array is passed to the MAX function, which in this case returns a 9, giving the desired result.

Another Method for Finding the Bottommost Cell in a Range

Let's look at another application of using the bottommost cell in a range (see fig. 7.9).

Fig. 7.9

Using array formulas to find the last used row in a range to determine future appointments.

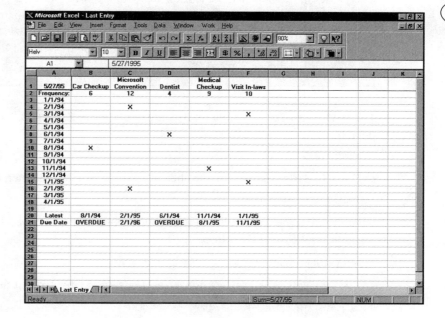

Cell A1 contains a date that would usually represent today's date. Row 1 contains the type of recurring event and row 2 contains the number of months that event should be repeated. For example, Column D indicates that every four months the dentist should be visited. The Xs in B3:F18 indicate the completion of the events. So the X in cell D8 means the dentist was visited on 6/1/94. This value shows in cell D20. Because the dentist should be visited every four months, 6/1/94 + 4 months is 10/1/94, and this is earlier than today's date, so the event is overdue. This is indicated in cell D21.

Similarly, the X in cell F15 means the in-laws were visited on 1/1/95. Ten months later (cell F2) is 11/1/95, and this date hasn't happened yet, so cell F21 indicates the due date, rather than the word OVERDUE.

Let's examine the formulas here. This time, we're not interested in the bottommost row in the worksheet, but the bottommost row in range B3:B18 through F3:F18 (*not* B3:F18). This is done in row 20. Cell B20 contains the formula

```
=INDEX($A:$A,MAX((B3:B18="X")*ROW(3:18))).
```

 Note

The INDEX function returns the value of an element in an array, selected by the row and column number indices. For example, INDEX({6,3,87,3,12},4) returns the 4th item in the array {6,3,87,3,12}, or 3 (the commas indicate that this is a horizontal array). An example of a two-dimensional array might be INDEX(A1:C4,2,3), which means the 2nd row of the range, 3rd column, and the INDEX function would return whatever is in cell C2.

The MAX part of the formula returns the last X in range B3:B18. Notice this is multiplied by

```
ROW(3:18),
```

so the X in B10 results in the number 10 in the formula. This then becomes

```
INDEX($A:$A,10),
```

which returns the date to which the X corresponds. The $A:$A is absolute so that the formula can be filled right to cell F20.

The formula in cell B21 is

```
=IF($A$1>DATE(YEAR(B20),MONTH(B20)+B2,1),"OVERDUE",DATE(YEAR(B20),MONTH(B20)+B2,1)).
```

 Note

The DATE function returns the serial number of a date, and has the syntax
```
DATE(year,month,day).
```

This formula compares today's date to the correct number of months beyond the date in the cell above, B20. The DATE function is used because it's easy to "parse" out the year, month, and day, and add the number of months to the month part.

```
YEAR(B20)
```

refers to the same year as the cell above (in cell B21, the reference to YEAR(B20) is the reference to the year of the date in cell B20),

```
MONTH(B20)+B2
```

is the same month as the cell above (in cell B21, the reference to MONTH(B20) is the reference to the month of the date in cell B20) *plus* the number of months the event recurs, and the 1 indicates the first day of the month.

Searching Strings for Errors

In figure 7.10, range A4:A12 is supposed to contain names in the form First name, space, Last name. Cells A7 and A12 have errors—there is no space between the names. This technique explores a way to determine which names, if any, are in error.

Fig. 7.10

The array formula described in this section finds errors in a range of strings.

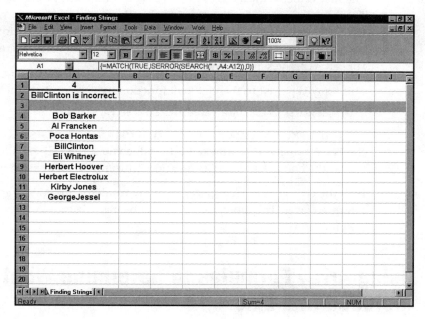

Cell A2 contains the formula

```
=IF(NOT(ISERROR(A1)),INDEX(A4:A12,A1)&" is incorrect.","")
```

which says that if cell A1 is not an error, then display the offending cell and the text is incorrect. The offending cell is indicated as the

```
INDEX(A4:A12,A1).
```

Therefore, cell A1 must contain the location of the cell that contains an error within the range A4:A12. Cell A1 contains the formula

```
=MATCH(TRUE,ISERROR(SEARCH(" ",A4:A12)),0).
```

This is an interesting formula in that one does not usually use a MATCH(TRUE…) in Excel. You will find that this (as well as MATCH(FALSE…) has very powerful applications.

The inner part of the formula is unusual in that the SEARCH function usually examines a cell, not a range:

```
SEARCH(" ",A4:A12)
```

Therefore, it's this usage that requires the formula to be array-entered. The function in this example returns

```
{4;3;5;#VALUE!;4;8;8;6;#VALUE!}.
```

The first value, 4, means that there's a space in the 4th position of cell A4: Bob Barker. The same holds true for the second value, 3, which indicates a space in the third position, and the third value, 5. The #VALUE! error in the 4th position of the array corresponds to cell A7, which contains BillClinton, and indicates there is no space in the cell. For cell A12, the same is true—there is no space.

This array is passed to the ISERROR function, which converts the array to

```
{FALSE;FALSE;FALSE;TRUE;FALSE;FALSE;FALSE;FALSE;TRUE}
```

where the TRUE corresponds to the #VALUE! errors. The MATCH function, then, finds the TRUE value in this array, and the value you see in cell A1, 4, is the result of that (the ",0" at the end of the MATCH function indicating that an exact match is to be found).

If all the cells contained a space, the array would be all FALSEs, and the MATCH would return an error. Therefore, cell A2 would be blank because it's testing for an error condition in cell A1.

Using Array Formulas to Determine What's *Not* Included in a List

Suppose you need to set up a tournament schedule where there are six players, but only four players play at any given time. You need to determine which of the players are *not* playing once you know which ones *are* playing. Obviously, with just six players this is a trivial task, but the technique used can be expanded to any number of players.

The list of valid players is in row 2, and the four players selected currently are in A5:D5 (see fig. 7.11). The players who did not play are in E5:F5. These cells contain the formulas used to determine the results. A5:D5 are entered manually, and the remaining players must be selected from the list in A2:F2. The array-entered formula in cell E5 is

```
=INDEX(Names,MATCH(TRUE,ISNA(MATCH(Names,$A5:D5,0)),0)).
```

Fig. 7.11

This is an array formula that returns values that are not in a list.

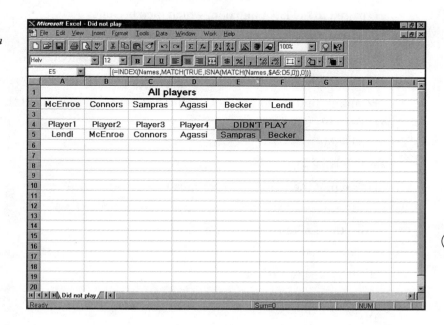

Note

The ISNA function returns TRUE if its argument is #N/A, or FALSE, otherwise.

Notice that the inner MATCH contains a mixed reference from $A5:D5. This is so that when the formula is entered, you can fill right to F5, where $A5:D5 becomes $A5:E5, and so on if this extended further to the right.

The inner MATCH is

```
MATCH(Names,$A5:D5,0),
```

where "Names" is A2:F2. This evaluates to

```
{2,3,#N/A,4,#N/A,1}.
```

Each item in Names is compared against the array A5:D5. Therefore, when McEnroe, the first item in Names, is MATCHed against A5:D5, the match is found in the 2nd position, hence the 2 in the array. The 3 comes from matching Connors against A5:D5. The #N/A is when Sampras is matched. Sampras does not appear in A5:D5. This array,

```
{2,3,#N/A,4,#N/A,1},
```

is passed to the ISNA function, which then becomes

```
{FALSE,FALSE,TRUE,FALSE,TRUE,FALSE}.
```

The TRUEs correspond to the #N/A. The formula now reduces to

```
=INDEX(Names,MATCH(TRUE,{FALSE,FALSE,TRUE,FALSE,TRUE,FALSE},0))
```

meaning "find the location of the first TRUE." This is position 3. The formula now reduces to

```
=INDEX(Names,3),
```

which is Sampras.

Let's repeat the steps for the formula in F5,

```
=INDEX(Names,MATCH(TRUE,ISNA(MATCH(Names,$A5:E5,0)),0)).
```

Now, the innermost MATCH reduces to

```
{2,3,5,4,#N/A,1},
```

the ISNA changes that to

```
{FALSE,FALSE,FALSE,FALSE,TRUE,FALSE},
```

the

```
MATCH(TRUE,...
```

becomes 5, and the

```
INDEX(Names,5)
```

is now Becker.

Matching More Than One Column Against a String

Examining figure 7.12, you can see that there are duplicate names running down column A. To find an amount (Column C) for a name must depend on some other factor, like a code (Column B). For example, you can look at the spreadsheet and find that the amount for John with code 3 is found in row 9, and is 158. But how can you find that using Excel formulas?

Fig. 7.12

Using MATCH to compare two fields against a two-column range.

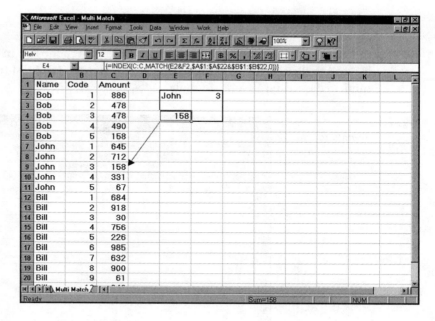

If columns A and B were combined, for example, by entering =A2&B2 in cell D2 and filling down, you'd have a unique set of values to search. That is, in column D you could see Bob1;Bob2;Bob3, and so on. John3 would appear in cell D9. Then you could use

```
=MATCH(E2&E3,D2:D20,0)
```

to find the row the result is in.

Using array formulas, you can simulate the combining of columns A and B. Cell E4 contains the array-entered formula

```
=INDEX(C:C,MATCH(E2&F2,$A$1:$A$22&$B$1:$B$22,0)).
```

Because you are ANDing A1:A22 with B1:B22, this gives you

```
{"NameCode";"Bob1";"Bob2";"Bob3";"Bob4";"Bob5";"John1";"John2";"John3";"John4";"John5";
"Bill1";"Bill2";"Bill3";"Bill4";"Bill5";"Bill6";"Bill7";"Bill8";"Bill9";"Bill10";
"Bill11"}.
```

MATCHing "John3" to this gives the result you want: 9. Passing this to the INDEX function gives the number 158.

Calculating the Sum of the Digits

In figure 7.13 you see a value in cell A1 and the digits added up in cell B1. If you can make each digit in cell A1 occupy its own cell, you can just SUM the results. This can be simulated by using an array formula.

Fig. 7.13

An array formula to add up the digits in a number.

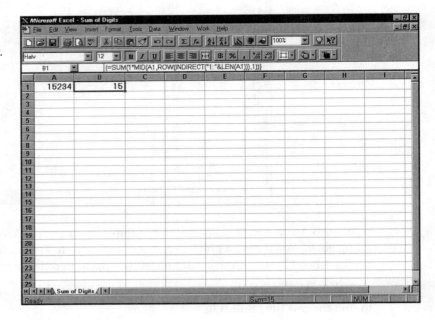

Cell B1 contains the array formula

```
=SUM(1*MID(A1,ROW(INDIRECT("1:"&LEN(A1))),1)).
```

 Note

The MID function returns a specified number of characters from a text string. Its syntax is MID(text,starting from, number of characters).

The LEN function returns the length of a string of characters. LEN("abc") is 3.

Let's look at the formula to use if you knew the length of cell A1 was 5:

```
=SUM(1*MID(A1,ROW(1:5),1)).
```

This expands to

```
=SUM(1*MID(A1,{1;2;3;4;5},1))
```

which becomes

```
=SUM(1*{"1";"5";"2";"3";"4"})
```

which becomes

```
=SUM({1;5;2;3;4})
```

which is 15.

But, as you saw earlier, Excel won't allow you to enter

```
ROW(1:LEN(A1)).
```

You can simulate this formula by using the INDIRECT function,

```
INDIRECT("1:"&LEN(A1)).
```

This becomes

```
INDIRECT("1:5")
```

which Excel "understands," and passing this to the ROW function gives us the array

```
{1;2;3;4;5}.
```

Another attempt might be to just use an array that is large enough to cover any number entered. So try

```
=SUM(1*MID(A1,ROW(1:30),1))
```

This formula gives a #VALUE! error because once Excel evaluates MID(A1,6,1), the result is null, (""), and when a null value is multiplied by 1 it becomes an error. SUMming arrays with errors results in an error.

Finding the Last Part of a String

Frequently you may want to know the name of a file without its path, as in figure 7.14.

Cell A1 contains the text of the path to a file. The backslash is used as a delimiter, separating the various "fields." Cell A1 could also contain *any* text, like "Now is the time for all good men to come to the aid of their country" where the "delimiter" is a space, and this technique extracts the word "country," the last "field" in the string.

Fig. 7.14

A formula to extract the last field in a string. This is especially useful for getting a file name from a path.

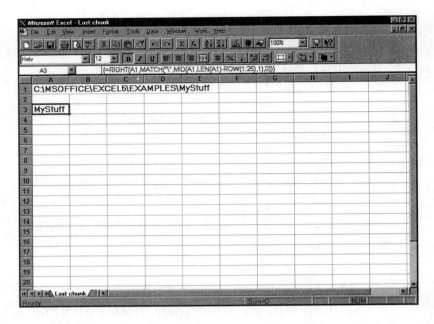

The formula in cell A3 is complicated, so let's see what it needs to contain rather than just reveal it.

The task would be easy if what you needed to find was the *first* backslash: you could use the SEARCH function. If the text were reversed, then you *could* find the first backslash. So, your job will be to reverse the text. It turns out that reversing the text in one formula is not possible, but it *is* possible to reverse the text as single characters rather than as one string. For example, suppose cell D7 in a separate spreadsheet contained the text "abc". You've used techniques earlier to change that to the array {"a","b","c"}. How can that be changed to the array {"c","b","a"}? Well, that can be done fairly easily. Because the technique that makes it {"a","b","c"} is done by array-entering

```
=MID(D7,ROW(1:3),1),
```

look at what this function does:

```
=MID(D7,4-ROW(1:3),1).
```

The 4- subtracts the array {1;2;3} from the value 4, which produces the array {3;2;1}. Now,

```
=MID(D7,{3;2;1},1)
```

produces {"c","b","a"}.

Now that you see the approach, let's look a bit further. Instead of using a constant, 4, use the LEN(D7)+1. Instead of just reversing the string, you also need to MATCH the delimiter against this string to find the *first* one.

The formula

```
MATCH("\",MID(A1,LEN(A1)+1-ROW(1:25),1),0)
```

used in figure 7.14 becomes

```
MATCH("\",{"f";"f";"u";"t";"S";"y";"M";"\";"S";"E";"L";"P";"M";"A";"X";"E";"\";"5";"L";
"E";"C";"X";"E";"\";"E"},0).
```

You are searching *backward* for the occurrence of the backslash. This evaluates to 8.

So, what about this 8? You actually want one fewer character from the end because you don't want to include the backslash. You need to take the last seven characters of the cell. Taking the last seven characters of the cell lends itself to the RIGHT function. Therefore, subtracting 1 from the formula does the trick. Array-enter:

```
=RIGHT(A1,MATCH("\",MID(A1,LEN(A1)+1-ROW(1:25),1),0)-1).
```

It turns out that adding 1 and then subtracting 1 cancels itself out, and the more compact formula is

```
=RIGHT(A1,MATCH("\",MID(A1,LEN(A1)-ROW(1:25),1),0)).
```

To ensure you will find the last part of cell A1 (it *may* be more than 25 characters), you should change the

```
ROW(1:25)
```

to

```
ROW(1:255).
```

7

Adding the Last N Values in a Range that Has Blank Cells

Adding values in a range usually consists of the simple SUM(range) formula, even when the range has blanks in it. It's a little more difficult if you don't want to start at the beginning. Then you often need to use a formula such as

```
=SUM(INDEX(Range,x):INDEX(Range,y))
```

where x and y can be determined. For this example, you want to start somewhere in the range (the harder part) and finish at the end of the range (the easier part). A horizontal range is used in this example. The end of the range is indicated by

```
INDEX(Range,COLUMNS(range)).
```

Now y is known. How do you find x? X, remember, represents the location in the range of the Nth value. That is, if cells A6:V6 contain numbers and blanks, and you want to add the last three values, you need to find the column that contains the third nonblank *counting from the right.*

With a range of column numbers corresponding to the nonblanks, SMALL(Range,1) is the "leftmost" value, SMALL(Range,2) is the next one to the right, and so on. How about using the LARGE function? LARGE(Range,1) is the "rightmost" value (in a vertical orientation this would be the bottommost value), LARGE(Range,2) is the next one to the left, and so on. Look at this array-entered function:

```
=LARGE(IF(ISBLANK(Range),"",COLUMN(Range)),1).
```

If Range were A6:E6 and cell C6 were blank you would have

```
=LARGE(IF({FALSE;FALSE;TRUE;FALSE;FALSE},"",{1,2,3,4,5}),1)
```

which is

```
=LARGE({1,2,"",4,5},1)
```

which is 5, the column for the last value in the range.

But if you wanted to find the 3rd nonblank value,

```
LARGE({1,2,"",4,5},3)
```

would return 2.

See figure 7.15 for a specific example.

Fig. 7.15

Summing the last N values in a range containing blank cells.

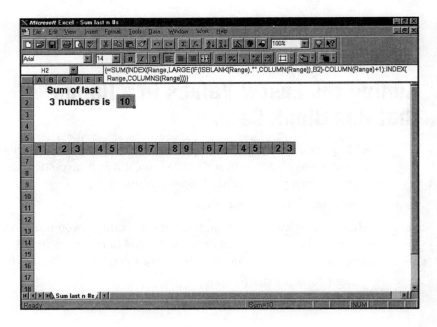

Let's assume that Range here is A6:V6. The last three numbers are 5, 2, and 3, as seen in cells S6:V6. The function

```
=LARGE(IF(ISBLANK(Range),"",COLUMN(Range)),B2)
```

becomes

```
LARGE({1,"",3,4,"",6,7,"",9,10,"",12,13,"",15,16,"",18,19,"",21,22},3),
```

which is the third largest number, or 19. This 19 is then used as in

```
=SUM(INDEX(Range,19):INDEX(Range,COLUMNS(Range))).
```

COLUMNS(Range) is 22, so the formula now becomes

```
=SUM(INDEX(Range,19):INDEX(Range,22)),
```

which is

```
=SUM({5,0,2,3}),
```

which is 10.

Putting it all together in one formula, you have

```
=SUM(INDEX(Range,LARGE(IF(ISBLANK(Range),"",COLUMN(Range)),B2)):INDEX(Range,COLUMNS
(Range)))
```

If the range does not begin in column A, you still have one more adjustment to make. You have to adjust for the starting column of the range. When the range starts in column A, you need to add the start column and subtract 1 (this has the effect of adding zero, but it works for all columns). If the range started in column C, you need to add 3 and subtract 1. The final formula is

```
=SUM(INDEX(Range,LARGE(IF(ISBLANK(Range),"",COLUMN(Range)),B2)-
COLUMN(Range)+1):INDEX(Range,COLUMNS(Range)))
```

and this is what is found in cell H2 of figure 7.15.

Extracting Just the Numeric Portion of a Cell

If you have a column of cells that contains alphanumeric data, such as a part number, you may want to be able to sort by the numeric portion. But extracting the numeric portion may not be easy if the numeric size varies. For example, if one part number is ABC123 (see fig. 7.16) and another is PART0772, finding the 123 and the 772 is not a trivial task. This section explores one method to do it. The first part is to determine how to find the location of the first digit.

Fig. 7.16

Getting at the numeric portion of a cell with alphanumeric data. Useful for sorting by the numeric part.

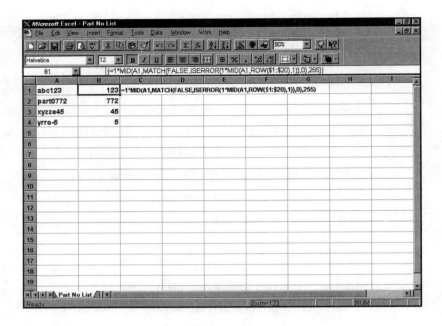

You can change the string into an array by an array-formula such as

    =MID(Ptno,ROW(1:10),1).

The function ROW(1:10) is used for the array portion, the 10 being an arbitrarily large enough number to "parse" each string (assuming no part will have a numeric section longer than 10 characters). Using ABC123 as an example, this formula would give the array {"A","B","C","1","2","3","","","",""}. You still can't distinguish a real difference between letters and numbers here, but if you multiply this array by 1:

    =1*MID(Ptno,ROW(1:10),1)

you get the array

    {#VALUE!, #VALUE!, #VALUE!,1,2,3, #VALUE!, #VALUE!, #VALUE!,#VALUE!}.

Notice that there are values 1, 2, and 3 embedded in the resulting array. Now pass this array to the ISERROR function.

    =ISERROR(1*MID(Ptno,ROW(1:10),1))

This gives the array

    {TRUE,TRUE,TRUE,FALSE,FALSE,FALSE,TRUE...}

and here you can find the first FALSE condition (the position that corresponds to the first digit in the part number) by using MATCH:

    =MATCH(FALSE,ISERROR(1*MID(Ptno,ROW(1:10),1)),0)

which returns a 4.

You now need to extract that part of the part number using MID:

```
=MID(Ptno,MATCH(FALSE,ISERROR(1*MID(Ptno,ROW(1:10),1)),0),255)
```

But that returns the numeric portion *as text*, which won't sort the way you want (2 sorts after 123 because as text "2" is after "1"), so to convert it back to a number you need to multiply it by 1:

```
=1*MID(Ptno,MATCH(FALSE,ISERROR(1*MID(Ptno,ROW(1:10),1)),0),255)
```

Fill this down and sort by the result.

Determining If the Contents of a Range Are Unique

Suppose you want to determine if the items in a worksheet's ranges are unique. For example, look at figure 7.17.

Fig. 7.17

Using COUNTIF to help determine whether a range consists of unique values.

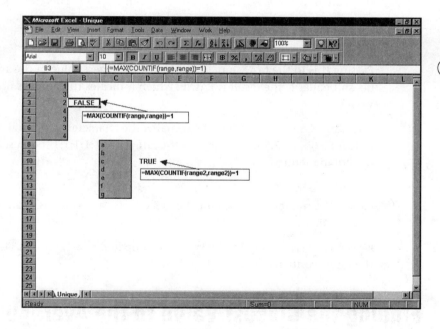

Cells A1:A7 are defined as "range", and the COUNTIF function is used to return an array of values. Usually, the COUNTIF function takes two arguments: a range, and a criteria, where the criteria is a simple test. This case uses the range itself as the criteria, and therefore the function must be array-entered.

Note

The COUNTIF function returns the count of items in a range that meets a criteria. If A1:A6 contains {1,0,3,0,0,7}, then COUNTIF(A1:A6,0) would be 3.

How does this COUNTIF function help determine the uniqueness of the range of values? Well, each value in the range is used as the criteria in turn. When the range A1:A7, which evaluates to {1;3;2;4;3;3;4}, is used twice in the COUNTIF function, the first test is

```
=COUNTIF({1;3;2;4;3;3;4},1)
```

which counts the number of times the range is equal to 1. This is 1. The second test is

```
=COUNTIF({1;3;2;4;3;3;4},3)
```

which counts the number of times the range equals 3. The reason the criteria is 3 is that this is the second value in the range. There are three 3s. Similarly, for the other five tests there are one 2, two 4s, three 3s, three 3s, and two 4s. Therefore,

```
=COUNTIF({1;3;2;4;3;3;4},{1;3;2;4;3;3;4})
```

produces the array {1;3;1;2;3;3;2}.

Passing this to the MAX function returns the largest value of the array, or 3. Because this doesn't equal 1, the result is FALSE, which indicates the range is not made up of unique values.

The range C8:C14 in figure 7.17 contains the characters a through g. The COUNTIF(Range2,Range2) returns the array {1;1;1;1;1;1;1} because each of the items in the criteria returns a 1:

```
=COUNTIF(Range2,"a")
```

counts the number of times the Range2 equals "a", which is 1, and similarly for "b", "c", and so on.

MAX({1;1;1;1;1;1;1}) is 1, which, when compared to a 1, returns TRUE, indicating that the range contains unique values.

Finding the Closest Value to the Average

When you use the AVERAGE function, the result will not necessarily be one of the values in the range. There may be times when you want to know which value is the closest. For example, in figure 7.18, you can see that cell B8 returns the value 23, which is the closest value to the average of 21.8, shown in cell B7.

Fig. 7.18

Determining the closest number to an average of values.

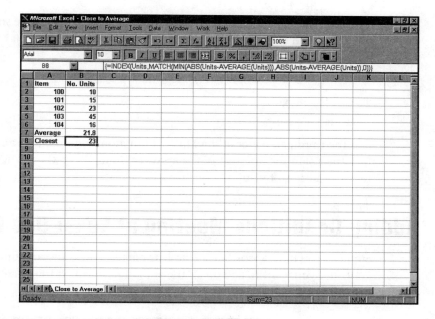

When you need to find a close value, you're not interested in whether the value is on the high side or low side. That is, for the average of 21.8, 22 is closer than 21—subtracting the average from these values produces a .2 and a negative .8. Because you're not interested in positive or negative, you can't just take the minimum value, but you can take the minimum value of the absolute differences. To get the absolute differences, you take each value and subtract the average, then pass this calculation to the ABS function. So far, then, you have

```
=ABS(Units-AVERAGE(Units)).
```

 Note

The ABS function returns the absolute (unsigned) value of a number.

Using figure 7.18, the ABS part of the function produces the array

```
{11.8;6.8;1.2;23.2;5.8}:
```

(10–21.8 is –11.8, 15–21.8 is –6.8, and so on. The negative sign disappears because of the ABS function).

Now there is a range of differences, but you are interested in the smallest of these, so this array is passed to the MIN function, which returns 1.2. Now you have to find *where* the 1.2 is in the range, so we MATCH

```
MIN(ABS(Units-AVERAGE(Units)))
```

against the range

```
ABS(Units-AVERAGE(Units)),
```

and the third parameter of the MATCH function, zero, requests an exact match, so you find the 1.2 in the 3rd item of the array. Pass this "3" to the INDEX function, and Excel returns the closest value.

Adding Conditions Meeting at Least One Criteria

Suppose you have a worksheet that lists names, dates, and amounts, as shown in figure 7.19, and you want to add up all the amounts for which the name is Bob or the date is before 5/1/95.

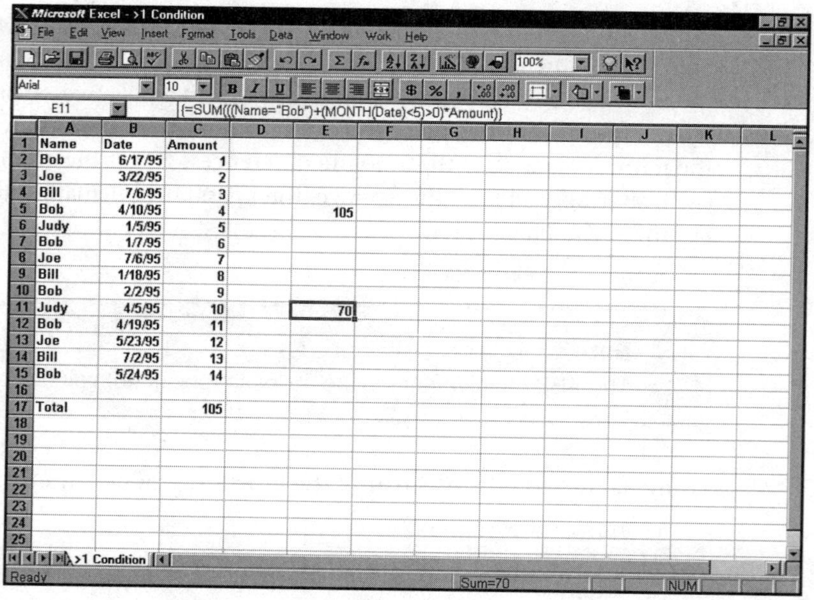

Fig. 7.19

A formula for summing values that meet more than one criteria.

If you use an OR function of some sort, you will meet with failure because if *any* of the items returns TRUE, then the entire OR function will return TRUE, and you will probably add up *all* the amounts. For example, if you try

```
=SUM(IF(OR(Name="Bob",Month(Date)<5),Amount))
```

in figure 7.19 you'll get 105, as shown in cell E5, which is the same as the total indicated in cell C17. This is because Name="Bob" evaluates to

    {TRUE;FALSE;FALSE;TRUE;FALSE;TRUE;FALSE;FALSE;TRUE;FALSE;TRUE;FALSE;FALSE;TRUE},

and

    Month(Date)<5

evaluates to

    {FALSE;TRUE;FALSE;TRUE;TRUE;TRUE;FALSE;TRUE;TRUE;TRUE;TRUE;FALSE;FALSE;FALSE},

and when these arrays are ORed together, the result is simply TRUE, not an array consisting of TRUE/FALSE. Therefore, the formula reduces to

    =SUM(IF(TRUE,Amount))

which, of course, is the sum of all the amounts.

The formula for the solution is shown in the formula bar for cell E11. Array-enter:

    =SUM(((Name="Bob")+(MONTH(Date)<5)>0)*Amount).

Let's see how this works.

If you ADD the two TRUE/FALSE arrays detailed previously, you get the array

    {1;1;0;2;1;2;0;1;2;1;2;0;0;1}.

 Tip

TRUE + TRUE evaluates to 2, TRUE + FALSE evaluates to 1 and FALSE + FALSE evaluates to 0.

What does the preceding array represent? Well, each 1 corresponds to a TRUE+FALSE or FALSE+TRUE, meaning one of the conditions was met (Name was "Bob" or Month(Date) was less than 5). 2 means both conditions were met, and zero means neither condition was met. You're interested in the non-zeros. Therefore, comparing this array to zero,

    {1;1;0;2;1;2;0;1;2;1;2;0;0;1}>0

evaluates to

    {TRUE;TRUE;FALSE;TRUE;TRUE;TRUE;FALSE;TRUE;TRUE;TRUE;TRUE;FALSE;FALSE;TRUE},

and when this is multiplied by Amount, it evaluates to

    {1;2;0;4;5;6;0;8;9;10;11;0;0;14}.

When this is passed to the SUM function, you get 70.

If you had wanted to add the amounts together when *both* conditions are met, you could use the array-entered formula:

```
=SUM((Name="Bob")*(MONTH(Date)<5)*Amount).
```

If you had wanted to add the amounts together when *only one* condition was met (not both), you could use the array-entered formula:

```
=SUM(((Name="Bob")+(MONTH(Date)<5)=1)*Amount).
```

Using One Array Formula to Create a Calendar

This chapter ends with a fairly intricate example of using array formulas, but by now you should be familiar with the evaluations and steps involved. You are going to create a calendar for any month for the years that Excel understands to be "valid." That is, any date from 1/1/1900 through 12/31/2078 (see fig. 7.20).

Fig. 7.20

A single array formula that creates a calendar.

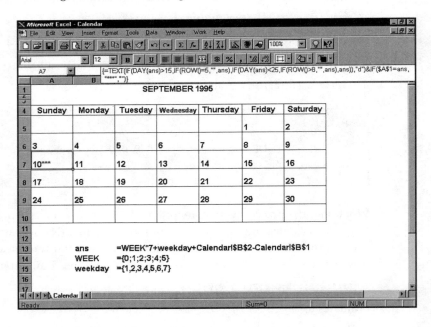

Figure 7.20 shows the month of September, 1995. Before examining the formulas used to make this worksheet, let's look at a beginning step of making this worksheet. In figure 7.21 you see an array-formula in cell A5 of

```
=WEEK*7+weekday.
```

In fact, this formula was entered by first selecting cells A5:G10, entering

    =WEEK*7+weekday,

and pressing Ctrl+Shift+Enter. The definitions of WEEK and weekday are shown at the bottom of the figure.

Fig. 7.21

A first step in constructing the calendar.

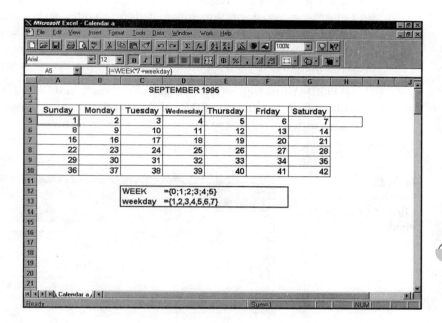

WEEK is a vertical array,

    {0;1;2;3;4;5}

and weekday is a horizontal array,

    {1,2,3,4,5,6,7}.

The formula contains WEEK*7, which produces a vertical array

    {0;7;14;21;28;35}

and when this is added to the horizontal array

    {1,2,3,4,5,6,7},

you get the array shown, namely the numbers from 1 to 42. Don't forget to press Ctrl+Shift+Enter to enter this formula.

In fact, cells A4:G4 contain a single array formula, =weekday, formatted as dddd. The number 1 formatted with dddd as Sunday, because 1/1/1900 was a Sunday.

There are many steps between the display in figure 7.21 and what is in figure 7.20. You want to get serial numbers into range A5:G10, which represents the current month. If you take the serial number of the first day of the month (September 1, 1995 is serial # 34943) and add it to each number already in cells A5:G10 (1–42), you would get 34944 through 34985, which correspond to September 2, 1995 through October 13, 1995. This isn't quite what you want. September 1 falls on a Friday, so you want the first date of September to be on Friday. The first Friday already has a 6 in it, so somehow you have to add 34937 to the numbers already in A5:G10. Where does this number come from? You are 6 too high (34943 [9/1/95] minus 34937 [the number you want] is 6).

The WEEKDAY function returns the day of the week, and WEEKDAY (a Friday date) is 6. What if you subtract the WEEKDAY of the first day of the month from this new array (the one created by adding in the first day of the month)?

In fact, this is *exactly* what you should do (see fig. 7.22).

Fig. 7.22

Using defined names to simplify a complex formula.

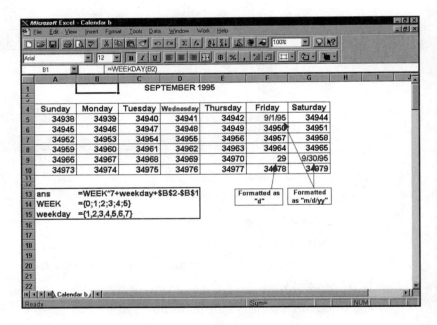

The formula in A5:G10 is the array-entered =ans, where ans is defined to be

`=WEEK*7+weekday+$B$2-$B$1`.

$B$2 (formatted as ; to not show) contains the formula for the serial number of the first day of the month wanted:

`=DATE(YEAR(A1),MONTH(A1),1)`

Cell A1 (formatted as ; to not show) contains the month wanted. In this example it contains 9/10/95.

Cell B1 (formatted as ; to not show) contains =WEEKDAY(B2).

Therefore, cell B1 calculates to a 6, cell B2 calculates to 34943, and the first element of "ans" calculates to 1+34943–6, or 34938, a serial number.

As you can see from figure 7.23, cells F5 and G9 are formatted as m/d/yy, and cell F9 is formatted as "d", which corresponds to the day of the month. (It's the same "d" as in "m/d/yy"). If you were to format *all* the cells in range A5:G10 as "d", you would have figure 7.23, in which the last few days of the month before (August), and the first few days of the month after (October) also show. The last thing to do is to blank these extras out.

Fig. 7.23

A formula for a calendar that includes the end of the previous month and the beginning of the following month.

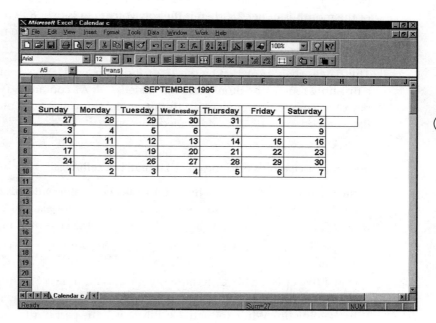

Instead of formatting the cells, the TEXT function was used, because you can format just the cells you want to show and blank the cells you don't want to show. The first part of the formula is:

```
=TEXT(IF(DAY(ans)>15,IF(ROW()=5,"",ans),IF(DAY(ans)<25,IF(ROW()>8,"",ans),ans)),"d").
```

Let's look at this in detail.

In row 5 of figures 7.20 to 7.23, you are faced with the possibility of some of the cells containing the latter days of the previous month. Therefore, you can test both conditions. This part of the formula:

```
IF(DAY(ans)>15,IF(ROW()=5,"",ans...
```

tests that if the day of the month is over 15 and if the row you are in is 5 (the key row), then show nothing. But if the day is over 15 and you are in any other row, show the day of the month.

This part of the formula:

```
IF(DAY(ans)<25,IF(ROW()>8,"",ans),ans)
```

is looked at if the DAY(ans) is *not* over 15. The days of the month in rows 9 or 10 *might* contain the early days of the following month, so this piece checks to see that if the day of the month is under 25, then if the row you are in is over 8 (9 or 10), then also show nothing, otherwise show the day of the month. If the day of the month is *not* under 25, then show the day of the month.

This date is then formatted by the TEXT function as "d". This completes the calendar. As a finishing touch, one more piece was added. Cell A1 contains =TODAY(), which has a day of the month component. In this example, this cell is September 10, 1995 and the day component is 10. The added piece,

```
...&IF($A$1=ans,"***","")
```

appends three asterisks to the day that matches cell A1.

Some interesting effects are achieved if you click in different cells of the calendar and then click the formula bar and press F9 (recalculate). For example, if you select any cell in row 5, click in the formula bar (or double-click the cell) then press F9, you see

```
{"","","","","","1","2";"3","4","5","6","7","8","9";"10***","11","12","13","14","15","";
"","","","","","","";"","","","","","","";"1","2","3","4","5","6","7"}
```

The first five cells are blank because the selection is in row 5, but the numbers only go up to 15! These are followed by several blanks, then the series 1 through 7! What's going on? While the active cell is row 5, the part of the formula, IF(DAY(ans)>15,IF(ROW()=5,"",ans) produces TRUE for ROW()=5 *for all cells* because the active cell is row 5. Therefore, any day greater than 15 shows as blank. (Notice that the day 10 still has the "***" attached.)

If you click a cell in rows 6, 7, or 8, the recalculation of the formula bar shows

```
{"27","28","29","30","31","1","2";"3","4","5","6","7","8","9";"10***","11","12","13",
"14","15","16";"17","18","19","20","21","22","23";"24","25","26","27","28","29","30";
"1","2","3","4","5","6","7"},
```

and if you click a cell in rows 9 or 10, you see

```
={"27","28","29","30","31","","",;"","","","","","","";"***","","","","","","16";"17","
18","19","20","21","22","23";"24","25","26","27","28","29","30";"","","","","","",""}
```

Summary

As you can tell by now, array formulas are an extremely powerful set of tools that, when understood, can increase your productivity using Microsoft Excel. This set of examples is by no means exhaustive of the uses for array formulas. This chapter barely touches on multiple-cell array-entered formulas (such as those LINEST takes advantage of), and there are many other examples possible to discuss.

But with the set of examples in this chapter, you have a great start on mastering these array formulas and becoming a power user.

chapter 8

Using Defined Names for Worksheet Formulas

by Donna Payne

In this chapter

◆ **How to apply defined names to formulas**
To better work with defined names, this chapter looks at the rules, advantages, and disadvantages of applying defined names to complex formulas.

◆ **Tips for working with defined name formulas**
This chapter shows you how to use naming conventions as you would with your Visual Basic for Applications declarations.

◆ **Use dynamic named ranges with worksheet functions**
You learn how to create dynamic intersections, unions, and use the offset function.

◆ **Create your own named formulas to solve complex analytical problems and apply advanced formulas for everyday use**
Learn how to use named formulas to return the sheet name of the active cell, create simple to complex running totals, create named directional range formulas, and use named formulas to create extensible charts.

One measure of good computer programming is how well you have documented what each line of your code does with comment lines. This is standard practice in Visual Basic for Applications as well as most high-level programming languages. Using names for worksheet formulas and other objects is really just an extension of this practice, and can be just as vital to your success and sanity as comment lines are to a C programmer. Like comments, defined names are vital for debugging or making future modifications to a document. They can also speed the development of new spreadsheets by allowing you to quickly and easily adapt pieces of work you've already done for other projects.

The idea here is not to overlook the most important user of your user-friendly spreadsheets—that is you, the developer. Six months from now how easy will it really be for you to decipher what your worksheet actually does? If you wrote the formula =(AC146-AD146) an hour ago, would you know now that this formula represents January sales minus January expenses?

And don't just think of yourself. If you are developing documents that others need to understand, defined names can serve to accurately and clearly describe the purpose or function of formulas.

This chapter explains how to use the naming capabilities of Excel not only to make life easier for you, but also to harness the power of named formulas and other objects. Using defined names with formulas can actually provide solutions to problems that are not otherwise easy to solve. The emphasis in this chapter is on defined names for formulas, as this is the most effective and powerful use for Excel's defined names feature.

Understanding Defined Names

This chapter jumps pretty quickly into advanced defined name formulas so it may be a good idea to briefly review some things about defined names. A *defined name* is a unique, descriptive string of characters, created by the user, that is applied to reference cells, formulas, arrays, a range, or constants. An example showing each type, and how the defined name can appear is shown here:

Type	Defined Name	Defined Name Refers To
Range	Bob_stats	=Sheet1!A1:D10
Formula	Now	=Today( )
Arrays	Directions	={"Up,""Right,""Down,""Left"}
Constants	Desired_rate_of_return	=.28

Here are some rules for creating defined names that you need to be aware of:

▶ The first character must be a letter or an underscore.

▶ A defined name can have as many as 255 characters.

▶ A defined name cannot resemble a cell reference, for example A1.

▶ There can be no spaces in defined names.

▶ The only character punctuation allowed is a period or an underscore.

▶ Defined names are not case-sensitive. The name JanRevenue is the same as janrevenue (although Excel remembers the case of the characters when you initially define the name).

As you can see, these constraints still leave a lot of room for naming possibilities.

Defined names can have global or local scope. *Global names* are available to the entire workbook structure. There is no need to specify where or on what sheet the defined name is located.

By default, all defined names in a workbook are global. To reference a global name, just type an equals sign (=) followed by the defined name. An example of a global defined name is =myname.

A local defined name requires that the sheet name and an exclamation point be added before the descriptive part of the name. This directs Excel to use the defined name on a specified sheet in the reference. You can reference a local name from anywhere in the workbook as long as you include the sheet name that the local name resides on. An example of a local defined name is =Sheet1!myname. In the preceding example, myname is a local name to Sheet1. If Sheet1's name is changed to Sales95, the defined local name will change also to Sales95!myname.

Note

Excel experts often refer to the exclamation point in a defined name as a *Bang*. For example, a local name may be described verbally as "Sheet One Bang MyRange."

8

Note

Local names have a higher priority than global names. When a local name is used on the sheet it is local to, and there is a global name that is the same as the local, the local name takes priority.

Creating Defined Names

There are several ways to create defined names. The drop-down Name Box located at the far-left portion of the formula bar can be used to create a defined name that refers to a range. Select the range that you want to name, place your cursor in the Name Box, type the defined name, and press Enter. If you want to create a local defined name in the drop-down Name Box, remember to add the sheet name and exclamation point prior to the defined name.

Note

When creating local names programmatically, the safest method is to always wrap the sheet name in single quotation marks. An example of this is shown here:

```
ActiveWorkbook.Names.Add Name:="'"& ActiveSheet.Name&"'!Name1", RefersToR1C1:
➥= "1.56"
```

If the single quotes were not placed around the ActiveSheet.Name and ActiveSheet.Name had spaces, the code above would fail.

For clarity, instead of literally typing a single quote ('), some programmers prefer to use the character code 39, which returns the same result.

```
ActiveWorkbook.Names.Add Name:=Chr(39) & ActiveSheet.Name & Chr(39) &
➥"!Name1", RefersToR1C1:= "1.56"
```

This is preferable because single quotation marks and double quotation marks can easily be confused in the code.

 Tip

The Name Box displays a maximum of the first 100 defined names. This limitation is not true when you create a defined name in the Define Name dialog box. The amount of Defined Names in a workbook is limited only by available memory.

There may be a situation where you will need to create a locally defined name and a global name with the same name. For instance, if you have on Sheet 1 a locally defined name of Sheet1!total and a global name of total, when the defined name total is used on Sheet1, the local name takes precedence over the global name. You can reference the locally defined name of total from anywhere in the workbook by including the name where the locally defined name exists followed by the exclamation point and defined name. If you are on a sheet other than Sheet 1 and type **=total**, the globally defined name's value would be returned. Additionally, when using the drop-down Name Box and there exists a local name with the same name as a global name, the local name has priority and will be displayed. Additionally, it is not possible to determine whether the defined name is a local name or a global name from the drop-down Name Box because the drop-down Name Box does not precede local names with the sheetname and exclamation point as it does in the Define Name dialog box.

Another way to create a defined name is to choose Insert, Name, Define. This displays the Define Name dialog box that is shown in figure 8.1. Type a name in the edit box for Names in Workbook (Excel will attempt to guess the new name and place it in the edit box; if the name is incorrect, simply type over it). In the Refers To edit box, enter a range that corresponds to the defined name, a formula, an array, or a value. Click OK to add the define name and close the dialog box. If you want to add several defined names while the Define Name dialog box is displayed, click the Add button after each entry.

Fig. 8.1

The Define Name dialog box can be used to add and edit defined names. Here the name InterestRate is set to equal 6.75 percent.

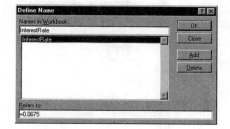

Caution

Changes made in defined names through the Define Name dialog box cannot be undone. For example, you cannot undo a delete, an addition, or an edit of a defined name.

8

It is possible to define a name based on existing labels of a selection on a worksheet. Choose Insert, Name, Create and Excel creates a name based on the right, left, top, and/or bottom of the current range if these ranges are labels. The labels will not be included in the definition of the name, but the labels will be used to name the created defined names. These names will be global in scope unless a global name with the same defined name already exists. If any of the labels are invalid for use as names, Excel replaces invalid characters so the defined name will be valid. An example of creating defined names from existing column or row headers is shown in figure 8.2. Defined names will be created named Jan, Feb, Mar, Part_1, Part_2, Part_3, Part_4, and Part 5. (Excel will automatically fill in the spaces between the words with an underscore.)

Fig. 8.2
Since the Top Row and Left Column check box options are selected, defined names will be created based on the labels in the top and left portion of the selection.

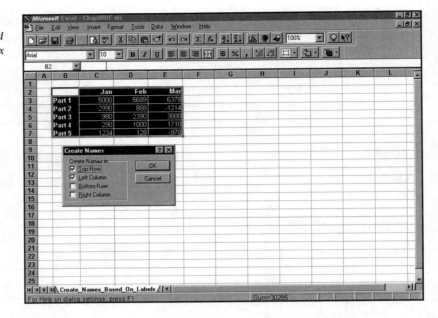

Constants and Formulas

In the Define Name dialog box, you can set the value of a name equal to a constant value. For example, the retail sales tax in Seattle, Washington is 8.2 percent. By creating a defined name of SalesTax, and assigning a value of .082 to the name, you can reference SalesTax anywhere in the current workbook and have it perform calculations or return the value of 8.2 percent. An example of this is =20000*(1+SalesTax), which returns the value of 21,640, given the predefined value of SalesTax in the Define Name dialog box.

1. On a new worksheet, choose Insert, Name, Define.

2. In the Names in Workbook edit box, type **SalesTax**.

3. Delete any reference in the Refers To edit box and type **.082** and click OK to close the Define Name dialog box.

4. In a cell on the worksheet, type **=20000*(1+SalesTax)** and press Enter. The value of 21,640 is returned, which reflects a $20,000 purchase with 8.2 percent sales tax added.

An advantage to assigning a defined name to a constant value is that the value can quickly be changed in the Define Name dialog box, and it will automatically update formulas that reference the name SalesTax to reflect any value change. This saves you from finding and replacing any reference to the sales tax throughout the workbook.

Likewise, assigning a defined name to a formula can be extremely powerful. Two reasons to use defined names in formulas are

▶ A name can provide information on what function the formula performs.

▶ Named formulas are stored formulas, available to plug in wherever needed and can be used in building larger formulas.

Caution
There are several problems that can occur when using defined names. Defined names can be difficult for the inexperienced user to edit or maintain. Also, some defined name formulas cannot be audited using standard Excel auditing procedures.

Naming a formula creates a programming function that is similar to "buckets," or subroutines used by developers. When a formula is given a defined name, that stored information can be used in another statement. For example, the formula =3^2 can be named "ThreeSquared" and =4^2 can be named "FourSquared." Then, the formula =ThreeSquared*FourSquared would return the value 144. You can see that named formulas hold the potential for simplifying much more complex formula solutions, as will be shown later in this chapter.

Relative Referencing and Potential Problems

A powerful use of defined names is to use them in place of formulas inside of a formula. An example of this is shown in figure 8.3 where the values are summed by quarter. The action required is to sum the four cells to the left. Instead of typing the formula =SUM(B3:E3) in cell F3, =SUM(B4:E4) in cell F4, and so on, or filling down, you can create a defined name that will sum the four cells to the left of the active cell, no matter the location. Follow these steps:

1. Enter the data from figure 8.3 into a blank worksheet.

Fig. 8.3

Using defined names inside of formulas can be both self-documenting and powerful.

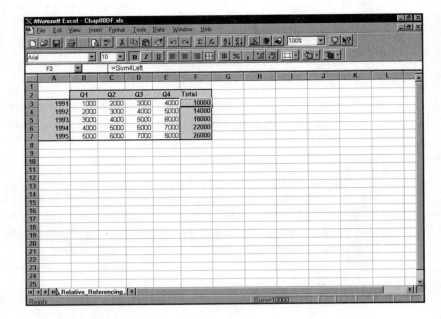

2. Select cell F3, choose <u>I</u>nsert, <u>N</u>ame, <u>D</u>efine. In the Names in <u>W</u>orkbook edit box, type ***TheActiveSheetsName!Sum4Left***.

3. In the <u>R</u>efers To edit box, type **=SUM(B3:E3)**. Click the <u>A</u>dd button. Note that Excel immediately converts this formula to =SUM(*TheActiveSheetsName*!B3:E3). Click OK to close the Define Name dialog box.

4. Select cell F3 and type **=Sum4Left**. The summing occurs just as before; however, it is now more readable and understandable.

5. Select cell F4. Choose <u>I</u>nsert, <u>N</u>ame, <u>D</u>efine. Select the name, Sum4Left and look at its formula. The formula is now =SUM(*TheActiveSheetsName*!B4:E4). This is because relative references in a defined name are based on the active cell or where the defined name is placed, in this case, the four cells to the left.

 Tip

Relative referencing is a bit easier to understand if you've set the reference style to R1C1 notation.

Getting the Most from Defined Name Formulas

By using named formulas, you are already tapping into one of Excel's most powerful and most under-used features. You can substitute defined names for ranges to make the formula more readable, and you can name constants and set them to a predefined value. Now it's time to move on to the next level and apply these same techniques to more advanced formula problems.

Naming Schemes

You've probably already adapted naming conventions for your VBA code, whether it's a 9-prefix notation or perhaps just a single character before the object name. You can do the same with your defined names.

It's not uncommon for a custom application to contain hundreds of defined names. If you use a standard naming convention for your defined names, the names will be more descriptive, and they will be arranged alphabetically in the Define Name dialog box.

It may seem like it's just adding a level of bureaucracy to your work, but it's definitely worth it, especially if there is no easy way to differentiate closely related formulas without using text strings for names that are long enough to fly kites with.

One method of naming conventions is to prefix all defined names that refer to ranges with the letters "nr," all names that refer to formulas as "nf," and defined names that refer to constants as "nc." An example of this is: nrStateList. This name refers to a named range, (nr) that contains a list of states (StateList). This can be extremely useful in finding and debugging problem defined names.

Dynamic Defined Names

A common way for developers to point to an area on a worksheet that may change, based on certain conditions, is by creating dynamic named ranges. The following procedure illustrates how this is done:

1. Enter the data from figure 8.4 on a blank worksheet.
2. Name cells C3:F3 **PriorYear**.
3. Name cells C4:F4 **CurrentYear**.
4. Name cell C6 **Criteria**.

Fig. 8.4

A sum of prior and current years occurs dynamically, based on the user's selection.

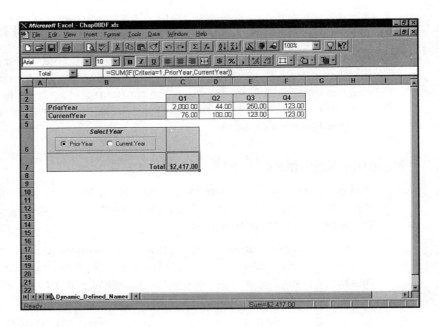

5. Name cell C7 **Total**.

6. Enter the following formula in cell C7:

   =SUM(IF(Criteria=1,PriorYear,CurrentYear)).

7. Choose <u>V</u>iew, <u>T</u>oolbars, select the Forms toolbar and click the OK button.

8. Using the Forms toolbar, create two option buttons within a group box. Set their cell link as cell C6. You can set the cell link of the option button one of two ways. The first way is by selecting the option button (Ctrl+right-click), and then double-clicking the object. The Format Object dialog box with the Control tab is displayed. The second way is to select the option button and choose F<u>o</u>rmat, Obj<u>e</u>ct selecting the Control tab in the Format Object dialog box. Place your cursor in the Cell <u>L</u>ink edit box and type **$C$6**. Click the OK button to close the dialog box.

   By following these steps, you have created a cell link to the option buttons placed on your worksheet. Note that the two option buttons that were placed on the worksheet must be completely inside of the group box in order for them to work together so that only one is selected at one time.

Now it's time to test the dynamic range that you've set up. Toggling between the Prior Year and Current Year option buttons automatically changes the value displayed as the total, based upon the defined criteria.

Note

Dynamic names are not displayed in the Name Box or the Go To dialog box. If you want to select a dynamic name, choose Edit, Go To. In the Refers To edit box, type the dynamic name and choose OK. If the name points to a valid range, that range will be selected.

Dynamic Intersection

You may find it necessary to find the intersection of two ranges that have defined names by using a dynamic name. This is useful when the location of several parts of your spreadsheet may change. By creating a couple of anchors that have defined names assigned to them, you are able to quickly find the intersection of two points. Follow these steps:

   1. Enter the data from figure 8.5 into a blank worksheet.

Fig. 8.5

The Intersection Method is a good way to find the intersection of two ranges when the ranges themselves are subject to change.

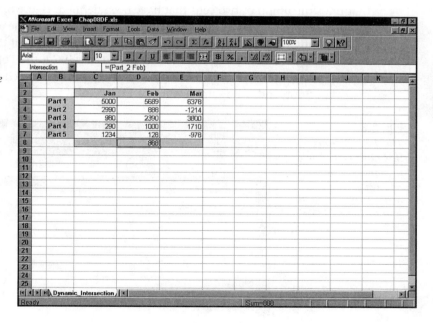

2. Select cells B2:E7.

3. Choose Insert, Name, Create. Select the Top Row and Left Column options.

4. Type the following formula in cell D8:

   =(Part_2 Feb)

   The space between the two defined names is the intersection operator.

5. Press Enter.

Tip
Parentheses are added for clarity and are recommended when using the intersection operator.

Dynamic Unions

Rather than hardwiring a formula, you might want instead to create a flexible formula that finds the union of two cells that have been defined. Figure 8.6 shows a file that was created using dynamic named ranges to find the union of a table and return a sum in the cell that contains the Total. In the dynamic table in figure 8.6, if the position of TopLeft is cell C3 and the BottomRight handle is moved to cell G4, the Total in cell B12 will be 26. If the BottomRight handle is dragged to cell G10, the Total changes to reflect the moved position and will return a value of 152.

Fig. 8.6

The defined name of this table is dynamic, it changes with the relative position of TopLeft and BottomRight.

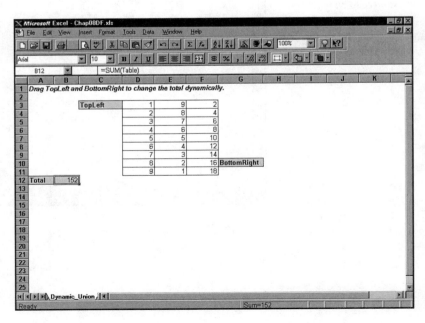

I've dubbed this example the "elevator formula." By dragging and dropping the TopLeft or the BottomRight handle, the summed total value changes dynamically in cell B12.

Here is how this example showing dynamic unions was created:

1. Enter the data from figure 8.6 on a worksheet.
2. Create Define Names **TopLeft** in C3 and **BottomRight** in G11.
3. Choose Insert, Name, Define and in the Names in Workbook edit box, type **Table**.
4. In the Refers To edit box type **=(TopLeft:BottomRight)**. Click the OK button to close the Define Name dialog box.
5. In the Total cell (using this example, cell B12), type **=Sum(Table)**.

Now you can move TopLeft or BottomRight and the Summation will change dynamically because Table is based on a dynamic union.

OFFSET

There will be occasions when you know the top-left cell of a range, but the number of rows and columns are dynamic or else unknown. To create a dynamic name that uses these values, use the OFFSET function.

The OFFSET function returns a reference of a specified height and width, offset from a known cell reference by a specified number of rows and or columns. You might use the OFFSET function when you are adding records to a database and you need to move down to select the next available row. Consider that you have two defined ranges, nf.NumRows and nf.NumCols. The following formula is an example of how this might be done:

```
=OFFSET(TopLeft,0,0,nf.NumRows,nf.NumCols)
```

Returning the Sheet Name of the Active Cell

One shortcoming in Excel is the lack of a built-in functionality to return the sheet name of the active cell. Perhaps future versions of Excel will correct this, but for now, you can use the following formula in any blank cell on a worksheet.

1. Enter the following formula in a workbook that has previously been saved:

    =MID(CELL("filename"),FIND("]",CELL("filename"))+1,255)

2. Select the cell containing the formula.
3. Highlight the entire formula in the formula bar.

    This step is important because if you just select the active cell with the formula and copy the contents, it will not paste correctly in the Define Name Refers to edit box.

4. Choose <u>E</u>dit, <u>C</u>opy and then press Enter.

5. Choose <u>I</u>nsert, <u>N</u>ame, <u>D</u>efine.

6. Type **sheetname** as the defined name, and select the Re<u>f</u>ers To edit box and then choose <u>E</u>dit, <u>P</u>aste. The formula from step 1 is assigned to the defined name of sheetname. Click OK to close the Define Name dialog box.

7. In any cell, type **=sheetname** and press Enter.

   Excel uses the <u>R</u>efers To formula of *sheetname*, evaluates it, and returns the sheet name. This can be used in a worksheet in the workbook in which you create the defined name. You can now delete the original formula.

Let's break down this formula and see how it works. Excel first evaluates the Cell("filename") portion of the formula. Next, Excel looks for the location of the end bracket and adds one to it. Here's where the MID function comes into play. The MID function takes the first argument string and then sets the number that it counted and returns as many as the next 255 characters, resulting in the sheet name.

Running Totals

A common use of spreadsheets is the process of keeping a running total of sums or data from an adjacent column. This is easily done, as shown in figure 8.7. The formula that resides in cell B2, =SUM(A2,B1) is copied down the column of data.

Fig. 8.7

To keep a running total in an adjacent column, create a formula that adds the adjacent column value to the last summed value. In this case, the value from the cell above.

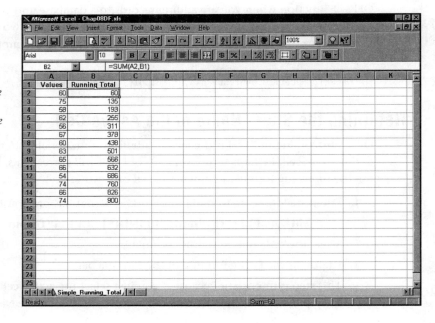

It would be ideal if this formula could be given a defined name such as "rtotal," but doing so will cause several problems. Relative references in defined names can cause an increase in file size, and when a formula containing a worksheet reference is assigned a defined name, the sheet name is appended to each reference in the formula. So, if =SUM(A2,B1) was defined as "rtotal," on reexamination of the tname, it will refer to =SUM(Sheet1!A2,Sheet1!B1) if the active cell is in the same location. Thus, "rtotal" could then only be used on Sheet1 for running totals.

If a formula is to be globally available in a workbook and it operates on worksheet ranges, it must be constructed such that it does not refer to those ranges with an explicit reference. This can be accomplished by using several building block functions to create the following formula:

```
=SUM(OFFSET(INDIRECT(ADDRESS(ROW(),COLUMN()))),
➡-1,0),OFFSET(INDIRECT(ADDRESS(ROW(),COLUMN())),0,-1))
```

Figure 8.8 shows an example of using a named formula to create a running total where the defined name rtotal is assigned the formula just given.

Fig. 8.8

The defined name rtotal is assigned to a formula containing several worksheet functions.

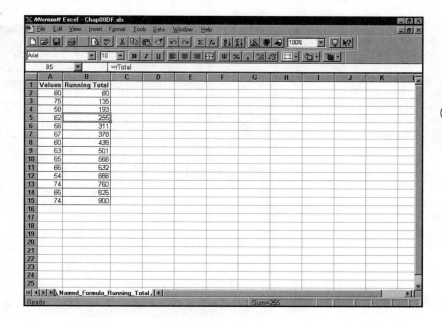

Here is how to interpret the formula, assuming it is placed in cell D5.

The intermediate formula INDIRECT(ADDRESS(ROW(),COLUMN())) is used twice. This intermediate formula is used to create a reference that points to the cell in which the formula is placed. ROW() returns 5 and COLUMN() returns 4 (Column D is the 4th column). The ADDRESS function then interprets these values and creates a cell address as text, returning $D$5. This argument is then interpreted by the INDIRECT function, which converts it to a true address. So, in conclusion, you get the following when the formula is placed in cell D5:

```
INDIRECT(ADDRESS(ROW),COLUMN()))=$D$5
```

An intermediate version of the original formula is in cell D5.

```
=SUM(OFFSET($D$5,-1,0),OFFSET($D$5,0,-1))
```

This can be translated to mean the sum of the cell to the left of D5, which is D4, and the sum of the cell above D5, which is D4.

When this formula is defined as "rtotal," it can be used in any cell on every worksheet in the workbook.

An example of a more useful running total is presented in figure 8.9. The formula used in this example calculates the running total of a banking account. The formula is:

```
=SUM(INDIRECT("RC[-2]",FALSE),-INDIRECT("RC[-1]",FALSE),INDIRECT("R[-1]C",FALSE))
```

Fig. 8.9

A more useful formula for running totals where =balance is entered into cells D2:D10. This example shows a transaction register with a running total column.

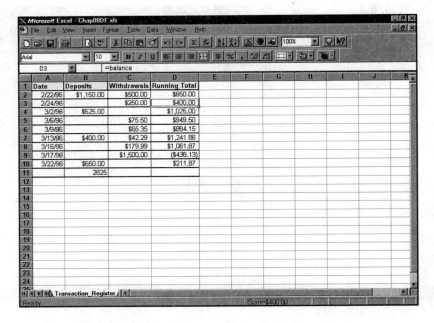

This formula, when placed in cell D3, subtracts the value in the cell one cell to the left of D3, or cell C3 from the value in the cell that is two cells to the left of cell D3, which is cell B3, and adds it to the previous total, which is one cell up from cell D3, or cell D2. Because the formula is based on relative references, this will still work if the list was located anywhere in the worksheet.

When defined with a name such as "balance," it can be used globally as well, because Excel does not detect any reference in text form, which is again converted to a reference by the INDIRECT function when the second argument in INDIRECT is assigned as FALSE.

 Note

The INDIRECT function is a powerful spreadsheet function but should only be used when a problem can't be solved without using INDIRECT. The INDIRECT function enables you to create references "on-the-fly," although the speed is greatly affected. The syntax of the INDIRECT function is as follows:

```
INDIRECT(ref_text,A1)
```

`ref_text` is a reference to a cell that contains either an A1-style reference, an R1C1-style reference, or defined name that contains a value that can be evaluated as a reference.

`A1` is a logical value that specifies what type of reference is contained in the `ref_text`. If `A1` is TRUE or omitted, `ref_text` is interpreted as an `A1` style reference.

It's important to note that `ref_text` can also be the name of a defined name that points to a range. In this case, `A1` or R1C1 does not matter.

8

 Tip

Use the INDIRECT function only when other functions cannot be used (such as OFFSET or INDEX) as INDIRECT is slower to recalculate than other referencing types of functions.

Both of the formula methodologies presented here for calculating running totals for global use in a workbook can be modified for a myriad of uses.

Creating Named Directional Range Formulas

The AutoSum tool in Excel can be used to create automatic SUM formulas and it can "sense" what range of cells you would like to include in your total. However, users can be very particular in what they want out of a formula. If a column of data contains blank cells, the AutoSum tool will return a formula containing only those cells below the first blank cell.

In figure 8.10, the result of using the AutoSum tool when cell D11 is selected returns =SUM(D7:D10), the total that is shown in cell D11. As you can see, only the four cells below the blank cell were included in the range selected by AutoSum to give a value of 25. In this instance, you want to sum all of the cells from cell D2:D10 and have the formula =SUM(D2:D10), so you end up entering the formula manually. By using named ranges that perform this function, this job becomes much easier and straightforward.

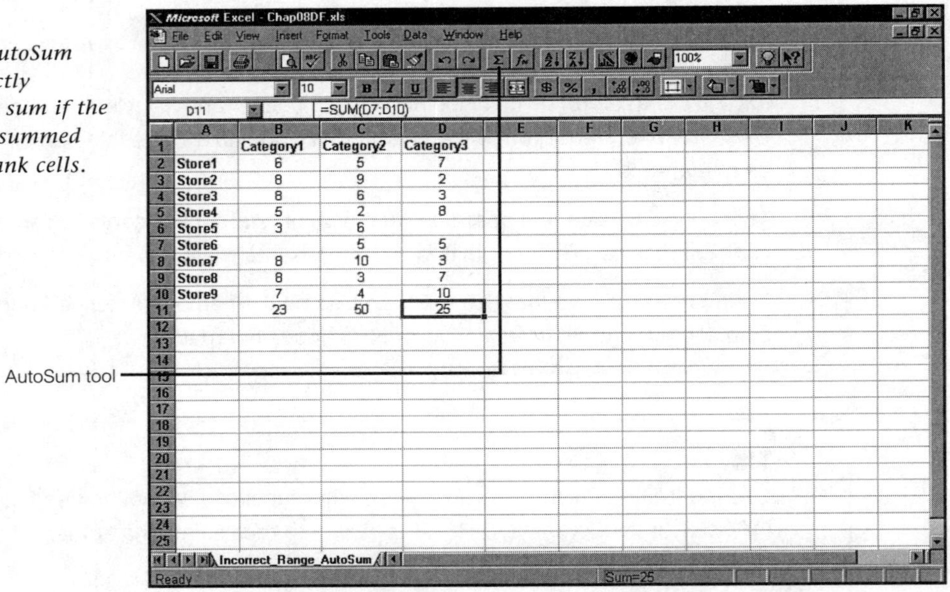

Fig. 8.10

Using the AutoSum tool incorrectly calculates a sum if the range to be summed contains blank cells.

AutoSum tool

Before the cells above D11 are summed, a reference to that range must be constructed. The following formula returns the range of cells above the cell where the formula is written.

```
=OFFSET(INDIRECT(ADDRESS(1,COLUMN())),0,0,ROW()-1,1)
```

Here's how the formula works. Because the formula is entered into cell D11, the COLUMN() and ROW() functions return 4 and 11 respectively, so the intermediate evaluation of the formula is

```
=OFFSET(INDIRECT(ADDRESS(1,4)),0,0,10,1)
```

The formula INDIRECT(ADDRESS(1,4)) returns "$D$1", so the second intermediate evaluation of the formula is

```
=OFFSET(D1,0,0,10,1)
```

The arguments of the OFFSET function return a range of cells offset from D1 by zero rows and zero columns (or D1), with the size of the range to be 10 rows down by one column. In A1 reference notation, the range is D1:D10.

```
=(D1:D10)
```

Now that there is a formula that returns a reference to all of the cells above where it is placed, the sum can be created in cell D11 with the following formula:

```
=SUM(OFFSET(INDIRECT(ADDRESS(1,COLUMN())),0,0,ROW()-1,1))
```

No matter what cell this formula is placed in on a worksheet, it will always return the sum of the cells above it. To use this type of formula effectively, a defined name is called for.

In this case, it is useful to assign only the OFFSET function to a name. It can then be used with all of Excel's worksheet functions. A good descriptive name to use here is "up." The formula =SUM(up) is placed in cell B11 then filled to cell D11 in the example shown in figure 8.11. Using the naming procedure discussed previously, "up" now refers to:

```
=OFFSET(INDIRECT(ADDRESS(1,COLUMN())),0,0,ROW()-1,1)
And in cell D11:        =SUM(up)
```

Fig. 8.11
Replacing the AutoSum formula with a summed defined named range is a preferred technique for calculating ranges.

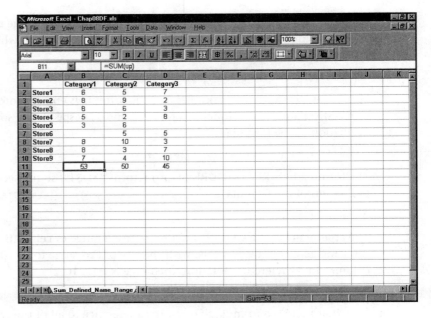

Another example of how "up" can be used is in a formula for finding the 3rd smallest values in Column B of the table in figure 8.12. The formula =SMALL(up,3) placed in cell B11.

Fig. 8.12
The worksheet function SMALL is used to return the 3rd smallest value in the table specifying the named range "up."

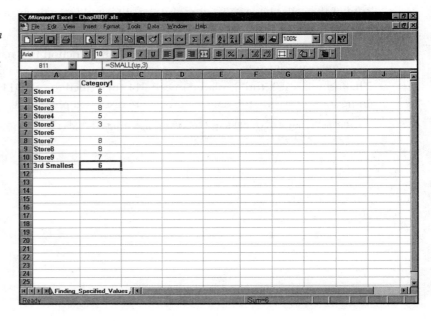

A very particular Excel user would still not be happy with this formula, and perhaps for a very good reason. If on a worksheet as shown in figure 8.13, there happens to be two tables of data occupying the same column (although not good practice), the formula =SUM(up) could not be placed below the second table and return the total only from that table. However, in most data tables, there are column and row headings in text. That fact can be put to good use in constructing a formula that will "sum up" until it encounters a cell containing text.

To do that, a formula is needed to find the row number of the text cell closest to the cell containing the formula. A formula that accomplishes this task is shown here. For this formula to return the desired value in a cell, it must be array-entered. But one of the beauties of defining formulas as names is that the names can function as array formulas without having to use Ctrl+Shift+Enter.

The following formula returns the row of the first cell going up that contains text.

```
=MAX(ISTEXT(INDIRECT(ADDRESS(1,COLUMN())):INDIRECT(ADDRESS(ROW()-
1,COLUMN()))))*ROW(INDIRECT(ADDRESS(1,COLUMN())):INDIRECT(ADDRESS(ROW()-1,COLUMN()))))
```

Let's examine how this array formula works. The formula returns the maximum value from an array formed by the multiplication of a logical and a numerical array. The first array is

```
ISTEXT(INDIRECT(ADDRESS(1,COLUMN())):INDIRECT(ADDRESS(ROW()-1,COLUMN())))
```

With the formula entered in cell F16, the range referred to by the INDIRECT function is F1:F15. So this array simplifies to ISTEXT(F1:F15). When evaluated by Excel, Excel returns the array:

```
{TRUE;FALSE;FALSE;FALSE;FALSE;FALSE;FALSE;FALSE;FALSE;FALSE;FALSE;TRUE;FALSE;FALSE;FALSE}
```

The TRUE values indicate cells that contain text. The second array is

```
ROW(INDIRECT(ADDRESS(1,COLUMN())):INDIRECT(ADDRESS(ROW()-1,COLUMN())))
```

Again, the range is F1:F15, so the formula evaluates to ROW(F1:F15) and finally to

```
{1;2;3;4;5;6;7;8;9;10;11;12;13;14;15}
```

When the two arrays are multiplied together, the resulting array is

```
{1;0;0;0;0;0;0;0;0;0;0;12;0;0;0}
```

and the maximum value of that array is 12, which is the row number needed in the next formula (note that multiplying FALSE to a number gives a result of zero). Now, the MAX formula is given a defined name of "matchutext." This named formula is used in a formula that returns a range from the cell containing the formula to the closest text cell above that cell in the column.

```
=OFFSET(INDIRECT(ADDRESS(ROW(),COLUMN())),matchutext-ROW(),0,ROW()-matchutext,1)
```

The formula that is defined as "matchutext" is quite long, and it is used twice in the OFFSET formula. Without using a defined name, the entire formula is excessively long and difficult to edit.

The final step is to define the OFFSET formula as "up_to_text." If the formula =AVERAGE(up_to_text) is entered in cell F16, the resulting answer comes from the three cells from the second table only.

The preceding examples showed formulas that operate in an up direction. The following is a list that contains the formulas that perform the same operations but in other directions.

```
Down  =OFFSET(INDIRECT(ADDRESS(ROW()+1,COLUMN())),0,0,16384-ROW(),1)
Right =OFFSET(INDIRECT(ADDRESS(ROW(),COLUMN()+1)),0,0,1,256-COLUMN())
Left  =OFFSET(INDIRECT(ADDRESS(ROW(),1)),0,0,1,COLUMN()-1)
```

The row number of the first cell below the cell in which the formula is placed, matchdtext:

```
=MATCH(1,N(ISTEXT(INDIRECT(ADDRESS(ROW()+1,COLUMN()):INDIRECT(ADDRESS(ROW()+6549,
➥COLUMN())))),0)-1
```

The column number of the first cell to the right containing text, matchrtext:

```
=MATCH(1,N(ISTEXT(INDIRECT(ADDRESS(ROW(),COLUMN()+1)):INDIRECT(ADDRESS(ROW(),256)))),0)-1
```

The column number of the first cell to the left that contains text, matchltext:

```
=MAX(ISTEXT(INDIRECT(ADDRESS(ROW(),1)):INDIRECT(ADDRESS(ROW(),COLUMN()1)))*COLUMN(INDIRECT
➥(ADDRESS(ROW(),1)):INDIRECT(ADDRESS(ROW(),COLUMN()-1))))
```

Returns a reference from the cell below the cell in which the formula is placed to the first cell going down that contains text, down_to_text:

```
=OFFSET(INDIRECT(ADDRESS(ROW()+1,COLUMN())),0,0,matchdtext,1)
```

Returns a reference to the right, right_to_text:

```
=OFFSET(INDIRECT(ADDRESS(ROW(),COLUMN()+1)),0,0,1,matchrtext)
```

Returns a reference to the left, left_to_text:

```
=OFFSET(INDIRECT(ADDRESS(ROW(),COLUMN())),0,matchltext-COLUMN(),1,COLUMN()-matchltext)
```

Figure 8.13 displays an example of using the preceding formulas with the defined name up_to_text to find the AVERAGE of the contents of the cells until text is present.

A final example demonstrates the flexibility in the use of these named auto-ranges. In figure 8.14, the data table contains quite a few blank cells. These cells interfere with our theoretical user's desire to obtain the average of the last four values in each column. Observe that each column has a different size range that includes those values. For this job, the following formula can be used to return the correct range (if nvalues has been defined as =4).

```
=INDEX(up,LARGE(IF(ISBLANK(up),"",ROW(up)),nvalues)-ROW(up)+1):INDEX(up,ROWS(up))
```

Fig. 8.13

Cell B16 calculates the average for all cells above it until it reaches a cell that contains text. In this example, cell B12 contains text so the average is generated from cells B13:B15.

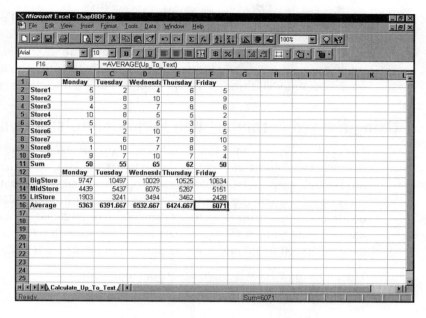

Fig. 8.14

The calculations are dynamic, based on whether a cell contains values.

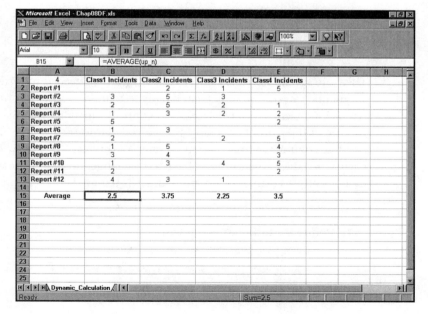

If this formula is defined as "up_n," then =AVERAGE(up_n) will return the correct answer for each column of data. For convenience, the name "nvalues" can be assigned to a worksheet cell (in this example, A1), and the value can be changed by entering a new value. As you can now appreciate, there are many opportunities for enhancement of spreadsheet models through the application and modification of these techniques.

Using Named Formulas with Form Controls: A Dynamic Table

The application of named formulas to create dynamic data tables is a powerful technique that uses worksheet form controls to aid in data lookup. To understand the process behind building such a model, a simple data lookup table is illustrated in figure 8.15. In this example, where the data table might represent information kept for a video store distributor, if the name of a client is entered in cell A2, and a column heading (field name) is entered in cell A10, the data point corresponding to that intersection will be returned in cell A18. Thus, the data point in this example is P. Campos's phone number.

The following steps were used in setting up this model:

1. Define the formulas as follows:

```
Name = MATCH($A$2,OFFSET($C$4,1,0,3,1),0)

Field = MATCH($A$6,OFFSET($C$4,0,1,1,4),0)

d_point = OFFSET($C$4,Name,Field)
```

2. Type the formula "**=d_point**" into cell A10.

There are several necessary improvements that are needed to turn this simple model into a dynamic working system. First, having to manually enter information into cells A2 and A10 is inefficient given the worksheet controls capability that Excel provides. Second, the size of the current data table is hard-coded into the formulas for only three clients and five columns of information. Because of this, each time new fields of information or clients are added, the formulas have to be changed to reflect the growth. A technique for dynamically adjusting information arrays is required and is displayed in figure 8.16.

To revise this model, take the following steps:

1. Define the formulas as follows:

```
NameArray = OFFSET($D$8,1,0,COUNTA($D:$D)-1,1)

FieldArray = TRANSPOSE(OFFSET($D$8,0,1,1,COUNTA($8:$8)-1))

data_point = OFFSET($D$8,$B$1,$B$9)
```

Fig. 8.15

A lookup table will generate information that is associated with other information from the same table.

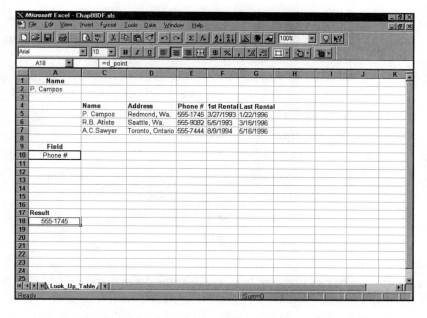

Fig. 8.16

Utilizing the built-in worksheet controls adds ease, utility, and a professional appearance.

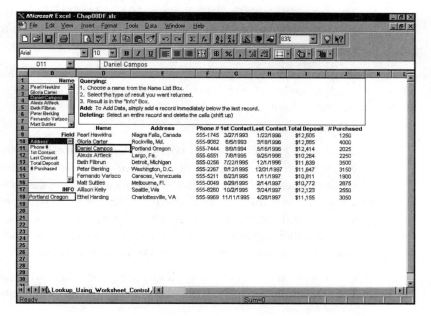

8

2. Assign the named arrays to populate the list boxes. Choose <u>V</u>iew, <u>T</u>oolbars, Form.

3. Select the List Box toolbar button and place the cursor control over cell B2. The same process was used for a control over cell B10.

4. Select the list box control that is over cell B2 and double-click to reveal the Format Object dialog box. Select the Control tab from the dialog box.

5. Enter the following information:

   Input Range: **NameArray**

   Cell Link: **$B$1**

6. Select and double-click the list box control over cell B10.

7. Enter the following information:

   Input Range: **FA** (see the following paragraphs)

   Cell Link: **$B$9**

There was a problem in assigning a dynamic array for the list of column headings to the list box in that it only accepts a vertical array. The TRANSPOSE function can be used to transform a horizontal array to a vertical array. It was envisioned that this formula (named as FieldArray) could be used to populate the list box, but it did not work! Excel form controls do not recognize arrays transposed in this manner. A workaround is necessary. The following was entered into cell $A$12 and filled down to cell $A$262.

```
=INDEX(FieldArray,ROW()-ROW($A$12)+1
```

This effectively produced a transposed vertical array of the column headings with enough formulas added to anticipate the addition of many new columns. Next, the formula shown here was defined as "FA" and used in the input range for the Field list box.

```
=OFFSET($A$16,0,0,COUNTA($8:$8),1)
```

Choices are made in the two list boxes by clicking the desired criteria. To make the dynamic table more presentable, column A, which contains the transposed vertical array of the column headings, was hidden. Also, notice the active cell is $B$1 and the formula bar indicates that the value in that cell is 3 (the returned position of the selection in the Name Box, and not "Name," as it appears in the cell). This cell, as well as cell $B$9, has a custom number format that is simply text. For cell $B$1, this was done by choosing Format, Cells, Number, and entering "Name" in the edit box.

The dynamic table is now ready. Adding rows and columns of data will automatically update the list boxes to allow the user to quickly locate and display (in cell $B$18) any piece of information that is requested.

Using Named Formulas to Create Extensible Charts

If you analyze data, you know that charting is a very effective way of presenting data. As the saying goes, "a picture is worth a thousand words." Creating charts from data in Excel is very easy, but there is one catch. In most cases, users are dealing with a constantly growing data set. Thus, they must repeat the job of creating a new chart when new data needs to be viewed. Previously, it was shown that dynamic range formulas of the form =OFFSET($A$1,1,0,COUNTA($A:$A),1) can be used to correctly size arrays based on the number of occupied cells in a column.

This type of formula can also be used for dynamic charting, but it does have one serious drawback that limits its use for this application. The problem occurs when data is not contiguous; that is, when there are blank spaces in a list as a result of missing data. The example in figure 8.17 illustrates this problem.

Fig. 8.17

When there are non-contiguous cells in a list, dynamic charts may become a problem.

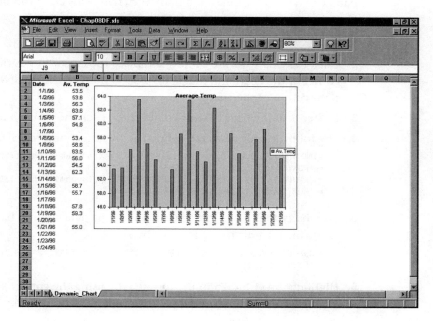

Note that in the range B1:B25, B8, B15, B18, B21, and B23 to B25 are blank. Because there are only 17 cells that contain entries, the OFFSET formula returns an array that contains the first 17 elements in B1:B25, or B1:A17. To circumvent this problem, a formula of the following form can be used:

```
=MAX(($A$1:$A$4000<>"")*ROWS($A$1:$A$4000)))
```

This array formula returns the row number of the last occupied cell in the specified range (in this case, range A1:A4000). When this formula is used in combination with the INDIRECT function, the following dynamic array formula is created:

```
=INDIRECT("$B$1:$B$"&MAX(($B$1:$AB4000<>"")*ROW($B$1:$A$1:$B$4000)))
```

This formula returns the column array of all of the values in the range B1 through the last occupied cell in B1:B4000.

> **Note**
>
> α A range of 4,000 cells is used to conform with an array formula size limitation in Excel 7.

Figure 8.17 illustrates this technique. In this example, data is being collected on the average daily temperature, with the date in Column A and the data in Column B. The key to making a dynamic chart is to create the chart as you normally would with a set amount of data. Use named formulas to modify the chart. This chart can be constructed by following these steps.

1. Select cells A1:B25 of the worksheet.

2. Click the Chart Wizard button and place the cursor in position for the upper-left corner of the chart and drag it across the sheet to the desired location of the lower-right corner of the chart.

3. In Step 1 of the Chart Wizard dialog box, click the Finish button.

4. The following formulas are defined as "x_range" and "data_range" respectively:

   ```
   =INDIRECT("'Dynamic_Chart'!$A$2:$A$"&MAX((Dynamic_Chart!$B$2:$B$4000<>"")
   ➥*ROW(Dynamic_Chart!$B$2:$B$4000)))
   =INDIRECT("'Dynamic_Chart'!$B$2:$B$"&MAX((Dynamic_Chart!$B$2:$B$4000<>"")
   ➥*ROW(Dynamic_Chart!$B$2:$B$4000)))
   ```

5. To modify the chart, double-click one of the data column bars. You will see the following formula in the formula bar.

   ```
   =SERIES('Dynamic_Chart'!$B$1,'Dynamic_Chart'!$A$1:$A$10,'Dynamic_Chart'!
   ➥$B$1:$B$10,1)
   ```

6. Highlight $A$1:$A$25 in the formula (by using the cursor) and type **x_range**. Highlight $B$1:$B$10 and type **data_range**. Enter the formula.

7. Deactivate chart editing by double-clicking in a worksheet cell and your dynamic chart is ready!

Now, whenever a new value is entered in Column B, the chart will automatically update to reflect that new value. It is important to note that when you deactivate the workbook containing the dynamic chart, the SERIES formula will change to reflect the workbook, rather than the sheet name, when named ranges are used,

```
=SERIES(Dynamic_Chart!$B$1,'Chap08DF.xls'!x_range,'Chap08DF.xls'!data_range,1)
```

so the named formulas must include the correct sheet name, as they did in this example.

Caution

Do not rename the worksheet containing the dynamic chart. It may be very difficult to readjust worksheet names in the dynamic formulas.

 Note

Robert Affleck, a contributor to this book recently posted a message on the MS Excel forum on CompuServe that described a new discovery that some XLM information functions can be used in worksheets if they are used through defined names. For example, a defined name named "AllFiles" can be created that refers to =DOCUMENTS(). If in a worksheet, you can then access the list of all open Excel workbooks with =INDEX(AllFiles,1) for the 1st file, =INDEX(Allfiles,2) for the 2nd file, and so on.

This functionality was previously only available through custom functions and may be a resource to developers. Three caveats:

▶ It is only available in Excel 5 and Excel 7.

▶ It is an undocumented "feature" and may not be supported in future versions of Excel.

▶ Define names that refer to XLM information function may not update when a recalculation occurs.

Developers may consider this undocumented feature in their development, but should use it only if no other workaround is available.

The XLM functions that are available include EVALUATE, FILES, WINDOWS, DOCUMENTS, and NAMES.

Summary

Wouldn't it be great if we could just talk to the computer and describe what we wanted it to do in plain English, like Scotty in *Star Trek*? Well, we are probably still light years from that capability, but we can get the computer to talk to *us* about how and what it is doing in an Excel worksheet. Defining names for formulas, if used properly, tells the complete, unabridged story of your workbook, not only to us, but to other formulas and objects. Naming your formulas allows you not only to peel away the layers of complexity in your worksheets for you and other users, but allows formulas to communicate and interact with each other in more powerful ways.

Hopefully the examples presented in this chapter have been ones that you can use in your everyday work. You don't have to understand how they work to be able to use them. Of course, we hope you have taken the opportunity presented through the explanations and examples in this chapter to master using defined names for formulas, one of the many powerful features of Microsoft Excel.

chapter 9

The Power of Custom Functions

9

by Donna Payne and Robert Affleck

In this chapter

◆ **An overview of custom functions**
Learn what a custom function is, along with differences between a Sub procedure and a Function procedure.

◆ **Design and use of custom functions**
This chapter helps you understand the process of creating and debugging a custom function and gives you advanced tips for doing both.

◆ **Examples of custom functions**
Discover the custom functions that will allow you to check for the existence of an item in a collection, check for an intersection, changing page fields, sum dynamically, sum an array cumulatively, and create a drawing object.

uilt-in functions are basic to spreadsheet development; therefore, you may be intrigued by the prospect of creating your own custom functions. Creating and maintaining a library of custom functions, tailored to your specific needs, can certainly speed development in the same way that built-in functions can. However, you may not be aware of some features and applications of custom functions that reach beyond the capabilities of built-in functions, or even VBA Sub procedures, for that matter. This chapter shows you not only how to design and use custom functions that act like the functions you are accustomed to, but also how to use the full capability of this powerful feature of Excel.

Overview of Custom Functions

There are two types of procedures available in Visual Basic for Applications, Sub procedures and Function procedures. Function procedures begin with the keyword "Function" and end with the keywords "End Function." A function procedure can return values to the procedure or worksheet formula that called it (Sub procedures cannot do this). The value returned can be a number, Boolean, string, array, or object. Function procedures also can be called through formulas entered in a worksheet.

The simplest type of function is demonstrated in Function Foo shown here. Function Foo accepts one required argument named MyArgument, which, because it is not explicitly typed, is treated as a variant.

```
Function Foo(MyArgument)
VBA Statements
Foo = Result of Statements
End Function
```

 Tip
For a detailed description of the syntax of a function, refer to Online VBA Help under the keyword "Function."

Function Procedures

Function procedures are not used by many developers because some believe, incorrectly, that a function cannot perform any action that changes the Excel environment. While this is true if a function is being called from a spreadsheet formula, it is positively untrue if a function is being called from another VBA procedure. In other words, when a custom function is used in a VBA procedure, it can do *anything* a subroutine can do.

Part of the confusion arises from the fact that most people are introduced to using custom functions as replacements for complicated spreadsheet functions. While this is an entirely useful purpose of a function, it leads people to the mistaken belief that functions can only be called from spreadsheet cells.

A function that is specifically designed to be called from a formula in a worksheet is called a *user-defined worksheet function*. Many developers call these UDFs (although UDWF would perhaps be a clearer acronym). Unlike functions created through function procedures, UDFs cannot change properties or execute processes that alter the Microsoft Excel environment. In other words, UDFs cannot:

▶ Format, insert, or delete rows

▶ Change cell values (other than the cell(s) in which the formula is used)

▶ Change display options such as displaying the formula bar, tabs, and so on

▶ Move, add, delete, or change the names of sheets

▶ Call any other procedure that changes the Excel environment

Excel does permit the developer to enter custom functions that *attempt* to change the Excel environment. These functions return the #Value! error to the calling formula. Excel does attempt to run these functions, but at the first line of code that attempts to change the environment, the function aborts and returns the #Value! error. Additionally, Excel "fails silently" when an action is attempted by a function called from a formula, returning only the error value, and does not produce an error message.

Debugging User-Defined Worksheet Functions

As mentioned previously, when testing a UDF, run-time errors do not always result in error messages to the user. If an error does occur, Excel aborts the function and returns an error value. Here are some recommended debugging approaches:

▶ Place breakpoints at critical points and step through the questionable part of the code.

▶ Place message boxes (MsgBox) at critical points in the function to monitor important values. Message boxes are displayed when a function is run from a spreadsheet formula. After debugging, remove the MsgBox calls from the function or add code to turn off the MsgBox when not debugging.

▶ Call the function from a subroutine. Run-time errors normally occur when a function is called from another VBA procedure.

Example of a User-Defined Worksheet Function

Suppose you have to create a spreadsheet that will calculate labor costs at a construction site. A laborer is paid dRate dollars per hour for up to the first 8 hours of work, dRate *(multiply) 1.5 for the hours greater than 8 but less than 12, and then paid dRate * 2 for 12 or more hours.

If the number of hours worked is in cell A2, the wage is in cell B2, and the calculation is in cell C2, the formula to calculate the salary would be something like:

    =IF(A2<=8,A2*B2,8*B2+IF(A2<12,(A2-8)*1.5*B2,4*B2*1.5+(A2-12)*B2*2)).

It's complicated, yet manageable. But what about changes? If overtime is changed to the nine-hour mark, you must edit each instance of this formula and change the formula accordingly. An alternative solution is to use a custom function that is called CalcSalary. CalcSalary is a UDF that is passed two arguments: the hours worked (dHours) and the base hourly rate (dRate). In figure 9.1, cell C2 then has the following formula:

```
=CalcSalary(A2,B2)
```

Fig. 9.1

Cell C2 has a formula containing the user-defined function CalcSalary. CalcSalary requires the arguments Hours(A2) and Rate(B2) to calculate the salary.

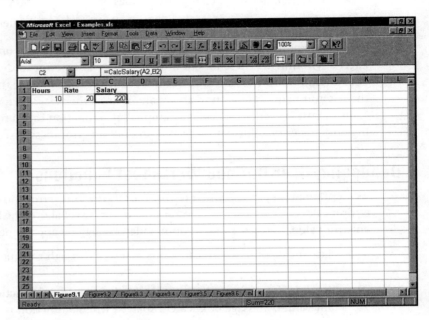

The CalcSalary function looks like this:

```
Function CalcSalary(dHours As Double, dRate As Double) As Double
    Select Case dHours
        Case 0 To 8
            CalcSalary = dRate * dHours
        Case 8 To 12
            CalcSalary = dRate * 8 + (dHours - 8) * (1.5 * dRate)
        Case Is > 12
            CalcSalary = dRate * 8 + (dHours - 8) * (1.5 * dRate) + (dHours - 12) *
            ➥(2 * dRate)
    End Select
End Function
```

CalcSalary takes two arguments: dHours and dRate. (The d indicates that the variables have a data type of Double, or double-precision floating-point.) It is obvious that CalcSalary is much less complicated than the spreadsheet function and easier to edit. In addition, note that CalcSalary can also be called from a VBA subroutine. The following example is of calling the function CalcSalary from the subroutine InputCalcSalary().

```
Sub InputCalcSalary()
    Dim dHours As Double
    Dim dRate As Double
    dHours = CDbl(InputBox("Enter the Number of Hours: "))
    dRate = CDbl(InputBox("Enter the Base rate: "))
    MsgBox "Hours: " & dHours & Chr(10) & _
        "Base Rate: " & dRate & Chr(10) & _
            "Salary is: " & CalcSalary(dHours, dRate)
End Sub
```

Figure 9.2 shows the result when the Sub procedure InputCalcSalary is called, and 10 hours are entered with a base rate of 20.

Fig. 9.2

The message box displays the result of the subroutine InputCalcSalary() calling the user-defined function CalcSalary.

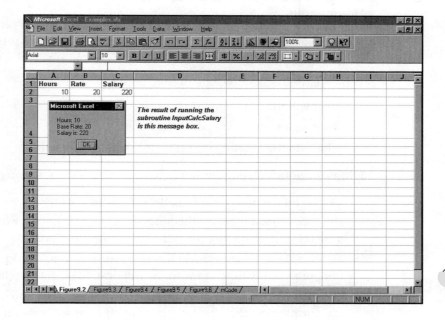

> ## α Note
> While in most cases it is best to specifically name a data type, when the argument of a function in a user-defined worksheet function is a cell or a range, you must use the Object data type. If you type the argument as a Range, the function will fail when called from a worksheet formula.

Accessing the UDF from a Worksheet Formula

After a UDF is created, it is available to be used in any open workbook, as long as the function has not been declared private. To access the function, select the cell(s) where the function is to be placed, then choose Insert, Function, User-Defined, and then select the function. Arguments can be cell references, defined names, other functions, or constants.

Designing Custom Functions

The best functions are those that perform a specific process and perform it well. Create lots of general purpose functions rather than a few functions that try to do everything. Short functions are usually more reusable than complicated multipurpose functions.

When designing a function, you need to decide:

- ▶ What will the function do?
- ▶ What arguments, if any, does the function need?
- ▶ What will the function return to its caller on completion?

Additional tips for creating custom functions include the following:

- ▶ Use descriptive names for functions and their arguments.
- ▶ Use specific data types for the function and its arguments where practical, without unnecessarily restricting the flexibility of the function.
- ▶ To access built-in spreadsheet functions such as Sum, Average, and so on, in a function, precede the function with the Application object qualifier.
- ▶ Use the Object Browser - Options to classify a function into one of a variety of classifications so the function can be easily accessed from the Function Wizard.
- ▶ If a function's scope is not explicitly declared, the default is Public. (This is the same as a subroutine.)
- ▶ If a function's scope is Private, it will not appear in the Function Wizard's list of functions. A Private function can only be called from within the module in which it resides.
- ▶ Do not reinvent the wheel by re-creating a function that already exists in Excel (such as SUM and AVERAGE). A custom function is always much slower than a built-in function, so replicate an existing built-in function only when absolutely necessary.
- ▶ Require only the arguments absolutely necessary. If an argument is not absolutely necessary, make it optional.

▶ When creating a function, think about reusability and maintainability. While developing an application, if you create a function that is reusable, copy the code to a library workbook so it can be used again on another project.

▶ When calling a function from a VBA procedure, use the named arguments (MyArgument = "Hello"). While this may seem a nuisance at first, it will pay great dividends in the long run.

User-Defined Categories

There is no way to manually create a user-defined category for a custom function that is written in Visual Basic for Applications without first inserting a Microsoft Excel 4.0 macro sheet. To create a user-defined category, you can use the following subroutine:

```
Sub CreateNewCategory()
    Dim NewCategory As String
    NewCategory = InputBox("Enter Name of New Function Category: ")
    Workbooks.Add xlExcel4MacroSheet
    ActiveWorkbook.Names.Add Name:="Test1", RefersToR1C1:="=Macro1!R1C1" _
        , Category:=NewCategory, MacroType:=xlFunction
End Sub
```

After the subroutine CreateNewCategory has been run, a new category has been added to the Function Category list. To add the function to the new category, in a module sheet, choose <u>V</u>iew, <u>O</u>bject Browser, select the function, click <u>O</u>ptions, and then select the newly added category. After you add a function to the new category, the workbook with one Excel 4 macro sheet in it can be closed and not saved. (Do not close it before you add a function to the category or the added category is lost.)

 Tip

To add a function category without using the subroutine CreateNewCategory, look up the Microsoft Knowledge Base article Q137526 titled "How to add a new function category to a function category list."

 Note

The Microsoft Knowledge Base is a database of more than 40,000 articles on Microsoft products that includes answers to common questions, technical product information, and bug lists. You can access the MS Knowledge Base through several electronic services and through the Internet.

If you are a CompuServe member and wish to access the MS Knowledge Base, type **GO MSKB**. On America Online, choose the Go To menu, type **Microsoft** in the Keyword box, and then click Knowledge Base in the Microsoft Resource Center. Access the Knowledge Base on Genie by typing **m505** at the Genie system prompt. If you use The Microsoft Network (MSN), choose Edit, Go To, Other Location and in the Go To Service dialog box type **MSKB** and click OK.

The Microsoft World Wide Web site is located at **http://www.microsoft.com**. The Microsoft Gopher site is located at **gopher.microsoft.com**. The Microsoft FTP site is located at **ftp.microsoft.com** and can be accessed via anonymous logon.

Calling a Function

If a function resides in a module in the same workbook from which it is called, calling the function is simple—just enter the function and its arguments in either a worksheet formula or in a VBA module. For example, the function CalcSalary can be called from a cell by typing (or entering via the Function Wizard) the following formula:

```
=CalcSalary(10,20)
```

where 10 and 20 are the arguments for the hours and rate, respectively.

To call the function from another module in the same workbook, something such as `Result = CalcSalary(10,20)` is correct, while `Result  = CalcSalary(dHours:=10, dRate:=20)` is preferable, as using a named argument makes code more readable and reduces the chance of passing the wrong value to an argument.

To call a function from a worksheet formula from a different workbook than the one in which the function resides, there are two approaches: a tools-reference or a link. In both cases, the workbook containing the function must be open (or an installed add-in). If you create a tools-reference from the calling workbook to the function's workbook, the result is the same as shown previously. Assuming the function CalcSalary is in your personal.xls, you can refer to CalcSalary in a cell by entering it as a standard link. The following code is an example of entering a standard link to a function in your personal.xls.

```
=Personal.xls!CalcSalary(10,20)
```

To call a function from a VBA procedure in a different workbook than the one in which the function resides, you can use a tools-reference or Application.Run. If a tools-reference has been established, the function in the separate workbook can be called as if it is in the same workbook that the calling procedure resides. The Application.Run approach does not require establishing references. The following code is an example of calling the function CalcSalary from another workbook.

```
Result = Application.Run("Personal.xls!CalcSalary",10,20)
```

Some references have been observed to have caused extremely long opening times for workbooks in Excel 5.0, so developers often choose to avoid applications that require establishing references. The opening times for workbooks with Tools, References has decreased substantially in Excel 7, so the Tools, Reference problem is of less concern. When Application.Run is used to call a function, that function cannot return an object.

Sample Function Development

You need a function that sums all the cells in range, but only if the cell's row is not hidden (the Hidden property of the entire row is false). This cannot be done with a normal spreadsheet function because many of the properties of the range object, such as the Hidden property, are not exposed to spreadsheet functions. So you must create a custom function for this kind of summation. The function will have one argument, the range to be summed, and will return the sum of all the unhidden cells in the range.

The function SumVisibleRows shown here demonstrates one method of summing the values of the visible rows in a range.

```
Function SumVisibleRows(oRange As Object) as double
    Application.Volatile
    Dim oCell As Range
    Dim vTemp as Variant
    For Each oCell In oRange
        If Not oCell.EntireRow.Hidden Then
            vTemp = vTemp + oCell.Value
        End If
    Next oCell
    SumVisibleRows = vTemp
End Function
```

An explanation of the preceding function follows:

```
Function SumVisibleRows(oRange As Object) as Variant
```

The function has been given a very descriptive name so the name of the function is self-documenting. The function accepts one argument, which in this case must be an Object.

 Note

If a function is to be used as a user-defined worksheet function, you must use the Object data type, not the more specific Range data type.

The function SumVisibleRows returns a Double data type. In the absence of a declared data type, all custom functions return a Variant data type.

```
Application.Volatile
```

The Volatile Method marks this function to be recalculated any time a recalculation occurs on the worksheet in which the formula that calls the function resides. Note that this function will not automatically recalculate when rows are hidden or unhidden since changing this does not prompt Excel to automatically recalculate. Whenever rows are hidden or unhidden, the user must force a recalculation of the worksheet. The Application.Volatile method has no effect when used in a function that is not called from a worksheet cell.

```
Dim oCell As Range
Dim vTemp as Variant
```

These are variable declarations. oCell is used to loop through each cell in the passed Range oRange. vTemp is used to accumulate the summation.

```
For Each oCell In oRange
    If Not oCell.EntireRow.Hidden Then
        vTemp = vTemp + oCell.Value
    End If
Next oCell
```

Loop through each cell in the passed range; if the cell's row is not hidden, add the cell's value to vTemp, otherwise continue.

```
SumVisibleRows = vTemp
End Function
```

Assign the value of vTemp to the function SumVisibleRows and return this value to the calling procedure or formula.

SumVisibleRows is a relatively simple function that does one thing: sums the numeric values in a range where the cell's row is not hidden. Note that SumVisibleRows can be called from a spreadsheet or from another procedure. See figure 9.3, where the SumVisibleRows example demonstrates calling the function from cell A5 (note that cell B1's row is hidden).

The subroutine shown here is an example of how to call the SumVisibleRows function from another procedure.

```
Sub DisplaySumVisibleRows()
    Dim oRange As Range
    Set oRange = Selection
    MsgBox "Sum of Visible Cells is :" & SumVisibleRows(oRange)
End Sub
```

If the user selects the cells A1:A4 as shown in figure 9.4, and runs the procedure, the result is displayed.

Fig. 9.3
This is an example of a use of the SumVisibleRows function in a formula.

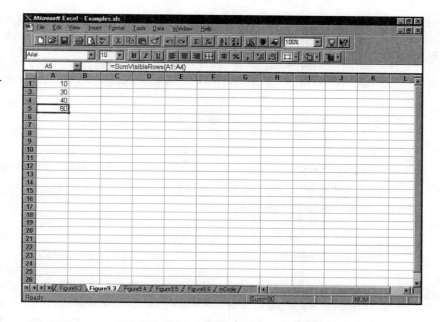

Fig. 9.4
This message box is the result of calling a custom function from a subroutine.

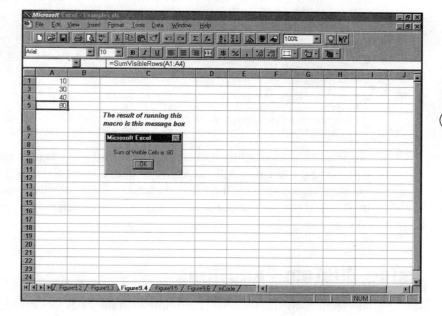

9

Functions that Cannot be Called from Spreadsheet Formulas

The function NameSheetDOW is a function that changes the name of the active sheet to the day of the week passed in the argument. This function is a perfectly legitimate function that cannot be used in a formula in a worksheet. When called from a cell, the value returned by the formula is #Value!.

```
Function NameSheetDOW(tDate As Date)
    ActiveSheet.Name = Format(tDate, "DDDD")
End Function
```

The function NameSheetDOW can easily be called from another procedure as shown in the subroutine ChangeSheetName().

```
Sub ChangeSheetName()
    NameSheetDOW #1/1/96#
End Sub
```

Because 1/1/96 is a Monday, the subroutine ChangeSheetName changes the name of the ActiveSheet to "Monday." Note that while a function can return a value, it does not have to explicitly do so, nor does the calling procedure have to use a returned value. An example of this is the function NameSheetDOW, which does not explicitly return a value, nor does the subroutine ChangeSheetName attempt to use any value returned by the function NameSheetDow.

A function can return any data type except for user-defined data types. When the returned data type of a function is not declared, Excel assigns it as a Variant, just as it treats an undeclared variable. Thus, the following functions are acceptable:

```
Function FooBoolean(MyArg as Double) as Boolean
Function FooDouble(MyArg as Object) as Double
Function FooObject(MyArg as String) as Object
Function FooString(MyArg as string, MyArg2 as range) as String
```

The default values of a function are the same as those in regular variables. If not explicitly assigned, a function will return the default value of the data types. For example, if a function FooBoolean() will return False and (the default value of a Boolean) is not explicitly changed to True, function FooString() will return an empty string ("") (the default value of a string) if not explicitly changed, and so on.

Using Custom Functions

This section discusses several commonly used methods for creating a custom function. While some of these methods are not always required for some custom functions, they can be used to make a custom function more powerful.

Use of Application.Caller

The method Application.Caller is frequently used in VBA procedures. Application.Caller returns information about how a Visual Basic procedure was called. If Application.Caller is used in a custom function called from a cell formula, Application.Caller returns the range specifying the calling cell.

 Note

For additional information on Application.Caller, see on-line help.

The function SheetName returns the name of the calling sheet when placed in a formula in a cell. While the sheet name can be determined by using a complicated spreadsheet formula, the function SheetName is a simple and elegant replacement. The function SheetName is an example of a function that would primarily be called from a formula in a cell.

```
Function SheetName() as String
        Application.Volatile
        SheetName = Application.Caller.Parent.Name
End Function
```

As with any function that is potentially called from a spreadsheet cell, SheetName has Application.Volatile in it to ensure it updates whenever a recalculation occurs. Application.Caller returns the calling cell, and the parent property returns the worksheet of the calling cell, thus SheetName is assigned to the name of the sheet in which the function resides. Note that SheetName will fail if called from another VBA procedure. This is because Application.Caller does not return a usable value when the called routine is called from another VBA procedure.

9

Use of Optional Arguments

Optional arguments are common in spreadsheet functions and can be extremely useful in custom functions. They allow users to use functions flexibly, pass some arguments, and ignore others and use defaults. Optional arguments are always Variants. The VBA function IsMissing is used to test if an optional argument has been passed. The function IsMissing returns True if the arguments were not passed, False otherwise. The function DaysSinceJan1 is designed to return the number of days from Jan 1 to an optional passed date argument. If the argument is not passed, the function uses the current date to perform the calculation.

```
Function DaysSinceJan1(Optional vdDate) As Integer
    If IsMissing(vdDate) Then vdDate = Now
    DaysSinceJan1 = Int(CDate(vdDate) - DateSerial(Year(vdDate), 1, 1) + 1)
End Function
```

Use of ParamArray

In general, the number of arguments passed to a procedure must be the same as those specified by a procedure. Using the ParamArray keyword allows the developer to specify a function with an arbitrary number of arguments. The function CustomConcatenate takes an arbitrary number of arguments, concatenates them, and places a passed string, such as a comma, between each passed argument.

```
Function CustomConcatenate(sConnect As String, ParamArray sElements())
    Dim sTemp As String
    Dim v As Variant
    For Each v In sElements
        sTemp = sTemp & v & sConnect
    Next v
    'take out last sConnect
    CustomConcatenate = Left(sTemp, Len(sTemp) - Len(sConnect))
End Function
```

So, calling the function CustomConcatenate with the following subroutine, RunCustomConcatenate will result in the message box shown in figure 9.5.

```
Sub RunCustomConcatenate()
        msgbox CustomConcatenate(",","A","B","C","D")
End Sub
```

Fig. 9.5

This shows the result of the CustomConcatenate function.

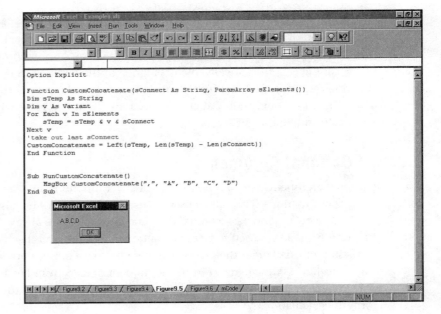

Using the Returned Value to Trap Errors

One of the best uses of the value returned by a function is in error trapping, especially if the function performs an action that may fail, but you want to trap the failure so a run-time error does not occur. In the example function DoesAction(), Boolean returns True if it is successful, and returns a value of False otherwise. Calling the procedure tests what the function DoesAction returns and responds accordingly:

```
Sub RunsDoesAction
        If DoesAction() then
                Code if DoesAction returned True
        Else
                Code if DoesAction returned False
        End If
End Sub

Function DoesAction() as Boolean
.. VBA Code
   If Successful
           DoesAction = True
   else
        DoesAction = False
End Function
```

Some Useful Custom Functions

This section presents functions that were developed in conjunction with "real world" applications. You may want to add these functions to your personal library or change them as necessary to suit your needs. As with any library of functions, some of these functions will evolve over time and should be updated when new techniques are learned or discovered.

Check for the Existence of a Name in a Collection

Excel developers frequently must check for the existence of a specific object in a collection. For example, if a procedure needs to check for a sheet by the name of "Sheet1" in the ActiveWorkbook, a common method is to use code such as:

```
        Dim oTest as Object
 Set oText = Nothing
 On Error Resume Next
 Set oText = Activeworkbook.sheets("Sheet1")
 On Error goto 0
 If oTest is nothing then
       Code if Sheet1 does not exist
 else
       Code if Sheet1 does exist
 end if
```

While this is an acceptable way to handle this situation, having similar blocks of code throughout an application can be wasteful. Instead, use a custom function to test if Sheet1 exists within the ActiveWorkbook. You can create a custom function such as the function Sheet1Exists that is shown here.

```
Function Sheet1Exists() As Boolean
      Dim oTemp As Object
      On Error Resume Next
      Set oTemp = ActiveWorkbook.Sheets("Sheet1")
            On Error GoTo 0
       If Not (oTemp Is Nothing) Then Sheet1Exists = True
End Function
```

The function Sheet1Exists attempts to set oTemp to the potential object ActiveWorkbook.Sheets("Sheet1"). If this fails, the On Error Resume Next procedure prevents a run-time error and the oTemp value is not changed— it remains as the default value of an object—Nothing. If the Set does not fail, oTemp will not be Nothing—it is set to Sheet1. Then, after turning On Error Resume Next off with the On Error Goto 0 line of code, the code tests if oTemp is Nothing. If oTemp is Nothing, the function returns the default value of a Boolean (False), otherwise, Sheet1Exists will be set to True.

While this is an acceptable solution, the function is very inflexible. It only checks for the existence of Sheet 1 in the active workbook. It would be preferable to have a more flexible function.

To describe this situation in a more abstract way, you want to test if a given sheet name exists within an ActiveWorkbook sheet collection. A more flexible function is shown in the function SheetExists.

```
Function SheetExists(sSheet as String) As Boolean
      Dim oTemp As Object
      On Error Resume Next
      Set oTemp = Activeworkbook.sheets(sSheet)
      On Error GoTo 0
      If Not (oTemp Is Nothing) Then SheetExists = True
End Function
```

This function accepts the sSheet argument, which is the name of a potential sheet, and checks if that sheet's name exists in the ActiveWorkbook. Again, while this function is more flexible than Sheet1Exists, it still only works with the ActiveWorkbook. To allow the function to work with any workbook, you have to pass an argument that points to a particular workbook. An example of this is shown in the function SheetExistInWorkbook.

```
Function SheetExistInWorkbook(oBook as Workbook, sSheet as String) As Boolean
      Dim oTemp As Object
      On Error Resume Next
      Set oTemp = oBook.sheets(sSheet)
      On Error GoTo 0
      If Not (oTemp Is Nothing) Then SheetExistInWorkbook = True
End Function
```

This function tests for the existence of a particular named sheet in an open workbook. Note that since this function accepts an object variable (oBook as Workbook), it cannot be called from a worksheet formula.

To raise this to an even higher level of abstraction, you can test if a given name exists within a given collection. The function IsNameInCollection returns True if a given name is in a collection, otherwise False.

```
Function IsNameInCollection(sObjectName As String, oCollection As Object) As Boolean
    Dim oTemp As Object
    On Error Resume Next
    Set oTemp = oCollection(sObjectName)
    On Error GoTo 0
    If Not (oTemp Is Nothing) Then IsNameInCollection = True
End Function
```

The beauty of the function IsNameInCollection is that it can be used with any collection that uses the .Name property as a unique descriptor of each of its elements. So the function IsNameInCollection can be used for testing for the existence of a specific workbook in the workbooks collection, a sheet in the sheets collection, or a PivotTable with a PivotTables collection.

Because the function IsNameInCollection uses the general object, it may be slightly slower than an equivalent function that has been designed to test if a specific name in a specific collection, such as a given workbook, is open. If an application that needs to test for a given workbook name is opened thousands of times in an application, you might want to fine-tune the function to just test for a workbook being open:

```
Function IsWorkbookOpen(sBook as String) As Boolean
    Dim oTemp As Workbook
    On Error Resume Next
    Set oTemp = Application.workbooks(sBook)
    On Error GoTo 0
    If Not (oTemp Is Nothing) Then IsWorkbookOpen = True
End Function
```

Note that the structure of the function IsWorkbookOpen is identical to the function IsNameInCollection. It has just been fine-tuned to test for the workbook.

Check If Two Ranges Overlap (or Intersect)

Developers often want to know if two ranges intersect in one or more cells. A reusable Boolean function to accomplish this is the IfIntersection function, which takes two objects as arguments.

```
Function IfIntersecting(oRange1 As object, oRange2 As object) As Boolean
    Application.Volatile
    Dim oIntersection As Range
    On Error Resume Next
    Set oIntersection = Application.Intersect(oRange1, oRange2)
```

```
      On Error GoTo 0
      If Not (oIntersection Is Nothing) Then IfIntersecting = True
End Function
```

Note that the function IfIntersecting can be used in a worksheet formula or from another VBA procedure. In this example, a formula such as =IfIntersecting(A1:D4,D4:F10) returns True because A1:D4 and D4:F10 intersect in at least one cell, D4. A routine to call IfIntersecting from a Sub procedure is:

```
Sub CheckIntersecting()
      If IfIntersecting(Range("Range1"),Range("Range2")) then
            MsgBox "Ranges Intersect in at least one cell"
      Else
            MsgBox "Ranges Do not intersect"
      End if
End Sub
```

Change a Page Field's CurrentPage Property

The function ChangeCurrentPage changes (if necessary) the .CurrentPage property of a PivotTable page field to a specified value. If successful, the function returns True, otherwise False. The function first tests if the page field's CurrentPage property is already equal to the sChangeTo value, and if so, it exits with True. If the preceding test fails, the code attempts to change the CurrentPage to sChangeTo. If this succeeds, the function returns True, or else it returns the default False value.

```
Function ChangeCurrentPage(oPivotField As PivotField, sChangeTo As String) As Boolean
With oPivotField
    If .CurrentPage = sChangeTo Then
        ChangeCurrentPage = True
    Else
        On Error Resume Next: .CurrentPage = sChangeTo: On Error GoTo 0
            If .CurrentPage = sChangeTo Then ChangeCurrentPage = True
    End If
End With
End Function
```

ChangeCurrentPage cannot be used as a worksheet function because it would attempt to change the workspace and because it requires a PivotField object passed as an argument. The only object that can be passed to a function called from a worksheet is a range object.

ChangeCurrentPage also demonstrates an anomaly that exists with certain objects and properties in the Excel Object Model. For example, if the CurrentPage property of a page field is "X," and you execute code that sets the CurrentPage property of that page field equal to "X," the PivotTable does a recalculation, even though nothing changed! This can slow down applications that manipulate PivotTable page fields to a considerable degree. This is why the function ChangeCurrentPage checks if the CurrentPage is already equal to sChangeTo prior to changing the CurrentPage property to sChangeTo.

Summing a Cell Dynamically

One of the more difficult things to maintain in Excel is functions that sum ranges that are dynamic, especially if inexperienced users may be changing the range that is being summed. In Chapter 8, "Using Defined Names for Worksheet Formulas," you are shown how to do this with defined names that refer to formulas. Here the function SumUpToText is an alternate way of summing all the cells up from a cell with a custom function. Function SumUpToText sums all the cells up from a starting cell and stops at the first cell that contains text. The starting cell can be passed in an optional argument called vcell. If vcell is not passed from the calling formula, the cell containing the formula that calls SumUpToText is used as the starting cell.

```
Function SumUpToText(Optional vCell) As Double
    Dim I As Integer
    Dim dSum As Double
    Application.Volatile
    If IsMissing(vCell) Then Set vCell = Application.Caller
    For I = 1 To vCell.Row - 1
        If Application.IsText(vCell.Offset(rowoffset:=-I)) Then Exit For
        dSum = dSum + vCell.Offset(rowoffset:=-I).Value
    Next I
    SumUpToText = dSum
End Function
```

Note

SumUpToText can be called from either a worksheet formula or another VBA routine. However, if it is called from a VBA routine, the vCell argument must be passed because Application.Caller causes a run-time error when a procedure containing it is called by another VBA routine.

9

Handling Arrays with Functions

The function CumulativeByRow demonstrates using and returning arrays from a function. This function accepts a two-dimensional array that can be either a range or a regular two-dimensional array.

The function accepts an array, and then returns an array of the identical size that represents the cumulative total for the values in the passed array, summing by row.

```
Function CumulativeByRow(vIn As Variant) As Variant
    Dim iRow As Integer
    Dim iCol As Integer
    Dim iRowSize As Integer
    Dim iColSize As Integer
    Dim vInputArray As Variant
    Dim vTemp()
```

```
        vInputArray = vIn
        iRowSize = UBound(vInputArray, 1)
        iColSize = UBound(vInputArray, 2)
        ReDim vTemp(1 To iRowSize, 1 To iColSize)
        For iRow = 1 To iRowSize
            vTemp(iRow, 1) = vInputArray(iRow, 1)
            For iCol = 2 To iColSize
                vTemp(iRow, iCol) = vTemp(iRow, iCol - 1) + vInputArray(iRow, iCol)
            Next iCol
        Next iRow
        CumulativeByRow = vTemp
End Function
```

Figure 9.6 demonstrates the use of this function. Range B3:D6 is the range that is used as the source for creating a cumulative range in E3:G6. To use the function, you must array-enter it. Here is how:

1. Select E3:G6.

2. Enter **=CumulativeByRow(B3:D6),** and then press Ctrl+Shift+Enter.

Fig. 9.6
An array-entered custom function.

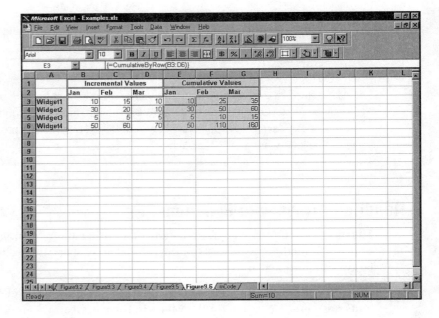

Returning an Object from a Function

The function CreateRectangleOverRange accepts a Range argument and then creates a rectangle that fits perfectly over the range. If the function is successful, an object variable is returned from the function that points to the rectangle. If the Add Method fails (such as if the sheet was protected), the On Error Resume Next will prevent a run-time error. In this case, the function will return the default value of an object, which is Nothing. This is a convenient way to error-trap a failing function.

```
Function CreateRectangleOverRange(oRange As Range) As Rectangle
      On Error Resume Next
      With oRange
            Set CreateRectangleOverRange = ActiveSheet.Rectangles.Add(.Left, .Top,
         ➥.Width, .Height)
      End With
End Function
```

 Note

Developers often place a rectangle with no pattern fill or borders over ranges and then assign a macro to them because there is not an On Click event for the Range Object in the current Excel Event model.

The Subroutine CreateRectangleOverSelection calls CreateRectangleOverRange, tests if a rectangle was created, and displays an error if an error occurred; otherwise, it performs a custom format on the created rectangle. A use of the subroutine CreateRectangleOverSelection is to create a rectangle with no pattern fill or borders that fits perfectly over a selected range while developing an application.

```
Sub CreateRectangleOverSelection()
      Dim oRectangle As Rectangle
      Set oRectangle = CreateRectangleOverRange(Selection)
      If oRectangle Is Nothing Then
            MsgBox "Could Not Create Rectangle"
      Else
            With oRectangle
                  .Border.LineStyle = xlNone
                  .Shadow = False
                  .RoundedCorners = False
                  .Interior.ColorIndex = xlNone
                  .Placement = xlMoveAndSize
                  .PrintObject = False
            End With
      End If
End Sub
```

Summary

Custom Functions are often the building blocks of power Excel applications. The best Custom Functions are those that do a specific task, are easy to maintain, and can be reused in other applications.

In this chapter, you have learned the differences between Sub procedures and Function procedures. Tips for working with and debugging user-defined functions were given and the process of creating a new category for custom functions was explained. Finally, you were shown useful custom functions that can be a starting point for future development projects.

chapter 10

Ensuring Quality Using Advanced Error Checking

by David Bellamy

In this chapter

◆ **Excel error messages**
What the Excel error messages are and how to interpret them.

◆ **Pro-active error trapping**
Finding errors before they find you.

◆ **Using the Edit Go To Special dialog box**
Finding the source of errors by using Edit Go to Special.

◆ **The Auditing toolbar**
How to use these helpful tools to trace the source of errors.

◆ **Checksums**
Beyond Excel's built-in features, how to assure quality with special error checking formulas.

◆ **Numeric methods**
Give the spreadsheet numbers you can work with easily to make errors stand out.

t has always amazed me that, in 30 years of working with computers, people seldom question the accuracy of my work if it's presented in computer output format. If I give them the same data handwritten, they will almost invariably ask if I checked it carefully. Yet, in all those years, I have seen more mistakes, larger mistakes, made much more quickly with a computer than could ever have been done by hand. Computers not only make doing calculations easier, but they make doing incorrect calculations easier too!

If you create spreadsheets, you'll make mistakes. Mistakes in formulas, logic, typos, entry errors, and all kinds of other errors. No one writes formulas perfectly, any more than they can write programs or even sail a boat perfectly. Alas, imperfection is the human condition!

In electronic spreadsheets, unlike the old pencil and paper spreadsheets, errors can proliferate, and one small mistake can become enormous somewhere else. Or an error that was insignificant at one time can become much larger as the spreadsheet changes over time. You need to know that your answers are correct at the time you create the sheet, and as the sheet changes and grows.

Excel provides error checking for certain kinds of errors, primarily syntax errors. But spreadsheets contain many other kinds of errors that software cannot detect. It is vitally important in creating spreadsheets to be sure that the results are correct. And the more important the decisions made based on the spreadsheet, the more important it is that the numbers are correct! Contracts, bid documents, and other papers often contain spreadsheet data, if not the spreadsheet itself, and the accuracy of this data makes the difference between profit and loss. It may even be the difference between being in business or being on the street! To ensure that your calculations are correct, you will have to use many of the Excel features, and add additional checks to the spreadsheet.

This chapter explains Excel's error checking features and how to use them. But it goes further than that, showing you how to put your own checking features into your spreadsheets to increase your assurance (and your boss's or client's assurance) that the results are correct. This chapter helps you to ensure that if there is an error, you will be notified in a such a way that you can't miss it.

The SALES BONUS.XLS workbook is used as an example throughout the chapter (see fig. 10.1). This workbook is for an imaginary sales organization with four sales people. The first columns show their gross sales for two months and the total sales by salesperson. Additional columns show the percentage each contributed, and a monthly bonus calculated on a percentage based on the gross sales figure. The bonus percentage is taken from the Commission Table (in the lower part of the figure) by using a VLOOKUP function. The columns and rows have been given appropriate range names such as Joe, Don, Jan, Feb, Base, Gross Sales, and so on. The workbook contains several versions of the same spreadsheet on the different pages. The "Standard" sheet contains the formulas without error checking, as most users would probably create it. Each additional sheet contains the same information, but the formulas include error checking, of different kinds, built in to trap errors and give a more desirable result when errors occur.

Fig. 10.1
*This is the SALES
BONUS workbook.*

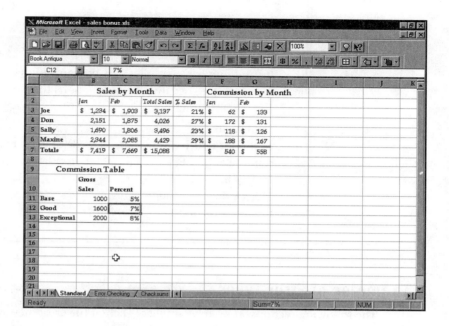

Excel Error Messages

There are a number of common error messages Excel uses to warn you of problems. Table
10.1 lists these error messages, defines them, and offers suggestions about how to deal
with each.

Table 10.1   Types of Error Messages

Error	Definition	Recommendation
#REF	Illegal cell reference	Usually cells needed by formulas have been deleted. Check all cell references in the formula.
#DIV/0!	Division by zero	Check denominators in all calculations.
#NAME	Illegal name in formula	Check all range and function names.
#NULL	Intersection of two ranges which does not exist	Check all range intersections.
#VALUE	Function cannot be evaluated	Check all function arguments (for example, text in place of a number).

10

continues

Table 10.1 Continued

Error	Definition	Recommendation
#NUM	Invalid number in a function (e.g., negative 1 in a SQRT function)	Compare your numbers with the functions they are used in
#N/A	"Not Available," formula could not return a valid result (e.g., trying a lookup in which the index value is outside the range of values in the lookup table)	Check your formulas for values outside of expected ranges or inappropriate numbers.

Examples of Error Types

The following sections show an example of each of the error messages and a suggested fix. Remember, there are many circumstances that can trigger each message, so you may find rather different situations causing these errors in your spreadsheets.

#REF Error

Cell reference errors are often caused when cells referred to in formulas are deleted (not cleared) from the spreadsheet. As an example, go to the SALES BONUS workbook, Standard sheet, and select the Feb column. Then do a Delete from the menu (not the Delete key). The formulas, formerly in column G, move into column F and become #REF errors (see fig. 10.2).

Make sure you choose Edit, Undo to remove the cell reference error before continuing to the next section.

#DIV/0! Error

To get a division by zero error, change the denominator in one of the percent formulas, column E, to a blank cell. More realistically, this error might result if when the first percent formula was created, a relative cell address was chosen for the denominator instead of an absolute address. Then, when the other percentage formulas are created using an Autofill down the column, division by zero errors occur in each of them (see fig. 10.3).

Fig. 10.2

An Excel spreadsheet with Cell reference errors.

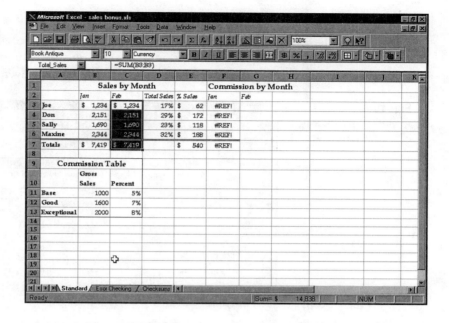

Fig. 10.3

An Excel spreadsheet showing a Division by zero error.

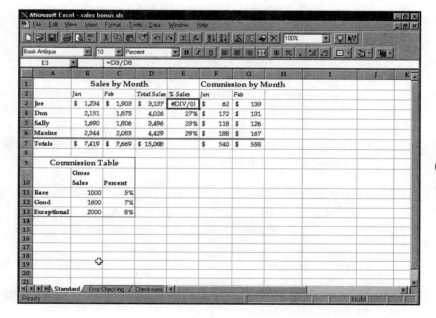

Make sure you Undo the error before proceeding to the next section.

#NAME Error

If you enter a function name that doesn't exist, Excel cannot recognize it, and will return a #NAME error (see fig. 10.4). For instance, if you enter a paste function called "averag," Excel won't recognize it because the correct function name is "average."

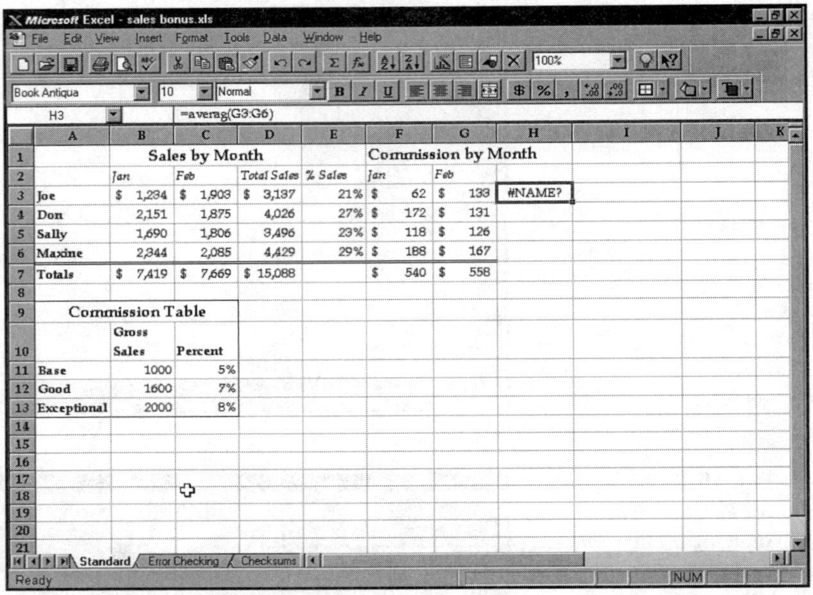

Fig. 10.4

A spreadsheet showing a #NAME error.

Excel gives you help with this. When you enter a paste function using lowercase letters, Excel converts it to uppercase when you enter the formula, if it recognizes the function. If the function name does not convert to uppercase, it is not an Excel paste function. If you correct the "averag" function name to "average," the name goes automatically to uppercase, and the error message goes away (see fig. 10.5).

> ⚛ **Tip**
>
> Using the Function Wizard eliminates errors such as misspelled function names, because only existing functions can be selected.

Excel does not capitalize range names. This helps you to differentiate between range names and functions.

Fig. 10.5

This is a demonstration of how the Automatic Uppercase for recognized functions feature works.

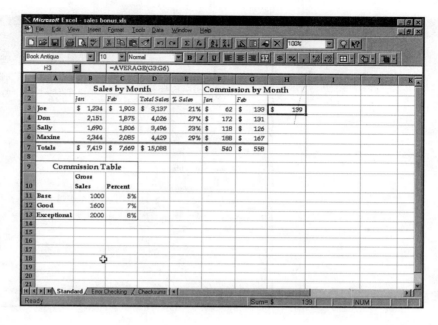

Make sure you undo the name error before continuing.

#NULL Error

Null errors occur when a formula refers to the intersection of two named ranges that do not intersect. In the SALES BONUS worksheet, create a formula making such a reference. Select cell F11, and enter the following formula.

```
=jan base
```

Because the ranges Jan, cells B3 to B6, and Base, cells B11 to C11, do not intersect, you get a #NULL error in cell F11 (see fig. 10.6).

Delete the formula before continuing.

#VALUE Error

There are error checking paste functions to help you find various kinds of mistakes. Some may not really be errors, but may cause error messages if misinterpreted. For example, certain cells can contain either text or numbers, but if the cell contains text, and a formula uses that cell thinking it contains a numeric value, the formula will return a #VALUE error. This means Excel cannot evaluate the function properly.

Fig. 10.6

A spreadsheet with a
#Null error.

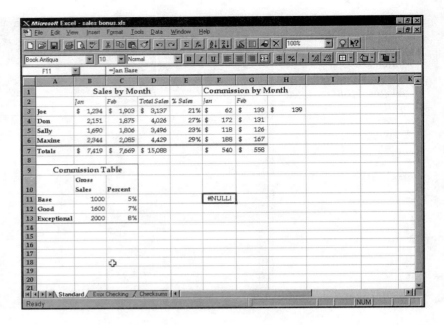

Of course, if the cell isn't supposed to contain text, the #VALUE error is returned. To see
this error, put text into cell C11, the Base Percent. The formula in cell F3 is expecting a
numeric value from the table, not text, and returns the error (see fig. 10.7).

Fig. 10.7

A spreadsheet showing
a #Value error.

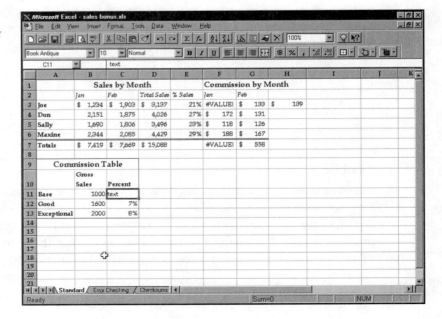

#NUM Error

Certain functions cannot work on certain values. The SQRT (square root function) doesn't work on negative values (unless you're an electrical engineer!), so if you try to take the square root of a negative number, you'll get a #NUM error.

#N/A Error

#N/A means that the value Excel needs to calculate something is not there, and therefore, not available. To replicate this kind of error, simply clear a cell (use the Delete key) that contains a value referred to in a formula. Cell C3, Feb sales, will work for this example (see fig. 10.8).

Fig. 10.8

A spreadsheet with a #N/A error message.

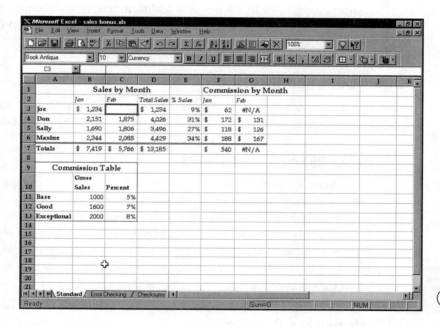

If you substitute a text value in cell C3, you'll get a #N/A error. It simply means that the kind of value the paste function or formula needs is not available in that location.

Other Considerations

You may already have noticed that when you have an error in a cell that is then referred to in another formula, the cell containing that formula shows the same error. For example, when you created the #VALUE error by changing the base percent to a letter, not only did cell F3 return a #VALUE error, but cell F7 returned a #VALUE error, because it is summing F3 and doesn't know how to sum an error message.

Unfortunately, there is some overlap in error messages. I have often seen, in Excel classes, different error messages on different computers after people entered the same change to a formula. I haven't figured this one out myself.

If you are rearranging a spreadsheet, moving sections around to put them in more accessible places, keep a look out for the sudden appearance of error messages, usually #REF, in an entire section of the worksheet. This is caused when Excel loses track of the source data for the formula. If this occurs, execute an undo immediately! When doing this sort of rearranging, save many times as you go, making sure each time that the spreadsheet is still correct.

If you are having trouble figuring out which function is causing the error message in a complex formula or in a series of linked formulas, type the error message exactly into the Find field in the Help box. The functions that can return that kind of error message are listed in box 3 at the bottom of the Help dialog box.

Other Common Errors

Other kinds of errors yield message boxes rather than error messages in the cell. Some of these and their common causes are listed in the sections that follow.

Space Character in Formula

If you place a "space" character in a formula, you may get an error message. Which error message you see depends on where you enter the space. Each successive version of Excel is more tolerant of spaces, which is a mixed bag. It gives you more flexibility in entering formulas with spaces in them, but it makes it harder to find the offending space when there is a problem. Maybe I'm lucky that I learned spreadsheets when they allowed no spaces, so I don't put any in, at least not on purpose, so they're easy to find and remove when they occur.

Mismatched Parentheses

When entering long formulas involving many sets of parentheses, it is easy to get a Parentheses do not match error message when you try to enter the formula (see fig. 10.9). This one's a frustrating one because Excel does not let you clear the entry line until it thinks the problem is fixed. You must make the parentheses match before you can go on.

This is one of the areas where Excel error messages are not always consistent. Sometimes, when there are too many parentheses in a formula, Excel returns an error in formula message instead of a mismatched parentheses message. This makes the error a little harder to find, since error in formula is less specific.

Fig. 10.9

This is a mismatched parentheses error message.

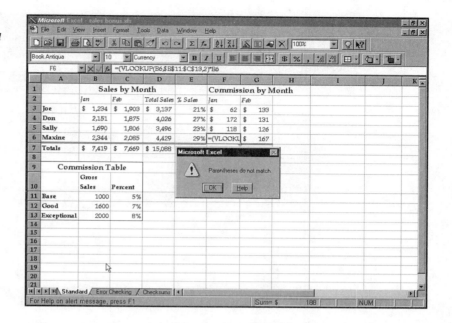

Excel does help with matching parentheses. When you enter a closing parenthesis, it and its matching opening parenthesis appear in boldface for a fraction of a second. You have to watch closely on the entry line, but you can see which parenthesis Excel thinks it is matching (see fig 10.10).

(10)

Fig. 10.10

A spreadsheet showing how Excel helps to match parentheses.

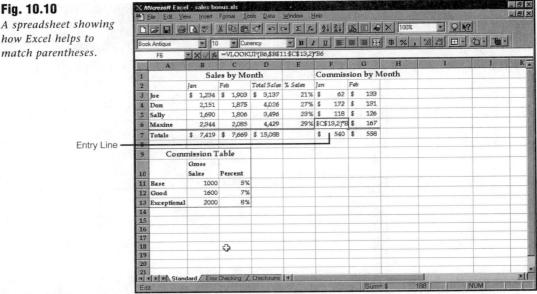

Entry Line

⚛ Tip

If you're still getting a `Parentheses do not match` error message, try this fix. Start counting parenthesis, but count positive one for each opening parenthesis, and negative one for each closing parenthesis. For example, in the following formula;

`=(A6+B7)*(D6-D5*(E5+B7)/(F9+F6+E8)+A4)`

the first parenthesis, =(, would give you a count of +1

the second parenthesis, =(A6+B7) would give a count of 0,

the third parenthesis, =(A6+B7)*(, would give a count of +1

the fourth parenthesis, =(A6+B7)*(D6–D5*(, would give a count of +2

the fifth parenthesis, =(A6+B7)*(D6–D5*(E5+B7), would give a count of +1

the sixth parenthesis, =(A6+B7)*(D6-D5*(E5+B7)/(, would give a count of +2

the seventh parenthesis, =(A6+B7)*(D6–D5*(E5+B7)/(F9+F6+E8), would give a count of +1

the eighth parenthesis, =(A6+B7)*(D6–D5*(E5+B7)/(F9+F6+E8)+A4), would give a count of zero

When you finish, you should get zero. If you get +1, you have one too many opening parentheses, or one to few closing parentheses. Conversely, if you get –1, you have one too many closing parentheses or one too few opening parentheses.

Incorrect Number of Arguments

A paste function has a certain number of required arguments. (Remember, required arguments are boldface in the Function Wizard, optional arguments are not boldface) If you put in too many or too few arguments, you will get the Too many arguments error message box. Check all paste functions for the correct number of arguments. Also, check for unintentional commas. If you accidentally format a numeric entry in a formula with a comma, Excel assumes it's an argument separator. It then assumes the numbers following the comma are the next argument, and usually thinks there are too many arguments in the formula.

Go to cell F3 and insert two additional commas after the final argument. This causes a Too many arguments error message (see fig. 10.11).

Fig. 10.11

A spreadsheet showing a Too many arguments *error.*

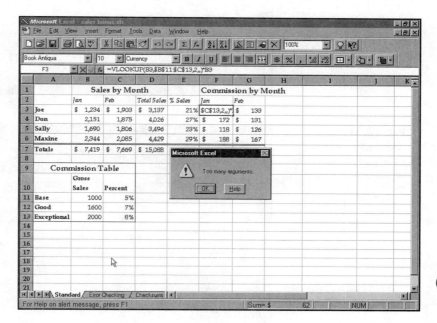

Circular Cell References

If a formula in one cell refers to a cell that refers back to the original cell, you will get the circular cell reference message Cannot resolve circular references. In the spreadsheet used as an example, type **=F3** in cell B3 and press Enter (see fig. 10.12).

F3 contains a formula that uses the value from B3. Because B3 depends on F3, and F3 depends on B3, you get a circular reference error when you enter the formula in B3.

When you click OK in the error message box, Excel puts a value of 0 in the cell, and a Circular: F7 message on the status line to warn you that the error still exists (see fig. 10.13).

Fig. 10.12
This is the circular reference message box.

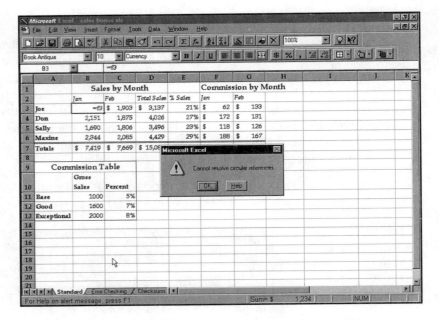

Fig. 10.13
A spreadsheet with a circular reference message in the status line.

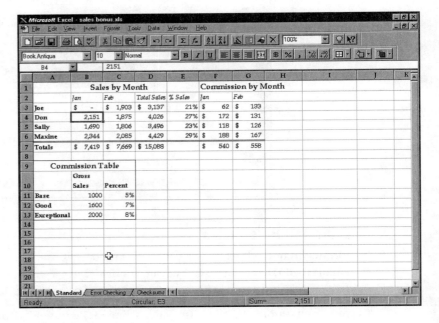

This warning remains until you fix the circular reference. Remember a circular reference can and often does involve more than two cells. If there was a formula in cell C2 that referred to cell B2, and B2 referred to D7, and D7 referred to C3, there would be a circular reference. This one involves three cells instead of two. The more complex the spreadsheet, the more likely circular references appear.

Remember to remove the circular reference by changing cell B3 back to a value of 1234.

Incorrect Logic

Logic errors cover a lot of territory. A *logic error* is simply an error in your thinking. A common error logic is a circular cell reference, which is discussed in the previous section.

Another common logic error occurs when you nest paste functions, putting a function or argument in the wrong place. For example, if you want to round off the Total Sales for Jan to the nearest hundred dollars, you would put the ROUND function outside the SUM function (see fig. 10.14).

Fig. 10.14

A spreadsheet using nested ROUND and SUM functions.

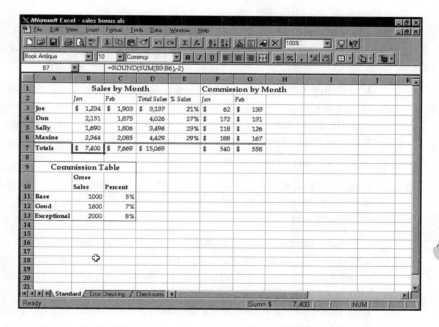

If you confused the nesting, and put the ROUND function inside the SUM function, you'd get an #VALUE error because of your logic error (see fig. 10.15).

You'll get a #VALUE error because the ROUND function doesn't know what to do with the cell range as an argument.

Make sure you change the formula back to its original form before continuing.

Fig. 10.15

A spreadsheet with incorrectly nested round and sum functions.

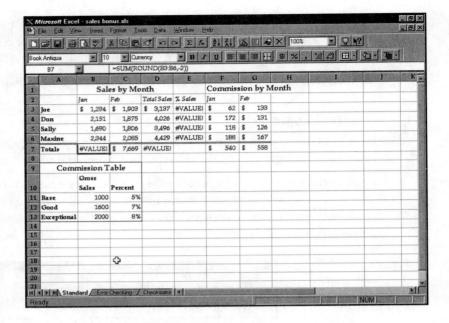

IF statements are another common place for logic errors. Let's say your company pays their sales people a 5 percent bonus for selling $1,000 or more worth of widgets in a month. You create a formula to determine who gets the bonus and who doesn't. Your formula might look like this:

```
=IF(B3>1000,B3*5%,"No Bonus")
```

If it does, you will face some disgruntled sales people when the bonuses come due. If anyone sold exactly $1,000 worth of widgets, they won't get a bonus because you used a "greater than" (>) instead of a "greater than or equal to" (>=) comparator.

It's even easier to make a mistake in nested IF statements, when you try to get all the arguments in all the right places and all the commas and parentheses correct. Always check your formula at the boundary conditions, that is at the exact value you are testing, and make sure the result is what you envisioned. And when nesting functions, use the Function Wizard; it makes it a lot easier to keep track of exactly where you are in the various functions and to keep track of the arguments. Even better, try using a VLOOKUP or HLOOKUP function instead of nested IFs. You're less likely to make an error.

Entry Errors

There are two kinds of entry errors; errors in entering values, and errors made entering formulas.

Errors made when entering data are among the hardest to find. The software simply can't do much here. It can help some if you allow data entry only in custom forms and apply "masks" to the data so that it must be in some standard format and/or within a specified range. Setting that up can be a lot of trouble. Unless the data is crucial, it may not be worth the time and effort.

The best entry error checking is to have a second person check the entries carefully. If this is done too routinely by the same person, it is difficult to get consistently good checking. You may want to change the checker regularly.

Errors you make when entering formulas can be tricky. If you type in C4 instead of C3, this kind of error may be rather difficult to find. One of the first things I do when I know something is wrong in a spreadsheet and can't find it right away, is to switch to Formula mode. If you aren't familiar with this option, try it now. Follow these steps:

1. Choose Tools, Options.

2. Select the View tab (see fig. 10.16).

3. Choose Formulas, then choose OK.

Fig. 10.16

This is the Tools Options dialog box with formulas selected in the View tab.

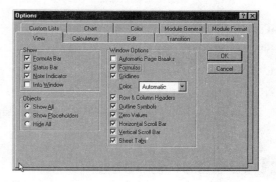

Wherever a formula resulted in a value in the worksheet, now the formula appears (see fig. 10.17). Usually the first thing to look for in formula mode is breaks in patterns across rows or columns. For example, in column D, the percentage formulas follow a precise pattern, the numerator (a relative address) being one cell address further down in the worksheet as formulas go down the column. The denominator is an absolute address and stays the same down the column. If one of the formulas deviates from this pattern, it would be cause for suspicion that there was an error. Of course, patterns do change, so you have to look at the cell and decide if the pattern should break at that point or not. By following across rows and down columns through the spreadsheet, you can look for deviations in the patterns and check carefully any deviation.

Fig. 10.17

The SALES BONUS spreadsheet in Formula mode.

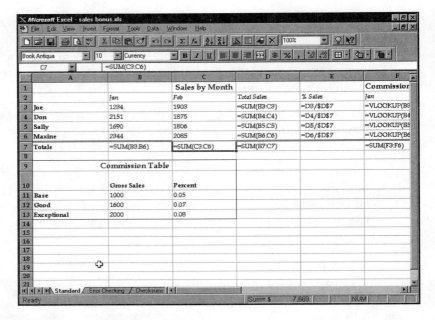

You should turn off Formula mode when you are done looking at the spreadsheet in this mode. Follow these steps:

1. Choose Tools, Options.
2. Select the View tab.
3. Choose Formulas (to deselect the option), then choose OK.

Pro-Active Error Trapping

You can take a more pro-active approach to errors. Instead of waiting for them to happen, and reacting to them, you can prevent error messages from occurring in the first place by using special paste functions designed for this purpose. In programming, this is called *error trapping*. It is especially helpful if other, less knowledgeable people will be using the spreadsheet, and wouldn't know how to interpret or handle Excel's error messages.

IS Functions

Excel has paste functions that can be used to detect errors or situations that might cause errors. They can be found in the Function Wizard under Information Functions and are called IS functions. They are listed in table 10.2.

Table 10.2   Excel IS Functions Table

Function	Returns true if:
ISBLANK	Value refers to an empty cell.
ISERR	Value refers to any error value except #N/A.
ISERROR	Value refers to any error value (#N/A, #VALUE!, #REF!, #DIV/0!, #NUM!, #NAME?, or #NULL!).
ISLOGICAL	Value refers to a logical value.
ISNA	Value refers to the #N/A (value not available) error value.
ISNONTEXT	Value refers to any item that is not text. (Note that this function returns TRUE if value refers to a blank cell.)
ISNUMBER	Value refers to a number.
ISREF	Value refers to a reference.
ISTEXT	Value refers to text.

For example, one of these functions, ISERROR, can detect if a formula returns an error message. A formula can include this test to detect the error in the particular cell, and to change what the formula does if an error is found, usually by using an IF statement and the ISERROR function nested inside it.

Using the ISERROR Function

For example, in the SALES BONUS workbook example, the boss wants you to put "No Sales" in any month a sales person didn't sell at all. Maybe they were on vacation that month. If you enter text in place of the sales amount for Don's January sales (cell B4) in the Standard sheet, you get #N/A errors in Don's January commission and in Total January Commissions (see fig. 10.18).

You can modify the formula to account for this eventuality by adding an IF statement and an ISERROR function.

```
=IF(ISERROR(VLOOKUP(B3,$B$11:$C$13,2)*B3),"No   Bonus",VLOOKUP(B3,$B$11:$C$13,2)*B3)
```

This formula has been entered in the Error Checking sheet. The "value if true" argument of the IF statement is the VLOOKUP nested inside an ISERROR statement. If the VLOOKUP returns an error message—and it will if the value it is trying to look up is text—the ISERROR function returns TRUE. The "value if true" in the IF statement is text, "No Bonus." If the VLOOKUP does not return an error, the "value if false" argument is the VLOOKUP, and it returns the value from the formula.

Fig. 10.18
The Sales Bonus spreadsheet with text in B4.

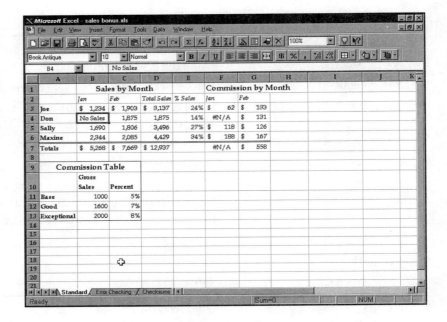

Change cell B4 to text, No Sales in the Error Checking sheet and see what happens (see fig. 10.19).

In the error checking version of the worksheet, you get a text message, designed to handle just such an event.

Fig. 10.19
A spreadsheet showing the VLOOKUP formula with error testing.

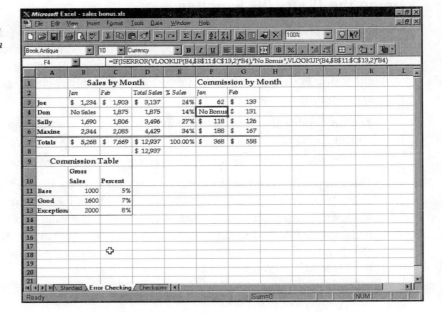

Caution

This error detection scheme also detects and traps other kinds of errors in the spreadsheet, such as text in the Commission Table itself. When using this kind of error trapping, make sure it gives the desired result in all cases. That is, if you don't want to report "No Bonus" if there is text in the Commission Table, you'll need some additional error trapping in your formulas for that eventuality.

Using the ISBLANK Function

Blank cells can lead to formula errors. In most calculations, blank cells are treated as zeros. In some cases this is fine, in others, it may cause problems. If you think that certain cells may be blank, and that it may cause errors, use ISBLANK to detect and trap. Remember that in statistical functions, such as AVERAGE and COUNT, blank cells are not treated as zero, but as text, and are not counted into the result.

Using the ISLOGICAL Function

The ISLOGICAL function tests to see if a cell contains a logical value, that is, TRUE or FALSE. If a formula requires a logical value, but the referred to cell may not always contain a logical value, use the ISLOGICAL function to trap the error.

Using the ISTEXT and ISNONTEXT Functions

The ISTEXT and ISNONTEXT functions test to see if a cell contains text and return a TRUE or FALSE value. Use these when text is expected but may not be in the cell, or if the presence of text in the cell may be a problem.

Using the ISNUMBER Function

This function determines if a cell contains a numeric value. Use it whenever a numeric value is needed or could cause problems in a formula.

Using the ISREF Function

ISREF determines if the argument is a valid cell reference (cell address or range name). In formulas, you would know if you were using a valid cell reference, so this function is usually used in macros to detect the presence of a range name before doing a routine that depends on the range being there. It is not often seen in formulas.

10

Using the ISNA Function

This function determines specifically if an #N/A error is present.

Using the Edit Go To Special Dialog Box to Find Errors

Another useful way to track down errors in your spreadsheets is the Edit Go To Special dialog box. It can help you find constants, formulas, blank cells, and other kinds of cells that might be causing errors. This dialog box also can give you clues as to where the error might be.

To access the Go To Special dialog box, follow these steps:

1. Choose Edit, Go To. The Go To dialog box appears (see fig. 10.20).
2. Choose Special. The Go To Special dialog box appears (see fig. 10.21).

Fig. 10.20

The Go To dialog box.

Fig. 10.21

The Go To Special dialog box.

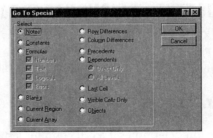

The options in the Go To Special dialog box that can be used to find spreadsheet errors are discussed in the following sections.

Constants

In large spreadsheets or spreadsheets you didn't create, selecting Constants will show you which cells contain numeric values (see fig. 10.22). This is primarily used for finding entry errors.

Fig. 10.22

The spreadsheet showing constants in SALES BONUS.XLS.

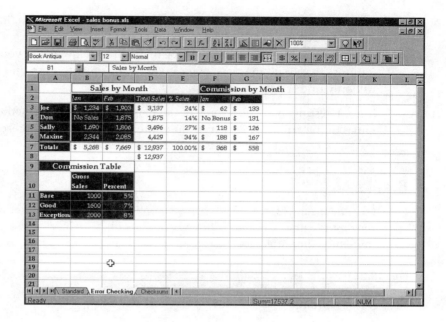

Formulas

If you select Formulas in the Go To Special dialog box, the cells containing formulas are highlighted. These formulas are ones that you should check for various kinds of errors such as those errors listed in the previous sections (see fig. 10.23).

Fig. 10.23

The spreadsheet with formulas highlighted in SALES BONUS.XLS.

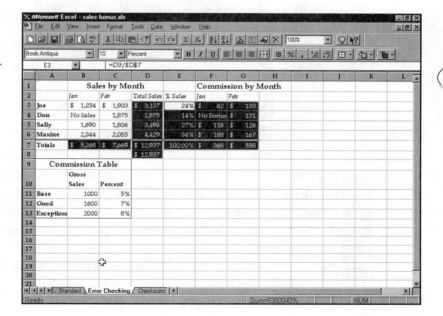

10

Under the Formulas option, there are additional options used to find particular results of formulas. These options are Numbers, Text, Logicals, and Errors. If you select all four, all formulas in the spreadsheet will be highlighted. However, if you are looking only for formulas that result in errors, you can deselect Numbers, Text, and Logicals and then you will only find errors.

It is interesting to see how some of these options are affected by the error trapping formulas in the Error Checking version of the sheet. Cell B4 has already been changed to text, let's see what other errors result from other inputs.

Blanks

In some instances, blank cells can be a problem. Blanks are sometimes interpreted as zeros, sometimes ignored by functions. Knowing which cells are blanks helps to determine how they affect formulas, especially in ranges or arrays (see fig. 10.24).

Fig. 10.24
*SALES BONUS with
blank cells highlighted.*

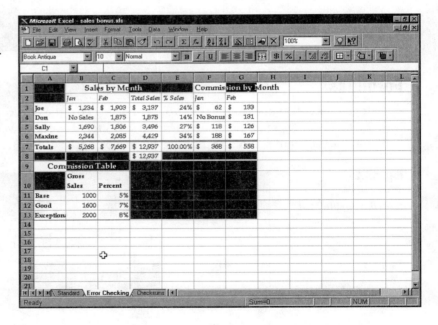

Caution

There is a shortcut that is a holdover from the early days of Lotus that often causes problems in spreadsheets. In early versions, it took four keystrokes to clear a cell. Many users started using a shortcut, which was to put a space in the cell, rather than do the four keystrokes. They thought they were clearing the cell. In fact,

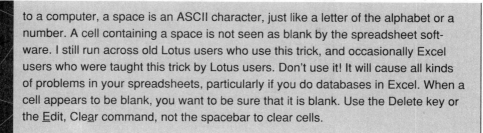

to a computer, a space is an ASCII character, just like a letter of the alphabet or a number. A cell containing a space is not seen as blank by the spreadsheet software. I still run across old Lotus users who use this trick, and occasionally Excel users who were taught this trick by Lotus users. Don't use it! It will cause all kinds of problems in your spreadsheets, particularly if you do databases in Excel. When a cell appears to be blank, you want to be sure that it is blank. Use the Delete key or the Edit, Clear command, not the spacebar to clear cells.

Precedents

If you need to know which cells are used in a formula, follow these steps:

1. Select a cell with a formula in it, such as F3.
2. Choose Edit, Go To.
3. Choose Special.
4. Choose Precedents, and choose OK

The cells used to calculate the formula in cell F3 are highlighted (see fig. 10.25). Note that the sales figure for the appropriate sales person as well as the entire Sales Commission Table are highlighted. All these cells are used in some way to calculate Joe's January Sales Commission. Cell B3 is highlighted because this is the figure for Joe's January sales. The entire Commission Table is highlighted because the VLOOKUP function refers to it, not to a particular cell within it.

 Note

There are two additional options below Dependents: Direct Only and All Levels. These apply to both Precedents and Dependents. Direct Only, the default, means that only cells directly preceding or depending on the selected cell will be highlighted. All Levels means that *all* cells preceding the cells immediately preceding the selected cell will be highlighted, or all cells dependent on the dependent cells will be highlighted. Try these options to familiarize yourself with how they work and when you might use each of them

10

Fig. 10.25

SALES BONUS with precedents to F3 highlighted.

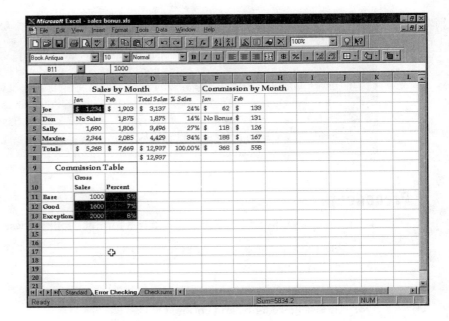

Dependents

The Dependents option works the same as the Precedents option, except that it highlights cells that depend on the selected cell. To see how it works, do the following:

1. Select cell C4, Don's February Sales.

2. Choose Edit, Go To.

3. Choose Special.

4. Choose Dependents, and choose OK.

The cells whose formulas refer to cell C4 are highlighted.

It's easy to accidentally, within a formula, refer to an incorrect cell. You can use the Precedents feature to graphically show which cells are referred to, and to help find an incorrect one.

Similarly, you may wonder what cells are using a particular cell to calculate a value. The Dependents feature helps you to find such cells. Try each of these options to get a feel for how they work and when you might use them.

As seen in the next section, there are other ways to show Precedents and Dependents as well.

The Auditing Toolbar

Excel has special auditing features to help track problems through large, complex spreadsheets. These features relate primarily to the precedents and dependents discussed in the previous section.

Accessing the Auditing Toolbar

To bring up the Auditing toolbar follow these steps:

1. Right click on any toolbar.
2. Select Auditing.

The Auditing toolbar appears on-screen (see fig. 10.26).

> **Tip**
> You can also access the Auditing toolbar and the Auditing functions in the menu by choosing Tools, Auditing.

Fig. 10.26
The Auditing toolbar.

Auditing Tools

The Auditing toolbar helps to find potential error sources in the worksheet. Some of these tools, the Trace Precedents and Trace Dependents tools, overlap with the Edit, Go To, Special features mentioned previously. Using the Auditing toolbar is a little faster than going through the menus.

Trace Precedents

In this section, the auditing tools will be applied in the SALES BONUS spreadsheet. Follow these steps:

1. Select cell D3.
2. Click the Trace Precedents button on the Auditing toolbar (see fig. 10.27).

Blue arrows appear on the worksheet, showing the cells used to calculate the formula in cell D3 (see fig. 10.28).

Fig. 10.27
*Trace Precedents
Button.*

Fig. 10.28
*SALES BONUS
spreadsheet showing
precedents arrows.*

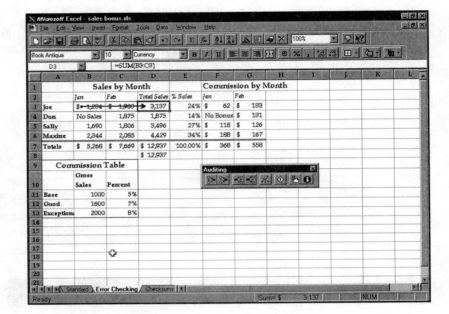

To use Trace Precedents on other cells follow these steps:

1. Select cell C7.
2. Click the Trace Precedents button.
3. Select cell G4.
4. Click the Trace Precedents button.

Each time you trace precedents on another cell, additional blue arrows indicate the precedent cells for that new cell. After a while, the spreadsheet becomes rather crowded with blue arrows. You can remove some of them shortly. First, let's talk about how to interpret the arrows.

Each arrow starts with a small blue circle, and ends with a blue arrow. The circle indicates the first cell along that arrow whose value is included in the selected cell's formula. Each additional circle along the line indicates that that cell is included in the formula. The arrow shows the cell selected to trace its precedents.

You may have noticed that some of the arrows are thicker than others. The horizontal arrow from cell B3 through C3 to D3 is thicker than the arrow from C4 over to G4. The thicker arrow indicates that all values along that line are included in the formula in the selected cell. The formulas that depend on the Sales Commission Table all have arrows coming from the first cell in the table, B11. And the table has a blue box around it to indicate that the entire table is used in the selected formula.

Remove Precedent Arrows

To remove specific precedence arrows, use the second tool on the Auditing toolbar, the Remove Precedence Arrows tool. Follow these steps:

1. Select cell C7.

2. Click the Remove Precedent Arrows button (see fig. 10.29).

The arrows to cell C7 are gone.

Fig. 10.29

The Remove Precedent Arrows button.

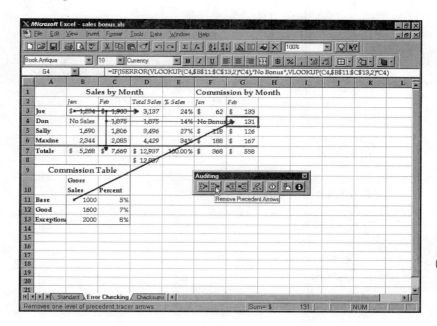

Trace Dependents

To show which cells are dependent on a particular cell use the Trace Dependents button on the Auditing toolbar. Follow these steps:

1. Select cell B6.

2. Click the Trace Dependents button (see fig. 10.30).

Fig. 10.30

The Trace Dependents button.

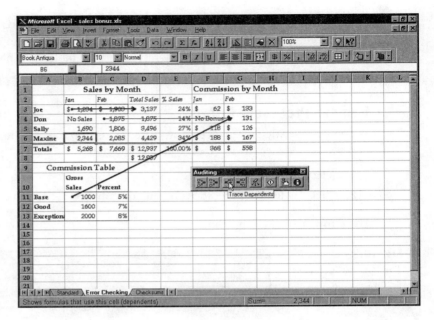

Arrows now run from B6 to B7, because B6 is used in the total in B7, and from B6 to D6 for the same reason, and from B6 to F6 because B6 is used to calculate Maxine's January commission. Notice that you can have multiple arrows on the same line if a cell is used in more than one formula in the same row or column.

Remove Dependent Arrows

To remove the dependent arrows, use the Remove Dependent Arrows tool. Follow these steps:

1. Select cell B6.
2. Click the Remove Dependent Arrows button (see fig. 10.31).

The arrows from B6 are gone.

Remove All Arrows

To remove all arrows of both kinds all at once, click the Remove All Arrows button (see fig. 10.32). If you don't have any arrows on your spreadsheet, turn some on and then click the Remove All Arrows button. All dependent and precedent arrows are removed.

Fig. 10.31
The Remove Dependent Arrows button.

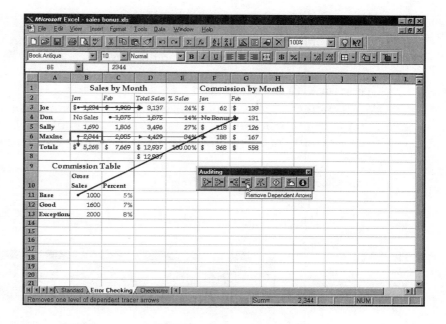

Fig. 10.32
The Remove All Arrows button.

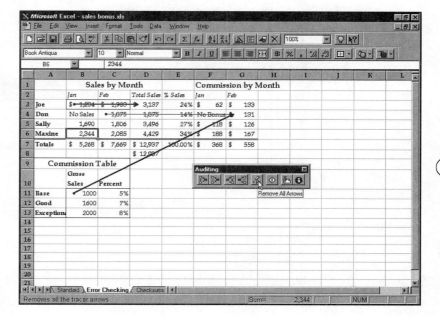

Trace Error

The next button on the Auditing toolbar is used to trace the source of errors. It can be applied on a single sheet, or across multiple sheets.

Tracing Errors in a Single Spreadsheet

When errors occur in your spreadsheet, you may have trouble finding the source, especially because certain kinds of errors cause cascading errors, as discussed in the earlier section "Other Considerations." The Trace Error feature can help in this. Follow these steps:

1. Select C11 in the Standard sheet.
2. Type **Text.**

    #VALUE errors appears in cells F3 and F7 (see fig. 10.33).

Fig. 10.33

Spreadsheet with #VALUE errors.

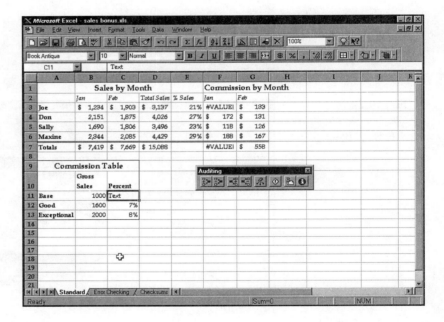

3. Select cell F3.
4. Click the Trace Error button to find the source of this error (see fig. 10.34).
5. Click the Remove All Arrows button.

Note

The formula in F3 takes Joe's January sales and looks up an appropriate multiplier in the Sales Commission Table. Because it finds text rather than a numeric value in cell C11, it returns a #VALUE error in cell F3. This causes the #VALUE error in cell F7 when the formula tries to sum the January Commissions and finds the #VALUE error. In a relatively small and simple spreadsheet like SALES BONUS, it might be obvious where to look for the source of this error. In a larger, more complex spreadsheet, with many tables and nested functions, it is more difficult to manually track the source of such an error.

Fig. 10.34

The Trace Error button.

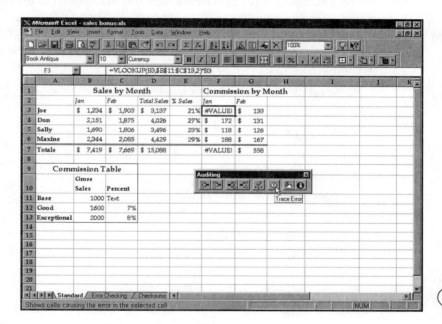

 Note

Blue arrows appear starting with a circle in cell B3 and in cell B11. Both arrows go to cell F3. The arrow from B11 is heavier because it indicates that it represents the relationship between the entire Sales Commission Table and F3. The table has a blue box around it to further show that the entire table is involved, not just cell C11.

Now let's see what happens if you select cell F7 and trace errors from there. Remember, F7 shows an error because it is trying to sum F3, which has the #VALUE error. This can be called a secondary error.

1. Select cell F7.
2. Click the Trace Error button.

The same blue lines appear connecting cell B3 and B11 with F3, but instead of an arrow in F3, there is see a blue circle. In addition, there is a red circle in F3, a red line from F3 to F7, and a red arrow in F7. This tells us that the source of the error in F7 is the error in F3, and that the source of the error in F3 in either in B3 or the Sales Commission Table. It certainly narrows the field over which you must search to find the problem.

Tracing Errors Across Multiple Spreadsheets

What happens if the error occurs across worksheets? Follow these steps to create that scenario:

1. Select the Error Checking spreadsheet.
2. Select cell E9.
3. Enter **=E6***.
4. Select the Standard worksheet.
5. Select cell F7.

   Your formula in E9 should be:

   ```
   =E6*Standard!F7
   ```

   The result is a #VALUE error.
6. Select the Error Checking worksheet.
7. Select cell E9.
8. Click the Trace Error button.

A blue arrow appears connecting cell E6 with E9, and an icon representing a spreadsheet appears with a dotted line connecting it to E9 (see fig. 10.35). This tells you that another worksheet is involved in the formula. Double-click the dotted line (not the spreadsheet icon). The Go To dialog box appears, with the address of the connected cell (see fig. 10.36). Double-click the address in the Go To box, and you'll go to that cell.

Fig. 10.35

An Error Checking worksheet with cross worksheet error trace.

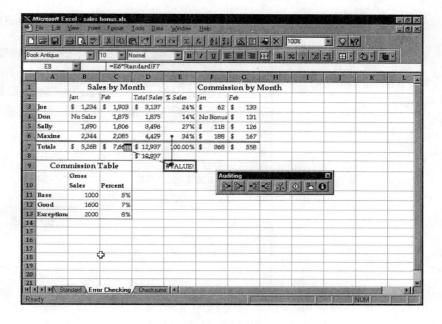

Fig. 10.36

The Go To dialog box with error trace location.

In this case, the error already existed when you created the formula, but the Trace Error function works just the same if the error appears after the formula was created.

Remove all arrows and the formula in cell E9 before continuing.

Attach Note

I'm not sure why the Attach Note button is on the Auditing toolbar, other than the Notes feature could be used to note errors and suspected causes. It's a nice feature in any case!

Show Info Window

The Show Info window has many uses, including finding errors. Actually, most of its error finding capabilities already have been discussed under "Trace Precedents" and "Trace Dependents." This section shows you how to access it and what's available there.

To display the Show Info window, use the Show Info Window button (see fig. 10.37).

Fig. 10.37
The Show Info Window button.

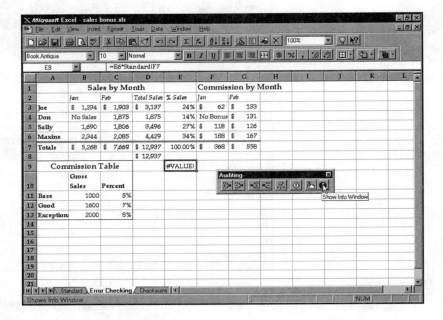

The Show Info box appears, covering your spreadsheet. Reduce its size as you would any other window so you can see it and the worksheet at the same time.

Initially, the Show Info box shows the cell address, formula, and any notes for the selected cell. To see data for other cells, you just click on any cell. When you do that, the Show Info box disappears. You can choose Window, Arrange Tiles to get both the worksheet and the Show Info box on-screen side-by-side (see fig. 10.38).

Now just click on different cells to see the data for that particular cell.

You can add to the information in the Show Info box. Click on the Show Info window, and look at the menu. You'll see a special menu containing File, Info, Macro, Window, and Help. Except for the Info option, the others work the same as in other menus.

The Info option lets you add or remove information from the Show Info box. Click Info to see what is available (see fig. 10.39).

Some of these options, precedents and dependents, have already been discussed in other formats, such as the Go To Special box and the Show Precedents and Show Dependents buttons on the Auditing toolbar.

The other option that's useful for error tracking is the Names option. Select it and you'll see all named ranges that contain the selected cell. This is useful if you suspect range name problems in your spreadsheet.

Fig. 10.38

*A standard worksheet
and Show Info box.*

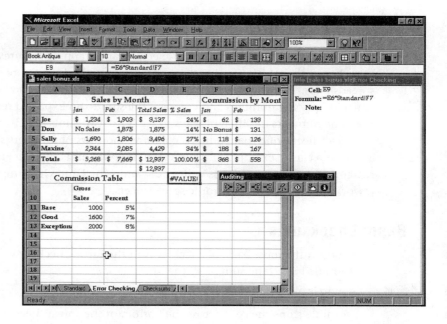

Fig. 10.39

Info menu.

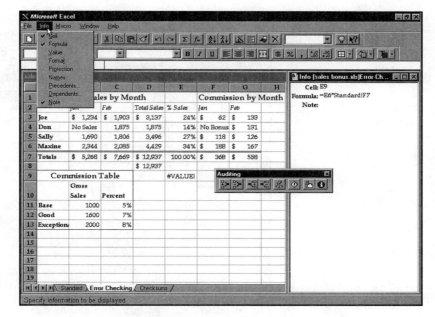

Using Checksums

While Excel has a lot of useful error checking and trapping features, sometimes you have to go beyond what is offered and use your own methods to assure the accuracy of your spreadsheets. The principle way to check for errors is called a *checksum*. With checksums, you add up some numbers and compare the sum to an expected result, or you add up the same numbers in different ways to see if the two sums match. The most basic of all spreadsheets, one that contains columns and rows of numbers summed down and across, is a classic example of a checksum. If your hair is turning gray, like mine, you'll remember doing spreadsheets with paper and pencil and checking them this way. Well, it works just as well on electronic spreadsheets.

Basic Checksums

Let's look at the most basic of checksums in the Error Checking worksheet. First, look at the formula in D7, the sum of all the sales.

```
=SUM(B7:C7)
```

The formula sums the cells across the bottom of the spreadsheet, the monthly totals (see fig. 10.40).

Fig. 10.40

SALES BONUS grand total.

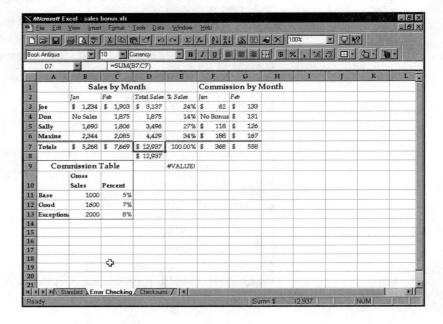

In the "good old days" before electronic spreadsheets, you would have manually totaled both these numbers and the sums across the sales people's total sales and compared the results. If they disagreed, you went back and started adding them all up again and again, until they agreed. You still need to do this, but the spreadsheet software makes it much easier. Just put the sum down in cell D8 (see fig. 10.41).

=SUM(D3:D6)

Fig. 10.41

The SALES BONUS spreadsheet with checksum.

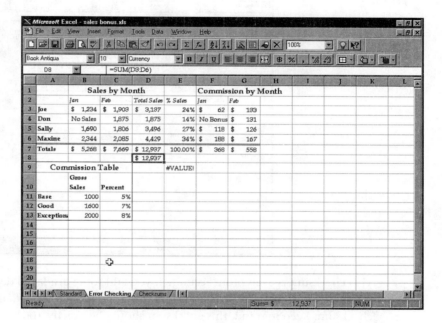

Notice that cells D8 and D7 match. This indicates that there are probably no formula errors previous to this point in the spreadsheet. This checksum can't check for every kind of error, but it certainly raises my confidence that the results are correct. It definitely won't check for entry errors, so you're on you own there.

If there is a difference between the two, that difference usually gives us a clue as to where the error might be. If the difference is 100, look for a value in the spreadsheet of 100. Then check the summation formulas in that column and that row to see if they include that cell.

When you prepare to print the spreadsheet, you can hide or remove the checksum, no one else needs to see it. Usually, I do this by hiding the column or row in which the checksum appears. A later section discusses how to hide the checksum so you don't have to hide the row or column, in case this is inconvenient.

You can add an additional checksum to this spreadsheet to check the percentage calculations. Select cell E7, click the AutoSum button, and press Enter. The result should be 100%. If it isn't, there is an error in the calculations (see fig. 10.42).

Fig. 10.42

A checksum for percentage.

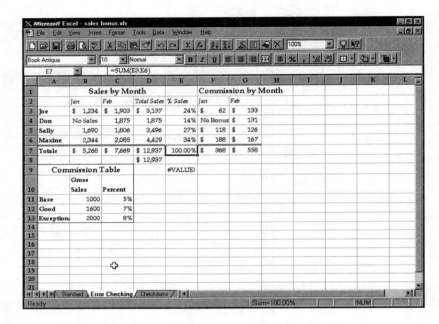

This checksum is even more accurate if you add some displayed decimals. Click twice on the Increase Decimal tool (on the Formatting toolbar) to add two decimal points to the checksum. Keep in mind, this checksum should be exactly 100%, even to many decimals. Even if the numbers in the column above don't add up to 100%, the checksum will because it is not the sum of the rounded numbers above, but the sum of the much more accurate numbers Excel is tracking. If the checksum is 100.01%, or 99.99%, there is an error in the spreadsheet. While it may be a small error now, as the spreadsheet changes, the same error could become more significant. If the checksum is not 100.00%, you need to find the source of the error and fix it.

Usually, if the first checksum checks out, but the percentage checksum is off, the error will be in the percentage column. Going to the Formula mode by choosing Tools, Options, as described previously, is a good way to look for errors in this kind of column. Look for inconsistencies between the formulas in the column.

If you wanted to check the bonus totals, you could sum the bonuses across, for each sales person, then sum them both down and across, as you did the sales amounts, and compare the two totals.

Use checksums wherever you can to assure yourself and others that there is little likeli-hood of errors in the spreadsheet. And the more critical the numbers, the more checks and checksums you want on the results.

Advanced Checksums

What if you don't want to hide and reveal checksums each time you work on a spread-sheet? What if there are many checksums throughout a large workbook? Do you have to hunt through each worksheet, checking each checksum in turn? How do you remember where they all are?

All of these problems can be dealt with using self-hiding checksums, remote checksums, or a checksum table. *Self-hiding checksums* only appear on-screen when the checksum indicates an error. A *remote checksum* is located somewhere away from the numbers it checks, usually a common area to check for errors. It doesn't need to be hidden when you print because it's not in the print area. A *checksum table* puts all the results of the checksums in one place, and controls the status of a single self-hiding error message indicating a problem, usually in a very prominent place. Then, all you have to check is that one obvious place to be sure no checked-for errors occur in the spreadsheet.

Local Hidden Checksums

To hide a checksum locally, simply add an IF function to the checksum to test for a true result. If the checksum returns a TRUE condition, the result appears in the cell. If there is no error, the cell is blanked.

Let's change the sales totals checksum to be a hidden one.

In cell D8, enter this formula.

```
=IF(SUM(D3:D6)=D7,"",SUM(D3:D6))
```

After you enter the formula, cell D8 is blank because the checksum finds no discrepancy. To test if the checksum is working, put a number, other than the correct one, in any of the cells between D3 and D6. The checksum appears and is different than D7 (see fig. 10.43). It's time to go hunting!

The IF statement tests to see if the sum of cells D3 to D6 (the sum down) equals D7 (the sum across). If they are equal, it "thinks" it's putting in text, which would be identified by the quotation marks. Because there is no text between the quotation marks, the cell is blank. If the test is FALSE, the IF statement puts in the sum of cells D3 to D6 to show there is a difference between the two sums. Using this hidden checksum, the checksum only appears if there is a discrepancy, and is hidden as long as there isn't.

Fig. 10.43
*Hidden checksum
result displayed.*

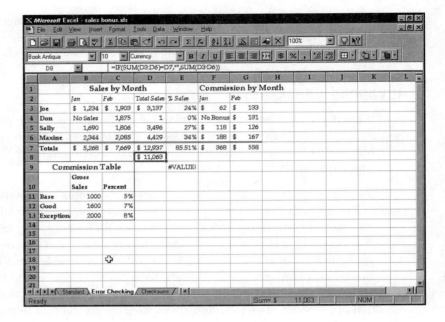

Remote Hidden Checksums

On the rather small SALES BONUS spreadsheet, the entire spreadsheet can be seen
at once. What if the spreadsheet were much larger, and the checksum(s) were not always
on-screen. Maybe your memory is better than mine, but I won't remember to look at
the checksum every time something changes in the spreadsheet that might affect the
checksum. In such a case, I move the checksum to a prominent area of the spreadsheet,
usually cell A1 or close by, so that if there's a discrepancy, it gives an almost unmistak-
able error message.

The simplest and most obvious way to do this is to move the checksum formula to cell
A1. Try it. If there's no error, the cell is blank. If an error occurs, the checksum appears in
cell A1—pretty hard to miss.

This may cause other problems, however. Cell A1 contains a number, but no obvious
explanation of what it means or where it came from. And what if the spreadsheet contains many checksums? You can't put them all in cell A1, or even in the cells adjacent
to it. What if someone else uses the spreadsheet? How will they know what the sudden
appearance of this number means?

The answer to these problems is a checksum table.

Checksum Tables

A checksum table, located anywhere on the spreadsheet, puts all error checking of this kind in one convenient place. And after you create a checksum table, you can put a single warning that there is an error in cell A1, referring to the checksum table. See figure 10.44 for such a table in SALES BONUS on the Checksums sheet.

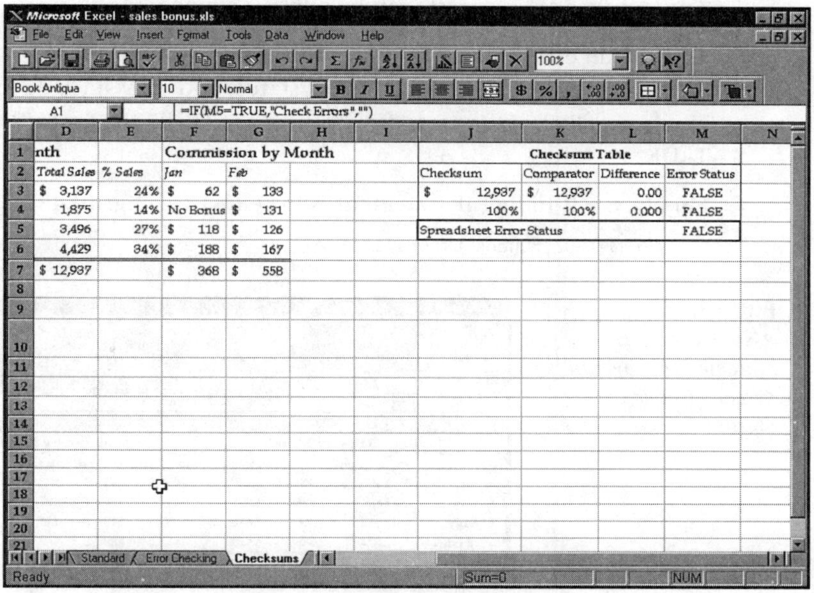

Fig. 10.44

A checksum table.

The first column, Checksum, contains the checksums moved from various locations throughout the worksheet (they could be from around the workbook, or even from different workbooks). The second column, Comparator, contains the value to which you want to compare the checksum. This could be a cell, as in the first comparator in K3, or a set value, as in the second comparator in K4. The third column, Difference, is the difference between the two, formatted to whatever degree of accuracy is deemed necessary. The last column, Status, is the status or the error. TRUE indicates an error is present, FALSE means there isn't. I've used a simple comparison formula to determine if there is an error greater than a allowable amount, whatever the user thinks is acceptable. Note that you must compare absolute values so that if the error is positive or negative, the result will be TRUE.

```
=ABS(L3)>0.001
```

If the absolute value of the difference between the checksum and the comparator is greater then the allowable error, the Status changes to TRUE.

> **Tip**
> Place the allowable error in a separate column, between Difference and Error Status, if you want it to show or want to be able to change it a little more easily.

Any number of these tests can be put in a single table.

The overall error status of the spreadsheet appears in cell M5. An OR function tests the cells containing the individual error status, and gives a FALSE as long as none as the errors are TRUE. As soon as any of them are TRUE, the Spreadsheet Error Status becomes TRUE.

Finally, a self-hiding IF statement is in cell A1 (see fig. 10.45).

```
=IF(M5=TRUE,"Check Errors","")
```

Fig. 10.45

A spreadsheet IF statement for overall spreadsheet error status.

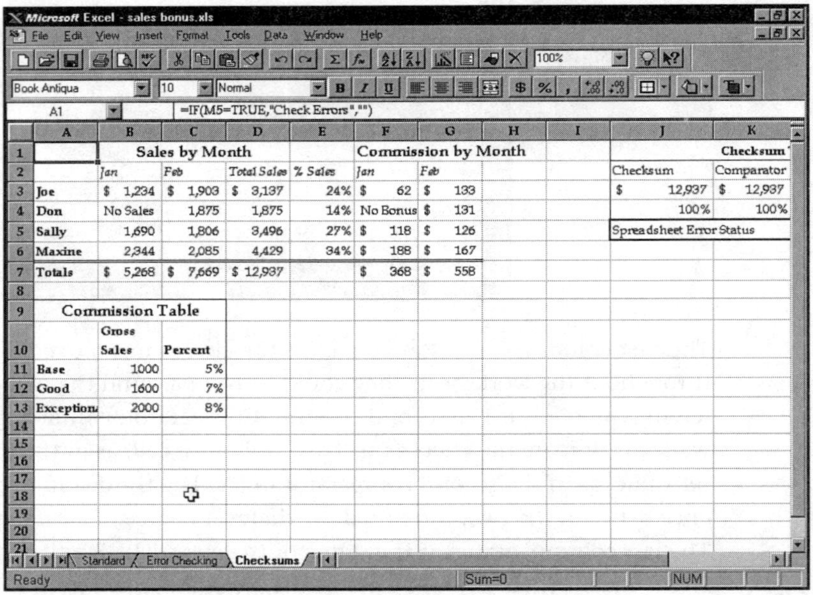

The self-hiding IF statement checks if cell M5 is TRUE. If it is, a message Check Errors appears in A1. The cell is formatted for text to be in red to make the message hard to overlook. If cell M5 is FALSE, the IF statement in A1 is hidden by the double quotation marks.

Numeric Methods

In some instances, there is no good way to check the correctness of your spreadsheet in the ways listed previously. Some spreadsheets don't lend themselves to these procedures. Many spreadsheets can be checked by numeric methods. These can be quite involved, depending on the complexity of the worksheet.

Basically, numeric methods involve putting dummy values into the cells that contain values. The most basic application is to put 1s in for every value. Then it is usually easy to check the results of formulas when they are operating only on values of one. In other cases, you might use tens, or one hundreds, whichever made it easiest to check the formula's results. Any kind of value that gives an easily calculated answer will work. Then you can check your work in your head, or with a calculator. If it's a very large spreadsheet, use the COUNT function to count how many ones there are. The COUNT of the cells and the SUM will be the same, if there are no errors.

Summary

Errors are just as possible in electronic spreadsheets as they were with paper and pencil. But just as creating a spreadsheet is faster and easier with software, so is finding and trapping errors. The single biggest hurdle is to realize that you should do error trapping! Once you understand that, the rest is, as usual, a matter of learning what's there and how to best use it.

Finally, remember the best error trapping tool on earth is the human brain! I have seen major errors left in spreadsheets, some of them financially significant, because the user simply forgot to look at the numbers. As you create your worksheet, keep looking at the results to see if they make sense. When you are done, before you submit, take an extra minute to look the entire piece over to see if any glaring errors show up.

10

chapter 11

Advanced Data Manipulation Tricks and Techniques

by Bob Umlas

In this chapter

◆ **Problems you can solve**
Explore interesting variations for the Paste Special dialog box, useful techniques in using relative-range defined names, techniques for double-spacing a worksheet, and learn how to create random test data.

◆ **Tricks for finding data**
Learn how to find strings that begin a cell, rather than just exist inside the cell.

◆ **Fancy F5 tricks**
Did you know you could type OFFSET(A4,3,1,5,3) inside the reference box of the Edit, GoTo dialog box? Here you will learn many other options.

◆ **Formatting for fun and profit**
You will learn how you can make a picture appear in your worksheet simply by entering text.

◆ **Advanced data table techniques you can use**
One cell is used for a column (or row) input cell in a data table, but sometimes you need more than one cell to solve a particular problem. We'll cover when those times occur and how you can use more than one cell.

◆ **Using interior series**
Discusses how to increment a value inside a formula, such as the 1 in =IPMT(rate,1,nper,pv,fv,type) becoming =IPMT(rate,2,nper,pv,fv,type), then 3, and so on, as you fill down the formula.

◆ **Fill Handle tricks**
Learn how you can alter the way the Fill Handle works depending on your initial selection or by using the right-mouse button.

There are as many tips and tricks in Excel as there are users. This chapter is full of tips and techniques designed to make your data entry, formatting, and moving ranges around much easier.

By the end of this chapter you will probably discover other interesting tips and techniques on your own simply by trial and error.

Finding Strings Using Formulas

There are times when you want to be able to find, dynamically, where text, or portions of text, is on your worksheet. Traditionally, the way to find the text is by using the MATCH function, or perhaps the various LOOKUP functions. The problem with doing this, however, is that these won't work if the text you're looking for is embedded in other text, or if you want to find the text *only* if it appears at the end of any text it's associated with, and so on (see fig. 11.1).

Fig. 11.1

Finding strings in certain positions of other strings.

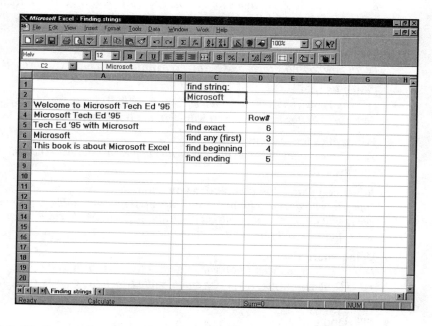

Notice that in cell C2, the search string is "Microsoft," and column A is the column being searched. Cells D5:D8 contain the locations of the word "Microsoft" in column A.

To find "Microsoft" as an exact match (cell A6), the formula used in cell D5 is

```
=MATCH(C2,A:A,0)
```

> **Note**
>
> The MATCH function returns the position of an element in an array that matches a specified value in a specified way. Its syntax is MATCH(lookup value, lookup array, type). The type used here, 0, indicates *exact* match. For example, MATCH("X",{"F","X","W","Q"},0) returns 2, the position of the "X."

This formula simply finds an exact match (the third parameter of the MATCH statement, the zero, indicates an exact match). Using the 0 at the end of the MATCH function is also the most common use of the finding of text, but there are other methods.

Let's say that you want to find the first cell containing the word "Microsoft," no matter where the word lies in the cell. The formula in cell D6 contains the solution:

```
=MATCH("*"&C2&"*",A:A,0)
```

This formula uses the wildcard character, an asterisk (*), and appends it to the contents of cell C2. That is, the search string now becomes "*Microsoft*". This tells Excel to find *any* cell containing the word, anywhere in that cell. It seems a little odd to then ask for an *exact* match (the zero as the third parameter of the MATCH statement), but the instructions are effectively "find the first cell that contains any characters, plus the word Microsoft, plus any other characters, and find it *exactly!*"

Suppose you want to find the cell containing the word "Microsoft" only if the cell *begins* with that word, as in cells A4 and A6. The formula in cell D7 finds the first occurrence of text:

```
=MATCH(C2&"*",A:A,0)
```

This formula uses the wildcard character, appended with the search string. That is, C2&"*" becomes "Microsoft*" as the search string, which is any cell beginning with the word "Microsoft," followed by any number of characters.

By now, you should be able to figure out the formula in cell D8, the one which will find the row of the cell which *ends* in the word "Microsoft." It is:

```
=MATCH("*"&C2,A:A,0)
```

This formula instructs Excel to find any characters appended with "Microsoft," or that end in "Microsoft."

You now have more tools to use to search for strings. Chapter 7, "Using Array Formulas," shows how you can find strings (or error conditions) using the SEARCH function.

11

Making and Using Interior Series

Interior series refers to the idea of a series (like 1, 2, 3...) *inside* a formula. For example, if A1 contained =INDEX(B3:B44,1), A2 contained =INDEX(B3:B44,2), C3 contained =INDEX(B3:B44,3), and so on, you can see that the second parameter is changing from 1 to 2 to 3, etc. This is an interior series.

There are many formulas in Excel that use some sort of counter inside the formula, such as LARGE(range,1) followed by LARGE(range,2). The 1 or 2, being a constant, cannot be used to fill down the formula because the constant doesn't change as you fill down =LARGE(range,1). It would be nice to be able to enter a formula with embedded counters that change as you fill down (or right).

Another such formula is PPMT, which returns the principal portion of a payment on a loan depending on which payment it is. The function's syntax is

```
=PPMT(rate,per,nper,pv,fv,type)
```

 Note

The PPMT function returns the payment on the principal for a given period for an investment based on periodic, constant payments and a constant interest rate. The per argument, specifies the payment number for the principal. So when per is 5, this function refers to the principal amount of the 5th payment.

The second parameter, per, is the one which would be nice to change (see fig.11.2).

Cells B7:B20 are the principal amounts for the first 14 payments. The total payment, $1,153.37 (in cell B4), is a constant payment amount for $150,000 paid over 30 years at 8.5% interest. The formula in cell B4 is

```
=PMT(B3/12,B2*12,-B1)
```

Cell B7's formula (using named ranges) should be

```
=PPMT(Rate/12,1,Years*12,-Principal)
```

and the formula in B8 should be

```
=PPMT(Rate/12,2,Years*12,-Principal)
```

and so on (notice the second parameter changed from 1 to 2).

You can use the ROW function to alter the number of the period being paid. The formula might start out as

```
=PPMT(Rate/12,ROW(),Years*12,-Principal)
```

but when this is entered in cell B7, the ROW function returns 7. Because this is the first payment, you need to subtract 6. If you try

```
=PPMT(Rate/12,ROW()-6,Years*12,-Principal)
```

in cell B7, you see that it works. If you fill this down to cell B20, in fact, it also works, for in cell B20, ROW()–6 is 20–6, or 14, which corresponds to the label in A20.

Fig. 11.2

Using an increasing value inside a formula (an interior series).

	A	B	C	D	E	F	G	H	I
			=PPMT(Rate/12,ROW()-ROW($B$7)+1,Years*12,-Principal)						
1	Principal	$150,000							
2	Years	30							
3	Rate	8.5%							
4	Payment	$1,153.37							
5									
6		Principal	Interest	Payment					
7	Payment 1	$90.87	$1,062.50	$1,153.37					
8	Payment 2	$91.51	$1,061.86	$1,153.37					
9	Payment 3	$92.16	$1,061.21	$1,153.37					
10	Payment 4	$92.81	$1,060.56	$1,153.37					
11	Payment 5	$93.47	$1,059.90	$1,153.37					
12	Payment 6	$94.13	$1,059.24	$1,153.37					
13	Payment 7	$94.80	$1,058.57	$1,153.37					
14	Payment 8	$95.47	$1,057.90	$1,153.37					
15	Payment 9	$96.15	$1,057.22	$1,153.37					
16	Payment 10	$96.83	$1,056.54	$1,153.37					
17	Payment 11	$97.52	$1,055.85	$1,153.37					
18	Payment 12	$98.21	$1,055.16	$1,153.37					
19	Payment 13	$98.90	$1,054.47	$1,153.37					
20	Payment 14	$99.60	$1,053.77	$1,153.37					

⍺ Note

The ROW function returns the row number of the reference. If the reference is missing, then it refers to the row of the cell containing the ROW() formula. So if ROW() is entered in cell F66, the function returns 66.

A problem arises, however, if you decide to insert (or delete) a row above row 7. Now, all those –6s should be –7s, or –5s, or some other number. The formula is not really "safe" to use.

Here's the trick you can use to get the correct results in all cases:

```
=PPMT(Rate/12,ROW()-ROW($B$7)+1,Years*12,-Principal)
```

The second parameter in the formula `ROW()-ROW($B$7)+1`, when entered in cell B7, is 7–7+1, or 1. In cell B8, this is 8–7+1, or 2. The absolute reference to cell B7 is necessary so that it doesn't change when you fill down. B7 was chosen because it is the first cell in the series of formulas used.

But now what happens if you insert two rows at row 5? Well, the formula in B7 (moved to B9 because of the insert) now reads:

```
=PPMT(Rate/12,ROW()-ROW($B$9)+1,Years*12,-Principal)
```

and the `ROW()-ROW($B$9)+1` becomes 9–9+1, or still 1! In row B22, this is 22–9+1, or 14 again.

This is what I refer to as an interior series because inside a formula it translates to 1, then 2, then 3, and so on.

Using Intermediate Formulas

An *intermediate formula* is one which hadn't been resolved by Microsoft Excel. To create one, enter ="=SUM(B1:B3)" in A1. You see the text, =SUM(B1:B3) in the cell, not the sum of B1:B3. Now copy that formula and paste special values back into the same cell. You see =SUM(B1:B3) *both in the cell and the formula bar*, but it still doesn't evaluate to the sum of the values in B1:B3. This is called an intermediate formula. The formula has yet to be resolved. You can resolve it by clicking in the formula bar and pressing Enter, or by double-clicking the cell (if you have in-cell editing turned on) and re-entering it, or by pressing the F4 key and the Enter key. It now functions like the SUM formula you've come to know and love.

Suppose you have a large worksheet, something like figure 11.3 and you need to add up all the products, as in =SUM(Prod1), =SUM(Prod2), and so on. (Remember this example only goes through row 18, but suppose it is a worksheet which goes through row 2000). Let's further assume that the ranges Prod1 through Prod18 are defined as B1:G1 through B18:G18, respectively. It would seem that you need to enter =SUM(Prod1) and =SUM(Prod2), and so on, typing each reference. (In the case of it going to row 2000, imagine typing all the formulas through to =SUM(Prod2000)!)

Fig. 11.3

The formula in H1,
="=SUM("&A1&")",
produces the inter-
mediate formula,
=SUM(Prod1), as text.

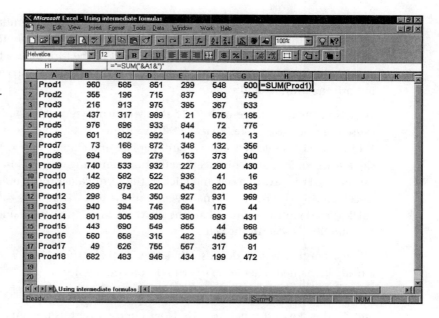

I will show two ways you could do that *without* all the typing. First, create the formula as text so the Fill Handle will come to the rescue.

 Note

The *Fill Handle* is the area at the bottom, right corner of any range selection. When you move the cursor over the Fill Handle, it becomes a large crosshair and when you drag the Fill Handle down, it replicates patterns. For example, if you enter Monday in A1, =B2 in A2, and Jan in A3, then select A1:A3, drag the Fill Handle down to A6, you will see Tuesday in A4, =B5 in A5, and Feb in A6.

In cell H1, you enter

```
="=sum("&A1&")"
```

What you will *see* in the cell will be =sum(Prod1), but not the *result* of the sum. By entering the formula in this manner, you can use the Fill Handle down to cell H18 where you'd have the formula ="=sum("&A18&")" but which looks like =sum(Prod18).

11

What is this? The text "=sum(Prod18)" is the *text* result of a formula entered as text. =SUM is *very* different from ="=SUM." The first begins a function, the second is text. So how can you use this? You can change this text to the formula itself. Select H1:H18 and copy and paste special values in place, and you'll have =sum(Prod1) through =sum(Prod18) in both the formula and value.

Why isn't the formula resolving? That is, why isn't =sum(Prod1) producing 3,743? Because the value was pasted in *as text*. There's one more step to get what you really want. While H1:H18 is selected, choose <u>E</u>dit, <u>R</u>eplace and change = to =. Yes, replace all equal signs with equal signs. This has the effect of reentering each cell in the range. If you have =sum(Prod1) as text in a cell and click in the formula bar (or double-click the cell while in-cell editing is turned on), then reenter it, the text will resolve to the formula. You see =SUM(Prod1) in the formula bar (the word "SUM" is in all capital letters) and the *value* of the function is seen in the cell.

There is another way to do this. Obviously, for =SUM(Prod1) to work, the ranges must already be named. Therefore, in cell H1 you could enter

    =SUM(B1:G1)

and fill this down through row 18. Now, choose <u>I</u>nsert, <u>N</u>ame, <u>A</u>pply, accept the default selections, and click OK.

 Note

When you use <u>I</u>nsert, <u>N</u>ame, <u>A</u>pply immediately after naming ranges, those names are all selected in the dialog box. If you do this sometime later, you will have to select all the names, in this case Prod1 through Prod18.

Each range is replaced by its name. That is, =SUM(B1:G1) is now =SUM(Prod1), and so on.

Filling Blanks to Manipulate Surrounding Data

Suppose you have a worksheet with data in it like you see in cells A1:C13 of figure 11.4.

Fig. 11.4

A range of cells that presents a problem when sorting by name.

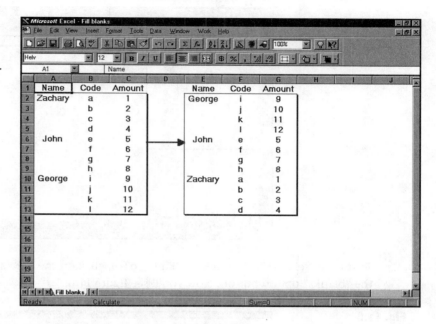

You see that the "groups" of names are not alphabetical. Your task is to convert it to be sorted, like you now see in cells E1:G13.

Obviously, if you select A1:C13 and sort it, you don't get what you want; it looks like figure 11.5, which, of course, sorts blanks to the end. You need to be able to keep the groups together. The technique involves filling in the blanks, then sorting, then removing the additional cells that were just filled in.

11

Fig. 11.5
A normal sort produces this undesired result.

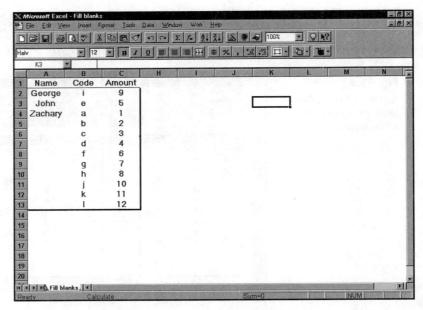

To do this, select A2:A13, press F5 (Edit, GoTo), click on the Special button, then select the "blanks" option button. Now you'll see figure 11.6.

Fig. 11.6
Selecting the blanks in preparation for sorting the range by names.

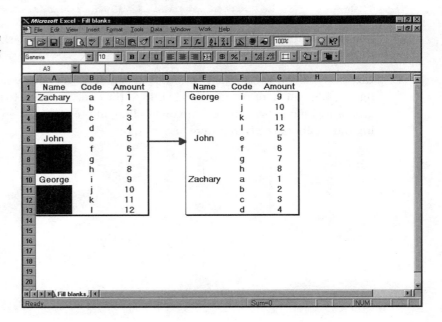

These are the blank cells that need to be filled in. Type an equal sign and press the up-arrow, which will enter the formula =A2, then press Ctrl+Enter. This will *fill* the blank cells with the cells above. It will now look like figure 11.7.

Fig. 11.7

The formula =A2 entered from cell A means "copy from the cell above." Ctrl+ Enter makes all the cells copy from the cell above.

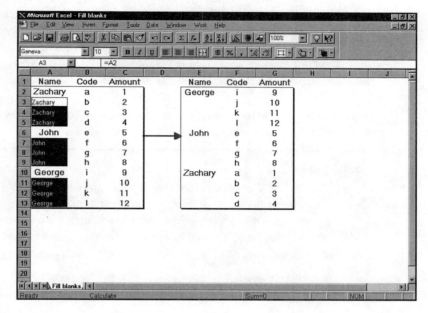

Now by sorting on column A, they're in the right sequence. All that's left to do is select A1:A13, use F5 again, click the "special" button, click on the Formulas option button, then choose Edit, Clear, All, and you're done.

Fancy F5 Key Tricks

Usually, you use the GoTo command (F5 key) to go to either a cell reference or a named reference. But you can go to the INDEX of a reference, or an OFFSET of a reference. For example, if you have a range named MyRange, which is cells $A$1:$G$20, then after you issue the GoTo command, you can type in **INDEX(MyRange,3,)** (notice the trailing comma) which will select the entire third row of MyRange, or cells A3:G3. Or, you can enter INDEX(MyRange,,6) (notice the 2 commas) which will select the entire sixth column of the range, or cells F1:F20.

11

Note

The INDEX function returns the value of an element in an array, selected by the row and column number indices. For example, INDEX({6,3,87,3,12},4) returns the 4th item in the array {6,3,87,3,12}, or 3. This used only a horizontal array (the commas indicate this). An example of a 2-dimensional array might be INDEX(A1:C4,2,3), which means the 2nd row of the range, 3rd column, and the INDEX function would return whatever is in cell C2.

You can also type `offset(MyRange,1,3,4,2)` in the GoTo dialog box to select a range which is 4 rows by 2 columns beginning with cell D2—this is D2:E5.

Note

The OFFSET function takes three or five parameters. When five are used, the last two refer to the *shape* of the result: number of rows by number of columns. The first parameter is the range (named or cell-reference), the second is how many rows down to start, and the third is how many columns over to start. The second and third parameters can be negative numbers, so you can have something like

```
OFFSET(MyRange,-3,-2,1,2)
```

Any or all of the numbers in the index or offset used in the preceding formula can also be already-defined variables. That is, you can type in

```
offset(D2,Myrow,Mycol,MyNumRows,MyNumCols)
```

and, if Myrow is 1, Mycol is 2, MyNumRows is 3 and MyNumCols is 4, this is the same as offset(D2,1,2,3,4), or range F3:I5.

Formatting for Fun and Profit

You are usually restricted to formatting a number as positive, negative, and zero, or to ranges like less than 10, more than 30, and anything between 10 and 30 by using the format [<10][Red]General;[>30][cyan][General];General.

There's a way to get practically unlimited formatting depending on a value of a cell. As you can see from figures 11.8 and 11.9, the value in cell B6 is either bold and centered (when the number entered is less than 100), or aligned to the right, italicized, and red for values between 100 and 200. How is this accomplished?

Fig. 11.8
This cell's value, 50, displays 50 as centered and bold.

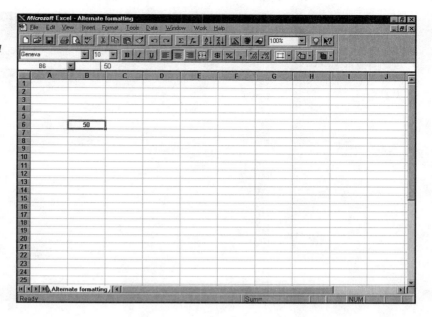

Fig. 11.9
This cell's value, 150, displays 150 as right-aligned, italic, and bold.

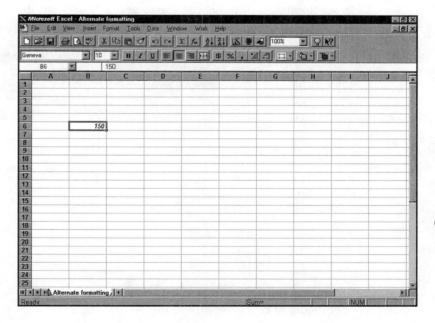

The formatting is hidden (see fig. 11.10).

Fig. 11.10
Showing the source of the overlapped picture objects. The value is italic, bold, and right-aligned.

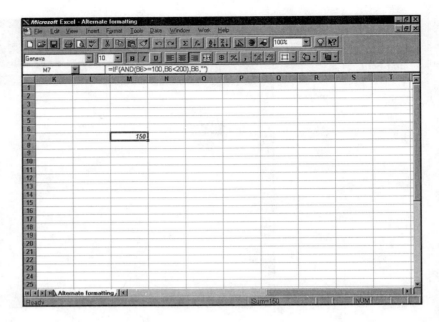

Cells M6 through M10 contain all the formats which could show up in cell B6. The formulas are shown in figure 11.11.

Fig. 11.11
The underlying formulas and formatting for the overlapped pictures on cell B6.

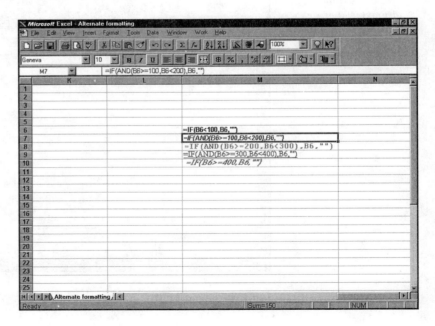

The formulas in M6:M10 are mutually exclusive. That is, if there is something shown in cell M9, the others are blank. If there is something in cell M6, the others are blank. Each of these cells is formatted differently. Cell M6 is bold and centered; M7 is aligned to the right, italic, and red. The formatting of *these* cells will determine the format of cell B6.

The "trick" is that each cell in turn from the range M6:M10 was selected, and the camera tool was used to take a picture.

 Note

To get the camera tool, choose View, Toolbars, click the Customize button, select the Utility category, and the camera tool is the fourth button in the top row. Clicking the camera tool takes a "picture" of the selected cells, and then clicking anywhere on a sheet shows that picture. (For an interesting effect, take a picture of a range of cells—like four rows by four columns—then click just slightly to the right and down of the upper-left corner. You will see multiple images of the source cells in the area you clicked.)

Each picture was "developed" on cell B6, holding the Alt key down to make sure the picture aligns exactly with the cell border. The Objects were all formatted to contain no border and no fill by choosing Edit, GoTo, Special, then clicking the Objects option button. Additionally, cell B6 was formatted as ;; in the number format so nothing would show in the cell.

 Note

The two semicolons is a custom number format. Usually, number formats have three sections, separated by semicolons. The first is for the format of positive values, the second for negative values, and the third for zero values. The successive semi-colons indicate that nothing should show for positive, negative, or zero since there's nothing in any of the three sections.

11

Because only *one* of the range M6:M10 is visible at any time, all the pictures show through each other, revealing the formatting depending on the value entered into the cell. Just make sure that the column width and height of the items in column M match the column width of column B or it will not look right.

Cell Editing

Suppose you have a worksheet that is very "busy," something like figure 11.12.

Fig. 11.12

A busy, crowded worksheet in which you want to change some text in one cell.

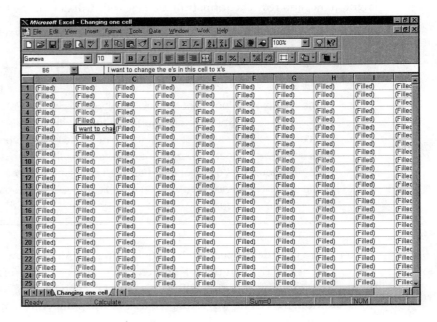

How can you change repeated text in only one cell where every cell in view has information in it and you need to change the contents of one cell, B6 in this case. In this example, B6 contains "I want to change the *e*'s in this cell to *x*'s." If you were to select B6 and issue the Edit, Replace command and change *e* to *x*, you would also change the *e*'s in all the other cells as well.

You could manually change the *e*'s to *x*'s in the cell, but that wouldn't illustrate the technique you can use here, namely: select the cell twice. If the selection consists of more than one cell, the replacement of characters is limited to those cells. You can select B6 twice by clicking on it, then holding the Ctrl key and clicking on it again. If, at this point, you were to issue the Insert, Name, Define command, you would see =Sheet1!$B$6,Sheet1!$B$6 in the Refers To box (assuming the sheet is called Sheet1).

You can also use this technique of selecting a cell twice to enter varying numbers to see the effect on other cells. For example, you may want to enter a 1 in cell A1, see what the result is on other cells which refer to A1, then try a 2 in A1, and so on. Usually, when you press Enter, Excel places you in the next cell down. By selecting the cell twice, the active cell doesn't change, and you can enter many test values into the same cell. Of course, you can override the setting by Tools, Options, Edit tab, and deselect the Move Selection after Enter check box, but you don't need to do that when you can take advantage of this tip.

A Look at Data Tables

This discussion assumes that you are familiar with basic usage of data tables. If that is not the case, you should review them in Microsoft Excel's documentation.

Suppose you have a list of vendors, amounts, and dates, as shown in figure 11.13.

Fig. 11.13

Cells F1:G8 summa-rize the data in cells A6:C165 where the amount is either under 300 or over 500, and the month is in the second quarter.

	A	B	C	D	E	F	G	H
1	Amount	Vendor				Vendor	2278	
2	<300		FALSE	TRUE		Karen Bush	2951	
3	>500		0	FALSE	TRUE	A. B. Properties	1131	
4						Ace Power & Light	2538	
5						City of Franklin	2045	
6	Vendor	Amount	Date			James Gregory	2178	
7	Karen Bush	530	1/6/95			Jim Parsons	796	
8	Karen Bush	696	1/30/96			Ralph Cook	602	
9	Karen Bush	976	3/19/96					
10	Karen Bush	749	3/20/95					
11	Karen Bush	364	3/21/95					
12	Karen Bush	530	4/2/96					
13	Karen Bush	696	5/17/95					
14	Karen Bush	364	5/24/95					
15	Karen Bush	749	5/30/96					
16	Karen Bush	976	6/18/95					
17	Karen Bush	468	7/3/95					
18	Karen Bush	729	7/10/95					
19	Karen Bush	261	7/17/95					
20	Karen Bush	442	7/19/95					
21	Karen Bush	418	7/21/95					
22	Karen Bush	114	7/29/95					
23	Karen Bush	912	9/13/95					
24	Karen Bush	980	9/27/95					
25	Karen Bush	939	10/14/95					

Suppose also, that you need to find out information about the total amounts spent by each vendor but only for those amounts that are under $300 or over $500. Additionally, you want only those amounts that were in the second quarter (dates between 4/1 and 6/30) even though the dates span more than one year.

> **α Note**
>
> To create the unique Vendor names listed in F2:F8 (the list of Vendor names with-out duplication), click anywhere in the list A6:C165, and issue the command Data, Filter, Advanced Filter. Choose Copy to another location, make sure the List Range is pointing to the correct range—in this case A6:A165 (*not* A6:C165), leave the Criteria reference box empty, enter F1 as the copy to range, click Unique Records Only, then click OK. This will place the unique vendors (and the title "Vendor") in column F.

Data tables require a column input cell and/or a row input cell. Yet this criteria requires three rows (one being a title row) because of the OR restriction necessary (under 300 or over 500).

What would be the input cell? How would it work even if you found the "correct" cell for the input cell?

Cells A1:D3 represent the criteria range—the range of cells used by the data table in the calculation of the values. Cells A1:A3 determine that the amounts must be under 300 or over 500. When used in DSUM formulas (or any D-formulas), you "OR" conditions by listing them down in a column, and you can "AND" conditions by listing them across in rows. Let's skip column B for a moment and look at what the formulas are in C2:D3.

Notice that C1 and D1 are blank. This is because you are going to use a "computed criteria" which implies that the data doesn't exist in the list in the form needed. For example, because you are interested in amounts, you can use the word "Amount" as in cell A1 because the field in the list has a title of "Amount" also (cell B6). However, you need to examine the *months* in the list (months of 4, 5, or 6), not the exact dates because they span two years, and the months aren't listed, so you can't put the word "Date" in C1 or D1. Leave it blank or put in any text *not* found in the top row of the list.

Cell C2 contains =MONTH(C7)>3 and cell D2 contains =MONTH(C7)<7.

 Note

The reason C7 is used for the MONTH function is that C7 is the *first* date in the list. When you use computed criteria on a list, you refer to the first item in that list to retrieve all the records that match the criteria.

Because they're in the same row (row 2) the conditions are ANDed and the data table is restricted to those records that have months over 3 and less than 7, independent of the year (which is months 4, 5, or 6).

You could have done away with column D and used the following formula in cell C2:

```
=AND(MONTH(C7)>3,MONTH(C7)<7)
```

It would have worked as well.

So, row 2 restricts the data table to all records with amounts under 300, any vendor, and dates in the second quarter. The formulas in C3 and D3 are the same as in C2 and D2. What appears as a zero in cell B3 is actually a key formula in using the data table. It is simply =$B$2. Why is this necessary?

If cell B2 becomes the column input cell for the data table, then as it places each value of the vendor in cell B2 (it doesn't really put anything into the cell, but it calculates the result of the D-formula *as if* each value from range F1:F8 were placed in cell B2 "behind the scenes"), it effectively places the same value into cell B3 because of its formula. Therefore, cells A3:D3 also restrict the data table to all amounts larger than 500 for months 4, 5, or 6, and whose vendor is the same as the vendor from B2.

All this is done for the calculation of the data table. Cell G1, by the way, has =DSUM(A6:C165,2,A1:D3) which means to sum all the values in column 2 of the range A6:C165 which meet the criteria defined by cells A1:D3.

 Note

All the D-functions (Database functions) have the same syntax: Dfunction(database or list,field,criteria). The criteria *must* be a range *reference*. For example, if the criteria were A1:A2 and the range contained {"Amount";">500"}, you could not use {"Amount";">500"} as the criteria.

Why is cell G1's value only 2278? Usually the cell containing the formula =DSUM(Database,field,Criteria) is the total of the rest of the data table's cells (G2:G8 in this case). The value seems incorrect because of the zero showing up in cell B3, part of the criteria. Since there is no vendor of zero, row 3's criteria is never found in the list, so the 2278 represents all vendors with amounts under 300 in the second quarter.

Well, this all works for data tables as described, but is there an easier way to get the same information? In fact, there is, depending on your definition of easier. It can be done with a simpler criteria range, but with a more complex formula as one of the computed criteria. The advantage is that there's one cell which can represent the column input cell for the data table (see fig. 11.14).

Fig. 11.14

The computed criteria (I1:J2) indicating any vendor with amounts less than 300 or more than 500, and months in the second quarter (months 4, 5, or 6).

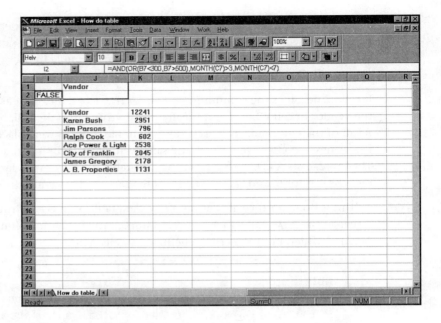

The values in the data table are the same as before with the exception of cell K4, that contains

```
=DSUM(A6:C165,2,I1:J2)
```

The only difference is the criteria range is now I1:J2 instead of A1:D3. Cell J2 is the column input cell, the cell through which each vendor name is "passed" to calculate the data table values. Cell I2 contains:

```
=AND(OR(B7<300,B7>500),MONTH(C7)>3,MONTH(C7)<7)
```

which has three parts to the AND function:

OR(B7<300,B7>500)

MONTH(C7)>3

MONTH(C7)<7

This says that three things must be true for the values in the data table: the amount must be less than 300 or greater than 500, and the month must be greater than 3 and less than 7. Notice also that cell I1 is empty because this is a computed criteria. It is a computed criteria because what you are looking for is not found directly in the list A6:C165.

Note

In referencing records from a list in a criteria range, the reference should be a relative reference to the first actual item in the list aside from the list column headers, hence the references to B7 and C7.

Date Manipulation

You may at times receive an Excel file which was uploaded by some source other than Excel, such as data from a mainframe computer, or from a Lotus 1-2-3 file, and find that you have dates that are like text values (see fig. 11.15).

Fig. 11.15

A worksheet as it may look imported from a mainframe or a text file. Note the text dates in column A.

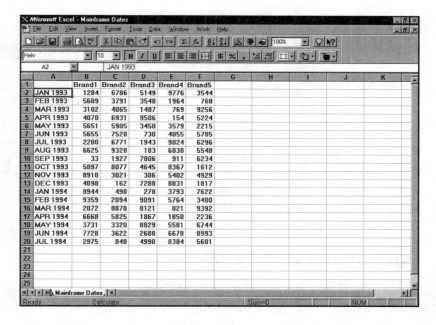

There is nothing special about this data except that the dates in column A are text, and no amount of formatting will change their appearance. However, if you simply selected cell A2, clicked in the formula bar and pressed Enter, the value would become a valid Excel date. Therefore, you might think that reentering each cell could be achieved by forcing Excel to recalculate each cell by perhaps multiplying each cell by 1 because they *do* represent valid dates. You could do this by entering the number 1 in a cell and copying it, then paste special into range A2:A17 and also click multiply (or divide). If you do this you see a worksheet that looks like figure 11.16.

11

Fig. 11.16

Intermediate result of changing text dates to serial numbers (how Microsoft Excel stores dates).

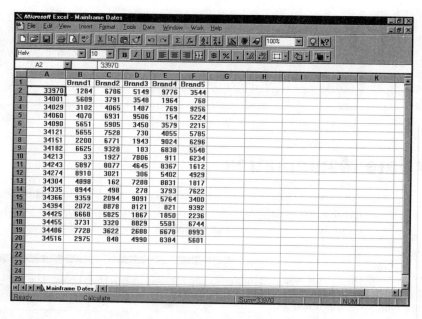

Now all you need to do is reformat the cells because they're valid dates in serial number form. Or, you may save a step by taking the original values and having Excel reenter them all by changing them to themselves! That is, each of these cells in range A2:A17 contains a blank (as well as the text "199," but using the blank is easier). So, if you issue the Edit, Replace command and change a blank to a blank, you'll get dates in all the cells in the format mm-yy (like Jan-93). If that's the format you want, you've saved a step! Actually, this saves more than one step because you don't need to enter a 1 into a cell first to multiply by and then remove afterward.

Formatting and Spacing

Figure 11.17 shows three lists of identical numbers, differing only in their formatting. Usually, when you have numbers in a list involving decimals you want to align the numbers on that decimal point. Column A is the "default" spacing, but you may find that it sometimes looks too close to the column on the right (when there are values there).

So you decide to center the values (column C). Well, these values are certainly distanced from the text in column D, but look at the alignment of the decimals. This is not acceptable because the decimal points do not line up. The solution is shown in column E. Notice the decimal points are aligned and the values are away from the text in column F. The simple solution is the formatting of something like 0.00_M which means two places to the right of the decimal, plus leave space as wide as the letter *M* in the current font.

Fig. 11.17

A worksheet showing a variety of alignments for numbers. Notice that column A's alignment, the default for numbers, is right up against the column boundary.

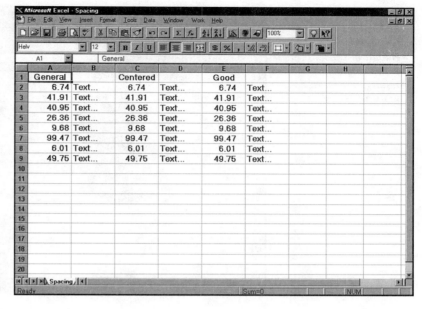

> **α Note**
>
> In cell formatting, the underscore character, (_) means to leave room in the cell as wide as the *next* character. So, _M means to leave room as wide as an M.

M was chosen because it is fairly wide, but you could have chosen other custom formats, such as a "_," a "W," or even a smaller spaced letter, like "I." These formats would have been 0.00__, 0.00_W, and 0.00_I, respectively.

Another Look at the Fill Handle

Sometimes it looks like the Fill Handle creates more problems than it solves, specifically when the referenced data does not appear in every line (see fig. 11.18).

Cell E3 contains the formula =AVERAGE(B3:D3) and its value is accurate. Using the Fill Handle to bring the formula down to cell E13 creates the #DIV/0! errors you see (as does a simple Edit, Fill, Down). The solution to avoid the errors is to *first* select cells E3:E4— selecting the initially blank cell E4 as well. Now, when you use the Fill Handle through cell E13 the blank in the Average/Blank/Average/Blank pattern is repeated, giving only the answers you want, as in figure 11.19.

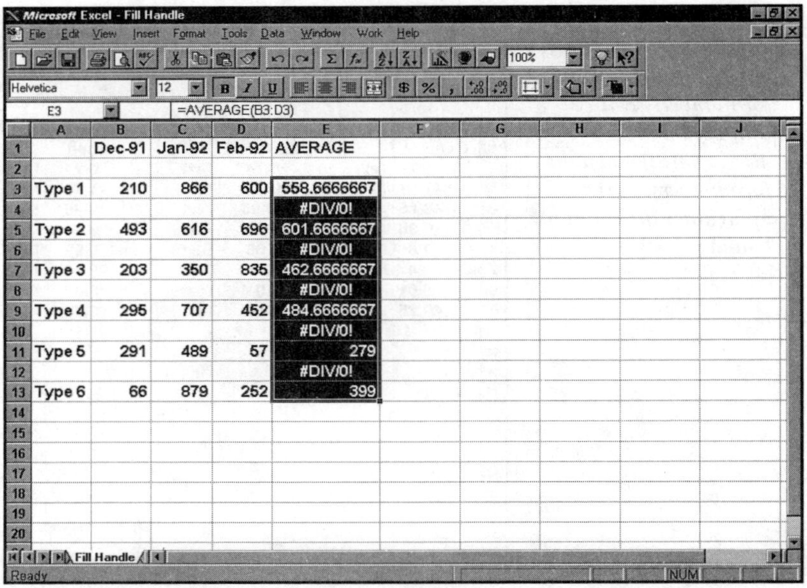

Fig. 11.18
Filling E3 down to E13 (either by the Fill Handle or the Edit, Fill Down command) results in the series of #DIV/0! Errors.

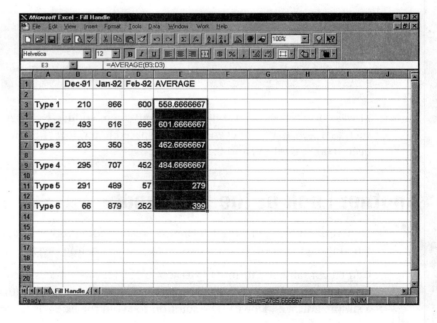

Fig. 11.19
By first selecting cells E3:E4 and using the Fill Handle, the empty cell (E4) is replicated, avoiding the #DIV/0! Errors.

Rearranging Data

Suppose you have data that looks something like figure 11.20. How can you arrange these values into a single list representing first A2:G2, then A3:G3, A4:G4, etc.?

Fig. 11.20

Data to be arranged into a single list.

	A	B	C	D	E	F	G
1							
2	2	4	6	8	10	12	14
3	3	6	9	12	15	18	21
4	4	8	12	16	20	24	28
5	5	10	15	20	25	30	35
6	6	12	18	24	30	36	42
7	7	14	21	28	35	42	49
8	8	16	24	32	40	48	56
9	9	18	27	36	45	54	63
10	10	20	30	40	50	60	70
11	11	22	33	44	55	66	77
12	12	24	36	48	60	72	84
13	13	26	39	52	65	78	91
14	14	28	42	56	70	84	98
15	15	30	45	60	75	90	105
16	16	32	48	64	80	96	112
17	17	34	51	68	85	102	119
18	18	36	54	72	90	108	126
19							
20							

Your task is to make the values appear in a single column so that cell I2 contains the 2 from cell A2, I3 contains 4 from B2, and so on through cell I8 which contains 14 from cell G2, then cell I9 contains 3 from A3, and so on, until cell I120 contains the 126 from cell G18.

2;4;6;8;10;12;14;3;6....

How can you do that? Your first attempt might be to find the pattern that represents the layout of these cells, so in cell I2 you enter =A2, in cell I3 you enter =B2, and so on through cell I8 where you enter =G2. Now you have the first row of the data, so you select I2:I8 and use the Fill Handle down a few rows to see if the pattern is picked up. You notice that cell I9 now contains =A9, I10 has =B9, and so on. No, that didn't do it—you want =A3, =B3, =C3, and so on, followed by =A4, =B4, and so on.

You're still stuck for the solution. Well, here's one fairly easy way to do it: In cell I2 enter xa2 (no "=" sign), in I3 enter xb2, and so on through cell I8 where you enter xg2. Now you can use the Fill Handle down to cell I120.

11

Note

An alternative to dragging the Fill Handle in long lists is to figure out the last cell (in this example we are using 7 columns × 17 rows, or 119 cells). Starting with I2, the last cell is then I120. You select I2:I120 by using the GoTo command and entering I2:I120, then use Edit, Fiil, Series and click on the AutoFill option button, and press OK. This is just like using the Fill Handle through cell I120 with all the first contiguous cells (I2:I8) selected. This makes cells I9:I15 contain xa3, xb3, ... xg3, then I16:I22 contains xa4, xb4, ... xg4, and so on. See cells I2:I18 (goes to I120) in figure 11.21.

Fig. 11.21

When the x's in column I are changed to =, the formulas reflect a single column list of the range A2:G18.

	A	B	C	D	E	F	G	H	I	J	K	L
1												
2	2	4	6	8	10	12	14		xa2			
3	3	6	9	12	15	18	21		xb2			
4	4	8	12	16	20	24	28		xc2			
5	5	10	15	20	25	30	35		xd2			
6	6	12	18	24	30	36	42		xe2			
7	7	14	21	28	35	42	49		xf2			
8	8	16	24	32	40	48	56		xg2			
9	9	18	27	36	45	54	63		xa3			
10	10	20	30	40	50	60	70		xb3			
11	11	22	33	44	55	66	77		xc3			
12	12	24	36	48	60	72	84		xd3			
13	13	26	39	52	65	78	91		xe3			
14	14	28	42	56	70	84	98		xf3			
15	15	30	45	60	75	90	105		xg3			
16	16	32	48	64	80	96	112		xa4			
17	17	34	51	68	85	102	119		xb4			
18	18	36	54	72	90	108	126		xc4			
19									xd4			
20									xe4			

Now use Edit, Replace and change *x* to = and you're done!

Using the letter *x* (any character would do that's not in the formulas, like *a* or *g* or *2*, except the equal sign) is a technique you can use to "fool" the Fill Handle's logic in filling formulas, then you can replace it with the equal sign to get the formulas you need.

Mastering the Paste Special Command

Suppose you have a worksheet that looks something like figure 11.22. How can you insert "Product 1," "Product 2," ... in the cell above each product?

Fig. 11.22

A worksheet into which you want to insert Product 1, Product 2 ... above each product.

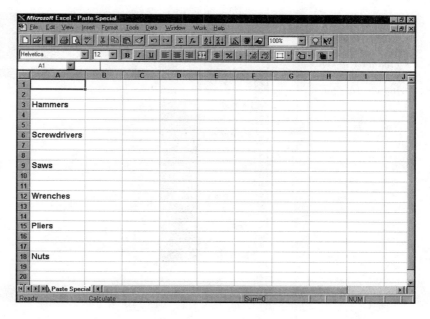

Now you want to insert "Product 1" in cell A2, "Product 2" in A5, and so on, through "Product 6" in cell A17. Granted, this is not too tough to enter into each cell, but suppose the list went through to row 2000 or so. By using the Fill Handle appropriately along with Paste Special, you can do the job.

First, enter Product 1 in cell B2, then select cells B2:B4, and use the Fill Handle down far enough to correspond to the row of the last item in column A.

 Note

If the range really went to cell B2000, you could still use the Fill Handle but it would take a lot of dragging to get the right cell. Using the Edit, Fill, Series, AutoFill command would also not work because it would fill *every* cell, not every third cell. You could fake it by entering a formula such as =1 or =NA() into cells B3 and B4, then use the AutoFill option button of the Series command. This would give you Product 1;1;1;Product 2;1;1;Product 3;1;1...and so on.) Then you could GoTo, Special, select the formulas and remove them via Edit, Clear.

Your worksheet now looks like figure 11.23.

Fig. 11.23

A step toward the desired result. Enter Product 1 in cell B2, select B2:B4, then use the Fill Handle.

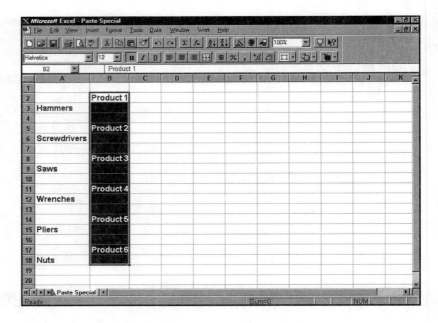

At this point, select B2 through B17 (or B18), and copy the cells. Then click cell A2 and issue the Edit, Paste Special command being sure to select the Skip Blanks check box. Now your worksheet looks like figure 11.24.

Fig. 11.24

By selecting Skip Blanks in the Paste Special dialog box, the original text in column A is untouched.

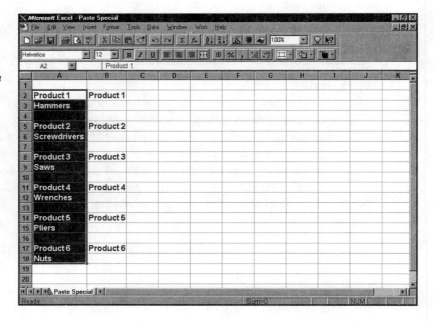

All that's left to do is clear column B.

A New Use for Relative Defined Names

Have you ever had to enter data in nonconsecutive columns, like in the columns indicated by the Xs in figure 11.25?

In figure 11.25, how can you easily get from column E to column J, and column M to column Z?

Fig. 11.25

Here the Xs represent the columns into which you want to enter data down this spreadsheet.

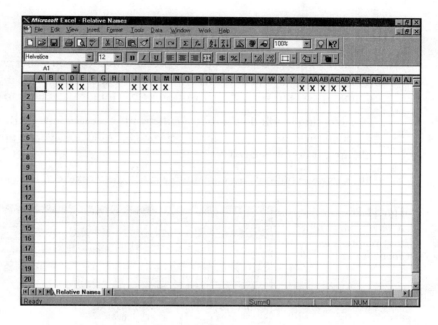

With a little trickery in defining names, you can do it quite easily. If you define a name, such as aa (use a simple name which will be easy to type or that will show up in the top of the GoTo dialog box and have it *relatively* reference the cells indicated), you should have no trouble. For example, *while the cursor is in row 1*, define a name to be

```
=$J1:$M1,$Z1:AD1,$C1:$E1
```

There are a few things to notice about this definition. All references to row 1 are relative (no $), and the area that you want to be selected *first,* must be defined *last.* That is, you might think you should define the name to be

```
=$C1:$E1,$J1:$M1,$Z1:AD1
```

11

with the $C1:$E1 coming first. But if you do that, when you issue the GoTo command and select the name aa (or whatever you called it), you will see cell Z1 selected.

After the name is defined, for each row you are entering data, you can issue the GoTo command and select aa, and the columns in the *active row* will be selected. That is, if you were in row 4 when you issued the GoTo command, you'd see C4:E4,J4:M4,Z4:AD4 selected with C4 as the active cell.

Double-Spacing a Range

If you're like most users, to double-space a worksheet you either write a procedure to do it or manually insert blank lines where you need to. This is fine if you have a few lines to double-space. But what if your worksheet has hundreds of lines to double-space?

One *very* simple solution is to make the worksheet *seem* like it's double-spaced: simply select all the rows and double the row height! As long as you're not printing gridlines, it'll appear double-spaced.

But suppose you must *actually* double-space the worksheet. Let's look at figure 11.26.

Fig. 11.26

A single-spaced range that you want to double-space.

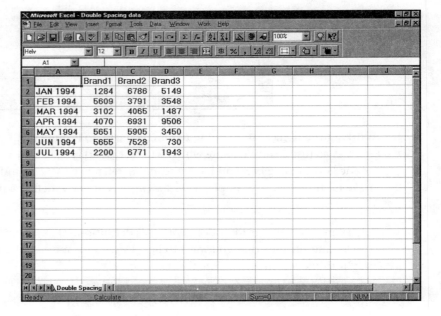

This is only a small worksheet, so the illustrations can be shown in one figure. The methodology works for very large worksheets. The procedure involves entering a series in a parallel range, like E1:E8. Enter the number 1 in cell E1, then you can select E1:F1 and double-click the Fill Handle.

 Note

If you selected only E1 and double-clicked, you'd get a list of 1s. By selecting E1:F1, Microsoft Excel will increment the value.

Now select E1:E8 and copy the cells, click in E9 and paste. Your worksheet now looks like figure 11.27.

Fig. 11.27

Preparing to double-space by entering a repeating series.

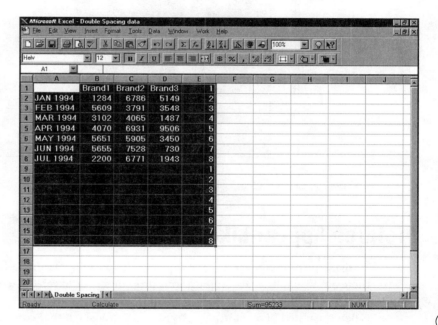

Notice you have two sets of 1 through 8. (To triple-space, repeat the paste starting in cell E17 and you'll have three sets of 1 through 8.) Select A1:E16. The quickest way to do this is click on any cell with information in it, then press Ctrl+*, the shortcut for selecting the current region, then either use Data, Sort and sort by column E (no header), or make a cell in column E active (start by selecting E1 and drag down and left to A16—this will make E1 the active cell) and click the sort tool.

Your worksheet now looks like figure 11.28.

Fig. 11.28

Sorting on the repeating series double-spaces the range.

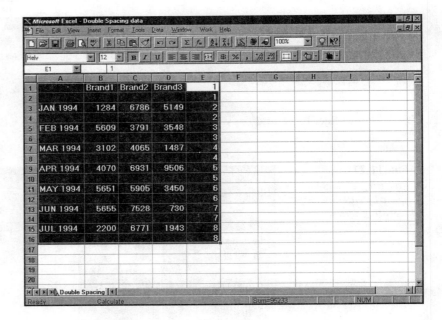

All there is to do is clear column E.

Pictures Appear Like Magic

To make pictures appear in your worksheet by typing text into a cell makes it seem like there are Visual Basic for Applications procedures (or Excel 4 macros) running in the background, but there are no macros or procedures of any kind needed to duplicate what is demonstrated here. Basically, envision a spreadsheet that contains part numbers, descriptions, etc. It's not difficult to set something up in which you enter a part number and the description shows up in the next cell. That's a simple matter of having LOOKUP formulas or MATCH formulas. But what about also having a *picture* of the part show up as you enter the part number? But first, look at an illustration (see fig. 11.29).

Fig. 11.29

Changing a pictorial display using a list box and without using any macros or VBA code.

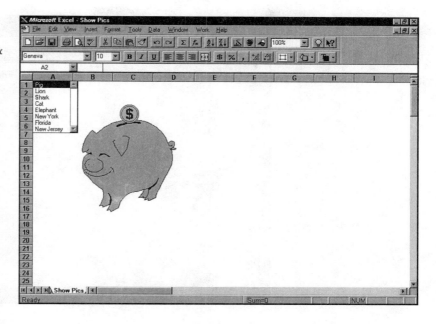

Here, simply by selecting an item from the list box, the picture of the item appears! Let's see in detail how this is accomplished. Rather than using potentially boring pictures of parts, you can see that pictures of a pig, lion, shark, cat, elephant, and three states: New York, Florida, and New Jersey were used.

First, all the pictures that *could* be shown were imported into the worksheet in column AA, each picture taking 20 rows and 9 columns, allowing for the maximum size picture used. Under *each* picture was the formula =NOW(). "Under" means in a cell that is covered by the picture. This step is important because when you change something on the worksheet, the =NOW function forces a recalculation, which changes the value of a defined name we will be using (and showing later).

Figure 11.30 shows a reduced snapshot of some of the pictures.

Then, using the camera tool, a picture of the pig was taken. Cells AA1:AJ19 were selected, and then the camera tool was clicked.

11

α **Note**

If the camera tool is not on your toolbar, you can get it by right-mouse clicking any tool, drag down to Customize, click the Utility menu, and then drag the fourth tool on the top row into your toolbar (or anywhere on the worksheet).

Fig. 11.30

*The stored pictures
kept out of view.*

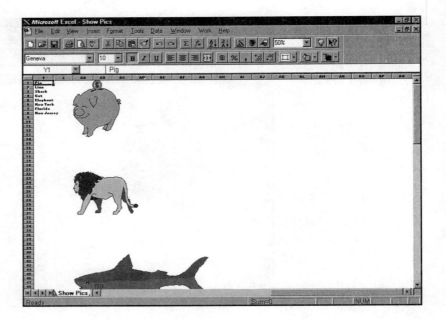

Now, go back to cell B4 and click, and you'll have the picture of the pig. This picture has a border, however, so you need to format the selected object, and select No border, No fill. To make this not always be the picture of the pig, you need to change the formula now showing in the formula bar. Replace the contents of the formula bar with =MyPic. The picture disappears because MyPic is not defined, so you have to define MyPic. It is

```
=OFFSET($AA$1,$A$1*20-20,0,19,10)
```

This formula means some offset from cell AA1, the column where all the pictures are stored. The last two parameters are the number of rows and columns, so MyPic is a 19×10 range. The $A$1*20–20 is how far down this offset starts. If A1 were 1, this would be 1*20–20, or 20–20, or 0. Then we are referring to

```
OFFSET($AA$1,0,0,19,10)
```

which is a 19×10 range starting from AA1. This is where the picture of the pig is. When A1 is 2, this is 2*20–20 or 40–20, or 20; this overlays the lion. When A1 is 3, this is 40, the shark, and so on. That is, when A1 is 1;2;3;4;5..., the calculation is 0;20;40;60;80....

This is why each picture needs to be 20 rows from the previous picture. Okay, how does cell A1 get its value? That's from the Cell Link of the list box which you see over A1:A8. Where does the list box get its values? From range Y1:Y8, shown in figure 11.31.

Fig. 11.31

The list of possible picks from the picture set.

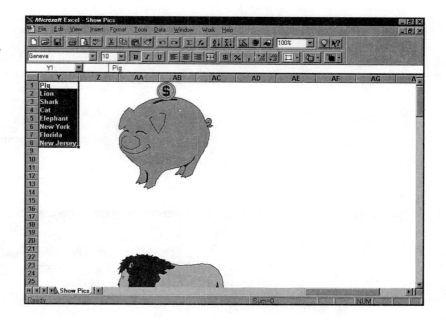

> α **Note**
>
> To enter a form onto a worksheet, use <u>V</u>iew, <u>T</u>oolbars, select the Forms Toolbar, click on the List box toolbar button, then drag the tool from the upper left of cell A1 to the lower right of A8 (in this example). After you draw it, while it's still selected, you can double-click it, and assign the input range to Y1:Y8 and the cell link to A1.

As you can see, this range contains the names of the pictures, in order, which are possible selections. Of course, you would normally replace these names with the part numbers, or part numbers and names, and so on, rather than pictures of pigs and sharks!

If you omit entering the formula =NOW() under each picture, then sometimes the pictures won't redraw when you choose a different item from the drop-down list.

Just click an item in the list and watch the picture appear.

You can have another item labeled "none" which is a picture of empty cells in column AA. But to have nothing show up while you enter =NOW() underneath the blank cells, you would have to format that =NOW() with ";;" (no quotes) so nothing shows in the cell.

11

Creating Test Data

Have you ever needed to test your worksheet and wanted some test data which was representative of your information? Here are some techniques which you can use.

Random Dates

A simple way to create test values of dates can be done by the formula

```
="1/1/95"+INT(RAND()*365)
```

Look at figure 11.32.

Fig. 11.32

Test dates created by the formula shown in cell B2.

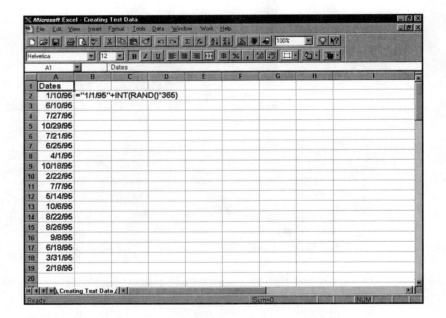

As you can see, the dates in column A represent a random range of dates from 1/1/95 through 12/31/95 (actually, in this small sample size, the dates range from 1/10/95 through 10/29/95). The formula gives a starting date as text, then adds a random number between 0 and 364.

Note

The RAND() function returns a random decimal between 0 and 1, but less than 1, then multiplying this by 365 gives a random number between 0 and 365, not including 365. The INT function removes the fractional part, giving random integers between 0 and 364. This is added to the text "1/1/95" which forces it to be calculated as a number.

After you fill cell A2 down as far as you'd like, you have your series.

After the values are in place, you can copy them and paste special values only in place.

Random Names

To create a list of random names you can enter the names in a list or directly in a formula, then use the RAND function again to pick from the list. For example, look at figure 11.33.

Fig. 11.33

Creating a random occurrence of names by using the formula shown in cell K2.

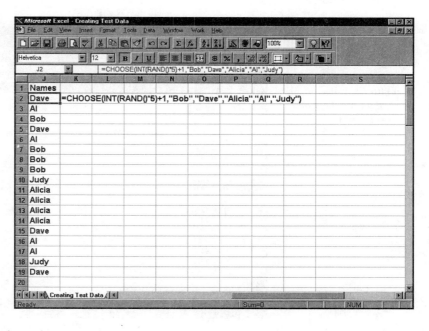

In this case, the formula

```
=CHOOSE(INT(RAND()*5)+1,"Bob","Dave","Alicia","Al","Judy")
```

does the trick for five names.

Note

The CHOOSE function picks an item from a list of items.
CHOOSE(3,A1,V3,D6,35.67,"Bob") returns the value from cell D6, the third in the list (not counting the "chooser"). The syntax is CHOOSE(INDEX,value1,value2,...).

Again, the RAND function returns a decimal less than 1, multiplied by 5 returns a decimal less than 5, giving this to the INT function returns an integer of 0, 1, 2, 3, or 4, adding 1 to it (because the CHOOSE function doesn't like a 0 as its first argument) gives random integers 1, 2, 3, 4, or 5, and then, depending on the value, picks an item from the list of names. =CHOOSE(3,{list}) will pick the third item from the list.

Numbers from 1 to 100 in a Random Sequence

Perhaps there have been times when you needed to create a list of values where the numbers don't repeat, like all the values between 1 and 100 but not in sequence (see fig. 11.34).

Fig. 11.34

Creating a random sequence of integers from 1 to 100 by using a parallel range of random numbers and sorting on it.

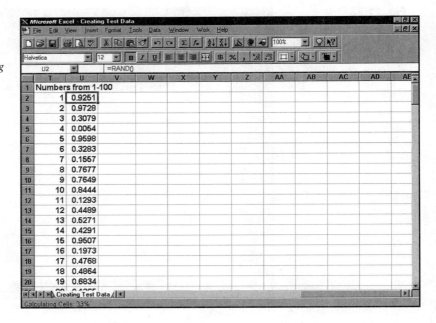

To create this random sequence in range T2:T101, do the following:

1. Enter 1 in cell T2.

2. Select T2:U101 (easiest by pressing T5 and then typing in T2:U101). Choose Edit, Fill, Series and select AutoFill, then press OK.

3. Select U2, and enter =RAND(). This places a random number in cell U2.

4. Double-click the Fill Handle in cell U2. This fills the formula =RAND() down through cell U101.

5. Select any cell in the range T2:U101, choose Data, Sort, and sort by column U (the column of random numbers). Column T is now randomly sorted as well.

6. Select all of column U, and choose Edit, Clear to remove this formula from the column.

Your worksheet now looks something like figure 11.35.

Fig. 11.35

The result of sorting the integers by the random number range.

	T	U	V	W	X	Y	Z	AA	AB	AC	AD	AE
1	Numbers from 1-100											
2		24										
3		8										
4		21										
5		97										
6		14										
7		20										
8		100										
9		73										
10		19										
11		25										
12		10										
13		45										
14		29										
15		71										
16		40										
17		83										
18		86										
19		35										
20		56										

11

As you can see, the values in column T are rearranged according to the random sort sequence in column U. If you have your calculation set to automatic, then column U will *not* appear to be sorted, but that's because the =RAND() was recalculated and new numbers were inserted. All that's left to do is to remove column U and you have your list.

Random Numbers within a Given Range

Don't forget that there's a function, RANDBETWEEN, which takes two arguments, a bottom number and a top number, and returns a random integer between the two values, inclusive. So, the function

```
=RANDBETWEEN(5,25)
```

returns a random integer between 5 and 25.

Using Data Filtering

Figure 11.36 shows a filtered list. The name was filtered on the occurrence of Bob, the date was filtered by clicking on the arrow in cell C1 and choosing Custom, then selecting dates which are greater than 6/1 AND less than 9/1, and the State was filtered to be NY only.

What you may not be aware of is that to copy the resulting filtered cells to another location (cells A22:E162), you don't need to first select the visible cells only, you can drag across the cells to copy (in this case you would see 121R×5C in the name box to the left of the formula bar as you dragged), click somewhere else on your worksheet at say, G1, and then paste, and you will only see the cells you see in figure 11.36, that is, a 4×5 cell range.

Tip
To select visible cells only, issue the GoTo command (or press F5), click the Special button, then select the Visible Cells Only option button and click OK.

Fig. 11.36

A filtered range is copyable by a simple Ctrl+drag (or Copy, Paste). The filtered (hidden) rows are not copied.

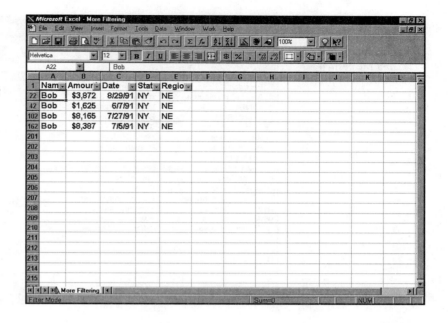

 Note

If you select cells B22:B162 in figure 11.36 and then create a chart, Microsoft Excel shows either 4 data points or 121 data points, depending on a setting in the Tools, Options, Chart tab: the Plot Visible Cells Only check box.

Rearranging Data in Cells for Sorting

If you've ever received (or created) a worksheet with a list of names where both the first and last name were in one cell and you needed to sort them, you know it isn't an easy task. For example, in figure 11.37, suppose you want to change the values in column A to be like those in column B so that you can sort them correctly.

Fig. 11.37

A worksheet showing a column of names in A, and the desired rearrangement in column B.

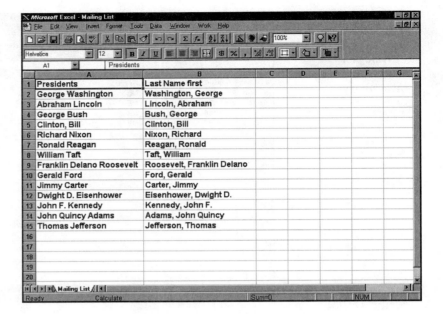

There are a few points to notice. First, notice that column B is last name, comma, then the rest. Also notice that some names in column A (such as A5 and A10) are already in the desired format. Not every name in column A is first name followed by last name. For example, cell A5 has "Clinton, Bill." Furthermore, some cells contain three names, like A9, and A12 through A14. You can see that column B contains the names ready for sorting.

In fact, this was all done by a formula in cell B2 which was filled down. This section takes apart the formula. Actually, you'll *build* the formula!

Because there may be some cells with a comma already in them, like cell A5, you need to assume that if a name has a comma in it, then it already is in the correct form. Therefore, the formula in cell B5 will have some form of:

```
=IF(ISERROR(SEARCH(",",A5)),…,A5)
```

 Note

The ISERROR function returns TRUE if the argument is any error (#N/A, #DIV/0!, #REF!, etc); otherwise, it returns FALSE.

Note
> The SEARCH function returns the position of a string within another string, or returns #VALUE if not found. For example, SEARCH("e", "abcdefg") returns 5, but SEARCH("ez", "abcdefg") returns #VALUE.

That is, the SEARCH(",",A5) is looking for a comma. If there is one, it will return a number, not an error, therefore

```
ISERROR(SEARCH…
```

will be FALSE. So, if it's FALSE, then you'll use the contents of cell A5 as is.

It's the "…" part (the TRUE part) of the formula which is not easy. First, let's look at the formula assuming there are always exactly two names, first and last. Therefore, there is only one space. You can look for the space and break the cell according to where the space is.

A space is found (from cell B2) by

```
=SEARCH(" ",A2)
```

Remember, you're assuming there is a space, so this does not produce an error condition. The =SEARCH(" ",A2) gives the position of the space. In this example, the space in A2 is found in position 7 ("George Washington").

Now you can take the eighth position (the space + 1) to the end, add a comma and a space, then take the first six positions (the space − 1) from the left. This piece is

```
=MID(A2,SEARCH(" ",A2)+1,255)&", "&LEFT(A2,SEARCH(" ",A2)-1)
```

 Note
> The "&" function attached whatever is to the left of it with whatever is to the right of it. For example, "Data" & "Manipulation" returns "DataManipulation."

 Note
> The LEFT function returns the leftmost n-characters in a string. For example, LEFT("ABCDE",2) returns "AB."

11

Translated, this is the middle of cell A2, starting with the position of the blank plus 1, to the end (the 255 means to the end) and ", " and the leftmost characters of A2 until the blank position less one.

If there were only two names in column A the completed formula is:

```
=IF(ISERROR(SEARCH(",",A2)), MID(A2,SEARCH(" ",A2)+1,255)&", "&LEFT(A2,SEARCH(" ",A2)-
➥1),A2)
```

But, there is a possibility of three names. How can we tell when that's the case? Well, there's a tip you can use to find how many specific characters there are in a cell, like how many blanks in the text. If there are two blanks, there must be three names, and that's what you can test for.

Examine this formula:

```
=LEN(A2)-LEN(SUBSTITUTE(A2," ", ""))
```

 Note

The SUBSTITUTE function substitutes certain text for other text. This is a *case-sensitive* function. The syntax is SUBSTITUTE(text,old text,new text,instance num). For example, SUBSTITUTE("Bob", "b", "n") returns "Bon." If the instance num is omitted, then *all* occurrences will be substituted.

The above formula returns the number of blanks in cell A2! How does it work? Notice that the SUBSTITUTE function is changing all occurrences of a space to a null (there's no space in the second pair of quotes, only in the first). So, if A2 contained "aaa bb ccc dddd," then LEN(A2) would be 15, the substitute of A2 of nulls for blanks would be "aaabbcccdddd," and the LEN of that is 12. When you subtract the 12 from the 15 you get the number of blanks.

You want to know if the count is 2, because with two blanks you have to use a different formula.

Use this formula:

```
MID(A2,SEARCH(" ",A2)+1,255)&", "&LEFT(A2,SEARCH(" ",A2)-1)
```

and instead of searching for a space in the cell (which would return the position of the *first* space) *mask* the first space by replacing it with a character that wouldn't be found in a name, like a CHAR(3). This is arbitrary—a backslash or any other character not found in names could be used.

Look at this formula and compare it with the one previously shown:

```
MID(A2,SEARCH(" ",SUBSTITUTE(A2," ",CHAR(3),1))+1,255) & ", "&LEFT(A2,SEARCH(" ",
➥SUBSTITUTE(A2, " ",CHAR(3),1))-1)
```

The only difference is that the search of a blank in cell A2 is replaced by a search of a blank in cell A2 with A2's first blank being changed to a CHAR(3). The fourth parameter of the SUBSTITUTE function, which is optional, specifies that you want to change only the *first* occurrence of the blank. So the function searches for the position of the blank in the cell with the first blank gone. This returns the position of the second blank, which is what you wanted.

The final formula is:

```
=IF(ISERROR(SEARCH(",",A2)),IF(LEN(A2)-LEN(SUBSTITUTE(A2," ",""))=2,MID(A2,SEARCH(" ",
➥SUBSTITUTE(A2," ",CHAR(3),1))+1,255)&", "&LEFT(A2,SEARCH(" ",SUBSTITUTE(A2," ",
➥CHAR(3),1))-1),MID(A2,SEARCH(" ",A2)+1,255)&", "&LEFT(A2,SEARCH(" ",A2)-1)),A2)
```

The following table breaks down the formula into easy to understand pieces.

Part of Formula	Meaning
IF(ISERROR(SEARCH(",",A2))	If there's not already a comma in the cell
IF(LEN(A2)-LEN(SUBSTITUTE (A2," ",""))=2	Then if there are three names in the cell (2 blanks)
MID(A2,SEARCH(" ", SUBSTITUTE(A2," ", CHAR(3),1))+1,255)& ", "&LEFT(A2,SEARCH(" ", SUBSTITUTE(A2," ",CHAR(3),1))-1)	Then change the first blank to CHAR(3), then find the position of the blank and use it to rearrange the names
MID(A2,SEARCH(" ",A2)+1,255)& ", "&LEFT(A2,SEARCH(" ",A2)-1))	Otherwise, find the position of the blank and use it to rearrange the names
A2	Otherwise, leave the cell alone

11

Another Look at Grand Totals

Suppose you have a worksheet like that shown in figure 11.38.

Fig. 11.38

Selecting blanks in preparation for using the Sum tool.

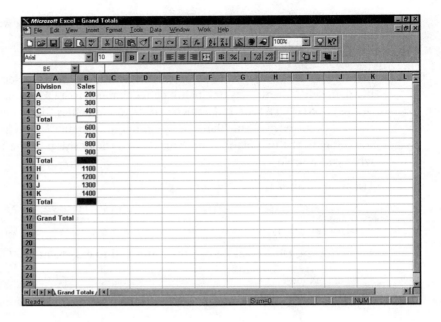

You may have already filled in the totals in cells B5, B10, and B15, but if you haven't, there's an easy way to do them simultaneously. If you drag across the range B1:B15, then press F5 to bring up the GoTo dialog box and press Special, you can select the Blanks option and you will have those cells selected (remember that in this example it's quite easy to select these directly, but suppose this worksheet went to cell B1000?).

Now, if you click on the sum tool, even though the ranges don't consist of the same number of cells, the correct formula is entered!

If you now select B1:B17 (or even A1:B17) and click the sum tool, the formula

```
=SUM(B15,B10,B5)
```

is entered into cell B17. You may have been afraid to use the sum tool here because of the notion that it would enter the formula =SUM(B2:B15) which would return incorrect results, but, as you can see, the sum tool is intelligent.

But suppose you wanted to simulate the functionality of the sum tool in a Visual Basic for Applications procedure? Duplicating the intelligence of the Sum tool would be quite difficult. Fortunately, there's another technique which you can use both in the worksheet or in your VBA procedure. If you enter

```
=SUM(B1:B15)/2
```

in cell B17, you would also get the correct result. Why is this? Because each "section" of data (such as B2:B4, or B6:B9) is totaled in the cell below, the section plus its total is twice the total! For example, B2:B4 adds to 900. The total in B5 is, therefore, reported as 900. If you add the cells to their total (B2:B5) you get 1,800, twice the total. Each section works like this, so

```
SUM(B1:B15)
```

is twice the total of the sections. Therefore, by dividing by 2, you have the answer you want.

This technique can be extended if there are subtotals, totals, and grand totals—the grand total would be

```
=SUM(range)/3
```

and so on.

Summary

In this chapter you learned new techniques for finding strings inside cells by varied uses of the MATCH formula, how to make and take advantage of Interior Series, how to take advantage of intermediate (unresolved) formulas, how to manipulate data by temporarily filling the blank cells in the surrounding area, how to use the F5 (GoTo) key in various new ways, such as using OFFSET and INDEX, new ways to format cells, Advanced Data Table techniques, how to manipulate dates, special formatting for desired spacing, new uses for the Fill Handle, new techniques for rearranging your data, new techniques for the Paste Special command, mastering relative referenced defined names, techniques for double-spacing your worksheet, how to have pictures appear when you enter text into a cell without using a macro, various ways to create test data for your spreadsheet, looking at data filtering, using formulas to manipulate data for sorting, and new techniques for producing grand totals.

Using these techniques will greatly enhance your mastery of Microsoft Excel.

chapter 12

More Formula Power

12

by Shane Devenshire

In this chapter

◆ **Warming up with basic formulas**
Common problems such as rounding can be simplified by employing seldom used functions or novel approaches.

◆ **A check writing application**
Constructing formulas to convert numbers to text provides the centerpoint for a check writing application.

◆ **Tracking rolling data**
Formulas that track rolling data automate the comparison of year-to-year figures.

◆ **Automating formula entry**
If the AutoSum toolbar button is useful, consider designing your own buttons to automatically enter other functions.

◆ **Summarizing data with arrays**
Array formulas can solve complex problems, increase flexibility, and reduce the need for criteria ranges.

F ew spreadsheet users take full advantage of the functionality built into Excel, and in the area of formulas and functions this cannot be overemphasized. This chapter looks at formulas that solve everyday problems. It begins with some simple function and formula solutions and moves to more complex situations. One thing to keep in mind—there are many acceptable solutions to a given task, although some may be better than others, if you get the correct result, that may be sufficient. Nevertheless, this chapter encourages the design of more efficient and elegant formulas.

Warming Up with a Few Basic Formulas

To start the creative juices flowing, this section addresses a few common concerns using approaches that introduce functions that are seldom used, or that use common functions in unusual ways. Understanding the functions introduced in simple problems will help your understanding later when the functions appear as components of more complex formulas. Three common spreadsheet problems—rounding, finding a specific value in a set, and saving memory are examined.

Improving and Extending the Rounding Process

Rounding is a very important part of the business process. Rounding, as compared with formatting, is often a problem that doesn't seem to have a simple solution. This section introduces some simple rounding techniques that can save time, improve accuracy, and shorten formulas.

The most widely used rounding function is ROUND(*number,digits*), which you can use to round 1.685 to 1.69 if the digits argument is set to 2. But not everybody is aware that you can round to the left of the decimal point as well as to the right, that is, the digits' argument can be positive or negative. For example, suppose you want to round the value in cell A1 to the nearest thousand, you would use ROUND(A1,–3). If cell A1 contained 123456.78, this function would return the value 123000. The digits argument of the ROUND function can range from about –10E308 to +10E308, a tad larger than most of us need.

Rounding Numbers Using ROUNDUP and ROUNDDOWN

Sometimes you don't want to employ typical rounding procedures. For example, if the cost of something from the wholesaler is $123.02, you may want to consider the cost to the next higher ten cents or $123.10. In other words you never round down, even if the value is only one penny over the nearest dime, instead you always round up to the next higher dime. The ROUNDDOWN and ROUNDUP functions accomplish these tasks. The syntax of these functions is =ROUNDUP(*number,digits*), where digits may be a positive or negative whole number. Figure 12.1 shows the results of these types of rounding.

Fig. 12.1

The results of rounding up or down to the nearest number of digits.

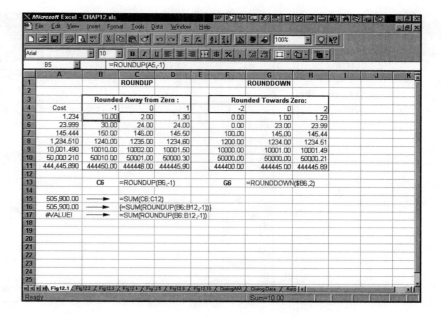

Rounding Numbers Using CEILING and FLOOR

You may find that your work requires you to round values in another nonstandard way. For example, you may need to round up or down to the nearest nickel, dime, or quarter. You could design a formula to do this, but Excel has the CEILING and FLOOR functions just for this purpose. The syntax for these functions are CEILING(*number,significance*) and FLOOR(*number,significance*). Figure 12.2 shows examples of the CEILING function. It also demonstrates the FLOOR function for rounding down in a manner analogous to the way the CEILING function rounds up.

While the ROUND function requires an integer for the digits argument, the CEILING and FLOOR functions do not, which allows you to round fractionally.

 Tip

Also consider using the EVEN or ODD functions to round up to the nearest even or odd integer.

Excel also contains an add-in function that is similar to FLOOR and CEILING, called MROUND(*number,significance*). This function rounds to the nearest multiple as ROUND would, but it also allows fractional significances as do FLOOR and CEILING.

12

Fig. 12.2

In this spreadsheet we have rounded sales figures up to the nearest nickel, dime, and quarter using the CEILING function.

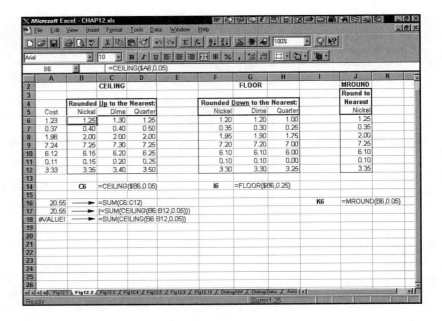

> ## Note
> MROUND is only available if you attach the Analysis ToolPak add-in by choosing Tools, Add-Ins, and checking Analysis ToolPak on the Add-Ins Available list.

> ## Note
> Consider the TRUNC function if you want to truncate a number to its integer portion, for example, TRUNC(–12.95) equals –12. You also can use INT to round down to the nearest integer, for example, INT(–12.95) equals –13.

Using Arrays for Rounding

Rounding is usually the first step leading to a final result. Often in that final result you want to sum a set of rounded numbers. One problem with all the rounding functions considered is that they seem to be designed to round one cell at a time. This means that if you want to sum a collection of rounded numbers, you need to enter one rounding function for each cell you want to round and then sum these rounded numbers. This wastes room and may even disrupt the structure of the spreadsheet. The solution is to replace all the rounding functions with a single array function. See Chapters 9, 10, and 11 for more discussions of array functions.

Suppose you want to round all the values in the range A1:A15 to zero decimal places and then sum the rounded numbers. Instead of entering 15 ROUND functions in cells B1:B15 and summing them, you can enter the formula =SUM(ROUND(A1:A15,0)), as an array, by holding down Shift+Ctrl when you press Enter. The resulting formula appears as {=SUM(ROUND(A1:A15,0))} on the formula bar.

You can employ an identical approach for the other four rounding functions presented in the previous section. For example, the formula to round each of the values in the range A1:A15 up to the nearest quarter and sum that result would read {=SUM(CEILING(A1:A15,.25))}. Examples using an array function approach with each of the four round functions are shown in figures 12.1 and 12.2. If you do not enter the formulas as arrays, you will get a #VALUE! error message, which is also demonstrated in both figures.

Tip

You can use EVEN, ODD, TRUNC, and INT within array formulas of the type {=SUM(FLOOR(A1:A15,.25))}.

Note

The MROUND add-in function is the only rounding function that cannot be incorporated into an array formula.

Determining Ending Balances

In many business situations the current ending balance of an account is needed, but because both debits and credits are concerned, a simple sum is not appropriate. This section demonstrates the use of a number of functions to find ending balances. The main purpose is to introduce functions with which you may not be familiar, within the framework of a real life problem. These solutions demonstrate that each problem may have many equally acceptable solutions.

Suppose you decide to create a check register in Excel such as the one shown in figure 12.3.

12

Fig. 12.3

The check register shown here demonstrates a number of possible solutions to the ending balance problem.

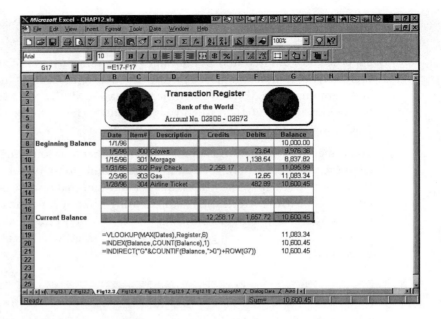

Follow these steps to set up the check register shown in figure 12.3:

1. Enter the labels you want for your check register. For example, enter **Date**, **Item**#, **Description**, **Credits**, **Debits**, and **Balance** in the cells across the top of your register, as is shown in cells B7:G7 of figure 12.3.

2. Add any desired formatting. For figure 12.3 the range B7:G17 was formatted by choosing Format, AutoFormat, and by choosing List1 in the Table Format list.

3. Add borders as desired.

4. If your check numbers will be sequential, you can enter a formula of the form **=IF(B10="","",C9+1)** in the Item# column and copy it down. In figure 12.3 this formula is entered in cell C10, and copied down to C16.

5. In the Balance column you can enter an array formula. Cell G9 contains the array formula **{=IF(AND(E9:F9=0),"",G8+E9-F9)}**, which is copied down to G16. The starting balance is entered on the first line of the balance column, here that is cell G7.

6. For convenience, you should consider naming the ranges containing the transaction dates, the ongoing balances, and the check register data. For the example, the ranges B8:G16, B8:B16 and G8:G16 were named Register, Dates, and Balances, respectively.

The array formula in cell G9 checks to see if both E9 and F9 are empty. The standard formula is =IF(AND(E9=0,F9=0,""),G8+E9-F9). The array was used here to illustrate one of its many uses, making formulas shorter.

Now the question arises of how to calculate the ending (current) balance shown in cell G17. One standard way is to total the debits and credits in cells E17 and F17, and then to subtract the results in cell G17, as shown in figure 12.3.

If you always keep your check register in date order, you could enter the following formula in cell G17 and leave cells E17 and F17 empty:

```
=VLOOKUP(MAX(Dates),Register,6)
```

This formula finds the row of the latest date entered, MAX(Dates), and looks this value up in the first column of the range Register. Then it returns the value in the sixth column in that range.

But, if you don't enter your checks in date order this method fails, as shown in cell G19.

See "Constructing a Text Conversion Formula," later in this chapter, for more uses of the VLOOKUP function.

An alternative formula that disregards the order of the entries is

```
=INDIRECT("G"&COUNTIF(Balance,">0")+ROW(G7))
```

This formula counts the number of non-zero rows in the Balance range, COUNTIF(Balance,">0"), and adds this to the row number of the top row of the register G7. The result is the row number of the last entry in the Balance column. This is then concatenated with the column letter G to produce the cell address of the latest balance, in the example, G13. The INDIRECT function returns the value located at that cell address. In other words, the formula resolves to =INDIRECT(G13).

A slightly shorter formula, which is also independent of the order of the entries, is

```
=INDEX(Balance,COUNT(Balance),1)
```

The syntax of this function is INDEX(*Range*,*Row*,*Column*). The COUNT function counts the number of cells in Balance that contain numbers. The INDEX function looks down the first column of Balance, the only column in this example, to the row calculated by COUNT and returns the value in that cell. In the present example, this would amount to =INDEX(G9:G16,6,1) or the sixth entry of the balance column.

12

Saving Memory When Using Linking Formulas

With Windows 95 comes the possibility of long file and directory names. This means that spreadsheet formulas linked to external spreadsheets may be quite long, especially if the file and directory names are long. The longer a formula is the more memory it takes, so if you have a lot of these linked formulas, you can use a lot of memory. So let's look at an alternative that may reduce this problem in some circumstances.

Suppose you have a spreadsheet that contains multiple links to other spreadsheets. For example, suppose you have 1,000 formula links of the type:

```
='[Customer Database.xls]Customer Information Database'!J4      [A]
```

This formula is 58 characters long. One thousand of these formulas, not an unusual number in today's spreadsheets, use about 50K. You can reduce this by more than 50 percent by using the INDIRECT function. To do this you would enter the text:

```
''[Customer Database.xls]Customer Information Database'!
```

in one cell, say E1, and replace formula [A] with the formula:

```
=INDIRECT(E1&CELL("address",J4))      [B]
```

Caution
The text entered in cell E1 must be preceded by two single quotation marks.

If you want a still shorter formula, you can do better by using:

```
=INDIRECT(E1&"J4")      [C]
```

To make these formulas more useful, the E1 reference should be absolute. Formula [B] lends itself to copying, while formula [C] does not because the J4 portion is quoted text. If you copy formula [C], it appears that you would have to manually modify each and every copy, which is certainly an unwelcome prospect. With a little ingenuity you can eliminate this tedious endeavor.

Suppose you want to create a set of references in cells A2:A202 that link to cells B2:B202 of an external spreadsheet such as the one shown in formula [A]. Follow these steps to create a collection of formulas using the INDIRECT function:

1. Enter "**[Customer Database.xls]Customer Information Database**'! in cell E1. Note the use of two single leading quotation marks.

2. Enter the formula **=INDIRECT($E1&B2)** in cell A2.

3. Copy this formula to the desired range, for example, cells A3:A202. All the formulas will return the #REF! error.

4. Now convert all the formulas to text. Select the range A2:A202 and choose Edit, Replace and enter **=** in the Find What box and **x=** in the Replace With box, and then choose Replace All.

5. With the same range selected choose Edit, Replace and enter **&** in the Find What box and **&"** in the Replace With box, and then choose Replace All.

6. Repeat step 5, but enter **)** in the Find What box and **)"** in the Replace With box, and then choose Replace All.

7. Convert the text back to formulas. Repeat step 5 but enter **x=** in the Find What box and **=** in the Replace With box.

While this multiple search and replace approach may seem unusual, it can be a real time-saver. (In fact, it is used later in this chapter in a macro.) The results of this process are shown in figure 12.4.

Fig. 12.4

When you employ the INDIRECT formula, you can reduce the length of formulas linked to external references. The longer the filename and sheet name, the greater the memory savings.

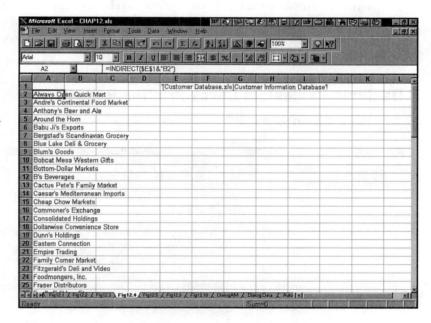

 Note

The INDIRECT function only works with open files, when you close the source file all the formulas return #REF! if the spreadsheet is allowed to recalculate.

12

This use of the INDIRECT function also can be employed between sheets in a single workbook, but will only be useful if the sheet names are quite long. For example, with a sheet name such as Projected 1998 - Budget Figures, you could reduce formula length by 50 percent.

Building a Check Writing Application

This section discusses more complex formulas. The first problem to solve is to automate a check writing process using Excel.

If you have ever considered using Excel to generate checks, you might have rejected the concept because you would have to enter the text for the amount of the check by hand. You might decide that if this step cannot be automated, the whole process might as well remain manual. But it is possible to have Excel convert the numerical check amounts to text via formulas. For example, if you write a check for $1234.56 you would want Excel to convert this to One Thousand Two Hundred and Thirty Four dollars and Fifty Six cents.

Designing a Custom Check Printing Range

Figure 12.5 shows a possible custom check you could design in Excel.

Fig. 12.5

The final check with data entered and the conversion formula in operation.

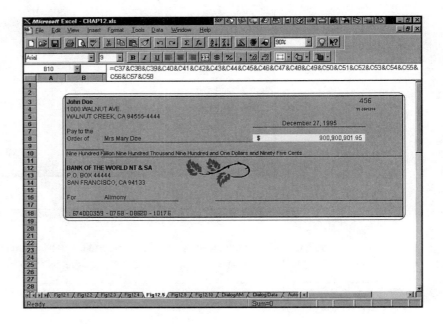

Follow these steps to create a custom check:

1. Enter labels as needed in the check range and add all necessary formatting. For figure 12.5, the customer's name and address are entered in B3:B5, **Pay to the** and **Order of** in cells B7:B8, the bank name and address in the range B12:B14, **For** in B16, the account number in B18, and check numbers in I4:I5.

2. Lines can be created by formatting the cells with bottom borders.

3. To create an automatic dating formula, enter the formula **=IF(G8>0,NOW(),"")** in cell G6, and format G6:I6 using the Center Across Columns button. Format G6 with the date format of your choice.

4. Add any graphical formatting you want. The leaf in figure 12.5 is a Microsoft ClipArt file. To add clip art choose Insert, Object, and choose Microsoft ClipArt Gallery from the Object Type list. After you bring the clip art in, you can choose Format, Object, select the Patterns tab and set the Border and Fill to None.

Constructing a Text Conversion Formula

Now you want to construct a formula that converts the amount entered in G8 into text to show on row 10. You can construct formulas that can deal with values between one cent and $999,999,999.99. This is no simple task. The best way to deal with a problem of this complexity is to break it into smaller pieces. To create the conversion formula follow these steps:

1. In a blank area of your spreadsheet enter the data as shown in table 12.1 and give the range a name such as T. All the items in the conversion text column of the table have a single space following the text, which is used to space the converted text within the final formula.

 Note

Table 12.1 shows the layout of one of the lookup ranges used by the conversion formula. In the following formulas this range has been named T.

Table 12.1   The Lookup Table Enteries for the Text Conversion Formula

Table Lookup Value	Conversion Text
0	
1	One
2	Two

12

continues

Table 12.1   Continued

Table Lookup Value	Conversion Text
3	Three
4	Four
5	Five
6	Six
7	Seven
8	Eight
9	Nine
10	Ten
11	Eleven
12	Twelve
13	Thirteen
14	Fourteen
15	Fifteen
16	Sixteen
17	Seventeen
18	Eighteen
19	Nineteen
20	Twenty
30	Thirty
40	Forty
50	Fifty
60	Sixty
70	Seventy
80	Eighty
90	Ninety

2. Enter the data shown in table 12.2 into the spreadsheet and name the cells in the second column with the names shown in the first column.

 Note

Table 12.2 shows five ranges that will be used within the conversion formulas to shorten the length of the formulas.

Table 12.2   Range Names for Cells Containing the Corresponding Text

Range Name	Text
H	Hundred
K	Thousand
M	Million
L	Dollar
S	Cent

3. Enter the formulas shown in table 12.3 into your spreadsheet. For this example the formulas are in the range C37:C58.

 Note

Table 12.3 shows the formulas for each of the parts of the text conversion calculation. The table is divided into sections—the top section handles numbers between 1 and 999 Million, the next section deals with the numeric portion between 1 and 999 Thousand, the third section converts the portion of an entry between 1 and 999 Dollars, and the last section works with the Cents portion of the number.

Table 12.3   Text Conversion Formulas and the Location

Cell	Text Conversion Formulas
C37	=VLOOKUP(N/10^8,T,2)
C38	=IF(N>=10^8,H,"")
C39	=IF(MOD(N,10^8)>=10^6,"and ","")
C40	=VLOOKUP(MOD(N,10^8)/10^6,T,2)
C41	=IF(MOD(N,10^8)>=2*10^7,VLOOKUP(MOD(N,10^7)/10^6,T,2),"")
C42	=IF(N/10^6>=1,M,"")
C43	=VLOOKUP(MOD(N,10^6)/10^5,T,2)
C44	=IF(MOD(N,10^6)>=10^5,H,"")
C45	=IF(MOD(N,10^5)>=10^3,"and ","")
C46	=VLOOKUP(MOD(N,10^5)/1000,T,2)

continues

12

Table 12.3   Continued

Cell	Text Conversion Formulas
C47	=IF(MOD(N,10^5)>=20000,VLOOKUP(MOD(N,10^4)/1000,T,2),"")
C48	=IF(MOD(N,10^6)>=1000,K,"")
C49	=VLOOKUP(MOD(N,1000)/100,T,2)
C50	=IF(MOD(N,1000)>=100,H,"")
C51	=IF(AND(MOD(N,100)>=1,N/100>=1),"and ","")
C52	=VLOOKUP(MOD(N,100),T,2)
C53	=IF(MOD(N,100)>20,VLOOKUP(MOD(N,10),T,2),"")
C54	=IF(N>=1,L,"")&IF(N>=2,"s","")&" "
C55	=IF(AND(N>=1,MOD(MOD(N,10),1)>0),"and ","")
C56	=VLOOKUP(ROUND(MOD(MOD(N,10),1)*100,1),T,2)
C57	=IF(ROUND(MOD(MOD(N,10),1),2)>0.2,VLOOKUP(ROUND(MOD(MOD(N,10),0.1),2)*100,T,2),"")
C58	=IF(MOD(MOD(N,10),1)>0,S,"")&IF(ROUND(MOD(MOD(N,10),1),2)>0.01,"s","")

4. In the text conversion cell, here B10, enter the following formula:

```
=C37&C38&C39&C40&C41&C42&C43&C44&C45&C46&C47&C48&C49&C50&
C51&C52&C53&C54&C55&C56&C57&C58
```

5. Name the cell containing the numerical amount of the check N. In the example, this is cell G8.

Let's examine some of these formulas. Let's start with the simplest.

```
=IF(N>=1,L,"")&IF(N>=2,"s","")&" ")
```

This formula checks to see if the amount of the check, N, is greater than or equal to one dollar and if so returns the word Dollar, the text in the range L. It concatenates this result with the letter *s* if the value N is greater than or equal to two dollars. Finally, it concatenates these results with a space that is needed if N contains any cents.

```
=VLOOKUP(MOD(N,100),T,2)
```

This formula, in cell C52, looks up any portion of N between 1 and 99 dollars. The MOD function does this by calculating the remainder after dividing N by 100. The VLOOKUP formula then looks in column 1 of the T table for the value returned by the MOD function, and returns the text equivalent in the second column. For example, the remainder after dividing $1234.56 by 100 is 34.56. For this value, the VLOOKUP function returns the text Thirty from the T table. If N does not have values between 1 and 99 the lookup function returns the first value in the T table, which is an empty cell.

```
=IF(MOD(N,100)>20,VLOOKUP(MOD(N,10),T,2),"")
```

The formula in cell C53 is checking to see if N contains values between 21 and 99 dollars. If it does, the VLOOKUP(MOD(N,10),T,2) portion finds the remainder after dividing N by 10 and looks this up in the T table. For example, if N is $1234.56, the first MOD(N,100) is equal to 34.56, which is greater than 20; therefore, the VLOOKUP formula is calculated. MOD(N,10) returns 4.56, which the VLOOKUP formula checks in the T table and returns the Four.

```
=IF(AND(MOD(N,100)>=1,N/100>=1),"and ","")
```

The formula in cell C51 returns and if N has a portion greater than or equal to 100 dollars and also a portion between 1 and 99 dollars. For example, if N is $1234.56 the MOD(N,100) returns 34.56, which is greater than one dollar. Also, N/100 is 12.3456, for twelve hundred dollars, which is greater than or equal to one hundred dollars. Therefore, this formula would return and.

The formulas for thousands and millions work in similar ways, however, it would be good to examine one.

```
=VLOOKUP(MOD(N,10^8)/10^6,T,2)
```

This is the formula in cell C39. 10^8 means 100,000,000 or a hundred million. Again the MOD function returns the remainder when dividing N by 10^8. For example, if N is 435,000,000.00, the result of this step would be 435,000,000/100,000,000 or 35,000,000.00. This value is divided by 10^6 or 1,000,000 to give 35. The VLOOKUP function then looks up 35 in the T table and returns Thirty.

 Tip

Use exponents to reduce the length of formulas if you feel comfortable with them; otherwise, write the values out in full.

Let's turn our attention to the formulas that deal with the cents portion of N. Consider the formula in cell C56:

```
=VLOOKUP(ROUND(MOD(MOD(N,10),1)*100,1),T,2)
```

Suppose the number is $12.34. For that value of N, MOD(N,10) returns 2.34. The outer MOD function then returns .34, the remainder after division by 1. The value .34 is then multiplied by 100 to give 34.00, which is then rounded. The rounded value is then looked up in the T table. The result in the this calculation is rounded because the MOD function returns an approximation of the remainder, which, if looked up in the T table, might return an incorrect result. Rounding to one or two decimals is satisfactory to deal with this problem.

Caution
For values greater than 134,217,727, MOD(N,1) returns the error #NUM!. The MOD function returns #NUM! at different values depending on the second argument. To work around the problem discussed in the caution above you can employ the trick demonstrated in the previous formula, that is taking the MOD of the result of a MOD.

The MOD function is an extremely useful function, as demonstrated by its repeated use in this section. If this function is new to you, try to use it enough to develop a good comfort level with it.

Now all you need to do to write a check is to enter the numeric amount and let Excel calculate the text equivalent. If you connect this range to a database that lists each check, its amount, and to whom it should be written, you can have Excel generate a series of checks for you. The next section, although dealing with a separate issue, will present an approach that could be employed here to automate the entire process.

Creating a Rolling Variances Report

In business, it is often necessary to calculate and compare variances for the current month's sales figures with profits, current-month current-year figures with current-month prior-year figures or the year-to-date numbers with the prior year's year-to-date figures. You can design a formula approach that solves all these calculations automatically each month as new data is added to your database.

This example assumes that your data areas include current and prior year's figures in a month-by-month format, and that you add data to the database as it comes in each month. You will not need to run a macro, rename ranges, modify the formulas each month, or make adjustments as you roll into a new year. In addition, this application will allow you to display these figures for each of your customers, departments, or products depending on what you are tracking. This example looks at sales and profits by customer.

Setting Up the Database Ranges

The first step in developing any kind of automated approach is planning. You should consider what your report area needs to look like, and how you will lay out the data storage area. Remember, the setup of the data area limits what methods you can exploit to automate the final report. The database area probably should not include any calculations, and should be as simple as possible. In other words you should minimize the complexity of the database storage area and leave the intricacies for the report areas. For example, you might create a different data area for each year's data, but it would be better to use one range that continues to grow from year to year. Of course if you don't intend to retain history, your approach may be slightly different.

For this demonstration, let's assume you track sales and profit numbers by customer and that you will retain history. Also, you will keep the sales, profits, and customer information on three separate sheets called Sales, Profits, and Accounts, respectively. To create the database warehouse follow these steps:

1. Set up the Sales sheet as shown in figure 12.6. Column A is the record number column. To create this column after you have entered the account numbers in column B, enter **1** in cell A5 and **2** in A6, select the two cells and double-click the fill handle. Enter your sales figures by period, extending to the right of the account number column as far as necessary. The months used as titles across the top of the database can be entered quickly using the fill handle.

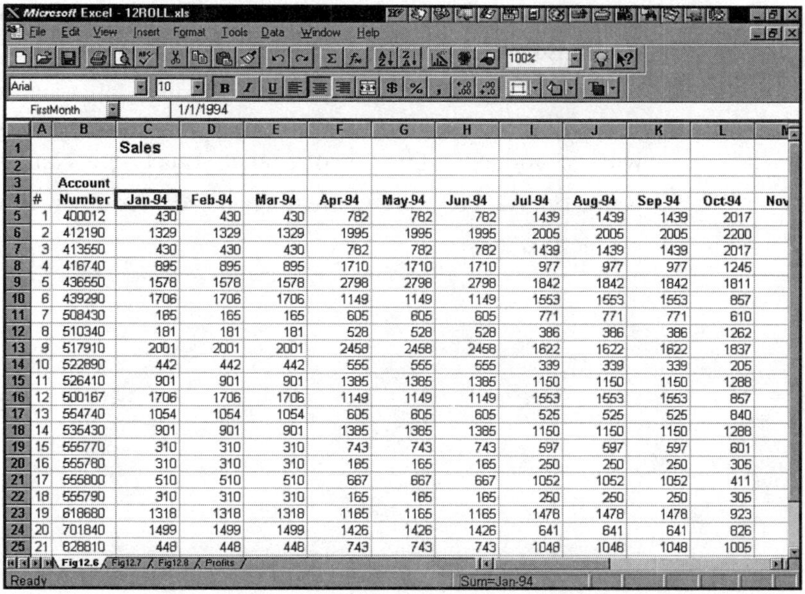

Microsoft Excel - 12ROLL.xls
File Edit View Insert Format Tools Data Window Help
100%
Arial
10
FirstMonth
1/1/1994
A B C D E F G H I J K L M
1 Sales
2
3 Account
4 # Number Jan-94 Feb-94 Mar-94 Apr-94 May-94 Jun-94 Jul-94 Aug-94 Sep-94 Oct-94 Nov
5 1 400012 430 430 430 782 782 782 1439 1439 1439 2017
6 2 412190 1329 1329 1329 1995 1995 1995 2005 2005 2005 2200
7 3 413550 430 430 430 782 782 782 1439 1439 1439 2017
8 4 416740 895 895 895 1710 1710 1710 977 977 977 1245
9 5 436550 1578 1578 1578 2798 2798 2798 1842 1842 1842 1811
10 6 439290 1706 1706 1706 1149 1149 1149 1553 1553 1553 857
11 7 508430 165 165 165 605 605 605 771 771 771 610
12 8 510340 181 181 181 528 528 528 386 386 386 1262
13 9 517910 2001 2001 2001 2458 2458 2458 1622 1622 1622 1837
14 10 522890 442 442 442 555 555 555 339 339 339 205
15 11 526410 901 901 901 1385 1385 1385 1150 1150 1150 1288
16 12 500167 1706 1706 1706 1149 1149 1149 1553 1553 1553 857
17 13 554740 1054 1054 1054 605 605 605 525 525 525 840
18 14 535430 901 901 901 1385 1385 1385 1150 1150 1150 1288
19 15 555770 310 310 310 743 743 743 597 597 597 601
20 16 555780 310 310 310 165 165 165 250 250 250 305
21 17 555800 510 510 510 667 667 667 1052 1052 1052 411
22 18 555790 310 310 310 165 165 165 250 250 250 305
23 19 618680 1318 1318 1318 1165 1165 1165 1478 1478 1478 923
24 20 701840 1499 1499 1499 1426 1426 1426 641 641 641 826
25 21 828810 448 448 448 743 743 743 1048 1048 1048 1005
Fig12.6 Fig12.7 Fig12.8 Profits
Ready
Sum=Jan-94

Fig. 12.6
The layout of the Sales sheet of the database warehouse area. The Profits sheet, discussed in steps 3 and 4, will be laid out with an identical structure.

12

2. Name the cell containing the first date title FirstMonth. In the example, that would be cell C4. Name the sales data Sales. In figure 12.6 this range name would begin at cell A5 and extend down as far as your accounts extend or beyond. It would extend as far to the right as you foresee a need. In other words, your Sales range needs to include all the data and can extend beyond the data, as far as you want, to allow for future data.

3. On a separate sheet called Profits, set up an area identical in structure to the sales area, for your profits data, as you did in step 1.

4. Repeat step 2, naming the profits range Profits.

Setting Up the Customer Accounts Range

Following good relational database design strategies, set up a separate sheet where you will keep customer-related information. One advantage to this approach is that you can easily bring data in from or send data out to a set of relational database tables. Mainframe data is often stored in relational database structures and therefore can be downloaded as separate files that match the structure of your spreadsheet.

To setup a customer accounts information sheet follow these steps:

1. Create a customer data area similar to the one shown in figure 12.7 and name the sheet Summary. If necessary, review step 1 under "Setting Up the Database Ranges." The account numbers are entered in column B, the account names, street addresses, city, state, zip code, country, and account opening date are entered in columns C:I.

2. Name the range starting at A5 and extending down and to the right, Accounts, as you named the ranges Profits and Sales. Also name the column C range beginning with C5 and extending down as far as you choose, Names.

3. Name cell A2, Pick, and name range B5:B50 (or down as far as you need) Nums.

Fig. 12.7

Here is the possible data layout for your customer information area. You might also choose to include other fields for Contact Name, Contact Phone, FAX, and E-Mail.

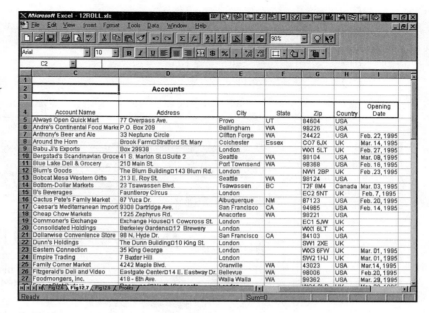

Designing the Report Area

After you have created the database areas you should design the report area. The design of the report area is dictated by the needs of you and your users, not by the database or the approach you will use to automate the process. Figure 12.8 shows a possible final report area.

To create the report area shown in figure 12.8 follow these steps:

1. On a blank sheet, enter the labels listed in table 12.4

Table 12.4   The Text Entries Needed To Add to the Summary Page

Cell Address	Text Entry
B6	Monthly Business Evaluation
B10	Customer ID
C10	Location
B13	Account Opening Date
B16	Current Month
F16	Year to Date
D17 and H17	% Variance

continues

12

Table 12.4   Continued

Cell Address	Text Entry
E19	Sales
E20	Profits
E21	% Profit/Sales

Fig. 12.8

Here is the completed report area including the dynamic formulas and a pick list.

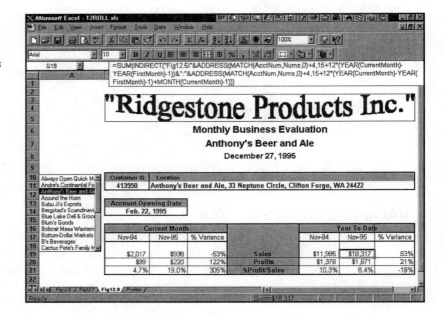

2. Add any custom formatting you want. For example, in figure 12.8 the following ranges have been formatted to center across columns: B6:H8, B13:C14, B16:D16, and F16:H16.

3. Now you need to enter the formulas to automate the report area. Use table 12.5 as a guide to enter the formulas in the indicated cells.

Table 12.5   Formulas that Automate the Report Area

Cell Address	Formula
B7	=VLOOKUP(Pick,Accounts,3,TRUE)
B8	=NOW()
B11	=VLOOKUP(Pick,Accounts,2,TRUE)

Cell Address	Formula
C11	=VLOOKUP(Pick,Accounts,3,TRUE)&", "&VLOOKUP(Pick,Accounts,4,TRUE)&", "&VLOOKUP(Pick,Accounts,5,TRUE)&", "&VLOOKUP(Pick,Accounts,6,TRUE)&" "&VLOOKUP(Pick,Accounts,7,TRUE)
B14	=IF(VLOOKUP(Pick,Accounts,4,TRUE)=0,"",VLOOKUP (Pick,Accounts,4,TRUE))
B17	=EDATE(CurrentMonth,-12)
C17	=EDATE(NOW(),-1)
F17	=B17
G17	=C17
B19	=VLOOKUP(Pick,Sales,2+MONTH(CurrentMonth)+12* (YEAR(CurrentMonth)-YEAR(FirstMonth)-1),TRUE)
C19	=VLOOKUP(Pick,Sales,12+2+MONTH(CurrentMonth)+ 12*(YEAR(CurrentMonth)-YEAR(FirstMonth)-1),TRUE)
D19	=IF(B19,(C19-B19)/B19,)
F19	=SUM(INDIRECT("Sales!"&ADDRESS(MATCH(AcctNum, Nums,0)+4,3+12*(YEAR(CurrentMonth)YEAR(FirstMonth) -1))&":"& ADDRESS(MATCH(AcctNum,Nums,0)+4,3+12*(YEAR (CurrentMonth)-YEAR(FirstMonth) 1)+MONTH(CurrentMonth)-1)))
G19	=SUM(INDIRECT("Sales!"&ADDRESS(MATCH(AcctNum, Nums,0)+4,15+12*(YEAR(CurrentMonth)- YEAR(FirstMonth)-1))&":"& ADDRESS(MATCH(AcctNum,Nums,0)+4,15+12*(YEAR(Curren tMonth)-YEAR(FirstMonth)- 1)+MONTH(CurrentMonth)-1)))
B20	=VLOOKUP(Pick,Profits,2+MONTH(CurrentMonth)+12* (YEAR(CurrentMonth)-YEAR(FirstMonth)-1),TRUE)
C20	=VLOOKUP(Pick,Profits,12+2+MONTH (CurrentMonth)+12*(YEAR(CurrentMonth)- YEAR(FirstMonth)-1),TRUE)

12

continues

Table 12.5 **Continued**

Cell Address	Formula
F20	=SUM(INDIRECT("Profits!"&ADDRESS (MATCH(AcctNum,Nums,0)+4,3+12*(YEAR(CurrentMonth)- YEAR(FirstMonth)1))&":"&ADDRESS(MATCH(AcctNum, Nums,0)+4,3+12*(YEAR(CurrentMonth)YEAR(FirstMonth)- 1)+MONTH(CurrentMonth)-1)))
G20	=SUM(INDIRECT("Profits!"&ADDRESS (MATCH(AcctNum,Nums,0)+4,15+12*(YEAR(CurrentMonth)- YEAR(FirstMonth)1))&":"&ADDRESS(MATCH(AcctNum, Nums,0)+4,15+12*(YEAR(CurrentMonth)- YEAR(FirstMonth)-1)+MONTH(CurrentMonth)-1)))
B21	=IF(B20+B19,B20/(B20+B19),)

4. Copy the formula in cell D19 to the cells D20:D21 and H19:H21. Also copy the formula in cell B21 to C21 and F21:G21.

5. Name the cells B11 and C17 AcctNum and CurrentMonth, respectively.

Now add the pick list onto the spreadsheet. To do this follow these steps:

1. Display the Forms toolbar by choosing View, Toolbars and check Forms on the Toolbars list.

2. Click the List Box tool and then drag a range of the size you want the list.

 Tip

If you hold the Alt key down as you drag, the list box will fit exactly within the selected cells. If you hold the Shift key down as you drag, the list box will be a perfect square. If you hold both the Shift and Alt keys down as you drag, the list box will form a perfect square that fits exactly within the selected cells.

3. To get the list box working, double-click it to display the Format Object dialog box.

4. Select the Control tab and in Input Range box enter the range name **Names**, and in the Cell Link box enter the range name **Pick**.

5. Close the dialog box and click off the list box control and you should be in business.

The list box allows you to see the report area for whichever customer you pick.

Now let's examine some of the formulas to see how they work. The formulas in B7 and B11 are standard VLOOKUP functions and were discussed earlier in this chapter. The NOW function in cells B8 and C17 return the computers current data and time.

The EDATE(*startdate,months*) function in B17 and C17 calculates the number of *months* before or after the *startdate*. This function is only found in the Analysis ToolPak - VBA add-in.

See the note earlier in this chapter in the section "Rounding Numbers Using CEILING and FLOOR," on how to attach an add-in.

The function in cell C11:

```
=VLOOKUP(Pick,Accounts,3,TRUE)&", "&VLOOKUP(Pick,Accounts,4,TRUE)&", "&
VLOOKUP(Pick,Accounts,5,TRUE)&", "&VLOOKUP(Pick,Accounts,6,TRUE)&" "&
VLOOKUP(Pick,Accounts,7,TRUE)
```

is just our old friend VLOOKUP concatenated many times with itself, spaces, and commas. Each VLOOKUP is returning parts of the addresses, which are located in a columns 3 through 7 of the Accounts range.

The formula:

```
=IF(VLOOKUP(Pick,Accounts,4,TRUE)=0,"",VLOOKUP(Pick,Accounts,4,TRUE))
```

in cell B14 demonstrates one way to check for and handle the situation where the VLOOKUP function finds no matching information in the lookup table. This formula checks to see if the desired information is missing, and if it is enters a blank, "" in B14, otherwise the second VLOOKUP function returns the account opening date.

The formula in cell D19:

```
=IF(B19,(C19-B19)/B19,)
```

and a similar one in B21 are simple IF functions that illustrate some unusual modifications. First, the formula demonstrates that if you want to test to see if a cell contains a value other than zero or blank, you don't need to use the test B19="" or B19=0, you can just test for B19. The result of this test is TRUE if B19 contains a value other than zero or blank. The second point that this formula illustrates is that you don't have to enter all arguments in the IF function. In the preceding case there is no argument after the comma following (C19–B19)/B19. The result is that the function returns a zero if the test is FALSE. To exclude the TRUE argument you could enter something of the form =IF(B19,,(C19-B19)/B19), in which case the formula would return a zero when the test was TRUE.

Now let's turn to the workhorse formulas for this application. The formula in cell B19 is

```
=VLOOKUP(Pick,Sales,2+MONTH(CurrentMonth)+12*(YEAR(CurrentMonth)-YEAR(FirstMonth)
-1),TRUE)
```

12

This formula is just our VLOOKUP friend again, but with a dynamic column argument: 2+MONTH(CurrentMonth)+12*(YEAR(CurrentMonth)–YEAR(FirstMonth)-1). The first thing to keep in mind while trying to interpret this formula is that the first month with sales figures in the Sales range is January 1994, which is in column 3. The first part of this formula 2+MONTH(CurrentMonth) returns the month number of the month we are interested in and adds that to 2. For example, for January it returns 2+1 or 3, which means that the VLOOKUP formula looks in the third column of the range Sales, which is in fact January data. Remember that you are trying to retrieve data for the prior year in cell B19, so you really want 1994 data when the current year is 1995, which is exactly what the formula does to this point. But this only works when the prior year is 1994. In 1996 the prior year will be 1995, and January 1995 data is in column 15, that is, it is 12 columns to the right of January 1994. The second portion of the formula: +12*(YEAR(CurrentMonth)–YEAR(FirstMonth)-1) handles this situation. This formula determines how many years have gone by since the first year of data and adds 12 months for each of those years. For example, suppose the current month is January 1996, then this portion of the formula becomes +12*(1996-1995) or +12. In that case the VLOOKUP function will look in column 3+12 or 15 to find the prior January's data. In January 1996, the prior January's data should be in column 15, which it is.

The same basic approach is used in the formulas in cells C19, B20, and C20.

The formulas in cells F19, G19, F20, and G20 also are similar to each other. In F19 the formula is

```
=SUM(INDIRECT("Sales!"&ADDRESS(MATCH(AcctNum,Nums,0)+4,3+12*
    (YEAR(CurrentMonth)YEAR(FirstMonth)-1))&":"&ADDRESS(MATCH(AcctNum,Nums,0)+4,3+12*
    (YEAR(CurrentMonth)-YEAR(FirstMonth)-1)+MONTH(CurrentMonth)-1)))
```

Here the problem is to sum a variable range, something that the VLOOKUP formula can't do because the *column* argument only allows digits not variables.

 Note

It is possible to get a single VLOOKUP function to lookup the values in more than one column, but the column argument cannot be a variable. For example, the array formula {=SUM(VLOOKUP(Pick,Sales,{3,4,5,6}))} will sum the values in columns 3 through 6 for the record that matches Pick.

To understand this formula you must take it apart. The ADDRESS(*rownumber,columnnumber*) returns an address in the A1 notation if you provide the row and column numbers. The *rownumber* is calculated using the following formula: MATCH(AcctNum,Nums,0)+4. The

MATCH(*lookupvalue,lookuparray,matchtype*) function looks up a value in an array and returns its relative location in that array. In the preceding formula, MATCH looks up AcctNum in the Nums column for the first exact match and returns the number of the row within that range on which the value is found. For example, if the AcctNum you are trying to match is on row 5 of the Nums array, it returns 5. It adds this value to 4, which is the number of rows above the top row of the Nums range.

> **Note**
> The way this formula is written assumes that the Nums range on the Accounts page is on the same rows as the account numbers on the Sales and Profits pages. If not, you will need to make some adjustments to the formula.

The second argument of the ADDRESS function, *columnnumber,* is identical in principle to the column argument of the VLOOKUP function just discussed. The end result of this portion of the formula is INDIRECT("Sales!"&ADDRESS(9,3)&":"&ADDRESS(9,15)) or INDIRECT(Sales!C9:O9). The values in this range are then summed.

With this you have a dynamic reporting range. As new data comes in each month, your figures update to reflect the changes. In addition you can click any customer name in the spreadsheet list box and see all the figures specifically for that customer. Thus your report range is doubly dynamic.

Creating AutoAnything Tools

Everybody loves the AutoSum button, but it seems a pity that the only function that can be input at the click of a button is SUM. If you use another function regularly, you may want to create a button to auto enter it in a manner analogous to the AutoSum procedure. The example in this section creates a button to AutoAverage, and by way of that example, introduces you to a method that can automate the entry of many of the functions Excel contains. This section looks at a method for creating a tool to allow you to auto enter any one of many functions via a single button.

Creating One Macro for One Auto Function

In this section, you create a VBA solution for automating some formula construction. The section addresses the creation of one button for one function. This method can be applied to many of Excel's functions, but not all of them.

12

Suppose you want to automatically enter averages for a range of data, such as that shown in figure 12.9, at the press of a toolbar button. Follow these steps to create an AutoAverage macro and button:

1. Choose Insert, Macro, Module.

2. Enter the following code:

```
Sub AutoAverage()
    SendKeys "%={Enter}"
    Application.OnTime Now, "Avg"
End Sub
Sub Avg()
    Cells.Replace What:="sum", Replacement:="average", LookAt _
        :=xlPart, SearchOrder:=xlByRows, MatchCase:=False
End Sub
```

3. Choose View, Toolbars, Customize and select Custom from the Categories list.

4. Drag any button to any toolbar and the Assign Macro dialog box will appear. From the Macro Name/Reference list, select AutoAverage and press OK.

Fig. 12.9

Averages can be entered for the selected range as easily as sums.

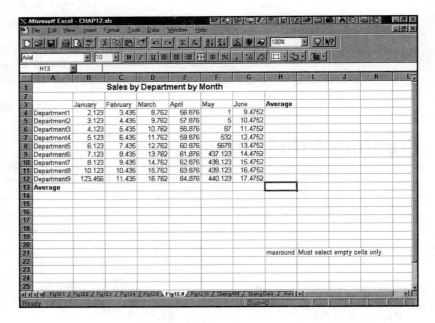

With the exception of the Replace command, none of this macro can be recorded. This is a short but elegant macro. How does it work? First the macro runs the AutoSum command. You cannot record this because the AutoSum command records a specific range, instead the SendKeys command executes the AutoSum keyboard shortcut of Alt+ =, and does not require a predefined range. At this point your spreadsheet contains SUMs where you want AVERAGEs. Then the macro ends and immediately runs the second macro. This is done using the Application.OnTime command with a delay of zero, NOW(). The second macro replacing SUMs with AVERAGEs. Why call a subroutine, that is, the second macro, rather than make it a single macro? Because SendKeys must complete its action before the Replace command acts, otherwise, Replace finds nothing to replace.

To make other AutoAnything buttons, all you need to do is modify the replace line. If you have more than one of these AutoAnything macros, each replace macro needs to have a different name. Also, the OnTime commands of each need to call a different Replace macro.

Most functions that have only one argument can be made into an AutoAnything macro, that means about 25 percent of Excel's functions. Some of the functions you might consider, depending on your line of work, are listed in the following table. To automate some of these functions would require more than just modifying the replace commands as you will see.

Function	Name	Text
ABS	ACOS	AVEDEV
BIN2DEC	CHAR	CODE
COUNT	COUNTA	COUNTBLANK
DATEVALUE	DAY	DEGREES
EVEN	EXP	FACT GEOMEAN
HARMEAN	HOUR	
INT	LEN	LN LOG10 LOWER
MIN		
MAX	MEDIAN	SQRT RADIANS
STDEV	VARP	

With some ingenuity, you can create Auto macros that can handle functions with more than one argument and even formulas with more than one function. For example, the ROUND function has two arguments but can be automated. The Visual Basic code to create an AutoRound function is shown here.

```
Sub AutoRounded()
    SendKeys "%={Enter}"
    Application.OnTime Now, "Rnd"
End Sub
Sub Rnd()
    Selection.Replace What:="=sum", Replacement:="x=round", LookAt _
        :=xlPart, SearchOrder:=xlByRows, MatchCase:=False
    Selection.Replace What:=")", Replacement:=",2)", LookAt:=xlPart, _
        SearchOrder:=xlByRows, MatchCase:=False
```

12

```
         Selection.Replace What:="x=", Replacement:="=", LookAt:=xlPart, _
             SearchOrder:=xlByRows, MatchCase:=False
     End Sub
```

Caution

This program is designed to round one number to two decimals. You must select the number you want to round and one empty cell before running the macro. You also can select a range of single numbers and a range of blank cells in which you want the rounded values placed. For example, in figure 12.10 you might want to round the number in the range A2:A16 to two decimals and put the results in B2:B16, therefore, you should select the range A2:B16 before running the macro. Or you can select just the range B2:B16 if there is only one row of values.

Fig. 12.10

You must select the appropriate range when using this function, for example, to round the figures in the range A2:A16 you should choose the range shown here.

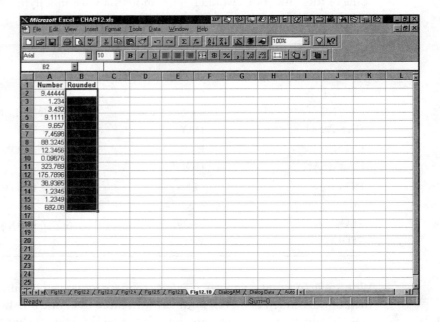

As mentioned, you can create multifunction Auto macros. For example, earlier in this chapter the array formula {=SUM(ROUND(*range,digits*))} was discussed for which you can create an Auto macro. The code for this is shown here.

```
     Sub AutoSumRounded()
         Set Here = Selection
         SendKeys "%={Enter}"
         Application.OnTime Now, "SR"
     End Sub
```

```
Sub SR()
    ActiveCell.Select
    Selection.Replace What:="=sum", Replacement:="x=Sum(round", LookAt _
        :=xlPart, SearchOrder:=xlByRows, MatchCase:=False
    Selection.Replace What:=")", Replacement:=",2))", LookAt:=xlPart, _
        SearchOrder:=xlByRows, MatchCase:=False
    Selection.Replace What:="x=", Replacement:="=", LookAt:=xlPart, _
        SearchOrder:=xlByRows, MatchCase:=False
    SendKeys "{F2}+^{Enter}", False
    Application.OnTime Now + TimeValue("00:00:01"), "CopyIt"
End Sub
Sub CopyIt()
    Selection.Copy
    Here.Select
    ActiveSheet.Paste
End Sub
```

> **Caution**
>
> To run this macro you must first select a single empty cell or a range of empty cells, but do not include the data. You cannot use this program in a manner identical to the AutoSum.

Designing One Auto Macro for Many Functions

To create the AutoMany macro follow these steps:

1. Enter the following code:

```
Sub AutoMany()
    DialogSheets("DialogAM").Show
This command displays the dialog box DialogAM.
    If Range("response1").Value = 1 Then
    AutoSumRounded
    ElseIf Range("response1").Value = 2 Then
```

The If and ElseIf commands determine which function the user has chosen from the dialog box, and then runs the appropriate subroutine.

```
    AutoAverage
    ElseIf Range("response1").Value = 3 Then
    AutoRound
    ElseIf Range("response1").Value = 4 Then
    AutoMax
    ElseIf Range("response1").Value = 5 Then
    AutoMin
    ElseIf Range("response1").Value = 6 Then
    AutoStdev
Else
    End If
End Sub
```

12

2. Add the following subroutines, so there is a number of Auto functions.

```
Sub AutoMax()
    SendKeys "%={Enter}"
    Application.OnTime Now, "Max"
End Sub
Sub Max()
    Cells.Replace What:="sum", Replacement:="max", LookAt _
        :=xlPart, SearchOrder:=xlByRows, MatchCase:=False
End Sub
```

 Note

This macro and the next two do not require any special considerations, they run in a manner identical to the AutoSum feature. That is, you can select any range you might choose for running AutoSum and run these macros.

```
Sub AutoMin()
    SendKeys "%={Enter}"
    Application.OnTime Now, "Min"
End Sub
Sub Min()
    Cells.Replace What:="sum", Replacement:="min", LookAt _
        :=xlPart, SearchOrder:=xlByRows, MatchCase:=False
End Sub

Sub AutoStdev()
    SendKeys "%={Enter}"
    Application.OnTime Now, "Stdev"
End Sub
Sub Stdev()
    Cells.Replace What:="sum", Replacement:="stdev", LookAt _
        :=xlPart, SearchOrder:=xlByRows, MatchCase:=False
End Sub
```

To run the AutoMany macro, select a range appropriate for the formula you want to enter and then choose Tools, Macro, select AutoMany from the Macro Name/Reference list and press Run. You will see the Auto Functions dialog box shown in figure 12.11, double-click your choice. Better yet, add a toolbar button to run this macro.

 Note

If you do not enter the subroutines in the same module as the calling routine and you assign a value to a variable in one module that will be used in another module, remember to declare the variable as Public.

Fig. 12.11

Here is a sample of what the AutoMany dialog box looks like if you choose to use the suggested functions.

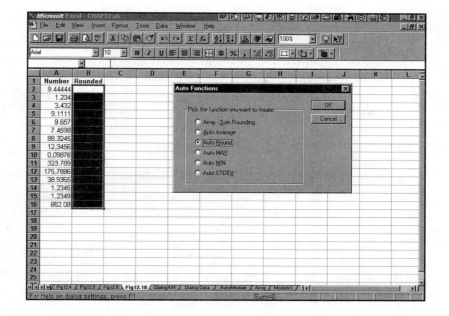

Using Array Formulas to Simplify Solutions

Array functions can often be used to find simple solutions to problems that would otherwise require quite complex solutions. This section examines a formula solution that demonstrates this concept. The situation can be approached with a large number of DSUM functions, each with its own criteria range, but an array formula leads to a simpler solution.

The Database and Report Areas

Suppose you have a database of all the books your company printed in the past five years. This database tracks the category of each book, whether it is hard cover or soft, which series it belongs to if any, and for each of these books you break out the cost by author fees, production costs, marketing cost, technical support cost, and any number of other categories. Now you want to roll up totals based on all of these breakouts. The entire process can be handled with a single formula!

12

A sample database is shown in figure 12.12.

You could use a DSUM function approach; however, you would need a different criteria for each breakout and you would need to modify each DSUM formula both for the column it summed and the criteria range it used. In the small database shown in figure 12.12, which has only two kinds of covers, four series, and five subjects with four cost breakouts, you would need 40 criteria ranges and 160 different DSUM formulas! Instead, you decide on an array formula approach which, with a few tricks, can be done with only one formula.

Fig. 12.12

Here is the data you want to analyze. Notice that each book falls into three subcategories and that expenses are broken down into four categories.

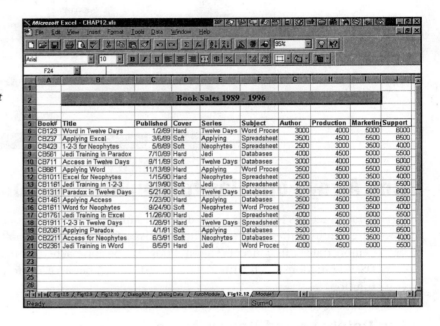

Suppose your database area is similar to the one shown in figure 12.12 and you want to produce a summary area similar to the one shown in figure 12.13.

Fig. 12.13

The layout of the final report area summarizes your data.

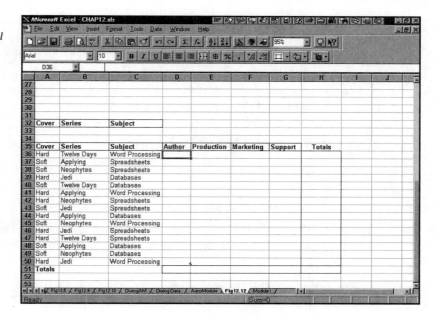

Creating the Basic Array Formula

Instead of approaching the development of this formula from the final product and dissecting it, the basic formula is introduced and developed in to the end result. Suppose you have worked to a point where the formula looks something like:

```
{=SUM($D6:$D21="Hard")*($E6:$E21="Applying")*($F6:$F21="Spreadsheets")*($G6:$G21))}
```

This formula multiplies four arrays, three of which produce arrays of True and False and one of which returns a collection of cost figures. The first three arrays evaluate to sets that look like:

```
{TRUE;FALSE;FALSE;TRUE;FALSE;TRUE;TRUE;FALSE;FALSE;TRUE;FALSE;TRUE;TRUE;FALSE;FALSE;TRUE}
```

and the fourth array evaluates to:

```
{3000;3500;2500;4000;3000;3500;2500;4000;3000;3500;2500;4000;3000;3500;2500;4000}
```

12

For each element in the arrays there is either something of the form TRUE*TRUE*TRUE*1000, which is equivalent to 1*1*1*1000 or 1000, or of the form TRUE*TRUE*FALSE*1000, which is equal to 1*1*0*1000 or 0. The only elements in the array formula that return non-zero values are those for which all three conditions are TRUE. Therefore, this array is summing a series of 0s and non-zero values, resulting in the total of all values that simultaneously meet the three criteria.

Making the Formula More Dynamic

The first step toward a dynamic formula is to replace ranges with names, and doing that the formula becomes:

    {=SUM(Cover="Hard")*(Series="Expert")*(Subject="Excel")*(Author))}

To name all the columns in the database range using the titles at the top of each column, select the range D5:J21 and choose Insert, Name, Create and check Top Row in the Create Names In list.

The problem with this formula is that it won't adjust if it is copied. If you had a listing of all the existing combinations of conditions in the columns to the left of our formulas, you could reference those cells in the formulas, thus allowing you to copy the formulas in the vertical direction. The current report area is set up in exactly that way. With the current report area you can modify the formula as follows:

    {=SUM(Cover=$A28)*(Series=$B28)*(Subject=$C28)*(Author))}

This formula can now be copied in the vertical direction and it automatically adjusts. However, the formula still cannot be copied to the right for each cost category. To add this level of flexibility, you need to make the last argument dynamic. To do this you can resort to your old friend the INDIRECT function. You already have column titles above each column of summary area that are the same as the range names of the columns in your data area. Because of this, you can modify our formula to read:

    {=SUM(Cover=$A28)*(Series=$B28)*(Subject=$C28)*INDIRECT(D$27))}

Now you have one formula that needs no adjustments and that can be copied over the entire range. After adding a Totals row and column the end result is shown in figure 12.14.

Fig. 12.14

The completed summary area. Note the array formula on the formula line.

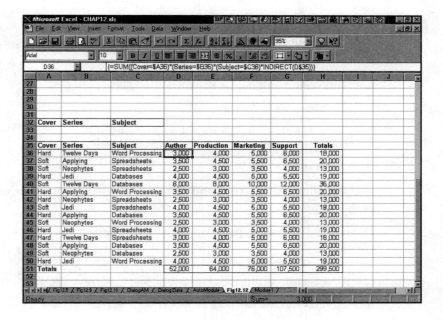

Automating Creation of the Report Area

Suppose you use this approach repeatedly but with ever-changing ranges, field titles, and combinations of categories. Because of this you decide to automate the entire process of producing the summary area. The code for this macro is shown here.

```
' Summary Macro
'
' Keyboard Shortcut: Ctrl+e
'
Dim ArrayRows As Integer
```

It is good programming practice to declare all variables. The Dim command declares the variable ArrayRows as an integer. It is not necessary to declare the data type of a variable, but if you know it, declare it. If you don't declare a variable's type, Excel will use the variant data type. Variant data types may slow down the execution of your code.

```
Sub Summary()
    Range("B6").Select
    Selection.CurrentRegion.Select
```

The Selection.CurrentRegion.Select is the VBA equivalent of the Edit, Go to, Special, Current Region command. This command selects all the data bounded by the edge of the spreadsheet or empty rows and columns.

12

```
Selection.CreateNames Top:=True
```

This command is the equivalent of the <u>I</u>nsert, <u>N</u>ame, <u>C</u>reate, <u>T</u>op Row command.

```
ActiveWorkbook.Names.Add Name:="SData", RefersToR1C1:=Selection
```

AddName command names the currently selected range SData.

```
Range("D5:J5").Select
Selection.Copy
ActiveCell.SpecialCells(xlLastCell).Select
ActiveCell.Offset(5, 0).Range("A1").Select
Selection.End(xlToLeft).Select
ActiveSheet.Paste
```

The preceding six lines copy and paste the titles at the top of the data area to the top row of the summary area.

The next eight lines prepare the output and criteria ranges for the AdvancedFilter copy command.

```
Range(ActiveCell, ActiveCell.Offset(0, 2)).Select
ActiveWorkbook.Names.Add Name:="SOut", RefersToR1C1:=Selection
Selection.Copy
ActiveCell.Offset(-3, 0).Range("A1").Select
ActiveSheet.Paste
Range(ActiveCell, ActiveCell.Offset(1, 2)).Select
ActiveWorkbook.Names.Add Name:="SCrit", RefersToR1C1:=Selection
Application.Goto Reference:="SData"
```

The AdvancedFilter command copies Cover, Series and Subject information from the SData range to the Sout range, but only for unique combinations of those three columns.

```
Range("SData").AdvancedFilter Action:=xlFilterCopy, CriteriaRange _
    :=Range("SCrit"), CopyToRange:=Range("Sout"), Unique:=True
Application.Goto Reference:="Sout"
TopArray = ActiveCell.Row
ActiveCell.Offset(1, 3).Range("A1").Select
```

The first array formula is entered, and then the formula is copied to the entire summary area.

```
Selection.FormulaArray = _
    "=SUM((Cover=RC1)*(Series=RC2)*(Subject=RC3)*INDIRECT(R" + TopArray + "C))"
Selection.Copy
Selection.CurrentRegion.Select
ArrayRows = Selection.Rows.Count - 1
Application.Goto Reference:="Sout"
ActiveCell.Offset(1, 3).Range("A1").Select
Range(ActiveCell, ActiveCell.Offset(ArrayRows - 1, 3)).Select
ActiveSheet.Paste
Application.Goto Reference:="Sout"
Selection.End(xlToRight).Select
ActiveCell.Offset(0, 1).Range("A1").Select
Application.CutCopyMode = False
```

A title is added for the Totals column, the formula to sum the first summary row is entered and then copied down for as many rows as needed.

```
ActiveCell.FormulaR1C1 = "Totals"
Selection.Font.Bold = True
ActiveCell.Offset(1, 0).Range("A1").Select
ActiveCell.FormulaR1C1 = "=SUM(RC[-4]:RC[-1])"
Selection.Copy
Range(ActiveCell, ActiveCell.Offset(ArrayRows - 1, 0)).Select
ActiveSheet.Paste
Selection.BorderAround Weight:=xlThin, ColorIndex:=xlAutomatic
Application.Goto Reference:="Sout"
```

A Totals row is added at the bottom of the summary. A title is added, the formula to sum the first summary column is entered and then copied to the right for as many columns as needed.

```
Selection.End(xlDown).Select
ActiveCell.Offset(1, 0).Range("A1").Select
ActiveCell.FormulaR1C1 = "Totals"
Selection.Font.Bold = True
ActiveCell.Offset(0, 3).Range("A1").Select
ActiveCell.FormulaR1C1 = "=SUM(R" & (ArrayRows + 1) & "C:R[-1]C)"
Selection.Copy
Range(ActiveCell, ActiveCell.Offset(0, 4)).Select
ActiveSheet.Paste
Selection.BorderAround Weight:=xlThin, ColorIndex:=xlAutomatic
End Sub
```

To get this macro to work as written, you have to have your data area set up as discussed earlier. Although some of this macro can be recorded, much must be written. Recording a macro is easy, but writing VBA is quite a challenge. Run the macro and then read through the code to see exactly how things have been managed.

Summary

In this chapter you have seen a number of ways to expand your use of formulas within the context of real-world situations. In addition, many of these formulas were integrated into the fabric of larger applications to provide a more global perspective of their use. Finally, VBA code was added to a number of these applications to illustrate the potential for automation and to help build your library of programming skills.

In other chapters you will see how to apply formulas in graphing and database situations.

12

Effective Data Access and Sharing

chapter 13

Automating Database Access

13

by Shane Devenshire

In this chapter

◆ **Warming up with some database tricks and techniques**
Common database problems such as inconsistent capitalization, unparsed data, and sorting can be solved easily with some simple techniques.

◆ **Querying databases using formulas**
Formula and functions can be used to return desired data to a report or display area. Such approaches can be enhanced with dynamic formulas and VBA.

◆ **Automating downloads of data from Microsoft Access**
Data stored in Access can be quickly and easily downloaded into Excel. Automating the process with VBA can simplify the process further.

◆ **Using Microsoft Query to perform multitable queries of Excel ranges.**
Microsoft Query is designed to query external databases, but it can query Excel spreadsheets to solve problems that cannot normally be addressed in Excel.

◆ **Downloading data from Mainframes**
By employing Visual Basic for Excel, mainframe data can be automatically downloaded, cleaned up, and reported on quickly and easily.

Anyone can collect and store large volumes of data, but the key to a database is data access. With modern technology, large volumes of data are everywhere. So, what you need to be able to do is to get to it, digest and analyze it, and then summarize your analysis in a succinct manner. Excel can assist you by automating many of the steps of this process, thereby freeing you to spend more time understanding the results and formulating actions to take based on those results. Certainly, accessing data should not be the most time consuming part of the process of data management. The primary purpose of this chapter is to introduce new techniques to help you in your use of database information.

The process of automating database access can be as simple as knowing how to use a spreadsheet function or as complex as an extensive macro. In this chapter you will be introduced to techniques that span the range from quick-and-easy to time consuming and intricate. Just because a technique is simple doesn't mean that it is well-known, so hopefully, even quick tips will prove new and useful.

A large part of this chapter also is dedicated to using VBA to solve database problems. Programming of complex problems usually requires quite a bit of labor, but once complete, pays big dividends. To understand VBA you need to work with it extensively. To that end, this chapter provides an extensive look at the code needed to generate a report based on information contained in fourteen separate files.

Warming Up with Some Useful Database Tricks and Techniques

To get you into the database frame of mind you will look at some spreadsheet techniques that can be quite useful in the database area. In particular, database cleanup, calculated criteria ranges, and database related functions will be covered.

Cleaning Up Your Excel Database

The old saying "Garbage in, garbage out" is nowhere more applicable than in databases. Unfortunately, databases are seldom clean. This section looks at solutions to two common database cleanup chores: consistent capitalization and compound fields.

Creating Consistent Capitalization

Although Excel is not case-sensitive, many programs are (Microsoft Query, for example). Furthermore, sometimes you want Excel to be case-sensitive, and even if you don't, you would like your data to at least maintain consistent capitalization.

For example, suppose various people had entered data into your spreadsheet and there was no consistent capitalization. See the Contact Name column in figure 13.1 for an example.

If you want to convert all the data in the range C2:H1000 to uppercase, lowercase, or proper case you can do it quickly. The PROPER function converts a text reference to proper case, that is, the first letter of each word is capitalized. To clean up a range of entries using this technique, follow these steps:

1. Suppose you want to clean up the range K2:P1000. In an empty area of your spreadsheet select a range of equal size (for example, Q2:V1000) type the formula **=proper(K2)** in cell Q2, and hold down the Ctrl key and then press Enter. This fills the entire range with the PROPER function.

2. With the entire formula area still selected, choose the Edit, Copy command and then select the first cell in your database that you are cleaning up, K2 in this example. Choose the Edit, Paste Special, Values command.

3. Finally, erase the range where the original formulas were placed.

To convert text to upper- or lowercase, use the UPPER and LOWER functions, respectively.

Fig. 13.1

The Contact Name column of this database is a real nightmare. You can clean this mess up quickly and easily.

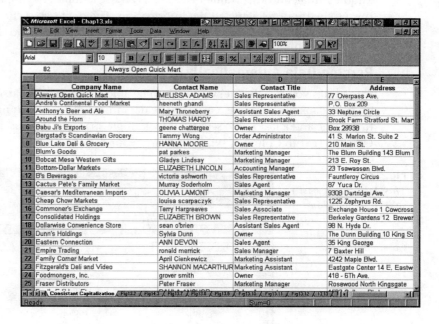

> ### α Note
>
> If you need to do case conversion using VBA you will find the following two functions available: LCase and UCase. There is not a PCase function; however, you can use the following command to convert text to proper case in VBA: Application.proper(x). For example, the following code converts the text in the current cell into proper case:
>
> ```
> ActiveCell.Value = Application.proper(ActiveCell.Value)
> ```

Breaking Database Fields into Their Smallest Logical Units

A second major problem with databases created by non-database people is that they combine fields that should have been separated. For example, they may choose to create a field called Name that contains the first, middle, and last name. Among other things, this makes sorting by last name difficult.

To rectify this situation it is best to break up the compound field into a number of separate fields, a process called *parsing*. In general, compound fields should be broken into their smallest logical units. For example, a name field might be broken into First Name, Middle Initial, and Last Name fields. You can use a number of approaches to accomplish this task without rekeying all the information. The next two sections, "Parsing Data Automatically" and "Using Formulas to Parse Fields," discuss two of those methods.

Parsing Data Automatically

Sometimes you may be lucky enough to be able to use Excel's parsing command to break up your data. For example, consider the data in figure 13.2; each name is composed of a first name and a last name separated by a single space. In this case, you can employ the Convert Text to Columns Wizard to parse your data.

Fig. 13.2

This data can be easily split into First Name and Last Name fields using Excel's Text to Columns Wizard.

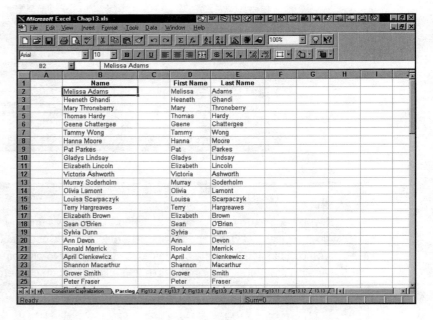

Data is delimited when a specific separator is used between the components of data. For example, the first name and last name may be in one column, but they are always separated by a space or a comma. The alternative is fixed-width data. With fixed-width data the first name would occupy a predetermined number of characters. For example, the first name data might always occupy the first fifteen characters of data, the last name the next fifteen, regardless of how long any given name actually is. To parse data follow these steps:

1. Select the data and then choose the <u>D</u>ata, T<u>e</u>xt to Columns command, which displays the first step of the Convert Text to Columns Wizard dialog box shown in figure 13.3.

Fig. 13.3

This is the first dialog box you see when using the <u>D</u>ata, Text to Columns command. It allows you to specify whether the data is delimited or fixed-width.

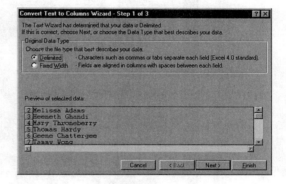

2. If the data is delimited, choose <u>D</u>elimited and the Next button to advance to the second step of the Wizard where you can specify the type(s) of delimiters in your data. Figure 13.4 shows the Step 2 dialog box after checking the <u>S</u>pace delimiter.

Fig. 13.4

Step 2 of 3 in the Convert Text to Columns Wizard lets you indicate what type(s) of delimiters are used with your data.

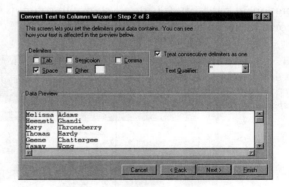

3. Choose Next to move to the final step of the Wizard, which allows you to indicate where you want the results placed, which column(s), if any, you want excluded, and what formats you want for each column. The result of this operation is shown in figure 13.5.

If you cannot use the <u>D</u>ata, T<u>e</u>xt to Columns command you may need to consider a formula approach to parsing data. The next section addresses the use of formulas to parse data.

13

Fig. 13.5

The Convert Text to Columns Wizard is the method of choice for parsing, provided the data is set up as delimited or fixed-width.

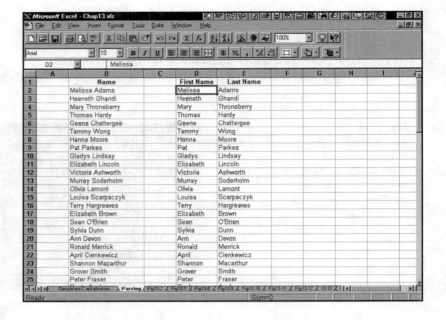

Using Formulas to Parse Fields

Suppose you want to parse the address data shown in column B of figure 13.6 into its component parts. These parts are shown in columns C:F. One formula approach is shown in the bottom half of the figure.

Fig. 13.6

Parsing a field into its components using a formula approach.

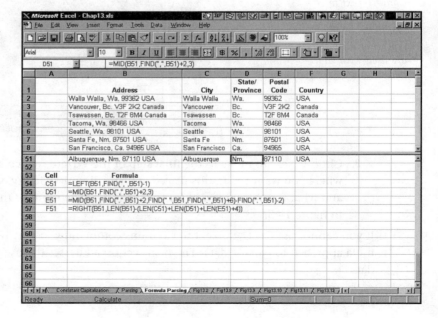

How do these formulas work? Notice that every city name is followed by a comma. So the first formula:

```
=LEFT(B51,FIND(",",B51)-1)
```

uses the FIND(*find_text,within_text,start_number*) function to locate the position of the comma after the city name. Note that the default *start_number* is 1, so if you want the FIND function to check from the beginning of the *within_text* you don't need to enter this argument. Suppose the comma is the twelfth character, then the LEFT(*string,characters*) function returns the first eleven characters, that is, the city name. Next notice that each state or province follows two spaces after the comma and is three characters long including the trailing period. So the formula to extract the state or province portion of the address is

```
=MID(B51,FIND(",",B51)+2,3)
```

which uses the FIND function to find the position of the comma. The function MID(*string,start_position,number_of_characters*) returns the three characters starting two characters after the comma, that is, the state or province abbreviation. To find the formula necessary to extract the postal code, notice that each postal code begins two spaces after a period, which can be found with the formula =FIND(".",B51)+2. Secondly, note that the postal codes are either five or seven characters long. Therefore, if you can find the end position of this code, you can calculate the length of the address field out to that point and subtract from it the length of the address field out to the beginning of the postal code. The difference in these two lengths is the number of characters in the postal code. Consider the address in cell B51. To find the blank space after the postal code, start searching six characters after the period; if you start earlier and the postal code has a space, as Canadian ones do, the formula will find the space in the middle of the postal code, not the one at the end. In the following formula:

```
=MID(B51,FIND(".",B51)+2,FIND(" ",B51,FIND(".",B51)+6)-FIND(".",B51)-2)
```

the FIND(".",B51,FIND(".",B51)+6) portion finds the end position of the postal code and FIND(".",B51) locates the position of the period. From the difference between these two positions subtract 2, which is the number of spaces occupied by the period and its following space. With this information the MID function returns the postal code. Notice that this formula could be simplified if all the postal codes had five digits, or more complicated if postal codes could be three sets of two digits each, separated by spaces, as in X2 R3 Q4.

To extract the country from the address, notice that if you subtract the length of all the previous elements from the length of the entire address, you can find the number of characters in the country portion. There are three spaces and a comma that must be counted. With this information, the formula:

```
=RIGHT(B51,LEN(B51)-(LEN(C51)+LEN(D51)+LEN(E51)+4))
```

13

returns the country by using the RIGHT(*string,number_of_charcters*) function. The formulas you employ depend on the structure of the field you are trying to parse. Sometimes the data may seem too complex to design a reasonable formula approach to parsing; however, if you attack the problem in a stepwise manner it may prove less intractable. For example, using the same data as in the previous example, you could employ six shorter formulas. To extract the city, you would employ the same type of formula as in the prior example: =LEFT(A51,FIND(",",A51),-1). The second formula, =RIGHT(A51,LEN(A51)-FIND(",",A51)-1), is used to return all of the address field minus the city portion. The third step is to pull the state portion of the address out of the result of the second formula, rather than deal with the entire address field. The formula to accomplish this is =LEFT(C51,3), a dramatic simplification over the formula used in the first method. The next step uses a formula that is structurally identical to the second formula of this approach: =RIGHT(C51,LEN(C51)-FIND(",",C51)-1). Because of this, the second formula can be copied. This formula returns everything from column C except the state. Next, the zip code is extracted from the result of the last formula with the formula =LEFT(E51,FIND(" ",E51,5). This formula searches for the first space in cell E51 beginning at the fifth position, and then returns all characters to the left of that position, which is the postal code. The last formula you need extracts the country from the results of the formula in column E, which contains the zip code and the country. The formula to accomplish this is =RIGHT(E51,LEN(E51)-LEN(F51)), which subtracts the number of characters in the postal code from the length of the postal code and country. With this number the RIGHT function can extract the country. Figure 13.7 shows the formulas and results of using this stepwise approach.

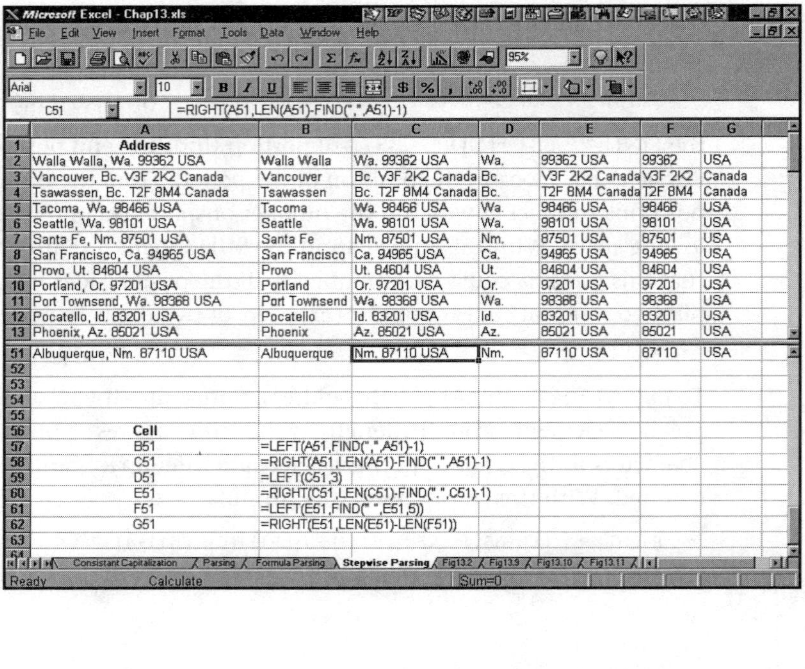

Fig. 13.7

A stepwise approach to parsing a complex field may employ simple formulas.

By attacking a problem in a stepwise fashion you can often reduce its complexity, although it may require more steps. When you have finished parsing the data with formulas you can convert all the formulas to values and then remove any unnecessary columns.

Using Calculated Criteria Ranges

Criteria ranges can enhance the scope of almost all database commands. To add more power to the criteria ranges you use, you should master calculated criteria ranges. This section gives five examples of this special type of criteria range.

There are a few basic points regarding calculated criteria that you should be aware of. Unlike all other criteria ranges, the title above a calculated criteria must *not* match any titles in your database. Second, the calculated cell should always refer to the first row of data below the titles in the database.

Excel's criteria ranges are not case-sensitive. This means that, if your criteria cell contains "mary," Excel will find not only "mary," but also "Mary" and "mAry," as well as all other case combinations of mary. Excel also would find "Mary Ann." With the following calculated criteria, both of these problems are solved:

    =EXACT(B2,"mary")

To make this formula dynamic, the second argument can refer to a cell. Figure 13.8 shows this criteria range in cells D1:D2, and cell E4 displays D2's criteria formula. Note that the second argument in the formula, =EXACT(B2,$E$2), is absolute.

Fig. 13.8

Here are some useful calculated criteria ranges. Each criteria range refers to cell B2, and if they reference any other cell, that reference is absolute.

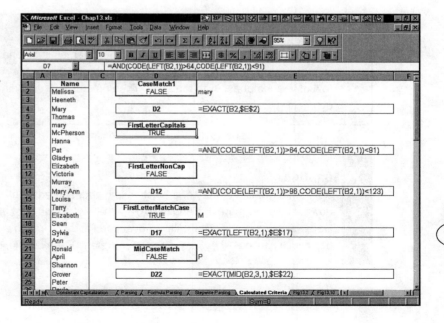

If you are interested in finding all items that begin with a capital letter, the next calculated criteria will accomplish that. The second calculated criteria in cell D7 is shown in E9 in figure 13.8.

```
=AND(CODE(LEFT(B2,1))>64,CODE(LEFT(B2,1))<91)
```

To understand this formula remember that all characters are represented by ASCII codes, and that the codes for A to Z run from 65 to 90. Hence, this formula checks to see if the first letter of each word is greater than 64 and less than 91—that is, if it is in the range 65 to 90. The next calculated criteria shown in the figure, cells D11:D12, finds each item whose first letter is lowercase:

```
=AND(CODE(LEFT(B2,1))>96,CODE(LEFT(B2,1))<123)
```

Sometimes you may want to find all items that begin with a certain first letter and you want the search to be case-sensitive only for that first letter. In that case, you can employ the following formula, which is shown in cells D16:D17 of figure 13.9:

```
=EXACT(LEFT(B2,1),$E$17)
```

Lastly, you might want to find all the items that have an exact match at a certain position. For example, you want to find all people whose last name has a capital P in the third position, such as McPherson. The calculated criteria shown in cells D21:D22 accomplishes that:

```
=EXACT(MID(B2,3,1),$E$22)
```

With calculated criteria you can find records that meet almost any conditions imaginable. These techniques will be helpful in the latter parts of this chapter.

Tip

Except for calculated criteria ranges, the field names in criteria ranges and output ranges must match the database field names. To ensure this, reference the title row of your database with formulas. Then not only will they match, but they will be dynamic.

Caution

Very seldom will the entry of a function into your spreadsheets bring your system down; however, there is a bug in Excel 7 that will do just that. If you use Excel 7's Data functions or the Data, Filter, Advanced Filter command with calculated criteria, do so with caution—they may crash your system. For example, if you use the DGET function with calculated criteria that use relative references, Excel will crash. To solve this problem, use absolute cell references in the calculated criteria.

Consider the example shown in figure 13.9. If you enter the function =DGET(A1:D11,4,F1:F2) into the spreadsheet and use a calculated criteria with relative references, such as =A2=MAX(A2:A11) shown in cell F5, Excel will crash. In all earlier versions of Excel you will have no problems. To use the D functions shown in figure 13.9 with calculated criteria, you should change the calculated criteria to absolute cell references. In figure 13.9, the correct calculated criteria in cell F2 is shown in cell F7:=A2=MAX($A$2:$A$11).

Fig. 13.9

If you enter any of the functions shown in cells F10:F22 or the Advanced Filter command using relative calculated criteria, Excel 7 will crash.

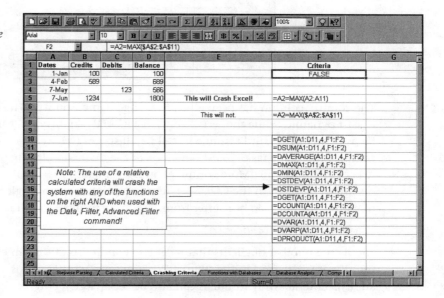

Applying Spreadsheet Functions to Database Tasks

When you are working with databases, don't forget the spreadsheet functions. Some of these functions are particularly useful when you're trying to analyze the data in a database. For example, suppose you want to know how many employees' Social Security numbers are missing from your database. You can use the COUNTBLANK(*range*) function to quickly answer this question. The closely related function COUNTIF(*range,condition*) can be useful for counting all the items in a range that meet a given condition. For example, suppose you want to know how many clients you have in each country. Figure 13.10 shows three formulas that could be used to calculate that information.

13

Fig. 13.10

If you want to count the number of clients in the USA, Canada, and Great Britain, you have a number of approaches available. Three approaches are shown here.

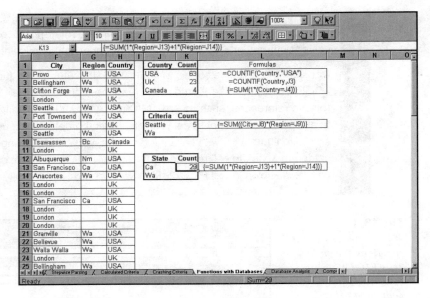

The country column has been given the range name Country. The first countif formula is least dynamic, while the second one, =COUNTIF(Country,J3), can be copied down as far as desired. The third formula in cell L4 illustrates the use of an array formula to accomplish the same task. You should look at the discussion in Chapters 7 and 12, "Using Array Formulas" and "More Formula Power," for additional uses of array formulas. The *condition* argument in the COUNTIF function is limited to a single criteria, a limitation that array formulas do not suffer from. The array formula in cell K8:

```
{=SUM((City=J8)*(Region=J9))}
```

counts the number of clients that meet two conditions at the same time—they live in the city of Seattle and in the state of Washington. In other words, this is what is called an AND criteria. Array formulas can also be set up as OR criteria. For example, the formula in cell K13 of figure 13.10

```
{=SUM(1*(Region=J13)+1*(Region=J14))}
```

counts all the clients in California or Washington. This calculation could be done using two COUNTIF functions. However, here it is employed to illustrate the process of creating an OR criteria. By combining the AND and OR array criteria approaches you can create complex search conditions, which would not be possible with the COUNTIF function. If COUNTIF is a useful function for your database work, you should also look at the SUMIF(*range,criteria,sum_range*) function.

Sometimes the solution to an apparently complicated problem can be unbelievably simple. Suppose you have a database listing the date of each sale and you want to know on what day the most sales occur. If the date of each sale is in a range named SalesDates, then the formula =MODE(MOD(SalesDates,7)) will return the number of the day of the week with the largest number of sales. Format the cell with the custom format dddd and you will have what you need. If the distribution is bimodal, that is, two days are tied with the greatest number of sales, then the first one in the SalesDates range will be returned.

You can take this one step further by totaling the sales for the day with the largest number of sales. One approach is to use the array formula:

```
{=SUM((MOD(SalesDates,7)=MODE(MOD(SalesDates,7)))*Sales)}
```

This formula assumes that the sales figures are located in a range named Sales. Both of these formulas are displayed in figure 13.11.

Fig. 13.11

By using the MOD and MODE functions you can determine the most frequent date in a range of dates and the total sales for that day of the week.

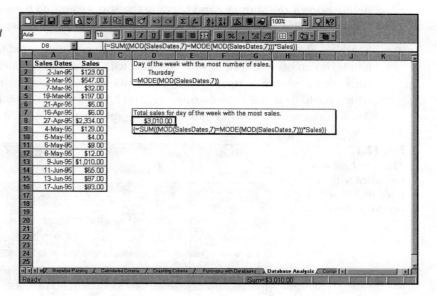

Simple Shortcuts to Increased Productivity

Sometimes simple tricks save more time than sophisticated techniques. To wrap up this warm-up section, consider the following simple techniques to save you time when working with Excel databases.

You do not need to use the Data, Sort command for multilevel sorts. Instead, you can use the Sort Ascending and Sort Descending buttons to perform these types of sorts. Start by sorting on the least important field first and working towards the most important. For example, if you want to sort by last name, and then first name, place the cursor in the First name column and hit the Sort Ascending button, then place the cursor in the Last name column and repeat the sort.

13

You can use the Sort Ascending and Sort Descending buttons even when you need to highlight the sort range. After you select the sort range, use the Tab or Shift+Tab keys to move the cursor to the column you want to sort on and click the appropriate sort button.

If you add more tools to your toolbars you can improve the access to Excel's features. For example, Excel has a button for applying an AutoFilter based on the contents of the currently selected cell. This tool is not on any toolbar, but you could add it. Suppose you do not have any extra space on your toolbars, and you need to remove something that you find useful. One solution is to remove redundant tools. To save space on the Standard toolbar, remove the Sort Descending button. You can still do descending sorts by holding down the Shift key and pressing the Sort Ascending button. Excel has many dual function toolbar buttons, all of which work by using the Shift key with the button.

There are also timesaving formatting techniques you might want to consider. For example, if you need to format your database with alternating shaded and non-shaded rows such as shown in figure 13.12, you could manually format the entire database, which could be rather time-consuming. An alternative solution is to choose the Format, AutoFormat command, and pick the List 1 Table Format.

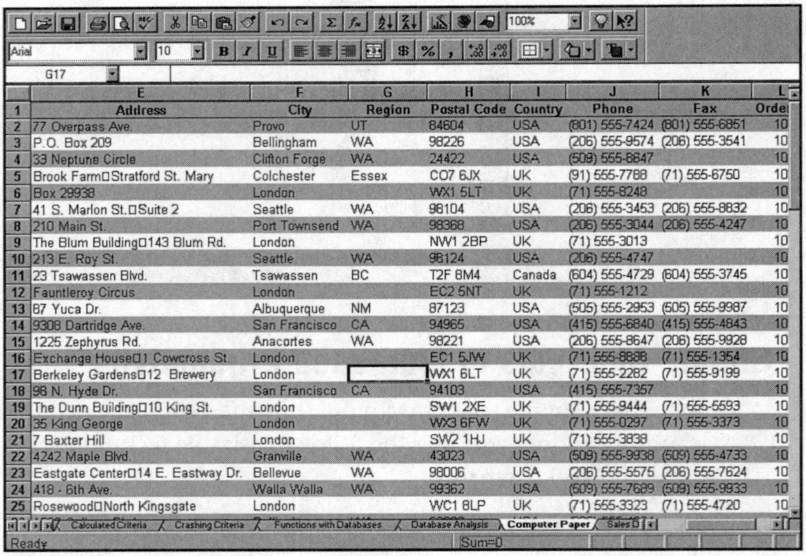

Fig. 13.12
This database was formatted with one command to look like computer paper.

Each of the preceding techniques is a simple solution to speed up your database work. Mastering the simple shortcuts often saves you as much time as advanced techniques. The following sections move beyond the quick solutions and introduce you to sophisticated techniques for solving complex problems.

Automating Excel Database Queries with Formulas

Although you can write code or use various Data commands to retrieve data from an Excel database, you can also design an automated formula approach to accomplish the same task even in complex situations. This section develops a formula-based Excel application for bringing data to a predesigned output range using the database functions. What makes this approach unique is the complex nature of the criteria.

Examining the Database Layout

Your database contains sales figures by year for your company and many other companies. These figures are broken down into five different groupings, which you will want to query on. A sample database is shown in figure 13.13.

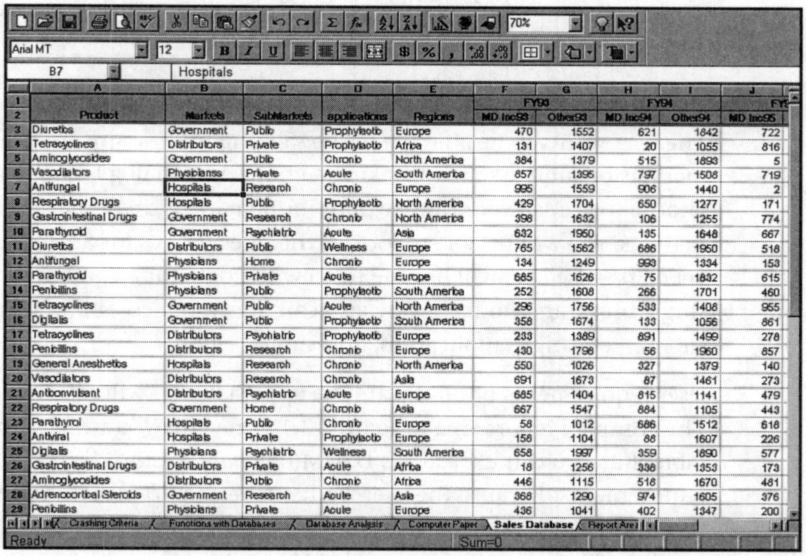

	A	B	C	D	E	F	G	H	I	J
1						FY93		FY94		FY
2	Product	Markets	SubMarkets	applications	Regions	MD Inc93	Other93	MD Inc94	Other94	MD Inc95
3	Diuretics	Government	Public	Prophylactic	Europe	470	1552	621	1842	722
4	Tetracyclines	Distributors	Private	Prophylactic	Africa	131	1407	20	1055	816
5	Aminoglycosides	Government	Public	Chronic	North America	384	1379	515	1893	5
6	Vasodilators	Physicianss	Private	Acute	South America	857	1395	797	1508	719
7	Antifungal	Hospitals	Research	Chronic	Europe	995	1559	906	1440	2
8	Respiratory Drugs	Hospitals	Public	Prophylactic	North America	429	1704	650	1277	171
9	Gastrointestinal Drugs	Government	Research	Chronic	North America	398	1632	106	1255	774
10	Parathyroid	Government	Psychiatric	Acute	Asia	632	1950	135	1648	667
11	Diuretics	Distributors	Public	Wellness	Europe	765	1562	686	1950	518
12	Antifungal	Physicians	Home	Chronic	Europe	134	1249	993	1334	153
13	Parathyroid	Physicians	Private	Acute	Europe	685	1626	75	1832	615
14	Penicillins	Physicians	Public	Prophylactic	South America	252	1608	266	1701	460
15	Tetracyclines	Government	Public	Acute	North America	296	1756	533	1408	955
16	Digitalis	Government	Public	Prophylactic	South America	358	1674	133	1056	861
17	Tetracyclines	Distributors	Psychiatric	Prophylactic	Europe	233	1389	891	1499	278
18	Penicillins	Distributors	Research	Chronic	Europe	430	1798	56	1960	857
19	General Anesthetics	Hospitals	Research	Chronic	North America	550	1026	327	1379	140
20	Vasodilators	Distributors	Research	Chronic	Asia	691	1673	87	1461	273
21	Anticonvulsant	Distributors	Psychiatric	Acute	Europe	685	1404	815	1141	479
22	Respiratory Drugs	Government	Home	Chronic	Asia	667	1547	884	1105	443
23	Parathyroi	Hospitals	Public	Chronic	Europe	58	1012	686	1512	618
24	Antiviral	Hospitals	Private	Prophylactic	Europe	158	1104	88	1607	226
25	Digitalis	Physicians	Psychiatric	Wellness	South America	658	1997	359	1890	577
26	Gastrointestinal Drugs	Distributors	Private	Acute	Africa	18	1256	338	1353	173
27	Aminoglycosides	Distributors	Public	Chronic	Africa	446	1115	518	1670	481
28	Adrenocortical Steroids	Government	Research	Acute	Asia	368	1290	974	1605	376
29	Penicillins	Physicians	Private	Acute	Europe	436	1041	402	1347	200

Fig. 13.13
Here is a sample database that tracks sales figures by year and by many other levels of breakout.

Constructing the Database Formulas

Many users want to display the data as shown in figure 13.14. Each product line is on the left with subtotals for each major product group with a grand total at the bottom. Horizontally, the data is shown by year, with your company's figures, the numbers for the entire market, and the figures as a percent of the total market.

Fig. 13.14

Here is the report area that will be designed to display only the data the user requests. Notice the formula for cell B10, which is showing on the edit line.

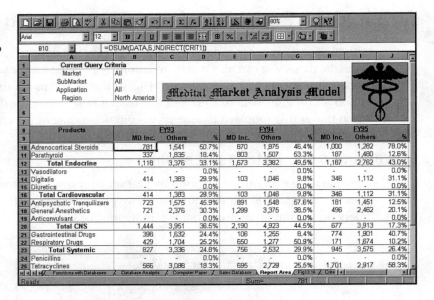

The user wants to be able to see the sales figures for any application, region, or set of markets or submarkets by making a choice in a dialog box. This means that she may choose to see sales for one, two, or more markets at a time. Therefore, if you have ten markets, she will be able to look at the sales figures for any combinations of those markets. Likewise, she will be able to view the date for a combination of regions or any other single breakout you have. She also can query any combinations of a single market, single submarket, single application, and single region.

User requirements often dictate the approach you will take in creating an application. The complex report area in figure 13.14 prevents you from employing a simple pivot table. But you can use Excel's DSUM(*database,column,criteria*) function to meet the user's requirements. Because the user wants to be able to pick more than one item from a particular breakout, the criteria range must be variable. For example, the user may choose to see the sales figures for Europe and North America, which means that there must be two rows below the titles in the criteria range to accommodate an OR criteria.

The formula in cell B10 is

```
=DSUM(DATA,6,INDIRECT(CRIT1))
```

This formula assumes that you have named the database in figure 13.13 DATA and that there is a cell named CRIT1 that contains a reference to a criteria range. This criteria range is examined shortly, but first look at the subtotal and grand total lines. On the edit line in figure 13.15 you see that the formula used for the grand total on line 31 is the SUBTOTAL(*function_number,range*) function. All the subtotal rows (12, 16, 20, 23, and 29) also use this function. This eliminates the need for a formula of the form =B12+B16+B20+B23+B29. The SUBTOTAL function ignores other subtotal functions in the *range* so there is no double counting. The *function_number* argument of nine tells Excel to sum the range. There are ten other functions for which you can run subtotals, including average, count, and standard deviation.

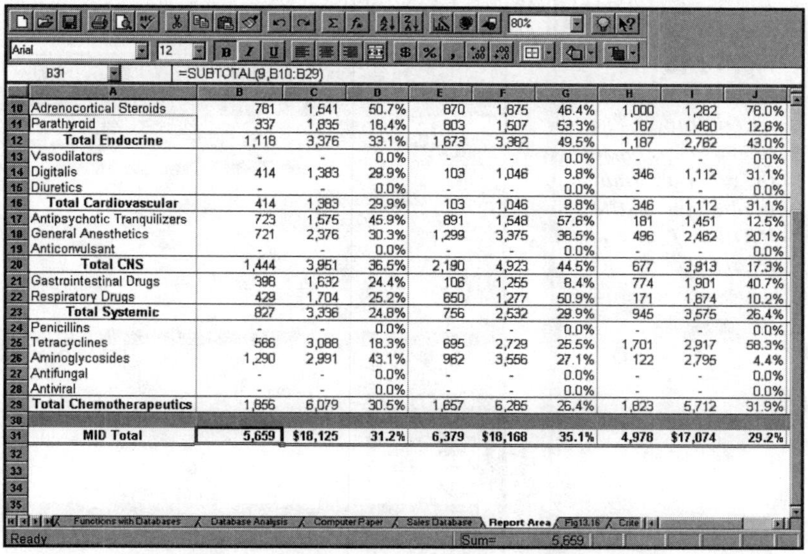

	A	B	C	D	E	F	G	H	I	J
10	Adrenocortical Steroids	781	1,541	50.7%	870	1,875	46.4%	1,000	1,282	78.0%
11	Parathyroid	337	1,835	18.4%	803	1,507	53.3%	187	1,480	12.6%
12	**Total Endocrine**	1,118	3,376	33.1%	1,673	3,382	49.5%	1,187	2,762	43.0%
13	Vasodilators	-	-	0.0%	-	-	0.0%	-	-	0.0%
14	Digitalis	414	1,383	29.9%	103	1,046	9.8%	346	1,112	31.1%
15	Diuretics	-	-	0.0%	-	-	0.0%	-	-	0.0%
16	**Total Cardiovascular**	414	1,383	29.9%	103	1,046	9.8%	346	1,112	31.1%
17	Antipsychotic Tranquilizers	723	1,575	45.9%	891	1,548	57.6%	181	1,451	12.5%
18	General Anesthetics	721	2,376	30.3%	1,299	3,375	38.5%	496	2,462	20.1%
19	Anticonvulsant	-	-	0.0%	-	-	0.0%	-	-	0.0%
20	**Total CNS**	1,444	3,951	36.5%	2,190	4,923	44.5%	677	3,913	17.3%
21	Gastrointestinal Drugs	398	1,632	24.4%	106	1,255	8.4%	774	1,901	40.7%
22	Respiratory Drugs	429	1,704	25.2%	650	1,277	50.9%	171	1,674	10.2%
23	**Total Systemic**	827	3,336	24.8%	756	2,532	29.9%	945	3,575	26.4%
24	Penicillins	-	-	0.0%	-	-	0.0%	-	-	0.0%
25	Tetracyclines	566	3,088	18.3%	695	2,729	25.5%	1,701	2,917	58.3%
26	Aminoglycosides	1,290	2,991	43.1%	962	3,556	27.1%	122	2,795	4.4%
27	Antifungal	-	-	0.0%	-	-	0.0%	-	-	0.0%
28	Antiviral	-	-	0.0%	-	-	0.0%	-	-	0.0%
29	**Total Chemotherapeutics**	1,856	6,079	30.5%	1,657	6,285	26.4%	1,823	5,712	31.9%
30										
31	**MID Total**	**5,659**	**$18,125**	**31.2%**	**6,379**	**$18,168**	**35.1%**	**4,978**	**$17,074**	**29.2%**
32										
33										
34										
35										

Fig. 13.15
The subtotal and grand total lines use the SUBTOTAL function to simplify formula construction.

Setting Up Variable Criteria Areas

There must be a separate criteria range for each product or row of the display range in figure 13.14. Also each criteria range is set up to allow as many as ten items under it. Figure 13.16 shows part of two of the criteria areas.

To make the process easier to interpret, three formulas are set up to determine the size of the dynamic criteria range. The formula in cell named CRIT1, and shown on the edit line, helps to determine the size of the criteria range in conjunction with the formulas in cells F25 and B25:E25. The formulas in cells B25:E25 are

```
=COUNTA(B15:B24)
```

The COUNTA function counts the number of items under a particular category; in other words, it determines how many items the user requested from any one category. The other formulas in this range are identical. The formula in cell F25:

```
=FIXED(MAX(A25:E25,1)+CELL("ROW",F14),0)
```

uses the MAX function to find the largest value in the range A25:E25 or 1. For example, if the values in the range A25:E25 are all zero, the function returns 1. The formula adds this value to the row number of cell F14, which is 14, returning the row number of the last row of the dynamic criteria range. Although you could just enter 14, if you did so, the formula could not be copied. The FIXED(*number,decimal_places*) function converts the numeric result of the MAX and CELL calculations into text displayed with zero decimal places. This result is used by the formula in cell F15:

```
=MID(CELL("Filename"),FIND("]",CELL("Filename"),1)+1,50)&"!"&CELL("Address",A14)&":E"&F25
```

Fig. 13.16

Part of a dynamic criteria range. The edit line displays one of the criteria formulas used by the DSUM's INDIRECT criteria reference.

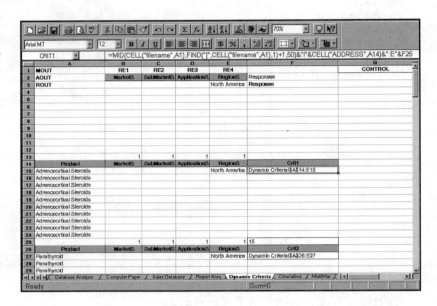

The CELL("Filename") portions of the formula return the drive, path, filename, and sheet where the formula is located. An example is D:\QUE\Chap 13 Expert\ [Market.xls]Fig13.1. From this you can extract just the sheet name. Notice that the sheet name follows the] symbol. The MID portion of the formula returns as many as 50 characters beginning one character after the] symbol. This is then concatenated with the CELL("Address",A14) portion of the formula, which returns the cell address of cell A14. Again you have used a formula where you could have entered a text value because you want to be able to copy the formula. This portion of the formula is concatenated with the text ":E" and then with the text result of the calculation in cell F25.

The result of all of these calculations is a dynamic reference. The absolute notation around the A14 is an irrelevant artifact of the CELL("Address",A14) function. You may wonder if the sheet name portion of this formula is necessary—it is. Remember, the formulas that use this reference are on another sheet. If you did not include a sheet name the INDIRECT functions on the display page would reference the display page and not the criteria page.

All three of these formulas were designed to be copied for as many criteria areas as necessary.

Creating Dialog Boxes

You might choose to create a set of five dialog boxes, three of which are shown in figures 13.17 through 13.19. The first dialog box the user sees is shown in figure 13.17. In this dialog box the user has two types of choices. He can pick one item in each category to create an AND criteria. For example, he could choose to see all the sales of drugs for chronic care to private hospitals in North America. Alternatively, the user can select any number of items under one category. For example, he can select any combination of hospitals, physicians, distributors, and government. The dialog box for this option is shown in figure 13.18.

Fig. 13.17

This is the first dialog box that the user sees when he wants to see the sales for a particular subset of the data.

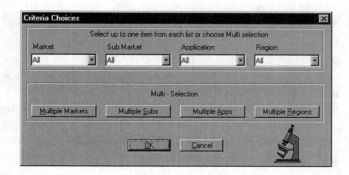

Fig. 13.18

This dialog box appears when the user clicks the Multiple Markets button in the Multi-Selection area.

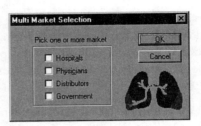

Fig. 13.19

The Multi Region dialog box incorporates a little trickery to create a graphic watermark and formatted text, but otherwise is identical to the three other Multi-Selection dialog boxes.

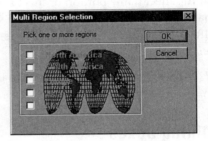

To construct a dialog box follow these steps:

1. Choose the Insert, Macro, Dialog command to add a blank dialog box to a new dialog sheet. This command will also display the Forms toolbar.

2. Add controls by choosing the desired tool on the Forms toolbar and dragging on the dialog box.

3. To modify the default properties of each control, select the control and then choose the Format, Object command and set the desired properties.

4. To attach a macro to a control, select the control and choose the Tools, Assign Macro command, and then pick the desired macro or record a new one.

5. To add a graphic picture to a dialog box, choose the Insert, Object command, and pick the type of object from the Object Type list on the Create New tab. When the object appears on the dialog sheet, resize and reposition it as necessary. To construct the first dialog box, figure 13.17, add four drop-down boxes, four buttons, two group boxes (which are used to outline the two main sets of options), a number of labels, and a graphic object. All items except the graphic object are added using the Forms toolbar. To enhance your dialog boxes with graphics, choose Insert, Object and then pick the Object Type you want and click OK. All the objects in the dialog boxes of this application can be found in the Microsoft ClipArt Gallery. To keep the graphic object in the correct proportion, size it by holding down the Shift key and dragging one of the corners. The four multi-selection buttons are attached to macros. These macros are discussed in the next section.

Dialog box controls such as drop-down lists can be linked to cells in a spreadsheet or controlled entirely with VBA code. For many situations, it is easier to work with spreadsheet links. Figure 13.20 shows the ranges used with the four drop-down lists. Each drop-down box displays the items you store in an input range from a spreadsheet and returns the user's response to a link cell as is shown in figure 13.20. For example, the input range for the first drop-down list is in cells B2:B6 of figure 13.20, named MarketList. The user's response is returned to cell H4, named MResponse.

Fig. 13.20

You can link dialog box controls to spreadsheet cells. Here are the ranges used in the drop-down lists in the opening dialog box.

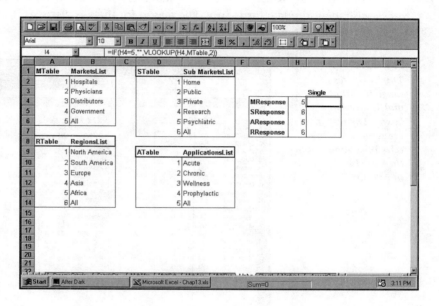

Excel returns a number to the link cell that represents the position of item on the list. This number must be converted to the name of the item chosen. To do this, you can use a VLOOKUP function. In figure 13.20 the formula in cell I4, shown on the edit line, is

```
=IF(H4=5,"",VLOOKUP(H4,MTable,2))
```

This formula checks to see if the user chose All and, if so, returns a blank; otherwise, VLOOKUP returns the item name from the second column of the range named MTable. MTable is the range A2:B6 in figure 13.20. The items the user chose in all four list boxes are located in the range I4:I7, and are named Single, a range that will be copied to the criteria area by VBA code.

To select more than one item, you can employ a set of check boxes as is done here or set up a list box with a selection type of Multi or Extend. This second approach is substantially more complicated. To set up a multi-selection dialog box like the one shown in figure 13.18, you add four check box controls, a group box, one item of text, and a graphic. Check boxes only require a link cell in which to indicate the user's response.

13

Figure 13.21 shows part of the link cell range for all the check boxes in each of the four multi-selection dialog boxes. Column A shows the range names of the cells in column B. The entire set of response cells in column B has been named Initial. Column C contains formulas to determine the user's response. For example, the formula in cell C21 is

```
=IF(MultiReg1,B9,"x")
```

This formula determines whether the check box was checked. If it is, cell MultiReg1 will contain TRUE, which causes the IF statement to return the value North America; otherwise the formula returns an x. The reason for the x is discussed later in this chapter in the section "Automating the Entire Process with VBA."

Fig. 13.21

This is the response range for all of the multi-selection check boxes. The responses are returned to the cells in column B and then used by formulas in column C.

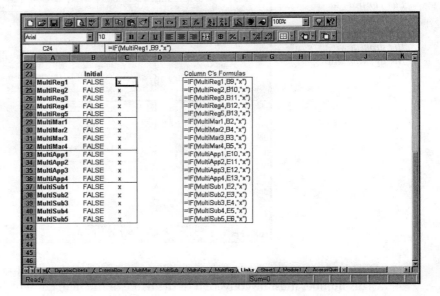

Figure 13.19 was created exactly the same way as all the other multi-selection dialog boxes except for a little trickery to create the watermark effect and the formatted text. Although you cannot format text in a dialog box, you can paste a picture of formatted text from the spreadsheet. To create this type of dialog box, delete the default labels on each check box and then resize the label portion of the control to its minimum by dragging the right-hand edge to the left. The check box labels are entered into spreadsheet cells and can be formatted as desired. They are then copied as pictures to the dialog box. The graphics are positioned three-dimensionally by using the Send to Back and Bring to Front tools on the Drawing toolbar.

Caution

Positioning is the key to allowing controls to function when graphics are added to dialog boxes. If a control overlaps a graphic completely, the control will be nonfunctional, even if you have sent the graphic to the back. If the control partially overlaps the graphic, the graphic may redraw every time the control is selected, a process that will slow down response time considerably. In figure 13.19, the check boxes and their default labels do not overlap the graph map or the picture labels. Because the default label could overlap the graphic even if it does not contain text, you want to shrink the label portions to the minimum.

Initializing the Response Ranges

To automate the process of querying the database, you can present the user with a series of dialog boxes. These dialog boxes will allow the user to pick the criteria for a given query. The responses of the user are then placed in the criteria ranges that the DSUM functions use to return the appropriate data from the database.

The code to accomplish these tasks is shown here with explanations. This code has been assigned to the graphical title button on the data display page shown in figure 13.14.

The CriteriaDialog subroutine initializes the response areas and opens the first dialog box:

```
Sub CriteriaDialog()
  Range("MResponse").Value = 5
  Range("AResponse").Value = 5
  Range("SResponse").Value = 6
  Range("RResponse").Value = 6
```

These lines initialize all the list boxes to display the choice All.

This command enters False in every cell of the range Initial, thus unchecking all the multi-selection check boxes:

```
Range("Initial").Value = False
```

These lines open the dialog box and, if the user presses OK, runs the subroutine EnterCriteria; otherwise the code ends:

```
If DialogSheets("CriteriaBox").Show Then
  EnterCriteria
End If
End Sub
```

Automating Criteria Entry

The following subroutine handles user responses when the user has chosen from the drop-down lists at the top of the initial dialog box:

```
Sub EnterCriteria()
    Application.ScreenUpdating = False
```

To make the code run faster, screen changes are suppressed:

```
Calculate
Range("Response").ClearContents
```

Because of the large number of complex functions in the workbook, recalculation is set to manual and so the spreadsheet is recalculated at various steps in the macro. The second command clears the contents from the range Response on the criteria page:

```
Application.Goto Reference:="Single"
Selection.Copy
Application.Goto Reference:="RE1"
Selection.PasteSpecial Paste:=xlValues, Operation:=xlNone, _
  SkipBlanks:=False, Transpose:=True
```

These commands present one way to copy data. There are more efficient methods, but they cannot be recorded. The more efficient methods are shown in the later section "Adding Code for the Remaining Multi-Selection Dialog Boxes." The PasteSpecial command transposes copied data and pastes it as values. So, you are taking a vertical range of formulas, Single, and entering them as a horizontal range of values in the range RE1.

These lines copy the range B2:E13 in figure 13.16 to the range B14:E205. By doing this, the criteria is copied to all the criteria ranges with one command. There's a lot to be said for consistency of design!

```
Range("SingleCrit").Select
    Application.CutCopyMode = False
    Selection.Copy
    Range("AllCrit").Select
    ActiveSheet.Paste
    Application.CutCopyMode = False
```

The spreadsheet is recalculated and the cursor returned to the page data display page:

```
Calculate
    Application.Goto Reference:="Top"
End Sub
```

Coding for the MultiReg Dialog Box

This is the code assigned to the Multiple Regions button in the opening dialog box. This can be done either by right-clicking the button on the dialog sheet and choosing Assign Macro or by choosing the Assign Macro from the Tools menu.

```
Sub MultiRegions()
   If DialogSheets("MultiReg").Show Then
     Application.SendKeys "{esc}", True
     Application.OnTime Now, "RNow"
   End If
End Sub
```

This code displays the MultiReg dialog box. If the user clicks the OK button, the SendKeys command sends the Esc key command to Excel. This is done to close the first dialog box without executing its code. At this point, you want the code to process the query by executing the subroutine Rnow. Unfortunately, if you try to execute the Rnow subroutine immediately, the action of SendKeys command will not have been completed, so the stack is not empty before the Rnow subroutine attempts to execute. To give Excel time to execute the SendKeys command, the OnTime command is used. This command tells Excel to execute another subroutine at some future time. At this point, the subroutine ends. But, the delay before execution of the Rnow subroutine has been set to Now and, therefore, execution continues immediately. The slight delay gives Excel just enough time to process the SendKeys command and everything works as desired.

Caution

If you do not use the OnTime command, you will get inexplicable errors. For example, Excel many tell you that it cannot execute an Application.GoTo or Range.Select command. In addition, because Excel's stack has not been cleared, you may find that a simple command such as pressing F5 in a spreadsheet will open the Macro dialog box instead of the GoTo dialog box.

This subroutine takes the response to a multi-selection dialog box and updates the criteria range:

```
Sub RNow()
   Application.ScreenUpdating = False
   Calculate
   Application.Goto Reference:="RESPONSE"
   Selection.ClearContents
   Application.Goto Reference:="MultiRegCrit"
   Selection.Copy
```

These steps are similar to previously discussed code:

```
   Application.Goto Reference:="RE4"
   Selection.PasteSpecial Paste:=xlValues, Operation:=xlNone, _
     SkipBlanks:=True, Transpose:=Falsed
```

The user responses to the multi-region dialog box are copied into the region portion of the criteria area, RE4. As before, the values are pasted, but in this case there is no need to transpose the results.

13

```
Selection.Replace What:="x", Replacement:="", LookAt:=xlWhole, _
SearchOrder:=xlByRows, MatchCase:=False
```

The response range contains either x or the appropriate criteria value for each check box. The x's need to be replaced with blanks for the criteria range to work properly.

Caution

You may be tempted to have the formulas that determine the value of the user's responses enter a blank, using something of the form =IF(MultiReg1,B9,"") instead of =IF(MultiReg1,B9,"x"). However, when you paste the values of these results, the target cell is not truly empty. Because of this, the criteria will fail to work properly. You need to enter something that can be replaced by a truly empty cell using the Replace command.

```
Selection.Sort Key1:=Range("RE4"), Order1:=xlDescending, Header:= _
   xlGuess, OrderCustom:=1, MatchCase:=False, Orientation:= _
   xlTopToBottom
```

The response range must be sorted in descending order to move all the empty cells to the bottom of the selection.

```
Application.Goto Reference:="SingleCrit"
Selection.Copy
Application.Goto Reference:="AllCrit"
ActiveSheet.Paste
Application.Goto Reference:="Top"
Application.CutCopyMode = False
Calculate
End
End Sub
```

These steps are similar to previously discussed code.

Adding Code for Remaining Multi-Selection Dialog Boxes

The following subroutine performs the same functions for the Multiple Applications button and dialog box as the previous code did for the Multiple Regions button.

```
Sub MultiApps()
   If DialogSheets("MultiApp").Show Then
     Application.SendKeys "{esc}", True
     Application.OnTime Now, "ANow"
   End If
End Sub
Sub ANow()
   Application.ScreenUpdating = False
   Calculate
   Range("Response").ClearContents
   Range("MultiAppCrit").Copy
```

The last two lines demonstrate a method of affecting spreadsheet ranges without moving the cursor. These commands execute faster than their equivalents in the prior code, but they must be typed. This presents two problems: you must know the commands and their proper syntax and you must take care to avoid typographical errors.

```
        Application.Goto Reference:="RE3"
        Selection.PasteSpecial Paste:=xlValues, Operation:=xlNone, _
          SkipBlanks:=True, Transpose:=False
        Selection.Replace What:="x", Replacement:="", LookAt:=xlWhole, _
          SearchOrder:=xlByRows, MatchCase:=False
        Selection.Sort Key1:=Range("RE3"), Order1:=xlDescending, Header:= _
          xlGuess, OrderCustom:=1, MatchCase:=False, Orientation:= _
          xlTopToBottom
        Range("SingleCrit").Copy
        ActiveSheet.Paste destination:=Range("AllCrit")
        Application.CutCopyMode = False
        Application.Goto Reference:="Top"
        Calculate
        End
End Sub
Sub MultiMarket()
    If DialogSheets("MultiMar").Show Then
        Application.SendKeys "{esc}", True
        Application.OnTime Now, "MNow"
    End If
End Sub
Sub MNow()
    Application.ScreenUpdating = False
    Calculate
    Range("Response").ClearContents
    Range("MultiMarCrit").Copy
    Application.Goto Reference:="RE1"
    Selection.PasteSpecial Paste:=xlValues, Operation:=xlNone, _
      SkipBlanks:=True, Transpose:=False
    Selection.Replace What:="x", Replacement:="", LookAt:=xlWhole, _
      SearchOrder:=xlByRows, MatchCase:=False
    Selection.Sort Key1:=Range("RE1"), Order1:=xlDescending, Header:= _
      xlGuess, OrderCustom:=1, MatchCase:=False, Orientation:= _
      xlTopToBottom
    Range("SingleCrit").Copy
    ActiveSheet.Paste destination:=Range("AllCrit")
    Application.Goto Reference:="Top"
    Calculate
    End
End Sub
Sub MultiSubMarket()
    If DialogSheets("MultiSub").Show Then
        Application.SendKeys "{esc}", True
        Application.OnTime Now, "SNow"
    End If
End Sub
Sub SNow()
    Application.ScreenUpdating = False
    Calculate
    Range("Response").ClearContents
    Range("MultiSubCrit").Copy
    Application.Goto Reference:="RE2"
```

13

```
        Selection.PasteSpecial Paste:=xlValues, Operation:=xlNone, _
          SkipBlanks:=True, Transpose:=False
        Selection.Replace What:="x", Replacement:="", LookAt:=xlWhole, _
          SearchOrder:=xlByRows, MatchCase:=False
        Selection.Sort Key1:=Range("RE2"), Order1:=xlDescending, Header:= _
          xlGuess, OrderCustom:=1, MatchCase:=False, Orientation:= _
          xlTopToBottom
        Range("SingleCrit").Copy
        ActiveSheet.Paste destination:=Range("AllCrit")
        Application.Goto Reference:="Top"
        Calculate
        End
End Sub
```

Automating Access Downloads Inside Excel

If you have to download data from Access on a regular basis, the easiest way may be to use Access' Tools, OfficeLinks, Analyze It with MS Excel command. However, you may not want to open Access, so an alternative way is to use Excel's Data, Get External Data command. You can automate this process with VBA. This section looks at the process of querying Access by using the Data, Get External Data command (Microsoft Query) and then automates the process with VBA code.

Querying Access Using Microsoft Query

Before trying to record the process of querying an external database, you should step through the entire process noting all the steps involved; in other words, plan. The following example uses Microsoft Access' Northwind database, so if you want to follow the discussion with the same examples, you should make sure that you have this sample database installed.

Suppose you want to query Access' Northwind database to see a year-to-date listing of all the orders that have been placed. You want this listing to show the company that placed the order, the date of the order, the product name, the quantity ordered, and the unit price. The information you need resides in four tables: Customers, Orders, Products, and Order Details.

Because there are quite a number of steps involved in this process and because Microsoft Query may be new to you, the following steps show this process:

1. Choose Data, Get External Data, which opens Microsoft Query and displays the Select Data Source dialog box shown in figure 13.22.

Fig. 13.22

The Microsoft Query opening screen automatically displays the Select Data Source dialog box.

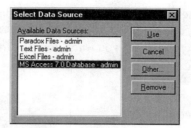

α Note

Microsoft Query and its drivers are not installed automatically when you install Microsoft Office; you must specify during a Custom install that you want these features added. Assuming that you have installed all the appropriate drivers but don't find the Data, Get External Data command available, you will have to turn on the add-in or show Excel where it is. To add MS Query to Excel, choose Tools, Add-Ins, check MS Query Add-In, and then choose OK. If MS Query Add-In is not on the Add-Ins Available list, choose Browse to locate Xlquery.xla. Most likely, this file will have been installed in the MSOffice\Excel\Library\MSQuery\ directory. After you have installed the add-in, you will be able to query closed external database files.

---

2. If the Available Data Sources list contains your data source, here MS Access, select it and click Use and then skip to step 6. If your data source is not on the Available Data Sources list proceed to step 3.

3. If you do not see the MS Access data source in the Select Data Source dialog box, choose Other to display the ODBC Data Sources dialog box (see fig. 13.23). Then select the data source from the Enter Data Source list.

Fig. 13.23.

The ODBC Data Sources dialog box enables you to see the types of drivers you have installed and enables you to pick the file type you want to use.

13

4. If the ODBC driver you want is not displayed in the ODBC Data Sources dialog box, choose New to display the Add Data Source dialog box shown in figure 13.24. Select the driver you want from the Installed ODBC Drivers list and then choose OK.

Fig. 13.24
The Add Data Source dialog box lets you select the ODBC driver you need.

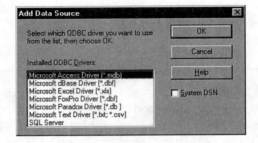

5. For Microsoft Access Driver(*.mdb), this will display the ODBC Microsoft Access 7.0 Setup dialog box shown in figure 13.25. The only item you need to enter is the Data Source Name, which will be the name displayed in the ODBC Data Sources dialog box.

Fig. 13.25
The ODBC Microsoft Access 7.0 Setup dialog box.

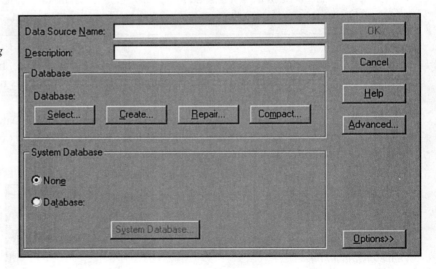

6. Assume for this discussion that you only specify a name for the data source in step 5. When you click OK twice you will be in the Select Database dialog box, which is where you would be if you had found MS Access in the Select Data Source dialog

box at step 2. Find and select the database you want, in this case Northwind, and choose OK. The Northwind database is usually installed in the Samples folder of Access 95.

7. The Add Tables dialog box is displayed. From this dialog box, add the tables you want to query. For example, suppose you want to add the Customers, Orders, Order Details, and Products tables. Select each table in turn from the Table list and then choose Add. When you've added all the desired tables, close the Add Tables dialog box.

8. Choose View, Criteria to display the query by example (QBE) grid.

9. To specify which fields of data you want returned to Excel, choose them using the Records, Add Column command and then pick the field from the Field list and choose Add, or simply by double-clicking the field name in the tables above the grid. For the current example, add the CompanyName field from the Customers table, the ProductName field from the Products table, the OrderDate from the Orders table, and the Quantity and UnitPrice fields from the Order Details table.

10. To add criteria to the QBE grid, you can manually enter them: click the Criteria Equals toolbar button, or choose Criteria, Add Criteria. In the Add Criteria dialog box, choose the Field you want to query on, the query Operator you want to use, and the Value you want. Suppose, for example, that you want to see all orders placed between 1/1/93 and 8/31/93. Choose Orders.OrderDate from the Field list, Is Greater Than or Equal To from the Operator list, and enter 7/1/93 in the Value box and choose Add.

11. The Add Criteria box remains open until you close it. In the current example, you want to add a second criteria. Make sure the Add option button is selected and then leave the Field Orders.OrderDate, and choose Is Less Than or Equal To from the Operator list, and 8/31/93 for the Value. When you close the Add Criteria dialog box your screen will look something like figure 13.26.

Caution

Clearing criteria within Microsoft Query may crash the program depending on how you do it. If you clear a criteria using the Backspace key, the Delete key, or the Edit, Delete command, the program may crash. The only way I have not crashed the system is to choose the Criteria, Remove All Criteria command. Hence, if you are going to try the other methods, save your query first. This problem can be quite a nuisance.

Fig. 13.26

Microsoft Query with a four-table query of the Northwind database. Because Northwind's tables are keyed, you do not have to add any joins.

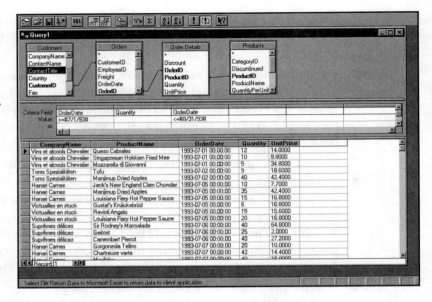

12. When you add fields and criteria to the grid, the results of the query will be displayed immediately if the Records, Automatic Query command is on. If it is not, choose Records, Query Now or the Query Now toolbar button to display the results of the query.

13. To return the data to Excel, choose File, Return Data to Microsoft Excel. This returns you to Excel and displays the Get External Data dialog box.

14. You can choose Keep the Query Definition with Excel, or not. The advantage to retaining it is that you can refresh the query results with a single command from Excel. If you do not retain the query definition but want to rerun the query, for example, from other spreadsheets, you might choose to create VBA code for use by many individuals or in new spreadsheets.

> **Note**
>
> When you return data to Excel, the Get External Data dialog box gives you the option Keep Query Definition. If you choose not to keep the definition, the definition will not be brought into Excel and it will be removed from Microsoft Query, without prompting you to save it. When you choose to keep the query definition, the definition is retained in Excel but, again, it is discarded from Microsoft Query. If you keep the query definition with Excel, you can always return to it by choosing the Data, Get External Data, Edit Query command. However, if you want to retain the query but not return it to Excel, you should save the query while in Microsoft Query before you return the data to Excel.

One of the real beauties of using the <u>D</u>ata, Get E<u>x</u>ternal Data command is that you can query programs whose data you can't easily import. For example, you can query both the DOS and Windows versions of Paradox. On the other hand, if you do not intend to retain the Excel spreadsheet with all the query data you may need to code the process. In either case, you may want to code cleanup and analysis procedures.

Constructing and Examining the VBA Code

Suppose you do decide to use VBA code to automate your query of Microsoft Access. Here is what that code might look like:

```
Sub MonthlyRollUp()
    QueryAccess
    FormatData
End Sub
```

The main subroutine calls two other subroutines. The first subroutine, shown here, runs Microsoft Query. These are not the types of commands that you should consider typing. In addition, you will be extremely hard pressed to find useful information on the Application.Run command in the help system or the manual. This is one more reason to use the recording feature. Because of the way Excel records the query it may seem somewhat difficult to determine where one aspect of the query ends and another begins.

In this example, the path to the Northwind database is C:\MSOFFICE\ACCESS\SAMPLES\NORTHWIND, the default path created during a typical install. If you installed Access in any other location, you should modify the appropriate lines of code. The following lines tell Microsoft Query which tables and fields are to be used in the query:

```
Sub QueryAccess()
  Range("A1").Select
  Application.Run "QueryGetData", "", _
    "SELECT Customers.CompanyName, Orders.OrderDate, Products.ProductName, `Order
    ➡Details`.Quantity, `Ord" _
    , , , , , False
  Application.Run "QueryGetData", "", _
    "er Details`.UnitPrice FROM `C:\MSOFFICE\ACCESS\SAMPLES\NORTHWIND`.Customers
    ➡Customers, `C:\MSOFFICE\ACCESS\SAMPLES\NORTHWIND`.`" _
    , , , , , False
```

These lines identify the joins in the query and begin defining the criteria:

```
  Application.Run "QueryGetData", "", _
    "Order Details` `Order Details`, `C:\MSOFFICE\ACCESS\SAMPLES\NORTHWIND`.Orders
    ➡Orders, `C:\MSOFFICE\ACCESS\SAMPLES\NORTHWIND`.Pro" _
    , , , , , False
  Application.Run "QueryGetData", "", _
    "ducts Products WHERE Orders.CustomerID = Customers.CustomerID AND `Order
    ➡Details`.OrderID = Orders." _
    , , , , , False
  Application.Run "QueryGetData", "", _
```

13

```
        "OrderID AND Products.ProductID = `Order Details`.ProductID AND
       ➡((Orders.OrderDate>={ts '1993-01-01 0"  _
        , , , , , False
```

These lines finish defining the criteria, which, in this example, returns all sales on or after 1/1/93 and on or before 8/31/93:

```
    Application.Run "QueryGetData", "", _
        "0:00:00'}) AND (Orders.OrderDate<={ts '1993-08-31 00:00:00'}))"  _
        , , , , , False
    Application.Run "QueryGetData", "DSN=MS Access 7.0
        Database;DBQ=C:\MSOFFICE\ACCESS\SAMPLES\NORTHWIND.mdb;DefaultDir=C:\MSOFFICE\ACCESS\
       ➡SAMPLES;DriverId=25;FIL=MS Access;UID=admin;", _
        "", True, True, False, Range("Sheet1!$A$1"), True, False
    End Sub
```

The database, program, and drivers are also passed to Microsoft Query. The location where the data will be placed in the spreadsheet and the notation whether to save the query definition complete this code.

The following code messages the incoming data. Much of this code cannot be recorded. Whenever you want your code to maintain flexibility you have to write or modify recorded code.

```
    The cursor is placed at the top of income data in column B and then moved to the
        ➡bottom of the column's data: Sub FormatData()
      Range("B2").Select
      Selection.End(xlDown).Select
    The variable LastRow is assigned the row number of the cursor, that is, the last row
        ➡of the data: LastRow = ActiveCell.Row
    The range from B2 to the cursor is selected, hence, all the data in the second
        ➡column, excluding the title: Range("B2", ActiveCell).Select
    The dates in the range are formatted. The original data came in displaying date and
    time: Selection.NumberFormat = "m/d/yy"
    Best fit is applied to column B: Columns("B:B").EntireColumn.AutoFit
    A title is entered in cell F1:    Range("F1").Select
      ActiveCell.FormulaR1C1 = "Total Charge"
    A formula which calculates the total cost of an order by multiplying the unit cost
        ➡times the quantity is entered into cell F2: Columns("F:F").EntireColumn.AutoFit
      Range("F2").Select
      ActiveCell.FormulaR1C1 = "=RC[-2]*RC[-1]"
    The formula in the active cell is copied: ActiveCell.Copy
    A range extending from F2 as far down in column F as the data extends is selected:
        ➡Range(ActiveCell, "F" & LastRow).Select
    The formula is pasted, the range formatted to currency, and the spreadsheet
        ➡recalculated: ActiveSheet.Paste
      Selection.NumberFormat = "$#,##0.00_);($#,##0.00)"
      Calculate
    End Sub
```

Using Microsoft Query to Query Excel

There are a number of reasons to consider using Microsoft Query to query your Excel tables. First, Microsoft Query is the only reasonable way to perform a multi-table query on Excel tables. Also, if you are comfortable with Access' query techniques, Microsoft Query has many similar features. Microsoft Query provides query-by-example and SQL, both of which provide you with greatly enhanced and simplified tools for querying Excel.

Opening a Query on Two Excel Tables

Suppose you run a mail-order company. You have two ranges in Excel, one containing employee information and the other containing order related data. Each range is set up with titles in the row above the first line of data, and the two ranges, including titles and data, have been named Employees and Orders, respectively. You would like to see all the orders placed during a given interval, taken by those employees who were hired before a given date. A portion of the two Excel tables you will be working with in this example are shown in figures 13.27 and 13.28.

Fig. 13.27

The employee table contains information about each employee including his or her ID number.

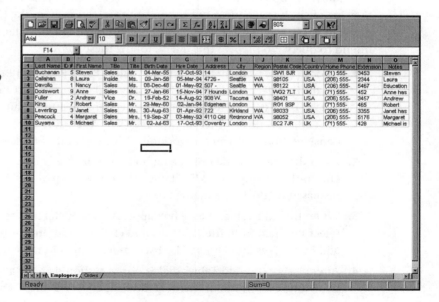

Fig. 13.28

The Orders table contains data about each order that is placed, including the ID number of the employee who took the order.

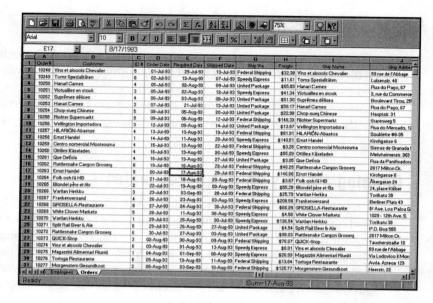

If you have set up your files to <u>A</u>llow Multi-User Editing, you can query the files even if they are open. If you choose not to turn on this feature from the <u>F</u>ile, <u>S</u>hared Lists command in Excel, the first thing you must do is close the files containing the tables you intend to query. To prepare this query, follow these steps:

1. Choose <u>D</u>ata, Get E<u>x</u>ternal Data and select Excel Files in the <u>A</u>vailable Data Sources list of the Select Data Source dialog box and choose <u>U</u>se. If the Excel Files choice is not on the list, choose <u>O</u>ther and proceed in a fashion similar to that discussed in the earlier section, "Querying Access Using Microsoft Query," steps 3-5, taking into consideration that you are working with Excel and not Access.

2. From the Select Workbook dialog box, find the file you want to query and choose OK. In this example, the two tables are in the Chap13 Databases.xls file. This will display the Add Tables dialog box.

3. When the Add Tables dialog box appears, add the tables you want to query by selecting them from the <u>T</u>able list and clicking <u>A</u>dd. In this example, you would add Employees and Orders, the two named ranges in the Chap13 Databases.xls file.

4. After closing the Add Tables dialog box you should create a relationship linking two tables on a common field. To do this, choose Ta<u>b</u>le, <u>J</u>oins, and select the common field in one table from the <u>L</u>eft list and the field containing the same

information for the other table in the Right list. Make sure that the Operator is the equal sign, and then choose Add and Close. Since you are querying the Employees and Orders tables, you can link them to the ID # fields, which are common to both tables.

5. Next, you tell Microsoft Query which fields you want returned to Excel either by double-clicking them or by dragging and dropping them on the first row of the grid. For the current example, you could add the First Name and Last Name fields from the Employees table and the Customer, Ship City, and Ship Country fields from the Orders table.

Setting Up a Complex Criteria

Suppose you want to see all the orders placed on or after June 1, 1994, for employees who were hired in 1992 and where the freight charges were less than $10.00, and you want to see all orders for the same employees but for the orders which had freight charges of $50.00 or more. To create the criteria area for this query, follow these steps:

1. After you have chosen all the fields you want to see in the results, you are ready to enter the conditions that you want the results to meet—that is, the criteria. To add criteria, choose Criteria, Add Criteria to display the Add Criteria dialog box. Choose a field you want to query on from the Field list and a condition operator from the Operator list, and then enter a value in the Value box or pick it from the Values list. In the current example, you want to see all orders made by employees hired in 1992, so you would choose Employees.Hire Date from the field list and the Is Between operator, enter **1/1/92 and 12/31/92** in the Value box, and click Add.

2. In the current example, you also want to display only those orders that meet the additional condition that they were made on or after June 1, 1994. In the preceding step the Add Criteria dialog box was not closed, so you can easily add the second criteria. For this example, make sure the And option button is selected, and then choose Orders.Order Date from the Field list and Is Greater Than from the Operator list, enter **6/1/94** in the Value box, and then click Add.

3. Orders that meet the condition in step 2 must also have a freight charge of less than $10.00. You continue in the Add Criteria dialog box by making sure the And option button is selected, and then choose Orders.Freight from the Field list and Is Less than from the Operator list, enter **10** in the Value box, and then click Add.

4. To complete the criteria, continue as in the preceding steps or manually enter the criteria shown in figure 13.29.

13

Fig. 13.29

A relational database query against two Excel tables. The criteria involve both AND and OR conditions.

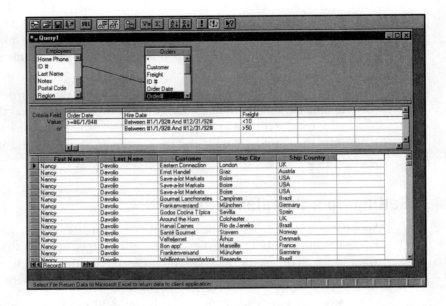

Tip
Remember, unlike Access, Microsoft Query's criteria are case-sensitive.

In the criteria range all conditions on the same row represent AND conditions; that is, they must all be true for the condition to be met. In figure 13.29, the Hire Date criteria Between #1/1/92# And #12/31/92#, the Order Date >=#6/1/94#, and the Freight <10 are one set of AND conditions. The second set is Hire Date Between #1/1/92# And #12/31/92# and Freight >=50.00. Because these two AND conditions are on different lines they are OR criteria. With OR criteria, either condition may be true for the query to display the records.

If the Automatic Query option is on, the query runs as soon as you enter a condition. When you have added all the conditions, the final results are displayed in the bottom of the Query window. To return the data to Excel, choose File, Return Data to Microsoft Excel. In the Get External Data dialog box, choose the desired options and click OK. The results of the query are shown in figure 13.30.

Fig. 13.30

The results of a multi-table query using two Excel tables.

	A	B	C	D	E	F	G	H	I
1	First Name	Last Name	Customer	Ship City	Ship Country				
2	Nancy	Davolio	Eastern Connection	London	UK				
3	Nancy	Davolio	Ernst Handel	Graz	Austria				
4	Nancy	Davolio	Save-a-lot Markets	Boise	USA				
5	Nancy	Davolio	Save-a-lot Markets	Boise	USA				
6	Nancy	Davolio	Save-a-lot Markets	Boise	USA				
7	Nancy	Davolio	Gourmet Lanchonetes	Campinas	Brazil				
8	Nancy	Davolio	Frankenversand	München	Germany				
9	Nancy	Davolio	Godos Cocina Típica	Sevilla	Spain				
10	Nancy	Davolio	Around the Horn	Colchester	UK				
11	Nancy	Davolio	Hanari Carnes	Rio de Janeiro	Brazil				
12	Nancy	Davolio	Santé Gourmet	Stavern	Norway				
13	Nancy	Davolio	Vaffeljernet	Århus	Denmark				
14	Nancy	Davolio	Bon app'	Marseille	France				
15	Nancy	Davolio	Frankenversand	München	Germany				
16	Nancy	Davolio	Wellington Importadora	Resende	Brazil				
17	Nancy	Davolio	Drachenblut Delikatessen	Aachen	Germany				
18	Nancy	Davolio	Hanari Carnes	Rio de Janeiro	Brazil				
19	Nancy	Davolio	The Big Cheese	Portland	USA				
20	Nancy	Davolio	Comércio Mineiro	São Paulo	Brazil				
21	Nancy	Davolio	Rancho grande	Buenos Aires	Argentina				
22	Nancy	Davolio	LILA-Supermercado	Barquisimeto	Venezuela				
23	Nancy	Davolio	Berglunds snabbköp	Luleå	Sweden				
24	Nancy	Davolio	Vaffeljernet	Århus	Denmark				
25	Nancy	Davolio	White Clover Markets	Seattle	USA				

 Note

On some occasions, when you are returning data to Excel and the Get External Data dialog box is displayed, if you have Keep Query Definition checked and click OK, Excel will warn you that the query definition will not be saved. By choosing Cancel, you are returned to the Get External Data dialog box, where you can click OK again.

Assuming that you have chosen the Keep Query Definition option, you can refresh the query results almost any time either by using the Data, Refresh Data command or by clicking the Refresh Data button. Keep in mind the following warnings regarding refreshing data.

 Caution

If you attempt to refresh a query using the Data, Refresh Data command while Microsoft Query is open and after you have performed query on another file, Excel will appear to lock up. The hourglass appears and nothing happens. Actually, Microsoft Query is waiting for you to let it know what file to query. You should toggle to Microsoft Query where you will find the Select Workbook dialog box open and waiting for you to select the appropriate file. Note that this problem does not occur if Microsoft Query is closed when you attempt to refresh the data.

13

If you assume that Excel has frozen and you shut down Excel and then attempt to open the file you were attempting to query you will receive the message `This program has performed an illegal operation and will be shut down`. After shutting down Excel you should also shut down Microsoft Query, and if this does not work you will have to restart your entire system.

If you attempt to use the Data, Refresh Data command while the Excel data source file is open, you may lock Excel or get the message `Unrecognized database format`. So, make sure the source spreadsheet is closed or that you have turned on the Allow Multi-User Editing before attempting to refresh a query.

It is possible to copy and paste data from Microsoft Query into Excel using either Edit, Paste or Edit, Paste Special, Paste Link. However, these approaches are not very satisfactory. If you paste data into Excel, you cannot update automatically. If you paste a link into Excel, you are creating an array. When you update the query in Microsoft Query, the Excel array will not resize. If the refreshed query has more records than the original query, Excel will not display the extra records. If the refreshed query has fewer records, Excel will display a lot of #N/A's.

If you create a query using the Paste Link command, the links update automatically until you close the query. When you open a query in Microsoft Query that was linked to Excel via the Paste Link command, those links will not update automatically until you choose Excel's Edit, Links command and choose the appropriate Source File, and then choose Update Now.

Microsoft Query or the Data, Get External Data command provides you with the capability of doing relational database queries against Excel ranges. The next section discusses the issue of handling mainframe downloads with Excel.

Downloading Mainframe Data into Excel

Because mainframe downloads are a common source of Excel data, it is useful to know how to import data from either a fixed-length or delimited file. It would also be helpful to know how to automate this type of process with VBA code. The example in this section develops the VBA code to import, cleans up, and messages downloaded data automatically with the goal of producing a final report. Although the Import Wizard is introduced, and a number of techniques to manipulate and analyze data are demonstrated, the main emphasis is on the VBA code.

Using the Import Wizard to Bring in Your Downloaded Data

When it comes to importing data from mainframes, Excel has some excellent tools. As you have seen in the previous section, you can use the Data, Get External Data command to access external data without importing the actual files into Excel. If you want to open the files, Excel provides the Import Wizard, a tool to quickly and easily step you through the process of bringing in data that is in fixed-length or delimited formats. The Import Wizard appears during the file open process if the file is a non-Excel file. Because the Import Wizard will be used in the small application developed in this section, it is briefly examined here.

As you step through the Import Wizard you are first asked to indicate whether the file is in a fixed width or delimited format. Figure 13.31 shows the first screen of the Import Wizard. You can also exclude as many of the top lines of the file to be imported as you want. This is great for removing header records or useless information that appears at the top of some database downloads.

The Import Wizard will appear anytime Excel cannot open the file you want to open as an Excel file. Excel can import files that are fixed width or delimited and, on some occasions, files that meet neither of these conditions.

Fig. 13.31

The first step of the Import Wizard allows you to see all the records of the import file and decide what type of file format they are in.

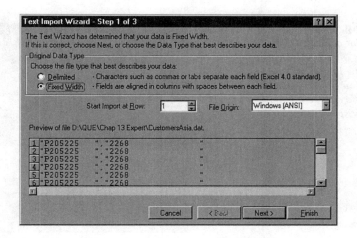

After you have made your choices from Step 1, you click the Next button to advance to the second step, which will be different depending on whether you indicated a fixed-width or delimited file format. A completed Step 2 for fixed-width files is shown in figure 13.32. At this point, Excel takes a guess where the fields should be split, but you have complete control. If you want to move a line break, drag it to the left or right. To add a line break, click at the desired locations. To remove an unwanted line break, double-click it.

13

Fig. 13.32

This is the second step of the Import Wizard for a file type of fixed width. In this step, you show Excel where fields begin and end by moving, adding, or removing line breaks.

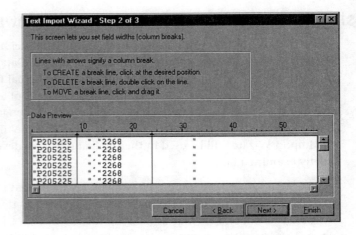

The second stage of the Import Wizard is different if you choose a delimited file type. In that case, you are asked to specify the types of delimiters your file contains and to indicate the type of character that encloses text. For example, text is often enclosed in quotation marks and fields are often separated by commas. Figure 13.33 shows the second stage of the Wizard for delimited files.

Fig. 13.33

For delimited files, this is the second stage of the Import Wizard. You can choose one of the common delimiters or specify your own.

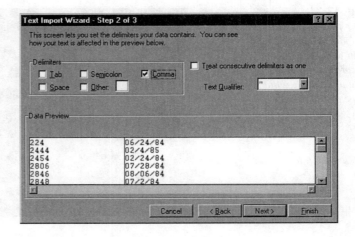

At the third stage of the Import Wizard, you can specify which fields are to be imported and which are to be skipped. The dialog box for this step is shown in figure 13.34. This dialog box is identical regardless of the file format chosen during the first stage of the Import Wizard.

In the application developed in this section, you will import both fixed-length and delimited file types.

Fig. 13.34

The last step in the Import Wizard is the same for both delimited and fixed-length files. You can also specify some field formats at this stage.

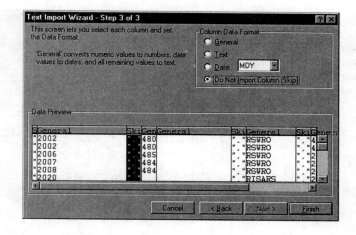

Cleaning Up Downloaded Data

Database downloads often require some cleanup. For example, many programs download packed fields. This means that a field will contain trailing blanks when the data does not fill the entire field. This may have little or no visual impact on the data, but you may discover problems in handling such data unless the extra spaces are removed. In other cases, an empty database field may contain a null field character when it is imported into Excel. These characters are invisible and occupy no space but, nevertheless, can cause problems during data analysis. Some techniques for dealing with these problems will be demonstrated in the discussion of the VBA code in the later section entitled "Creating Code to Open and Clean Up a Text File."

Analyzing the Intended Task

All programming tasks should be analyzed before you begin writing or recording code. In fact, the analysis stage is often the most time-consuming when done properly. The task is to bring data from thirteen separate files into the single report shown in figure 13.35.

Fig. 13.35

The is the final objective: a report showing information from 13 mainframe downloaded files.

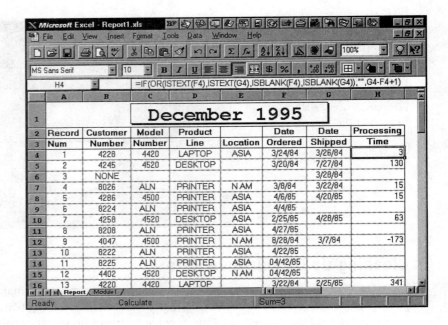

Most imported files should be cleaned up before they are used, which is the case in the following application. After the data files have been opened and cleaned, the data needs to be integrated into the report. This process may be as simple as copying and pasting, or it may require some sophisticated techniques. In the application that is presented here, a number of methods are used to get data into the final report. For example, you may have to use one of Excel's Data commands to limit the data to unique records. You may have to retrieve only the data for certain items. Or, perhaps, you'll need to see the address for all the employees in a given department. If the addresses are stored in a company-wide database you will only have to return data for those employees in the given department. Sometimes the data you need will be in two or more files, so you will need to check each file. For example, suppose you want to know the date each purchase was made, but if you don't know that date, you need to use the second best thing, which might be the date the item was ordered.

The following application will demonstrate some techniques you can choose to use to solve such problems. Hopefully, these techniques will give you ideas for manipulating and analyzing your own data.

All the download files for this application are included on the enclosed disk.

Automating the Entire Process with VBA

In the following program, the Main subroutine's primary purpose is to call other subroutines. A subroutine call requires only the name of the called subroutine. For example, to call the subroutine that imports the list of customers who made purchases this month in Europe, you add the line OpenTextCustEur, which runs the subroutine of that same name.

Creating the Main Subroutine

These lines name the subroutine and set the working directory:

```
Sub Main()
    ChDir "D:\QUE\Chap 13 Expert"
```

This is a good idea if your code saves or opens a lot of files in the same directory. The File, Open and File, Save commands do not need to specify the path, in which case the default will be used. If you need to reset the path you need to modify only one line of code. The next line stops screen redrawing:

```
Application.ScreenUpdating = False
```

When you set ScreenUpdating to False, you tell Excel not to redraw the screen as the program runs; this substantially speeds up the running of most code. All the remaining lines in the Main program are calls to other subroutines. A subroutine call runs the code in the subroutine and then returns to the calling program and continues execution at the line following the call. These are the subroutine calls:

```
        OpenTextCustEur
        OpenTextCustNa
        OpenTextCustAsia
        OpenTextCustO
        CreateCustomersxls
        ExtractUniqueSNs
        PrepReportPage
        CopySNtoReportPage
        OpenTextModels
        OpenTextOrderDate
        OrderDateToReport
        OpenTextProduct
        AddProductLine
        OpenTextLocation1
        OpenTextLocation2
        LocationToReport
        OpenTextShippedDate1
        OpenTextShippedDate2
        CombineShippedDates
        OpenTextTransactionDate1
        OpenTextTransactionDate2
        CombineTransactionDates
        ShipDateToReport
        ReformatReport
    End Sub
```

13

Creating Code to Open and Clean Up a Text File

The first subroutine that is called opens the text file CustomersE.DAT and then it calls a subroutine that cleans up the file.

```
Sub OpenTextCustEur()
    Workbooks.OpenText Filename:="CustomersE.DAT", Origin:= _
        xlWindows, StartRow:=1, DataType:=xlFixedWidth, FieldInfo:= _
        Array(Array(0, 9), Array(1, 1), Array(9, 9), Array(14, 1), Array(24, 9))
```

This is the code that tells the Import Wizard to import a fixed-width file. You should always record this command. When you record it, Excel will include the full path in the Filename argument. You can then remove the path portion of the argument and retain only the filename, as shown previously.

```
    CleanUpABCD
    Selection.End(xlDown).Select
```

This command is the equivalent of pressing Ctrl+down arrow. The command shown here is the simplified version of the recordable command ActiveCell.Offset(1,0).Range("A1").Select, which allows you to move a given number of columns and rows away from the current cell.

```
    ActiveCell.Offset(1, 0).Select
End Sub
```

This subroutine cleans up incoming files and removes leading, trailing spaces, and null characters. This particular cleanup program works specifically for a file containing two columns. With some work, you can write a program to deal with any number of columns.

```
Sub CleanUpABCD()
    Range("C1").Select
    ActiveCell.FormulaR1C1 = _
        "=IF(LEN(RC[-2])>0,""xxx""&Trim(RC[-2])&""xxx"",""xxx"")"
```

This is the most important single line of this subroutine. The formula uses the TRIM function to remove all leading or trailing spaces. If the cell is zero length, it may still contain a null character. To get rid of it, you enter xxx in the cell, which you will replace with nothing later. Note that if the FALSE argument of the IF statement is "", the cell will not be empty when you convert the formula to a value, and this will cause problems at later stages.

```
    Selection.Copy
    Range("A1").Select
    Selection.End(xlDown).Select
    Range("D1", "C" & ActiveCell.Row).Select
```

With the cursor on the last row of data, this command selects the range from column C of this row to cell D1. This is the range where the formula is copied once for each cell of incoming data. This dynamic version of the Range(x,y).Select command cannot be recorded. The ActiveCell.Row command returns the row number of the cursor and concatenates that with the column letter C.

```
   ActiveSheet.Paste
     Selection.Copy
     Selection.PasteSpecial Paste:=xlValues
```

This command converts formulas to values, before replacing the xxx's with nothing in the following lines. When you record the Replace command, Excel enters all the arguments, but in most cases, many of these arguments can be removed as in the following line.

```
   Selection.Replace What:="xxx", Replacement:=""
     Selection.Cut
     Range("A1").Select
     ActiveSheet.Paste
```

The last three lines cut and paste the results of the cleaned up command over the imported data.

```
   End Sub
```

Creating Code to Open, Clean, and Combine Fixed-Width Files

The following subroutine opens and cleans another text file. Then it calls the Combine subroutine to appended data to the first opened file.

```
Sub OpenTextCustNa()
   Workbooks.OpenText Filename:="CustomersNA.DAT", Origin:= _
     xlWindows, StartRow:=1, DataType:=xlFixedWidth, FieldInfo:= _
     Array(Array(0, 9), Array(1, 1), Array(9, 9), Array(14, 1), Array(24, 9))
   CleanUpABCD
   Combine
```

This line calls the Combine subroutine:

```
   Windows("CustomersNa.DAT").Activate
     ActiveWindow.Close savechanges:=False
```

Because the data from the second DAT file has been appended to the first file, you don't need to save this file.

```
   End Sub
```

The following subroutine, which is called many times by different subroutines, cuts the selected cells and pastes them to the first blank cell in column A of CustomersE.DAT file:

```
Sub Combine()
   Selection.Cut
   Windows("CustomersE.DAT").Activate
   ActiveSheet.Paste
```

After pasting the information into the file, the cursor is repositioned in the first empty cell below the data.

```
   Range("A1").Select
     Selection.End(xlDown).Select
     ActiveCell.Offset(1, 0).Select
End Sub
```

13

This subroutine performs the same function as the OpenTextCustNA subroutine, but for the data received from the Asia division. It uses both the CleanUpABCD and Combine subroutines.

```
Sub OpenTextCustAsia()
  Workbooks.OpenText Filename:="CustomersAsia.DAT", Origin:= _
    xlWindows, StartRow:=1, DataType:=xlFixedWidth, FieldInfo:= _
    Array(Array(0, 9), Array(1, 1), Array(9, 9), Array(14, 1), Array(24, 9))
  CleanUpABCD
  Combine
  Windows("CustomersAsia.DAT").Activate
  ActiveWindow.Close savechanges:=False
End Sub
```

This subroutine completes the process of opening, cleaning, and appending the customer orders files.

```
Sub OpenTextCustO()
  Workbooks.OpenText Filename:="CustomersOther.DAT", Origin:= _
    xlWindows, StartRow:=1, DataType:=xlFixedWidth, FieldInfo:= _
    Array(Array(0, 9), Array(1, 1), Array(9, 9), Array(14, 1), Array(24, 9))
  CleanUpABCD
  Combine
  Windows("CustomersOther.DAT").Activate
  ActiveWindow.Close savechanges:=False
End Sub
```

Reorganizing Data with VBA

This subroutine sorts, adds titles to,and saves the customer data as an Excel file.

```
Sub CreateCustomersxls()
  Selection.CurrentRegion.Select
```

This is one of the most useful selection commands in Excel, and is the equivalent of the Ctrl+* command. It selects the current region, which is defined as the range bounded by the edges of the spreadsheet, or by rows and columns that are completely empty.

```
  Selection.Sort Key1:=Range("A1"), Order1:=xlAscending, Header:= xlGuess
```

The following two commands select row 1 and insert a blank row. You can manually code this with one command, as you will see later.

```
  Rows("1:1").Select
  Selection.Insert Shift:=xlDown
```

These two lines demonstrate two ways to enter a value in a cell, but there are many others. Because the B1 argument is not quoted, you can enter a variable, which allows greater flexibility.

```
  Range("A1").Value = "ProdCode"
  [B1].Value = "SerialNum"
```

The following line suppresses alert dialog boxes such as the one that appears during the File, Save operation if a file of the same name already exists. Use this command with caution, and always turn the display of alerts back on, or else it will remain off until the program ends, which is definitely not a good idea.

```
    Application.DisplayAlerts = False
    ActiveWorkbook.SaveAs Filename:="Customers.XLS", FileFormat:=xlNormal
    Application.DisplayAlerts = True
End Sub
```

Handling Advanced Filter Commands with VBA

The next subroutine extracts unique customer numbers. An order may be composed of many items, each of which has its own line in the data. Therefore, a customer number may appear many times, but you only want to report it once.

```
Sub ExtractUniqueSNs()
    Range("B1").Copy
    ActiveSheet.Paste destination:=Range("F1")
```

The title at the top of the customer number column is copied to the cell F1. By writing the command this way, the cursor does not move to cell F1. In many cases, this technique would perform faster than the recorded equivalent. You cannot record this form of the Paste command.

The following lines name the current region Data for use in the AdvancedFilter command. The recorded version of the add names command enters a cell reference for the RefersToR1C1 argument, such as "=Sheet1!R3C2:R11C4". To make this command dynamic, edit the command as shown here.

```
    Selection.CurrentRegion.Select
    ActiveWorkbook.Names.Add _
      Name:="Data", _
      RefersToR1C1:=Selection
    Range("F1").Select
    ActiveWorkbook.Names.Add _
      Name:="Extract", _
      RefersToR1C1:=Selection
      Range("Data").AdvancedFilter Action:=xlFilterCopy, CopyToRange:= _
      Range("Extract"), Unique:=True
```

The previous command extracts unique records from the range named Data to the range named Extract. Notice that you do not need to enter a criteria range for this command if you want to check all records.

```
    Range("F1").Select
    ActiveCell.Clear
    Range("F2").Select
End Sub
```

13

Preparing a Report Area with VBA

Each month, the program uses the prior month's spreadsheet as a template. Because of this, the program must clear out the old data in preparation for the new. The file containing the report and the VBA code is called REPORT1.XLS. The following subroutine prepares the Report sheet of that file for the new month's data.

```
Sub PrepReportPage()
    Windows("REPORT1.XLS").Activate
    Sheets("Report").Select
    Range("A4").Select
    Selection.End(xlDown).Select
```

The next line demonstrates the use of a variable to hold the row number of the cursor.

```
    Bottom = ActiveCell.Row
```

 Note

It is strongly advised that you declare all your variables at the beginning of a module. To force variable declaration, enter the line Option Explicit at the top of each module, or, better yet, choose the Tools, Options command and select the Module General tab and turn on Require Variable Declaration.

Three of the following lines can use the variable Bottom to select various ranges. The next line clears the contents of the variable range. Of course, when you use variables, you must write or edit your code manually.

```
    Range("B4", "G" & Bottom).ClearContents
        Range("A" & Bottom + 1, "A300").Select
        Selection.EntireRow.Insert
```

The next line demonstrates a different method for inserting rows than was used in the CreateCustomers.xls subroutine.

```
    Range("A" & Bottom, "A300").Select
```

The remainder of the subroutine inserts and numbers all the rows down to row 300, a large enough range to handle any month's incoming data.

The DataSeries command enters a series of record numbers on the report.

```
    Selection.DataSeries _
        Rowcol:=xlColumns, _
        Type:=xlLinear, _
        Date:=xlDay, _
        Step:=1
End Sub
```

This subroutine copies the unique customer numbers to column B of the Report page.

```
Sub CopySNtoReportPage()
    Windows("Customers.XLS").Activate
    Selection.CurrentRegion.Select
    Selection.Copy
    Windows("REPORT1.XLS").Activate
    ActiveSheet.Paste destination:=Range("B4")
    Range("B4").Select
    Selection.End(xlDown).Select
```

The last two lines of the preceding code move the cursor to the bottom of the incoming data. The following lines will delete all the extra lines, bringing the bottom of the report up to the bottom of the data, and close the Customers.XLS file without saving it.

```
    Range(ActiveCell.Offset(1, 0), "A300").Select
    Selection.EntireRow.Delete
    Windows("Customers.XLS").Activate
    ActiveWindow.Close savechanges:=False
End Sub
```

Bringing Data into a Report Area Using VBA

The next piece of information you want to add to the report is a model number. This macro uses the same approach to open and clean the Models.DAT text file. The incoming data includes four columns of information so the CleanC subroutine must accommodate this change.

```
Sub OpenTextModels()
    Workbooks.OpenText Filename:="Models.DAT", _
        Origin:=xlWindows, StartRow:=1, DataType:=xlFixedWidth, _
        FieldInfo:=Array(Array(0, 9), Array(1, 1), Array(19, 9), Array(22, 1), _
        Array(40, 9), Array(43, 1), Array(53, 9), Array(56, 1), Array(66, 9))
    CleanC
```

At a later time, you will need the first three digits of the fourth column of incoming data. However, not every cell in the fourth column contains exactly three digits, so the following steps add a new column that contains the left three characters converted to value. The incoming data in the fourth column always starts with three numbers but in some cases may be followed by text. When this happens, Excel's LEFT function returns the first three digits as a label and not a number. The VALUE function makes the proper conversion. The formulas are then converted to values and the entire data range is named Table.

```
    Range("E1").Select
    ActiveCell.FormulaR1C1 = "=VALUE(LEFT(RC[-1],3))"
    Selection.Copy
    Range("D1").Select
    Selection.End(xlDown).Select
    Range("E1", "E" & ActiveCell.Row).Select
    ActiveSheet.Paste
    Selection.Copy
    Selection.PasteSpecial Paste:=xlValues
    Selection.CurrentRegion.Select
    ActiveWorkbook.Names.Add Name:="Table", _
        RefersToR1C1:=Selection
```

13

The file is saved as Models.xls. Notice that the SaveAs command can be written on one line or many lines. Here, each argument is on its own line. You may find this easier to read but, unfortunately, it takes longer to create because it must be manually edited.

```
Application.DisplayAlerts = False
   ActiveWorkbook.SaveAs _
     Filename:="Models.xls", _
     FileFormat:=xlNormal
   Application.DisplayAlerts = True
End Sub
```

The CleanC subroutine is identical to the earlier clean routine except that it addresses four columns of incoming data.

```
Sub CleanC()
  Range("E1").Select
  ActiveCell.FormulaR1C1 = _
    "=IF(LEN(RC[-4])>0,""xxx""&RC[-4]&""xxx"",""xxx"")"
  Selection.Copy
  Range("A1").Select
  Selection.End(xlDown).Select
  Range("E1", "H" & ActiveCell.Row).Select
```

When you perform an action on a very large area of an Excel spreadsheet, you will be warned that if you continue, Excel will not be able to undo the action. In a macro, this means that the user will need to respond to each of the alert dialog boxes. To eliminate the need to respond to these alerts, the DisplayAlerts is turned off, but only for the one command that would cause the problem. If you turn alert boxes off for the entire macro, you may miss important messages.

```
Application.DisplayAlerts = False
  ActiveSheet.Paste
  Application.DisplayAlerts = True
  Selection.Copy
  Application.DisplayAlerts = False
  Selection.PasteSpecial Paste:=xlValues
  Application.DisplayAlerts = True
  Selection.Replace What:="xxx", Replacement:="", LookAt:=xlPart, _
    SearchOrder:=xlByRows, MatchCase:=False
  Selection.Cut
  Range("A1").Select
  Application.DisplayAlerts = False
  ActiveSheet.Paste
  Application.DisplayAlerts = True
```

In many imported files you will find garbage in the last row of data. The next two lines move to and then delete this garbage at the end of imported data:

```
Selection.End(xlDown).Select
  Selection.EntireRow.Delete
  Range("A1").Select
  Selection.CurrentRegion.Select
```

Be careful with the Sort command: Excel does not always correctly guess whether a header is present. If Excel guesses incorrectly, you can rerecord the code or change the Header argument to xlNo or xlYes.

```
   Selection.Sort Key1:=Range("A1"), Order1:=xlAscending, Header:= _
      xlGuess
End Sub
```

Using Spreadsheet Functions to Retrieve Specific Data

Your next concern is the model number. Adding the model number illustrates a technique for using spreadsheet functions to check more than one file for data. The model number may be found in one of two files: the Models file or the OrderDate file. If the model number is in the OrderDate file, have Excel use that model number; if not, Excel will check the Models file. The following subroutine opens and cleans the OrderDate file. Notice that this file is delimited.

```
Sub OpenTextOrderDate()
   Workbooks.OpenText Filename:="OrderDate.dat", _
      Origin:=xlWindows, StartRow:=1, DataType:=xlDelimited, _
      TextQualifier:=xlDoubleQuote, ConsecutiveDelimiter:=False, Tab _
       :=False, Semicolon:=False, Comma:=True, Space:=False, _
      Other:=False, FieldInfo:=Array(Array(1, 1), Array(2, 1), Array(3, 1 _
      ), Array(4, 1))
   CleanC
   Selection.End(xlDown).Select
   Selection.EntireRow.Delete
   Range("A1").Select
   Selection.CurrentRegion.Select
```

Many of the commands in this section have been rewritten with each argument occupying a separate line.

```
   Selection.Sort _
      Key1:=Range("A1"), _
      Order1:=xlAscending, _
      Header:=xlNo
   ActiveWorkbook.Names.Add _
      Name:="Table", _
      RefersToR1C1:=Selection
   Application.DisplayAlerts = False
   ActiveWorkbook.SaveAs _
      Filename:="OrderDate.xls", _
      FileFormat:=xlNormal
   Application.DisplayAlerts = True
End Sub
```

Order dates as well as model number are found in the OrderDate file. In the following subroutine, both are added at the same time because they come from the same files.

```
Sub OrderDateToReport()
    Windows("REPORT1.XLS").Activate
    Sheets("Report").Select
    Range("C4").Select
    ActiveCell.FormulaR1C1 = _
        "=IF(ISERROR(VLOOKUP(RC[-1],OrderDate.xls!Table,2,0)),IF(ISERROR(VLOOKUP
        ➥(RC[-1],Models.xls!Table,2,0)),"""",VLOOKUP(RC[-1],Models.xls!Table,2,0)),
        ➥VLOOKUP(RC[-1],OrderDate.xls!Table,2,0))"
```

The preceding formula checks the range named Table in the OrderDate file to see if the customer number on the Report sheet is in the OrderDate file. If there is no match the VLOOKUP(B4,OrderDate.xls!Table,2,0), which checks for exact matches, returns an error. The ISERROR function detects this error and returns TRUE to the IF function, which tells Excel to check the Table range in the Models.xls file. If this function also returns an error, a blank is entered in the cell. If either ISERROR function did not return TRUE, a VLOOKUP function returns the model number from the appropriate file.

```
    Range("F4").Select
```

The following formula checks the Table range of the OrderDate.xls file for an order date for the given customer. Again the VLOOKUP function is looking for an exact match. The zero in the last argument of this function forces the match to be exact. For the order date only one file is checked.

```
    ActiveCell.FormulaR1C1 = _
        "=IF(ISERROR(VLOOKUP(RC[-4],OrderDate.xls!Table,3,0)),"""",VLOOKUP
        ➥(RC[-4],OrderDate.xls!Table,3,0))"
```

Both sets of formulas are copied into the appropriate cells of columns C and F on the report page. The formulas then are converted to values. When you run macros that enter complicated formulas such as these, keep the files that the formulas are referencing open when the formulas are being entered. If the files are closed, the code will run a lot more slowly. After the formulas are converted to values, you can close the subordinate files.

```
    Range("C4:F4").Select
    Selection.Copy
    Range("B4").Select
    Selection.End(xlDown).Select
    Range("C4", "F" & ActiveCell.Row).Select
    ActiveSheet.Paste
    Selection.Copy
    Selection.PasteSpecial Paste:=xlValues
    Windows("Models.xls").Activate
    ActiveWindow.Close
    Windows("OrderDate.xls").Activate
    ActiveWindow.Close
End Sub
```

The following subroutine adds the product line information to the Report sheet. The product line is in a file containing only model numbers and the corresponding product line information. If Excel cannot find an exact match between the model numbers on the report page and in the Product file it will compare the first two digits of the model numbers.

```
Sub OpenTextProduct()
   Workbooks.OpenText Filename:="Product.DAT", Origin:= _
      xlWindows, StartRow:=1, DataType:=xlDelimited, TextQualifier _
      :=xlDoubleQuote, ConsecutiveDelimiter:=False, Tab:=False, _
      Semicolon:=False, Comma:=True, Space:=False, Other:=False, _
      FieldInfo:=Array(Array(1, 1), Array(2, 1))
   CleanUpABCD
   Selection.CurrentRegion.Select
   ActiveWorkbook.Names.Add _
      Name:="Table", _
      RefersToR1C1:=Selection
   Selection.Sort _
      Key1:=Range("A1"), _
      Order1:=xlAscending, _
      Header:=xlNo
```

The following lines insert a new column and enter a formula to return the left two digits of the contents in column B if they are numbers; otherwise, it returns everything in column B. Two range names are created for the two ranges that are used to bring the data to the Report1 file.

```
   Range("A1").Select
   Selection.EntireColumn.Insert
   ActiveCell.FormulaR1C1 = _
      "=IF(ISERROR(VALUE(LEFT(RC[1],2))),RC[1],LEFT(RC[1],2))"
   Selection.Copy
   Range("B1").Select
   Selection.End(xlDown).Select
   Range("A1", "A" & ActiveCell.Row).Select
   ActiveSheet.Paste
   Selection.Copy
   Selection.PasteSpecial Paste:=xlValues
   Selection.CurrentRegion.Select
   ActiveWorkbook.Names.Add _
      Name:="Table2", _
      RefersToR1C1:=Selection
   Application.DisplayAlerts = False
   ActiveWorkbook.SaveAs _
      Filename:="Product.XLS", _
      FileFormat:=xlNormal
   Application.DisplayAlerts = True
End Sub
```

The next subroutine adds the product line information to the Report1 file.

```
Sub AddProductLine()
   Windows("REPORT1.XLS").Activate
   Sheets("Report").Select
   Range("D4").Select
   ActiveCell.FormulaR1C1 = _
      "=IF(ISERROR(VLOOKUP(RC[-1],
   ➥'Product.XLS'!Table,2,1)),IF(ISERROR(VLOOKUP(VALUE(LEFT(RC[-1],2)),
      ➥'Product.XLS'!Table2,3,1)),"""",VLOOKUP(VALUE(LEFT(RC[-1],2)),
      ➥'Product.XLS'!Table2,3,1)),VLOOKUP(RC[-1],'Product.XLS'!Table,2,1))"
```

13

This complex formula attempts to find a match between the model number on the Report sheet with the model number in the range named Table of the Product file. It first checks the entire model number. If this fails, the formula looks for an exact match on the first two characters of the model numbers on the Report sheet and in the range named Table2 of the Product file. If both attempts at a match fail, the formula enters a blank; otherwise, it returns the result of the match.

The formula is copied to the appropriate range of the Report sheet and then converted to values.

```
Selection.Copy
Range("C4").Select
Selection.End(xlDown).Select
Range("D4", "D" & ActiveCell.Row).Select
ActiveSheet.Paste
Selection.Copy

Selection.PasteSpecial Paste:=xlValues
```

Keep in mind that when you record VBA code, Excel includes all the arguments, whether they are needed or not. If the value of those arguments would be the default value, you can edit them out of your code. There are two good reasons to do this: first, it makes the code shorter and easier to read and, second, in some cases the code will execute more quickly.

```
Windows("Product.XLS").Activate
ActiveWindow.Close


End  Sub
```

Deciding to Write or Record VBA Code

A great deal of VBA code can be recorded, but on occasion you should consider the benefits of writing or modifying code even when it could be completely recorded. The following discussion uses additional code needed for the application, as a way of demonstrating this idea.

The next set of items that needs to be added to the report is the locations of the customers. This information is contained in two delimited files, which are opened and cleaned by the next two subroutines.

```
Sub OpenTextLocation1()
   Workbooks.OpenText _
   Filename:="Locations1.dat", _
   DataType:=xlDelimited, _
     TextQualifier:=xlDoubleQuote, Comma:=True, _

   FieldInfo:=Array(Array(1, 1), Array(2, 1), Array(3, 1))
```

If you remove recorded arguments or manually enter code, you can place the arguments in any order you want, provided that you use the argument name. For example, in the OpenText command, the DataType:=xlDelimited can be after the Comma argument, as long as you include the DataType:= portion to tell Excel to which argument you are referring. If you don't include the argument names, you must include at least the comma separators where each argument would be. For example, the preceding command might begin Workbooks.OpenText Locations1.dat",,,, xlDelimited, xlDoubleQuote,,,,,, Array(Array(1, 1), Array(2, 1), Array(3, 1)).

```
    Range("B1").Select
    Selection.EntireColumn.Delete
```

Because of the file structure you can use the CleanUpABCD subroutine again.

```
    CleanUpABCD
    Selection.End(xlDown).Select
    ActiveCell.Offset(1, 0).Select
End  Sub
```

The subroutine opens, cleans the second location file, and combines it with the first location file.

```
Sub OpenTextLocation2()
    Workbooks.OpenText Filename:="Locations2.dat", _
      Origin:=xlWindows, StartRow:=1, DataType:=xlDelimited, _
      TextQualifier:=xlDoubleQuote, ConsecutiveDelimiter:=False, Tab _
       :=False, Semicolon:=False, Comma:=True, Space:=False, _
      Other:=False, FieldInfo:=Array(Array(1, 1), Array(2, 1))
    CleanUpABCD
    CombineLocations
End  Sub
```

Caution

If you manually enter code on multiple lines be careful to include a space before the underscore at the end of each continuing line. When you read code it is difficult to tell if there is a space, but it is needed.

This subroutine appends the data from one location file to the other one and saves the combination as an Excel file.

```
Sub CombineLocations()
  Selection.Cut
  Windows("Locations1.DAT").Activate
  ActiveSheet.Paste
  Selection.CurrentRegion.Select
  ActiveWorkbook.Names.Add _
    Name:="Table", _
    RefersToR1C1:=Selection
  Selection.Sort _
    Key1:=Range("A1"), _
    Order1:=xlAscending, _
    Header:=xlNo
```

13

If you record the pressing of the Ascending Sort button, sometimes Excel cannot guess correctly whether the sort range has a header. In such cases, it will be necessary to record the Data, Sort command or manually modify the Header argument to read xlNo.

```
Windows("Locations2.DAT").Activate
ActiveWindow.Close savechanges:=False
Application.DisplayAlerts = False
ActiveWorkbook.SaveAs Filename:="Location.XLS", FileFormat:=xlNormal
```

It is not necessary to save the combined file as an Excel file for the data to be added to the report. It is being done here so that the user can examine the source data files easily if any questions arise.

```
    Application.DisplayAlerts = True
End Sub
```

The location files do not contain the customer numbers; instead, they contain a list of all location codes and the corresponding locations. The Models file contains location codes and customer numbers. So, check a customer number on the Report sheet against the customer number in the Models file and get the corresponding location code. This code is checked against the Location file to find the matching location.

One way to solve this problem is to create a new column in the Models file that looks up the location in the Location file. After this is done, a formula is entered on the Report sheet to look up the location for each customer in the Models file.

```
Sub LocationToReport()
   Workbooks.Open Filename:="Models.xls"
   Range("F1").Select
   ActiveCell.FormulaR1C1 = _
     "=IF(ISERROR(VLOOKUP(RC[-3],Location.XLS!Table,2,0)),"""",VLOOKUP(RC[-
3],Location.XLS!Table,2,0))"
```

This formula compares the location code in the Models file to the location codes in the range named Table in the Location file and returns the matching location. This data is entered as a new column in the Models file.

```
   Selection.Copy
   Range("E1").Select
   Selection.End(xlDown).Select
   Range("F1", "F" & ActiveCell.Row).Select
   ActiveSheet.Paste
   Selection.Copy
   Selection.PasteSpecial Paste:=xlValues
   Windows("Location.XLS").Activate
   ActiveWindow.Close savechanges:=False
```

The location information has been transferred to the Models file, so the Location file is no longer needed.

```
   Selection.CurrentRegion.Select
   ActiveWorkbook.Names.Add _
```

```
   Name:="Table", _
   RefersToR1C1:=Selection
Windows("REPORT1.XLS").Activate
Sheets("Report").Select
Range("E4").Select
ActiveCell.FormulaR1C1 = _
   "=IF(ISERROR(VLOOKUP(RC[-3],Models.xls!Table,6,0)),""",VLOOKUP(RC[-
3],Models.xls!Table,6,0))"
```

The VLOOKUP function checks customer numbers for exact matches in the Table range of the Models files.

```
Selection.Copy
Range("D4").Select
Selection.End(xlDown).Select
Range("E4", "E" & ActiveCell.Row).Select
ActiveSheet.Paste
Selection.Copy
Selection.PasteSpecial Paste:=xlValues
Windows("Models.xls").Activate
ActiveWindow.Close savechanges:=True
End Sub
```

Next, you want to enter the date the order was shipped. The shipping date is stored in two files, which will be opened, cleaned, and combined. Sometimes the shipping date information is not available, so a second set of files is used. These files contain a transaction date, which will be used in lieu of a shipping date. The transaction date is used only when no shipping date is available.

```
Sub OpenTextShippedDate1()
   Workbooks.OpenText Filename:="Ship1.dat", _
      Origin:=xlWindows, StartRow:=1, DataType:=xlDelimited, _
      TextQualifier:=xlDoubleQuote, ConsecutiveDelimiter:=False, Tab _
       :=False, Semicolon:=False, Comma:=True, Space:=False, _
      Other:=False, FieldInfo:=Array(Array(1, 1), Array(2, 1))
End Sub

Sub OpenTextShippedDate2()
   Workbooks.OpenText Filename:="Ship2.DAT", _
      Origin:=xlWindows, StartRow:=1, DataType:=xlFixedWidth, _
      FieldInfo:=Array(Array(0, 9), Array(1, 1), Array(19, 9), Array(22, 1), _
      Array(30, 9))
End Sub

Sub CombineShippedDates()
   Selection.CurrentRegion.Select
   Selection.Cut
   Windows("Ship1.DAT").Activate
   Selection.End(xlDown).Select
   ActiveSheet.Paste
   Selection.End(xlDown).Select
```

When you record VBA, Excel often records multiple steps rather than the shortest single-step approach. You will need to write these alternate VBA approaches manually. Manually entered code often runs faster than Excel's verbose equivalent.

13

The Selection.EntireRow.ClearContents command demonstrates a one-step approach for clearing an entire range.

```
Selection.EntireRow.ClearContents
   Range("A1").Select
   Selection.CurrentRegion.Select
   Selection.Sort _
      Key1:=Range("A1"), _
      Order1:=xlAscending, _
      Header:=xlNo
   ActiveWorkbook.Names.Add _
      Name:="Table", _
      RefersToR1C1:=Selection
   Application.DisplayAlerts = False
   ActiveWorkbook.SaveAs _
      Filename:="ShippedDate.xls", _
      FileFormat:=xlNormal
   Application.DisplayAlerts = True
   Windows("Ship2.DAT").Activate
   ActiveWindow.Close savechanges:=False
End Sub
```

Completing the Import Process

The two transaction date files are opened and combined in the next three subroutines. If you are lucky, the files you import may need no cleanup, as is the case with these two fixed-width transaction files.

```
Sub OpenTextTransactionDate1()
   Workbooks.OpenText Filename:="Trans1.DAT", _
      Origin:=xlWindows, StartRow:=1, DataType:=xlFixedWidth, _
      FieldInfo:=Array(Array(0, 9), Array(1, 1), Array(19, 9), Array(22, 1), _
      Array(30, 9))
   Selection.End(xlDown).Select
End Sub

Sub OpenTextTransactionDate2()
   Workbooks.OpenText Filename:="Trans2.DAT", _
      Origin:=xlWindows, StartRow:=1, DataType:=xlFixedWidth, _
      FieldInfo:=Array(Array(0, 9), Array(1, 1), Array(19, 9), Array(22, 1), _
      Array(30, 9))
End Sub

Sub CombineTransactionDates()
   Selection.CurrentRegion.Select
   Selection.Cut
   Windows("Trans1.DAT").Activate
   ActiveSheet.Paste
   Selection.CurrentRegion.Select
   Selection.Sort _
      Key1:=Range("A1"), _
      Order1:=xlAscending, _
      Header:=xlNo
```

It is not always necessary to sort the range used by a VLOOKUP function. If you are searching for an exact match, no sorting is required. The fourth argument of the VLOOKUP function controls this option.

```
ActiveWorkbook.Names.Add _
    Name:="Table", _
    RefersToR1C1:=Selection
Windows("Trans2.DAT").Activate
ActiveWindow.Close savechanges:=False
Application.DisplayAlerts = False
ActiveWorkbook.SaveAs _
    Filename:="TransactionDate.xls", _
    FileFormat:=xlNormal
Application.DisplayAlerts = True
End Sub
```

The following subroutine enters the shipping date, or the transaction date in its stead, into the Report sheet.

```
Sub ShipDateToReport()
    Windows("REPORT1.XLS").Activate
    Sheets("Report").Select
    Range("G4").Select
    ActiveCell.FormulaR1C1 = _
        "=IF(ISERROR(VLOOKUP(RC[-5],ShippedDate.xls!Table,2,0)),IF(ISERROR(VLOOKUP(RC[-
5],TransactionDate.xls!Table,2,0)),"""",VLOOKUP(RC[-
5],TransactionDate.xls!Table,2,0)),VLOOKUP(RC[-5],ShippedDate.xls!Table,2,0))"
```

This VLOOKUP function works in a manner analogous to earlier ones.

```
    Selection.Copy
    Range("E4").Select
    Selection.End(xlDown).Select
    Range("G4", "G" & ActiveCell.Row).Select
    ActiveSheet.Paste
    Selection.Copy
    Selection.PasteSpecial Paste:=xlValues
    Selection.NumberFormat = "m/d/yy"
    Windows("TransactionDate.xls").Activate
    ActiveWindow.Close savechanges:=False
    Windows("ShippedDate.xls").Activate
    ActiveWindow.Close savechanges:=False
End Sub
```

Formatting the Final Report

Not all of the incoming data may be in the final report format. The final subroutine formats the report.

```
Sub ReformatReport()
    Range("A4").Select
    Selection.End(xlDown).Select
```

All the new data is selected in preparation for reformatting.

```
Range("A4", "G" & ActiveCell.Row).Select
```

The recorded Font command has been edited to eliminate unnecessary arguments, as has the Borders command shown here.

```
With Selection.Font
    .Name = "MS Sans Serif"
    .Size = 10
End With
With Selection
    .Borders(xlLeft).Weight = xlHairline
    .Borders(xlRight).Weight = xlHairline
    .Borders(xlTop).Weight = xlHairline
    .Borders(xlBottom).Weight = xlHairline
End With
Selection.HorizontalAlignment = xlCenter
Selection.End(xlDown).Select
```

The two columns containing dates are formatted to a consistent date format.

```
Range("F4", "G" & ActiveCell.Row).Select
Selection.NumberFormat = "m/d/yy"
End Sub
```

The final column of the report page contains a formula that calculates the number of days between the time the order was placed and when it shipped. If either date is not available, or if either date field contains text rather than numbers, the formula returns a blank. If the date field contains text, it means that one of the files contained bad data. The following formula accomplishes this task:

```
=IF(OR(ISTEXT(F4),ISTEXT(G4),ISBLANK(F4),ISBLANK(G4)),"",G4-F4+1)
```

The ISTEXT functions check to see if the date fields contain text. The ISBLANK functions test to see if those same fields are blank. The OR function returns TRUE if any of the four conditions is true, in which case the IF function enters a blank in the cell. Otherwise, the difference between the two dates is calculated.

Summary

Working with databases in Excel can be challenging and exciting. This chapter has introduced a number of techniques for handling databases efficiently. The intent was to present solutions that would stimulate your creativity. Many other chapters of this book will also provide information, ideas, and suggestions that have further applicability in an Excel database environment.

chapter 14

Mapping Your Data

by Heidi Sullivan-Liscomb

In this chapter

◆ **Install Data Map**
This chapter helps you confirm that you have the correct set-up and install Data Map in minutes.

◆ **Organize your data**
In this chapter you learn how to prepare your data so that Data Map can accurately interpret it for your map.

◆ **Create and edit a map**
Using your data or the data that comes with the program, you will learn how to display your information in a map and make changes whenever you need.

◆ **Customize your map**
This chapter introduces you to the world of custom application! Learn how to create a map that reflects your specific business goals.

◆ **Familiarize yourself with Data Map add-ins**
In this chapter you get to know the different programs that are available for use with Data Map.

◆ **Perform advanced tasks**
Learn the steps for creating sophisticated, complex maps.

◆ **Use Data Map in conjunction with MapInfo**
Finally, if you are a MapInfo user, you need to review this chapter to learn what you can and cannot do with Data Map and MapInfo data.

Anyone involved in business is familiar with the daunting task of managing vast quantities of data. Excel has always offered valuable tools to assist today's businessperson to effectively handle his or her data. Because the types and quantities of data are constantly evolving, so is Excel. Excel 95 offers the most updated data management tool yet, the capability to give your data geographic reference. This tool is called Data Map. Data Map allows you to take your data and put it on a map. You can embed your own worksheet data or the demographic data included in the Data Map package in any one of several maps. There also are Data Map add-ins that you can purchase to create impressive visual displays and presentations. When you use Data Map, your sales figures, age demographics, national housing numbers, and percentage of earnings can be displayed in ways that enable you to make better business decisions.

How Can Data Map Help Me?

Data is more readily available now than at any other time in history. How to use that data can be one of the most important business decisions made today. Effective and accurate usage is, of course, the most sought after goal for handling this abundance of data. Besides dealing with mass quantities of data, businesses are also using different types of data. Often, you run into situations where the data is directly linked to geographic information. Examples are sales figures that are reflected throughout the nation, age demographics, health statistics, and income by area statistics. The ideal way to display data that is intimately linked with a geographic region is to use a map. Excel's new feature, Data Map, offers you the capability to shade one or many variables in ranges, plot your data using dots or graduated symbols, create pie or column charts to display your data, or use the standard pin map.

How Does Data Map Work?

Data Map uses what is known as *thematic mapping*. This means that particular values in your data are displayed on a map using different colors, patterns, or symbols. Data Map provides you with six different ways to display your data:

- Pie charts
- Column charts
- Value shading
- Category shading
- Dot density
- Graduated symbols

Each of these methods is discussed in this chapter.

Installing Data Map

To install Data Map you must have Microsoft Excel 95, but this alone does not automatically provide you with access to Data Map. You must do a custom install to add Data

Map to your program. The minimum requirements for running Data Map are a 486/25 PC with 8M RAM and a VGA monitor. In addition, you will need the Windows 95 or Windows NT 3.51 operating system. Hard disk space requirements are approximately 15M and Data Map requires 6899K.

To install Data Map, follow these steps:

1. Follow the instructions in the Microsoft documentation to install Office or Excel 95.

2. During the install process, choose Custom Installation.

3. Highlight the Microsoft Excel option.

4. Click the Change Option button.

5. Check the Microsoft Data Map option.

If you have already installed Office or Excel 95 and did not run the Custom Installation to install Data Map, follow these steps:

1. Follow the instructions in the Microsoft documentation to add or remove components.

2. Highlight the Excel option.

3. Click the Change Option button.

4. Check the Data Map option.

Data Map is now ready to run on your system. Questions concerning Excel or Data Map should be directed to Microsoft technical support.

Creating a Map with Data Map

This section shows you how to organize your data for Data Map, familiarize yourself with the MAPSTATS.XLS file, find out what to do if Data Map doesn't recognize your data names, and create a map displaying your data. This section is the most important part of this chapter because it teaches you the basic skills for successful map making. After you have mastered these, you can create maps using any of your data in Excel 95.

Get to Know Your MAPSTATS.XLS File

Data Map recognizes many different regional names. To see a complete listing of those names, open the MAPSTATS.XLS file using the following steps:

1. In Windows 95, click Start and choose Find.

2. Select Files/Folders and enter MAPSTATS.XLS in the Named box.

14

3. Click F<u>i</u>nd Now. Double-click the file name to display the table of contents.

4. Select a tab from the bottom of the table of contents to display the regional information. The recognizable geographic and data names are shown across the tops of the columns.

Data Map recognizes regional names in the following places:

▶ Australia

▶ Canada

▶ Europe

▶ Mexico

▶ United Kingdom Standard Regions

▶ United States with Alaska and Hawaii inserts

▶ United States in North America

▶ World Countries

You can use the copy and paste functionality of Excel to copy data from the MAPSTATS.XLS file into your worksheet. Select the section of data that you want to use by clicking and dragging the cells, choose <u>E</u>dit, <u>C</u>opy. Go to your worksheet, choose <u>P</u>aste. The data from the MAPSTATS.XLS file displays. Now you can follow the basic map-making steps to display that data in map form.

Organizing Your Data

Data Map is a powerful addition to Excel's data manipulation tools. Like the Chart or Graph tool, Data Map takes your data and gives it form. To create a map, you must first organize your data so that Data Map can read it. In a few short steps you are on your way to viewing your data on a map.

To organize your data follow these steps:

1. Create a new worksheet in Excel. Enter your geographic region in the first column. (Don't forget to create a heading.)

 Note

Data Map must recognize a geographic indicator in one of the columns of your worksheet in order to select and display it on your map. Data Map operates on a *hit rate* system. This means that a certain number of text items must be recognized as geographic references. In Data Map's case the hit rate must reach 80 percent to recognize and map your data.

2. Insert your text data in the far-left column of your worksheet. The text can be county, state, or country names or abbreviations.

   When using county names it is important to also use state names or abbreviations because there is more than one county with the same name.

3. Put your numeric information regarding the text in the second column. For example, if you want to display a map that shows state population by age, the state names go in the first column and the age or population numbers go in the second column. Other numbers and textual information can follow in subsequent columns.

Note

If you are using postal codes they must be saved as text for Excel to accept them. To do this, select the cells in which a postal code occurs, choose Format, Cells, select the Number tab, select Text from the Category list, and then choose OK.

4. Select all of the columns that you want displayed in your map by clicking and dragging around the data. Include the headings in your worksheet because they provide Data Map with titles and legends for your data. Steps for editing your titles and legends are discussed later in this chapter.

Tip

If you are mapping fewer than five rows of geographic data, do not include the headings in your selection. Data Map includes the heading in its search and will not recognize it as a geographic region. This causes Data Map to return an unknown data screen.

Figure 14.1 shows you how your data looks with some cells selected. This example uses end-of-year sales figures and projected sales figures for some western states. This is the standard worksheet setup for your data with geographic regions in the first column and numeric data following it.

Note

Multiple columns of data can be used and displayed by Data Map, but you must have *at least* two columns of information.

14

Fig. 14.1

Data as it appears when it has been selected. Select the cells by clicking and dragging.

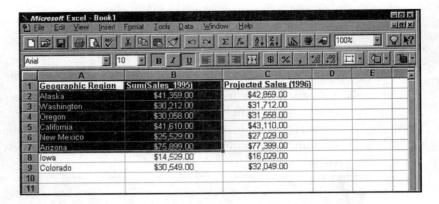

	A	B	C	D	E
1	Geographic Region	Sum(Sales_1995)	Projected Sales (1996)		
2	Alaska	$41,359.00	$42,859.00		
3	Washington	$30,212.00	$31,712.00		
4	Oregon	$30,058.00	$31,558.00		
5	California	$41,610.00	$43,110.00		
6	New Mexico	$25,529.00	$27,029.00		
7	Arizona	$75,899.00	$77,399.00		
8	Iowa	$14,529.00	$16,029.00		
9	Colorado	$30,549.00	$32,049.00		
10					
11					

Data Map must recognize your data to map it. To be sure that you are using the correct format, you should review the listing of all the regional terms that can be used. These terms are located in the MAPSTATS.XLS file. Click any of the tabs for the following geographic areas: World, USA, Mexico, or Europe. Each sheet has a listing of the terms.

Making Your Map

Now that you have entered data into the worksheet, you are ready to create your map. Follow these steps:

1. Select the data in your worksheet by clicking and dragging the cursor over cells you want. Click the Map button (it looks like a globe) in the Excel toolbar. The cursor becomes a cross-hair.

2. Click and drag the cursor in the worksheet where you want the map to display. Release the mouse button and let Data Map go to work creating your map. Don't worry about where you put it at first. You can move it later.

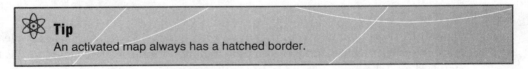

⚛ Tip

An activated map always has a hatched border.

3. Data Map selects and displays the map that best fits your data from a set of templates. In some cases it prompts you to decide which map best suits your needs. Data Map opens a dialog box and asks you if you need to use, for example, the United States standard map or the United States with an Alaska and Hawaii insert map. The map displays with your data embedded in it.

Caution
Make sure that you have geographic regions and numeric information in your worksheet—if you don't, your data will not appear on the map!

4. You can now size and format the map and add special features such as pop-up labels and push-pins. To format the map, you must double-click in the map to make it active. Making the map active allows you to make changes to the map. Clicking outside the map or pressing the Esc key deactivates the map.

 Tip
To move your entire map, place your cursor on one of the edges until it becomes a four-headed arrow. Drag your map to its new location.

 Note
Saving your map as a template is a great way to create personal standards for displaying your data! To save your map as a template choose M̲ap, S̲ave Map Template. Remember to change the name of your map—don't overwrite or delete an existing template!

When the map displayed, you probably noticed that it looked formatted. That is because Data Map uses the value shaded map as the default. You will learn more about value shading and how to change it later in this chapter.

Changing the data in your worksheet changes how the map appears. If, for instance, you need to update your numbers or change a geographic region, click outside the map to activate the worksheet. When you have finished entering your changes, you will see that your map has an exclamation point in the upper-left corner. This is the Map Refresh button. Click this button to update your map with the changes you made to your data. Figure 14.2 shows a map with the Map Refresh button.

14

Fig. 14.2
The Map Refresh button is a signal that something has changed in your data. Click this button to update your map with the changes.

Map Refresh button

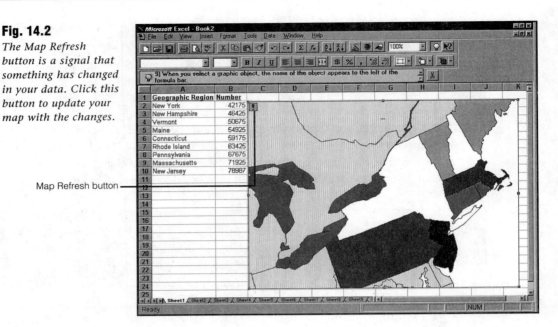

What If Data Map Doesn't Recognize My Region Names?

If Data Map does not recognize one of your region names, the Resolve Unknown Geographic Data dialog box appears, prompting you to insert a name it recognizes (see fig. 14.3). Use the Change To box to make changes to the region name. If you're not sure what to change it to, there is a Suggestions list from which you can select a region to replace the unrecognized entry. Choose Change to put the changes in place. You may also choose Discard or Discard All to ignore one or more rows that contain unidentified regions.

Fig. 14.3
The Resolve Unknown Geographic Data dialog box lets you know that Data Map does not recognize one or more of your geographic references. Use this box to make changes to the unknown data.

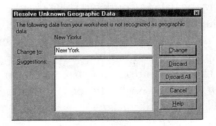

Using the Data Map Toolkit

Data Map provides one toolbar and a list of commands to assist you in creating and editing your map. This section focuses on the buttons and their uses.

Understanding the Tools

Data Map has a toolbar that allows you to change the appearance of your map. After the map has been created the Data Map toolbar replaces the Excel toolbar. Don't be alarmed—clicking in a worksheet cell brings the Excel toolbar back. Double-click in the map to display the Data Map toolbar. This function gives you great flexibility by allowing you to move rapidly between your map and the data worksheet. Figure 14.4 shows the toolbar buttons and their uses.

Fig. 14.4
The Data Map Toolbar has all of the buttons that you need to create and edit your maps.

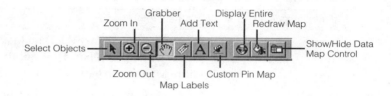

Table 14.1 defines the different buttons on the toolbar in the order in which they appear. Use this table as a quick reference guide until you become comfortable with the buttons.

Table 14.1   Toolbar Buttons and Their Uses

Button Name	Use
Select Objects	Allows you to select objects in your map.
Zoom In	Click and drag to see smaller sections of your map in better detail.
Zoom Out	Click and drag to see larger sections of your map in less detail.
Grabber	Click and drag to move the entire map.
Map Labels	Point and click on your map for instant labeling.
Add Text	Create text, remarks, or other textual references.
Custom Pin Map	Mark your map with push-pins for reference purposes.
Display Entire	Display your entire map by clicking this button.

continues

14

Table 14.1 Continued

Button Name	Use
Redraw Map	Refresh the display by clicking this button.
Show/Hide Data Map Control	Show or hide the data Map Control dialog box by clicking this button.

There are some additional commands that will make using your map a little easier. When your map is active, the Excel menu and toolbar are replaced with the Data Map menu and toolbar. Table 14.2 defines each new menu command in the order that it appears in the menu.

Table 14.2 Data Map Menu Commands

Menu Command	Function
View	Enables you to display the Data Map Control dialog box, Data Map Toolbar, Title, Subtitle, All Legends, Entire Map, or to Redraw Map.
Insert	Enables you to insert your spreadsheet Data or External Data.
Tools	Opens the Labeler, which enables you to label specific parts of your map. Opens the Options dialog box, which enables you to set up timed data matches, to determine a quick or thorough data search, to change the size of your units, and to determine whether legends will be compact by default.
Map	Features enables you to look at the features of the map. Add Features provides you with a list from which to choose new features. Save or delete a map template. Refresh your map. Open, close, or delete a Custom Pin Map. Value shading options enable you to make changes to your value shaded map.

Using the Data Map Control Dialog Box

When the map is active, the Data Map toolbar and the Data Map Control dialog box display. An important detail to remember is that your map must have at least one data column in order to activate the dialog box. Think of the Data Map Control dialog box as the command center for Data Map. It is in this dialog box that you can make changes to your map that determine how your data is interpreted. Later on, you'll see how to use all of the tools that are in this dialog box. You learn how to use and make changes to value and category shaded maps and pie and column charts on your map. Figure 14.5 shows the Data Map Control dialog box.

Fig. 14.5

The Data Map Control dialog box is the command center for your map. Use this dialog box to define how your data is displayed.

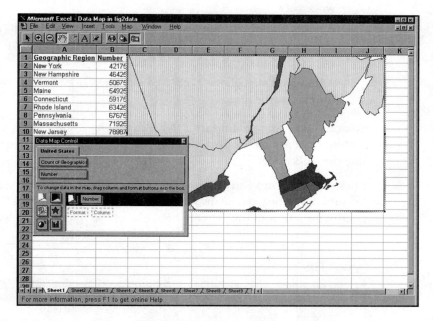

Inside the Data Map Control dialog box are the Column and Format buttons and a work space. These are the tools that you will use to make changes in your map. Clicking and dragging the map Format or Column buttons into an empty position in the dialog box workspace or out of the workspace allows you to change how your data is displayed.

For instance, if you want to change the format of a map so that it uses value shading as a backdrop and displays pie charts on top, you would follow these steps:

1. In the top half of the Data Map Control dialog box, the data that you selected to map will appear as a series of named boxes (for instance, Column A, Column B, and so on). Click and drag the box that contains your data into the Column button in the workspace.

2. Click and drag the value shading box from the left into the work area. Drop it into the Format button.

 Tip
The Format and Column buttons in the Data Map Control dialog box will display as gray boxes with hatched borders when they are not in use.

14

3. Data Map shades your map based on the values in your data.

4. To put pie charts on top of your value shaded background, simply click and drag the data from the top into the Column button in the workspace.

5. Click and drag the Pie Chart button from the left into the Format button in the workspace.

6. A new Column button will appear, indicating that you can add more data to your pie charts. As you do this the pie charts will get more complex and will add more colors to display the differences in data.

7. After each data column is entered into the workspace, an updated pie chart will display on the map.

You can make changes to the display by dragging a new Format button onto the old button. Changes can be discarded by selecting, dragging, and dropping the button outside the workspace.

Click, drag, and drop are the key steps to creating changes on your map. The Data Map Control dialog box can be displayed or hidden by choosing the Show/Hide Data Map control button from the extreme right end of the Data Map toolbar.

 Tip

Format or Column buttons can be removed by dragging and dropping them outside the workspace. A trash can icon will replace the Format button to indicate that the format of the map is being changed.

Figure 14.6 shows a map and its Control dialog box. The first row in the workspace shows you that the value shading refers to the number of houses sold in the state. The second row uses a symbol to represent the count for the area. You'll learn more about using symbols later. Familiarize yourself with the control box, you'll use it with every map!

Using Value and Category Shading

Value and category shading are two different ways to display data. *Value shading* displays numbers that fall within a range (for instance, 1–99, 100–199, and so on). On the map, higher numbers are represented by darker shades and lower numbers by lighter shades. *Category shading* enables you to display a number of ranges for one variable creating different regions on your map. You might need to display regions that are defined by yes/no responses. Displaying the percentage of registered voters in a geographic region is one example. You can display all the states where more than fifty percent of the residents are registered in one color—green, perhaps—and those states where fewer than fifty percent of the residents are registered in another color, such as red.

Fig. 14.6

The Data Map Control dialog box workspace is the area in which changes are made to your map. Select value and category shading, pie and column charts, and graduated symbols from inside the workspace.

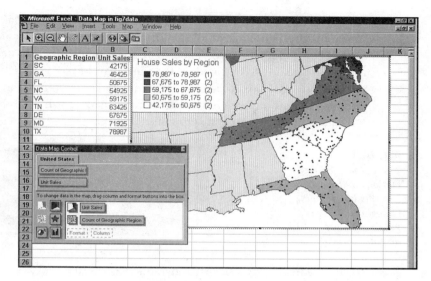

Value Shading

Value shading is used to display variations in the numeric data that is mapped. Your data is divided into two or more ranges and assigned colors. A common example of the use of value shading is the breakdown of demographic data such as population and income. It is also useful as a backdrop for other layers, such as pie charts and graduated symbols that display different sets of information.

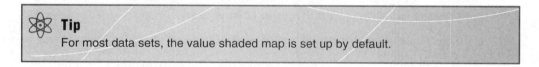

Tip

For most data sets, the value shaded map is set up by default.

Data Map creates value shading by taking your columns of data and sorting them into ranges. The data is then represented by shade variations. Greater data values are represented by darker shades and lesser data values by lighter shades.

You can change the colors and control the number of data ranges in your value shaded map by selecting Map, Value Shading Options, or by double-clicking the Value Shading format button in the work space in the Data Map Control dialog box.

The Value Shading Options dialog box provides a series of drop-down list boxes to implement changes to the map. If you want to create a map showing a range of high, medium, and low values, you will enter the number three in the Number of Value Ranges drop-down list box. The Define Value Ranges By dialog box determines how values are split into segments. In the case of a map value shaded with high, medium, and low ranges, this option determines how large the values will be for the high range and how low the

14

values will be for the low range. You can choose to have an equal number of map areas appear for the high range as for the low range or to have an equal spread of values in each range, 0–9, 10–19, 20–29, and so on. In addition, you can decide whether you want your value shading to be based on the sum or average of your data by clicking in the SUM or AVERAGE box located in the Summary Function box. Finally, you can change the color scheme and determine whether the shading will be visible in this box. Figure 14.7 shows the Value Shading Options dialog box.

Fig. 14.7
The Value Shading Options dialog box. Use this box to make changes to the way your ranges are displayed.

To create a map using value shading, follow these steps:

1. Select the data range in your worksheet.

2. Click the Map button and create your map.

3. In the Data Map Control dialog box, click and drag the Value Shading format button from the left into the work area. The map automatically updates with the data displayed in shaded ranges.

If you have a second set of data that you want to display in another format, you can select pie or column charts. You must initially select a column of data from your worksheet to associate with the pie or column charts.

To create pie or column charts on top of your value shaded map, follow these steps:

1. Click and drag the pie chart symbol over the grayed Format button in the workspace.

2. Click and drag the columns of data over the grayed Column button in the workspace. You can use as many as eight columns of data.

3. The map displays with the pie chart on top of the value shaded map.

 Note

Select Map, Value Shading Options to display the Value Shading Options dialog box. You can make changes to your map here.

Figure 14.8 shows a value shaded map with pie charts on top. This map was created using age demographic data for a selection of states.

Fig. 14.8

A value shaded map with pie charts. Use the legend to see what the pie charts represent.

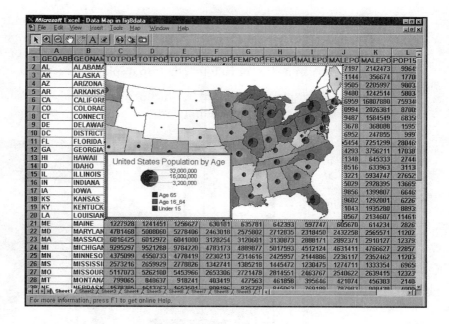

 Tip

Value and category shading cannot be used at the same time.

Category Shading

Sometimes it is necessary to differentiate one geographic region from another. If you have a number of different ranges for one variable, you could use the category shading option in Data Map.

Data Map displays a set of default colors that enable you to determine at a glance the differences in your data. You can change the colors associated with each region, as well as determining whether the color is visible, by selecting Map, Category Shading Options.

One possible business situation that could require you to divide your data into categories is if your company were trying to determine how well-known it was in a specific region. Using the results of a survey with yes/no columns, you could divide your regions into areas that were familiar with the company and areas that weren't. This might be useful in target marketing and sales programs.

Another example might be a company that offers a travel or bonus incentive for those departments that exceed their sales quotas for the fiscal quarter. As in the previous example, you will need to divide your data into yes/no columns for category shading to work. You can use pie or column charts to display the exact numeric data.

Figure 14.9 displays the regions in which red-tailed hawks were sighted. Category shading allows you to quickly determine where the sightings occurred.

Fig. 14.9

An example of a map created using category shading. Category shading is useful for differentiating geographic regions.

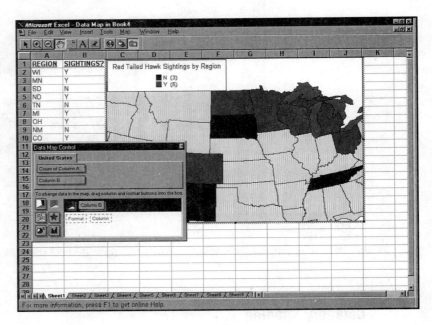

When and How Do I Use Graduated Symbols?

Graduated symbols are another method used to represent variations in numeric data. For instance, if you select the house symbol to represent average housing sales in a region, a larger house will represent more houses sold and a smaller house will represent fewer houses sold.

To use graduated symbols follow these steps:

1. Display the Data Map Control dialog box by clicking the Show/Hide button.
2. In the Data Map Control dialog box, click and drag the star icon from the left into the format button in the workspace.
3. Select the data column from the top of the box and drag it into the Column button in the workspace.

4. Changes such as shape, color, and size are made by selecting <u>M</u>ap, and then the <u>G</u>raduated Symbols Options.

In the Graduated Symbols Options dialog box you can set up the map so that the symbols display in various sizes by checking the <u>G</u>raduated box. To display symbols that are all the same size, deselect this box. Symbol size can be based on the data value sum or average for each map region, or you can assign a specific size by entering a number in the At <u>V</u>alue box. Larger numbers create larger symbols and vice versa. Figure 14.10 shows the Graduated Symbols Options dialog box.

Fig. 14.10

Click the symbol to select it. Click the Font button to change the color and size of the symbol.

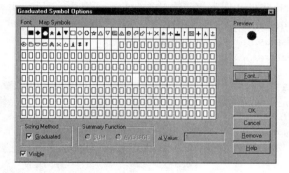

You have already learned that you can display several types of data by using more than one mapping format at a time. Another combination to consider is that of value or category shading and graduated symbols. Using value or category shading as a backdrop for a second data set that is represented by graduated symbols provides another level of information for your audience. By showing the relationship between the two sets of data, the map becomes a more useful tool for data interpretation. For example, if you are trying to determine where the highest and lowest automobile sales in a select region are, you can use a value shaded map. Add sales numbers for specific salespeople ordealerships and you could use pie or column charts.

When and How Do I Use Dot Density?

Dot density is also used to represent numeric data, such as units per square mile, relative to a regional area. Larger amounts of data are represented by large groups of dots, and smaller groups of data by smaller groups of dots. Data displayed in this manner makes variations in your data immediately obvious. The dot density theme allows your audience to view any regional patterns that exist in your data over a large geographic area.

To create a map using the dot density theme, follow these steps:

1. Display the Data Map Control dialog box by clicking the Show/Hide button.

2. From the Data Map Control box, click and drag the dot density button from the bottom left into the format button in the workspace.

3. Select the data column from the top of the box and drag it into the workspace.

4. Determine how many units each dot represents and the size of the dots by selecting Map, Dot Density Options.

The Dot Density Options dialog box is the place for formatting the appearance of the dots on your map. Choose to base your dots on summed or averaged data, make your dots invisible, and edit the size of each dot from within this box. The dot density option, when used in combination with value or category shading, provides another way to display more than one data set. Figure 14.11 shows a map made using the dot density feature.

Fig. 14.11
A dot density map that was created on top of a value shaded map.

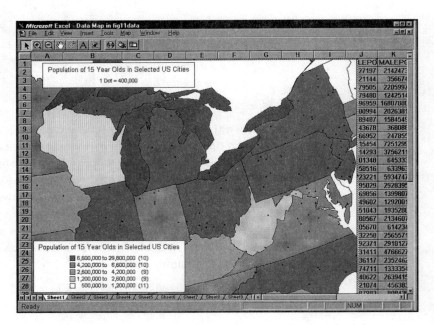

Defining Pie and Column Charts

Pie and column charts are two of the most widely used methods of displaying segments of data. If you have more than one data set that you want to display in a single region, pie and column charts are a good way to reach that goal. Suppose that you work on an experimental farm that is testing several different varieties of corn. You want to track which seeds have sprouted and how they fare in a variety of weather conditions. Furthermore, you want to set up the different quadrants of your farm. Place the numbers in your Excel worksheet and create pie or column charts to display them on your map.

Note

It is important to remember that pie and column charts require more than one column of data. If you drag the Pie or Column Chart button into the workspace and it goes gray, check to be sure that you have enough data.

To create a map using pie charts, follow these steps:

1. Display the Data Map Control dialog box by clicking the Show/Hide button.

2. From the Data Map Control dialog box, click and drag the pie chart button from the left into the Format area in the workspace.

3. Select the data columns and drag them into the Column area in the workspace.

4. You can make changes to your pie charts by choosing Map, Pie Chart Options.

Another business situation in which pie charts would be useful is if you were an architectural firm in New England interested in designing and building retirement communities. To determine where the largest communities of retirees live, you can select the results of your age demographics study and display them in pie charts. Figure 14.12 shows a map with graduated pie charts using that example.

Fig. 14.12

A map using pie charts to display age distribution. In this particular map we've chosen to show the pie charts in graduated form.

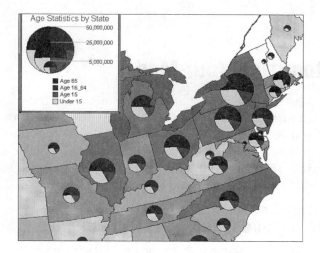

Multiple columns of data can also be displayed using column charts. Figure 14.13 is a map of the previous age demographics example using column charts. You can edit the look of your columns by choosing Map, Column Chart Options.

14

Fig. 14.13

A map using column charts to display age distribution. In some cases it is more effective to show your data using column charts. Try both pie and column charts and decide which works best for you.

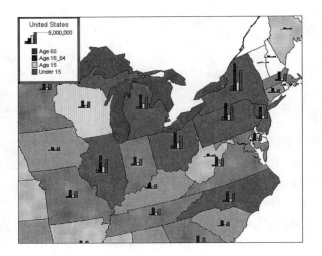

⚛ **Tip**

When creating column charts, several gray dashed lines appear in the workspace indicating that more columns are available. You may use as many as eight columns.

Customizing Your Map

Mastering the skills of map making may take a little time, but it is certainly worth the effort. Once you become comfortable with the steps already discussed in this chapter, you will be able to move on to custom-made maps. In this section you will learn to create and edit your own maps so that they display your data in exactly the right format for you. You will learn how to create and use a Custom Pin Map, and add, delete, or edit titles, legends, labels, and other text.

Creating and Using a Custom Pin Map

While Data Map has made the use of push-pins on a paper map obsolete, it has not made the use of push-pins any less desirable. Now you have an improved way to display your data electronically and you can create Custom Pin Maps in the same medium! Custom Pin Maps are useful for showing specific geographic locations that match your data. Figure 14.14 shows areas in the South where coffee is being grown as a cash crop. You can use the push-pin feature to display housing complexes, manufacturing plants, educational facilities, and so on.

Fig. 14.14

A Custom Pin Map showing areas growing coffee as a cash crop.

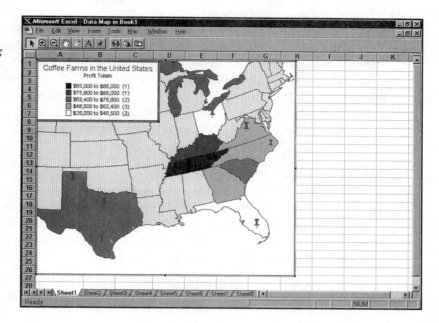

To create a Custom Pin Map, follow these steps:

1. Make your map editable by double-clicking in it. Select the Pin button from the Data Map toolbar. The Custom Pin Map dialog box appears. Type in the name of the new pin map that you are creating and click OK.

2. Press Enter. Your cursor becomes a push-pin.

3. Click the areas of your map where you want the pins to appear. In figure 14.14 the pins are placed wherever coffee is being grown as a cash crop.

4. You must select the pin by clicking it before you can make any changes to it. You can center the pin and change its size by clicking the edges of the gray box that surrounds the pin and dragging.

 Note

When you are finished adding pins to your map you must press the Custom Pin Map button.

5. If you place a pin where you don't need one, you can delete it by selecting it and pressing the Delete key.

Map Titles, Legends, and Labels

In most cases, you will want a textual reference to link your data to your map. This makes it easier for your audience to understand what it is seeing, as well as enhances the map's appearance. Adding labels, titles, legends, and additional text ensures that the map will deliver your information. Deletions and changes to your text are easily made. You can delete any of these text items by selecting them and pressing Delete. Changes are made by selecting the text and typing in the new information.

Titles

Titles are generally the first thing your audience will look at. The title defines the overall meaning of the map, what it is looking at, and what the map is trying to accomplish. Data Map creates initial titles from the row headings on your worksheet, and default titles if you don't select any row headings. These are not always appropriate map titles, however, and you may want to create your own.

To create or make changes to the map title, follow these steps:

1. Activate your map by double-clicking it.

2. Double-click the title box. You can now edit the text. Click outside the title box to accept the new text.

3. Click your right mouse button to open the editing window. Select Format, Font (see fig. 14.15).

Fig. 14.15

Use the Font dialog box to make changes to your titles.

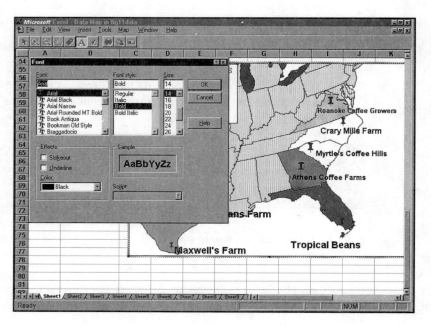

4. You can also choose to hide your title from this window. To hide your title, right-click and select <u>H</u>ide or select <u>V</u>iew, T<u>i</u>tle. To get your title back into view, choose <u>V</u>iew, T<u>i</u>tle.

Legends

Legends offer you the opportunity to present more details regarding the data in whatever map you are using. Your legend is directly linked to your data and any changes made to the data will be reflected in your legend. To create or make changes to your legend follow these steps:

1. If the legend is not displayed, select <u>V</u>iew, <u>A</u>ll Legends. Click in the legend to make it active. Double-click to display the Edit Legend dialog box (see fig. 14.16). Another way to display the Edit Legend dialog box is to right-click.

2. The Data Map default legend is the compact format. To see more detail in your legend, deselect the Use <u>C</u>ompact Format box in the Edit Legend dialog box. Deselecting this box also allows you to make changes to your legend text.

3. You can check the Use Currency Format box to accurately display monetary data.

4. Hide your legend by making it active and clicking the Delete key or right-clicking and selecting <u>H</u>ide. Legends can be restored by selecting <u>V</u>iew, <u>A</u>ll Legends.

Fig. 14.16

Use the Edit Legend dialog box to make all changes to your legend. Choose Edit, Legend Entries to edit individual columns.

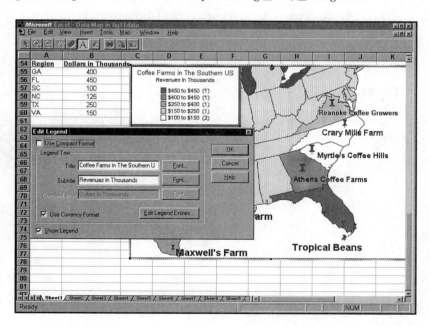

Labeling

Data Map offers labeling capabilities that simplify identifying key areas on your map. When you click the Map Labels toolbar button the Map Labels dialog box appears. Choose which feature Data Map should label and click OK. If you drag the icon over a geographic region, floating labels will automatically appear. Don't worry about the initial size of these labels—you can edit and move them. To make the floating label a part of your map, click on the area in which you want the label to display. You can edit the size and style of the font after you have created the label.

To create or make changes to your map labels, follow these steps:

1. Click the Map Labels button in the toolbar. The Map Labels dialog box appears.

2. Select the map feature you want to label, and then choose the source of the labels by selecting either the <u>M</u>ap feature names or <u>V</u>alues from radio buttons. (You cannot select both.) Click OK.

3. Place the cursor over the region you want labeled.

4. Click to position the cursor and the label appears.

5. To format your label, right-click and choose <u>F</u>ormat, Font. You can change the size of the label by clicking the label to make it active (an active label has a gray border) and dragging on the corners.

6. To delete your label, select the label and press the Delete key.

Figure 14.17 shows a map with the Great Lakes and some of the states in the central United States labeled.

Fig. 14.17
*A map with some
states and the Great
Lakes all named.*

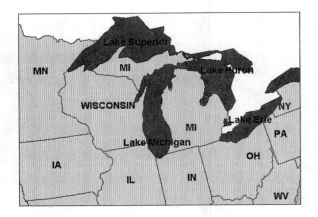

Tip
Change the font and size of your text by clicking the right-mouse button. Choose Format, Font and make your selections.

Note
Your label text can be dragged anywhere in the map. Simply click and drag.

Besides titles, legends, and labels, you can add text to your map to enhance its appearance. To create text in your map, select the Text button from the Data Map toolbar, position it on your map, and type. You can edit your font by clicking the text with the right mouse button.

Add-Ins Available from MapInfo

This section discusses the add-in package for Data Map that is available from MapInfo Corporation. This package is called Mapplets and consists of two wizards (Demographic Viewer and Territory Builder) and three tutorials (Great Maps!, Mastering Data Map, and Marketing Savvy). The package also contains a set of data called MasterPak. MasterPak can be used in conjunction with the wizards or even copied into your spreadsheet and used with Data Map.

The MasterPak data is broken into the following sections:

▸ *Banking*: Includes data for population, income, housing, and employment analysis.

▸ *Business-to-Business*: Includes data for market analysis.

▸ *Healthcare*: Includes data for age, income, and employment analysis.

▸ *Media*: Includes data for age, income, and consumer spending patterns analysis.

▸ *Neighborhood*: Population, income, occupations, number of businesses, housing values, median monthly rent, and mortgage rates are just some of the data included in this section.

▸ *Real Estate*: Analyze the area's housing values and median monthly rent and mortgage rates.

▸ *Retail*: Study the income and spending habits of customers in your trading area.

14

Table 14.3 shows some examples of the data and what it looks like in MasterPak.

Table 14.3   MasterPak Data Sample

Field	Description
COUNTY	County name
STATE	State name
FIPS_CODE	State and county FIPS code (federal code that uniquely defines each county—two-digit state code, three-digit county code)
TOTPOPHIS	1990 total population (historical)
POP_GROWTH	1990–1995 population growth shown as a percent
TOTHOUHIS	1990 total number of households (historical)
TOTHOUCUR	1990 total number of households (current year)
TOTFAMHIS	1990 total number of families (historical)
GRP_QTRS	1990 total population in group quarters (college dorms, nursing homes, military barracks, and so on.)

To install the wizards, tutorials, and MasterPak data, follow these steps:

1. Run the file called CDSETUP.EXE found on the CD-ROM that the program came on. Follow the instructions to complete the installation.

2. You are prompted for an installation path. Under the path that you specify, two folders are created. One folder is called MapData and contains all of the Excel 95 workbooks and Word documentation files describing each of the products. The other folder is called Mapplets and contains all of the Mapplet files.

3. The Mapplet Manager displays in your Tools menu.

4. To unload the Mapplet Manager, click Tools, Add-Ins and deselect Mapplet Manager. You cannot install these products on a network.

If you have any questions regarding the Mapplets or any of the data that you have purchased to use with Data Map, you can fax your inquiry to MapInfo at (518)285-6080 or you can e-mail messages to their technical support Internet address: **techsupport@mapinfo.com**.

After you have installed the program, the words "Mapplet Manager" appear in your Tools menu. Select Mapplet Manager and then the tutorial or wizard when using any of the following applications.

The following section discusses the wizards because they are programs that actually enable you to make maps using your own data or the MasterPak data.

Great Maps!

Great Maps! is a tutorial that provides you with the information you need to quickly become a Data Map expert. The tutorial is set up as a guideline with some steps for implementing what you learn. You learn how and why you want to utilize theme layering, value and category shading, when to use graduated symbols rather than dot density, and how to specify data ranges to effectively display your data. In addition, sections on custom pin maps; the accurate usage of legends, titles, and map annotation; and mapping changes over time are included. The tutorial ends with a checklist called, appropriately, the Great Maps! Checklist!, which summarizes what you have just learned. Take some time to use this tutorial; it will add to your Data Map knowledge base.

To run Great Maps!, click Tools, Mapplet Manager, and select Great Maps!

Marketing Savvy

People in marketing tend to have different needs than those in other aspects of the business world. Using an interactive tutorial, Marketing Savvy uses hypothetical business situations to show you how to customize your marketing data to work best with Data Map. You are guided through case studies that analyze marketing effectiveness and demonstrate how to use Data Map to track marketing campaigns. You also learn how to overlay pie and column charts on shaded maps to analyze response rates and compare regional leads. Marketing Savvy teaches you how to eliminate the guesswork in planning your marketing strategy.

To run Marketing Savvy, click Tools, Mapplet Manager and select Marketing Savvy.

Mastering Data Map

This tutorial is the perfect place for you to start if you are new to mapping. It introduces you to the concept of mapping with themes, how to determine which maps are best suited for your needs and directions to create them. Mastering Data Map is a tutorial that will have you producing impressive, professional maps in no time. Step-by-step instructions on creating powerful maps to display your data are used in conjunction with hypothetical business situations such as targeting market demographics (who are the potential customers?), displaying the distribution of customer accounts (where are the existing customers?), or determining sales or service by location (what volume and where?).

To run Mastering Data Map, click Tools, Mapplet Manager and select Mastering Data.

14

Territory Builder

Territory Builder is a wizard that automates the value and category shading mapping features in Data Map. It shows you how to create maps displaying your spreadsheet data aggregated by custom geographic territories in either category or value shaded maps. Included in this program are techniques for creating new territories in your map, instructions for combining boundaries, and steps to apply them to a new or existing map. Included in Territory Builder are detailed instructions on using value and category shading with your territories; applying titles, legends, and annotations; and methods for performing "what if?" analysis in your territories.

When you create a basic map in Data Map, you must first gather, prepare, and select the data that you want to map. You must go through the same procedure with Territory Builder. Before you can create your territories, you must have data from which you can select. One of the benefits of Territory Builder is that it allows you to select the data after you have opened the wizard, so don't worry if you've forgotten to make your selection! The important thing to remember is that you must select a valid range of data, which is determined by the following criteria: the range must be one contiguous block of cells, contain at least one column of recognizable geographic names, and contain at least one column of additional data.

To create a map using Territory Builder, follow these steps:

1. Choose Tools, Mapplet Manager and select Territory Builder. The step one dialog box appears. Select your data or click Example to display example data. Click Next.

   Caution
   The Example button in Territory Builder and Demographic Viewer will perform the data selection for you, but it chooses from a set of sample data. If you want to go back and choose your own data you must click Cancel and begin again.

2. In step two you will create new territories or modify existing ones. To create a new territory, click New and type in the name of the new territory. Click OK to add the territory to the Defined Territories box.

3. You can add or remove geographic regions, or "members," to or from the territory. To add geographic areas to a territory, select the territory from the Defined Territories box. Select geographic areas from the Available Geographic Names box and click Add or Add All to enter the name into the territory. To remove a geographic area, select the area from the Members Of list box and click Remove or Remove All.

Note

When adding or removing geographic areas from your territories, do not double-click the names; use the buttons. Double-clicking causes Territory Builder to accept the input and move on to the next step.

4. Click <u>N</u>ext to move on to step three. You must now specify the type of map that you want to create. You are given the choices of category or value shading. A category shaded map shows the territories as different colors. The value shaded map shows the territories as different shades of the same color and takes it one step further by assigning value to the colors. For example, a value shaded map could show dark-blue areas that represent the northeastern territory and high sales volume. Light-blue would represent the lower sales volume areas in the northeastern territory.

Enter a title and subtitle and click <u>F</u>inish to create the map. Figure 14.18 shows a category shaded map of the United States using sample data that comes with Territory Builder. It includes the numbers and row headings so you can see what the data looks like and pattern yours after it. Figure 14.19 shows a value shaded map of the same data.

Fig. 14.18

This category shaded map was created using the sample data that comes with Territory Builder. Category shading is useful for displaying data with fewer ranges.

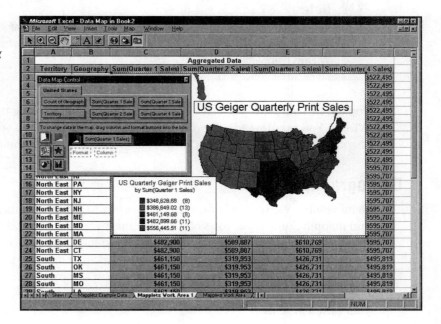

14

Fig. 14.19

Value shaded maps are better for displaying data that cover a wide range of values. Try category and value shading to decide which works best for your situation.

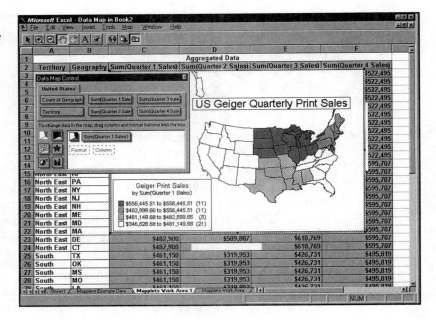

α **Note**

If you click Finish before you have completed all of the steps, the Territory Builder Wizard will use default settings to complete your map. Selecting Cancel stops the Wizard completely.

You did it! Your territories have been successfully mapped using the Territory Builder Wizard. You can now edit the contents using the skills that you acquired earlier in this chapter. Remember—the Data Control box is the command center!

Demographic Viewer

Demographic Viewer is a wizard that allows you to automate value shading by selecting and mapping only those rows of data that meet your criteria. Value shading can be used for analyzing age demographics or population trends across the nation and for targeting a particular market. If, for example, you are marketing a luxury item, it would be valuable to know where the population with the most disposable income is located. Demographic Viewer teaches you how to create maps that focus on business scenarios to meet your business goals.

Demographic Viewer comes with county-level data for the United States. Before you attempt to use Demographic Viewer, make sure that this data is installed on your hard disk. If you need data with a greater level of detail, there are other data products available from MapInfo. You can purchase census data and feature data such as roads, cities, airports, and waterways.

To create a map using the Demographic Viewer Wizard follow these steps:

1. Open the county demographics file that came with Demographic Viewer and select the data ranges that you want to map.

2. Choose <u>T</u>ools, <u>M</u>applet Manager and select the Demographic Viewer Wizard.

3. The Wizard now reviews the data that you have selected to map. If you have not selected any data from your worksheet, Demographic Viewer will prompt you to do so. If you are not sure which data to choose, you can click the Example button and Demographic Viewer will show you how. Remember, Demographic Viewer selects from a set of sample data for this example. You must choose Cancel and begin again if you want to use your own data. Data can be selected before or after opening the Demographic Viewer Wizard.

 Tip

You must select a valid range of data which is determined by the following criteria: the range must be one contiguous block of cells *and* contain at least one column of recognizable geographic names *and* contain at least one column of additional data in order for Demographic Viewer to map it.

4. Select <u>N</u>ext and go on to the Step 2 dialog box. This window prompts you to specify filter criteria for the data you have selected to map. For example, if you wanted to map only those areas with populations of more than 15,000, you would click the TOTPOPCUR (Current Total Population) in the Column In box. (An asterisk appears next to TOTPOPCUR in the list to let you know that it has been selected.) These abbreviations may seem difficult to manage, but fortunately, Demographic Viewer defines them for you within the dialog box. To see the definitions, click the abbreviation GEOABBR and look at the title bar of the Show Rows Column. The words Geographic Abbreviation will display.

5. You can either tab or mouse-click over to the Show Rows box to select the criteria statement. In this case "is Equal to" is selected. Enter the number you want to use. Figure 14.20 displays the Step 2 dialog box. At the bottom left of this dialog box is a check box labeled <u>D</u>ata Has Column Titles. Check this box if you want Demographic Viewer to ignore those cells that contain titles during its search.

14

Fig. 14.20

Demographic Viewer's Step 2 dialog box. Use this step to set up filter criteria.

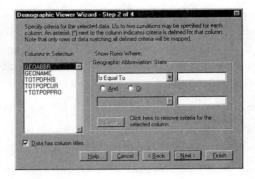

6. Select <u>N</u>ext to move to Step 3 or <u>B</u>ack to return to Step 1. In Step 3, you specify what geographic region column to use for the value shaded layer and what non-geographic columns to use for additional layers such as pie or column charts. You must select one column to be the value shaded layer. In this example the GEOABBR (geographic abbreviations) column is selected. The remaining non-geographic columns appear in the Columns in Selection box. Select and move to the Additional Data to Map area any columns of data you want to include in the Data Map Control Panel. You can select from these columns to create pie or column charts on the resulting map. Figure 14.21 shows the Step 3 dialog box. Click <u>N</u>ext to go on to Step 4.

Fig. 14.21

Demographic Viewer's Step 3 dialog box. This box prompts you to define your value shaded layer and any additional layers you want to use.

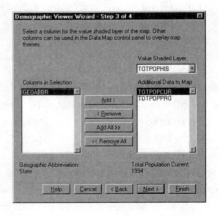

7. Create a title and subtitle for your map. Click <u>F</u>inish and Demographic Viewer creates your map in a separate Mapplets work area. Figure 14.22 is the completed map.

Fig. 14.22

Here is a completed Demographic Viewer map. You should have a value shaded map displaying your data or the example data.

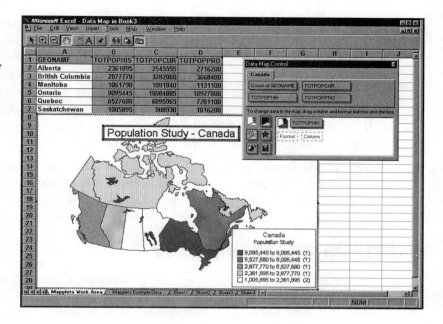

Some maps for Data Map contain thousands of boundaries that may take a little extra time to draw on the screen. For example, US Counties and US ZIP Codes display every county and ZIP code boundary for the entire United States. Besides taking extra time to draw, you may not need that much detail! You can change the default view of the map by following these steps:

1. Create a map.

2. Zoom in on the section of the map that you need to use.

3. Choose Map, Save Map Template. Click Save. When Demographic Viewer asks you if you want to overwrite the existing template, choose Yes, or type in a new name to create your own template. Keep in mind that if you overwrite the existing template, that data will not display again. It is a good idea to create your own template.

 Tip

If a map is taking too long to redraw, you can interrupt the redraw by pressing the Esc key.

14

After you have created a map, you can share it with other Data Map users, as long as they have installed Data Map and have the same data that you are using. You can insert the Data Map object into a workbook or document, copy it, and give it to your colleagues. For example, if you create a map using Canadian data files, make a copy of it and give it to a colleague, that person must have the Canadian data files installed to display the map. If they don't have the data installed the data will disappear from the document. If the map has been embedded in an Excel workbook the data will disappear from the workbook.

If the user has not installed Data Map he or she will not be able to edit the map. It will open as a Windows metafile or picture. If the user has Data Map installed, he or she can simply double-click the map to make it active and begin editing.

Expert Data Mapping Uses

Now that you have seen the potentially powerful relationship that can exist between data and geographic representation, you are probably eager to learn about other, more advanced tasks that Data Map offers. Practice working closely with the features of Excel, and you will find that Data Map offers you a variety of display capabilities. This section looks at maps that have added features such as roads and cities.

At the beginning of this chapter you were advised to explore the MAPSTATS.XLS file to familiarize yourself with the data that is recognized by Data Map. If you did that, you know that Data Map has much to offer in the way of data. There are more than boundaries for countries and counties here! You can create interest in your map by adding details such as major highways and roads, airports, and waterways. In Data Map, these are referred to as *features*. When you right-click in your map and look at the features list, you will see a box with all of the attributes of your map checked. You can add and delete features using Data Map's Add Features function.

Figure 14.23 shows an example of a map with added features. In this case, we have added highways and cities to a map of Canada.

Fig. 14.23
A map of Canada with highways and cities added to it.

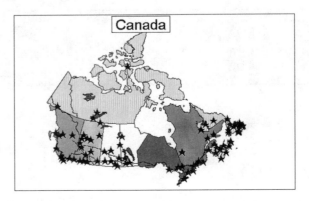

To add or remove features to your map, such as highways, cities, or airports, follow these steps:

1. There are a few ways to open the features list: right-click your mouse and select Features from the short-cut menu and double-click the map, or choose Map, Features to display the Map Features dialog box.

2. Click the box for each item that you want to display. A check mark will appear in the box. If an item is already selected and you wish to remove it, click the box to deselect it.

3. Click OK and return to your map to see the features that have been added or deleted.

Besides adding more details to the map, you can add other maps to your existing map. For instance, if you wanted to add the United States to your map of Canada, you can right-click your map and select Add Feature. Figure 14.24 shows the Add Map Feature dialog box.

Fig. 14.24

The Add Map Feature dialog box allows you to select data from your data files and add them to your current map.

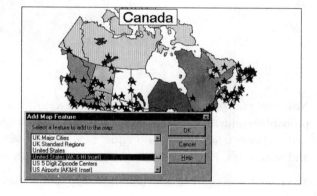

Select the feature that you want to add from the list and click OK. This example chooses the United States with Alaska and Hawaii inserts. Click OK. The map of Canada redraws with the United States map attached to it.

To delete a feature from the map, right-click your mouse in the map and select Feature. The Map Features dialog box appears (see fig. 14.25). To delete a feature, deselect its box in the Visible column.

You can also change the colors of the map in this dialog box. Simply select Custom for a drop-down list of colors. Click OK.

Figure 14.26 displays the final map of Canada with the United States as an added feature.

14

Fig. 14.25
Select which features will display in your map by selecting and deselecting them in this dialog box. You can also change the colors of your map by selecting Custom.

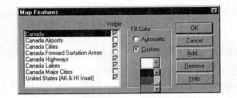

Fig. 14.26
The final map of Canada with the United States as an added feature. Add or delete features to your map until you find the one that best displays your data.

US Map with Canada as an Added Feature

Now that you've learned how to add and delete different features in your map, you are probably wondering how to label some of these new features. The same technique that you used when labeling your original map can be used to label added cities, highways, and waterways. Figure 14.27 is a map of Mexico with some of its cities labeled.

To create labels on your added feature map follow these steps:

1. Double-click your map to make it active.
2. Click the Map Labels toolbar button.
3. Drag the label over the city that you want to label. Cities are, by default, shown as small, black blocks on the map.
4. Click the mouse to insert the label.
5. Right-click the mouse to edit the font of your label.

Fig. 14.27

A map of Mexico with labeled cities as an added feature.

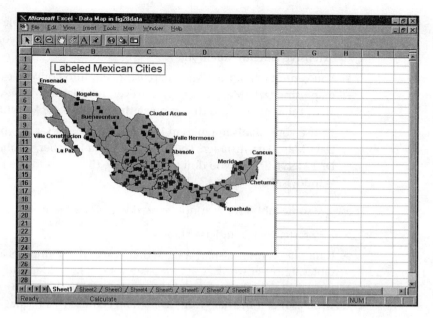

Tip

To change the city symbol, right-click the mouse and select <u>F</u>eatures. A drop-down list of the map features appears. Click inside the Mexico Cities check box and click Custom. The default symbol appears; click it to get a listing of all the symbols that are available to use.

Data Map and MapInfo

While Data Map allows you to create thematically shaded maps based on the data that you put in your worksheet, there are some differences between Data Map and MapInfo. Familiarize yourself with what you can and cannot do before trying to use Data Map and MapInfo at the same time.

▶ Data Map uses the data that you have in your worksheet or from sample files that come with the add-in packet. MapInfo uses data created in tables in MapInfo. The tables and the worksheets are set up differently.

14

▶ Data Map offers a selection of the features that are available in MapInfo. Don't get frustrated when you find that you cannot perform a geographic query or an extensive labeling function.

▶ You cannot edit a Data Map map using MapInfo and you cannot edit a MapInfo map using Data Map. You can, however, use MapInfo tables in Data Map. In fact, all of the sample maps that come with Data Map are MapInfo tables.

▶ To use your MapInfo tables in Data Map you must set up your table using the Data Map Data Installer. To launch the Data Installer, double-click the file DATAINST.EXE. If you don't know where this file is located, click Start, Find in Windows 95.

These are some tables that cannot be used with Data Map:

▶ Any raster image underlay tables.

▶ Data Map cannot display a table that is actually defined as a relational join of other tables. In other words, Data Map cannot display a MapInfo StreetInfo table. You must first save the street table in MapInfo using the Save Copy As command, which saves it in "flat" form. Data Map can use this format.

▶ It is not possible for Data Map to display point objects that use MapInfo's Custom symbol styles. If your map contains these points they will be invisible in Data Map.

Purchasing Add-In Packages

The Data Map feature in Excel is written by MapInfo Corporation. It offers the bundled package of wizards, tutorials, and data that enhance the mapping functions. You also can purchase other mapping packages and data.

To contact MapInfo Corporation:

MapInfo Corporation
One Global View
Troy, New York 12180-8399 USA
Telephone: (800)488-3552 USA
(518)285-7110 International
Fax: (518)285-6070
Internet: **sales@mapinfo.com**

Summary

At this point you should be comfortable with the functionality of Data Map. In the previous chapter we covered quite a bit of ground, but don't be discouraged if you didn't assimilate *all* of the details—that's the beauty of a book; it's always there for your reference.

We've covered the installation of Data Map on your system, including the setup on which Data Map will run best. We then reviewed how to organize your data so that Data Map can recognize and use it to create effective maps. You learned how to create those maps using your own data or the data that comes with the program. It might be useful just to experiment with the MAPSTATS.XLS data for a while before attempting to map any of your own data. Finally, we looked at the different ways to customize your map, use the add-in programs that are available separately, and use advanced functions in Data Map.

While Data Map is a very serious business tool, it can also be fun! Use it to explore different areas, plan trips, and get to know more about the world we live in.

chapter 15

Using Shared Lists

15

by Donna Payne

In this chapter

◆ **How to work with shared lists**
You learn the process for setting up a shared list, and how to use the different options in the Shared Lists dialog box.

◆ **The best types of lists for sharing**
Because there are limitations to what you can do after a list is shared, there are lists that should and should not be set up to be shared.

◆ **How Excel handles conflicts**
You learn how conflicts within the workbook are solved, and where these conflicts are stored. The Conflict Manager is explored in-depth.

◆ **Using VBA to control shared lists**
The properties and methods used to control shared lists are explained.

At one time or another, you've probably been tasked with maintaining a list of data for your entire department or company. As such, you entered the data, performed the edits, updated the list, and created all necessary reports. For a small list, this probably wasn't a big deal. However, if your list had many entries, if there were constant updates, or if others accessed the file, this could become a real nightmare.

Shared lists, a feature new to Excel 7, enable multiple people to access a file simultaneously over a network. Prior to Excel 7 and shared lists, only one person at a time could open a file and have read-write privileges. Now, with Excel 7, as many people as your network allows may open the shared list file simultaneously and have both read and write privileges.

Note

The process of how to set up and designate a list is very simple. This chapter emphasizes which normal Excel features are not available when lists are shared. Because the Shared Lists feature is new to Excel 7, more basics are covered in this chapter than what you will find in chapters covering features that have been around a while.

Working with Shared Lists

Because the shared lists feature is new to Excel 7, you may not have had much occasion to use it. And even if you were aware of this feature, you may not have thought about how much it could aid in your custom application development and in your everyday Excel use. The truth is, if you maintain lists that are used for a group or division within your company, you may find shared lists one of the best new features of MS Excel.

A *shared list* is a normal Excel worksheet within an Excel workbook that has been set up to be accessed and edited by more than one person at a time. Figure 15.1 shows a worksheet that has not yet been designated as shared. This chapter uses an example from a fictitious company called the ABC Company to show how to create a shared list, how to tell who is currently accessing the file, how Excel handles conflicts, and the limitations of using a shared list.

The ABC Company is small, but its operation is spread out over several geographical regions. For this reason, it needs to maintain a list of employees that indicates names, department, and location.

Note

If you would like to follow these examples, you will find a Chapter 15 example file on the CD that accompanies this book or you may choose to re-create this worksheet and follow the steps in the following sections. The first example, file START ABC COMPANY.XLS, has not been designated as shared. The file ABC COMPANY.XLS is the second of the two examples that has been designated as shared and shows a conflict history.

Fig. 15.1

The ABC Company has a network server to which all employees have access, and have decided to create a shared list.

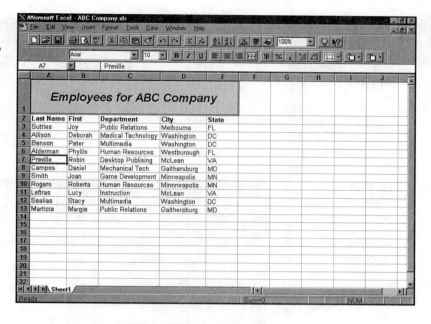

The file START ABC COMPANY.XLS is ready to be shared. Follow these steps to create a shared list:

1. Choose <u>F</u>ile, <u>S</u>hared Lists, and in the Editing Tab, check the option to <u>A</u>llow Multi-User Editing. Figure 15.2 shows the Shared Lists dialog box.

Fig. 15.2

The Shared Lists dialog box is used to designate the list as shared, to set options for editing the list, and to show which users have the workbook open at the same time.

2. Click OK. A warning dialog box appears, which tells you that the action of allowing multi-user editing requires that the file be saved (see fig. 15.3).

3. Click OK. The Save As dialog box is now displayed.

4. In the Save As dialog box, type a name in the File <u>N</u>ame edit box. The example file will be saved with the name, ABC Company (you can choose any name that you want). Save the file to a common directory on the network and click OK.

Fig. 15.3

You are asked if you want to continue. If you do not want a shared list, click Cancel.

Now that you've set the file up as a shared list, there are a few changes to the worksheet. Figure 15.4 shows the same worksheet shown in figure 15.1 but now the worksheet is available to be shared by multiple users.

Fig. 15.4

If the workbook is saved to a common network directory, anyone who has access to that directory is able to access this file.

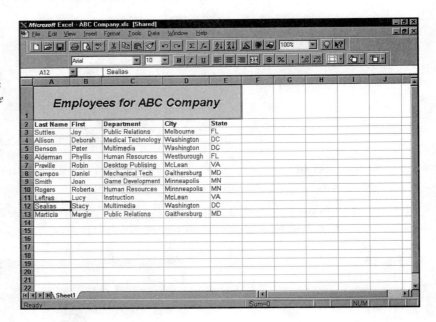

α Note

Notice that the title bar now has [Shared] next to the workbook name. This lets you know that the workbook is now available to anyone who has access to the shared directory on the network. If you were to remove the option to Allow Multiple Users from the Editing Tab on the Shared Lists dialog box and make the list exclusive, the word [Shared] would disappear from the title bar.

Limitations of Shared Lists

If you look at several of the menu options, you'll find that many submenu commands are disabled when the list is designated as shared. The menu items that are disabled in a shared list must be used either before the workbook is shared, or after the workbook is made exclusive again. The features that are not available once a list is shared are described in the sections that follow.

Formulas

Shared lists do not save formulas. However, if a formula is present before the workbook is designated as shared, the formula continues to save but cannot be edited and then the new formula is saved.

When the workbook is open, and a formula is edited, the formula appears to calculate as a normal Excel worksheet formula. In fact, if you try to enter a formula, or edit an existing formula on a shared list, you will see the dialog box that is displayed in figure 15.5.

Fig. 15.5

If you are new to shared lists, you might want this dialog box to appear each time you try to enter or edit a formula to remind you that it will not be saved on a list that is shared.

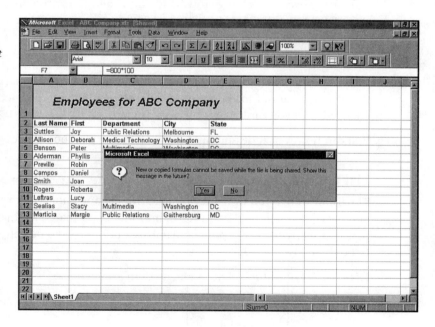

 Note

If you choose the <u>Y</u>es button displayed in figure 15.5, you will see the same warning each time you try to enter, copy, or modify a formula on a shared worksheet. This includes when you attempt to:

▶ Use AutoFill to drag the value returned from the formula

▶ Press the shortcut key combinations of Ctrl+D, Ctrl+R, or Ctrl+L

▶ Choose Edit, Fill, and choose any direction, Up, Down, Left, or Right

However, you do not receive the formula warning dialog box if you choose Edit, Fill, Series, and choose a Type option such as Growth.

Formatting

You cannot change the formatting of a shared list. This means that you cannot even make the contents of a cell bold. This same restriction applies when using formatting toolbar buttons. Choose Format and notice that the Cells command is disabled. If you click the Underline button on the toolbar, nothing will happen. You cannot do any formatting except to change row height and column width when the list is marked as shared. Additionally, AutoFormats and Styles cannot be used on a shared list.

Inserting and Deleting

Inserting and deleting sheets cannot be done while the list is marked as shared. Additionally, you cannot insert or delete cells, objects, names, or functions. Links cannot be changed, and you can't insert pictures or maps.

You can however, hide and unhide sheets in the workbook that contains a shared list.

List and Database Features

The list of things you can and can't do with list and database features is fairly long. If you have a list that tracks and stores information, a shared list may be ideal. If you need to access many of Excel's popular database options, you'd be better off not setting the list to be shared.

Here is a list of features that can be used on a shared list:

▶ You can sort by entire row or column.

▶ You can choose Data, Filter.

This list contains the features that cannot be used on a shared list:

▶ You cannot create scenarios in a shared list.

▶ AutoSum and AutoSubtotals are disabled.

▶ You cannot choose Data, Filter, Advanced Filter.

▶ You cannot use a PivotTable and you cannot use the group or ungroup commands.

▶ You cannot use the <u>T</u>able command on the <u>D</u>ata menu.

If you have a list that contains thousands of rows of data, you may want to consider maintaining your list in a relational database such as Microsoft Access that can be stored on a network. Because you cannot use the Advanced AutoFilter feature on a shared list, you will be unable to determine whether or not you have duplicates in your list, and if so, to remove them.

Macros and Modules

Macros run and record while a workbook is shared. Recording a new macro, however, defaults to recording to a new workbook. Furthermore, if you choose to record a new macro from a shared list, and you choose <u>T</u>ools, <u>R</u>ecord Macro, <u>R</u>ecord New Macro, and click the <u>O</u>ptions button, you only can choose to record to a <u>N</u>ew workbook, or record to your <u>P</u>ersonal macro workbook. Additionally, you cannot assign a macro to an object when the workbook is shared.

Help Menu

Lotus 1-2-3 Help is not available nor is the command to access The Microsoft Network. Other Help options are available as usual.

Protection

Protection is not available once the workbook is designated as a shared list. If you want to apply file-level, workbook, worksheet, or cell protection, you must do so while the file is exclusive.

Not All Lists Make Good Shared Lists

When a worksheet is designated as a shared list, some restrictions are set to protect the data, and protect the way the data is presented. Because you cannot edit formulas in a shared list, there doesn't seem to be any reason to share a list in which formulas will be edited often. Likewise, a file that contains a database option like a PivotTable will not function on a shared list. With this in mind, there are candidates for good shared lists and others that should not be shared.

Lists that work best for sharing are

▶ *Contact Lists.* Customer contact information, personal Rolodex, corporate directories, and the like.

▶ *Tracking Lists.* Part numbers, inventory, sales quotas (although you may not want this to be shared), RSVP information, outstanding proposals, fiscal budgets, costs, and so on.

Lists that are not good candidates for sharing include

▶ Lists that contain PivotTables

▶ Macros that need to be edited that are associated with the list data

▶ Lists that have formulas that may need to be edited

Understanding the Shared Lists Dialog Box

The Shared Lists dialog box has two tabs: Editing and Status. The Editing tab options are Allow Multi-User Editing, and Show Conflict History. When you check Allow Multi-User Editing, you designate that the list become shared (refer to fig. 15.2).

If you deselect Allow Multi-User Editing, you will make the workbook exclusive again and prevent any user currently accessing the shared list from saving any changes. After you make the workbook exclusive, however, you are able to format, edit, insert, delete, and perform all other operations as you would with any normal Excel workbook.

After a workbook is saved as shared, the Editing tab on the Shared List dialog box allows the second option, Show Conflict History, to be checked. The Conflict History is stored in a worksheet that by default is hidden. On this sheet, all conflicts that occur about the data that resides in the list are tracked and displayed.

The Status tab on the Shared Lists dialog box shows which users currently have the workbook open. Figure 15.6 displays the Status tab of this dialog box.

Fig. 15.6

Besides the names of the users that have the shared workbook open, the dates and times that they opened the file also are displayed.

 Note

Excel doesn't limit the number of users to a shared list, but your network may.

When a second or additional users log onto a shared list, after selecting the shared file and opening it, they are presented with the User Identification dialog box. The dialog box prompts the user to enter his or her name in the edit box so all users of the shared workbook may be identified in the Status portion of the Shared Lists dialog box. This is required to track conflicts and who is involved in each conflict. After entering your name, click the Close button and the information is stored. The information for the default user identification is taken from the User Name setting as shown by choosing Tools, Options, General, User Name. The General tab is displayed in figure 15.7.

Fig. 15.7

The default user identification is taken from the General tab after choosing Tools, Options.

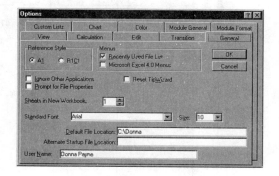

Handling Conflicts in Shared Lists

The Show Conflict History option on the Editing tab, if checked, displays a dialog box indicating a conflict that has occurred due to a second user changing data that has been entered and saved by the first user who placed data in the cell. This includes any data in the used range of the shared list. The *used range* is the range of cells that contains, or has contained, data.

Tip

You can find the used range of a worksheet by pressing Ctrl+End, or by pressing the F5 key, and choosing Special, Last Cell.

In the example shown in figure 15.8, any information that is changed in cells A1:E13 from a list that has been saved will result in a conflict.

Caution

Don't leave blank rows in the shared list. Either add rows between existing data, or at the bottom of the list (next record). Ctrl + +(plus sign) inserts a new row.

Ctrl + – (minus sign) deletes a row. If there are blank rows between the existing data, Excel cannot determine what area makes up the list.

Fig. 15.8

The last used cell on this worksheet is E13.

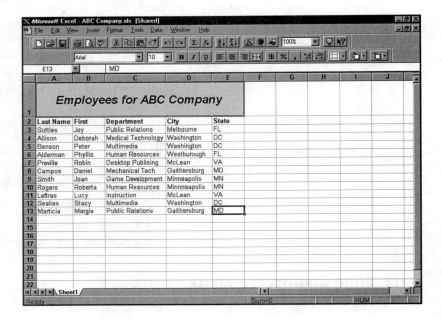

If existing data on a worksheet needs to be edited, a conflict will occur because Excel is being told that two different values should reside in the same cell. When a conflict occurs, a Conflict Resolution dialog box appears.

An example of when this might happen is when a person from the list of ABC Company employees shown in figure 15.8 changes jobs or location and the list must be updated. In cell D3, the city for the employee Joy Suttles is Melbourne. If she transfers to the Minneapolis office and the city is changed to Minneapolis in the cell after it has been saved, a conflict will occur because two different values occupy that cell.

Figure 15.9 shows the options presented to a user when a conflict occurs.

The Conflict Resolution dialog box has four buttons that do the following:

▶ Use your changes (the current user) to a cell on the named sheet. This includes the cell location and the date. If your change is to be used, press the Use My Changes button.

Fig. 15.9

Instead of overwriting the contents of a cell, Excel notifies the user of a conflict that has occurred and allows the user to choose which edits to retain.

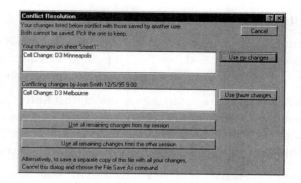

▸ Use the conflicting (other or previous edit) change cell location, user who changed it, and the date and time it was changed. If the conflicting changes should be used, press the Use These Changes button.

▸ Use All Remaining Changes from My Session, or the current user, if you want to save your changes as opposed to any other user's changes.

▸ Use All Remaining Changes from the Other Session.

If changes are made to the list by a second user, you will not immediately see the changes that have been made. Once you have saved and chosen to close the workbook, a dialog box will notify you that the save resulted in changes by other users.

Caution

When a conflict occurs, and when the Conflict Resolution dialog box as shown in figure 15.9 is displayed, Excel will not allow other users to save their changes to the shared file. When the conflict is resolved, the file can be saved as usual by other users accessing the file.

When there is a conflict and when the secondary user attempts to save the file, a dialog box will display informing them of a conflict and the person's name that is involved in the resolving of the conflict.

Tip

If the warning of a conflict is displayed, and you are unable to save the file until the second person resolves the conflict, you are permitted to save the file by a different name. The shared list version is not saved and you will need to go in later, after the conflict is resolved, and make and save your changes.

Storing Conflict History

Just because a user chooses to replace the value of a cell does not mean that the information that was entered into the cell prior to the edit is completely lost. This is where the option to Show Conflict History from the Editing tab comes into play.

When you choose not to display the conflict history, Excel stores the information anyway and hides the Conflict History worksheet. If you choose File, Shared Lists, Editing, and select the check box next to the option to Show Conflict History, a worksheet will unhide in your shared workbook with eight columns of information.

Even if there have been no conflicts in the shared file, you can still show the Conflict History worksheet. It's not very exciting but it may be more of a reassurance of no edits to the data when you're dealing with important numbers and profits. In figure 15.10, a Conflict History is shown where there have been no recorded conflicts. This will help you see which columns and headers are filled when there is a conflict in a shared list.

Fig. 15.10

The worksheet headings for each conflict category will be formatted in a bold, blue font style.

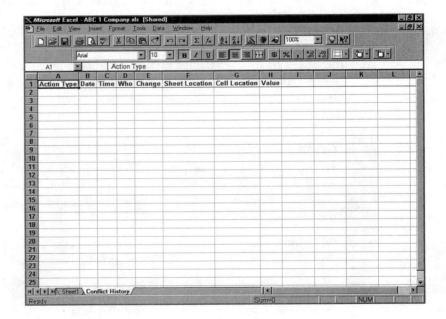

A comfort to many managers who express concern for the integrity of the data on the Conflict History worksheet is that the cells in this worksheet are locked. No manual edits can take place on the worksheet. Nor can there be any inserting or deleting of rows and columns. The only thing the user can do when they want to hide any conflicts is to either hide the sheet, or save the file as exclusive and then resave it as a shared list.

Caution

If you have a saved shared list and you decide to make it exclusive, even temporarily, the Conflict History worksheet will be deleted, *permanently*. All conflict history will be erased from the file.

15

The Conflict History worksheet stores the following eight columns of information:

▶ *Action Type*. This value will be either Won or Lost.

▶ *Date*. The date that the information that was entered was saved.

▶ *Time*. The time that the information was saved.

▶ *Who*. The user who made the change to the cell.

▶ *Change*. The action that took place—was a cell changed, a sheet renamed, the sheet sorted?

▶ *Sheet Location*. The name of the worksheet where the change or conflict took place.

▶ *Cell Location*. The address of the cell where the conflict occurred.

▶ *Value*. The value that was placed in the cell.

Figure 15.11 shows a record of conflict that occurred between two users.

Fig. 15.11

The conflicts shown here have been exaggerated to give you an indication of how the conflict history is stored.

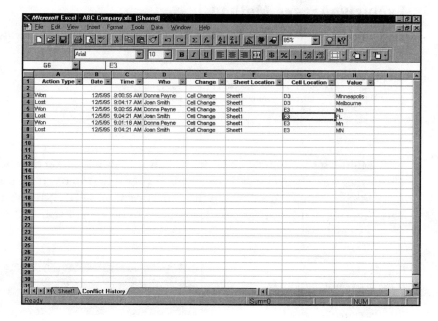

Note

Note that the AutoFilter option has automatically been implemented on the Conflict History worksheet when there are conflicts in the shared list.

Method and Properties of a Shared List

There is one method that represents actions that can be performed on a shared list. There are four properties that can be set or get a property setting from a list that is shared. The method and properties are

- ExclusiveAccess   (Method)
- MultiUserEditing   (Property)
- RevisionNumber   (Property)
- ShowConflictHistory   (Property)
- UserStatus   (Property)

ExclusiveAccess Method

If the current open workbook is designated as shared, the following subroutine will give the current user exclusive access to the file:

```
Sub AssignExclusiveAccessMethod()
    If ActiveWorkbook.MultiUserEditing Then
        ActiveWorkbook.ExclusiveAccess
    End If
End Sub
```

The subroutine, `AssignExclusiveAccessMethod` determines whether the option to Allow Multi-User Editing has been checked on the Editing tab on the Shared Lists dialog box. If True, your changes will be saved but anyone else who has the workbook open will have to save changes to a different file name by choosing File, Save As. Figure 15.12 shows the warning that is displayed when the subroutine AssignExclusiveAccessMethod is run from a shared list.

Fig. 15.12

If the active workbook is open as a shared list, the current user will now have exclusive access to the file.

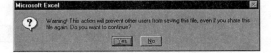

MultiUserEditing Property

This is True if the workbook is open as a shared list. To save a workbook as a shared list, use the SaveAs method. To change the workbook from shared mode to exclusive mode, use the ExclusiveAccess method. This applies to the workbook object.

The subroutine that follows, CheckForMultiUserEditingProperty, determines whether the active workbook is open as a shared list. If it is, a message box stating that this is a shared workbook will appear.

```
Sub CheckForMultiUserEditingProperty()

'''Checks to see if the option for multi-user is checked.
'''If it is, then it returns a message box below.

    If ActiveWorkbook.MultiUserEditing Then
        MsgBox "This is a shared workbook."
    End If

'''If the active workbook is not designated as a shared list, then it will
'''save the file with the full name of the active workbook, and set the argument
'''accessMode of the ActiveWorkbook to xlShared.

    If Not ActiveWorkbook.MultiUserEditing Then
    On Error Resume Next     ''' Prevent Error Message if Cancel Clicked
        ActiveWorkbook.SaveAs fileName:=ActiveWorkbook.FullName, _
            accessMode:=xlShared
    End If
End Sub
```

Figure 15.13 shows the message box that is displayed when this subroutine is run and the list is not a shared list.

Fig. 15.13

To trap an error when a user clicks the Cancel button, the line On Error Resume Next *has been placed after the IF Not ActiveWorkbook. MultiUserEditing procedure.*

RevisionNumber Property

The RevisionNumber property returns the number of times the local copy of the workbook has been saved. If the subroutine ShowRevisionNumberofList is run on an exclusive workbook, the file is saved as shared with the active workbook's full path as its name.

The number of times the local copy of the workbook has been saved is displayed in a message box.

If the workbook is opened in exclusive mode, the property of 0 (zero) is returned.

```
Sub ShowRevisionNumbersofList()
    If ActiveWorkbook.RevisionNumber = 0 Then
        ActiveWorkbook.SaveAs filename:=ActiveWorkbook.FullName, _
            accessMode:=xlShared, conflictResolution:= _
                xlOtherSessionChanges
    Else
        MsgBox xlOtherSessionChanges
    End If
End Sub
```

Caution

The RevisionNumber property is only updated for saved local copies.

ShowConflictHistory Property

When the ShowConflictHistory property is called on the ActiveWorkbook, as demonstrated in the subroutine shown here, the active workbook is checked to see if it is a shared list. If so, the Show Conflict History option on the Editing tab of the Shared Lists dialog box is checked and the worksheet Conflict History is unhidden and made active.

```
Sub ShowConflictHistoryProperty()
    If ActiveWorkbook.MultiUserEditing Then
        ActiveWorkbook.ShowConflictHistory = True
    End If
End Sub
```

UserStatus Property

The UserStatus property returns an array specifying information about all current users of the open, shared list file. In the following subroutine, ShowCurrentUsersNames, the current user names are determined by the UserStatus of the active workbook. A new workbook is created, and the name of each current user, the date and time, and the status of the shared file, whether it is shared or exclusive, are placed in the new workbook.

Caution

The UserStatus property doesn't return information about users that may have opened the shared list workbook as Read-Only.

```
Sub ShowCurrentUserNames()
    Dim CurrentUserNames As Variant
    Dim irow As Integer
    CurrentUserNames = ActiveWorkbook.UserStatus
    With Workbooks.Add.Sheets(1)
        For irow = 1 To UBound(CurrentUserNames, 1)
          .Cells(irow, 1) = CurrentUserNames(irow, 1)
          .Cells(irow, 2) = CurrentUserNames(irow, 2)
             Select Case CurrentUserNames(irow, 3)
                 Case 1
                     .Cells(irow, 3).Value = "Exclusive"
                 Case 2
                     .Cells(irow, 3).Value = "Shared"
             End Select
        Next
    End With
End Sub
```

Figure 15.14 shows the worksheet from the new workbook that is created when the subroutine, Sub ShowCurrentUserNames is run.

Fig. 15.14

Three columns of information are returned: the name of each current user of the file, the date and time, and the status of each.

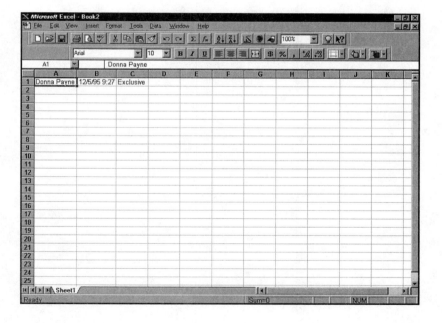

Summary

In this chapter, you have learned how to designate a Excel workbook that contains a list as a shared list, types of lists that are best suited for shared lists, and those that are not.

You have learned how Excel resolves conflicts in the shared workbook, about the Conflict History worksheet, and how properties and methods are used through VBA to control shared lists.

In the next chapter, you learn about another new feature to Excel 7, the Binder Object Model.

chapter 16

Using the Binder Object Model

16

by John V. Green

In this chapter

◆ **What Binder is all about**
Binder allows you to group and manage your files so you don't need to worry about loading the supporting files and software programs.

◆ **What limitations Binder imposes**
There is a trade-off between ease of use and access to all features.

◆ **The Binder Object Model**
The Objects, Methods, and Properties in the Binder Object Model.

◆ **Putting it all together**
Using VBA procedures, the power of Binder, Excel, Word, and PowerPoint can be harnessed.

Microsoft Office 95 introduced a number of exciting innovations. One of these is a new application called Binder. Binder provides you with the facility to hold all your Excel, Word, and PowerPoint files for a particular project in a single file. This has numerous advantages for maintaining and distributing applications.

Through extensions to the Excel Object Model and through the creation of a PowerPoint Object Model and Binder Object Model in the Office 95 versions of these products, you can now tap the full capabilities of this software via VBA code in an Excel module.

There is little documentation available on how you take advantage of these new capabilities. This chapter shows you how.

Why Use Binder?

Binder is a tool that allows you to group a number of Office files into a single file. This means that you can keep a number of related files grouped together as a single entity. It also makes it easier to exchange or share those files.

Grouping Documents

Say you needed to set up an Excel budget for your organization similar to the one in figure 16.1. The workbook contains four identically formatted sheets for the three international divisions of the company in the USA, Europe, Australia, and the Consolidated figures. Each sheet has a chart showing the projected Net Profits.

Fig. 16.1

The Excel workbook, BudSheet.xls, contains budget figures for the three divisions of Sheet Steel Enterprises.

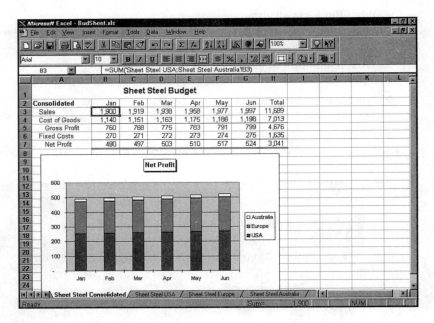

Having established your figures, you need to write a cover letter and summary using Word, with figures and charts from the Excel budget. Figure 16.2 shows the document that contains a copy of the consolidation table and chart from the Excel workbook.

Fig. 16.2

The Word document, BUDDOC.DOC, contains a report on the budget, including the Consolidated summary figures and chart from BUDSHEET.XLS.

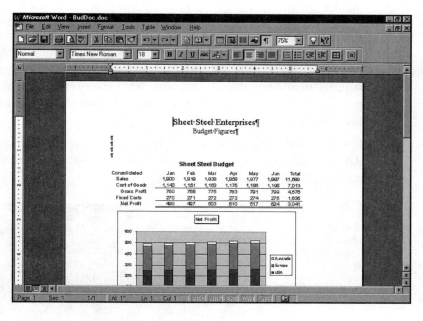

16

You also need to put together a slide show using PowerPoint that will assist you while presenting the figures to the board. Figure 16.3 shows the slides you will use with charts copied from the Excel workbook.

Fig. 16.3

The PowerPoint presentation, BUDPP.PPT, contains slides that have charts copied from the Excel workbook.

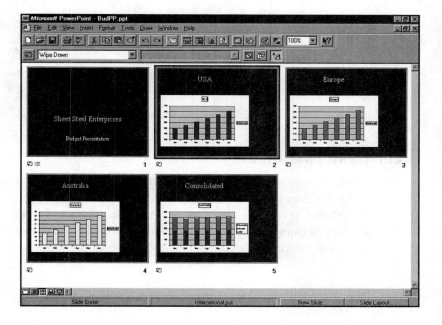

For convenience, you have decided to group the three files into a Binder file as shown in figure 16.4. Once you have done that, you can access all three components of the budget by loading just one file in Binder. Binder lets you switch from one component to another by clicking the icons, and it automatically loads the required software applications required to give you seamless access to what you need. As you move from one component to another, the environment changes accordingly to give you the correct context including toolbars and menus.

Binder makes it easy if you want to transport your application. When you transfer your data to your laptop computer, you only have to concern yourself with the one file instead of three.

Fig. 16.4

The three budget files have been placed in a single Binder file, SteelBud.obd.

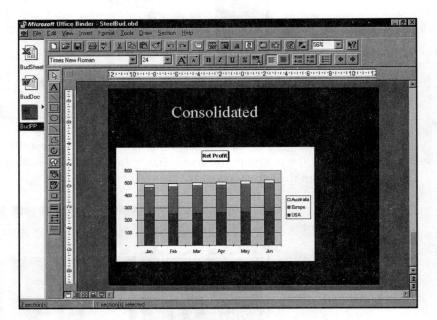

Early and Late Binding

You can create your Binder before or after you set up the individual sections. If you prefer, you can open a new, empty Binder file, add the required Excel, Word, and PowerPoint sections and then proceed to fill in the data. This early binding technique means you can work entirely within Binder without ever having to open the other applications. Binder does all that for you as you add sections and switch from one section to another.

The alternative is to use a late binding technique. You create your Excel, Word, and Powerpoint files using each application separately, or by opening documents already created using those applications. You then add the completed files to a Binder file.

To use the early binding technique, follow these steps:

1. Open a new Binder file.
2. Choose Section, Add menu item and, in the dialog box, choose the required type of section.
3. Repeat step 2 until you have all the required sections.
4. Choose File, Save Binder to save the Binder file.

To use the late binding technique, follow these steps:

1. Create your Excel, Word, and PowerPoint files using those applications in the usual way.
2. Click the Windows 95 Start button, Choose Programs and then Microsoft Binder. A new empty Binder will be created.
3. Choose the Section, Add from File menu item and, in the dialog box, choose a file to add to the Binder file, then click Add.
4. Repeat step 3 until you have all the required sections.
5. Choose File, Save Binder to save the Binder file.

Exchanging Documents

Another advantage of using Binder is that it makes it easier to exchange your multi-file applications with others. If you are connected to a network, you can directly mail the Binder file. If not, you can copy the one file to a floppy disk.

 Note

If you want to exchange Binder files with others, they will need to have the Office 95 programs installed on their computer.

To mail a Binder file, while you have it open, use the File, Send Binder menu item. This will take you into your mail system and automatically embed a copy of the application into your mail message. You can add any required text, specify the recipient, and send it off without having to manually swap between applications.

Note

If you send a Fax from Binder using the Microsoft Exchange Fax facility, it will send a separate fax for every section.

Binder Templates

As other Microsoft Office software products let you create templates, Binder also lets you create templates for frequently used combinations of files. You can set up a Binder file with as much or as little information in it as you need as a starting point for other versions of the application before saving it as a template. You can also use the templates that come with Office 95.

Using Templates

Binder behaves a little differently than the other Office applications in regard to handling multiple files. If you create a new Binder file using File, New Binder or File, Open Binder, you don't get a new window in the currently running instance of Binder. Instead, Binder opens an entirely new instance of itself in a new application window to hold the new file.

To create a new Binder file from a template, follow these steps:

1. Click the Windows 95 Start button, Choose Programs and then Microsoft Binder. A new, empty Binder will be created.

2. Choose File, New Binder menu item and, in the dialog box shown in figure 16.5, choose the General or Binders tab.

3. Select the required template.

4. Click OK or press Enter to open a copy of the template.

If you open Binder from the Start button, you automatically get a file based on the default Blank Binder template. If you then choose the File, New Binder menu item and choose Blank Binder, you will get a second instance of Binder opening. However, if you go to the Binders tab, shown in figure 16.5, and select one of the templates, you will find that it replaces the Blank Binder already opened, without opening a new instance of Binder.

Fig. 16.5

In the New Binder dialog box, you can see the templates that are supplied with Office 95.

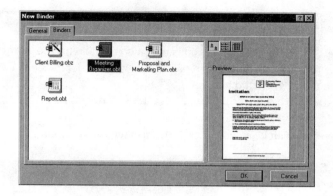

Creating Templates

Binder templates can be saved into the general Templates subdirectory under the MSOffice subdirectory, or in the Binders subdirectory underneath Templates. These locations correspond to the tab options in the New Binder dialog box. If you save the template anywhere else, it will not be available when you choose the File, New Binder menu item.

If you do save a template in any other location, you can still open the template file by choosing File, Open Binder, but you will get the original template file, not a copy. You can choose File, Open Binder on the template files saved in the Templates and Binders subdirectories when you want to edit the original templates.

Two file extensions are available for Binder templates, obt and obz. Normal templates are given obt as the extension, and it is the default if you do not specify it. obz identifies the file as a Wizard. This is intended for files that contain macros to guide a user through a customizing process. You have to manually add this extension. There is an example of a Wizard in the sample templates provided with Office 95 that is named Client Billing.obz.

To create a new Binder template, follow these steps:

1. With the file you want to make into a template open in Binder, choose the File, Save Binder As menu item. You will see the dialog box shown in figure 16.6.

2. Use the Save as Type drop-down list to select Binder Templates. The Templates subdirectory will be automatically activated.

3. Select the Binders subdirectory if you do not want to save the template in the general Templates directory.

4. In the File Name edit box, type in the name for the template. If the template is a Wizard, add the extension obz.

Note

The obz extension is only a convention to differentiate templates that contain macro code from those that do not. You are not forced to use a special extension to create a Wizard template.

5. Click <u>S</u>ave or press Enter to save the template.

Fig. 16.6

You can create your own Binder templates by saving a Binder file as a template in the Binders subdirectory.

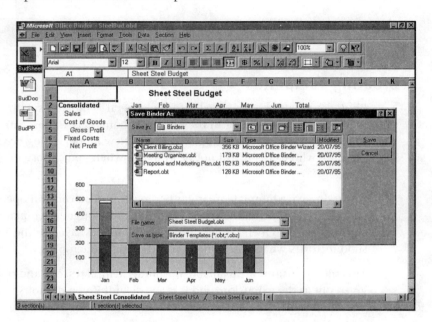

Working in Binder

Binder files provide you with many conveniences. We have already discussed some of the reasons why this is so. You only have to deal with a single file, and Binder automatically switches you to the correct application software as you click from one section to another. It is simpler to distribute copies of your application as it is kept in a single file.

Other advantages include the fact that you can print all the sections in your Binder file with a single print command and have continuous page numbers through the printout. You can organize consistent headers and footers throughout the printout, but these have to be set up individually for each section.

What You Can't Do in Binder

On the other hand, there are a number of features that are not available to you when you work in the Binder. If you need to use any of these, you can use the Section, View Outside menu item. This loads a copy of the Excel, Word, or PowerPoint section into the parent application.

You can return to Binder by closing the copy of the section. If you activate Binder while viewing a section outside, that section will be represented by an icon in Binder and cannot be edited in Binder until you return to the parent application and close it.

Status Bars

Binder has its own status bar at the bottom of its window. To avoid confusion, the normal parent application status bar is suppressed for all sections. You will not see the normal page information in Word for example, or the toggle key status information in Excel.

Print Preview

Print Preview does not work in Binder. You can't preview individual sections, and you can't preview the entire Binder file. You can see the section previews by viewing outside, but there is no method for previewing the entire Binder file.

Shared Lists

The powerful shared lists feature of Excel 7.0 does not work in Binder. Neither can you open Excel templates in Binder. Any view setting changes made in Binder are not saved with the Binder file.

Edit Macros

You can execute Excel and Word macros in Binder and you can even record Excel macros in Binder. However, you can't record Word macros, and you can't edit Excel or Word macros while in Binder. This is not a major limitation, but it is a nuisance when you are testing and debugging your macros.

To edit the macros, you have to view the file outside Binder. To some degree you can test the macros while outside Binder, but some actions require that the file be inside Binder, and some macro operations behave differently inside and outside Binder. Ultimately, you have to test your macros inside Binder. What this means is that you need to switch back and forth a great deal as you edit and execute your macros.

When you switch to the outside view, you have to activate the module containing the macros you want to edit. After editing, if you want to return to Binder, you have to activate a worksheet before closing the file in Excel. Binder will not let you return while a module is active.

Incorrect macro usage can also cause protection faults while in Binder. Fortunately, Windows 95 is fairly strong in this area. Although you might find that Excel has been terminated because of a macro crash, Binder will usually recover without losing the Excel section you are working on and automatically restart Excel.

Sharing Binders

Binder files can be shared with other users on a network in a variety of ways. You can electronically mail the Binder to one or more coworkers by choosing the File, Send Binder menu item. If you want the file to go to a series of coworkers for comment and have it return to you, you can route it using the File, Add Routing Slip menu item.

On a network, you can also use Microsoft Exchange to make a Binder file available to others, or you can simply copy it to a shared network directory. If each person places a copy of the shared file in the Briefcase on their desktop, they can share any updates by choosing the Briefcase, Update All menu item from the Briefcase menu.

Printing Binders

If you want to print an individual section of a Binder file as it would print in its parent application program, choose the Section menu that gives you access to Page Setup and Print. Alternatively, you can view it outside Binder and choose the normal File menu commands.

If you choose the File, Print Binder menu item in Binder, you can print the entire Binder file or any selected sections from it. The Print Binder dialog box is shown in figure 16.7. You can specify that page numbering is to be consecutive or restart in each section.

If you want to print only some of the sections, you need to select them before opening the Print Binder dialog box. You can select any number of sections by clicking the icons on the left-hand side of the screen while holding down Shift or Ctrl.

Fig. 16.7
*You can print an entire
Binder file or any selected
sections using the File,
Print Binder menu item.*

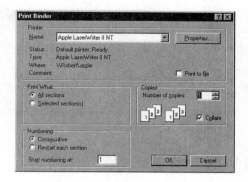

Working with Binder Using VBA

Binder supports Visual Basic for Applications. It exposes its objects, Binder objects and
Section objects, which you can manipulate from your Excel modules. The Binder Object
Model is very simple compared to Excel's Object Model, but you need to be aware of how
it is structured, and the available properties and methods of its objects to be able to access Excel, PowerPoint, and WordBasic objects in a Binder file.

You can't write VBA code in Binder directly. It has to be in an Excel module. Neither can
you write VBA code in Word or PowerPoint. However, PowerPoint exposes its objects to
VBA and Word exposes WordBasic to VBA, so the VBA code written in an Excel module
can manipulate everything contained in Binder.

Your Excel module can be contained in a workbook that is embedded in a Section of the
Binder file it is manipulating. It can also be in an independent workbook. We will look at
examples of both methods of operation.

In order to get access to the Binder and PowerPoint object libraries, you need to establish
references to them in your Excel file. To establish the references, follow these steps:

   1. In Binder, activate the Excel section that will contain your VBA macros. Choose the
   Section, View Outside menu item to activate Excel.

   2. In Excel, choose the Insert, Macro, Module submenu item to create a new module
   sheet.

   3. In the module, choose the Tools, References menu item to open the dialog box
   shown in figure 16.8.

   4. Select the check boxes for Binder and PowerPoint.

   5. Click OK or press Enter to save the updated references.

Fig. 16.8

You use the Tools, References menu item to establish references to the Binder and PowerPoint object libraries.

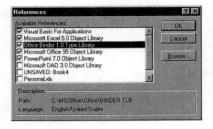

The Binder Object Model

You can get information about the Binder objects, properties, and methods from the Help screens in Excel, but there is no schematic representation of the model hierarchy as there is for the Excel Object Model. Figure 16.9 shows the relationship between the Binder and Section objects. In this figure, Object is not a specific object. It allows you to refer to the Excel, Word, or PowerPoint object embedded in a Section object.

Fig. 16.9

The Binder Object Model contains Binder, Section, and Object objects. Object is really a way of referring to the Excel, Word, or PowerPoint objects embedded in a Section object.

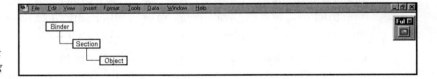

The Section object is contained in the Sections collection. The Sections collection has its own properties and a single method, the Add method.

 Note

The Binder Help file is an installation option in Office 95. If you can't find it via Excel's Help Topics, you will need to run the Office setup program to add the Help module to your hard disk.

Another way of getting information about Binder objects, properties, and methods is by using the Object Browser shown in figure 16.10. You can access the Object Browser in a module by pressing F2. Once you have highlighted an object and an associated property or method, you can get help by pressing the ? button in the bottom-left corner of the Object Browser dialog box.

Fig. 16.10

You can use the Object Browser to display the objects in the Binder Object Model and their properties and methods.

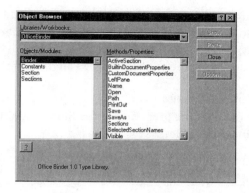

16

Binder Object

The Binder Help files list the properties and methods of the Binder object. Unfortunately, they give no clue as to how you generate a reference to a Binder object in the first place. The best way of doing this depends on the circumstances.

If you are referring to a Binder file from an independent Excel module, you can use the CreateObject function to create a new Binder object and an object variable that refers to it. For example

```
Set oBinder = CreateObject("Office.Binder")
```

Alternatively, you can use the GetObject function to open an existing Binder file and create an object variable referring to it.

```
Set oBinder = GetObject("C:\Data\SteelBud.obd")
```

 Note

You can also open an existing file using the Open method of the Binder object. However, it must immediately follow the use of the CreateObject function to create the Binder object. It is easier to use GetObject.

If you want to refer to the Binder that contains the Excel module, the following code is a convenient way to do it.

```
Set oBinder = ThisWorkbook.Container.Parent
```

This looks like a convoluted technique, but has the advantage that it is independent of the Binder file name and the names of the Section and the module. You can change the names of any or all of them without affecting the validity of the code.

Container is a property that only became available in Windows 95. It generates a reference to the object in which an OLE object is embedded. ThisWorkbook refers to the workbook containing the Excel macro code. ThisWorkbook.Container refers to the Section containing the workbook. The Parent of the Section is the Binder.

Binder Object Properties

Table 16.1 lists the properties of the Binder Object. You can also find this information in the Binder Help files.

Table 16.1   Binder Object Properties

Property	Description
ActiveSection	Returns a Section object that represents the active section in the Binder.
BuiltinDocumentProperties	Returns a DocumentProperties collection object that represents all the built-in document properties for the specified Binder. Read-only.
CustomDocumentProperties	Returns a DocumentProperties collection object that represents all the custom document properties for the specified Binder. Read-only.
LeftPane	True if the left pane of the Binder window is visible. The left pane, also called the Binder pane, includes the icons for all the sections in the Binder. Read-write.
Name	The filename of the Binder, not including its path on disk. Read-only.
Path	Returns the complete path of the Binder (as a string), without including the name of the Binder. Read-only.
Sections	Returns a Sections collection object that represents all the sections in a Binder. Read-only.
SelectedSectionNames	Returns or sets the array of selected section names. Read-write.
Visible	True if the Binder is visible. Read-write.

The ActiveSection property is similar to ActiveWorkbook and ActiveWorksheet in that it generates a reference to the currently active section in the Binder. The Builtin and

CustomDocumentProperties refers to the entries that can be made in the dialog box that is accessed by choosing File, Binder, Properties.

You can expose or hide the left-hand side Binder pane with the LeftPane property by setting it to True or False. To toggle the pane open and shut, you could use the following:

```
Sub TogglePane()
    Dim oBinder As Binder
    Set oBinder = ThisWorkbook.Container.Parent
    If oBinder.LeftPane Then
        oBinder.LeftPane = False
    Else
        oBinder.LeftPane = True
    End If
End Sub
```

 Note

You should be able to toggle a property such as LeftPane with the following:

```
oBinder.LeftPane = Not oBinder.LeftPane
```

However, this does not work in the first release of Binder.

The Name and Path properties define the Binder file location. Name is read-only. If you want to change the Binder file name, you use the SaveAs method.

The Sections property can be used to refer to the complete collection of Sections or to specify a particular Section. To activate the BudDoc Section of figure 16.4, for example, you could use the following:

```
Sub SelectSection()
    Dim oBinder As Binder
    Set oBinder = ThisWorkbook.Container.Parent
    oBinder.Sections("BudDoc").Activate
End Sub
```

Using the SelectedSectionNames property, you can specify which sections you want to select, for printing for example. You could print the BudSheet and BudPP sections from figure 16.4 with the following:

```
Sub SelectSections()
    Dim oBinder As Binder
    Set oBinder = ThisWorkbook.Container.Parent
    oBinder.SelectedSectionNames = Array("BudSheet", "BudPP")
    oBinder.PrintOut bindPrintSelectedSections
End Sub
```

The Visible property can be used to hide or show the Binder window. When you create a new Binder using VBA code, it is normally not visible. You can make it visible by setting this property equal to True.

Binder Object Methods

There are only four methods applicable to Binders. They are shown in table 16.2.

Table 16.2   Binder Object Methods

Method	Description
Open	Opens either an existing binder or a new binder based on an existing Binder template.
PrintOut	Prints every section, a subset of sections, or a single section in the Binder.
Save	Saves changes to the specified Binder.
SaveAs	Saves changes to the Binder or section in a different file. Returns True if the Binder is saved; returns False if it isn't saved. If the Binder isn't visible, an error occurs.

As has just been noted, you can use the Open method to open an existing Binder file but it is simpler to do this with the GetObject function. The Open method must be immediately preceded by the CreateObject function.

The PrintOut method has been illustrated in the last code example. There are many arguments available to control what is printed. You should consult the Excel Help menu for a complete listing of these.

You can use the Save and SaveAs methods to save updates to the Binder file or create a new file. The following would save the current file as NewBinder.obd in the active directory, without creating a prompt message if the file already exists:

```
oBinder.SaveAs "NewBinder.obd", bindOverwriteExisting
```

Section Object

The Section object is a member of the Sections collection, which each have their own properties and methods. They are discussed separately in the paragaphs that follow.

Sections Collection Properties

The three properties of the Selections collection are defined in table 16.3.

Table 16.3   Sections Collection Properties

Property	Description
Count	Returns the number of items in the Sections collection object. Read-only.
Item	Returns a Section object from the Sections collection object. Read-only.
Parent	Returns the parent object for the specified object. Read-only.

The Count property is standard for most collections and returns a count of the number of members in the collection. Item is equally standard and returns a member of the collection by referencing its index number or name. It is seldom used as the following lines of code all give the same result. The Set command is being used to create a reference to the BudDoc document in figure 16.4.

```
Set wwDoc = oBinder.Sections.Item(2)
Set wwDoc = oBinder.Sections.Item("BudDoc")
Set wwDoc = oBinder.Sections(2)
Set wwDoc = oBinder.Sections("BudDoc")
```

The Parent property creates a reference to the Binder object containing the Sections collection. It is a convenient way of getting a reference to the Binder object if you already have a reference to the Sections collection.

Sections Collection Methods

There is only one method that can be carried out on the Sections collection. It is the Add method as shown in table 16.4.

Table 16.4   Sections Collection Methods

Method	Description
Add	Creates a new section in the binder and returns a Section object that represents the new section. You can add a section by either creating a new object or inserting the section from an existing file.

The Add method creates a new Section object. The method returns a reference to the new Section, so you can use the Set command to create an object variable referring to the new Section as follows:

```
Set ppShow = oBinder.Sections.Add(Type:="PowerPoint.Show")
```

Section Object Properties

The properties of the Section object are listed in table 16.5.

Table 16.5 Section Object Properties

Property	Description
Index	Returns the index number of the Section object within the Sections collection object. Read-only.
Name	Returns or sets the name of the Binder or Section object. Read-write.
Object	Returns the OLE Automation object associated with this section. Read-only.
Parent	Returns the parent object for the specified object. Read-only.
Type	Returns a string containing the OLE long class name for the Section object. Read-only.
Visible	True if the section is visible. Read-write.

The Index property of the Section object returns the numeric position of the Section object in the Sections collection. The following code displays 2 in a message box if BudDoc is the second section in oBinder:

```
MsgBox oBinder.Sections("BudDoc").Index
```

You can get the name of a section with the Name property, or use it to change the name of the section. The following changes the name of BudDoc to Budget Document:

```
oBinder.Sections("BudDoc").Name = "Budget Document"
```

 Note

You can leave out the .Name in the example just given and get the same result. Name is the default property for a section.

The Object property is an important one to understand for successful manipulation of the section data. It provides a reference to the object model for the application embedded in the section. You need to be familiar with the Object Models for Excel and PowerPoint and with the commands in WordBasic to be able to work in each.

Note

The Object Model for PowerPoint 95 is not available in the standard PowerPoint documentation that comes with the software. It is not even accessible from PowerPoint, which does not have a VBA macro capability. The PowerPoint Object Model is available in Microsoft Solutions Development Kit for Windows 95, or can be downloaded from the PowerPoint forum on MSN or from Microsoft's World Wide Web site on **http://www.microsoft.com**.

The following code places the number 10 in the A1 cell of the Excel worksheet embedded in the section named BudSheet:

```
oBinder.Sections("BudSheet").Object.Range("A1").Value = 10
```

 Note

Be careful with the Object property for a workbook with many sheets. It refers to the first worksheet of a multi-sheet workbook. To refer to any other sheet requires the following:

```
oBinder.Sections("BudSheet").Object.Parent.Sheets(3).Range("A1").Value = 10
```

In a Powerpoint section, the Object property refers to the embedded presentation. To enter text into the first SlideObject on the second slide of the presentation embedded in the section called BudPP, use the following:

```
oBinder.Sections("BudPP").Object.Slides(2).Objects(1).Text = "SheetSteel Enterprises"
```

In a Word section you need to use the following code to access WordBasic:

```
oBinder.ActiveSection.Object.Application.WordBasic
```

In all cases, it is best to use the Set command and the With/End With construction to simplify the coding and increase its efficiency. You can find examples of this in listings 16.1 and 16.2, later in the chapter. For example, to insert text into a Word document in the section named BudDoc, you could use the following:

```
Set wwBasic = oBinder.ActiveSection.Object.Application.WordBasic
With wwBasic
        .FontSize 18
        .CenterPara
        .Insert "Sheet Steel Enterprises"
End With
```

The Parent property of the Section object returns the same result as the Parent property of the Selections collection. You get a reference to the Binder object containing the sections.

The Type property returns the OLE long class name of the embedded object. For example, the Type for the Word section might be Word.Document.6.

The Visible property of the Section object is similar to the same property for the Binder object. Setting it to False hides the section and True makes it visible.

Section Object Methods

Table 16.6 lists the methods that you can perform on the Section object.

Table 16.6   Section Object Methods

Method	Description
Activate	Activates the section in the Binder.
Copy	Copies the section to another location in the Binder. Returns the new Section object.
Delete	Deletes the Section object.
Move	Moves a section to another location in the Binder.
PrintOut	Prints every section, a subset of sections, or a single section in the Binder.
SaveAs	Saves changes to the Binder or section in a different file. Returns True if the Binder is saved; returns False if it isn't saved. If the Binder isn't visible, an error occurs.
Update	Saves changes made to the section.

The Activate method makes the specified section active. To activate the section named BudPP you could use the following:

```
oBinder.Sections("BudPP").Activate
```

You can use the Copy method to copy a section. To create a copy of the section named BudSheet, place it after BudSheet and name it ActualsSheet, you could use the following:

```
Set ActSheet = oBinder.Sections("BudSheet").Copy(After:="BudSheet")
ActSheet.Name = "ActualsSheet"
```

You can delete a section using the Delete method as follows:

```
oBinder.Sections("BudSheet").Delete
```

You can move the section named BudSheet after the section named BudPP with the following:

```
oBinder.Sections("BudSheet").Move After:="BudPP"
```

You can print a section using the PrintOut method, or you can use the appropriate print method from the Object Model for the embedded object. Using the section PrintOut method, you could print the section called BudDoc as follows:

```
oBinder.Sections("BudDoc").PrintOut
```

 Note

The PrintOut method does not work reliably on the Section object. You should select the sections you want to print using the SelectedSectionNames property of the Binder object and print them using the PrintOut method of the Binder object.

The Update method is used to update the Binder file after making changes to a section. The SaveAs method of the Section object is used to create a separate new file containing a copy of the object that is embedded in the section. This does not remove the section from the Binder file.

Example Applications

We have seen many small examples of VBA code used to process data in Binder. The following examples are more comprehensive and combine many of the techniques already discussed to provide a more coherent picture.

Creating a Binder from an Independent Excel Workbook

This example shows how you can create a Binder file entirely in VBA from an independent Excel workbook. Early binding is used to create the Binder sections before any data is entered into them.

The alternative would have been to create the Excel, Word, and PowerPoint files first and later bring them into a Binder file using the Add method of the Sections collection. This is actually a simpler process as far as the VBA coding is concerned, but would not give you an insight into how to work within a Binder.

The Binder file created by the code in listing 16.1 is shown in figure 16.11. This is how it appears at the end of the process. The sections have been assigned default names as no explicit naming is carried out in the code.

Fig. 16.11
This Binder file was created using the VBA code in listing 16.1.

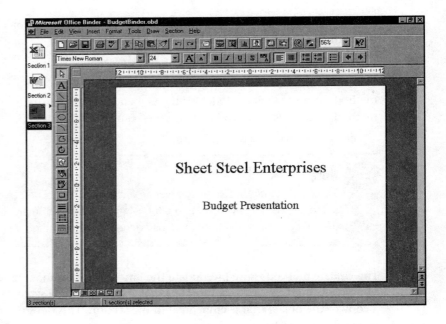

Listing 16.1   MAKEBINDER.XLS: Creating a Binder

```
Option Explicit
'Code to create a new Binder file with Sections containing _
    Excel, Word and PowerPoint data

Sub MakeBinder()
    Dim oBinder As Binder
    Dim xlSheet As Section
    Dim wwDoc As Section
    Dim ppShow As Section
    Dim wwBasic As Object
    Dim ppSlide As Slide

        'Create a Binder object
    Set oBinder = CreateObject("Office.Binder")
    With oBinder
        'Make Binder object visible
        .Visible = True
        'Add new Section objects
        Set xlSheet = .Sections.Add(Type:="Excel.Sheet")
        Set wwDoc = .Sections.Add(Type:="Word.Document")
        Set ppShow = .Sections.Add(Type:="PowerPoint.Show")
    End With

     'Activate Section with Excel worksheet
    xlSheet.Activate
    'Add data to worksheet
    With xlSheet.Object
        With .Range("A1")
```

```
            .Value = "Sheet Steel Enterprises"
            .Font.Bold = True
            .Font.Size = 18
        End With
        .Range("A1:G1").HorizontalAlignment = xlCenterAcrossSelection
        With .Range("A2")
            .Value = "Budget"
            .Font.Bold = True
            .Font.Size = 12
        End With
        .Range("A2:G2").HorizontalAlignment = xlCenterAcrossSelection
        .Range("B3") = "Jan"
        .Range("B3:G3").DataSeries Type:=xlAutoFill
        .Range("B3:G3").Font.Bold = True
    End With

    'Activate Section with Word document
    wwDoc.Activate
    'Create reference to WordBasic
    Set wwBasic = wwDoc.Object.Application.wordbasic
    'Enter data into document
    With wwBasic
        .FontSize 18
        .CenterPara
        .Insert "Sheet Steel Enterprises"
        .InsertPara
        .FontSize 14
        .CenterPara
        .Insert "Budget Papers"
        .InsertPara
        .Style "Normal"
    End With

    'Activate Section with PowerPoint presentation
    ppShow.Activate
    'Create reference to PowerPoint slide 1
    Set ppSlide = ppShow.Object.Slides(1)
    With ppSlide
        .Objects(1).Text = "Sheet Steel Enterprises"
        .Objects(2).Text = "Budget Presentation"
    End With

    'Save Binder and overwrite any old version of file
    oBinder.SaveAs "BudgetBinder.obd", bindOverwriteExisting
End Sub
```

The sub, MakeBinder, first declares the variable names it uses. It then uses the Set command and the CreateObject function to set up a new empty Binder object and assign a reference to the object to the object variable, oBinder.

A With/End With structure is then used to carry out a series of operations on oBinder. By default, the object is not visible, so its Visible property is set to True. The Add method of the Sections collection is used to add the required sections for Excel, Word, and PowerPoint and object variables are assigned to those Section objects.

The Excel section is then activated. This is not necessary for the following code, however it allows you to see what is happening. The outer With/End With structure refers to the Excel object embedded in the Section object referred to by xlSheet. Two inner With/End With structures are used to enter data into the worksheet following the Excel Object Model.

The Word section is then activated. Once again, this is not necessary to make the code work. A reference to WordBasic is assigned to the object variable, wwBasic, which is used to execute a series of WordBasic commands to enter text into the Word section.

The PowerPoint section is then activated and an object variable, ppSlide, is assigned a reference to the Slide object in the Presentation object embedded in the Section object. In the With/End With structure, text values are assigned to the SlideObject objects embedded in the Slide object.

Finally, the SaveAs method of the Binder object is used to save the binder contents to a file called BudgetBinder.odb. The bindOverwriteExisting constant specifies that there will be no alert message if an existing file is overwritten.

Manipulating Binder Sections from an Embedded Excel Workbook

This example shows how you can set up VBA procedures in an Excel module embedded in a Binder file. The file is identical to that presented in figures 16.1 to 16.4, apart from the addition of the macros. Figure 16.12 shows how two macro buttons have been added to the Excel section.

Fig. 16.12

SteelBud.obd contains Excel VBA macros to copy the latest data from the Excel worksheets and charts to the Word and PowerPoint sections of the Binder file.

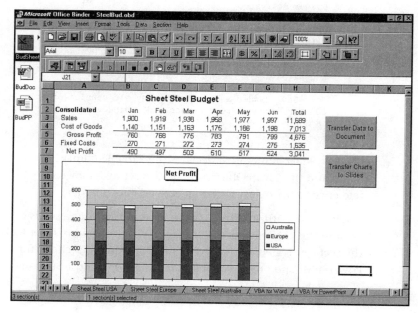

The purpose of the two buttons is to copy the latest data in the Excel section to the Word and PowerPoint sections, respectively. The macros are in the modules called VBA for Word and VBA for PowerPoint. The modules are visible at the bottom of the worksheet, but can't be accessed while you are in Binder. However, you can run the code in them by using the Tools, Macro menu item, clicking the Run Macro button on the VBA ToolBar, or, in this case, pressing the buttons embedded in the worksheet.

The code attached to the button entitled "Transfer Data to Document" is shown in listing 16.2, and the code attached to the button entitled "Transfer Charts to Slides" is shown in listing 16.3.

Listing 16.2   STEELBUD.OBD: Editing a Word Section in Binder

```
Option Explicit

Sub DataToDoc()
    Dim oBinder As Binder
    Dim wwBasic As Object

        'Create reference to Current Binder
    Set oBinder = ThisWorkbook.Container.Parent
    'Copy table and chart as a picture
    Sheets(1).Range("A1:H25").CopyPicture Appearance:=xlScreen, Format:=xlPicture

        'Activate the Section containing the Word document
    oBinder.Sections("BudDoc").Activate
    'Create a reference to WordBasic
    Set wwBasic = oBinder.ActiveSection.Object.Application.wordbasic
    'Execute WordBasic commands on active document
    With wwBasic
        .EditSelectAll
        .EditClear
        .FontSize 18
        .CenterPara
        .Insert "Sheet Steel Enterprises"
        .InsertPara
        .FontSize 14
        .Insert "Budget Figures"
        .InsertPara
        .Style "Normal"
        .InsertPara
        .InsertPara
        .InsertPara
        .InsertPara
        .EditPasteSpecial 0, 0, 0, "Excel.Sheet.5", "Pict"
    End With
End Sub
```

The first action of DataToDoc is to generate a reference to the Binder object it is embedded in using ThisWorkbook.Container.Parent and to assign the reference to the object variable, oBinder. It then uses the CopyPicture method of the Range object to copy the worksheet data to the Clipboard.

It then activates the Word section in the Binder file and generates a reference to the WordBasic object which it assigns to the wwBasic object variable. It can then issue the WordBasic commands to erase all the existing data in the document and insert new headings. It then uses the PasteSpecial command to paste the Clipboard picture into the document.

Listing 16.3 STEELBUD.OBD: Editing PowerPoint Slides in Binder

```
Option Explicit
Option Base 1

Sub ChartsToSlides()
    Dim oBinder As Binder
    Dim ppPres As Presentation
    Dim ppSlide As Slide
    Dim oChart As SlideObject
    Dim SourceArray
    Dim DestArray
    Dim i As Integer

        'Establish correspondence between Sheets and Slides
    SourceArray = Array(2, 3, 4, 1) 'Sheets with charts
    DestArray = Array(2, 3, 4, 5)   'Slides for charts

        'Create reference to Current Binder
    Set oBinder = ThisWorkbook.Container.Parent
    'Create reference to PowerPoint Presentation
    Set ppPres = oBinder.Sections("BudPP").Object
    'Copy charts from Sheets to Slides
    For i = 1 To 4
        Sheets(SourceArray(i)).ChartObjects(1).CopyPicture _
            Appearance:=xlScreen, Format:=xlPicture
        Set ppSlide = ppPres.Slides(DestArray(i))
        ppSlide.Objects(2).Delete
        ppSlide.Objects.Paste
        With ppSlide.Objects(2)
            .Top = 3240
            .Left = 360
            .Width = 10660
            .Height = 6360
        End With
    Next i
    oBinder.Sections("BudPP").Activate
End Sub
```

The ChartsToSlides macro procedure first defines two arrays that indicate the index numbers of the sheets containing charts to be transferred from the workbook and the corresponding slide numbers in the presentation.

As with DataToDoc, it creates oBinder referring to the Binder object. It then creates ppPres referring to the Presentation object embedded in the PowerPoint section.

In the For/Next loop, it copies the ChartObject objects from the worksheets. It creates another object variable, ppSlide, to refer to the corresponding slide and deletes the old chart from the slide. It then pastes the new chart into the slide and adjusts its dimensions.

Notice that the code does not activate anything until the final line where it activates the PowerPoint section so that you can see the results. By carrying out its operations without activating the sheets and slides involved, it operates in the most efficient manner.

Summary

In this chapter you have seen how the Office 95 Binder can be used to group files from Excel, Word, and Powerpoint to make them easier to manage and share. You have also seen that there are some features of the individual programs that are not available directly when working in Binder.

You have been shown how you can use the Binder Object Model to write VBA code in Excel to manage a Binder file and its components. You now have many examples of working code that you can adapt to your own applications.

Designing an Executive Information System

chapter 17

Building a Data Warehouse with Excel Lists

17

by John Lacher

In this chapter

◆ **Use Excel lists to create an electronic *data warehouse***
If your key management data is stored in Excel lists, you can improve your problem-solving abilities.

◆ **Make best use of Excel's built-in data entry form**
Excel provides a built-in data entry and update dialog boxes as part of the standard user interface.

◆ **Import data from text files, dBASE files, and Microsoft Access**
You can use Excel's Wizards to automate the process of importing data to your Excel lists.

◆ **Decide what to store in your lists**
If you carefully plan the content and structure of your lists, you produce a more effective data warehouse.

◆ **Use Microsoft Access to create data entry forms and linked lists**
You can integrate the features of Microsoft Access into your Excel workbook.

The corners of your office are no place to store data! Excel helps you clean out those corners by providing you with an "electronic warehouse" to store your data.

You can fill your electronic warehouse with key management indicators from Accounting, Production, Sales, Human Resources, the Marketplace, or other subject area. Excel provides built-in data entry and list management tools you can use to maintain your data.

When you move important management data from the corners of your office to the Excel *data warehouse*, you are able to focus on key measures, identify problems sooner, and "drill down" to analyze the details. As a benefit, you won't need to search through stacks of reports or directories of computer files. This means more time for problem solving—or for golf.

Why Use an Excel List?

Excel lists are easy-to-use databases. If you know how to put data in a worksheet, you already know how to enter data into a list. Adding a new data field is as simple as inserting a new column. A new data record is just another row in the worksheet. You don't need to hire programmers or learn to use a database package to use an Excel list.

When you store your data in an Excel list, you can use all of Excel's built-in tools to analyze the data. All of the tools are there, from addition to linear regression. You can use Excel's Function Wizard to help you find and use hundreds of mathematical, statistical, and financial functions.

To summarize your data and drill down to the details behind the summary totals, use an Excel PivotTable. You may link the powerful charting tools in Excel to a list or PivotTable. You can use all of Excel's formatting and worksheet publishing tools to present your data in reports.

When you use Excel's list management tools to build an electronic *data warehouse*, you can save time entering, importing, organizing, and querying your data.

Constructing a List

To construct a list in an Excel workbook, begin by inserting a blank worksheet. Each worksheet in the workbook can be a separate list. You can use the sheet tabs in the workbook to move from one list to another or to select multiple lists for reporting.

If you set up the list with a single heading row and columns of data beneath the headings, you can include titles, notes, or even buttons or listboxes above the headings. Enter data or formulas below the heading row. Formulas can refer to other columns in the list or be linked to other lists in the workbook.

When I construct lists in Excel, I identify the columns of data necessary to prepare summary reports. Then, I include additional columns that will be helpful in answering questions about the summary data. The additional columns contain details like location, product, time period, and so on.

You don't need to fill the Excel lists full of unnecessary details. Leave those details in the billing, payroll, accounting, production, and other transaction processing systems. To get the maximum return on your efforts, fill all of the space on the shelves of your *data warehouse* with key management data.

Excel lists let you store thousands of rows of data in each of over 200 worksheets. This capacity is more than adequate for most analysis and decision making tasks.

Creating a List

You can make your lists user-friendly by adding a title at the top and notes above each column. I leave a blank row above the single heading row so I can easily select the entire list by selecting any cell in the list and pressing Ctrl+Shift+* (asterisk). Use bold text for the heading row and consider leaving spaces out of the column headings to make them easier to use in formulas and list management functions.

To create a list like the one shown in figure 17.1, follow these steps:

1. Start with a blank worksheet. You can use Insert, Worksheet to add a new sheet to the workbook.

2. Double-click the sheet tab and give the worksheet a descriptive name.

3. Reserve the first three rows for heading information.

4. In row four, type the names of the data elements in the list.

5. Select the headings and format them as bold type—use Format, Cells, Font, Bold.

6. Enter data in the columns of the list.

7. Add a heading across the top of the worksheet with Format, Cells, Alignment, Center Across Columns.

8. Add explanations of each column in the second row.

Excel brings a whole set of "list sensing" abilities to the *data warehouse*. When you select one of the list management functions (sort, filter, and so on), Excel searches the worksheet to find a set of data with a single heading row. It uses this combination of rows and columns to apply the list function.

To exercise some control over this list sensing, name the range of cells in the list Database. When Excel sees that there is a range of cells named Database, it turns off autosensing. You can use the name Database in formulas and PivotTables.

When you add a new record to a list named Database, the built-in dataform automatically expands the range to include the new data. You can use this feature when you need the new data to feed automatically into a PivotTable.

If you need more than one list in a workbook, you can create a range named Database on each worksheet by including the name of the worksheet as part of the range name. Include the worksheet name from the sheet tab plus an exclamation point (!) and the name "Database" to form a full name—like PhoneData!Database.

Fig. 17.1

An Excel list is an easy-to-use database for storing key management data.

Title and notes

Blank row

Single row of headings

Data and formulas

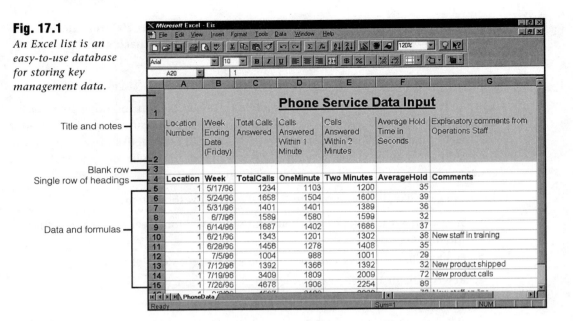

To name a list, follow these steps:

1. Select the entire list—including the data and one row of headings. Do not select the shaded area or blank rows above the single row column headings.

2. Choose Insert, Name, Define to name the list. Use a name with the worksheet name, an "!" and the special name Database, for example PhoneData!Database.

In figure 17.2 the name `PhoneData!Database` is assigned to the heading row and body of a list. Select the heading row and body by selecting any cell in the list and pressing Ctrl+Shift+*.

Fig. 17.2

Use the Define Name dialog box to create new range names and adjust the Refers To address for existing range names.

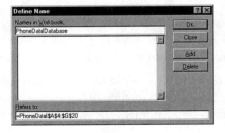

Figure 17.3 shows how to test the range name by selecting it from the formula bar names list. The selected area covers the entire data area and includes the single row of column headings.

17

> **⚛ Tip**
> Select the range of cells you want to include in the range before choosing Insert, Name, Define. The range you selected appears in the Refers To box in the Define Name dialog box.

Fig. 17.3

To quickly select a range, use the Names drop-down list on the formula bar.

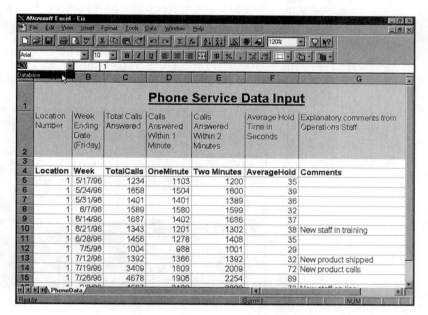

Phone Service Data Input

Location Number	Week Ending Date (Friday)	Total Calls Answered	Calls Answered Within 1 Minute	Calls Answered Within 2 Minutes	Average Hold Time in Seconds	Explanatory comments from Operations Staff
Location	**Week**	**TotalCalls**	**OneMinute**	**Two Minutes**	**AverageHold**	**Comments**
1	5/17/96	1234	1103	1200	35	
1	5/24/96	1658	1504	1600	39	
1	5/31/96	1401	1401	1389	36	
1	6/7/96	1589	1580	1599	32	
1	6/14/96	1687	1402	1686	37	
1	6/21/96	1343	1201	1302	38	New staff in training
1	6/28/96	1456	1278	1408	35	
1	7/5/96	1004	988	1001	29	
1	7/12/96	1392	1366	1392	32	New product shipped
1	7/19/96	3409	1809	2009	72	New product calls
1	7/26/96	4678	1906	2254	89	

> **Caution**
> Excel's tools for defining names require extra care. When you make a change to a range in the Define Name dialog box, click OK. Then use Insert, Name, Define to call up the Define Name dialog box again and make changes to the next range. Changes you make to a range will be lost without warning if you select another range without clicking OK.

Linking Lists with VLOOKUP

VLOOKUP is an addition to the Excel lists that speeds data entry and makes it easier to change data in your lists. To use VLOOKUP, you need a master list and a data list. The master list contains values used repeatedly—like location name. Enter a code on the data list and VLOOKUP retrieves the corresponding master list value.

You can avoid spelling mistakes and many keystrokes by using a master list value. If the master values change, all you need to change is the master list. The data lists will automatically update.

To link a master list to a data list with VLOOKUP, follow these steps:

1. Create a list of master data like that shown in figure 17.4. Start with a blank worksheet and add a descriptive name by double-clicking the sheet tab.

2. Enter values in the first column of the master list that match values in a column of your data list.

3. Name the master data list Database as described previously. The name Database is used to automatically add new locations to the range with the built-in data form.

Fig. 17.4

A master table contains a lookup code in the first column.

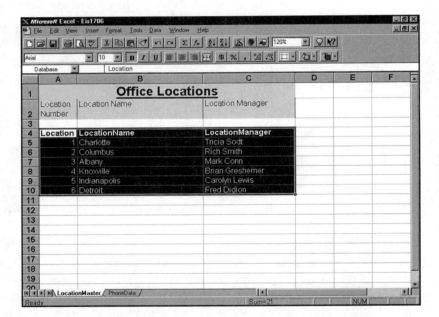

> **α Note**
>
> If the lookup key is a combination of two or more fields, you will need to create an extra column in your master list to hold a combination key value made up of values from two or more columns. Use the & operator to create a formula for the key value column like this: = B5 & F5.

4. Add one or more columns to the data list to hold lookup values. In each of these new columns, use the Function Wizard to create a VLOOKUP formula. Copy the

VLOOKUP formulas down the columns and check to see that the master table values appear in the data list.

Tell VLOOKUP which column on the data sheet holds the lookup code, where the master list is stored, and which column in the master list holds the value to retrieve to the data list. You also may tell VLOOKUP what to do if it cannot find the lookup code in the master list.

In the example in figure 17.5, VLOOKUP uses the location code in column A to look up a location name in the list named "LocationMaster!Database." If the location code matches a value in the first column of the master list, VLOOKUP will return the location name from the second column. range_lookup False tells Excel that if a match is not found, return the value #N/A. If you want VLOOKUP to return the next highest value from the list, you can set range_lookup to True.

Fig 17.5

Use the VLOOKUP function to link a data list to a master list.

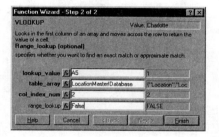

 Tip

Use the Formula Wizard to explore other lookup and reference functions. The MATCH and INDEX functions are two other functions that are useful when linking tables.

 Note

To ask VLOOKUP to return the next highest value when it cannot find a match, set the range_value parameter to TRUE. The master list must be sorted in ascending sequence by lookup code so that Excel can search the master list from the lowest lookup code to the highest.

You do not need to sort the master list if range_value is FALSE. VLOOKUP will search all the values in the list and return #N/A if it does not find a match.

The Vlookup formula in Figure 17.5 returns the location names as shown in Figure 17.6.

Fig 17.6

In column B, the VLOOKUP formula returns the location name from the master table of office locations.

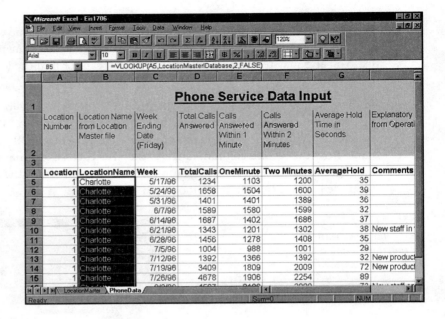

> **Tip**
> When you insert a row or column in a named range, Excel automatically expands the range to include the new row or column. When adding a row or column at the edge of the named range, you will need to redefine the range using Insert, Name, Define.

Adding Data to a List

Your Excel lists will be filled with information captured from other places in the organization. Often you can import the data by copying it directly to your list. Sometimes the data is less well behaved and you will need to enter it manually with Excel's built-in data form. You can put Excel's PivotTable tools to work directly on data contained in Microsoft Access or another external database. You learn more about accessing data from external sources in Chapter 19, "Analyzing Results with PivotTables and Charts."

Using the Data Form

If you need to enter data manually, use Excel's built-in data form. Choose menu options Data, Form to access this feature. Excel automatically creates a data-entry form that contains an input box for each of your columns of data. Formulas are shown as read-only fields. When you enter values in the data form, Excel recalculates the formulas and displays the result.

To enter data into a list, follow these steps:

1. Select any cell on the worksheet.

2. Choose Data, Form and a dialog box like the one shown in figure 17.7 appears.

3. Use the pop-up data form to create new rows, change existing data, or delete rows.

Fig. 17.7

You can use Excel's built-in data form to add, edit, and delete data in your list.

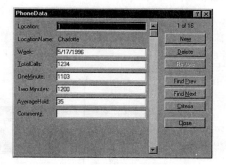

> **Tip**
> Use the Restore button on the data form to undo the changes you have made while editing a row in the list.

 Note
To change the width of data on the built-in data entry form, you can vary the width of columns on the worksheet. Excel uses the largest column width as the default size for the data entry form.

Automating the Data Form

You can use a very simple Visual Basic macro to add buttons that automate the data form.

Store the macro in a module page of your workbook. You can add a button anywhere in your workbook, give the button a name, and assign the macro "ButtonClick" to the button. Each time you click the button, the macro runs.

In the example shown here, the button is named "btnPhoneData." When you click the button, Excel makes a special value named "Application.Caller" equal to the name of the button. When the macro starts, it uses this value to decide which list to use for data entry.

To add a control button follow these steps:

1. Use Insert, Macro, Module to create a Visual Basic module page.

2. Type this subroutine at the top of the page:

```
Sub ButtonClick()
    Select Case Application.Caller
    Case "btnPhoneData"
        Worksheets("PhoneData").ShowDataForm
    End Select
End Sub
```

You can see the completed module page in figure 17.8.

Fig. 17.8

*Add a module page
and simple subroutine
for push button data
entry.*

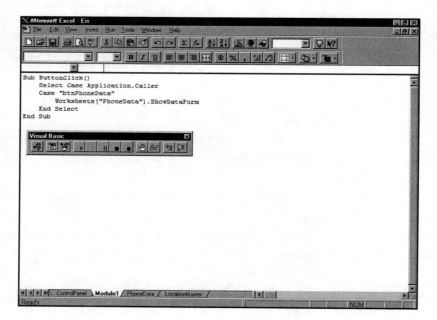

3. Create a new, blank worksheet with Insert, Worksheet. Label it "Control Panel."

4. Display the Forms toolbar by choosing View, Toolbars and selecting the Forms Toolbar check box. The screen should look like figure 17.9.

Fig. 17.9

Use the Forms toolbar to draw a button on the chart.

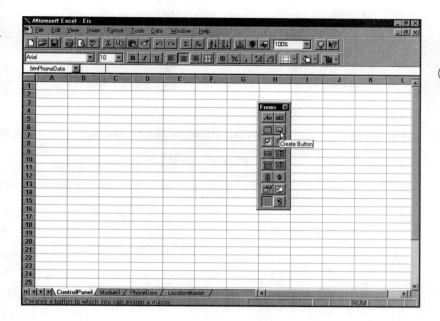

Tip

You can drag a toolbar to the edge of the screen and it will change shape to become part of the screen border. If you drag a toolbar to the middle of the screen it will float there and cover a portion of your worksheet.

5. Click the Create Button tool in the Forms Toolbar.

6. Position the crosshair cursor where you want the button to appear on the worksheet, click the mouse and drag to create a button.

7. When you release the mouse button, the Assign Macro dialog box appears as shown in figure 17.10.

8. Select the macro ButtonClick and click OK. A new button appears on the worksheet as shown in figure 17.11.

Fig. 17.10

*The Assign Macro
dialog box displays all
of the macros in the
workbook. Select a
macro to run when the
button is pushed.*

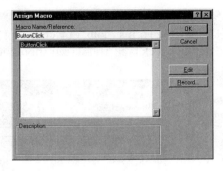

Fig. 17.11

*Excel assigns "Button
1" as a default button
name and caption.*

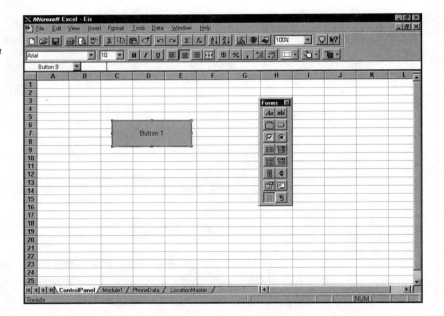

9. When the new button appears, click in the Names box on the formula bar and assign a new name to the button. Type in **btnPhoneData** and press Enter to create a name that matches the name in the Button Click subroutine.

10. Click the caption of the button and type **Phone Data Update** as a new caption. The screen appears as in figure 17.12.

11. Click outside the area of the button to complete the operation.

12. Test your new button—it should display the data form as shown in figure 17.7.

You can add new buttons by modifying the ButtonClick macro. Use one ButtonClick macro for all of the buttons in the workbook so that you can find and revise the logic behind any button. The Select...Case...End Select statements allow you to add and change the logic behind the buttons.

Fig. 17.12

Change the button name to a value you will test for in the ButtonClick macro. Change the caption to describe the button's action.

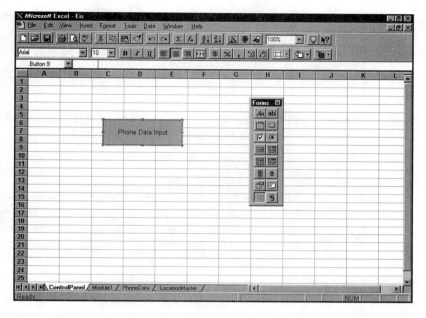

To modify the ButtonClick subroutine and add a button to update the Location Master list, follow these steps:

1. Modify the ButtonClick subroutine in your Visual Basic Module. Insert these lines of code in the Select…Case statement as shown in figure 17.13:

```
Case "btnLocationMaster"
        Worksheets("LocationMaster").ShowDataForm
```

Fig. 17.13

Modify the subroutine to display the built-in data form for worksheet "LocationMaster."

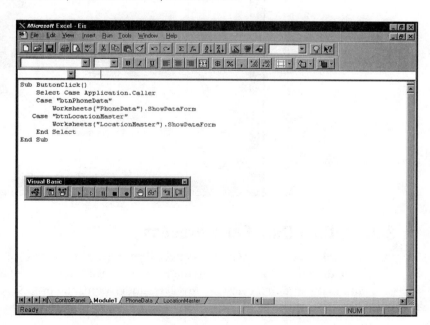

Tip

You can explore Visual Basic's on-line help by positioning the cursor on a Visual Basic statement and pressing F1.

2. Add a button to the ControlPanel worksheet, assign the macro ButtonClick to it, name the button **btnLocationMaster** and add a caption.

 Note

You can copy a button by dragging it with the mouse while holding down the Ctrl key. If you also hold down the Shift key, the new button will be lined up with the original button. The new button will be assigned the same macro as the original. You can right-click the new button to change its caption and name.

The completed button should look like the one shown in figure 17.14.

Fig. 17.14
The Control Panel worksheet contains a data update button for every list in the workbook.

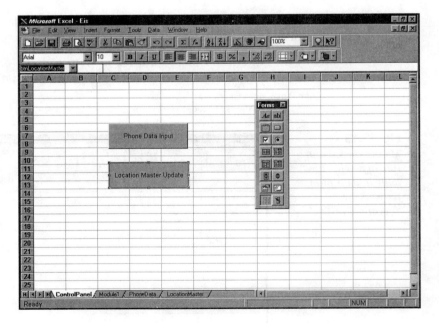

Setting Up a Data Entry Process

You can prevent the "Garbage In - Garbage Out" syndrome by eliminating input errors. Take time to define the requirements for the incoming data, set up a written procedure and make sure that everyone involved understands the process.

To set up a manual data entry procedure, follow these steps:

1. Determine how the data will arrive at the desk of the data entry person.

2. Establish two paper file folders—one for data that is yet to be entered, the other for data that has already been entered.

3. Decide how to balance the data. Set up a log to record date of receipt, entry date, and balancing results.

4. If the quantity of data is large, you may want to assign a batch number to each data report received. You could add a column to the Database range in the data worksheet to record this batch number.

 Tip

If your data repeats, as it does with a batch number, you can use the Ctrl+Shift+" shortcut keys to copy the value from the last row entered.

5. Add a new column to the Database range if you want to keep track of dates entered.

 Tip

To enter today's date in a worksheet of data form use the Ctrl+ ; (semicolon) short-cut keys.

6. Set up time frames for data entry. If your information is used weekly, you will need to arrange for rapid turnaround of the data.

Searching the List

Data is only valuable if you can find it. You can use the powerful search capability of Excel's built-in data form to find and edit individual rows in the list.

To search for data records in a list, follow these steps:

1. Activate the built-in Data Entry Form. You can use one of the custom buttons to do this, or select the worksheet and choose menu options Data, Form.

2. Click the Criteria button on the Data Form as shown in figure 17.15.

3. Enter a criteria value in any of the criteria fields. The value can include a comparison operator like "<" or ">". In the example shown in figure 17.16, the criteria value will find weeks with an ending date less than 6/14/96.

Fig. 17.15
*Excel's built-in data
entry form can search
for records.*

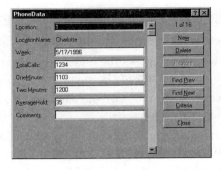

Fig. 17.16
*You can enter a search
value for any column
in the list.*

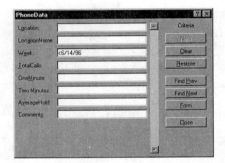

4. After filling in one or more criteria values, choose Find Prev or Find Next to display a record that matches your tests.

5. Continue to use the Find Prev and Find Next buttons to display other records that meet the test.

6. To clear the criteria, click Criteria and then click Clear.

Reading Data from Other Files

Most transaction processing systems such as the accounting system, payroll, production, and so on, are able to summarize information and write the summary to a file. Sometimes the file will be in dBASE format, but usually it is in a text format where data is separated by special delimiter characters like double quotation marks and commas.

You can copy the data from these files directly into your lists with the use of Excel's Text Import Wizard. You can successfully import a wide range of formats without hiring a single programmer.

Importing a Text File

Text files come in all variations. Each record is usually on a separate line, but the data on a line may be separated by spaces, semicolons, commas, and double quotation marks, or some other combination of characters.

You can handle any of these possibilities with Excel's Text Import Wizard. The Wizard is smart enough to select the right combination and shows you how it plans to interpret the data before it begins its work. If the text layout confuses the Wizard, use the text import preview to try different combinations of delimiters and column widths.

To import data from a text file follow these steps:

1. Open the text file using File, Open. Set Files of Type to Text Files and select the file just as you would any Excel file.

2. In Step 1 of the Text Import Wizard shown in figure 17.17 you select the type of delimiters used.

Fig. 17.17

Use the Text Import Wizard to automatically import many types of text files.

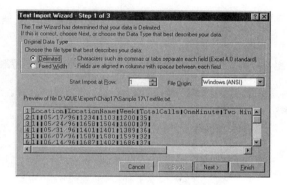

3. You can preview the data as shown in Step 2 of the Text Import Wizard (see fig. 17.18).

Fig. 17.18

You can review a preview of the text before completing the import.

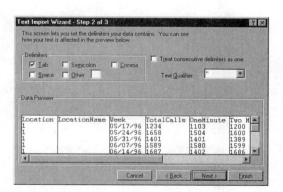

4. Use Step 3 of the Text Import Wizard as shown in figure 17.19 to fine-tune the formats of individual columns.

Fig. 17.19

*To change the format
of a column, use Step 3
of the Text Import
Wizard.*

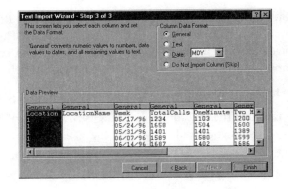

5. The Text Import Wizard produces a new file—separate from your original workbook. You will see your data displayed neatly in columns as in figure 17.20.

Fig. 17.20

*The Text Import
Wizard creates a new
workbook for imported
text.*

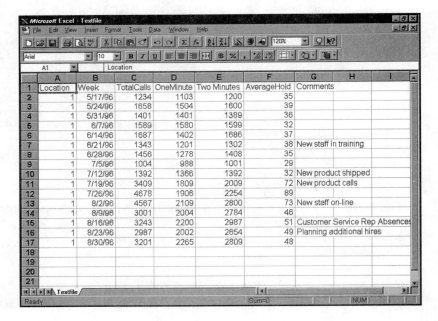

6. It may be necessary to add or rearrange columns of imported data so that they will match the layout of your workbook. In figure 17.21, a new column named Location Name has been added using Insert, Columns.

7. After the data is copied to the workbook, formulas can be inserted. In this example the VLOOKUP formula in column B is copied down the column.

Fig. 17.21

You can insert or rearrange columns before copying imported data to your list.

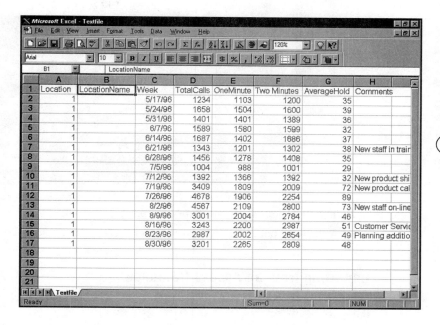

8. The final step is to include the new data in the named range Database. You can do this by choosing Insert, Names, selecting the name and editing the Refers To formula at the bottom of the dialog box as shown in figure 17.22.

Fig. 17.22

After copying data to a list, you can use the Define Name dialog box to include the new rows in the range named Database.

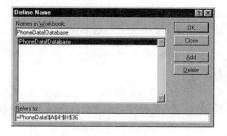

Importing from a dBASE File

dBASE files come with a predefined column width, data type, and column name. Excel uses these to automatically import the data.

To import data from a dBASE file, follow these steps:

1. Choose File, Open. Under Files of Type, select dBaseFiles (*.dbf). Figure 17.23 shows the file DBFFile.dbf selected for import.

Fig. 17.23
Excel automatically imports dBASE data.

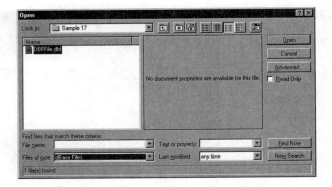

2. The file opens with one data field per column.

3. Adjust the data and copy to the data list in your workbook file.

Importing from an Access Database

You can use the Get External Data menu option to import data from an Access database.

To import data from an Access database, follow these steps:

1. Choose the menu option Data, Get External Data.

2. Choose the data source from the ODBC Data Source dialog box. If the Access database has not yet been set up as an ODBC Data Source, you can choose the New button on the dialog box and add the data source.

 Tip

If you have a copy of Access installed on your computer system, you can use the Tools, OfficeLinks, Analyze it with MS Excel option in Access to export an Access report to an Excel workbook. The totals on the report are copied to Excel as outline levels. Only the data selected by the report is exported.

3. Select the database tables you want to use from the Add Tables dialog. Click Close.

4. In the Microsoft Query form shown in figure 17.24, choose the data fields you want to import to Excel. Microsoft Query allows you to reorder columns, add calculated fields, and link multiple database tables.

5. When you have completed your Query design, choose File, Return Data to Microsoft Excel.

Fig. 17.24
Importing Access Data with Microsoft Query.

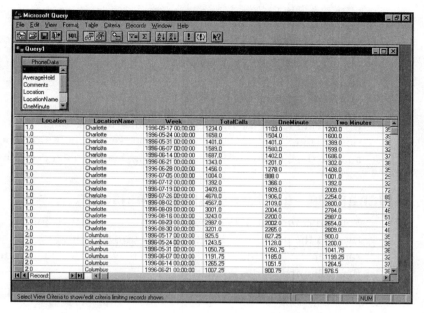

6. In the Get External Data dialog box shown in figure 17.25, you can choose the destination for the imported data. You can also choose the Keep Query Definition option to store the Query parameters in your Excel workbook. Later, you can update the imported data with the Data, Refresh Data menu option.

Fig. 17.25
Get External Data option to keep query definition.

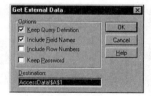

7. Click OK in the Get External Data dialog box and the imported Access data will appear in your Excel workbook.

α Note

You can drag-and-drop worksheet data from Excel to an Access table. Try this by creating a new Access table, selecting a range of cells on an Excel worksheet, and dragging the range to the Access table. Position the cursor arrow on the edge of the range of cells you want to copy, and hold down the Ctrl key while dragging.

Designing Lists for Your Organization

Now you should be convinced that Excel lists can do the job for your *data warehouse*. You may be wondering "What data should I capture?" You could look through the stacks of reports on your desk and in the corners of your office to answer that question, or you can take a more scientific approach.

If your *data warehouse* is to serve as a source of data for analysis and management decisions, it must contain data related to your key business indicators. You can use Excel to analyze the data and assist you in making management decisions.

Identifying Your Key Business Indicators

You can communicate management priorities to others in the organization by involving them in the process of identifying key business indicators. If others know what key indicators are being captured and analyzed, they will tend to focus their efforts on activities that will improve those indicators.

To involve a group in identifying a list of a key business indicators, follow these steps:

1. Meet with a cross section of managers. Limit the group to 12 or fewer participants. Include several supervisors in the participant list.

2. Use some type of brainstorming technique to generate a list of indicators. Invite a skilled facilitator to lead this part of the meeting.

3. Narrow the list by a secret vote with each participant voting for five to seven measures. This is not democracy in action—it is a way to develop a list for discussion. The process of voting ensures that each participant has time to think about the measurements.

4. Order the list by number of votes. One of the advantages of this process is that each participant will probably have at least one of his or her favorites in the top group of measurements.

5. Narrow the list to the top five to seven indicators. Don't accept the list as is but instead lead the group to consensus by asking each participant "What changes would I need to make to the list for you to be 80 percent in agreement?" Take time to discuss changes. Time spent reinforces understanding of the indicators.

6. Try to have the group leave the meeting room 80 percent in agreement and 100 percent in support of the list of key indicators.

Deciding What Data to Include in Your Lists

Now that you have key indicators defined, you can get down to details and plan each measurement. Often I find that the organization's accounting, production, payroll, and other transaction processing systems are missing data needed for several of the key measures. You can use Excel to begin entering this data manually, then switch over to importing as the transaction processing systems are modified to collect the data.

To decide what data to include in an Excel list, follow these steps:

1. Decide how often you want to review the measurement—daily, weekly, monthly, quarterly, and so on.

2. Select a time interval that will help you discover trends. Even if you plan to review the measurement on a monthly basis, you may be better able to uncover trends by storing daily data.

3. Choose the number of measures you need for each time interval. If you have two customer service units, you will want separate measures for each. If you are introducing a new product or service, you may want a separate measure during the introduction period.

4. Meet with others to determine where the data resides in your Transaction Processing Systems (Billing, Sales Tracking, Production, and so on).

5. Develop a strategy to import this data to an Excel list.

> ## α Note
>
> One of the advantages of using Excel is the ability to set up a separate store of data that can collect summary data from many different computer and manual sources. As the effort grows, you can replace manual sources with text or database import. Finally, you can replace the import with full integration.
>
> Excel was built to be a universal data client and it can be your front-end analysis tool for information stored in databases. Use Excel's PivotTable feature and Microsoft Query add-in to select data from Access and other types of databases. You can use Visual Basic macros with external databases through Data Access Objects or Open Database Connectivity (ODBC) tools.

Adding On to the Data Warehouse with Microsoft Access

The advent of Windows 95 has made the job of using Access and Excel together easier. Now is the time for Excel users who haven't yet explored Access to begin experimenting with the power of Access forms and reports.

You can learn about Access by using Excel's built-in Access Wizards. These new Access functions are listed on Excel's Data menu. The Access Form, Access Report, and Convert to Access options automatically make Access functions available to Excel users.

Access forms provide a more powerful interface than Excel for data entry and update. You can use the Access Query by Form to display selected records. Access provides many data validation functions not available in Excel.

The Access Conversion options provide you with a built-in migration path from Excel to Access. If you want to convert data to Access, you can use the wizard to define your database tables and do the conversion for you.

The Access Report Wizard assists you in building an Access report from an Excel list. You can use the grouping and formatting features of Access reports for data in a Microsoft Excel list.

 Note

The Access Wizard options are only available in Excel if you have a copy of Microsoft Access 95 installed on your computer system.

Powerful Access Forms

If you want an advanced Excel data entry form complete with drop-down lists and editing rules, you could develop it with Excel's dialog boxes and Visual Basic for Applications. Or, you could tap into the user-friendly features of Access forms and create advanced data entry and retrieval forms without programming.

The Access Form feature creates an Access Database with a .MDB file extension. The Access Database is linked to the Excel list and stores the data entry and retrieval forms.

To create an Access form for an Excel list, follow these steps:

1. Select the worksheet containing the list.
2. Select the entire list including the single row of headings.
3. Choose <u>D</u>ata, Access For<u>m</u>.

 Note

You might want to go get a cup of coffee while Excel and Access do their linking dance. It can take almost a minute on a fast machine—and there is no warning that the operation is in process. The cursor doesn't even change into an hourglass. But have faith; eventually the link will be completed and your system will respond again.

4. Choose New Database on the Create Microsoft Access Form dialog box and click the OK button. You can use the header row options at the bottom of the dialog box to tell Access that the first row of your Excel list contains field names.

5. Select all of the fields in the Excel Table as shown in figure 17.26.

Fig. 17.26

You can choose which columns you want Access Forms Wizard to use.

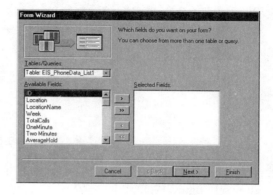

6. Choose a form layout and style as shown in figure 17.27 and 17.28.

Fig. 17.27

You can use the Access Form Wizard to design any type of layout.

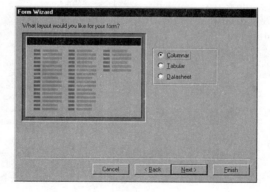

Fig. 17.28

Use one of the Access pre-defined styles.

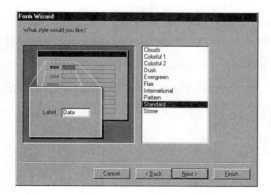

7. Choose the Open the Form to View or Enter Information option as shown in figure 17.29.

Fig. 17.29

Assign a form name and click Finish.

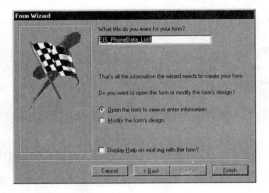

8. When you click Finish in the Form Wizard, the completed form will appear as shown in figure 17.30.

Fig. 17.30

The Access Form Wizard automatically creates a data entry form.

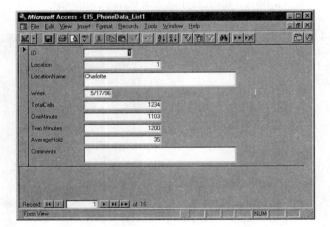

You can add powerful data entry features to the form using the features of Access. One of the modifications you can make is to replace a field with a drop-down list box.

To modify an Access form field, follow these steps:

1. Select Form View by clicking the button in the upper left corner of the Access Form View toolbar as shown in figure 17.31.

Fig. 17.31

Select the Form View button to switch to Design View.

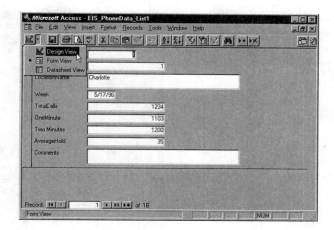

2. The form appears in Design view as shown in figure 17.32. Right-click the field you want to modify. Select Change To. In figure 17.33, the field is changed from a text field to a combo box.

3. You can right-click a field to change its properties. Figure 17.34 shows how properties are set for a combo box. The Row Source Type and Row Source are set to provide a lookup from a preset list of values.

Fig. 17.32

In Design view, you can modify the Access form to include advanced data entry and editing features.

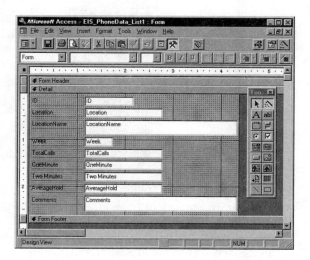

Fig. 17.33
You can modify a text field and change it into a drop-down list box.

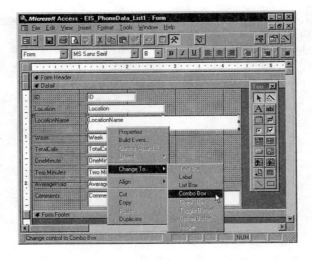

Fig. 17.34
Change the row source type and row source to create a simple table of values for the drop-down list box.

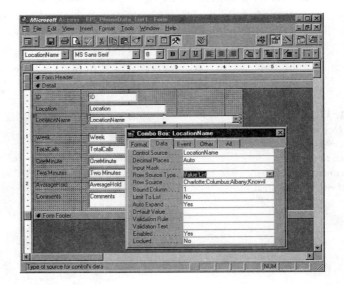

4. You can switch back to Form view and test the change. In figure 17.35 the combo box displays a pick list of locations.

You can use Access to develop advanced data entry forms for Excel lists. As your knowledge of Access grows, you can tap into the power of one of the best user-interfaces in the database world.

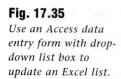

Fig. 17.35

Use an Access data entry form with drop-down list box to update an Excel list.

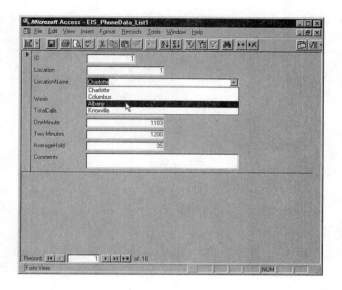

17

To use these features, choose <u>D</u>ata, Access <u>F</u>orm. Use the <u>D</u>ata, Access <u>R</u>eport menu option to start the Access Report Wizard and provide you with an easy way to tap into the rich reporting functions of Access. You can create publication quality reports with features that complement the extensive worksheet publishing tools of Excel.

Excel Tables Linked to Access

When you use the Access Form and Access Report options, Excel and Access automatically create a new Access Database that holds the form and report definitions. The Access Database is linked to the Excel list.

Figure 17.36 shows the Tables tab of the Access Database created using the Access form example shown previously. As you become familiar with Access, you will recognize this as the main entrance to Access. From this screen you can select a table of data in the database, define queries that filter and combine tables, define and run forms and reports for data entry and report printing, add macros in a user friendly form mode, or develop modules in Visual Basic for Application.

In the example, the EIS_PhoneData_List1 table is the only one in the Access Database named EIS.MDB. The symbol to the left of the table name tells you that the table is linked to the Excel list.

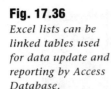

Fig. 17.36

Excel lists can be linked tables used for data update and reporting by Access Database.

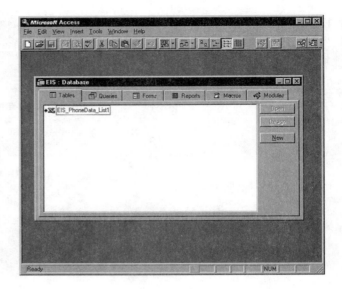

Converting a Linked Table to an Access Table

When you need to convert an Excel list to an Access Database, just ask Access to change the linked table to a table in the Access database.

To convert an Excel List to an Access database, follow these steps:

1. Select the Access Tables tab.

2. Choose File, Save As/Export and select Within the Current Database option as shown in figure 17.37.

Fig. 17.37

Copying the linked table to a new table within the Access Database.

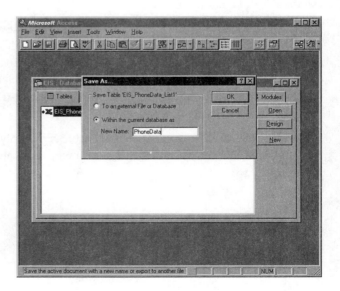

3. Access creates a new table in addition to the linked table. The new table is shown as "PhoneData" in figure 17.38.

Fig. 17.38

Linked table is still connected to Excel list. Copy of linked table created within Access Database.

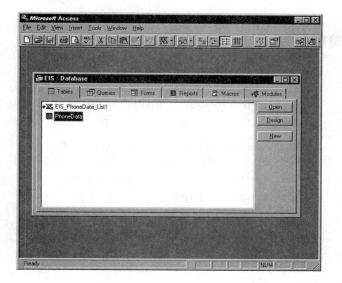

4. Change the record source of forms from the linked table to the new table. Display the properties of the form by right-clicking the small black square in the top-left corner of the Form Design window. Change the record source property to equal the name of the new table as shown in figure 17.39.

Fig. 17.39

Changing the Access data form to work with the internal Access table instead of the linked table.

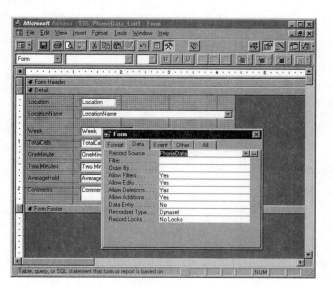

5. Delete the linked table by selecting the Tables tab, highlighting the name of the linked table and pressing the Delete key.

Summary

In this chapter, you have learned how to use Excel's lists to create a database. Lists can be maintained with Excel's built-in data entry form, or you can import data from external databases or text files. You can add the power of Microsoft Access data input forms to the Excel lists with the Access Forms Wizard.

Creating lists of data is just the first step in developing an information system. In the next chapter you will learn how to Outline and Filter the data in your lists. Chapter 19 explains how to link PivotTables to the lists. In Chapter 20, you will learn how to organize the lists and PivotTables into an Executive Information System.

chapter 18

Drilling Through the Data with Outlines and Filters

by John Lacher

In this chapter

◆ **Add a Current Month and Year to Date column to your Excel list**
With the Offset function, you can create worksheet formulas to calculate comparison values that automatically sum values in other columns.

◆ **Use AutoFilter to display selected detail**
With Excel's easy-to-use AutoFilter, you can display selected data with a click of the mouse.

◆ **Use Advanced Filters with Criteria Ranges and Scenarios to select data for display**
Advanced filters add more selection options and criteria options.

◆ **Create summary data totals using Outlining and Automatic Subtotals**
You can use outlining and subtotals to create a summary version of the data in your Excel worksheet.

◆ **Display outline levels using the View Manager**
With View manager, you can print or display summary totals from an Excel list.

◆ **Add database calculations to your worksheets**
Excel's powerful database functions can be used to summarize worksheet data.

D o your computer reports produce more back pain than useable data? Do you have trouble finding key detail data in towering stacks of computer reports? Excel searches through your data and displays the details you need. With Excel, you can focus on the details that are important and ignore the rest!

To make your Excel applications easy to use, you can design them so that the top worksheet shows exception or summary data. You can use buttons and other techniques described in

Chapter 21, "Forecasting in Excel," to provide ways for the user to display more detail by clicking these summary measures. Each level of detail provides a way to *drill down* (or search through) to more detail until finally the user sees the source data itself.

Once your Electronic Warehouse is filled with data, you can use Excel's powerful Outlining, Sorting, Filtering, and Subtotals functions to drill down through the data and analyze selected detail numbers. You can analyze data and prepare reports for any grouping in your detailed data.

Adding a Comparison Column to Your List

Use the OFFSET function to add comparison columns that automatically sum amounts from other columns. The Excel list shown in figure 18.1 contains one row of data for each combination of Location, Sales Unit, and Division. Each row contains a column of weekly sales data, starting with the most current week's data.

Fig. 18.1

A list of weekly detail numbers can be used as input to the filtering and outlining features of Excel.

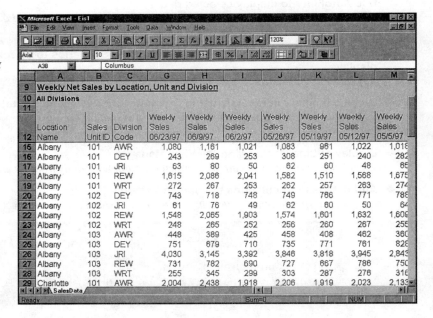

Location Name	Sales Unit ID	Division Code	Weekly Sales 06/23/97	Weekly Sales 06/9/97	Weekly Sales 06/2/97	Weekly Sales 05/26/97	Weekly Sales 05/19/97	Weekly Sales 05/12/97	Weekly Sales 05/5/97
Albany	101	AWR	1,080	1,161	1,021	1,083	961	1,022	1,018
Albany	101	DEY	243	269	253	308	251	240	282
Albany	101	JRI	63	80	50	62	60	48	65
Albany	101	REW	1,615	2,086	2,041	1,582	1,510	1,568	1,675
Albany	101	WRT	272	267	253	262	257	263	274
Albany	102	DEY	743	718	748	749	786	771	788
Albany	102	JRI	61	76	49	62	60	50	64
Albany	102	REW	1,548	2,065	1,903	1,574	1,801	1,632	1,609
Albany	102	WRT	248	265	252	256	260	267	255
Albany	103	AWR	448	389	425	458	408	462	360
Albany	103	DEY	751	679	710	735	771	761	828
Albany	103	JRI	4,030	3,145	3,392	3,846	3,818	3,945	2,843
Albany	103	REW	731	782	690	727	667	786	750
Albany	103	WRT	255	345	299	303	287	276	316
Charlotte	101	AWR	2,004	2,438	1,918	2,206	1,919	2,023	2,133

 Tip

Use SUM and OFFSET formulas to create summary rows or columns that total a variable number of weeks or other time periods.

If you add the Most Current Weeks, Same Period Last Year, and Increase or Decrease columns shown in figure 18.2, then you can sort, filter, and outline the data and display summary sales results. The value 10 in cell D11 of figure 18.2 is more than just a column label. It is used by the OFFSET function to sum the most recent ten columns of weekly data. To use a different comparison period, you can enter a different number in cell D11. Cell D15 in figure 18.2 contains the formula =SUM(G15:OFFSET(G15,,$D$11-1)). When D11 is equal to ten weeks, the formula tells Excel to sum the range G15:P15, which is the latest ten weeks of data.

Fig. 18.2

You can use formulas to insert summary columns in the detail list.

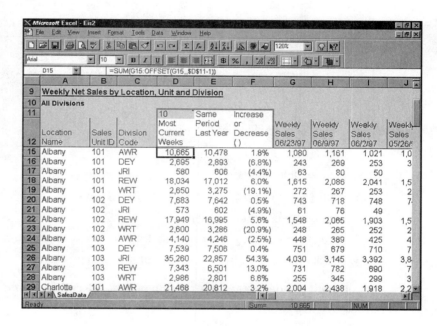

With a formula like =SUM(OFFSET(G15,,53):OFFSET(G15,,$D$11 +52)) as shown in cell E15 of figure 18.2, you can sum the ten weeks of data from the prior year. If D11 is 10 weeks, the formula will sum the range of 10 weekly sales numbers starting 53 columns from the latest column of sales numbers.

Drilling Down to the Detail with Filters

You can drill down to the detail you need with Excel's built-in filter capabilities. When you use AutoFilter, a filter button appears next to each column heading. If you click the button and select a value, the filter will hide all rows but those with the value you selected. AutoFilter is easy to use but cannot handle complex filter criteria with multiple "and" and "or" combinations.

When you use Advanced Filter, enter the filter criteria in a separate range of cells on the worksheet. You can enter multiple "and" and "or" criteria and even filter based on complex criteria.

Using AutoFilter

AutoFilter is Excel's automatic drilling machine. All the setup work is done for you. Click the AutoFilter button, select a value and then repeat the process for other columns. AutoFilter provides you with a custom criteria option you can use to specify a condition like `Amount >=100` or `Amount <= 2000`.

 Tip

Use AutoFilter to display the top ten values in a column of data. You can select Top Ten from the list of values in the AutoFilter drop-down list. The Top Ten option also provides for selection of the Top n or Bottom n values, where n is the number of items you want to display in the filtered list.

To use AutoFilter, follow these steps:

1. Select a cell in the list of data you want to filter.

2. Choose Data, Filter, AutoFilter.

3. Filter buttons will appear automatically next to each column heading in the list.

4. Click one or more filter buttons and select filter criteria.

If you want to filter on just one column of data, select the column heading and one row of data, as shown in figure 18.3.

To use AutoFilter's Custom criteria option follow these steps:

1. Click the Custom option as shown in figure 18.4.

2. Select a comparison operator and enter a value as shown in figure 18.5.

3. Choose And or Or to add an additional criteria for the column.

4. Click OK and the data will be filtered, as shown in figure 18.6. Rows that do not match the criteria are hidden and the message `Filter Mode` shows at the bottom of the screen in the status bar. If you have a color monitor, you will see that selected rows are labeled with blue row numbers while you are in filter mode.

Fig. 18.3
*Select column head-
ings and choose the
AutoFilter menu
option.*

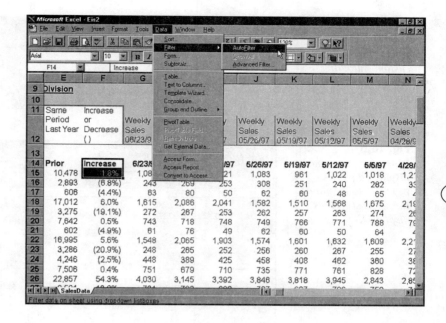

Fig. 18.4
*Use the custom
AutoFilter option to
use more than one
criteria.*

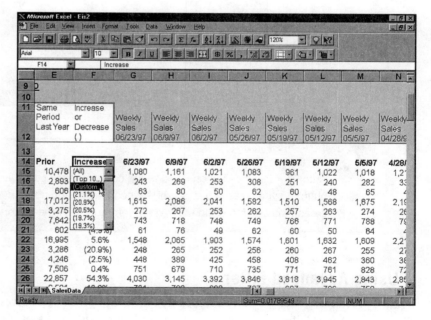

Fig. 18.5

You can specify two filter criteria in the custom AutoFilter dialog box.

Fig. 18.6

When the status bar displays the message Filter Mode, *only the selected records are displayed.*

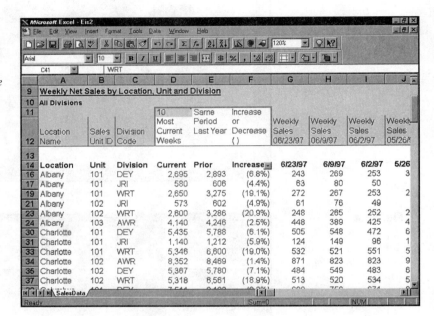

> α **Note**
>
> AutoFilter displays buttons next to the column headings on your worksheet. These buttons sometimes cover part of the heading, but do not print on your reports. Increase the column width to provide room to display the buttons.

Using Advanced Filter

Advanced Filter is a more complicated drilling machine that gives you more power than AutoFilter. In the example shown in figure 18.7, the Criteria Range in cells A2:A6 tells Excel to select rows with Division=AWR when the increase percentage is less than 0%. The criteria in range B2:B6 adds an additional selection: those rows that have

Division=JRI and an increase percentage less than 2%. If (Division=AWR and Increase<0%) or (Division=JRI and Increase<2%), then the row will be selected; otherwise, it will be hidden.

Fig. 18.7

Use a Query by Example Criteria Range to control Advanced Filter.

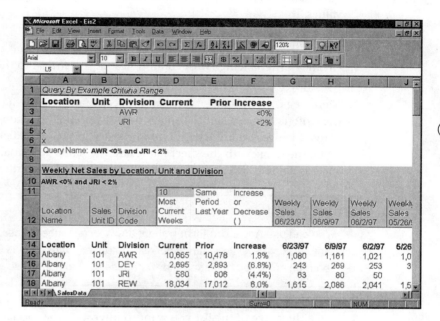

Note

To use Query by Example you can use Advanced Filter and a Criteria Range. Set up the Criteria Range with column headings that match the list of data. When you type a value in the Criteria Range, Excel filters out any rows of data that do not match the criteria values.

You must use Advanced Filter if:

▶ You want to use a formula in your criteria to reference a value outside the list you are filtering. By changing the reference value, the action of the filter changes.

▶ You need to use a formula to compare values in one column to values in another column.

▶ Your filter includes a set of conditions across multiple columns. The example in figure 18.7 illustrates this type of criteria.

▶ You want to copy the filtered data automatically to another range in your workbook.

▶ Your data contains duplicate values and you want to display or copy only unique values.

To use Advanced Filter follow these steps:

1. Create a Criteria Range with column headings identical to the column headings in the list.

2. Name the Criteria Range "Criteria," a special range name that Excel will use to find the Criteria Range when it displays the Advanced Filter dialog box. If you will have Criteria Ranges on more than one worksheet in your workbook, then you can name the range with the sheet name and the name "Criteria." For example: if your sheet is named "SalesData," name the range "SalesData!Criteria."

 Note

You can use Advanced Filter without any special range names. If you name your Criteria Range "Criteria" and your list "Database," then Excel will automatically use the ranges named "Criteria" and "Database" as input to the Advanced Filter.

---

3. Name the range of the list you want to filter with the special name "Database." Include the column heading in the named range. You can qualify this name with the sheet name as described in step 2. If your sheet is named "SalesData," you can name the range "SalesData!Database."

4. Select any cell in the Criteria Range or list range.

5. Choose Data, Filter, Advanced Filter from the menu.

6. Check to be sure that the List Range and Criteria Range contain the address of the ranges you named "Database" and "Criteria," as shown in figure 18.8.

7. If you want to select just unique records or copy the filtered data to another range on the worksheet, select those options.

8. Click OK and the filtered data will be displayed, as shown in figure 18.9.

Fig. 18.8

Advanced Filter provides options to filter or copy the data using a Criteria Range.

Fig. 18.9

Both AutoFilter and Advanced Filter display Filter Mode *in the status bar.*

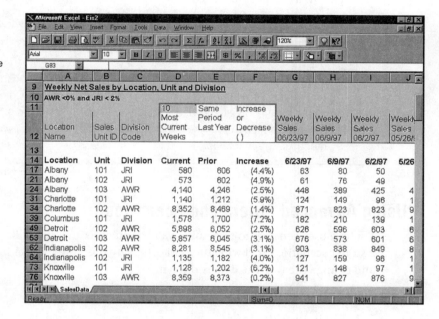

Location	Unit	Division	Current	Prior	Increase	6/23/97	6/9/97	6/2/97	5/26
Albany	101	JRI	580	606	(4.4%)	63	80	50	
Albany	102	JRI	573	602	(4.9%)	61	76	49	
Albany	103	AWR	4,140	4,246	(2.5%)	448	389	425	4
Charlotte	101	JRI	1,140	1,212	(5.9%)	124	149	96	1
Charlotte	102	AWR	8,352	8,469	(1.4%)	871	823	823	9
Columbus	101	JRI	1,578	1,700	(7.2%)	182	210	139	1
Detroit	102	AWR	5,898	6,052	(2.5%)	626	596	603	6
Detroit	103	AWR	5,857	6,045	(3.1%)	676	573	601	6
Indianapolis	102	AWR	8,281	8,545	(3.1%)	903	838	849	8
Indianapolis	102	JRI	1,135	1,182	(4.0%)	127	159	96	1
Knoxville	101	JRI	1,128	1,202	(6.2%)	121	148	97	1
Knoxville	103	AWR	8,359	8,373	(0.2%)	941	827	876	9

Controlling Advanced Filter with Formulas

If you use a formula in a Criteria Range, you can filter rows based on relationships between the fields in the list. For example, you can filter the list shown in figure 18.10 to select rows where the Current value is more than 10% higher than the Prior values. To add the formula to the Criteria Range, follow these steps:

1. Create a new column in the Criteria Range with a blank label or a label different from any of the field names. In this example, you can label the column **HighSales.**

2. Enter a formula that evaluates to True or False. In this example, the formula would be = D15 > (E15 * 1.1). D15 and E15 are the Current and Prior values in the first row of the list. Excel will automatically change the cell references to compare the values in each row in the list.

3. If your formula includes a reference to a cell outside the list, you need to use an absolute reference. For example, if instead of comparing to 10%, you want to compare to a percentage value in cell H1, use this formula instead of the one in step 2:
   = D15 > (E15 * $H$1).

 Note

Another way to use a formula in the Advanced Filter Criteria Range is to build it as a text string. You can reference a value outside of your list Criteria Range with a formula like ="<" & $G$12. Use a conditional criteria like =IF($G$12="Yes","A","B"). With worksheet controls like check boxes or drop-down lists, you can build powerful Criteria Range functions.

Using Advanced Filters and Scenarios

You can use Scenarios to remember values you enter in Criteria Ranges. When you select a stored Scenario, Excel will automatically copy the stored values into the Criteria Range and change the way the data is filtered.

To use a filter and Scenario together, follow these steps:

1. Fill in the Criteria Range as you want it to be restored by the Scenario.

2. Choose Tools, Scenarios and click the Add button.

3. Type a name for the Scenario as shown in figure 18.10.

4. Enter the Criteria Range address in the Changing Cells input box on the Add Scenario dialog box.

5. Click OK and click OK again to confirm the Scenario values, as shown in figure 18.11.

6. When you want to restore the criteria values from a Scenario, select the Scenarios from the Scenario Manager, as shown in figure 18.12.

Fig. 18.10

Store frequently used filter criteria values in a Scenario.

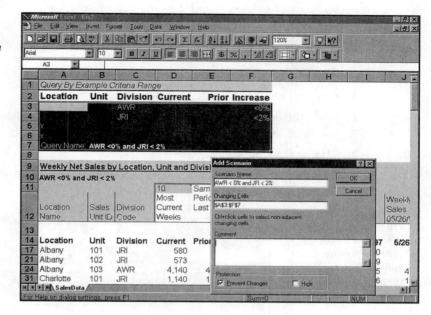

Fig. 18.11

Set the Scenarios Changing Cells values to the Advanced Filter Criteria Range.

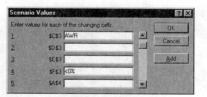

Fig. 18.12

Use the list of Scenarios to select values for the Advanced Filter Criteria Range.

Using Filters and Subtotals

You can add subtotals to filtered data with the automatic subtotal feature.

To add subtotals to filtered data, follow these steps:

1. Sort your data in the order you need for subtotals.

2. Select the data you want to subtotal. You do not need to select all columns, but you must include the columns heading row.

3. Choose Data, Subtotals.

4. As shown in figure 18.13, fill in the Subtotal dialog box with the name of the column that will control subtotal breaks.

Fig. 18.13

When you use the Subtotal feature, Excel automatically adds subtotals to the filtered data.

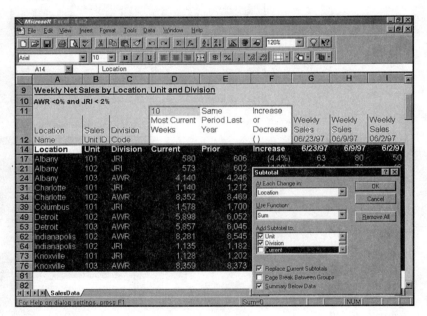

5. Select the type of function for the subtotal and the columns to be summarized. You can have one or more Sums, Counts, Averages, Maximums, Minimums, and other calculations at each subtotal break.

6. Excel automatically adds subtotals.

7. Add any additional formulas at the subtotal breaks. In the example in figure 18.14, the formula in column F was manually copied down across the new rows added by the subtotal function.

Fig. 18.14

When the Excel list contains formulas, you may need to add formulas to the subtotal rows. Percent increase formulas have been added to the subtotal rows in column F.

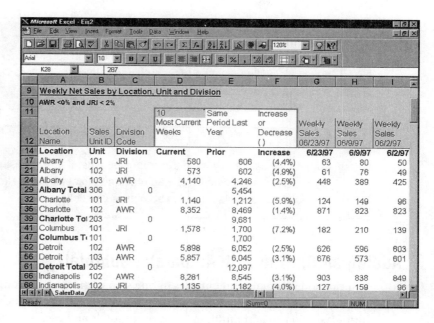

	Location Name	Sales Unit ID	Division Code	10 Most Current Weeks	Same Period Last Year	Increase or Decrease ( )	Weekly Sales 06/23/97	Weekly Sales 06/9/97	Weekly Sales 06/2/97
	Location	Unit	Division	Current	Prior	Increase	6/23/97	6/9/97	6/2/97
17	Albany	101	JRI	580	606	(4.4%)	63	80	50
21	Albany	102	JRI	573	602	(4.9%)	61	76	49
24	Albany	103	AWR	4,140	4,246	(2.5%)	448	389	425
29	**Albany Total**	306		0	5,454				
32	Charlotte	101	JRI	1,140	1,212	(5.9%)	124	149	96
35	Charlotte	102	AWR	8,352	8,469	(1.4%)	871	823	823
39	**Charlotte Tot**	203		0	9,681				
41	Columbus	101	JRI	1,578	1,700	(7.2%)	182	210	139
47	**Columbus T**	101		0	1,700				
52	Detroit	102	AWR	5,898	6,052	(2.5%)	626	596	603
56	Detroit	103	AWR	5,857	6,045	(3.1%)	676	573	601
61	**Detroit Total**	205		0	12,097				
66	Indianapolis	102	AWR	8,281	8,545	(3.1%)	903	838	849
68	Indianapolis	102	JRI	1,135	1,182	(4.0%)	127	159	96

Note

When you add a total using the Formula Wizard, Excel creates a SUM formula. When you add subtotals, Excel fills in the subtotal rows with the SUBTOTAL formula. SUBTOTAL can be used to count, average, sum, or return other mathematical and statistical functions. It does not include hidden rows in the summary total. Use online help to learn more about the differences between SUM and SUBTOTAL.

Creating Drill Down Levels with Outlines

You can drill down to the detail with Excel's built-in outline features. Like filters, outlines hide the detail you don't need and display the data in which you are interested. Filters always hide rows, but outlines can hide unneeded columns, too. Excel will automatically analyze your data for subtotal rows and then create its outline around that structure.

Caution

If you are in Filter mode when you add automatic subtotals, Excel will not add an automatic outline. If you add an automatic outline to a filtered list with subtotals, the outline may not reflect all of the subtotal levels in the data.

Tip

To help the user answer different types of "what-if" questions, provide multiple ways to drill down to the detail. You can provide both outline and filter drill down methods. Outlines can hide detail in both rows and columns.

Adding an Outline with Automatic Subtotals

You can add subtotals and outlines in one step with Excel's automatic subtotal function. When you add automatic subtotals, Excel creates new rows that contain SUBTOTAL formulas. You can add multiple levels of subtotals and each level becomes a level in the outline.

To use the Automatic Subtotals feature follow these steps:

1. Select a cell in an Excel list.

2. Choose Data, Subtotals.

3. Fill in the subtotal dialog box by selecting a field in the At Each Change In option. Select a Use Function value from the list of available functions. You can specify which columns in the list have subtotal values in the Add Subtotal to option. When you have selected these values click OK.

4. Your worksheet will appear with subtotals and an outline area at the left margin, like that shown in figure 18.15.

Click a + button in the outline and Excel will drill down and display the next level of detail in the outline. Click a – button and Excel will hide the detail and display the outline total. You can use the numbered buttons at the top of the outline margin to select a level of detail for every item in the list.

If you click the 2 button in an outline like the one shown in figure 18.16, then you will display the second level of totals in the outline.

Fig. 18.15
Use the outlining feature of Excel to hide the detail rows and display only the summary totals.

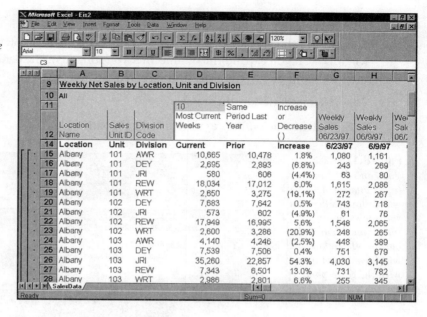

Fig. 18.16
You can use the outline buttons to hide detail rows.

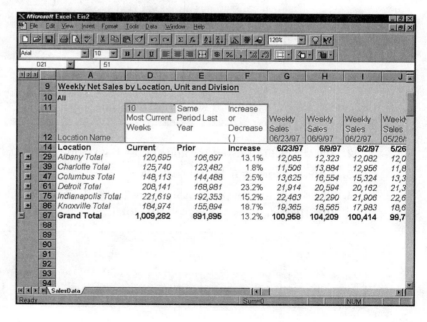

Sorting Outlined Data

You can sort the list based on the totals in an outline. When you sort the total, the detail will follow. If you expand the outline after you sort, all of the detail rows for the first total will have moved to the beginning of the list.

To sort subtotals follow these steps:

1. Collapse the outline, as shown in figure 18.17.

Fig. 18.17

You can sort summary totals and the detail will follow. When you sort the summary totals and expand the outline, the detail rows will have sorted along with the corresponding summary row.

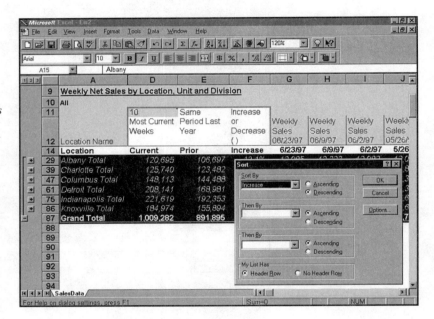

2. Select a cell in the outline and choose <u>D</u>ata, <u>S</u>ort.

3. Choose a sort by field and click OK.

4. The sorted total appears, as in figure 18.18. If you expand the outline, you will see that the detail has moved with the totals.

 Tip

Sort summary totals to change the order of the list. Detail rows will follow the sorted summary rows in outline view.

Fig. 18.18

Sorting summary totals reorders the list in descending order by totals in column F.

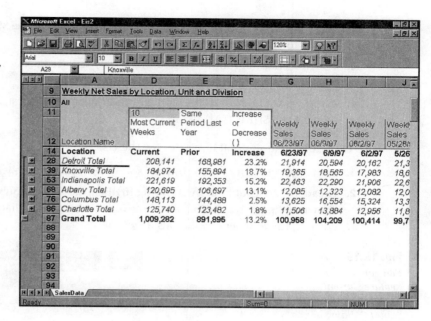

Adding Additional Subtotal Levels

You can add additional subtotal levels with Excel's subtotal feature. By nesting subtotal levels you can create subtotals within other subtotals. For example, you can create a subtotal by sales unit within department.

Caution

Don't trust Excel's nested subtotals—if you add more than one level of automatic subtotals, a bug in Excel's subtotal feature may cause an error. If you are using nested subtotals, use the Expert Solutions Subtotal add-in provided on the CD-ROM.

To install the Expert Solutions Subtotal add-in follow these steps:

1. Copy the file SUBTOTAL.XLA from the Expert Solutions CD-ROM to your hard disk. You can copy the file to your Excel/Library directory if you want to store the XLA file with other add-in files.

2. Use Tools, Add-Ins and use the browse button to select the SUBTOTAL.XLA file you copied to your hard disk.

3. The new subtotal routine will automatically replace Excel's standard subtotal routine on the Data menu.

4. If you want to return to the standard subtotal routine, choose Tools, Add-Ins, and deselect the SUBTOTAL add-in.

To create multiple subtotal levels, follow these steps:

1. Start with the first column in your sort order—usually the leftmost column.

2. Create the first subtotal by selecting the Replace Current Subtotals check box, as shown in figure 18.19. This will remove all existing automatic subtotals before creating the new set of subtotals. Click OK.

Fig. 18.19

You can use the Replace Current Subtotals option in the Subtotal dialog box to create nested subtotals.

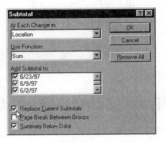

3. Create the second subtotal by deselecting the Replace Current Subtotals check box. The new subtotal will be added in addition to the previous set.

Applying Automatic Formats

Excel provides several built-in formats that automatically give your list a professional appearance. When you choose a built-in format, you can decide which elements of that format you want to apply to your list: Number Format, Borders, Font, Patterns, Alignment, and Width/Height. Use the Options button on the AutoFormat dialog box to select these options.

 Tip

Choose a built-in AutoFormat and make it your standard for publishing Excel results. Staying with a standard format will make it easy for you to format other reports identically.

To apply an automatic format, follow these steps:

1. Choose F̲ormat, A̲utoFormat.

2. Choose the built-in format you want.

3. If you want to pick and choose which element of the format to apply, click the Options button.

4. Click OK and the new format will appear (see the example in fig. 18.20).

Fig. 18.20

Automatic formatting may be applied to outlined lists.

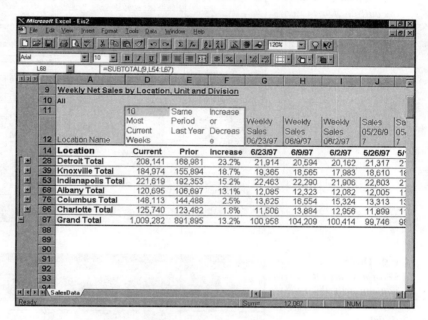

> **Note**
>
> Excel provides sixteen built-in formats. If you can't find one that meets your needs, you will be have to format your list manually. One way to store a format and re-apply it when subtotalling or outlining data is to write a Visual Basic macro that searches for SUBTOTAL or SUM functions and applies different formats to those rows or columns.

Drilling Down into an Outline

If you want to drill down into the detail of an outline like the one shown in figure 18.20, click the + button for the summary total you are interested in exploring. Excel will keep the other totals the same while showing you the next level of detail for the subtotal you selected. Different levels are shown in figures 18.21, 18.22, and 18.23.

Fig. 18.21

Drill down to the detail in outline by clicking the + button in a summary row of the outline. The button caption will change to - when the detail is visible.

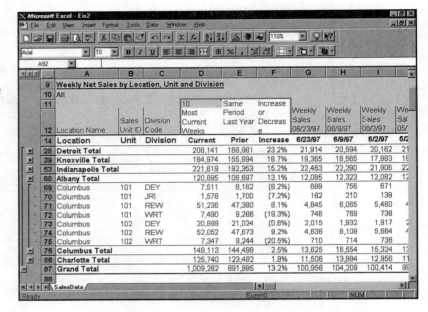

Fig. 18.22

With nested subtotals, you can drill down to an intermediate level of detail.

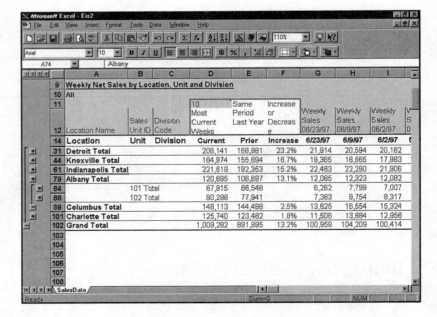

Fig. 18.23

Use the + button to show detail for just one intermediate total.

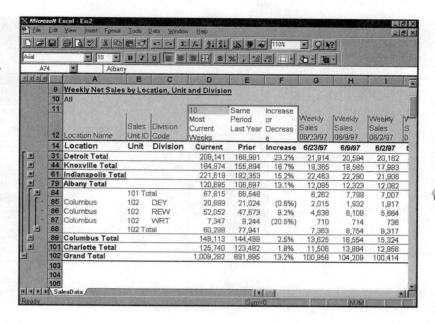

Using Outlines and Views

You can use a View to store the sequence of hidden rows or columns in an outline. With the View Manager, you can present a list of display options to the user.

> ⚛ **Tip**
>
> Use View Manager to store and retrieve views of outlines. A view will return the outline to a pre-set level of detail.

To create a view, follow these steps:

1. Arrange the outline as you want it to be stored in the View.

2. Choose View, View Manager, and click the Add button.

3. Assign a name to the view and choose View Includes Hidden Rows and Columns, as shown in figure 18.24.

Fig. 18.24

You can store outline settings in a View. By selecting a View, you can quickly display stored summary levels.

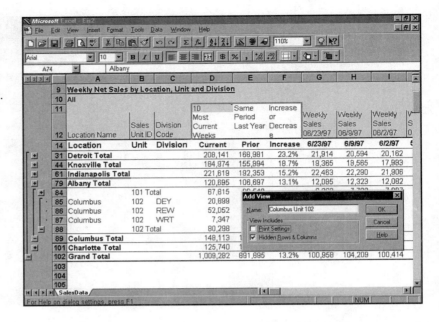

> ## α Note
>
> The View Manager is an Excel Add-In and must be installed before you can use it. Use Tools, Add-Ins to install the Views.XLA file from the EXCEL\LIBRARY folder.

To select views, follow these steps:

1. Choose View, View Manager and select the view as shown in figure 18.25.

Fig. 18.25

When you select a View, Excel hides or displays rows depending on the outline in effect when the View was created.

2. Excel displays a worksheet with the pattern of hidden and visible rows and columns that was stored in the view. Figure 18.26 shows the outline as it was stored in the View named Columbus Unit 101.

Fig. 18.26

When you select a View, the Outline is returned to the level of detail stored in the View.

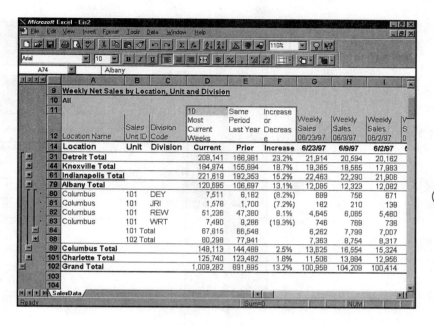

α Note

You can use the Report Manager add-in to print multiple views of a worksheet in one report. Report Manager keeps a list of the sheets, views, and scenarios to include in your report. You control the order of the printing and page numbering.

Creating Charts from Outlines

You can create a chart from an outline and change the way the chart looks by selecting different levels of detail in the outline. If you hide rows of data in the outline, those rows will not appear on the chart. You can select non-adjacent columns of data and use the outline to select the rows that will be included on the chart.

To create a chart from outlined data, follow these steps:

   1. Select the columns you want to include in the chart. Hold down the Ctrl key to select non-adjacent ranges. Figure 18.27 shows rows 14 through 101 for columns A, G, and H selected.

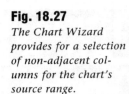

Fig. 18.27
The Chart Wizard provides for a selection of non-adjacent columns for the chart's source range.

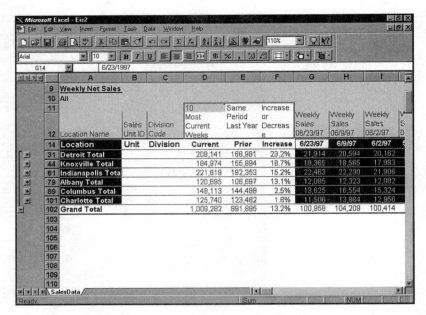

2. Select chart type and specify Data Series as Columns in Step 4 of the Chart Wizard.

3. Excel will produce a chart like the one shown in figure 18.28.

4. Change the chart detail level to display other rows in the chart automatically.

Fig. 18.28
A summary chart produced from an outline displays data from the visible rows. When you hide rows in the outline, the data from those rows disappears from the chart.

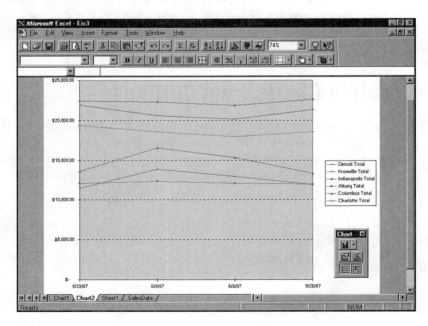

Adding Database Functions

Once you master the use of Criteria Ranges for the Advanced Filter, using the database functions is easy. The two simplest functions, SUMIF and COUNTIF, don't require you to use a Criteria Range. The more complex D... functions all require a separate Criteria Range. If you combine the Advanced Filter and D... functions, you can use the same Criteria Range for both. You can use a Scenario to save the criteria values for both the filter and database functions.

> **Tip**
> Use the database functions and Advanced Filter together. Both features can use the same Criteria Range. When you change the filter criteria, the database function will recalculate to include only the data shown in the filtered list.

18

Simple Calculations

The SUMIF and COUNTIF functions make it easy to sum or count without using a Criteria Range. The criteria can be stated in the formula—as long as the criteria are simple.

SUMIF(range,criteria,sum_range)

SUMIF sums the values specified by a criteria in the SUMIF formula. For example, SUMIF(E2:E44,"PRODUCT A",H2:H44) will return the sum of all of the values in column H of rows 2 through 44 where the value in column E equals PRODUCT A. The range contains the values to be evaluated. Criteria is a number or text value that determines which cells in the range will be included in the sum. sum_range is an optional parameter you can use when you want to evaluate a range and sum the values in a corresponding range.

COUNTIF(range,criteria)

COUNTIF is similar to SUMIF except that it counts the non-blank cells in the range specified by the criteria. For example, COUNTIF(H2:H44,">1000") will count all the values in column H of rows 2 through 44 where the value is greater than 1000. You can use comparison operators such as greater than or less than in the criteria.

More Complex and Powerful Database Function Calculations

The D... functions all require a Criteria Range. The criteria can be as complex as those used with the Advanced Filter. You can use multiple rows of criteria or formulas that refer to cells in your list or reference values somewhere else on the worksheet.

Each of the D... functions has the format:

```
D...(database, field, criteria)
```

where *database* is the range of cells in the list, *field* is the field number or column heading of the field you want to sum, average, and so on. *Criteria* is the Criteria Range. Both *database* and *criteria* should include a row of field headings.

Each of the D... functions performs the following operation on the field for rows in the database that match the Criteria Range.

DSUM(database, field, criteria)

DSUM is similar to SUMIF, except that it uses a separate Criteria Range to select values to include in the sum. You can use DSUM to create a total that will vary as the Criteria Range is changed. If DSUM and the Advanced Filter share a Criteria Range, DSUM will add all of the values displayed in the filtered range. If you change the filter's criteria, the value of DSUM will also change.

DAVERAGE(database, field, criteria)

DAVERAGE averages the numbers in a column of a list. This DAVERAGE formula calculates the average sale value in a database of sales transactions: `DAVERAGE(SalesDatabase, "Sale Amount",SelectionCriteria)`.

DMAX(database, field, criteria)

DMAX finds the largest value in a column of a database. For example, you can use DMAX to find the largest percentage increase in a database of production counts.

DMIN(database, field, criteria)

DMIN returns the smallest value in a column of a database. DMIN is similar in functions of DMAX. This formula would return the smallest percent increase in a production database: `DMIN(ProductionDatabase,"Percent Increase",SelectionCriteria)`.

DCOUNT(database, field, criteria)

DCOUNT counts cells containing numbers in a column of a database. If your database column contains both numbers and text, you can use DCOUNT to determine a count of numeric values that you can use to calculate an average of the numbers in the database column. For example, this formula calculates the average of the numeric values in the range "B1:B50": =DCOUNT(B1:B50,B1,CriteriaRange).

If you want to include all of the values in the range, your Criteria Range can consist of just two blank cells, one above the other. Excel requires you to specify a criteria range for each D... function, but an empty criteria range will select all data.

DCOUNTA(database, field, criteria)

DCOUNTA counts non-blank cells in a column of a database. DCOUNTA is useful when you need to count the number of occurrences in a database. For example, this DCOUNTA statement counts the number of non-blank data values in a list of experimental results: DCOUNTA(ExperimentalData, "Results Field", CriteriaRange).

Combining Filters and Outlines to Create an Executive Summary

You can use AutoFilter and AutoSubtotal to create simple Executive Summaries. If you use the Macro recorder to record the process of applying the outline or filter, then you can automate the process with a shortcut key or button on the worksheet.

You will learn more sophisticated ways to display Executive Summary data in Chapter 21, "Forecasting in Excel," but don't overlook the simple and powerful uses of AutoFilter and AutoSubtotals.

> **Tip**
> Use the macro recorder to create a Visual Basic subroutine that will automatically outline or filter your data at the click of a button on the worksheet or shortcut key.

Outlining by Geography

Figures 18.29, 18.30, and 18.31 illustrate an outline created with AutoSubtotal. The worksheet displays different levels of detail by region and product.

Fig. 18.29
When you select the first outline level, all but Grand Total is hidden.

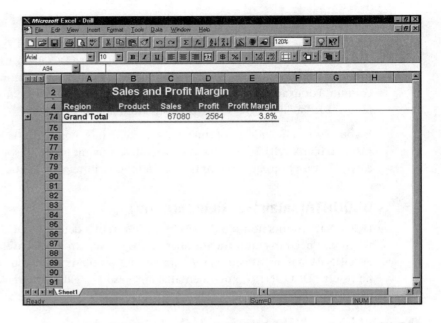

Fig. 18.30
By clicking on the + button or the 2 outline level, the list expands to show regions.

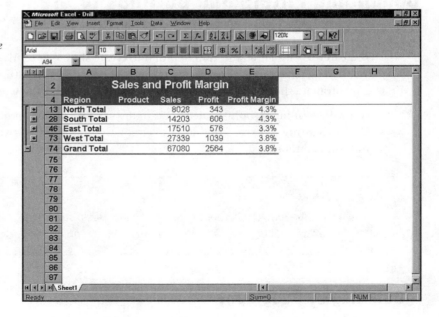

Fig. 18.31

*When you click the +
button next to the
South Total, the
outline expands to
show detail for the
South Region.*

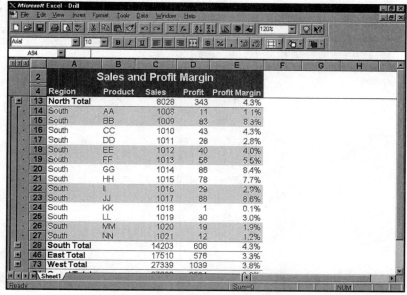

Analyzing by Product

You can show the largest or smallest values in a list by selecting the Top Ten option in the AutoFiter drop-down list. In figure 18.32, the ten largest profit percentages are shown. All other data is hidden.

To create an Executive Summary with your data, first decide what level of detail you need to see as you begin to analyze the data. Create an outline with subtotals at that level of detail and use the outline to expand the detail for totals that need further investigation. As you drill down through your data with the outline, you can use Excel's filtering features to narrow the focus of your analysis.

Fig. 18.32

AutoFilter can be used to provide a list of top ten profit percentages for all products and regions.

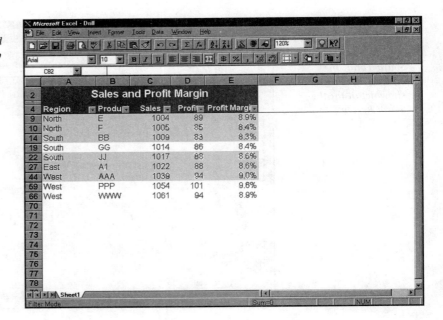

Summary

In the previous chapter, you learned how to construct Excel lists. In this chapter, you reviewed basic tools that can be used to analyze data in the lists. These tools include filtering and outlining, automatic subtotals, and the database functions. Two variations of filtering are available: AutoFilter and Advanced Filter. With Advanced Filter, you can use formulas and a Criteria Range to construct complex filters. The database functions also use a Criteria Range to calculate summary totals.

In the next chapter, you learn how to analyze the data in your lists with PivotTables. Chapter 20, "Running the Organization with an Excel Control Panel," explains how you can combine outlines, filters and PivotTables to create an *Executive Information System*.

chapter 19

Analyzing Results with PivotTables and Charts

by John Lacher

In this chapter

◆ **Create and modify PivotTables**
Use the PivotTable Wizard to create PivotTables from Excel lists and other data sources. PivotTables provide a wealth of summary functions you can include in your worksheets.

◆ **Group PivotTable rows and columns**
Create new categories of totals and automatically group date values by month, quarter, and year.

◆ **Link PivotTables and charts**
When you rearrange the totals in a PivotTable, a linked chart will automatically reflect the changes.

◆ **Use PivotTables with external data sources**
Analyze and report data stored in Microsoft Access and other database formats.

◆ **Create a user-defined function to use PivotTable totals in worksheet functions**
With Visual Basic for Applications, you can return a PivotTable total value to use a worksheet function.

Y ou know that key indicators in your data have changed, and you have some idea of the reasons why. Now, you can use PivotTables to do in-depth analysis. Linking your PivotTables to Excel charts presents your discoveries to others in a way that will convince them to take action.

Your worksheets come alive with PivotTables. With a click of the mouse, you can compare data in new ways. Drag a row heading to the top of the table, and it becomes a column heading. Drag a column heading to the top-left corner of the table, and it becomes a page heading. With PivotTables and charts you can build an effective executive information system.

What's the Point of a PivotTable?

A PivotTable is a table of totals. The automatic features of a PivotTable make it easy for you to create and arrange totals.

You can add totals and subtotals to your worksheet without using a PivotTable, but when new data is added to the worksheet, the total formulas have to be updated, generating more work and a chance for error. If you use a PivotTable, the PivotTable Wizard automatically creates the totals for you. If you have to change the totals, the PivotTable Wizard makes it an easy task.

> **Tip**
> Use PivotTable totals instead of subtotals and SUM formulas in your worksheet.

Imagine creating a set of totals by product and division with a column for each month—then deciding that you need totals by product and quarter with a column for each division. If you didn't use a PivotTable to do the job, you would be in for a late evening of formula rebuilding. Using a PivotTable, you can create a new set of totals in minutes rather than hours.

With PivotTables you can create sum totals as well as display maximums, minimums, counts, statistical functions, percentages, differences, running totals, and indexes.

Creating Instant PivotTables

You can create a simple PivotTable in seconds by following these steps:

1. Start with a range of data that contains field headings.
2. Use the PivotTable Wizard to calculate a PivotTable of summary values.
3. Add the PivotTable to a new worksheet or include it on an existing worksheet.

Figure 19.1 shows a simple PivotTable with its range of input data. The PivotTable displays totals for region and month.

Fig. 19.1

*You can create a
simple PivotTable
from a list of data.*

PivotTable by
Region and Date

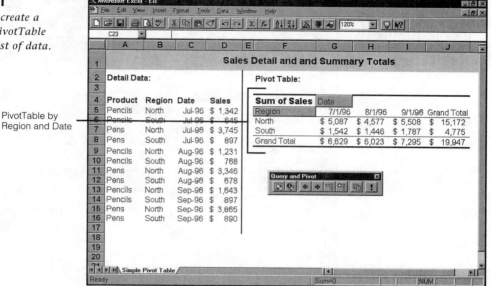

Structuring PivotTable Input Data

You can create a PivotTable from any range of data with column headings. In figure 19.1
the column headings are Product, Region, Date, and Sales. When you use the PivotTable
Wizard you specify which columns of data should be used as row headings, column
headings, and values. Region is shown as a row heading and Date as a column heading.

You can use the same range of input data to create a PivotTable like the one shown in
figure 19.2 with Product as row heading and Region as column heading.

Using the PivotTable Wizard

You can use the PivotTable Wizard to create PivotTables like those shown in figures 19.1
and 19.2. The Wizard is a series of dialog boxes that collect all of the information Excel
needs to construct a PivotTable. To create a new PivotTable, first select the range of data
you want to include in the table and then start the PivotTable Wizard. To make changes
to an existing PivotTable, select a cell in the PivotTable and start the PivotTable Wizard.

Fig. 19.2

The same input data can be used to create a PivotTable by Product and Region.

PivotTable by
Product and Region

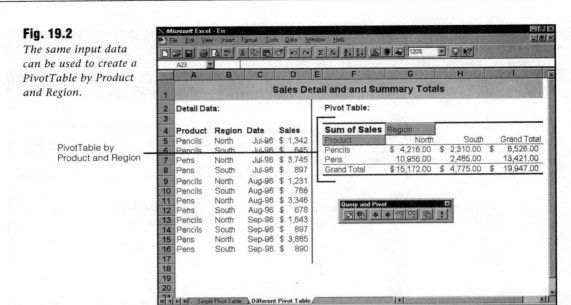

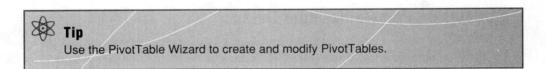

Tip
Use the PivotTable Wizard to create and modify PivotTables.

To create a PivotTable like the one shown in figure 19.1 follow these steps:

1. Select the range of data you want to summarize in the PivotTable.

2. Choose Data, PivotTable.

3. Select Microsoft Excel List or Database in Step 1 as the data source (see fig. 19.3) and click the Next button.

4. The PivotTable Wizard automatically uses the range of data you selected as the input range in Step 2 (see fig. 19.4). Click the Next Button to proceed to Step 3.

Fig. 19.3
Use the PivotTable Wizard to select a data source for the PivotTable.

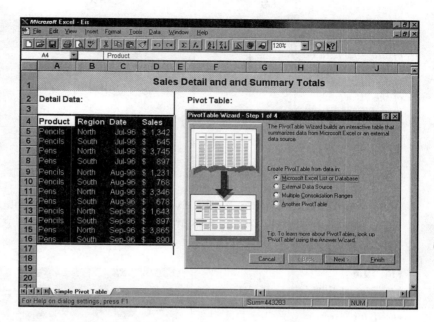

Fig. 19.4
Specify the address of the input data for the PivotTable.

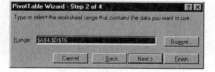

5. In Step 3 of the PivotTable Wizard, use the mouse to drag the field buttons to the PivotTable layout area. You can drag field buttons to Data, Column, Row, or Page field areas. Figure 19.5 shows the Region button in the Row area, the Date button in the Column area, and the Sales button in the Data area. When you drop the Sales button in the Data area, Excel assumes that you want to display a sum of sales and changes the label of the button from Sales to Sum Of Sales. Click Next to advance to Step 4 of the PivotTable Wizard.

Fig. 19.5

Create the PivotTable by dragging field labels to the Row, Column, Data, and Page areas of the PivotTable layout diagram.

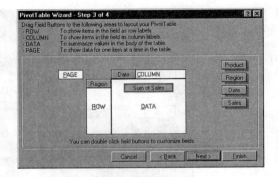

6. Choose a location for the PivotTable in Step 4 by positioning the cursor in the Starting Cell box and selecting a cell on the worksheet. In figure 19.6, the starting cell is F4 on the worksheet named Simple PivotTable.

Fig. 19.6

Choose a location for the PivotTable by specifying a starting cell address.

7. Click Finish and a PivotTable like the one in figure 19.7 appears on your worksheet. The Query and Pivot toolbar is automatically added to the toolbars that display on the worksheet.

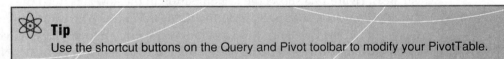

⚛ **Tip**

Use the shortcut buttons on the Query and Pivot toolbar to modify your PivotTable.

8. Select a cell in the PivotTable and choose Format, AutoFormat to apply styles to the PivotTable. The PivotTable shown in figure 19.7 was assigned the style "Accounting 2."

A PivotTable doesn't have to be on the same worksheet as the data input range. You can place your PivotTable anywhere in the workbook. Excel creates a new worksheet for the PivotTable if you leave the starting cell blank in Step 4 of the PivotTable Wizard.

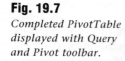

Fig. 19.7
Completed PivotTable displayed with Query and Pivot toolbar.

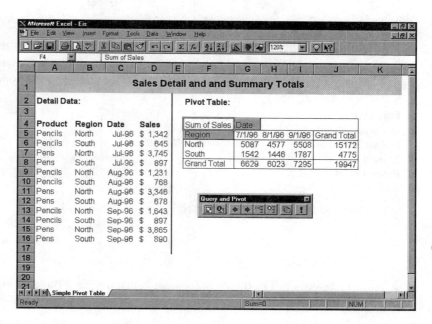

α Note

Data used by a PivotTable is stored in a hidden cache within the workbook file. If you make changes to the source data, the PivotTable will not reflect the changes until you refresh it. Use the Data, Refresh Data menu command or the Refresh button on the Query and Pivot toolbar to update the cached data.

If you remove the check mark from the Select the Save Data with Table Layout option in Step 4 of the PivotTable Wizard, the PivotTable's hidden cache of data will not be saved with the workbook. When you close the workbook, the cached data will be lost. Any change to the PivotTable causes Excel to read the source data and re-create a hidden cache.

Making Changes to a PivotTable

You can change any aspect of the table with the PivotTable Wizard or by dragging or clicking parts of the table itself.

Using the PivotTable Wizard Button

To start the PivotTable Wizard, choose <u>D</u>ata, <u>P</u>ivotTable or click the PivotTable Wizard button on the Query and Pivot toolbar. As shown in figure 19.8, each button on the Query and Pivot toolbar provides a shortcut for changing the appearance of a PivotTable.

Fig. 19.8

Query and Pivot toolbar buttons can be used to modify the appearance of a PivotTable.

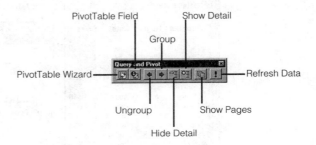

To make changes to a PivotTable with the Wizard, follow these steps:

1. Select a cell in the PivotTable and click the PivotTable Wizard button on the Pivot and Query toolbar.

2. As shown in figure 19.9, the first screen you see when changing a PivotTable is PivotTable Wizard Step 3 of 4. You can use the <u>B</u>ack button to change the input range in Step 2 of 4, or the type of data source in Step 1 of 4.

Fig. 19.9

Change PivotTables with the PivotTable Wizard.

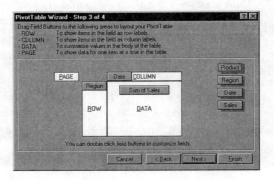

3. You can drag and drop the field button in Step 3 of 4 of the PivotTable Wizard. In figure 19.10, the field buttons have been moved from their original positions shown in figure 19.9. The Region field has been moved to the Column area, the Date field moved out of the PivotTable layout, and the Product field added to the Row area. Click <u>F</u>inish to redisplay the PivotTable.

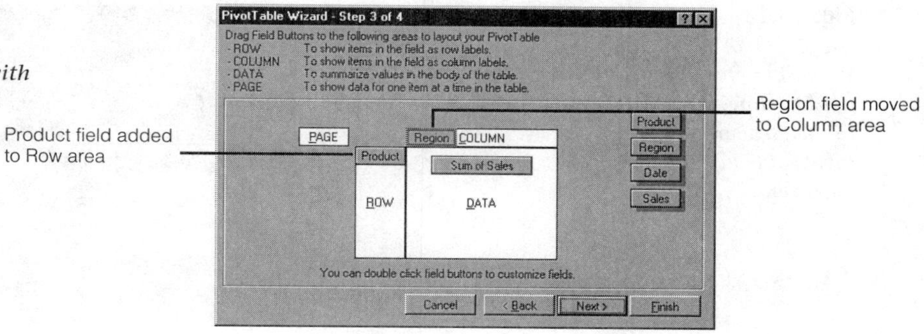

Fig. 19.10
Rearrange Row and Column headings with the PivotTable Wizard.

Product field added to Row area

Region field moved to Column area

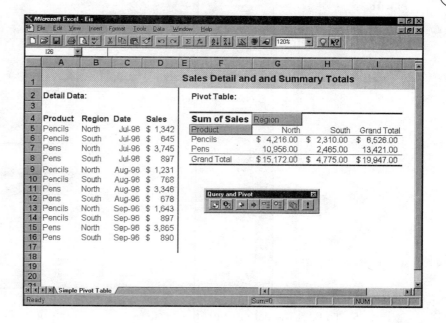

4. The changed pivot table is shown in figure 19.11. Notice that the PivotTable displays totals by Product and Region. The Date Field has disappeared from the PivotTable.

Fig. 19.11
PivotTable changed to display totals by Product and Region.

To add a page field to the PivotTable, follow these steps:

1. Select a cell in the PivotTable.

2. Click the PivotTable Wizard button.

3. Move a field to the Page area. In figure 19.12, the Date field has been dragged and dropped in the Page area.

Fig. 19.12

Use the PivotTable Wizard to create a Page field by dragging a field to the Page area of the PivotTable layout diagram.

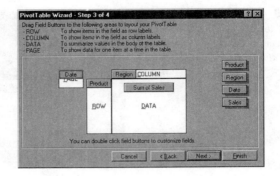

4. Click Finish to display the PivotTable as shown in figure 19.13. The Date field, shown earlier the PivotTable, is set for All dates.

Fig. 19.13

Page field set to show PivotTable totals for all dates.

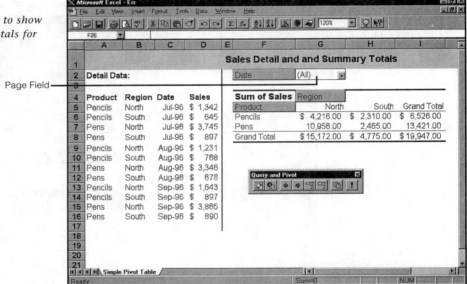

5. To filter the data in the PivotTable so that the totals only include one date, click the selection arrow in the Date field. Select a value from the drop-down list. Figure 19.14 shows the PivotTable with totals for date 8/1/96.

Fig. 19.14

Page field date set to 8/1/96.

Page field **Date** ——

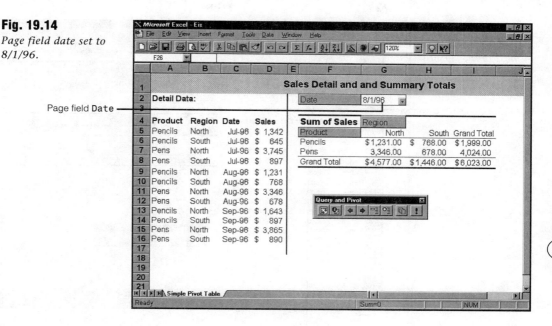

Making Changes on the Worksheet

You can rearrange Row, Column, and Page fields by dragging the gray field buttons right on your worksheet. As you drag the field buttons to different areas of the PivotTable, the cursor changes to show you whether it is over the Row, Column, or Page areas of the table. When you rearrange fields, the PivotTable will automatically recalculate all of the totals. You can also use drag-and-drop to change the sort order of multiple Row or Column fields.

To change the orientation of a PivotTable Field from Column to Row, follow these steps:

1. Click the gray field button in the Column heading area of the PivotTable. The cursor includes the Column Area shape as shown in figure 19.15.

2. Drag the field to the Row area. Notice how the shape of the cursor changes as shown in figure 19.16.

Fig. 19.15
*A symbol is displayed
next to the cursor when
selecting a Column
field.*

Column field symbol

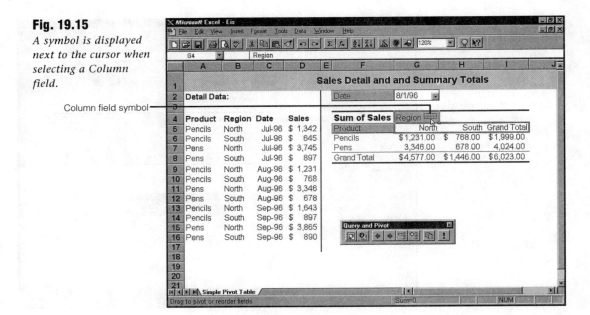

Fig. 19.16
*The Column field
symbol changes to a
Row field symbol as
the field is dragged
into the Row area of
the PivotTable.*

Row field symbol

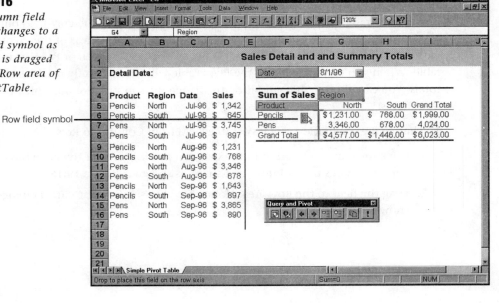

3. Drop the field by releasing the mouse button. The changed PivotTable is shown in figure 19.17.

Fig. 19.17

*PivotTable modified
by changing the
Region field from a
Column field to a Row
field.*

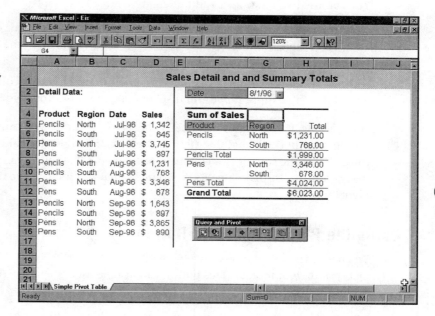

4. If you click the Region button and drag it to the left of the Product Button, the sort and subtotal order of the PivotTable will be changed as shown in figure 19.18.

Fig. 19.18

*Changing the sort
order of a PivotTable
by changing the order
of the Row fields.*

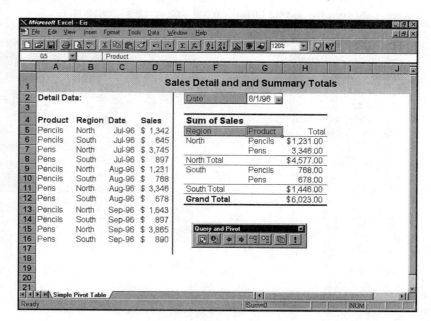

Adding Calculations to a PivotTable

You can use two methods to add calculations to a PivotTable:

▶ If you want to add standard calculations that are based on a column of data in the PivotTable input range, you can use options available in the PivotTable Field dialog box.

▶ To add more complex calculations, you can create a new column of formulas in the PivotTable input range and display that column in the PivotTable.

For example, if you want to add percentages to a column, you can select the % Of Column option in the PivotTable Field dialog box. If you need to add a special field—say the 120% of the sum of two columns in the PivotTable source range, you can add a new column with that value to the source range and include the new values in the PivotTable.

Using the PivotTable Field Button

To change the calculations for a PivotTable field, use the PivotTable Field button on the Query and Pivot toolbar. This button can also be used to change the number format options for the field.

The PivotTable Field button on the Query and Pivot toolbar is a shortcut that takes you directly to the PivotTable Field dialog box.

When you select a cell in a Page, Row, or Column Field and click the PivotTable Field button, the dialog box shown in figure 19.19 appears.

Fig. 19.19
PivotTable Field dialog box for a Row, Page, or Column field can be used to change orientation, subtotals, and hidden items.

You can use the PivotTable Field dialog box to change the name that is displayed in the Page, Row, or Column heading in the PivotTable. If you change the orientation, the PivotTable field will move to a new area of the PivotTable, just as it does when you drag and drop fields in Step 3 of 4 of the PivotTable Wizard.

If you have multiple Row fields or multiple Column fields, you can use the Subtotals option buttons to control subtotals shown in rows and columns of the PivotTable. Subtotals can be

▶ Sums of detail values or counts

▶ Averages, maximums, minimums, products

▶ Counts of numeric values

▶ Standard deviations

▶ Variances

The Hide Items option allows you to eliminate data from the PivotTable totals based on values in the PivotTable field. For example, in figure 19.19, you could eliminate all records with Product equal to Pens. The data temporarily disappears from the PivotTable. You can unhide items in the PivotTable Field dialog box by removing the highlight from the item's value in the Hide Items list.

When you select a cell in the Data area of the PivotTable and click the PivotTable Field button, you will see a dialog box like the one shown in figure 19.20.

Fig. 19.20

PivotTable Field dialog box for a Data field contains summary total and number formatting options.

The PivotTable Field dialog box for a Data Field differs from the dialog box for a Page, Row, or Column field. You can use the dialog box to change the name of the field as it is displayed in the top-left corner of the PivotTable.

To change the type of total, select a function in the Summarize By list box.

When you click the Number button, the Format Cells dialog box pops up—the same dialog box you see on the Number tab when you select menu options Format, Cells.

If you click the Options button, the dialog box will expand to present more calculation options as shown in figure 19.21.

Fig. 19.21

The PivotTable Field dialog box can be used to select from several different calculation options.

You can use the Show Data As option to change the displayed value from Normal to a percent or difference. For example, if you change the Show Data As option for a sum calculation from Normal to % of Column, then the totals in the PivotTable will be replaced by percentages.

To show data with both the calculated sum and a percentage, you can use the PivotTable Wizard to add two occurrences of the field to the data area of the PivotTable. You can set one of the occurrences to show the normal total and the other to display a percentage value.

Displaying Percentages

To add PivotTable percentages follow these steps:

1. Use the PivotTable Wizard to add another occurrence of the field to the data area of the PivotTable. Figure 19.22 shows a second occurrence of the Sales field added to the PivotTable.

Fig. 19.22

Add a second occurrence of a field to the data area to create a percentage column.

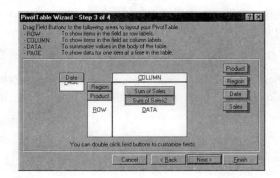

2. Double-click the button for the new occurrence of the field. Rename the field and click the Options button. The dialog box will expand to show calculation options as shown in figure 19.23. Select% of Column in the Show Data As drop-down list and click OK.

Fig. 19.23

Choosing % of Column in the Show Data As drop-down list will display PivotTable total with a percentage.

3. Click Finish in Step 3 of 4 of the PivotTable Wizard. The percentage values will be added to the PivotTable. Figure 19.24 shows the new values. To show the percentages next to the values, you may need to drag the gray Data button from the row area to the column area.

Fig. 19.24

Percentage values can be displayed next to totals in a PivotTable.

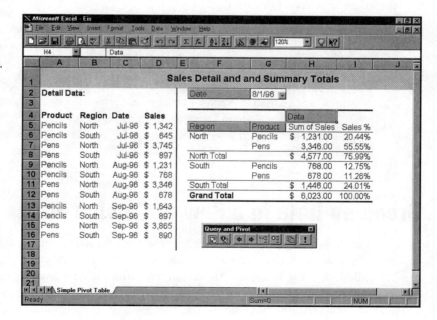

Other PivotTable Calculation Options

You can summarize data by:

- ▶ Total
- ▶ Count
- ▶ Count of Numeric Values
- ▶ Average
- ▶ Maximum or Minimum
- ▶ Product
- ▶ Standard Deviation
- ▶ Variance

Each of those summaries can be shown as:

- ▶ Normal, which is the value of the summary calculation
- ▶ Difference from, % of, or % difference from the summary value of a Row or Column field and item you select.
- ▶ Running total in
- ▶ % of row or column total
- ▶ % of PivotTable total
- ▶ Index

Note

If you want to use the built-in Pivot Data Functions Difference from, % of, or % difference from to compare two values such as Budget and Actual, the data values must be contained in the same column in the input range of the PivotTable. You may need to rearrange your input data to create a single column of values.

Grouping Data in a Row or Column Field

Excel's special grouping features show summary totals for groups of PivotTable values. If you have to create a total for three locations, you can use the grouping feature to create a group for those locations. The automatic grouping feature groups Row or Column fields that contain dates into monthly, quarterly, or annual groups.

Note

You can use the Hide Detail and Show Detail buttons on the Query and Pivot toolbar to hide detail in the PivotTable. For example, if your PivotTable contains totals for Location by Month, you can select a location, click Hide Detail, and the detail by month will be hidden. With this feature, you can show detail only for those items you want to analyze and hide unnecessary detail.

Creating Manual Groups

Group your detail data into reporting categories by selecting row or column items and clicking the Group button on the Query and Pivot toolbar.

If your data contains a Row field named Location and you need to manually add a grouping by Region, follow these steps:

1. Create a PivotTable by Location as shown in figure 19.25.

Fig. 19.25

PivotTable by Location can be used to group data by region.

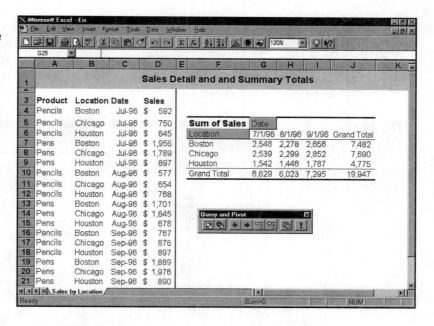

2. Click Boston and drag the mouse down; include Chicago in the selection. The two selected locations will appear as shown in figure 19.26. Click the Group button on the Query and Pivot toolbar.

Fig. 19.26
*PivotTable by Location
with North regions
Boston and Chicago
selected.*

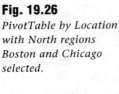

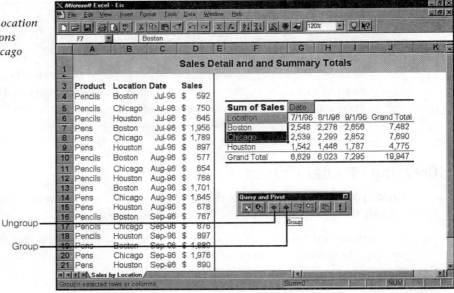

3. Excel adds a new Row field to the PivotTable. Figure 19.27 shows the new Row field renamed Region with the first group renamed North and the second group renamed South. You can rename a Row field with the PivotTable Field button on the Query and Pivot toolbar. Rename individual group items by changing item labels on the worksheet.

Fig. 19.27
*PivotTable creates a
new Row field for
Region. Boston and
Chicago are grouped
into the North region.*

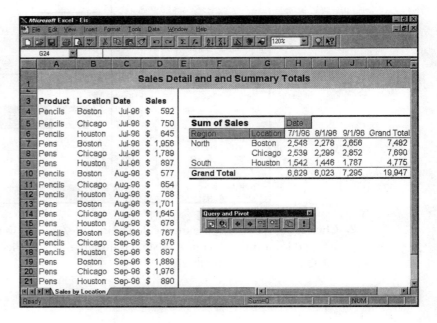

The new Row field Region can be used like any other PivotTable field. You can hide items or change it to a Column or Page Field. If you don't need to see detail by Location, you can remove the Location row field from the PivotTable and leave the Region field.

Using Automatic Grouping in a PivotTable

When you have a PivotTable with monthly data like that shown in figure 19.28, you can select one of the date column headings and use the Group button on the Query and Pivot toolbar to automatically group the dates by quarter and year.

Fig. 19.28
PivotTable with monthly dates can be used to automatically group dates by quarter and year.

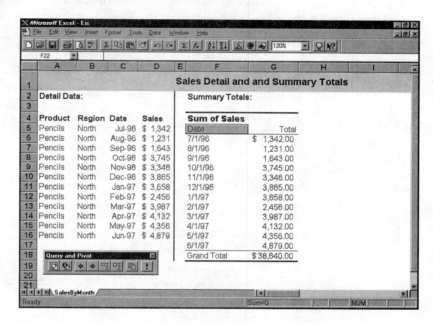

By clicking the Group button, you can select Group by Months, Quarters, and Years from the Grouping dialog box. Excel automatically displays this dialog box when it detects that the Row or Column field you are grouping contains date values. In figure 19.29 the Months, Quarters, and Years options are selected.

In figure 19.30, Excel has added the Years and Quarters row fields for you. The Date field now displays month name instead of mm/dd/yy. You can use the new row fields to hide items or change the orientation of the fields to Page or Column. Figure 19.31 shows the PivotTable after the Years field is changed from a Row field to a Page field.

Fig. 19.29
The Grouping dialog box presents choice of date and time grouping options.

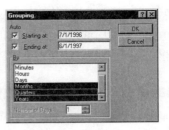

Fig. 19.30
Grouping creates two new PivotFields named Years and Quarters.

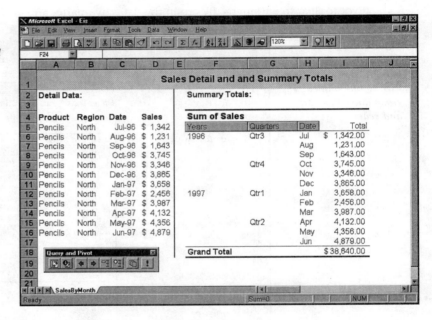

> ## α Note
> If you have a problem grouping Date fields in PivotTables, make sure that every row in the input data range contains a valid date. If one or more of the date values are missing, then Excel will not display the Grouping by Date dialog box.

Fig. 19.31
A PivotTable field created by grouping can be used as a Page field.

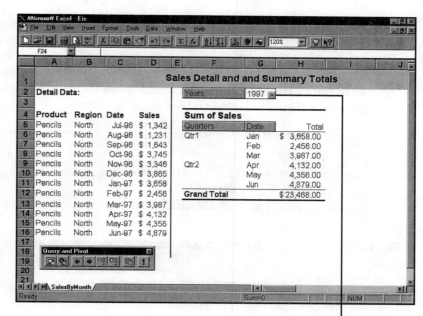

PivotTable field created by
grouping a date field

 Note

If you are unable to format your PivotTable dates with Date number formats, Excel may have converted your date values to text. To convert text values back to date format, enter a 1 in an unused cell and copy that cell over the date values in the pivot table using the Edit, Paste Special, Multiply. When it multiplies each cell by 1, Excel will convert the text value date to a number so that you can format the number as a date.

Linking Charts to a PivotTable

You can add the flexibility of a PivotTable to an Excel chart. If you link the chart to the PivotTable, when you change the structure of the PivotTable, the chart will automatically update and reflect the changes.

The PivotTable shown in figure 19.32 should be modified to remove the Grand Total row and Grand Total column before creating the chart. If the total values are left in the table, the chart will display the totals as data values. While this may be useful in some cases, usually you will not want grand total values to appear on the chart. You can delete the totals from a PivotTable using the Grand Totals for <u>R</u>ows and Grand Totals for <u>C</u>olumns options in Step 4 of the PivotTable Wizard.

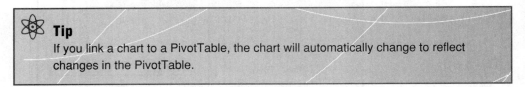

Tip

If you link a chart to a PivotTable, the chart will automatically change to reflect changes in the PivotTable.

Fig. 19.32

Grand Totals should be removed from PivotTable before creating a chart.

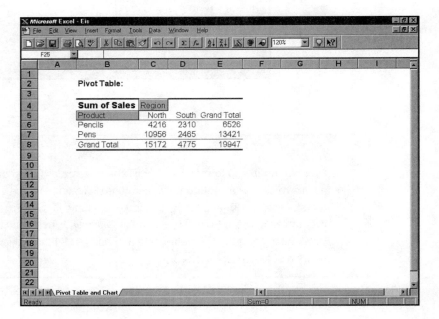

To create a chart from a PivotTable like the one shown in figure 19.33 follow these steps:

1. Use the PivotTable Wizard to eliminate the Grand Total row and column.

2. Select any cell in the PivotTable and press Ctrl+Shift+* (asterisk). This selects the entire range of the PivotTable excluding any Page fields.

3. Use the Chart Wizard to create a chart like the one shown in figure 19.33.

When you create the chart so that the source range of the chart includes all of the PivotTable except the Page fields, then Excel will automatically change the chart to include any changes in the PivotTable.

Fig. 19.33

Chart created from PivotTable. The source data range for the chart is the PivotTable's data range B4:D7.

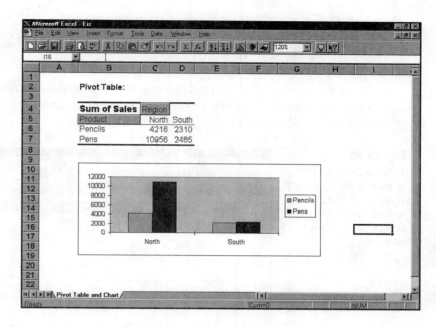

In figure 19.34, the PivotTable is changed to include Date as a Column field. Region has been eliminated from the table. Excel automatically adjusts the chart to reflect the new types of data.

Fig. 19.34

When PivotTable is rearranged by Product and Date, the chart automatically changes to show new PivotTable format.

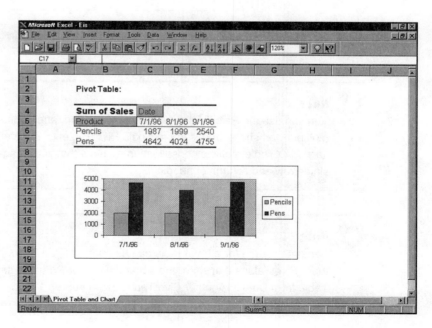

If you add a Page field to the PivotTable, you can link the title of the chart to the PivotTable Page Field Value. The Chart title in figure 19.35 contains the formula:

```
='PivotTable and Chart'!$C$2
```

When the value in the Page field changes, the chart title automatically shows the new value. To replace a chart title with a formula, select the chart title, press F2, and enter a formula on the Formula bar.

Fig. 19.35

When a Page field is used to filter the PivotTable, the chart will automatically redraw to show the new data.

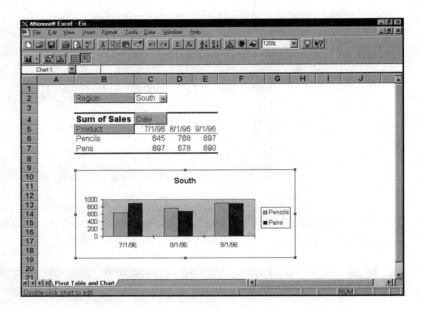

Note

You can use the PivotTable multiple consolidation range option to consolidate multiple worksheet ranges into a single PivotTable. Like Excel's consolidation feature, PivotTable multiple consolidation requires that your ranges be set up with a single row and column of headings.

Note

The data source for a PivotTable can be another PivotTable. If you need two or more PivotTables that share the same data range, you can select Create Pivot-Table from Data in Another PivotTable option in Step 1 of the PivotTable Wizard.

Creating PivotTables from External Data

PivotTables provide made-to-order capabilities for importing data from other sources. When you need to analyze a database stored in Microsoft Access, you can use the External Data option in the PivotTable Wizard to link the PivotTable to the database. The External Data link works for any of the many types of data you can link to using the Get External Data option in the Data menu. Both the Get External Data and the PivotTable External Data options use the Microsoft Query Add-In to select and access external data.

If your database is large, you can use the options in Microsoft Query to select only those records that you need to summarize in your PivotTable. When you want to combine data from two different database tables, Microsoft Query provides a point-and-click method of describing the relationships. Behind the scenes, Microsoft Query is creating SQL database access code.

To consolidate data into a PivotTable, follow these steps:

1. Select a blank cell on a worksheet and choose the Data, PivotTable option. In Step 1 of 4, choose the External Data Source option as shown in figure 19.36. Choose Next to advance to Step 2 of the PivotTable Wizard.

Fig. 19.36
The PivotTable Wizard can be used to access external databases.

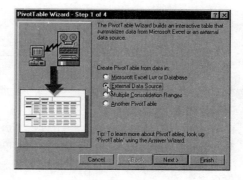

2. Click the Get Data button in Step 2 of the PivotTable Wizard as shown in figure 19.37.

Fig. 19.37
The PivotTable Wizard uses Microsoft Query to select and return data from the external database.

3. The Select Data Source dialog box will appear. Select the source of data from the Available Data Sources and click Use. You can see in figure 19.38 that the Select Data Source dialog box is part of Microsoft Query. The PivotTable Wizard starts Microsoft Query to access the external data source, and the Add Tables dialog box appears.

Fig. 19.38

The Select Data Source dialog box in Microsoft Query can be used to select an external source of data.

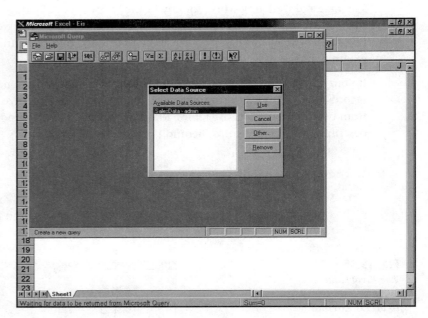

> **Note**
>
> If the source of the external data has not yet been added to the list of available data sources, you can use the Other button on the Select Data Source dialog box to add it to the list. This procedure is described in Chapter 13, "Automating Database Access."

4. The data source SalesData-admin is an Access database, and as shown in figure 19.39, you can select the database in the Add Tables dialog box. The example database has only one table, but you can choose two or more tables from a multiple table database and link the tables together with key fields. After selecting tables, click Close.

Fig. 19.39

You can select multiple tables from an external database.

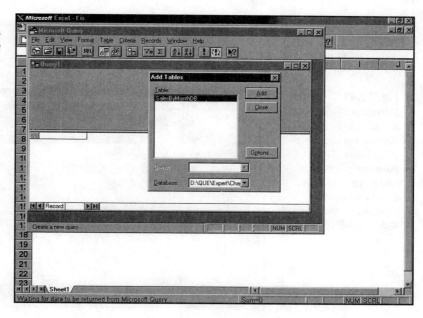

5. Choose the fields and enter selection criteria in the Microsoft Query dialog box. You can add all of the fields in the table to the selection by clicking the * (asterisk) in the field list, as shown in figure 19.40. The Query dialog box is similar to the Query dialog box used in Access. As you learn how to construct queries, you can use your skills in both Microsoft Query and Microsoft Access.

Fig. 19.40

All of Microsoft Query's field selection, calculation, and grouping features can be used to build a database query.

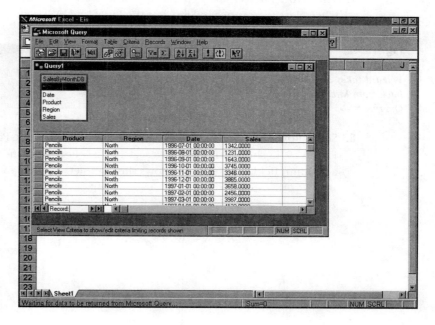

6. As shown in figure 19.41, when you click File, Return Data to Microsoft Excel, Microsoft Query gets the data specified in the query and returns control to the PivotTable Wizard.

Fig. 19.41

Microsoft Query returns the queried data to the Excel PivotTable. The parameters of the Query are stored in Excel and used to refresh the PivotTable data.

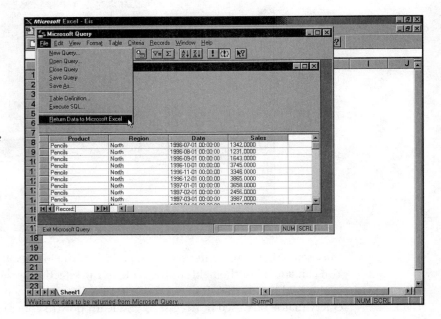

7. The PivotTable Wizard Step 2 now reports Data Retrieved as shown in figure 19.42. Click Next to advance to Step 3 of the PivotTable Wizard.

Fig. 19.42

The Excel PivotTable Wizard takes control back from Microsoft Query.

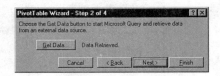

8. Select Row, Column, Page, and Data fields in Step 3 of the PivotTable Wizard. Figure 19.43 shows the Date area selected as a Row field and the Product area as a Column field. Figure 19.44 shows the completed PivotTable.

Fig. 19.43

Select PivotTable Row and Column Fields in Step 3 of the PivotTable Wizard. The fields selected from the external database are shown at the right edge of the PivotTable Wizard dialog box.

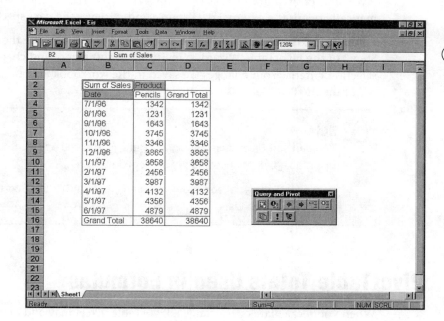

Fields selected from external database

Fig. 19.44

PivotTable created from an Access database.

Note

If you double-click a cell in the Data area of a PivotTable, Excel will create a new worksheet that lists all of the detail rows that make up the total. This *drill down* feature works for total cells, too. You can use the detail worksheet for further analysis of a PivotTable total. If you include a column of comments in your detail data, you can click a PivotTable total and read the comments on the detail worksheet.

Note

To create a report from PivotTable with a separate page for each Page Field value, you can use the ShowPages feature to create a separate worksheet and pivot table for each value in a Page Field. Each worksheet is named with the Page Field value. To start Show Pages, right-click any cell in the PivotTable and choose the ShowPages option or use the ShowPages button on the Query and Pivot toolbar.

Now that the PivotTable is created, you can make changes to it just as you do with a PivotTable created from worksheet data. When you refresh the PivotTable, Excel automatically opens the external data source and retrieves the data specified in the query.

If you want to change the parameters of the query, you can use the Get Data button in Step 2 of the PivotTable Wizard to revisit Microsoft Query and change tables, fields, and selection criteria. Your changes are saved in the workbook and are used automatically the next time the PivotTable is refreshed.

 Note

You can sort PivotTables using the Data, Sort menu option. Select a cell in the PivotTable before choosing the sort option.

If you need a special sort order, you can create a Custom Sort List with Tools, Options, Custom Lists.

PivotTable Totals Used in Formulas

When you recalculate or rearrange a PivotTable, Excel may add new data and shift the PivotTable columns and rows to make room for new totals. This can be a problem when you need to use a PivotTable total in a worksheet formula. Every time the PivotTable changes, you must modify your formula to point to the new location of the total.

You can use a Visual Basic for Applications function to extract a total value from a PivotTable. The function will find the new address of the total value when the PivotTable is recalculated or rearranged.

The user-defined function named PivotValue is also useful. It will find the value of a total in a PivotTable with one Row and one Column field. You can also use the function for a PivotTable with two Row fields and no Column fields. If the PivotTable contains more than one field in the Data area of the PivotTable, PivotValue will return the total for the first field.

 Tip

A user-defined function can return a value from a PivotTable based on Row and Column headings.

The PivotValue function contains only five lines of Visual Basic code. By reviewing this code you can learn how to access PivotTable total values with Visual Basic.

```
Function PivotValue(sPivotField1 As String, _
                    sPivotField1Item As String, _
                    sPivotField2 As String, _
                    sPivotField2Item As String)

        Dim oPivotTable As Object
        Set oPivotTable = ActiveSheet.PivotTables(1)

        PivotValue = Intersect( _
oPivotTable.PivotFields(sPivotField1).PivotItems(sPivotField1Item).DataRange, _
oPivotTable.PivotFields(sPivotField2).PivotItems(sPivotField2Item).DataRange, _
        oPivotTable.DataFields(1).DataRange)

End Function
```

The first line is a Function statement that defines the name of the function and the input values it needs to return the desired total. The name of the function is PivotValue. The function needs two input values for each of the two Row or Column fields in the PivotTable. The first value is the name of the field as shown on the PivotTable. The second value is the name of the item.

Figure 19.45 shows the result of using the PivotValue function in cell B17. The following formula,

```
=PivotValue("Region","North","Product","Pens")
```

tells the PivotValue function to find the total for Region=North and Product=Pens. The list of field and item names matches the list of input values in the first line of the PivotValue function.

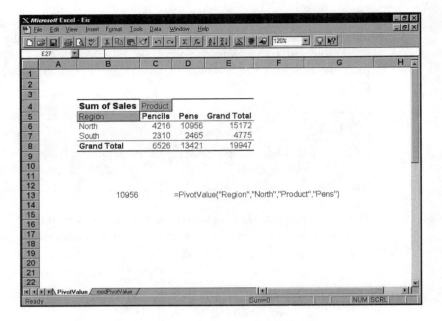

When the PivotTable is rearranged, as shown in figure 19.46, the PivotValue function returns the correct total value. The row and column heading are switched and the total value for North Region Pens shifts from D6 in figure 19.45 to C7 in figure 19.46.

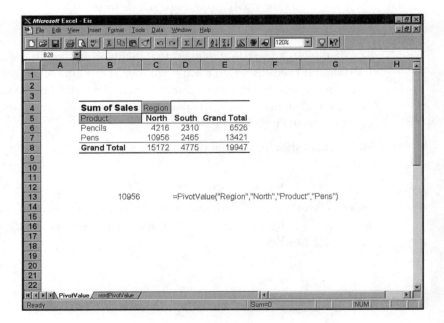

The following lines of this code define a variable named `oPivotTable` and set the variable to point to the first PivotTable on the active worksheet:

```
Dim oPivotTable As Object
Set oPivotTable = ActiveSheet.PivotTables(1)
```

The PivotValue function uses this variable to tell Excel which PivotTable to use to find the total values.

The next lines of code in the PivotValue function do the work of finding the PivotTable total:

```
PivotValue = Intersect( _
oPivotTable.PivotFields(sPivotField1).PivotItems(sPivotField1Item).DataRange, _
oPivotTable.PivotFields(sPivotField2).PivotItems(sPivotField2Item).DataRange, _
            oPivotTable.DataFields(1).DataRange)
```

The Intersect function uses three parameters to find the cell that contains the total. Figure 19.47 shows the intersection of the two data ranges—one for each PivotTable field and item specified in the input to the function. The value of the one cell intersection is assigned to the name of the function. This value is returned when the function is finished doing its work.

The Intersect function specifies a third Datafields(1).Datarange parameter that causes the function to ignore all but the first field in the PivotTable's Data area. You can add a percentage field as the second field in the Data area and the PivotValue function ignores it and looks only at the total values for the first field.

Fig. 19.47

The PivotTable function finds the intersection of the data ranges for the PivotTable items you specify in the function's input parameters.

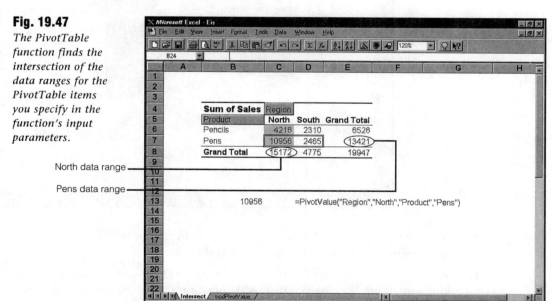

This last line of the user-defined function tells Excel that the Visual Basic code for this function is complete:

```
End Function
```

You can include several functions on the same module page, and Excel will use the Function and End Function statements to keep track of where one ends and another begins.

To use the PivotValue macro, follow these steps:

1. Copy the macro from the CD that accompanies this book or type it into a module page in your workbook. If you do not have a module page, you can use Insert, Macro, Module to create one.

2. Create a PivotTable where the total of Row and Column fields equals two. The PivotTable can have one Row and one Column field or two Row fields or two Column fields.

3. Enter the PivotTable formula. You can use the Function Wizard to enter the values as shown in figure 19.48.

Fig. 19.48

Use the Function Wizard to fill out parameters for the user-defined function PivotValue.

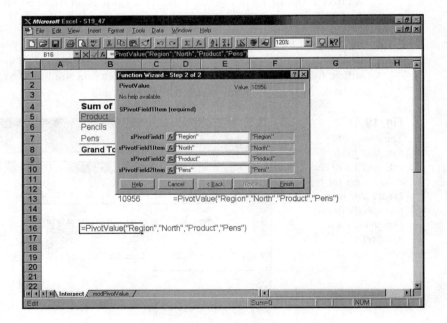

4. Rearrange the PivotTable by moving the Row and Column fields. The PivotValue function should find the value as the PivotTable changes.

5. Add some new items. For example, add West as a region. Refresh the PivotTable and the totals are rearranged. The PivotValue formula still returns the value from the Pivot items you specified.

In this section, you have learned how to access data in a PivotTable using Visual Basic. The example user-defined function was a simple one. A more complex version that will work with larger PivotTables is included on the CD that accompanies this book.

 Note

Another version of user defined function PivotValue is provided with the example files for this chapter. The enhanced version, named Lacher34.XLS, provides these features in addition to the PivotValue function described earlier:

▶ The enhanced PivotValue function will process larger PivotTables with multiple Row and Column fields.

If you have a PivotTable with Region, Product, and Date as Row fields, the function will allow you to specify a value for Region, Product, and Date. Any number of Row and Column field values can be input to the function.

▶ With the enhanced function, you can specify which field in the Data area you want to include in the total.

When you have multiple data values or data values with percentages, you can specify the field name of the data that should be included in the PivotValue total.

You can review the instructions in the example file and read the comments in the example's Visual Basic for Applications code to better understand how to use the enhanced PivotValue function with your PivotTables.

With Visual Basic you can control all aspects of a PivotTable from creation to formatting. You can learn more about using Visual Basic with PivotTables by reading about the PivotTable object in the on-line help system. If you enter a question such as "What can I do with the PivotTable object?" in the Answer Wizard, you can browse through all of the Visual Basic methods and properties that you can use to control PivotTables.

PivotTable Designs for Your Organization

You can use PivotTables to break out of the pattern of paper reports. Moving the key reports of your organization to PivotTables opens the door to new flexibility and power in data analysis. The sample PivotTables that follow are examples of ways to integrate PivotTables and graphs to communicate basic operating information.

Tracking Progress with PivotTables

The PivotTable in figure 19.49 shows the trend of average customer service phone time over a four-week period.

Fig. 19.49

A PivotTable and linked chart can be used to track time series data.

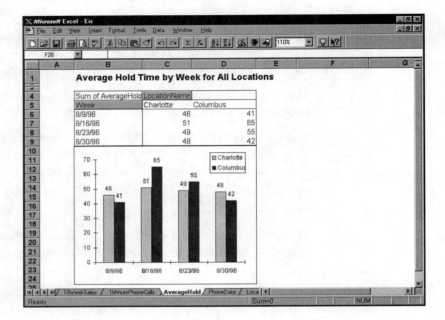

The chart in figure 19.49 is linked to the PivotTable so that changes in the table automatically update the chart. The source range of the PivotTable is a named range `PhoneData!Database`. You can update the range and then refresh the PivotTable to show the new data.

Only four of many weeks of data are shown in the Week Row field. The other weeks are hidden using the PivotTable Field dialog box described earlier, in the section "Using the PivotTable Field Button."

If the PivotTable is linked directly to an external data source like an Access database, every time the PivotTable is refreshed, it queries the database and updates its hidden cache of data.

You can use a chart to show percentage relationships as shown in figure 19.50. The bar graph shows percentage values for two of the three series of data in the PivotTable. The chart includes the third series (Call <=1 minute), but in the chart, the series' color and border is set to none so that the top of each bar in the chart is hidden.

Fig. 19.50

*A column chart and
PivotTable can be used
to show percentage
relationships.*

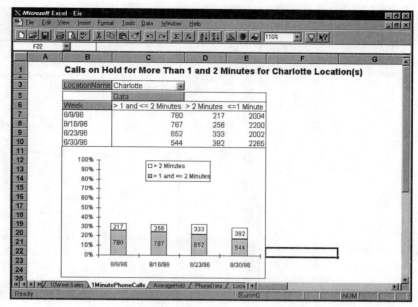

You can explore this example further by copying the file F49-52.XLS from the CD that
accompanies this book. If you select the chart and use the arrow key to select the <=1
minute series, you can review the settings in the Pattern tab that cause the series to be
hidden from view.

Projecting Future Values with PivotTables

Figure 19.51 demonstrates the use of a PivotTable and attached chart with a trend line.
When you select a different division or location, the chart automatically changes to
reflect the new data and updates the trend line.

 Note

You can learn more about trend lines in Chapter 21, "Forecasting in Excel." Charts,
PivotTables, and trend lines can be combined to create a powerful data analysis
feature.

You can add a trend line to a series in a chart by selecting the chart, right-clicking a series, and choosing the Insert Trendline option. Excel prompts you for the type of trend
line you want to add and asks how many periods into the future you want to project.

Fig. 19.51

Projecting future values with a PivotTable and chart.

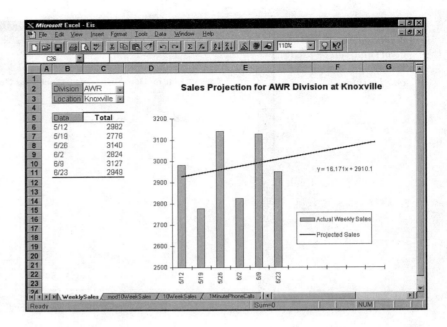

Linking PivotTables to Compare Operations

The pivot table in figure 19.52 shows how you can compare sales for the current ten week period to sales for the same period last year. The data range you use as input to the PivotTables contains formulas that use OFFSET to create totals for the current and prior year periods. This technique was described in detail in Chapter 18.

Fig. 19.52

Two PivotTables can be synchronized to the same page field.

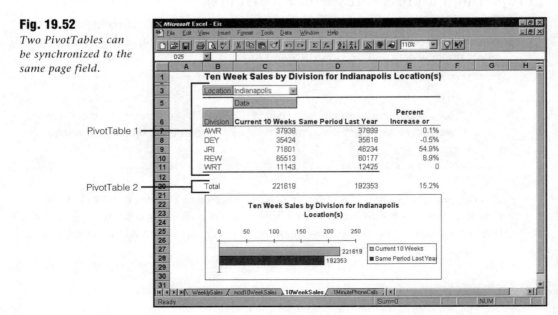

The chart in figure 19.52 shows totals by location. It ignores the totals by division. If you use the grand total row of a PivotTable as the input range for a chart, the chart will show invalid data when the PivotTable is refreshed or reorganized and the cell locations of the grand totals change.

> **Tip**
>
> Link two PivotTables with a Visual Basic macro that synchronizes the Page Fields from each PivotTable.

To link the chart to the grand totals, a second PivotTable is included on rows 13 through 20. In figure 19.52, you can see that rows 13 through 19 are hidden. They contain the page field location for the second PivotTable. The first PivotTable ends at row 11. Row 12 is a blank row between the tables.

If you want to use two PivotTables to display data about a location, you will need to link their page fields together so that when you change the location in the page field of the first PivotTable, the hidden page field is changed in the second PivotTable. In the example in figure 19.52, a simple Visual Basic macro assigns a new value to the hidden page field every time the worksheet is calculated.

In the code listing shown here, you can see that the Auto_Open subroutine assigns the macro SynchPivots to run each time the worksheet 10WeekSales is calculated. This macro runs each time the PivotTable is refreshed or rearranged.

The SynchPivots macro assigns the value of the location selected in the page field of the first PivotTable to the page field in the second PivotTable.

```
Sub auto_open()
    Worksheets("10WeekSales").OnCalculate = "SynchPivots"
End Sub

Sub SynchPivots()
    Dim oPivot1 As Object, oPivot2 As Object
    Set oPivot1 = Worksheets("10WeekSales").PivotTables("PivotTable1")
    Set oPivot2 = Worksheets("10WeekSales").PivotTables("PivotTable2")
    Worksheets("10WeekSales").OnCalculate = ""
    oPivot2.PageFields(1).CurrentPage = oPivot1.PageFields(1).CurrentPage.Value
    Worksheets("10WeekSales").OnCalculate = "SynchPivots"
End Sub
```

Summary

In this chapter, you learned how to use the many features of PivotTables. In Chapter 17, "Building the Data Warehouse with Excel Lists," you can learn how to create and maintain data in Excel worksheets, using Excel as a database. You can use those lists to summarize and drill down to the detail with the filters, outlines, and subtotals described in Chapter 18, "Drilling Through the Data with Outlines and Filters," or you can use PivotTables to automatically summarize the lists of data for you.

With Excel lists and PivotTables, you can build an executive information system that will help you to analyze the key factors in your data. In Chapter 20, "Running the Organization with an Excel Control Panel," you learn how to construct a Control Panel workbook that organizes Excel lists and PivotTables in a form that is easy to use. When your executive information system is complete, you can throw away many of your paper reports and use your Control Panel workbook to enhance your decision making and data analysis abilities.

chapter 20

Running the Organization with an Excel Control Panel

by John Lacher

In this chapter

◆ **Design a control panel workbook**

Display the key indicators for your organization in one workbook. The control panel workbook will replace many paper reports with one electronic data source.

◆ **Integrate Presentations and Word Processing documents into your Excel control panel workbook**

By combining the presentation capabilities of a presentation program such as Microsoft PowerPoint, the text processing capabilities of a word processor, and the analysis tools of Excel, you can add the power of integrated Microsoft Office applications to your Excel workbook.

◆ **Use IF statements and linked pictures to provide exception reporting**

Provide color exception messages to highlight important changes in key indicators. When you click on the exception data, Excel will automatically drill down to the detail data.

◆ **Link list boxes to PivotTable page fields**

With a list box and worksheet formulas, you can select different views of data and use list boxes to automate your workbook and make it easy to analyze data by location, division, date or other measure.

◆ **Create custom navigation controls**

It is easy to move through the data in your workbook—either down to the detail or to different measures. Use a custom navigation bar with Prior and Next buttons and a list box of worksheet ranges.

◆ **Publish the information in your control panel workbook**

Your key indicators can be available in electronic or printed form. Use the View and Report managers to create custom reports of the data.

All the key indicators of the organization can be combined in one workbook. You can design exception indicators that function like trouble lights on the dashboard of an automobile. A red light exception indicator pops up on the screen and with one click of the mouse, you can review and analyze the detail behind the indicator. Build a sophisticated *control panel workbook* for your organization using Excel's built-in features.

Your control panel workbook summarizes the results of outlines, filters, PivotTables, and charts to show the status of each key measure in your Executive Information System. Click a measure and drill down to the underlying detail.

A Tour of Control Panel Features

If you understand the types of controls you can include in the control panel workbook, then you are ready to invent one for your organization. The examples that follow introduce you to each of the features you can use in your applications. Each of the features is described from a user perspective in the first part of the chapter. You learn more of the details about each feature later in the chapter.

Most of the features require little if any Visual Basic code. You can create an effective control panel without using any Visual Basic code, or develop a custom designed interface and use Visual Basic to completely customize the look of your application.

The Home Page—a Starting Point

Key indicators are measurements of the most important factors in your organization, project, or data collection effort. If you put your key indicators on the first few screens of the control panel workbook, the user of the data can decide which indicators need attention and proceed to drill down through the data and review the detail for those indicators.

 Tip
Create a Home worksheet and provide ways for users to navigate to other worksheets from *Home*.

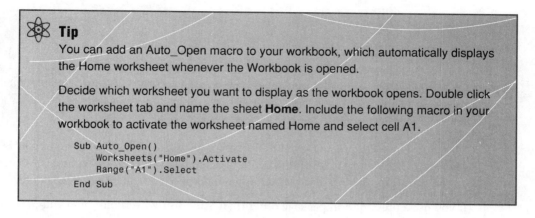

> ### 🜨 Tip
>
> You can add an Auto_Open macro to your workbook, which automatically displays the Home worksheet whenever the Workbook is opened.
>
> Decide which worksheet you want to display as the workbook opens. Double click the worksheet tab and name the sheet **Home**. Include the following macro in your workbook to activate the worksheet named Home and select cell A1.
>
> ```
> Sub Auto_Open()
>     Worksheets("Home").Activate
>     Range("A1").Select
> End Sub
> ```

In figure 20.1, the first screen in the control panel workbook provides choices to

▶ View Sales indicators

▶ View key indicators for Customer Service

▶ Display an embedded slide presentation that summarizes the week's sales and customer service results in presentation form

Fig. 20.1

Start your executive information system with a control panel.

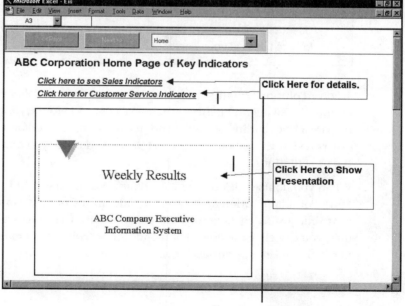

You can use text boxes and arrows to provide hints for new users.

Tip

If you provide too many options, the Home page can be confusing to new users. By providing just three or four options on the Home Page that lead to more options on other worksheets, the user can quickly select the options that are of interest without reading through a long list of choices.

Microsoft PowerPoint is the presentation graphics package that is a standard part of Microsoft Office and Microsoft Office Professional. PowerPoint for Windows 95 contains communication features that you can use to add power to your Excel workbooks.

If you use a presentation package other than Microsoft PowerPoint, you will probably be able to use the features of that package with Excel. Features of Lotus Freelance and other presentation packages that support the Object Linking and Embedding (OLE) standard can be added to your Excel control panel workbook. Most presentation packages support the OLE standard. Consult your presentation package user documentation for more information on your package. The following example uses Microsoft PowerPoint but can easily be adapted to Freelance or another presentation manager.

 Tip

Use a presentation package with Excel to provide overview information in outline form to users of your workbook.

A PowerPoint presentation provides the user of the control panel workbook with the option of viewing highlights of the week's results before reviewing the data. You can prepare a brief outline of results and make it into a PowerPoint presentation. As you and others review the data in the control panel workbook, you can easily make updates to the presentation.

When you double-click on the PowerPoint slide in figure 20.1, Excel will start the PowerPoint application and show the slides in the presentation. You can advance to the next slide just by clicking the mouse. If you want to record action items or meeting minutes, you can click the PowerPoint Slide Show Icon button in the bottom-left-hand corner of the screen or right-click with the mouse.

Note

It is easy to create an embedded PowerPoint presentation in your Excel Workbook with the menu option Insert, Object. The Object dialog box allows you to create a new object or copy an existing file.

If you choose the Link option when you choose an existing file, Excel updates the workbook everytime you change the PowerPoint file. Otherwise, the file will be embedded and changes to the original will not affect the embedded copy.

Displaying Key Indicators and Highlighting Exception Values

Figure 20.2 shows a presentation in progress with the Meeting Minder dialog box. You can record minutes of the meeting or action items as you view the slides. PowerPoint also provides a Pen feature you can use to mark the slides or add notes.

Fig. 20.2

PowerPoint Presentation features can be built into your Excel control panel.

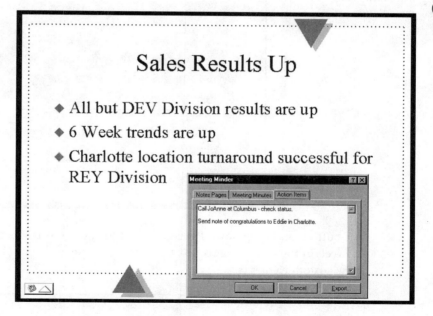

Tip

Use PowerPoint's Meeting Minder to keep track of action items and notes as you analyze the control panel workbook and discuss it with others.

The Click Here entries shown in figure 20.1 are colored blue, underlined, and high-lighted to resemble hypertext links on the World Wide Web. If you are a user of the World Wide Web, this format will be familiar.

When you click the link to Sales Indicators, you see the screen in figure 20.3.

Fig. 20.3

The Sales Indicators worksheet contains list boxes, links to other worksheets, and an embedded Word presentation.

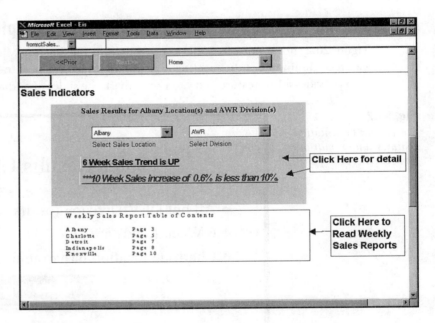

The buttons and drop-down list box at the top of each worksheet are not a standard part of Excel. In the upcoming section "Control Panel Navigation," you learn how to create these custom elements.

Tip

Create custom navigation controls to make it easy to find data in the workbook.

The Prior button shown at the top of the screen in figure 20.3 will return you to the first page of the control panel. The navigation system in this example is styled after the Prior and Next buttons found in many World Wide Web navigators.

Tip

You can use the Next button to move forward after backtracking with the Prior button.

The drop-down list box beside the Next button shows the name of the currently displayed worksheet. When you click the drop-down's arrow, you can select and move directly to any of the worksheets in the workbook.

You can control all navigation with the Prior button, Next button, and list box if you hide the worksheet tabs that show at the bottom of the screen. Choose <u>T</u>ools, <u>O</u>ptions, View, Window Options, Sheet Ta<u>b</u>s to hide the worksheet tabs.

Below the navigation buttons in figure 20.3 are two drop-down list boxes you can use to choose Sales Location and Division. When you choose a Location or Division, Visual Basic code automatically changes all of the sales PivotTables in the workbook so that their page fields are set to the same Location and Division.

In the later section "Using List Boxes to Select Information for Display," you learn the specifics of the Visual Basic code needed to synchronize PivotTable fields with list boxes.

Note

Use the example files for this chapter to learn more about how the controls in the example workbook are constructed. You can copy the example files to your computer, review the notes in Visual Basic code, and experiment with the control features.

The two text entries below the drop-down list boxes show the status of sales for the selected location and division. If the sales trend is up, the text is displayed in blue. If it is down, the text is red, indicating an exception. The ten-week sales increase for Albany, division AWR is below the expected ten percent, so the text is red. If the ten-week sales measure had shown an increase of ten percent or greater, the text would be blue.

Tip

Make your on-sheet controls more user friendly by designing them to operate like Excel or some other interface the user is already familiar with.

If you click the 6 Week Sales Trend is UP text, you see the screen shown in figure 20.4. The column chart of sales contains a trend line. The worksheet contains a formula just below the Slope of Sales Trend label that calculates the slope of the trend line using the LINEST function. If the slope is positive, then the six-week sales trend is up.

Fig. 20.4

Sales projection detail includes weekly data charted with a trend line.

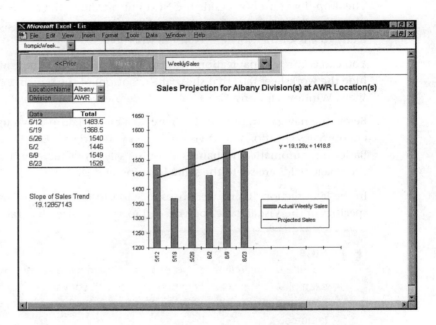

If you click the Prior button, the control panel returns you to the sales indicator screen shown in figure 20.3. Using the Prior button enables the Next button. You can use it to return to the screen shown in figure 20.4.

When you click the 10 week sales increase text in the Sales Indicator screen shown in figure 20.3, the control panel takes you to the screen shown in figure 20.5.

Fig. 20.5

Ten-week sales comparison contains a percent increase or decrease calculation and a bar chart comparing results to the previous year.

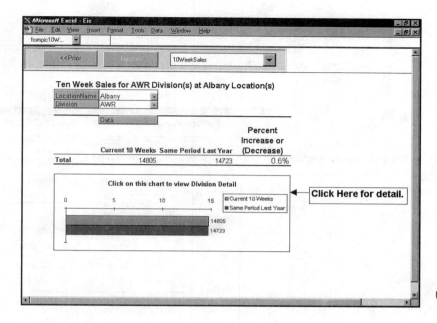

You can add a Percent Increase (or Decrease) value to the PivotTable with a worksheet formula. In figure 20.5, the `Current 10 Weeks` and `Same Period Last Year` are PivotTable totals and Location Name and Division are PivotTable page fields.

 Note

If you change the way your PivotTable is organized, formulas that reference PivotTable cells may become confused. You can prevent this problem by creating a one-line PivotTable that will not change as new data is added.

In Chapter 19, you learn how to construct a user-defined function that will adjust for changes in the PivotTable.

An IF statement can be used to select the text displayed on a worksheet. The IF statement can display an exception message in red when the Percent Increase (or Decrease) value does not meet requirements. When the percentage value is not an exception, the IF statement can display a differently worded and colored text message.

Clicking a Chart to Drill Down to More Detail

When you click the chart shown in figure 20.5, the screen in figure 20.6 appears. From this screen you can obtain percent increases for each of the product divisions at the Albany location.

Fig. 20.6

A PivotTable showing more detail about sales activity is displayed when you click the chart in figure 20.5.

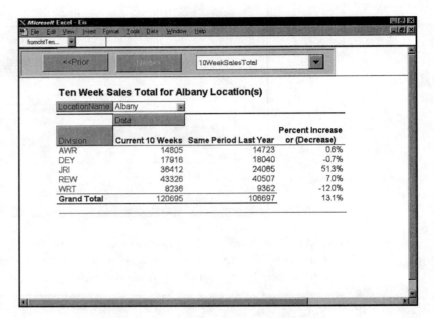

The chart object in figure 20.5 is assigned a Visual Basic macro that runs when you click the chart. The Visual Basic macro, called Click_On is described in the later section "Navigating by Clicking Worksheet Cells or Objects."

Using a Word Document as Part of the Control Panel

If you double-click Prior, you can return to the sales indicator screen shown in figure 20.3. If you right-click the Weekly Sales Report Table of Contents and select Document, Open, then Excel will open an embedded Microsoft Word Document.

While Excel does an excellent job of analyzing, storing, and presenting numbers, it is not designed to store large amounts of text. You can include written reports as part of your control panel by linking word processor files to an Excel worksheet. When you link a Microsoft Word document to Excel, you can access an entire set of weekly sales reports through the standard Word interface (see fig. 20.7).

You can embed many types of word processing documents into Excel. If you do not have a word processing package installed on your system, you can use the WordPad package that installs as part of Windows 95. Most major word processors such as Microsoft Word and Lotus AmiPro support linking and embedding. The example described in this chapter illustrates the use of Microsoft Word as an embedded document. You can easily adapt the examples to use WordPad, Lotus AmiPro, or another word processor.

> **Tip**
> Integrate a word processing document in your workbook to manage Reports, Memos, and other text related to the Excel data.

In the example shown in figure 20.7, weekly sales reports produced by the Sales Manager at each location are merged into one Word document that is copied into the Control Panel Workbook. Users of the workbook have all key information in one document—Excel numbers for analysis and reports from the field.

Fig. 20.7

If you click a linked Word document, a new window opens and you can review and edit the document.

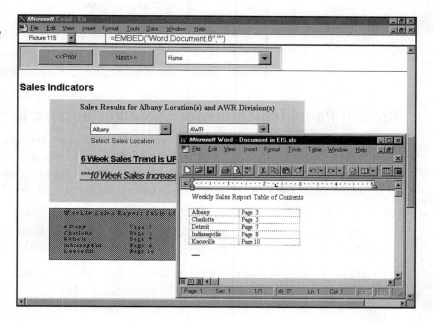

After you close the Word document and click the Prior button on the Sales Indicator screen, you will return to the home screen shown in figure 20.8. Because you have come back to the screen you started from, the Prior button is disabled and its caption dimmed.

Fig. 20.8

The Prior navigation button is dimmed when you return to the home screen.

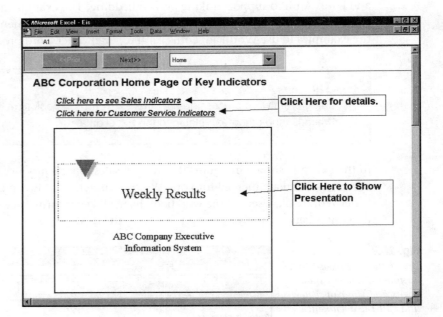

Control Panel Indicators for Customer Service Key Measures

When you click the Click here for Customer Service Indicators text as shown in figure 20.8, a Visual Basic macro will take you to the screen shown in figure 20.9. From this screen you can select a location from the drop-down list box and the two graphs will automatically update to show data from that location. You can also select the location All to view the total for all service locations.

The charts in figure 20.9 are linked to PivotTables. Visual Basic code synchronizes the PivotTable page fields to the drop-down list box in figure 20.9.

If you click the Calls on Hold chart on the right side of the screen in figure 20.9, a Visual Basic macro displays the screen shown in figure 20.10

Fig. 20.9

Two charts can be controlled with one drop-down list box.

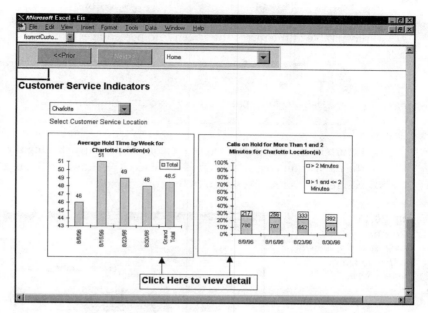

Fig. 20.10

The Calls on Hold chart uses a column chart to display percentages.

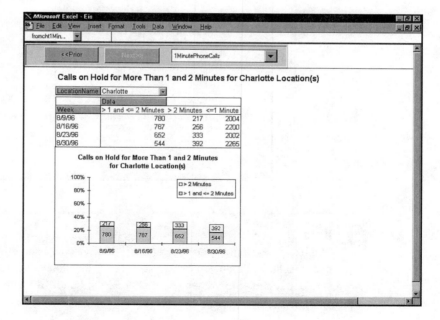

The Calls on Hold column chart shown in figure 20.10 translates the values in the PivotTable at the top of the screen into percentages.

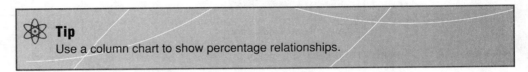

❅ Tip
Use a column chart to show percentage relationships.

Return to the starting screen of the control panel by clicking the drop-down list box in the navigation area at the top of the screen. As shown in figure 20.11, if you click Start, you return to the first screen in the control panel.

Fig. 20.11
Using the custom navigation drop-down list box to return to the Home screen.

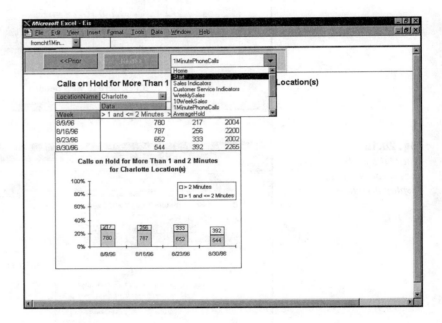

α Note
The example control panel worksheet uses a Visual Basic array to keep track of prior locations. When you move to a different location in the workbook, its address is added to the array. When you click the Prior button, a Visual Basic macro looks in the array to find the prior address.

When you have returned to your original starting location, the Macro disables the Prior button and dims its caption. If you haven't pressed the Prior button, the Next button is disabled and dimmed.

The example control panel workbook is with the Chapter 20 files. You may find that experimenting with a copy of the example will speed the process of learning to use control panel features.

You can build a control panel with exception reporting and navigation tools. Exception reporting helps the user of the system focus on the key factors of the process they are measuring. Navigation tools make it easy to navigate through the workbook. The next section explores exception reporting techniques. You learn how to construct a navigation system in the upcoming section "Control Panel Navigation."

Control Panel Exception Reporting Elements

To draw the reader's eye to the key indicators in your control panel, you can display text messages and show data in different formats. You can use a simple IF statement to highlight exception data or develop advanced exception reporting techniques in Visual Basic.

 Tip

To use exception reporting techniques in the control panel, highlight the information that needs to be attended to and hide as much of the other detail as you can. Only the information that demands action is presented to the user.

Simple Exception Reporting

One of the simplest exception reporting tools you can use is an IF statement that displays a warning message based on the value of other cells. If you have a column of percentages like those shown in Cells C5 through C15 of figure 20.12, and you want to highlight any percentage over ten percent, you can use the formula `IF(C5>.10,"EXCEPTION","")` in column D to display the caption EXCEPTION next to each percentage that exceeds ten percent.

Another simple exception reporting method is shown at the bottom of the screen in figure 20.12. You can use an IF statement to construct a text string that is displayed in cell D18. The IF statement used in cell D18 of figure 20.12 is displayed as text at the bottom of the screen. It uses the Text function to translate the values of the named ranges in cells D16 and D17 to percentage values. The last `""` in the formula will display an empty cell if the exception condition is not met. You could replace the `""` with another message. If you nest IF statements, you can assemble more complex message text.

20

Fig. 20.12
Exception messages can be displayed using IF statements.

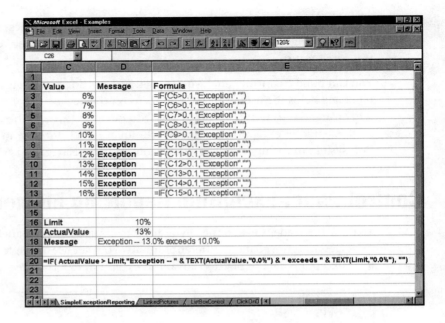

Adding Color to Exception Reporting

The exception reporting messages shown in figure 20.3 contain another element—color. The six-week sales trend message is either a blue 6 Week Sales Trend is UP or a red 6 Week Sales Trend is DOWN. The color red is used throughout the example to highlight exception conditions.

If you want to add color to your exception messages, you need to add either additional worksheet formulas or Visual Basic code. The built-in cell formatting capabilities of Excel do not provide a simple way to changing the color of a cell based on the value in another cell.

If you define an exception by comparing a cell's value to a constant, you can use Format, Cells, Number to display a number in a different color when its value exceeds the constant. The number format code: [>.1][RED]0.0%;[BLUE]0.0% will show the value of the cell in red if it exceeds 10%. Otherwise, the value will display as blue. If you want to change the constant you are testing against, use Format, Cells to re-enter the number format code values.

Displaying Exception Indicators with Pictures

Another way to add color to your control panel is to display a picture that is linked to a cell. You can create a named formula that changes the link depending on the value of an IF statement. When the IF statement detects an exception condition, it links the picture to a cell that contains an exception message. You can format the exception message with color and font style.

To link a picture to different cell values follow these steps:

1. Create two messages on your worksheet—one for the exception and one for the normal condition. See the example in cells E14 and E15 of figure 20.13.

Fig. 20.13

A linked picture is used to display an exception message.

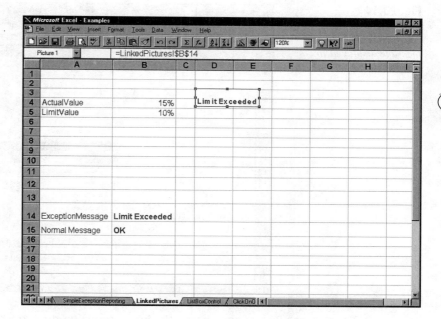

2. Create names for the messages and the test values. Add a label to the left of each value as shown in figure 20.13. Select the label and the value, and choose Insert, Name, Create to assign names to the values.

3. Select one of the message cells, B14 or B15, and press Ctrl+C to copy the cell value.

4. Select where you want the picture to appear. This can be a cell on a different worksheet. In figure 20.13, the top-left corner of the picture is aligned with cell D3 on the same worksheet.

5. While holding down the Shift key, choose menu options <u>E</u>dit, Paste Picture Li<u>n</u>k. A picture appears on your worksheet like the one in figure 20.13. The linking formula appears in the formula bar.

6. Choose <u>I</u>nsert, <u>N</u>ame, <u>D</u>efine to create a named formula. In figure 20.14, the formula is named PictureLink and the formula is

   ```
   =IF(ActualValue>LimitValue,ExceptionMessage,NormalMessage)
   ```

   If the Actual value exceeds the Limit Value, the formula returns the value in the cell named ExceptionMessage. Otherwise, the formula returns the value in the cell named NormalMessage.

Fig. 20.14

The named formula controls exception message displayed in the picture.

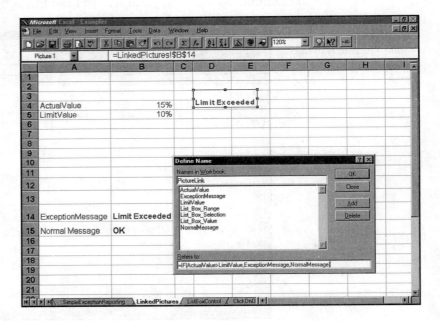

7. Select the Picture and change the link formula on the formula bar to the named formula. In the example in figure 20.14, change the value from `=LinkedPictures!$B$14` to `=PictureLink`. When the values on the worksheet change, Excel updates the formula PictureLink to point to the appropriate message value.

You can change the exception messages to include text and values from the worksheet using a formula. For example, the Exception message in cell B14 of figure 20.14 could contain the formula `="Exception - " & ActualValue & " exceeds the limit of " & LimitValue"`.

Another use for linked pictures is to display clip art images. The example in figure 20.15 shows how you can replace the `Limit Exceeded` message in figure 20.14 with a clip art image. The clip art will appear instead of the exception message.

Fig. 20.15

A clip art image is displayed instead of an exception message.

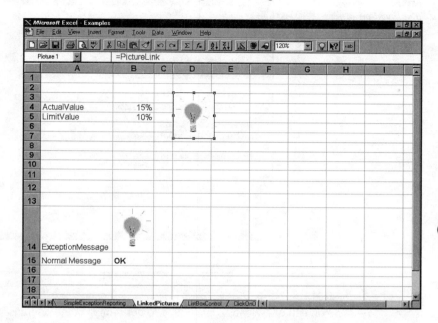

The formulas are the same in the examples in figure 20.13 and 20.14. The picture link formula shows the contents of the linked cell, even if those contents are part of another picture.

Add exception indicators like the ones in figure 20.3 with these techniques. The linked cells for figure 20.3 are contained on a hidden worksheet named Control, shown in figure 20.16.

The WeeklySalesIsException indicator value in figure 20.16 is set by an IF formula to values of TRUE, FALSE, or NoData. The formula WeeklySalesPicture returns the proper cell value to the picture on the visible worksheet. You can examine this formula in action in the Chapter 20 example files.

Fig. 20.16

The worksheet named ***Control*** *is used to store exception messages displayed on other worksheets in the workbook.*

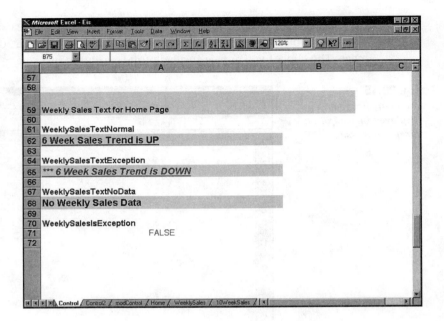

> α **Note**
>
> You can use Visual Basic Macro to perform all of the operations described in steps 1-7 in the previous list of instructions. With Visual Basic, you can set the Color property of a cell and construct a text message using a formula.

Using List Boxes to Select Information for Display

You can use a list box to control the information displayed on the control panel. The drop-down list boxes in figure 20.3 are examples of this feature. When you select a location and division, a Visual Basic macro updates PivotTable page fields and the PivotTable values are returned to the control panel.

The example in figure 20.17 shows all of the elements you need to use a list box to control a PivotTable. The top window contains a list box, list box controls, PivotTable, and data source for the PivotTable. The window at the bottom of figure 20.17 shows the one line of Visual Basic code necessary to change the page of the PivotTable to the value in the list box.

Fig. 20.17

A list box and VBA procedure are used to change the data displayed in a PivotTable.

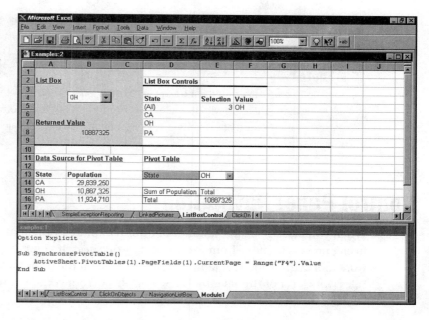

Cell B8 in figure 20.17 contains the formula =E16 and shows the value in the PivotTable total. If you want to return a value from a PivotTable with multiple rows and columns, you can learn in Chapter 19 how to create a user defined function that will return a value for a combination of row and column field values.

The list box in figure 20.17 is linked to the list of states in column D. When you select a value from the list box, Excel updates the number in cell E5 with the number of the item chosen. Cell F5 contains the formula =INDEX(D5:D8,E5) and returns the abbreviation of the state you select in the list box.

When you run the macro SynchronizePivotTable, one line of code assigns the value of cell F4 to the CurrentPage property of the PivotTable. The PivotTable changes and the new total value is displayed in cell B8.

If you want the SynchronizePivotTable macro to run automatically each time you select a new value from the list box, assign the macro SynchronizePivotTables to the list box. To assign a macro to a list box, right-click the list box, select Assign Macro, and choose the macro name from the list of macros in your workbook. The example in figure 20.17 synchronizes the PivotTable to the list box.

The Visual Basic code in figure 20.17 will work with the first page field in the first PivotTable on the active worksheet. You can store your PivotTables on different worksheets and update any page field by using some additional Visual Basic parameters. The example control panel found on the CDRom contains a working example of Visual Basic code that updates multiple PivotTables and page fields from a single list box.

 Note

Another way to control list boxes is to use Visual Basic to set the List values and return the selection with the ListIndex property. With this method, you do not need to create a range of list values or cell locations for the list's cell link.

Control Panel Navigation

When you package a large amount of information in a workbook, it can become a confusing process to move from worksheet to worksheet. If you fill up the bottom of the workbook with worksheet tabs, it is easy to forget if the information you need is on the Sales worksheet or the Sales by Week worksheet. Your computer screen becomes a tiny window into a confusing maze of data.

The navigation features of Excel make it easy to keep from getting lost while finding data in your workbook. Excel provides a powerful set of built-in navigation tools. You can build additional custom tools with Visual Basic for Applications.

Using Excel's Built-In Navigation

If you give each of your worksheets a descriptive name, then you can select a worksheet by clicking its sheet tab. If you have more worksheet tabs than can be seen at the bottom of your workbook, you can right-click the worksheet navigation buttons at the bottom-left corner of the workbook screen and select from a list of worksheets.

To give a worksheet a descriptive name, double-click its worksheet tab. A dialog box will appear and you can type a new worksheet name. The worksheet name appears on the worksheet tab and will print as part of the default page heading.

You can hide worksheets that you do not need to view. To hide a worksheet, use menu option Format, Sheet, Hide. When you need to access a hidden worksheet, it is easy to unhide it and include it with the other visible sheets. To make the worksheet visible use Format, Sheet, Unhide and select the worksheet name from the list of hidden sheets. You can hide and unhide module or dialog sheets using the Edit, Sheet menu option.

To go to a specific location in the workbook, you can use menu option Edit, GoTo and select the range name from a list of named ranges. You can use the shortcuts Ctrl+G or

F5 to jump directly to the GoTo dialog box. The Names drop-down list at the left-hand side of the formula bar provides another means of navigation. Select a named range from the drop-down list, press Enter, and you will go to that range.

Navigating by Clicking Worksheet Cells or Objects

You can use a very simple Visual Basic macro to go to another location in your workbook when you click a button, chart, or hidden rectangle. In figure 20.18, the button, rectangle, and chart are each assigned the macro Click_On. When you click the object, the Click_On macro uses the Application.Caller property and a Select statement to determine which object was clicked. Then the GoTo method displays the appropriate range.

Fig. 20.18

Buttons, rectangles, and charts can be used as navigation tools. When you click the object, a VBA procedure navigates through the workbook.

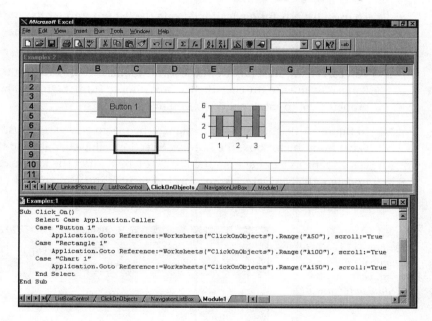

You can change the name of a worksheet object by right-clicking the object and entering a new name in the name box at the left side of the formula bar. Use the Drawing toolbar to add buttons and rectangles.

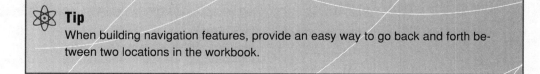

> ⚛ **Tip**
> When building navigation features, provide an easy way to go back and forth between two locations in the workbook.

If you want to move to a different location when you click a worksheet cell, you can position a rectangle object over that cell and use the Format Object options on the right-click menu to change the rectangle's border to None. The Rectangle will disappear, but still be positioned over the worksheet cell. If you assign a macro to the rectangle, when you click the cell, the macro will execute.

Rectangles are useful for clickable maps. If you position a picture of a map on your worksheet and then add rectangles over key locations, when you click that portion of the map, you can execute a macro and display detail lists or PivotTables.

Navigating with List Boxes

To use a list box for navigation, create the list box and set its control options. Then assign a macro to the list box that will go to different ranges in the workbook depending on the list box value chosen.

You can create a list box from the forms toolbar. To link the list box to the List Box Range of values, right-click the list box, choose Format Object, and enter the control properties of Input Range and Cell Link.

In figure 20.19, the list box is assigned the macro Navigation_ListBox. When you select a value from the list box, the List Box Selection value changes and the INDEX formula in cell F3 returns a name from the List Box Range. After the List Box Selection and Value are updated, the Navigate_ListBox macro executes and uses a Select statement to test the value in cell F3 and go to the appropriate worksheet range.

Fig. 20.19
A list box can be used to choose a range in the workbook. A VBA procedure automatically jumps to that location.

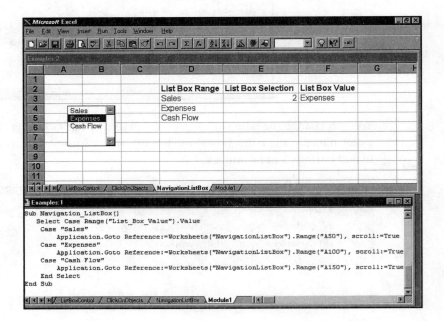

A Web Browser Navigation System

The custom navigation bar shown in figure 20.20 combines click-on buttons and a navigation list box. The Visual Basic macros assigned to the buttons and list box keep track of the last 25 ranges visited and allow you to move back and forth between worksheets in the workbook.

Fig. 20.20

A custom navigation bar can be added to each worksheet in the workbook.

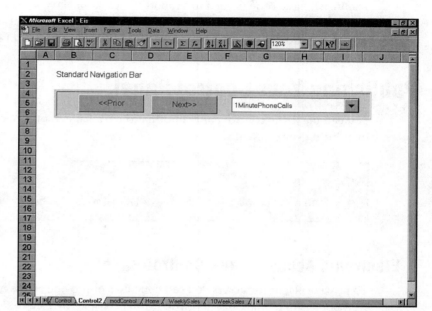

This arrangement of Prior and Next buttons is similar to the Back and Forward buttons at the top of most Web browser screens. If you want the user interface to resemble an Excel Wizard, you can position the buttons at the bottom of the screen.

The buttons and list box are on top of a grey rectangle. The three-dimensional effect is achieved by adding two black and two white lines on top of the rectangle. You can construct one copy of the navigation bar and copy it to each of your worksheets. If you assign macros to the buttons and list box, and then group all the objects together, you can copy them in a group to a worksheet. After you copy them, ungroup the objects so that the macros will function properly. You can group and ungroup sets of objects with buttons on the Drawing toolbar.

The navigation bar will stay visible at the top of the window if you use the freeze panes feature. Select the cell in column A just below the rectangle and choose Window, Freeze Pane. The navigation bar will remain at the top of the screen as you scroll through the worksheet.

The list box displays a list of all locations that you need to visit to get information out of the workbook. When you navigate by clicking other objects such as charts and rectangles in the workbook, Visual Basic adds these locations to the history list. You can click a chart, go to the range that contains the detail for the chart, and then use the Prior buttons to back up to the location you started from.

The Visual Basic code needed to support the Custom Navigation bar is contained in the Chapter 20 example files. You can copy the code from ModControl and the Control worksheet into your workbook and modify it for your navigation needs.

Publishing Your Control Panel

You can make the control panel information available to others, either electronically or by printing key elements on paper.

 Tip

Plan how you will publish the control panel workbook before you start building it.

Electronic Access to the Control Panel

To provide electronic access you can copy files or provide access on a network. If the workbook is of manageable size, you can send copies by Electronic mail to recipients within your network or to others over the Internet or on-line services like CompuServe.

If you want to reduce the size of the workbook file for transmission to others, you can compress the file with the WinZip file compression utilities on CompuServe or any on-line service. Copies are also available for purchase at your local computer store. Compression will reduce the file size and time required to transmit.

Use Windows 95 Briefcase features to copy the workbook file to your laptop. Briefcase makes it easy to take copies of files with you on your PC, make changes to the files on the laptop and update your desktop computer files.

Excel 95 supports the use of shared folders you can use to share access to your workbook on a network. Multiple users can access and update the same workbook file and Excel keeps track of changes. If two users are making changes to the same data, Excel will display a warning message and ask which change should be accepted and which should be discarded.

Printing Reports from the Control Panel

You can use View Manager in the View menu to create a series of views of the control panel workbook. Each view can contain a predefined print range. You can define multiple views of the same worksheet.

If you want to print the views in sequence, use Report Manager in the View menu to create a defined sequence of views. When you print the report, each view prints on a sequentially numbered page. You can define several reports and store the report definitions in the Report Manager.

 Note

The View Manager and Report Manager are add-ins that come with Excel. If the options do not appear on your menu, you can use Tools, Add-Ins to add the View Manager and Report Manager to your list of installed add-ins. Then you can choose their menu options from the View menu.

Summary

In this chapter you learned how construct a control panel workbook that contains all of the key indicators for an organization. You learned about exception reporting and navigation features that you can add to your workbooks. The example presented in the first part of the chapter illustrated an exception reporting workbook with the capability to drill down from an exception into the detail data.

With Excel's powerful Visual Basic macro language, you can completely customize the look of an Excel workbook. Or, you can use linked pictures and formulas to construct an effective control panel workbook without using Visual Basic.

High-Grade Reporting Techniques

chapter 21

Forecasting in Excel

21

by Conrad Carlberg

In this chapter

◆ **Forecasting basics**
  The general approach to forecasting in Excel.

◆ **Moving average forecasts**
  Forecasting from a baseline with both standard moving average and smoothing techniques. Finding the optimum smoothing constant.

◆ **Regression forecasts: linear and curvilinear**
  Using worksheet functions, chart trendlines, and the Analysis ToolPak to create least-squares forecasts.

◆ **Traps involving regression forecasts**
  The dangers of extended forecasts, forecasting one-time series from another and over-modelling the data.

At one time or another, most Excel users find it necessary to create a forecast. In this context, "forecast" does *not* mean "what-if" analysis, where you might project expenses by expressing them as a percentage of revenue, and then vary revenue to see what happens to expenses. Rather, the term as used here means the prediction of a future quantity on the basis of a past quantity.

There are several different ways to use Excel to create forecasts. Suppose that you have at hand a list of annual sales revenues for the past ten years, and you hope to use that information to forecast the most likely value of revenue for next year. Excel offers eight worksheet functions, 15 menu items, and three Analysis ToolPak add-ins that you can choose from to create that forecast.

The available approaches use least-squares techniques, linear and non-linear, criterion-related and autocorrelative, moving-averages, and smoothing techniques. It's even possible to combine these techniques in some extremely sophisticated ways.

If you don't understand these approaches, this chapter provides some fundamental information on how and why they work. If you do understand these approaches, this chapter explains how they are implemented in the Excel context.

 Note

You will find additional useful information pertaining to the forecasting process in Chapter 7, "Using Array Formulas." Several of Excel's worksheet functions that are used in forecasting require that you fully understand array formulas. Chapter 25, "VBA Arrays," provides information that can be helpful in overcoming some of the limits to Excel's worksheet functions and the Analysis ToolPak add-ins.

Forecasting Basics

Two terms used extensively in forecasting are *time series* and *baseline*. Forecasting deals in time series, which are observations of some process over time. Examples of time series include number of traffic accidents each day for six months, sales dollars each week for one year, and hourly bit error rates on a telecommunications line during a 24-hour period.

When you forecast the number of traffic accidents likely to occur tomorrow, next week's sales, or the number of bit errors that you expect to occur during the next hour, you generally use a time series as a basis for the forecast. In the forecasting context, the time series—the basis for the forecast—is often termed a *baseline*. Unless you're Nostradamus, you need a baseline of data to make a forecast.

It's best if your baseline has certain characteristics. The observations should represent time intervals that are as equal as possible, and they should come from the same location within the interval. For example, you might gather data each week, or each day, or every hour. By choosing one of these schemes, you will have equal time intervals. But if you obtained your weekly data on Monday during Week 1, Thursday during Week 2, and Tuesday during Week 3, your time intervals are not truly equal. Similarly, if you choose to make daily measurements, it's best if your observations can come from the same hour of each day.

Missing observations in a baseline can be a real problem. Although they are nearly inevitable, they throw off the mathematics that underlie the forecast. Try to have a complete baseline—but if that's impossible, consider replacing a missing measurement by the average of the prior and the subsequent observations.

For most forecasts, the longer your baseline the better. There are some complex mathematical reasons for this, but there are also some very practical ones. Suppose that a time series looks like the one in figure 21.1.

Fig. 21.1

Seasonal or cyclic time series can mislead you if your baseline is too short.

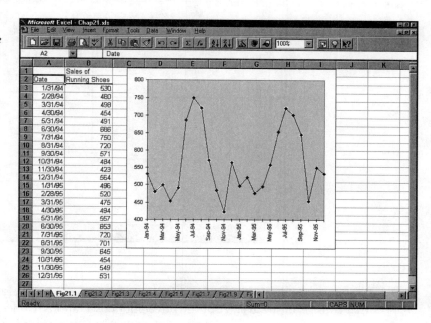

The time series in the figure is highly seasonal. Sales of running shoes peak during the summer months. If the baseline that you forecast from covered those months only, you might forecast a sale of 700 pairs of shoes during October. Or, if it covered only September through May, you might forecast a sale of 500 pairs during June. In either case, your forecast would be seriously off-base. Again, the longer the baseline, the better.

Once you have a usable baseline, you are faced with a choice among a large variety of forecasting techniques. These methods fall into two basic categories: Moving Averages (including the family of smoothing methods), and Regression (including linear, non-linear, and autoregressive).

Understanding Moving Averages

A moving average forecast makes a basic assumption: that recent observations in a baseline are the best estimate of the next observation—that is, the forecast. Moving averages are, computationally, a very easy method of forecasting, and might seem naive or simplistic. And they can be. But they also can be exactly the right approach to forecasting, and can become quite complex.

Figure 21.2 provides two examples of moving average forecasts.

Fig. 21.2

The moving average forecast tracks step functions well.

=AVERAGE(A1:A3)

Baselines

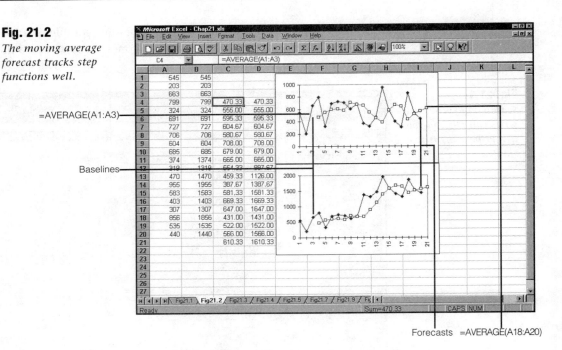

Forecasts =AVERAGE(A18:A20)

The upper chart in figure 21.2 contains a typical time series. It also contains a forecast that consists of the average of the three prior observations. Notice that the moving average tracks the actual time series fairly closely, but that it tends to lag behind the actual observations. This is as you would expect, because each forecast is the average of the three preceding actuals.

The lower chart in the figure contains a time series whose level increases suddenly and dramatically at time 10. The moving average forecast reflects that increase, shortly after it occurs. This effect is the principal strength of moving average forecasts. Other forecasting methods tend not to track sudden jumps, or *steps*, in a time series as well as do moving averages.

There is nothing magic about the choice of three observations for the moving averages: you could choose two, or five, or 25. Your choice would depend on the quality of the forecast. Sometimes, shorter averages work better, and sometimes the reverse. Keep in mind, though, that the shorter the average, the more quickly the forecast adjusts to changes in the level of the time series.

When a time series is subject to a change in level that tends to persist, moving averages are often the method of choice for a forecast. Examples include:

▶ *Inventory levels*. A major purchase to a company's inventory causes an increase in the value of that asset, and tends to persist for some time.

▶ *Crime statistics*. If an enforcement agency decides to focus its resources on a particular traffic offense, the reported incidence of some other offense is likely to decrease, and the new, lower level will persist until resources are reassigned.

▶ *Weather patterns*. If the El Niño effect is pronounced during a given year, the frequency and intensity of hurricanes and droughts is likely to increase and persist during that year.

Excel provides several ways to derive moving averages. You can enter the necessary formulas directly on the worksheet, or you can use the Analysis ToolPak's Moving Average add-in, or you can create moving averages on a chart using its Trendlines feature. Each method is illustrated in this chapter.

Understanding Regression Forecasts

The basis of a regression forecast is an equation that *minimizes the squared differences between a forecast and its corresponding observation.*

In years, how old will you be tomorrow? It's a trivial example, but it illustrates the concept. You could derive an equation like this:

```
Age[tomorrow] = AgeAtBirth + (1/365 × DaysLived[tomorrow])
```

This equation helps to illustrate some terminology. In the equation:

▶ Age[tomorrow] is the forecast. In Excel's terms, the *y-value*.

▶ AgeAtBirth is the starting level of the time series. In Excel's terms, the *intercept*.

▶ 1/365 is the change in the forecast for each change in time. In Excel's terms, the *coefficient* or the *slope*.

▶ DaysLived[tomorrow] is the time value. In Excel's terms, the *x-value*.

If you supply a few accurate values for Age[tomorrow] and for DaysLived[tomorrow], Excel derives an equation for you that includes the intercept and the coefficient. You can then plug a new value for DaysLived[tomorrow] into the equation, using the values Excel returns for the intercept and the coefficient, to forecast a new value for Age[tomorrow].

While this example is trivial, exactly the same concepts apply in much more meaningful situations. Suppose that your y-value is Revenue (instead of Age[tomorrow]) and that your x-value is Month (instead of DaysLived[tomorrow]). Figure 21.3 shows how you might forecast next month's Revenue.

Fig. 21.3

The worksheet functions INTERCEPT() and SLOPE() are two ways to get a regression forecast equation.

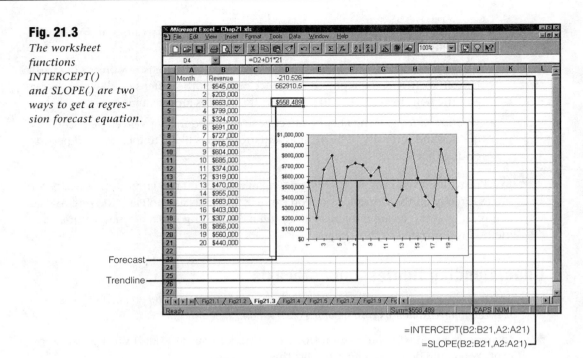

You can use Excel's INTERCEPT() and SLOPE() functions in an equation that forecasts both the existing, observed values of Revenue and next month's as-yet-unobserved Revenue. The main characteristic of the equation is that the sum of the squared differences between the observations and the forecasts is minimized. This is called the *least-squares* criterion, and it's a standard decision rule in many forecasting (and other statistical) situations.

Notice, in the chart in figure 21.3, that the trendline drawn through the observed revenues is a straight one. Contrast it with the trendlines in figure 21.2. A moving average trendline, and the forecasts it describes, responds directly to changes in the level of the time series or baseline. Although a regression trendline also responds to changes in the level of a time series, *all points in the time series contribute to the value of the intercept and the slope.* If you change any value in the time series, the entire trendline shifts. In contrast, changing a value would shift only the portion of the moving average trendline that uses that value.

When a time series depends on a value of some other variable, Regression is often the right forecasting approach. For example, Revenue might depend on Month or Advertising Expenses; or, water's boiling point might depend on barometric pressure. In these and similar cases, Regression can be a better approach than moving averages.

It happens that Regression also can be used when the forecasted variable also is the predicting variable. This sort of forecast is often called an *autoregressive* forecast—for example, Revenue can be regressed onto itself, instead of onto Month. Autoregressive forecasts are well beyond the scope of this chapter; for a brief discussion, refer to Que's *Business Analysis with Excel*.

Using Moving Average Forecasts

There are two principal types of moving average forecasts: the standard, traditional form, and the smoothing form. The standard moving average forecast is shown in figure 21.4.

Fig. 21.4

A moving average omits forecasts for as many time points as are used in each average.

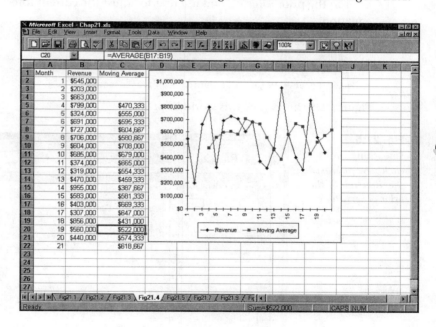

Moving Averages

At any time, the standard moving average forecast is based on the same number of observations. For example, the moving average forecasts in cells C12 and C13 of figure 21.4 are

```
=AVERAGE(B9:B11)
=AVERAGE(B10:B12)
```

So, as time passes, older observations drop out of the forecast and new observations enter it. Each observation in the time series that contributes to a particular moving average receives equal weight. All other observations in the time series receive no weight.

Smoothing

The second moving average approach, Smoothing, retains older observations in the forecast, but gives them less and less weight as they age. The Smoothing approach has broad applicability in forecasting.

The basic idea behind smoothing is to take into account the amount and direction of the error in the prior forecast, and use that to adjust the current forecast. Here's the basic equation:

```
New Forecast = Prior Forecast + Smoothing Constant × Prior Error
```

The prior error is defined as:

```
Prior Error = Prior Observation - Prior Forecast
```

Figure 21.5 shows how this works in practice.

Fig. 21.5

Smoothing "pulls" each new forecast in the direction of the prior observation.

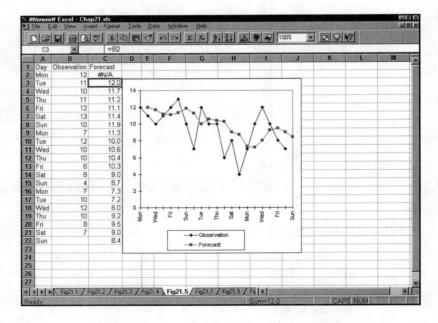

Tuesday's observation (cell B3) was 11 and Tuesday's forecast (cell C3) was 12. So the error in Tuesday's forecast is (11-12), or -1. Because Tuesday's forecast, 12, overestimated Tuesday's observation, 11, Wednesday's forecast uses that overestimate to improve (we hope) its accuracy:

```
Wednesday's Forecast = 12 + Smoothing Constant × (-1)
```

Suppose that the smoothing constant is .3. Then Wednesday's forecast is

```
Wednesday's Forecast = 12 + .3 × (-1)
Wednesday's Forecast = 12 + (-.3) = 11.7
```

Tuesday's forecast overestimated Tuesday's observation. So, the amount of forecast error is negative, and Wednesday's forecast is the result of subtracting a portion of the error in Tuesday's forecast from Tuesday's forecast.

In contrast, notice that Friday's observation was 12 and Friday's forecast was 11.1. Then, Friday's error is

```
12 - 11.1 = .9
```

and Saturday's forecast is

```
Saturday's Forecast = 11.1 + .3 × .9 = 11.4
```

Friday's forecast underestimated Friday's observation, so the amount of forecast error is positive. Saturday's forecast is the result of adding a portion of the error in Friday's forecast.

In other words, new forecasts are constantly self-correcting: they are the result of combining the prior forecast with some amount of the error in the prior forecast.

The formula is often rearranged to make its calculation a little easier:

```
New Forecast = Prior Forecast + Smoothing Constant × Prior Error
New Forecast = Prior Forecast + Smoothing Constant × (Prior Observation - Prior
➥Forecast)
New Forecast = Prior Forecast + Smoothing Constant × Prior Observation - Smoothing
➥Constant × Prior Forecast)
New Forecast = Smoothing Constant × Prior Observation + (1 - Smoothing Constant) ×
➥Prior Forecast
```

So, if the prior observation is in cell A5, the prior forecast is in cell B5, and the smoothing constant is .3, then the new forecast is

```
= .3 × A5 + (1 - .3) × B5
```

To create the forecasts and the chart shown in figure 21.5, use Excel's Exponential Smoothing add-in, which is part of the Analysis ToolPak. Follow these steps:

1. Choose Tools, Add-Ins. In the Add-Ins dialog box, fill the Analysis ToolPak check box, and choose OK.

2. Choose Tools, Data Analysis. In the Data Analysis dialog box, highlight Exponential Smoothing and choose OK. The dialog box shown in figure 21.6 appears.

Note

If you do not see the Analysis ToolPak as an option, you will need to run Add/Remove Software in the Windows 95 Control Panel. Use it to navigate to Excel components in the Setup routine, and be sure to choose to install the Analysis ToolPak component.

Fig. 21.6

Use the Exponential Smoothing dialog box to specify the input range (your baseline observations), the damping factor, and the output range.

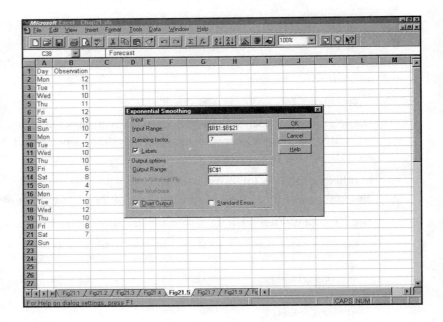

 Note

The *damping factor* referred to in the dialog box is 1 minus the smoothing constant. So, if you wanted to use a smoothing constant of .3, you would enter .7 as the damping factor. Yes, this is inconvenient. Most sources on forecasting discuss smoothing in terms of the smoothing constant rather than the damping factor, and this chapter follows that usage. It's easier to understand the rationale behind smoothing by thinking of it in terms of the smoothing constant rather than in terms of the damping factor.

3. In the Input Range box, enter **B2:B21**, or simply drag through that range with your mouse.

4. Enter **.7** as the damping factor.

5. In the <u>O</u>utput Range box, enter **C2**, and fill the <u>C</u>hart Output check box. Then, choose OK.

The result on your worksheet, shown in figure 21.7, will be similar to that shown in figure 21.5.

Fig. 21.7

The Exponential Smoothing add-in does not automatically provide the one-step-ahead forecast.

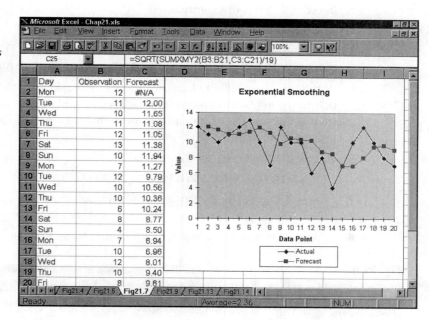

Tip

You can obtain the next forecast value of the series by selecting cell C21 and copying it down one row. That is the forecast for the next value in the series. Then, drag that value into the chart to extend the forecast data series.

It's probably occurred to you to ask, "What damping factor—or, equivalently, what smoothing constant—should I choose to create the best forecast?" There are many different decision rules available that can help answer this question, but probably the best both in theory and in practice is the least-squares criterion. This criterion was discussed previously in "Understanding Regression Forecasts."

In this context, the least-squares criterion states that the best smoothing constant is the one that results in the smallest value when the forecasting errors (the difference between each forecast and each observation) are squared and totalled.

To use the least-squares criterion as an aid to choosing the best smoothing constant for the data in figure 21.7, follow these steps:

1. Follow steps 1 through 5 in the list of steps just given to create a forecast by means of Exponential Smoothing.

2. In cell D25, enter the value **.3**.

3. In cell E25, enter this formula:

    =1-D25

4. Select the range C2:C21, and choose Edit, Replace. In the Find What box, enter **0.3**. In the Replace With box, enter **D25**. Choose Replace All.

5. With C2:C21 still selected, again choose Edit, Replace. In the Find What box, enter **0.7**. In the Replace With box, enter **E25**. Choose Replace All. The result of these steps is to cause the exponential smoothing formulas in C2:C21 to use cell values instead of constants.

6. Enter this formula in cell C25:

    =SQRT(SUMXMY2(B3:B21,C3:C21)/19)

7. Choose Tools, Solver. If you do not see the Solver item in the Tools menu, you will need to install it in the same way that you install the Analysis ToolPak.

8. In the Solver dialog box (see fig. 21.8), enter **C25** in the Set Target Cell edit box.

Fig. 21.8

Use the Solver to arrive at a value that minimizes the least-squares criterion.

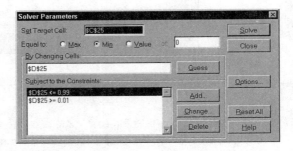

9. Click the Min option button. This establishes the least-squares criterion. The target cell, C25, contains the current total of the squared forecast errors. The Solver will seek to minimize that value.

10. In the By Changing Cells edit box, enter **D25**. The Solver will adjust the value in D25—the smoothing constant—to a value that minimizes the squared forecast errors in cell C25.

11. Click the Add button. The Add Constraint dialog box appears. In the Cell Reference box, enter **D25**. Choose the >= operator in the Constraint drop-down list, and enter **.01** in the edit box. Choose Add.

12. The Add Constraint dialog box reappears. In the Cell Reference box, again enter **D25**. Choose the <= operator in the Constraint drop-down list, and enter **.99** in the edit box. Choose OK. The Solver dialog box reappears.

13. The result of steps 9 and 10 is to constrain the smoothing constant to a value between .01 and .99. Values in this range are needed in order to obtain reasonable forecasts. You are now ready to start the solution process. Choose Solve in the Solver dialog box.

14. When the Solver notifies you that it has reached a solution, choose Keep Solver Solution.

The value in D25 will now be the smoothing constant that minimizes the squared forecast errors.

 Tip

As a practical matter, you cannot use the Goal Seek function in this instance. Goal Seek requires that you supply a specific value for the target cell. You do not know the minimum least-squares value before the fact, so use the Solver to set it to a minimum value for you.

21

Using Regression Forecasts

As was noted earlier in the section "Understanding Regression Forecasts," you generally need some *other* variable to create a forecast using regression. Excel refers to this other variable as the x-variable, and to the variable that you forecast as the y-variable.

It's quite common to forecast a y-variable using some measure of time. See figure 21.9 for an example.

In the figure, Revenue is forecast using Month as the x-variable. The trendline in the figure's chart is called the *regression line*. It has an intercept of 26227 and a slope of 2821.5. So you can make a forecast for the next period by using this equation:

```
Revenue[Month 20] = 26227 + 2821.5 × 20
```

How do you cause Excel to create the forecasting equation? There's a variety of options, discussed next.

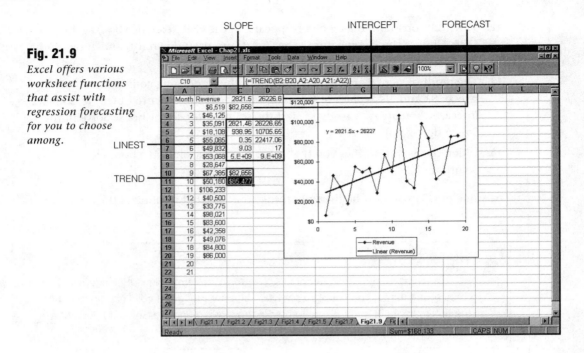

Fig. 21.9
*Excel offers various
worksheet functions
that assist with
regression forecasting
for you to choose
among.*

Using Chart Trendlines

To use a chart to create the forecast shown in figure 21.8, follow these steps:

1. Highlight cells A1:B20.

2. Choose Insert, Chart, On This Sheet (you can, of course, create the chart on a separate sheet if you want). The Chart Wizard starts.

3. Complete the Chart Wizard, choosing to create an XY (Scatter) chart. It's important to use an XY chart because only that chart type spaces the X-axis categories according to the numeric magnitude of the x-values. Other chart types space the X-axis categories equally, and this can cause the regression line to appear incorrectly.

4. When the Chart Wizard has finished, double-click the chart to open it for editing. Then, click once on the charted data series. The individual data markers become highlighted.

5. Choose Insert, Trendlines. This option is disabled unless the data series on the chart has been selected by clicking it.

6. The dialog box shown in figure 21.10 appears. Choose the Linear trendline option.

7. Click the Options tab. The dialog box shown in figure 21.11 appears. Fill the Display Equation on Chart check box, and choose to forecast forward 1 unit. This will give you a one-step-ahead forecast. Then, choose OK.

Fig. 21.10
The Trendline dialog box offers several different forecasting options.

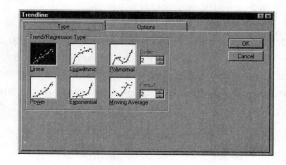

Fig. 21.11
Use the Options tab to specify your forecast horizon, and to display different statistics on the chart itself.

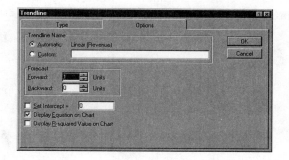

You should now see the chart, the equation, and the one-step-ahead forecast shown earlier in figure 21.9.

Using SLOPE() and INTERCEPT()

You have already met the SLOPE() and INTERCEPT() functions in the earlier section "Understanding Regression Forecasts." To use the SLOPE() function as shown in figure 21.9, just enter:

```
=SLOPE(B2:B20,A2:A20)
```

in, say, C1. Notice that SLOPE() returns the same value for the regression equation's coefficient, within rounding error, as is shown in the chart's regression equation.

To use the INTERCEPT() function, enter:

```
=INTERCEPT(B2:B20,A2:A20)
```

in D1. Again, the INTERCEPT() function returns the same value for the intercept as is shown on the chart. To create the forecast itself, you also need the next x-value. Because the next month is the 20th, you could enter in cell C2:

```
= D1 + C1 × 20
```

which is the regression-based forecast for the 20th month, given the relationship between the values in A2:A20 and the values in B2:B20.

Using LINEST()

LINEST() is an exceptionally powerful function, but one that's easy to use. It returns a variety of statistics pertaining to the regression forecast, including both the intercept and the slope of the regression line. To use it, first highlight a range two columns wide and five columns high. Then, array-enter this formula (shown in C4:D8 of figure 21.9):

```
=LINEST(B2:B20,A2:A20,TRUE,TRUE)
```

To array-enter a formula, you hold down Ctrl+Shift simultaneously after you have typed it, and then press Enter.

LINEST() returns these statistics in the range that you highlighted before entering the formula:

Column:	C	D
Row:		
4	Coefficient	Slope
5	SE of coefficient	SE of slope
6	R^2	SE of Y
7	F-ratio	Degrees of Freedom
8	SS, regression	SS, residual

Don't worry if you're unfamiliar with the statistics in rows 5 through 8. They pertain to the statistical significance of the regression equation. If you expect to do much forecasting by means of regression, you should consult an intermediate text on statistical methods, because the information in rows 5 through 8 of the LINEST() results can be important. Nevertheless, you can create useful forecasts without understanding things like standard errors (abbreviated SE in the preceding table), sums of squares (SS in the table), and so on.

The information really needed to create the forecast are the coefficient and the slope. You can derive a forecast for the next time period just as you did using INTERCEPT() and SLOPE(). Simply replace the references to the cells containing those functions with references to the cells that contain the first row of the LINEST() function.

Again, notice that LINEST() returns the same coefficient and slope as does the regression equation in the chart, and as do the INTERCEPT() and SLOPE() functions.

Using TREND()

The TREND() function is a convenient way to obtain a regression forecast without going through the intermediate steps of obtaining the slope and intercept. To use it to return two forecasts, first highlight a range one column wide and two rows high. Then, array-enter as shown in C10:C11 of figure 21.9:

```
=TREND(B2:B20,A2:A20,A21:A22)
```

As usual, B2:B20 contains the y-values, and A2:A20 contains the x-values. A21:A22 contains the values of the times to which you want to forecast. Notice that the first value from TREND() is the same as that found by using LINEST(), SLOPE(), and INTERCEPT(), and the one that is shown on the chart trendline.

Using the Regression Add-In

Excel's Analysis ToolPak provides a tool, Regression, that relieves you of the task of entering functions and their arguments directly on the worksheet. Using the Regression add-in, all you need to do is indicate the location of your y-values and your x-values, and to select the output options that you want to use.

To use the Regression add-in, first make sure that the Analysis ToolPak is installed, as described earlier in the "Smoothing" section. Then, choose Tools, Data Analysis and select Regression from the Analysis Tools list box. After you choose OK, the dialog box shown in figure 21.12 appears.

Fig. 21.12

The Regression add-in does most of the work involved in setting up a forecast for you.

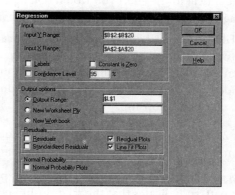

Not all the options and items in the dialog box are critical for forecasting purposes. Those that are, and those that can cause problems, are covered here:

▶ In the Input Y Range and Input X Range edit boxes, enter the forecast variable and time variable ranges, respectively.

▶ Unless you are certain of your grounds, do *not* fill the Constant is Zero check box. (Similarly, do *not* use FALSE as the third argument to the LINEST() function.) The Constant is another term for the intercept. If your data really do have a zero intercept, any departure from zero is due to sampling error and you might as well ignore it. If the data do not have a zero intercept, choosing this option introduces a statistical anomaly, making your regression equation appear more reliable than it really is.

▶ Fill the Labels check box if the first row in each range contains a text label for the x- and y-values.

Caution

If you are using Excel 5, be very careful of the Labels option. If you have numeric data in the first row of each range, and if you fill the Labels check box, Excel can terminate with a general protection fault.

▶ In the Output Range box, enter the address that you want for the upper left cell that the Regression output will occupy on the worksheet. Be careful when you choose the Output Range option button: when you choose it, the focus returns to the Input Y Range edit box.

▶ Fill the Line Fit Plot check box. This option creates a chart that plots the observed values and the predicted values over time periods. Apart from its formatting, it is identical to the chart you would obtain if you created an XY chart of the baseline against time periods, and included a linear trendline.

▶ Fill the Residual Plots check box. "Residuals" is a fancy term for the difference between the forecast values and the observed values—much like the error involved, in exponential smoothing, between the prior observation and the prior forecast. Ideally, when you view the chart of residuals by time periods, you should see a random relationship.

Figure 21.13 shows two charts containing residual plots. The first chart shows a random relationship between the size of the residual and its associated time period.

The second chart shows that there is a regular pattern to the residuals over time. This sort of pattern indicates that the relationship between time and the forecast variable is not linear, and a complication must be added to the regression model. This situation is discussed in more detail in the later section "Using Curvilinear Forecasts."

Fig. 21.13

Plots of residuals against time values offer clues to the adequacy of your forecasting model.

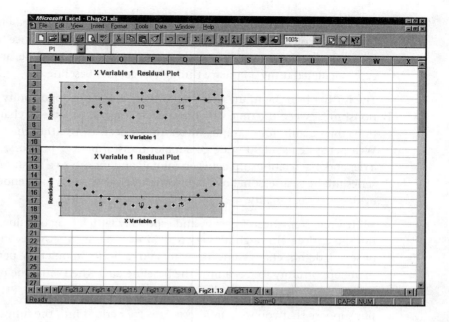

Extending Regression Forecasts

Thus far, this chapter has discussed one-step-ahead forecasts—that is, those that go only one time period beyond the end of the baseline. With simple exponential smoothing, you cannot forecast further than one step ahead. Recall that calculating an exponential smoothing forecast requires both the prior forecast and the prior observation. When you have reached the end of the baseline, you have a current observation and a current forecast from which to build the forecast for the next period. But to forecast two periods beyond the end of the baseline would require another observation that you don't yet have. The same point applies to standard moving average forecasts.

Using regression, you can forecast further than one period beyond the end of the baseline. Because the forecast depends on a number that represents a time period (for example, Month 1, Month 2,...Month 21), you can supply Excel the numbers that represent the next several time periods (in this case, Month 22, Month 23, and so on).

For example, you can use the Forecast option in the Trendline dialog box (refer to fig. 21.11) to forecast virtually any number of periods into the future. Or, you could use the third argument in the TREND() function to cause Excel to calculate the forecasts for the number of future periods that you want.

Doing so, however, extends an assumption that has so far been implicit. When you make a one-step-ahead forecast, you assume that the relationship between the time variable and the forecast variable will remain as it has been during the baseline period. Put another way, you assume that there would not be a major difference between the slope and intercept calculated using a January through November baseline, and the slope and intercept calculated using a January through December baseline.

The further into the future that you forecast, the more opportunity there is for the relationship between the time variable and the forecast variable to change. Market conditions might shift, for example, increasing or decreasing either the intercept or the slope. Weather systems might undergo a major transformation, temporarily changing what was a dependable relationship between rainfall and month to a random one. Or your time series might be a seasonal one, and your baseline was not long enough to capture the evidence of seasonality.

With a one-step-ahead forecast, and especially with a long baseline, this assumption is not too critical, although it's very real. Most systems, whether economic, meteorological, or social, do not change unexpectedly and radically in one time period. There is normally opportunity to reexamine the baseline data when only one period has been forecast, and an unusual shift subsequently occurs.

But suppose that you were to forecast twelve periods into the future and subsequently make important decisions on the basis of that forecast. Then, there is ample opportunity for the nature of the time series to change, and therefore, for your decisions to turn out badly. Be very cautious with lengthy forecasts, especially when your baseline is relatively short.

Using Curvilinear Forecasts

Time is linear. For each week that elapses, another seven days pass, and this is true for all weeks. A regression equation's intercept and slope are constants. When you multiply a linear quantity (time) by one constant (the coefficient) and add to that another constant (the intercept), you inevitably get a straight line.

But suppose that your baseline looked like the one shown in figure 21.14.

Here, the baseline shows that revenue is accelerating over time. There is no longer a linear relationship between revenue and time. And yet the first chart's trendline is linear. Regression itself is not capable of determining that the y-variable (here, Revenue) is nonlinear across a linear x-variable (here, time). You have to supply that information yourself. And you usually do so by changing the nature of the baseline's x-variable.

How might you change the x-variable, time, in the situation shown in figure 21.14? When the value of the y-variable is accelerating over time, it is usually because there is a linear relationship between the y-variable and the x-variable *raised to some power*.

Suppose that the x-variable in figure 21.14 were raised to the power of 3. You could do this by means of:

```
=A1^$D$1
=A2^$D$1
```

and so on, in B2:B21. Then, the chart would appear as does the second chart in figure 21.14.

Fig. 21.14

A linear regression line represents a curvilinear relationship poorly.

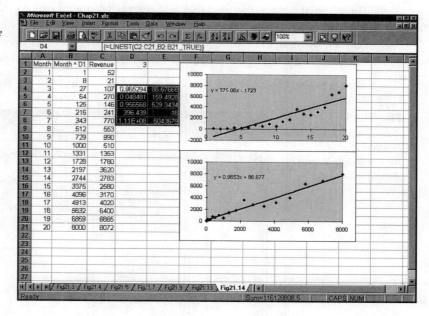

Notice that the linear trendline in the second chart in figure 21.14 tracks the baseline data values much more closely than does the trendline in the first chart. The x-values have been made non-linear, to correspond to the non-linearity in the y-values.

To get the next forecast, you would apply the regression equation to the next time value raised to the third power:

New forecast = Intercept + Slope * (New time value ^ 3)

How can you arrive at the optimum value for the exponent for the time value? Again, use the Solver. Enter the value 1.01 in D1, and then set up this array formula in D4:E8:

```
=LINEST(C2:C21,B2:B21,TRUE,TRUE)
```

Now, use the Solver to maximize the value in D6 by changing the value in D1. The value in D6 is the equation's R^2, which can vary from 0 to 1. The closer the R^2 value is to 1, the better the forecast. As noted in the earlier section on the LINEST() function, you can also use this array formula to obtain the slope and the intercept.

This approach is often preferable to using Excel's Exponential trendline. That type of trendline uses only the slope and power of the x-values to predict y-values: no intercept is used in the equation. But an intercept is frequently an integral part of the forecast equation, and should normally be included.

Therefore, it's recommended that you use the combination of LINEST() and the Solver to arrive at a forecast equation, rather than relying on the Exponential trendline option. Further, using the Polynomial trendline option includes all lower-order polynomials, as integers, in the equation. More often than not, this is neither necessary nor desirable.

Alternatively, the chart with the original values might look like the one in figure 21.15:

Fig. 21.15

A logarithmic trendline is often a good choice for a baseline whose growth slows over time.

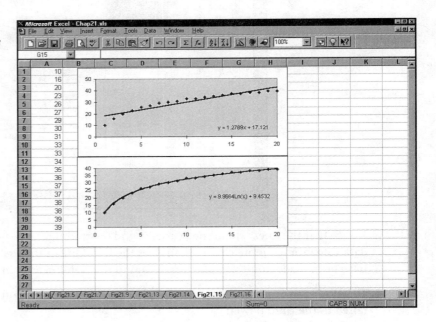

Here, the y-value's rate of increase slows over time. When you see a pattern like this one, it is often best to use the natural logarithm of the x-values to predict the y-values. You could set up this equation:

New forecast = Intercept + Slope * Ln(New time value)

In this instance, you could also use Excel's trendline feature to generate the best prediction equation. After setting up the chart of y-values against time values, insert a trendline and choose a logarithmic trendline. By opting to display the equation on the chart, you will obtain the prediction equation that you can use on the new time value.

The data shown in figures 21.14 and 21.15 are typical of the revenues associated with new products. In the very early stages of a successful product's life cycle, the revenues often display the explosive growth patterns illustrated in figure 21.14. But if you take a longer view—perhaps a year—the revenues might look like those in figure 21.15, where early and rapid growth changes to a more gentle rate of increase. This is yet another reason that it can be dangerous to forecast too far into the future from a relatively short baseline. Explosive growth doesn't continue forever.

What Are the Dangers of Forecasting with Regression?

As useful as regression forecasts are, there are some traps that you need to avoid. Two of the more common mistakes are discussed in the following sections.

Forecasting One Time Series from Another

Suppose that you wanted to forecast the usage of long-distance telephone access lines. On an intuitive basis, one good predictor variable is the demand for new telephone numbers. The more new phone numbers, the more opportunity there is for additional use of lines that connect a local phone company to a long-distance provider.

Suppose that you obtain historical data on monthly requests for new phone numbers as well as long distance access usage for the same time periods. Using one of the methods outlined in this chapter, you create a forecast of usage from requests. The result is a very strong prediction equation, as measured by the R^2 between the x-values and the y-values.

There are two problems with this approach. One is that in order to forecast usage, you must also forecast requests. This begs the question: you have replaced the problem of forecasting usage with the problem of forecasting requests.

The second problem is that both requests and usage are dependent on a time variable that is absent from your forecasting equation. The progression of time predicts increases in both usage and requests. It is not necessarily true that a change in requests *causes* a change in usage. If, by means of partial correlations, you removed the effect of time from both variables, you might find that usage bears no relationship to requests—and therefore you cannot forecast one from another.

Over-Modeling a Time Series

Casual users of Excel's trendline capability often find that choosing a polynomial trendline and increasing the order of the trendline from 2 to, say, 4 or 5 raises the R^2 of

21

the forecast equation. This increase in R^2 indicates a more accurate prediction, and they believe that their forecast equation is therefore better.

Unfortunately, this is not necessarily true. There is almost always some random error in the baseline. Adding more predictor variables, which is what happens when you increase the order of the polynomial equation, tends to capitalize on the chance variation in the baseline variable.

Although this increases the R^2, it does so because of the random variation in the baseline. This random variation is unlikely to display the same pattern in the future. Therefore, the forecast equation is predicting something that is not expected to recur.

There is a statistical test that you can use to determine whether you should add another predictor variable. Suppose that your data are laid out as shown in figure 21.16.

Fig. 21.16

A statistical test can tell you whether you should retain an extra polynomial in your forecasting equation.

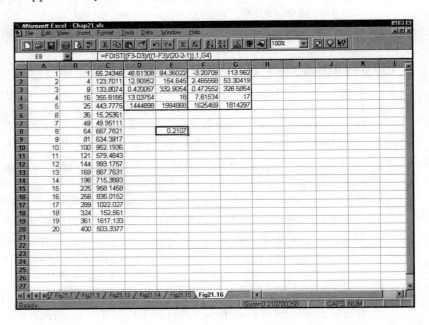

The forecast variable is in C1:C20. The time values are in A1:A20, and the square of the time values (the second order in a polynomial trendline) are in B1:B20. Array-enter this formula:

```
=LINEST(C1:C20,A1:A20,TRUE,TRUE)
```

in D1:E5. Then, array-enter this formula:

```
=LINEST(C1:C20,A1:B20,TRUE,TRUE)
```

in F1:G5. Then, this formula:

```
=FDIST((F3-D3)/((1-F3)/(20-2-1)),1,G4)
```

returns the statistical significance of associated with *adding* the second variable to the prediction equation. In the equation, the number 20 is the number of observations, and 2 is the number of predictors in the second equation. If the formula's result is, say, .05 or smaller, then you can be reasonably confident that it makes sense to use both the original time variable and its square.

Summary

Forecasting is an extremely complex topic, and it's not possible to cover—or even mention—many of its techniques in a single chapter. If you intend to make many forecasts, or to base a critical decision on the results of a forecast, you should first obtain a complete textbook on forecasting techniques and give it careful study.

Nevertheless, the methods discussed here are robust and useful. In fact, advanced forecasting techniques such as Box-Jenkins often simplify into simple exponential smoothing or single-variable regression, both of which were discussed here.

Excel makes it so easy to create forecasts that there is a temptation to over-model the data, or to ask more of the forecast than it can give. Be careful not to stretch the forecast too far out, or it might snap back at you.

chapter 22

Using Advanced Graphing Techniques

22

by Shane Devenshire

In this chapter

◆ **Creating impossible charts**
Dual-axis column, multi-series pie, and scale comparison charts, often considered impossible, are created here using a little trickery.

◆ **Graphing rolling data**
A rolling 12 month set of data is automatically updated monthly without VBA.

◆ **Automatically extending a chart series**
VBA can be used to have Excel add new data each month to a chart.

◆ **Controlling custom chart applications**
All aspects and properties of a chart can be managed by using VBA and form controls.

This chapter attempts to extend your charting skills beyond the basics. You've probably learned how to use most of Excel's basic graphing techniques by trial and error, reading the manual, or by exploring the Help system. Those basic techniques will handle 90 percent of all your routine business needs. But as spreadsheet users become more sophisticated and the demands of business extend beyond the basics, you will need to increase your skills. The techniques introduced in this chapter are intended to help you stay one step ahead in this race. In business, if you don't work to stay ahead, or at least abreast, of the competition, you quickly become a dinosaur. Nowhere is the danger of dinosaurism more prevalent than in computer-related fields. In the brief period since the introduction of the PC in 1981, companies have risen and fallen, seemingly overnight. Likewise, software has burst on the scene like a supernova, and just as quickly, it has flickered and died. So, will the skills you learn from this book actually help you survive? We hope so.

Creating Impossible Charts to Deal with Real Problems

Most real world charting tasks are solved easily and directly with Excel's powerful graphing tools. However, sometimes it seems that Excel can't create the chart you need. When this occurs, things become interesting.

To get your creative juices flowing, this chapter begins by addressing a number of interesting graph-related problems. For example, you will see how to make a dual-axis column chart and a multi-series pie chart, and how to format cells dynamically without using VBA.

Designing a Dual-Axis Column Chart

If you want to create a column chart with two series that are plotted on two separate Y-axes, Microsoft will tell you it's impossible. Yet, such a chart could be quite useful. For example, suppose you want a column chart that plots the national debt and the per capita national debt. If you try to do this, you will find that Excel puts one set of columns behind the other. Figure 22.1 shows the sample dummy data with the national debt expressed in billions of dollars, and the per capita debt shown in dollars. Because one series of values are four to ten times larger than the other, it would be best to display the data on different axes. If you plot both sets of data on the same scale, the larger values will overwhelm the smaller ones.

Fig. 22.1

Notice that this sample data for a dual-axis column chart is laid out in the typical row and column style.

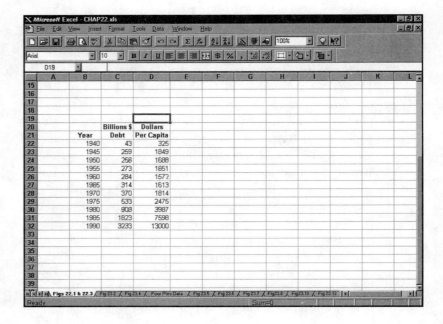

Year	Billions $ Debt	Dollars Per Capita
1940	43	325
1945	259	1849
1950	256	1688
1955	273	1651
1960	284	1572
1965	314	1613
1970	370	1814
1975	533	2475
1980	908	3987
1985	1823	7598
1990	3233	13000

To see what happens when you attempt to create a column chart that plots your data on two axes, follow these steps:

1. After selecting the data you want to plot, choose the Insert, Chart, As New Sheet command to start the ChartWizard.

2. At Step 1 of the ChartWizard click Next.

3. In the second step of the wizard, select the Combination chart type, and then click Next.

4. At the third step choose either format 2 or 3, and then click Next.

5. If you have entered the years as numbers, you will need to change the Use First Column(s) for Category (X) Axis Labels to 1, in Step 4 of the Wizard. Then choose Finish.

6. On the chart select the series that is plotted as a line and choose Format, Line Group. In the Format Line Group dialog box click the Chart Type button.

7. In the Chart Type dialog box select Column, and then click OK.

The result of these steps is less than rewarding, as figure 22.2 demonstrates.

Fig. 22.2

Although the legend and the second Y-axis indicate that you are plotting two sets of data, one set is obscuring the other.

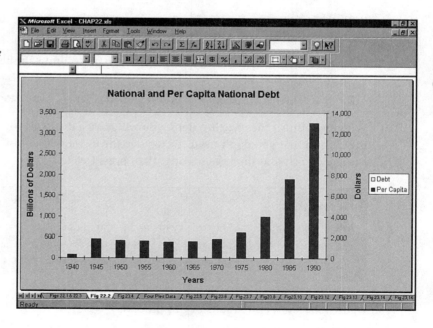

The solution to this sad state of affairs is to lay your data out in a rather unusual manner. What you need to do is to insert two empty dummy data columns between the Debt and Per Capita numbers, as shown in figure 22.3.

Fig. 22.3

By inserting empty columns, which Excel will graph, you set the stage for a useful column-column combination chart.

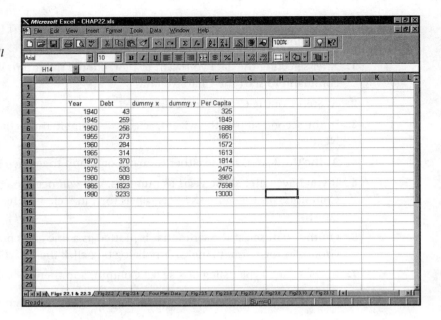

	Year	Debt	dummy x	dummy y	Per Capita
	1940	43			325
	1945	259			1849
	1950	256			1688
	1955	273			1651
	1960	284			1572
	1965	314			1613
	1970	370			1814
	1975	533			2475
	1980	908			3987
	1985	1823			7598
	1990	3233			13000

With the data laid out in this fashion you can overcome Excel's limitations. To create a dual-axis column chart, follow these steps:

1. Select a range that includes the dummy data columns. In figure 22.3 the range would be B3:F14.

2. Repeat steps 1 through 7 from the previous set of instructions.

When you finish the charting steps, you will have a dual axis bar chart, and two items in the Legend that you don't need. To remove the unwanted dummy legend entries, click the legend box and the LegendEntry, then press Delete.

Caution

If you choose the LegendKey instead of the LegendEntry you will delete the entire series, which you obviously don't want to do. You can tell which chart item is selected by observing the Name box on the left-hand side of the entry bar.

Figure 22.4 shows the results of this process.

Fig. 22.4

Note the enhanced border around the title of the "impossible" dual-axis column chart.

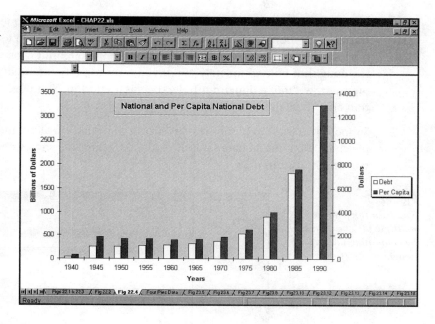

This technique works because you have created two sets of data. One series in each set will not display columns. Because of the placement of the dummy columns in the data range, the blank series from one set overlaps the series with data in the other set; hence, we can view both of the series that contain data.

 Note

The enhancement around the title is created by using the Group Box from the Forms toolbar. The title of the box is removed. Then, with the group box selected, you choose Format, Selected Object, select the Control tab, and check the 3D Shading box.

Creating a Four-Series Combination Pie Chart

Many users assume that you are limited to the types of charts that are found in the ChartWizard, but this is not so. The chart type created in this section should encourage you to explore beyond what Excel appears to provide.

Consider, for example, Excel pie charts; they only let you plot one series at a time. If you want to plot more than one series with a pie-like chart, you can use the doughnut chart type. There is only one small problem with using doughnut charts: you can't eliminate the doughnut hole completely. But if you want to plot more than one series on the same pie chart, without a doughnut hole, there is a solution. You need to create a combination chart type that is not listed.

Suppose you want to plot four years' worth of projected sales figures on one combination pie chart. No unusual data setup is required. Figure 22.5 shows some hypothetical data you might want to plot.

Fig. 22.5

The data range for a multiple pie chart created by combining pie and doughnut chart types.

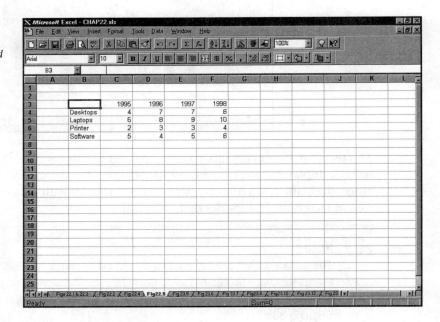

To create a multi-series pie chart follow these steps:

1. Select and plot the data as a combination chart type using the ChartWizard.

2. At the third step of the ChartWizard, choose the fourth format. Then complete the remaining steps of the wizard as needed.

3. With the completed chart on-screen, choose Format, 1 Area Group, click Chart Type, and select Pie.

4. Then choose Format, 2 Column Group, click Chart Type, and select Doughnut.

With some enhancements, you should have a multi-series pie chart similar to figure 22.6.

Fig. 22.6

A multiple pie chart is created by combining pie and doughnut formats.

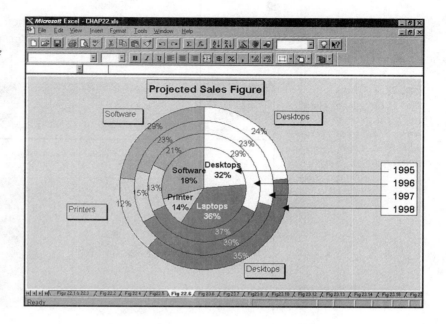

Caution

It is important to choose the correct series to convert to pies or doughnuts. If you reverse the choice, you will create a single pie that covers up all of the other series.

22

Tip

You can create straight lines, arrows, perfect squares, and circles by holding down the Shift key when you draw with the mouse.

This combination chart is not the only unlisted possibility. Create a combination chart and try changing the chart types to see what you can come up with. You may have applications for some of them.

Creating a Multiple-Line Scaling Chart

Many scientific disciplines and some businesses need to compare rankings on a number of test scales to determine the reliability of the individual tests. For example, one might choose to compare results from four intelligence tests for a number of individuals to see if the tests appear to measure similar factors—that is, to see if they are consistent. In other words, you want to create a chart similar to figure 22.7. This is not a straightforward line chart.

Fig. 22.7

This is the type of chart you want to create. The scores of four individuals on three tests are compared.

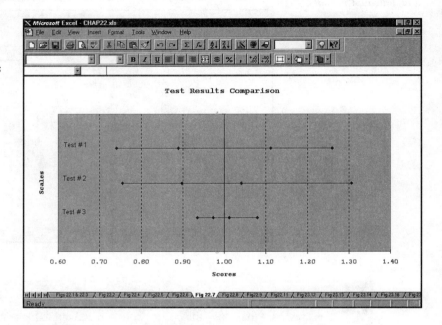

The key to creating this type of chart is the data layout. Figure 22.8 shows how you should lay out the data to produce the chart shown in figure 22.7.

If you try plotting the same data without a break between each set of dat, your results will look nothing like figure 22.7. In figure 22.9, the values in cells B4:E4 represent the test results from one test for four individuals. The values in cells C4:J4 are the test results from the second test for the same individuals. The values on the second row, row 5 in figure 22.8, control the positioning of each test vertically. Each value on the fifth row for any one test must be the same to create the straight lines; the actual values are arbitrary.

After you have laid the data out correctly, you can create the chart by following these steps:

1. Select the data and begin the ChartWizard.

2. At the second stage of the ChartWizard choose a XY (<u>S</u>catter) chart type, and click Next.

3. Choose the chart format 2, and then complete the remaining steps of the wizard.

   To reach the results in figure 22.7, you need to make some additional changes. For example, the X-axis starts at zero and the third data set sits at the very top of the chart, both of which may be unacceptable.

4. To adjust the X-axis, you select it and then choose Format, Selected Axis. Next, select the Scale tab and change the Minimum value as needed. You may also want to adjust the Maximum value in the Format Axis dialog box.

5. You can adjust the Y-axis by selecting it and proceeding as in step 4.

Fig. 22.8

This is the data layout that creates the chart in figure 22.7. Notice the empty range between each data set.

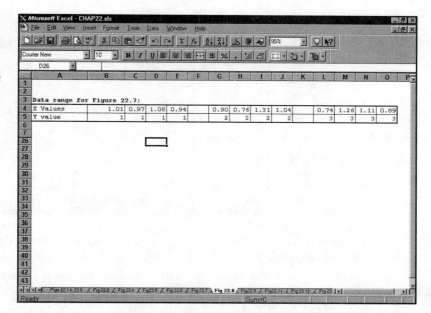

 Tip
You can move from tab to tab in a dialog box by typing the first letter of the tab's name, by pressing the left- and right-arrow keys or the up- and down-arrow keys, or by pressing Ctrl+PgDn or Ctrl+PgUp.

The legend on the chart provides you with a hint as to how Excel is treating your data, as a single series. Because of this, you are somewhat limited in the ways you deal with the various lines. For example, you can format all the data points or each individually, but not one set of test scores as a group. Also, you can't format the lines for each test differently, such as with a different weight, style, or color. If these limitations are unacceptable, you can overcome them with a little more trickery. By laying your data out in a different manner Excel will treat each test as a separate series. The result is shown in figure 22.9.

Fig. 22.9

With this chart you can format each line individually, but it requires a different data layout.

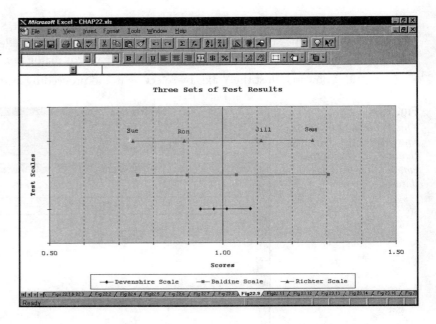

To create this chart, you need to arrange your data as shown in figure 22.10. The scores are entered on the first line of the data area without separation between each set. Then the numbers, which control the vertical positioning, are entered in a staggered layout. To create the chart, first select the data (in figure 22.10 that would be A13:M16), and proceed exactly as you did for the previous chart. Again, you will need to make adjustments to the X-axis and Y-axis scales. In figure 22.9, the data labels for the top line have been linked individually to the data range A10:D10 of figure 22.10.

To link data labels to spreadsheet cells, follow these steps:

1. Select the series you want to add data labels to, and then choose the Insert, Data Labels command. In the Data Labels dialog box, choose the Data Labels option Show Values.

2. Next, one at a time select each individual label and enter the cell reference for the label on the edit bar. For example, the data label for Sue is selected and then an equal sign is entered on the edit bar. Next, the tab for the sheet with the label's text is selected and then the appropriate cell is chosen. Finally, by pressing Enter, the label becomes a dynamic reference.

3. Each data label is selected and repositioned as necessary.

Fig. 22.10

This is the staggered data layout necessary to create the chart in figure 22.9. By using this staggered layout each scale has its own individual lines.

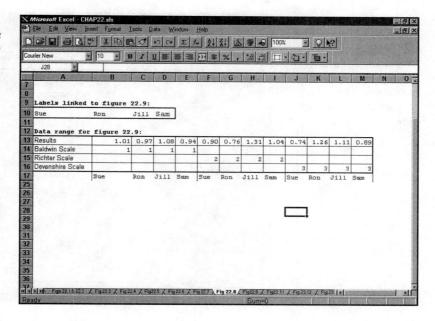

You may want all the scales to extend to the margins of the chart, possibly because you will be normalizing your data as shown in figure 22.11. To do so, you must modify the data area slightly by adding two data points to each series. These points will represent the left and right margin X-axis values. You are adding a maximum and minimum value to each set of results. The value of these endpoints will be the same for each of the series. In order to do this, you will have to arrange your data as shown in figure 22.12.

To create the chart shown in figure 22.11, follow these steps:

1. Select and plot the data as a scatter chart, as you did in the prior two examples.

2. To adjust the X-Axis scale as shown in figure 22.11, select the axis and choose Format, Selected Axis, and click the Scale tab and enter **0.4** for the Major Units and **0.2** for the Minor Units.

3. The individual data points at the margins are removed by selecting them one at a time, and then by choosing Format, Selected Data Point, and selecting the Patterns tab and choosing None for Marker.

4. The data labels are manually positioned above each data point.

Charts of this type are used to compare the results from a number of tests against each other. Such charts have long been used by scientists and engineers, but are now finding additional uses in the business community.

Fig. 22.11
Here is a modified scatter chart that extends all lines to the left and right margins. You might choose this type of chart for plotting normalized data.

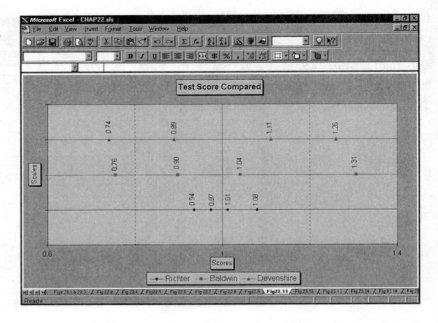

Fig. 22.12
Here is the data area for the chart in figure 22.11, showing the addition of endpoints.

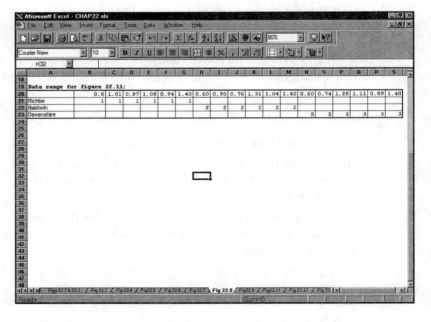

Using Charts to Format Cells Dynamically

Excel will automatically change the text color of values in a cell depending on that value. If you enter **-$5,000** in a cell that has been formatted to #,##0.00_);[Red](#,##0.00) the value will display in red. You can customize this automatic formatting to display colors other than red and to change color at a value of your choosing. However, this dynamic formatting is limited to changing text colors. You can't have Excel automatically change the cell's shading, borders, fonts, or font properties such as bold and italic. You also can't have Excel format based on a non-numeric entry in a cell. That is, Excel won't format the word "winter" to the color blue and "summer" to the color red automatically.

It is possible to create Visual Basic code to make these changes. But if you want to format a cell dynamically without using VBA code, you seem to be limited to changing the color of the entry based on its value. Of course, this must be untrue or this section wouldn't be here. Although it takes some work, it is possible to have Excel format a cell's contents, or the cell itself, based on the value of that cell. In other words, you can have Excel change the format of a cell to a gray background and a bold blue font depending on the value or text in the cell.

This can be done in at least two different ways. One uses graphs, and the other uses pictures. The following discussion pertains to using the picture approach; however, the graph approach can be found on the enclosed disk in a file entitled Chap22.xls, on the Cell Formatting sheet. Cell A1 of figure 22.13 shows the result of entering the text Completed in that cell. When you enter **completed** in cell A1, the cell automatically formats itself to a gray background and bold blue Arial font. If you enter **continuing** in cell A1, it will display as italicized red text on a light-blue background. If you enter anything else, it will display in the normal text font.

Because the process of setting up this automation is rather complicated, a step-by-step demonstration is called for. To set up a dynamically formatting cell, follow these steps:

1. Enter the following five formulas into the cells B9:B13:

```
=IF(A1="Completed","Completed","");
=IF(A1="Continuing","Continuing","");
=IF(A1="Completed",REPT(CHAR(219),8),"");
=IF(A1="Continuing",REPT(CHAR(219),8),"");
=IF(A1<>{"Completed","Continuing"}),(A1,"").
```

The last of these formulas employs an array in the test, which means that the words completed and continuing are enclosed in brackets ({ }). You can enter the values or text of your choosing in these formulas in place of the words completed and continuing.

22

Fig. 22.13

If you change the entry in cell A1, the cell's appearance changes. Note the Camera tool has been added to the Formatting toolbar.

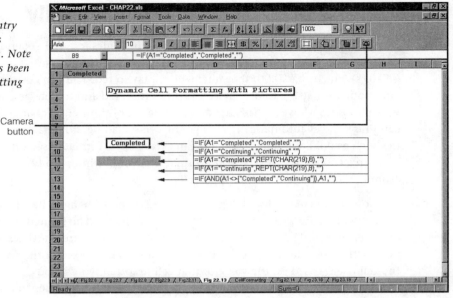

Camera button

2. Format the fonts in cells B9 and B10 to any combination you desire. In figure 22.13 the font in cell B9 is bold, dark-blue, Arial, and centered. The font in B10 is italic, bold, red, Courier, and left-aligned.

> **α Note**
>
> You should not format the font to a size larger than the row height of cell A1, because the font will overflow the cell. This happens because the cell will not change heights dynamically with the technique demonstrated here.

3. Format the font in cell B11 to MS LineDraw, 20 point, centered, and to the color you want as a background. In the example the color is gray.

4. Format the font in cell B12 to MS LineDraw, 20 point, centered, and to the color you want as a background. In the example the color is light-blue.

5. Set the row height for rows 11 and 12 back to the row height of the cell where you will create the dynamic formatting.

6. Because we need a dynamic picture, add the Camera tool to the toolbar by choosing View, Toolbars, Customize, and then pick Utility from the Categories list. The Camera tool is the fourth icon on the first row. Drag this tool to a toolbar.

Tip

You can make space on the Standard toolbar by selecting the Zoom Control box while in the Customize dialog box, and then by placing your mouse over the tool's right edge and dragging to the left.

 Tip

You can use the same technique as described in the previous tip with the Font and Font Size drop down lists on the Formatting toolbar.

7. Turn off Excel's grid lines temporarily.

8. Select cell B11 and click the Camera tool. Position and click the mouse cross hairs near the top-left corner of the cell where you are creating the dynamic formatting (in this case, A1). A dynamic picture will be placed in the cell.

 Tip

You can position the picture exactly in a cell by holding down the Alt key as you drag it.

22

9. Remove all formatting from the picture by choosing F<u>o</u>rmat, Obj<u>e</u>ct, and setting Border to <u>N</u>one and Fill to No<u>n</u>e.

10. Repeat steps 8 and 9 for cell B12. After that, repeat the same steps for cells B9, B10, and B13. It is important that the two cells with shading be placed in cell A1 before the other three pictures.

11. Move to the dynamically formatting cell, cell A1, and format its font to white so it won't display when you enter your data.

Now move to cell A1 and enter one of the labels or values you used in the formulas in cell B9 or B10. The cell will format dynamically. This technique works as follows: the function CHAR(219) returns the Û character which in some fonts (MS Line Draw, for example) displays as a solid fill pattern such as ■. The REPT(character,times) function repeats a character a certain number of times, which will allow us to create a ▬▬▬▬ solid fill pattern in a cell. When you enter text in the dynamically formatting cell the formulas in column B display or hide as appropriate. The dynamic pictures in cell A1 then update to reflect the items in column B.

Designing Dynamic Graphs: One Graph Fits All

In many business situations, large numbers of similar charts are prepared for individual budget items, sales products, revenue groups, geographic regions, and salesperson's results. It would be convenient if one graph could be designed to display any information you intend to graph. For example, suppose you have month-by-month sales and profit data from 50 states. You might need 50 charts to show all the results. This can be logistically complicated, memory intensive, and if a common change is needed, a large number of redundant changes may be necessary. If one chart can be used to plot each of the 50 states one at a time, the process might be greatly simplified. This is just one of the possible situations that may be attacked with dynamic graphing techniques. This chapter will examine five different techniques that can be used to improve your graphing power.

Automatically Charting Selected Data

The first technique to be examined enables the user to see a different chart depending on the location of the cursor. For example, suppose you have a list of individuals and their monthly sales figures. As you move the cursor down the list, a dynamic chart could show you the results for each salesperson.

If you have a data area similar to the one shown in figure 22.14, you can create a graph that charts the data one line at a time, as shown in figure 22.15. By moving the cursor to cell I16 and pressing F9, Excel recalculates the spreadsheet and displays the graph for that line (see fig. 22.16).

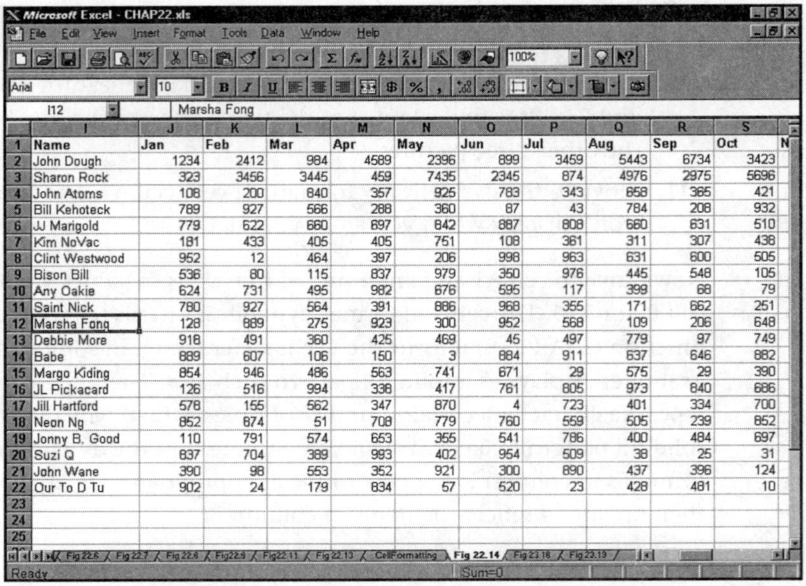

Fig. 22.14

Here is a sampling of some data you might choose to graph automatically.

	I Name	J Jan	K Feb	L Mar	M Apr	N May	O Jun	P Jul	Q Aug	R Sep	S Oct	N
2	John Dough	1234	2412	984	4589	2396	899	3459	5443	6734	3423	
3	Sharon Rock	323	3456	3445	459	7435	2345	874	4976	2975	5696	
4	John Atoms	108	200	840	357	925	783	343	658	365	421	
5	Bill Kehoteck	789	927	566	288	360	87	43	784	208	932	
6	JJ Marigold	779	622	660	897	842	887	808	660	631	510	
7	Kim NoVac	181	433	405	405	751	108	361	311	307	438	
8	Clint Westwood	952	12	464	397	206	998	963	631	600	505	
9	Bison Bill	536	80	115	837	979	350	976	445	548	105	
10	Any Oakie	624	731	495	982	676	595	117	399	68	79	
11	Saint Nick	780	927	564	391	886	968	355	171	662	251	
12	Marsha Fong	128	889	275	923	300	952	568	109	206	648	
13	Debbie More	918	491	360	425	469	45	497	779	97	749	
14	Babe	889	607	106	150	3	884	911	637	646	882	
15	Margo Kiding	854	946	486	563	741	671	29	575	29	390	
16	JL Pickacard	126	516	994	338	417	761	805	973	840	686	
17	Jill Hartford	578	155	562	347	870	4	723	401	334	700	
18	Neon Ng	852	874	51	708	779	760	559	505	239	852	
19	Jonny B. Good	110	791	574	653	355	541	786	400	484	697	
20	Suzi Q	837	704	389	993	402	954	509	38	25	31	
21	John Wane	390	98	553	352	921	300	890	437	396	124	
22	Our To D Tu	902	24	179	834	57	520	23	428	481	10	

Fig. 22.15

To plot the current line of data, the cursor was moved to the appropriate line, and then the F9 key was pressed.

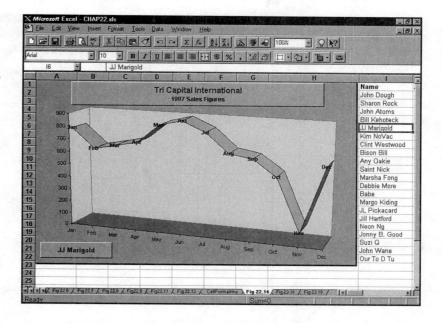

Fig. 22.16

This is a screen shot of the same graph after recalculations on a different row.

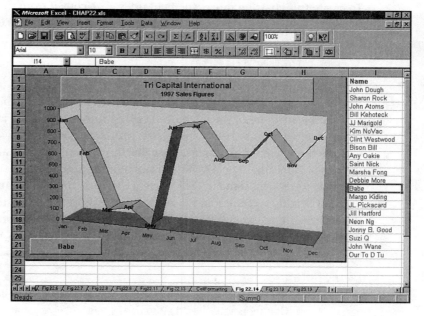

The key to this dynamic chart is the creation of a single charting range, which uses the data from the row on which the cursor is located. As the cursor moves, and the spreadsheet is recalculated, the charting range is updated. Figure 22.17 shows the range that is plotted by the chart.

Fig. 22.17

With a dynamic plot area you create a dynamic chart. The key to this range is a formula of the type shown in cell I32.

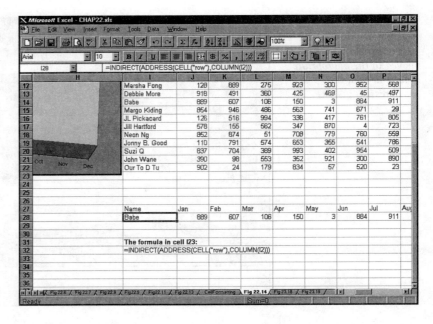

To create this charting range, the field titles were copied from the database area shown in figure 22.14 to row 27. Then the following formula was entered in cell I28 and copied to the right as far as necessary:

```
=INDIRECT(ADDRESS(CELL("row"),COLUMN(I2)))
```

Let's examine this formula. The COLUMN(cell) portion returns the column number of the referenced cell. For cell I2 this is column 9. The CELL("attribute",reference) function returns the attribute of the referenced cell. In this example, the attribute is row, which means the row number of the reference. Although not mentioned in the manual, if you exclude the reference argument, the CELL function returns the attribute of the cell where the cursor is located. The ADDRESS(row,column) function uses the row and column numbers to create a standard cell reference such as H5. Finally, our old friend, the INDIRECT(address) function, returns the contents of the cell at the location specified by the address argument. See the chapters dealing with building formulas for other examples of the use of the INDIRECT function.

 Note

There are alternatives to using the formula approach to set up a dynamic chart. One technique would be to use named relative references. To do this for the data area shown in figure 22.14, you would define the name Plot to be ='Fig22.14'!$J2:$U2 and Title to be the range J1:U1. The first of these names is a relative reference, notice that the absolute dollar signs have been removed from in front of the row numbers. You could then modify the series formula for the chart to read:

```
=SERIES('Fig22.14'!$I$28,CHAP22.xls!Titles,CHAP22.xls!Plot,1)
```

You can easily automate a print macro that will print the graph. Move the cursor down one cell, recalculate the spreadsheet, and print again. The print range and all page setup parameters will only need to be set once.

Caution

If you have a large enough number of print jobs, your computer can overload the print queue. If this happens, you can add a Wait command within a loop to slow things down.

Note

Excel's Visual Basic code, in many cases, runs substantially slower than the equivalent code written in the Excel 4.0 Macro language. This is particularly true for some of the print related commands. If speed is a critical issue, you should test the two languages against each other. Remember you can call VBA from the 4.0 Macro language and vice versa.

22

The example in this section uses a ribbon chart, also known in Excel as a 3-D Line chart. This type of chart is particularly well-suited for tracking a single time series, as was done here. The attractive three-dimensional look of the titles was created by using a button from the Drawing toolbar, but it is not attached to macros. Also, the dynamic text for the salespersons name was created with a linked formula. After you have created the button, a link can be added by selecting the button and typing an equals sign on the edit line. Then you must reference the cell containing the text you want linked. In the previous example, the link reads ='[CHAP23.xls]Fig 23.14'!$I$23.

Dynamically Graphing Different Columns of Data

Suppose that instead of graphing a particular line from a database, you decide you want to chart all the sales by region and by year for you and your company, and possibly even your competitors. The key to this graph, typical of most dynamic charts, is the setup of the dynamic data range. The database area and the desired graph are shown in figures 22.18 and 22.19.

You want to be able to have the graph change its display by some simple method, such as entering some code in a cell. For this graph, you will use a spinner to determine what you want to graph. Spinners are Windows' controls available in Excel for use in forms and charts, or embedded directly in the spreadsheet. When you click the spinner its value is incremented. Based on the value of the spinner, Excel can modify your spreadsheet.

The data in figure 22.18 is grouped by year and within one year by source—that is, by company (abbreviated Com) or competitors (abbreviated Mrk). When you want to plot the combination you must add the two sets of data together. Your database also breaks out the sales into a number of categories. For this graph you are only interested in the categories Market and Region.

To build a graph such as this, the first stage is to collect the data. For this process you will create a dynamic data range. The dynamic data range must accumulate the totals based on the year, market, and source.

Basically, you want to accumulate the total based on some conditions. There are a number of solutions to a problem of this type. For example, you might consider using DSUM functions, SUMIF functions, or Array formulas. There are subtle differences with each method.

The first method examined uses the DSUM function. With some work, you can come up with a single formula for the entire data area. Figure 22.20 shows how you could set up a dynamic data collection area, and a formula that could be employed.

Sometimes a lot of ingenuity is required to design one formula which can be copied over the entire data collection area. For example, the formula in C68 reads:

```
=DSUM(Data,COLUMN(C$67)*2,INDIRECT($B68))*(For<>"Competitors")+
DSUM(Data,COLUMN(C$67)*2+1,INDIRECT($B68))*(For<>"Company")
```

Fig. 22.18

The database area is broken into many categories. Notice that the sales figures are shown for the company as well as for the competition by year.

				FY93		FY94		FY95		FY96		FY97	
Markets	SubM	Applications	Regions	Com93	Mrk93	Com94	Mrk94	Com95	Mrk95	Com96	Mrk96	Com97	Mrk97
B	II	Fuel	West	350	1	420	569	46	1120	1050	8	50	918
SV	I	Communication	South	375	7	450	596	49	1180	1125	5	53	912
C	II	Electronic	East	50	19	60	245	10	400	150	440	14	990
ND	I	Transportation	South	333	33	400	551	44	1080	1000	32	48	922
C	III	Fuel	North	58	40	70	254	11	420	175	428	15	988
ND	IV	Pharmaceutical	North	400	87	480	623	52	1240	1200	8	56	906
SV	I	Transportation	West	242	129	290	452	33	860	725	164	37	944
ND	IV	Fuel	South	267	159	320	479	36	920	800	128	40	938
O	III	Fuel	East	392	159	470	614	51	1220	1175	7	55	908
A	IV	Communication	South	167	186	200	371	24	680	500	272	28	962
C	IV	Transportation	South	33	246	40	227	8	360	100	464	12	994
ND	IV	Communication	North	333	281	400	551	44	1080	1000	32	48	922
CE	II	Transportation	East	117	287	140	317	18	560	350	344	22	974
B	II	Transportation	West	283	289	340	497	38	960	850	104	42	934
C	I	Communication	West	208	292	250	416	29	780	625	212	33	952
C	I	Fuel	West	142	331	170	344	21	620	425	308	25	968
C	II	Communication	East	83	360	100	281	14	480	250	392	18	982
C	I	Transportation	West	75	365	90	272	13	460	225	404	17	984
O	III	Transportation	East	325	367	390	542	43	1060	975	44	47	924
AD	III	Fuel	North	225	401	270	434	31	820	675	188	35	948
SV	I	Fuel	South	308	455	370	524	41	1020	925	68	45	928
C	I	Pharmaceutical	West	275	464	330	488	37	940	825	116	41	936
C	I	Communication	West	42	481	50	236	9	380	125	452	13	992

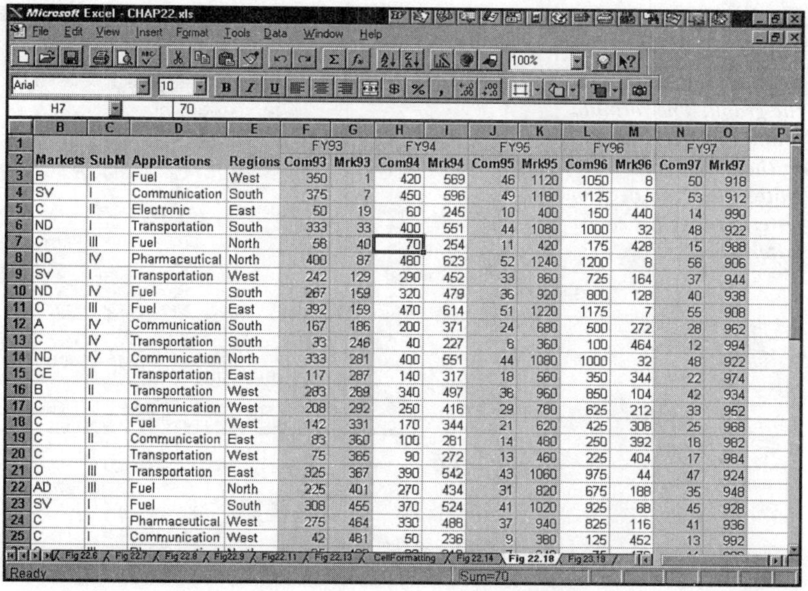

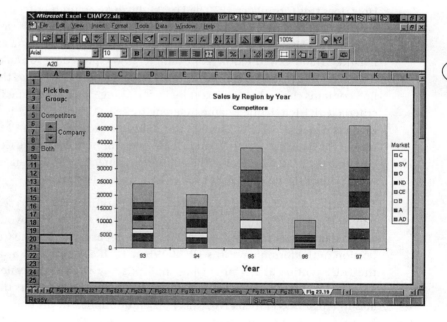

Fig. 22.19

The data for your company, the competition, or the combination of both can be shown by just clicking the spinner on the left.

Fig. 22.20

Here's how you might set up the formula area for the graph. The formula found in C68 is displayed in the box on row 81. Notice that you need one criteria range for each criteria.

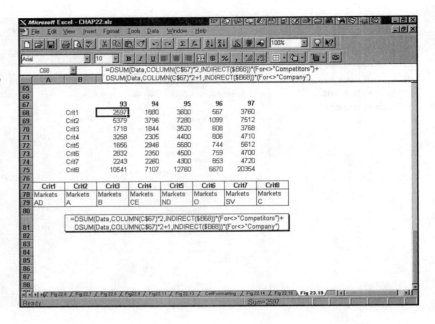

How does this formula work? The DSUM(database,column,criteria) function sums the specified column of the database base on a given criteria. In this case your database has been named Data. To make the formula more flexible, the criteria argument uses the INDIRECT(address) function. For example, in the preceding formula, INDIRECT($B68) tells Excel to use information in the cell referenced by cell B68 as the criteria. Since cell B68 contains the text Crit1, Excel looks for a range with the name Crit1 to use as the criteria. Crit1 is a defined name, referencing cells A78:A79. Crit1 is the condition that Markets equal AD. In this formula the column argument is COLUMN(C$67)*2. If you review the database layout, figure 22.18, you will notice that the Company data is in columns 6, 8, 10, 12, and 14. The column argument for 1993 data evaluates to 3*2 or 6, which is just the column of the database we want to sum.

The next portion of the formula (For<>"Competitors") checks to see if the text in the cell named For is not Competitors. The cell named For will contain your choice, indicating which data they want displayed. If you have not asked to see the Competitors data, this portion of the formula returns TRUE. When TRUE is multiplied by a value, Excel treats the TRUE portion as 1. Thus a value multiplied by TRUE is equivalent to the value times 1 or the value itself. If the contents of the cell For is Competitors then the formula evaluates to FALSE. Excel treats FALSE as 0 when multiplied by another value. Multiplying anything by zero returns zero. Thus the first half of the formula will evaluate to 0 when the text Competitors is in the For cell. In other words, the first half of the formula returns the sum of the company sales for the Market AD, if the user has not entered Competitors in the For cell.

The second half of the formula,

```
DSUM(Data,COLUMN(C$67)*2+1,INDIRECT($B68))*(For<>"Company")
```

works in an identical manner but sums all the competitor's data whenever the word Company is not in the cell For. Together, the two halves of the formula provide the dynamic features we were seeking.

Caution

This formula works just as advertised, but it may not give the correct results. The problem is the criteria range. Referring back to figure 22.20, notice Crit2. This criteria tells Excel to sum all values for markets whose names start with As. It does not sum just those that are equal to A. In the above example, this causes a major problem because the database contains an A and an AD market. If you use this approach, be sure that all criteria are mutually exclusive or change the criteria to indicate an exact match, by using: ="=a".

 Note

Never assume that formulas return the proper results. Although Excel may not make calculation errors, the logic of your formulas should be tested. It's imperative that you check the results of the formulas you construct. First, you can apply the test of reason, which, simply put, asks if the result is in the ballpark. Second, it's also a good idea to run at least one calculation with your formula for which you know the correct result.

One problem with using the DSUM function is the need for many criteria ranges. The next two approaches solve this problem. The first uses the SUMIF function:

```
=SUMIF(Markets,$A28,INDIRECT("Com"&B$27))*(For<>"Competitors")+
SUMIF(Markets,$A28, INDIRECT("Mrk"&B$27))*(For<>"Company")
```

The second approach employs a slightly shorter array formula:

```
{=SUM((Markets=$A50)*INDIRECT("Com"&B$49)*(For<>"Competitors")+
(Markets=$A50)*INDIRECT("Mrk"&B$49)*(For<>"Company"))}
```

Different ranges are used for each example, because these are actual ranges set up for each method in the file found on the disk included with this book.

Both of these formulas have a lot in common with the DSUM formula used above, and therefore need less analysis. However, to make these formulas work, we need to name the columns of our database. The easiest way to do that is to select the entire database, using the first row of titles, immediately above the data, as the top of the database. Then choose Insert, Name, Create and turn on only the Top Row check box. Next create a series of two digit numbers, representing the years, across the top of the location where the formulas will be entered. That is the range B27:F27 in figure 22.21.

How does the first formula work? The SUMIF(range,criteria,sumrange) function totals all items in the sumrange for which the value in range matches criteria. In our example, the market listed in cell A28 is checked against the range named Markets and, when they match the appropriate items in the range specified by the INDIRECT function, are totaled. The "Com"&B$27 argument of the INDIRECT function concatenates the value in cell B27 with the text Com returning Com93. The INDIRECT function uses this result to tell the SUMIF function that the range named Com93 is the range that should be summed. The (For<>"Competitors") portion of the formula was discussed in detail earlier in this section. The second SUMIF function works in an identical manner but sums a column whose range name is referenced in the function INDIRECT("Mrk"&B$27). In the example, this is the range named Mrk93. The results of these two portions of the formula are added to give a final result.

Fig. 22.21

Here is the formula range using the SUMIF approach. Notice that the years are across the top of the formula area for use by the INDIRECT function.

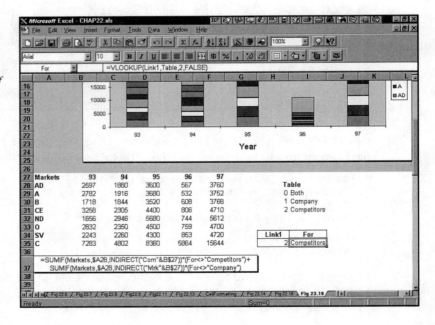

Remember that the reason for introducing this function was to eliminate the need for multiple criteria ranges. But this function has its limits as well. The major drawback of the SUMIF function is that its criteria portion cannot be very sophisticated. You are basically limited to a single condition.

Our third formula allows for more sophistication even though you don't need that in this example. This last approach, using an array formula, also is the shortest:

```
{=SUM((Markets=$A50)*INDIRECT("Com"&B$49)*(For<>"Competitors")+
(Markets=$A50)* INDIRECT("Mrk"&B$49)*(For<>"Company"))}
```

This is an array formula and works as follows. The (Markets=$A50) portion checks each cell in the range named Markets to see if it matches the value in cell A50. The result of this is an array of TRUE's and FALSE's, such as, {TRUE;TRUE;TRUE;FALSE;TRUE;FALSE}. This array is multiplied by an array of values in the range specified by the INDIRECT function. Notice that the INDIRECT function is being used in a manner identical to its use in the previous SUMIF formulas. In the current example, this portion of the formula would return an array of the form {100;200;150;194;163;50}. When Excel multiplies an array of values by an array of TRUE's and FALSE's it treats the TRUE's as 1's and the FALSE's as 0's; therefore, the product of these two arrays is équivalent to {1*100;1*200;1*150;0*194;1*163;0*50} or {100;200;150;0;163;0}. This array is multiplied by the result of the (For<>"Competitors") portion, which was discussed in detail earlier in this section. If the cell named For is not equal to Competitors then the first portion of the formula would be 1*{100;200;150;0;163;0} or simply {100;200;150;0;163;0}. The second portion of the formula works in an identical manner. The results of the two parts are then summed. For example, if For was equal to Company, the above formula would be SUM({100;200;150;0;163;0}+0) or 613. Figure 22.22 show the formula area when this last approach is used.

Array formulas have their limitations also. Their main limitation is their size—an array can contain a maximum of 5,458 elements in Excel 7 and 6,550 elements in Excel 5.

Once you have designed the data collection area, it is a simple matter to graph it. For the stacked column chart shown in figure 22.19, the range A27:F35 in figure 22.21, employing SUMIF functions, was graphed.

To make the graph easy to change, a spinner is added and linked to a range named Link1, cell H35 in figure 22.21. When the viewer wishes to see a different chart he or she simply clicks the spinner. Because there are only three different sets of data to be graphed—Company, Competitors, or Both—the spinner is a reasonable approach. To create the spinner shown to the left of the chart in figure 22.19, follow these steps:

22

1. Display the Forms toolbar by choosing View, Toolbars, and turning on the check box next to Forms in the Toolbars list.

2. Click the spinner tool and drag in the spreadsheet to create a spinner of any size you choose.

3. With the spinner selected, choose Format, Object, and select the Control tab. With only three possible charts, you could set the Current Value to 0, 1, or 2. Set the Minimum and Maximum Values to 0 and 2 respectively, and the Incremental Change to 1.

4. In the Cell Link text box, specify a cell in the spreadsheet where you want the value of the spinner to be placed. In this example you can link to the cell named Link1.

5. Turn on the 3D Shading; it adds a nice touch.

Fig. 22.22

This is what the formula area looks like if the array formula approach is being employed. The formula in cell B50 is displayed on the edit line and in a box below the formulas.

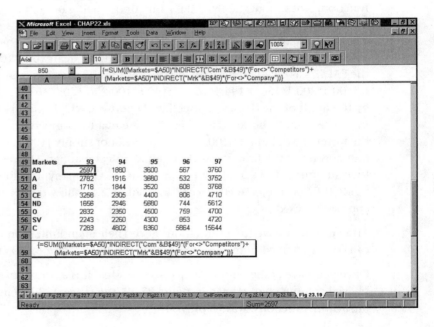

The results of the spinner could be sent directly to the For cell, but to illustrate other possibilities and techniques it is stored in a cell named Link1. A small table named Table showing the possible results of the spinner and their meaning is shown in cells H29:I31 of the same figure. Cell I35 is the For cell and contains the formula =VLOOKUP(Link1,Table,2,FALSE). The For cell also is linked to a text box on the chart directly below the main title. As the spinner changes, the result in the cell H35 changes. This result is used by the VLOOKUP function in the For cell, I35, as the key to look up in the range Table. The result in the For cell is used in all of the formulas in this section to control what data is looked up in the database and, hence, displayed on the graph.

The graphing techniques discussed in this section enable you to graph different columns of data at the click of a mouse without using any VBA code. They also illustrate the value of knowing a number of solutions to a given problem.

Dynamically Graphing Rolling Data

A third and quite different situation occurs when you need to track rolling data—that is, data ranges that change over time. For example, you may want to track the past twelve months of data for the current year and a prior year without having to reselect the data range every month. Or you may need to plot sales figures against profits for all your stores each month. You could delete or move old data and add new data onto the graph range each month, but that's not necessary. In fact, adding new data is often not desirable, for example, if you need to maintain historical data. What you really want Excel to do is graph your data, automatically changing the data range each month. Because tracking rolling data is a common business need, automating the task could save considerable time. And, of course, you can.

Figure 22.23 shows the result you are trying to achieve. Each month, this chart plots the current year's sales and profits up to the end of the prior month. It also allows you to pick which store's data is displayed by choosing from a listbox embedded in the spreadsheet.

Fig. 22.23

This chart automatically displays the year-to-date sales and profits for a store of the user's choosing.

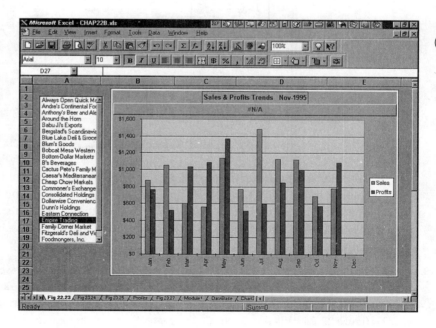

Following good database practices, the account information such as name, address, phone and so on, is maintained in separate areas from the Sales and Profits figures. By maintaining information in separate tables (ranges) you treat the data as you would in a relational database. With this type of arrangement you reduce redundant data entry, for example. Within the spreadsheet environment it could be useful if the data you work with is downloaded from a mainframe or PC database, which contains different files for account, sales, and profits figures.

The account area is shown in figure 22.24 and the sales information in figure 22.25. The profit information is laid out in a manner identical to the sales figures, but is not shown here.

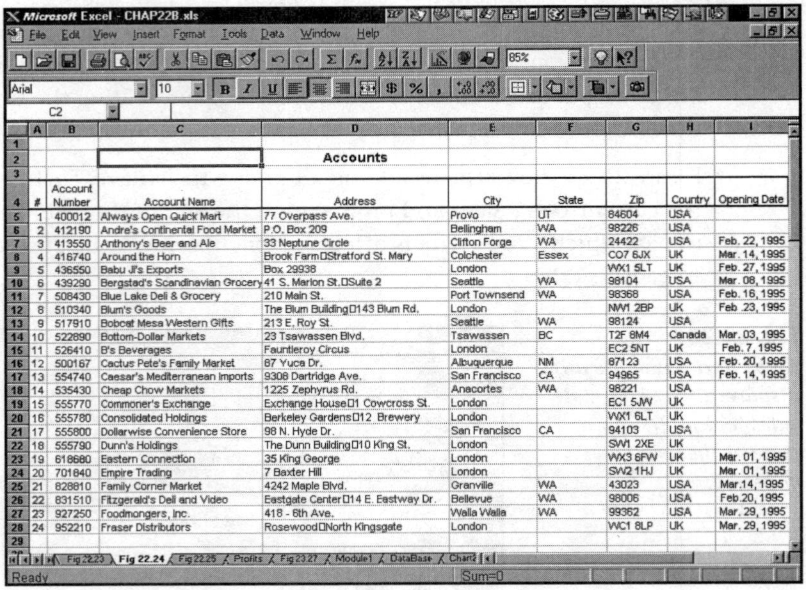

Accounts

#	Account Number	Account Name	Address	City	State	Zip	Country	Opening Date
1	400012	Always Open Quick Mart	77 Overpass Ave.	Provo	UT	84604	USA	
2	412190	Andre's Continental Food Market	P.O. Box 209	Bellingham	WA	98226	USA	
3	413550	Anthony's Beer and Ale	33 Neptune Circle	Clifton Forge	WA	24422	USA	Feb. 22, 1995
4	416740	Around the Horn	Brook Farm□Stratford St. Mary	Colchester	Essex	CO7 6JX	UK	Mar. 14, 1995
5	436550	Babu Ji's Exports	Box 29938	London		WX1 5LT	UK	Feb. 27, 1995
6	439290	Bergstad's Scandinavian Grocery	41 S. Marion St.□Suite 2	Seattle	WA	98104	USA	Mar. 08, 1995
7	508430	Blue Lake Deli & Grocery	210 Main St.	Port Townsend	WA	98368	USA	Feb. 16, 1995
8	510340	Blum's Goods	The Blum Building□143 Blum Rd.	London		NW1 2BP	UK	Feb .23, 1995
9	517910	Bobcat Mesa Western Gifts	213 E. Roy St.	Seattle	WA	98124	USA	
10	522890	Bottom-Dollar Markets	23 Tsawassen Blvd.	Tsawassen	BC	T2F 8M4	Canada	Mar. 03, 1995
11	526410	B's Beverages	Fauntleroy Circus	London		EC2 5NT	UK	Feb. 7, 1995
12	500167	Cactus Pete's Family Market	87 Yuca Dr.	Albuquerque	NM	87123	USA	Feb. 20, 1995
13	554740	Caesar's Mediterranean Imports	9308 Dartridge Ave.	San Francisco	CA	94965	USA	Feb. 14, 1995
14	535430	Cheap Chow Markets	1225 Zephyrus Rd.	Anacortes	WA	98221	USA	
15	555770	Commoner's Exchange	Exchange House□1 Cowcross St.	London		EC1 5JW	UK	
16	555780	Consolidated Holdings	Berkeley Gardens□12 Brewery	London		WX1 6LT	UK	
17	555800	Dollarwise Convenience Store	98 N. Hyde Dr.	San Francisco	CA	94103	USA	
18	555790	Dunn's Holdings	The Dunn Building□10 King St.	London		SW1 2XE	UK	
19	618680	Eastern Connection	35 King George	London		WX3 6FW	UK	Mar. 01, 1995
20	701840	Empire Trading	7 Baxter Hill	London		SW2 1HJ	UK	Mar. 01, 1995
21	828810	Family Corner Market	4242 Maple Blvd.	Granville	WA	43023	USA	Mar.14, 1995
22	831510	Fitzgerald's Deli and Video	Eastgate Center□14 E. Eastway Dr.	Bellevue	WA	98006	USA	Feb.20, 1995
23	927250	Foodmongers, Inc.	418 - 6th Ave.	Walla Walla	WA	99362	USA	Mar. 29, 1995
24	952210	Fraser Distributors	Rosewood□North Kingsgate	London		WC1 8LP	UK	Mar. 29, 1995

Fig. 22.24
One of the three data areas used by the chart in figure 22.23. This database maintains basic account information.

The sales and profits databases are set up to accept new data monthly by just adding a column to the right. Cell C4 on the Sales page (see fig. 22.25) should be named FirstYear. The sales and profits data areas are also designed to retain the historical figures. To maintain flexibility, the accounts, names, sales, and profits areas have been named with dynamic range names.

Dynamic range names use formulas rather than fixed cell addresses to define their ranges. In this example you need dynamic range names for the ranges Accounts, Sales, Profits, and Names. Names is the range where the names of each account are placed, in figure 22.24, this is column C. To create dynamic range names for these four ranges, follow these steps:

1. Choose Insert, Name, Define to open the Define Name dialog box.

2. Enter the name you want on the Names in Workbook box and the formula in the Refers to box, and then choose Add. In the present example repeat this process for each of the names Accounts, Names, Profits, and Sales, respectively, entering the following formulas:

```
=INDIRECT("'Fig 22.24'!$A$5:$I$"&COUNTA('Fig 22.24'!$A$5:$A$500)+4
=INDIRECT("'Fig 22.24'!$C$5:$C$"&COUNTA('Fig 22.24'!$C$5:$C$500)+4
=INDIRECT("'Profits'!$A$5:"ADDRESS(COUNTA(Profits!$A$5:$A$500)+4,COUNTA
➥(Profits!$A$4:$AA$4)))
=INDIRECT("'Fig 22.25'!$A$5:"ADDRESS(COUNTA('Fig
22.25'!$A$5:$A$500)+4,COUNTA('Fig 22.25'!$A$4:$AA$4)))
```

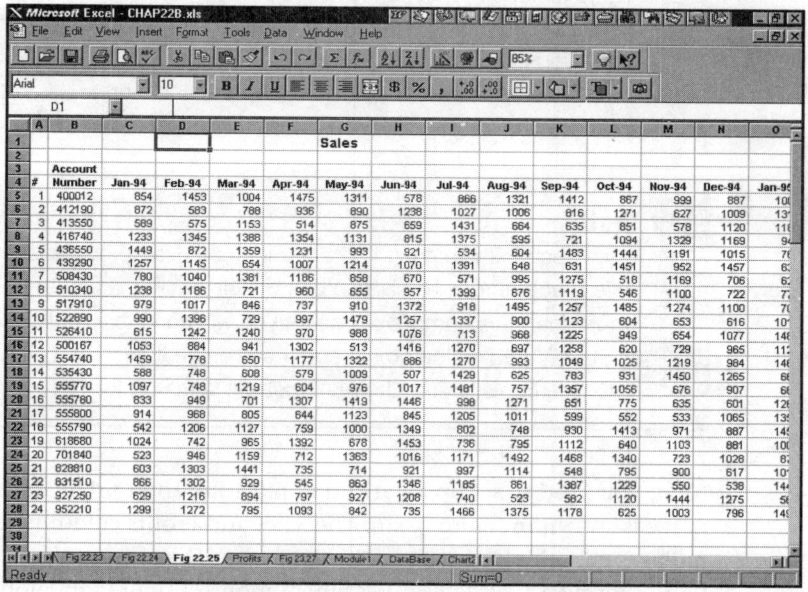

Fig. 22.25

The sales and profits figures are each maintained in separate database ranges.

#	Account Number	Jan-94	Feb-94	Mar-94	Apr-94	May-94	Jun-94	Jul-94	Aug-94	Sep-94	Oct-94	Nov-94	Dec-94	Jan-95
1	400012	854	1453	1004	1475	1311	578	866	1321	1412	867	999	887	100
2	412190	872	583	788	936	890	1238	1027	1006	818	1271	627	1009	13
3	413550	589	575	1153	514	875	659	1431	664	635	851	578	1120	11
4	416740	1233	1345	1388	1354	1131	815	1375	595	721	1094	1329	1169	9
5	436550	1449	872	1359	1231	993	921	534	604	1483	1444	1191	1015	7
6	439290	1257	1145	654	1007	1214	1070	1391	648	631	1451	952	1457	6
7	508430	780	1040	1381	1186	858	670	571	995	1275	518	1169	706	6
8	510340	1238	1186	721	960	655	957	1399	676	1119	546	1100	722	7
9	517910	979	1017	846	737	910	1372	918	1495	1257	1485	1274	1100	7
10	522890	990	1396	729	997	1479	1257	1337	900	1123	604	653	616	10
11	526410	615	1242	1240	970	988	1076	713	968	1225	949	654	1077	14
12	500167	1053	884	941	1302	513	1416	1270	697	1258	620	729	965	11
13	554740	1459	778	650	1177	1322	886	1270	993	1049	1025	1219	984	14
14	535430	588	748	608	579	1009	507	1429	625	783	931	1450	1265	6
15	555770	1097	748	1219	604	976	1017	1481	757	1357	1056	676	907	6
16	555780	833	949	701	1307	1419	1446	998	1271	651	775	635	601	12
17	555800	914	968	805	644	1123	845	1205	1011	599	552	533	1065	13
18	555790	542	1206	1127	759	1000	1349	802	748	930	1413	971	887	14
19	618680	1024	742	965	1392	678	1453	736	795	1112	640	1103	881	100
20	701840	523	946	1159	712	1363	1016	1171	1492	1468	1340	723	1028	8
21	828810	603	1303	1441	735	714	921	997	1114	548	795	900	817	10
22	831510	866	1302	929	545	863	1346	1185	861	1387	1229	550	538	14
23	927250	629	1216	894	797	927	1208	740	523	582	1120	1444	1275	5
24	952210	1299	1272	795	1093	842	735	1466	1375	1178	625	1003	796	14

To understand how the preceding formulas work, consider the last example. The COUNTA('Fig 22.25'!$A$5:$A$500) portion of this formula counts the number of cells in the range A5:A500, which contain items. In other words, it determines how many rows of data the range contains. It is assumed that every row of data has an Item # in column A, that all the row with data are contiguous, and that column A only contains Item #s down to row 500. The choice of row 500 is arbitrary; it just represents the maximum number of rows you expect to have containing data. The value 4 is added to the results of the COUNTA function because the Accounts range starts below the first four rows of the spreadsheet in this example. The second COUNTA function, COUNTA('Fig 22.25'!$A$4:$AA$4), counts the number of columns with titles. Again, the choice to end on column AA is arbitrary. This formula assumes that you will always enter a title above new months of data as they are added to the data range.

The results of both COUNTA functions are values that are passed to the ADDRESS function. If the data area is 25 rows by 20 columns, the ADDRESS function becomes ADDRESS(25+4,20) or $T$29. This result is concatenated with "'Fig 22.25'!$A$5:" to return the Accounts range, in this example, 'Fig 22.25'!$A$5:$T$29. When the completed formula has been entered into the Refers To box of the Define Name dialog box, you have a dynamic range name, one that will automatically resize depending on the amount of data in the given range. These types of range names are discussed in detail in Chapter 8, "Using Descriptive Names for Worksheet Formulas."

 Note

Keep in mind that dynamic range names will not appear in the Name box or the Go To dialog box; they will only be visible in the Define Name dialog box. Nevertheless, you can still enter this type of name into the Name box or Go To dialog box and Excel will take you to the appropriate location.

 Note

Just because you can't find a name in the Name box doesn't mean that it is a relative range name. The Name box will display a maximum of 189 names. If you have more than this number of names you will need to use the Go To dialog box or the Define Name dialog box to see them. Even if you can't pick a name from the Name box you can still enter it and Excel will take you to it.

Next, you need to set up an area that pulls the appropriate data in for graphing. This range is shown in figure 22.26. The Sales and Profits columns contain the dynamic formulas used to look up data in the databases. The area displayed in this figure also contains a formula that determines which month's figures are plotted, and others that create the dynamic titles for the chart. Dynamic titles are those that automatically change from month to month and store to store.

Cell A29 and C29 are named CurrentMonth and Pick, respectively. To set up this data area, follow these steps:

1. Enter the labels for the months in the range A31:A42. Enter the titles Month, Sales, and Profits in cell A30:C30, respectively. All other labels are for documentation.

2. Name the cells A29 and C29, and CurrentMonth and Pick, respectively.

3. Enter the formula following formulas in cells A29, B31, C31, D30, and D31, respectively:

```
=EDATE(NOW(),-1)

=IF(MONTH(CurrentMonth)>=COUNTA($A$31:$A31),
VLOOKUP(Pick,Sales,COUNTA($A$31:$A31)+2+12*(YEAR(CurrentMonth)-
YEAR(FirstYear)),TRUE),"")

=IF(MONTH(CurrentMonth)>=COUNTA($A$31:$A31),
VLOOKUP(Pick,Profits,COUNTA($A$31:$A31)+2+12*(YEAR(CurrentMonth)-
YEAR(FirstYear)),TRUE),"")

="Sales & Profits Trends  "&TEXT(CurrentMonth),"mmmm-yyyy")

=VLOOKUP(Pick,Accounts,3,FALSE)
```

4. Copy the formulas in cells B31 and C31 to the range B32:C42.

Fig. 22.26

This is the dynamic range that is used by the chart in figure 22.23.

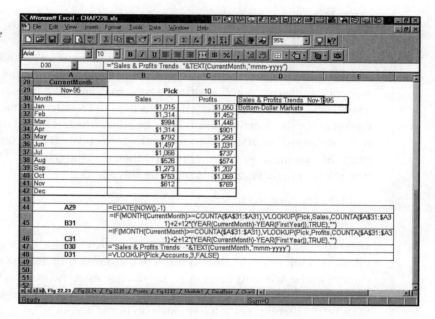

To understand how this dynamic data area works, start with the formula in the CurrentMonth cell, A29, which is =EDATE(NOW(),-1). The EDATE(startdate,months) function calculates the serial number of a date that is a stated number of months before, or after, the startdate. Since this function returns a date as a serial number, it has been formatted to a more useful display. Remember that this cell still contains a number. Because the NOW function returns the current date, the formula returns a date in the prior month. This is done because you only know the sales and profits figures after the month is complete.

Note

The EDATE function is available only if the Analysis add-in has been installed. To install the Analysis ToolPak, choose Tools, Add-Ins, and select Analysis ToolPak.

Cell C29, the range named Pick, is the link cell for the list box to the left of the chart in figure 22.23, of which we will have more to say later. For the time being, keep in mind that the Pick cell will contain the number of the item the user picks from the list box. That number corresponds to the first columns of the Accounts, Sales, and Profits databases.

Cell D30 contains this formula:

```
="Sales & Profits Trends  "&TEXT(CurrentMonth,"mmm-yyyy")
```

The TEXT(value,formattext) function formats a numeric value and converts it to text. We need to use this function because the CurrentMonth cell contains a number and when we concatenate that number with text we have something like Sales & Profits Trends 35467, which isn't user friendly. The & is used to concatenate the text portion of this formula with the function results. This formula, which is linked to the chart title, automatically adjusts each month to reflect the correct date. This is done by selecting the chart title, typing = on the edit line, and then clicking cell D30. Alternatively, you can type the formula =**'Fig22.23'!$D$30** on this edit line.

Cell D31 contains the function:

```
=VLOOKUP(Pick,Accounts,3,FALSE)
```

This function looks up the value of the cell named Pick in the range Accounts and returns the result from the third column of that range if there is an exact match. The third column of the Accounts range contains the names of the stores. This means as the user picks a name from the list box, and the link cell receives the items number, the VLOOKUP function looks that number up in the Accounts range and returns the store name. Finally, the contents of this cell are linked to a button control that has been added below the main title. To add a button control to a chart and link its title to a spreadsheet cell, follow these steps:

1. Click the Drawing tool on the Standard toolbar to display the Drawing toolbar.
2. Click the Create Button tool and drag on the chart to create a button of the desired size.
3. When you release the mouse, the Assign Macro dialog box appears; close it—you aren't using this button with a macro.
4. With the button selected, click the edit line, type =, and click to the cell containing the text you want displayed on the button. You also can manually enter a formula of the form ='[CHAP22B.xls]Fig22.23'!$D$31 on the edit line.

The formulas in columns B and C are virtually identical, differing only in the database range they use, so you only need to examine one of them. The formula in cell B31 is:

```
=IF(MONTH(CurrentMonth)>=COUNTA($A$31:$A31),VLOOKUP(Pick,Sales,COUNTA($A$31:$A31)+
2+12*(YEAR(CurrentMonth)-YEAR(FirstYear)),TRUE),"")
```

The first portion of this formula, MONTH(CurrentMonth)>=COUNTA($A$31:$A31)—which is the test used by the IF function—compares the month number of the range CurrentMonth with the number of items in a range extending from A31 to the same row that the formula is on. That is, for the formula in cell B31, the COUNTA formula counts the number of items in the range A31 to A31, and in cell B32 it counts the number of items in the range A31 to A32. Thus, this portion of the formula returns the numbers 1 through 12, depending on the row of the range B31:B42 that the formula is on. For example, if the CurrentMonth cell contains a date in June, the MONTH(CurrentMonth) function returns the number 6. So for the first six rows of formulas in column B, the test returns TRUE while the last six formulas return FALSE. The next portion of the formula, VLOOKUP(Pick,Sales,COUNTA($A$31:$A31)+2+12*(YEAR(CurrentMonth)-YEAR(FirstYear)),TRUE), looks up the value in the cell named Pick in the Sales table. The column that is returned by the VLOOKUP function is controlled by the last part of this formula.

If you notice the Sales database, you will see that the first column containing sales data is column three, which is for January 1994. The COUNTA function returns a number that represents the line and the month that the formula is on. For January, row 31, this formula returns 1. This is added to two, the number of columns in the database that are to be skipped over, returning the first January column number 3. So this portion of the formula determines which month's data is to be returned.

The second portion of this formula, 12*(YEAR(CurrentMonth)-YEAR(FirstYear)), determines the year of the date in the CurrentMonth cell, subtracts the year of the first set of data from that number, and then it multiplies this difference by 12. In other words, this portion of the formula determines which year's data should be returned. Remember that the range named FirstYear is the first title cell above data on the Sales database. These titles are dates, so the YEAR function returns the first year for which your database contains data. For example, if the current year is 1995, then the formula becomes 12*(1995-1994) or 12*1, which is 12. This tells the VLOOKUP function that the values for 1995 are found 12 columns further to the right than those for 1994. If the current month was in 1994, this formula would evaluate to 12*(1994-1994), or zero. The value of these two portions of the formula are added together, returning the column of the month and year for which data is being sought. In essence then, this portion of the formula has determined which column of the sales database to return data from. The formula in column C works in exactly the same way, but it returns data from the Profits database.

Now that you have a data area for your graph to plot, the construction of the graph is straightforward. After the chart is created, the titles are linked via formulas to the cells containing the dynamic titles, cells D30 and D31 in figure 22.26.

The creation of the list box is straightforward; the column containing the account names in the Accounts database should be named. In the example it is named Names. To create the list box, follow these steps:

1. Display the Forms toolbar by right-clicking any toolbar and choosing Forms.

2. Click the List Box tool and then drag in the spreadsheet to create a list box of the desired size.

3. With the list box selected, choose Format, Object and select the Control tab. In the Input Range box, enter the range where the items you want displayed in the list box are located. In the example, you would enter **Names** because the appropriate range has already been named.

4. In the Cell Link box, enter the cell where Excel will store the number of the item the user picks from the list box. For the example, that is the cell named Pick.

5. Choose the selection type Single to tell Excel that the user can only pick one item at a time.

6. To add some pizzazz to the list box, turn on the 3D Shading option.

Everything is done. Now when the user picks an item from the list box the graph will automatically display the appropriate data.

As you can see, dynamic graphing adds a great deal to Excel's basic charting commands. But you're not finished; there are more possibilities for creating dynamic graphs.

Automatically Adding New Data to a Graph

One of the common tasks facing cartographers is the need to add new data to a chart each month. If you do this with a standard approach you have two choices: you can define the data range to include blank range for future data or you can redefine the data range each month. If you choose the former approach, Excel will display a chart whose X-axis extends to the left for all potential data, while the data markers, such as columns, will only display to the currently available data. The result is a rather unsatisfactory chart, such as the one shown in figure 22.27.

In this section you will see how to create a chart that will automatically display just the data that is available, yet is prepared to accept new data without redefining the plot area each time. So, for example, when you enter a new month's data, the chart will automatically add one more data point to the plot. Also in this section, you will see that the form controls you have been using in the previous sections can be placed on a chart page just as easily as on a worksheet page.

Suppose you chart the number of crates of each type of fruit that your company ships each month. You want to put this chart on its own chart page and have it update automatically each month to include the newest data. Also, you want to be able to pick which product you are tracking. The resulting graph might look like figure 22.28.

Fig. 22.27

This chart is the result of plotting a range that is prepared for additional data.

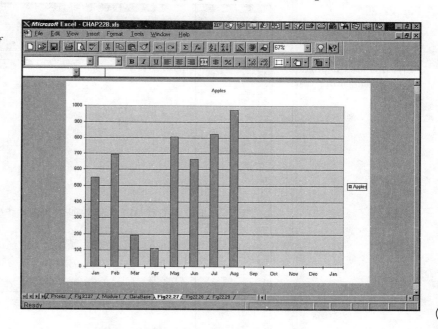

Fig. 22.28

A dynamic graph that will automatically display only the available data. You also can pick which category of data to view.

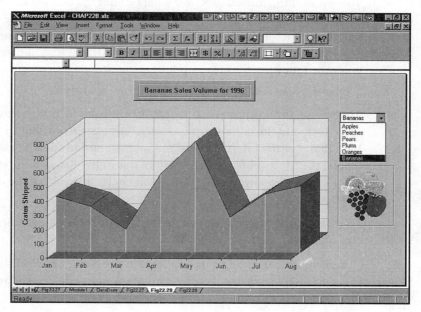

You have seen most of the techniques needed to accomplish this task earlier in this chapter, but not employed to these ends. To start you should set up a data area for the plot that might look like that shown in figure 22.29.

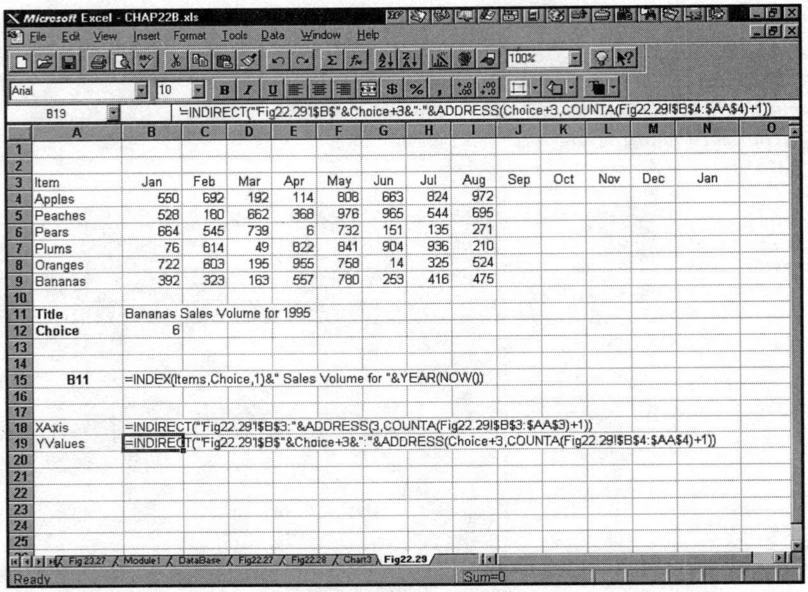

Fig. 22.29

Here is a sample data area of the type you might want to graph dynamically. It is used to produce the chart shown in figure 22.28.

There is nothing unusual about the data layout. As new data comes in you will add it to the empty columns on the right. For later use, you should name cells B11 and B12 Title and Choice, respectively, and the range where the item names are displayed Items. In this example the Items range would be A4:A9. If you want a dynamic title on your chart enter the following formula in cell B11:

```
=INDEX(Items,Choice,1)&" Sales Volume for "&YEAR(NOW())
```

This formula will concatenate the name of the product, the user choice to view with some text, and the current year. The INDEX(range,row,column) function returns the item that is at the intersection of row and column in the area range. In the current example, the function returns the item that is in the first column of Items and on the Choice row. The row named Choice will be the link cell for the drop-down list on the chart page.

To make the chart dynamic you need to define some names using formulas. To create this type of dynamic range name, follow these steps:

1. Choose Insert, Name, Define, and in the Names in Worksheet box enter the name you want to define. For the current example enter XAxis as the first name to be defined.

2. In the <u>R</u>efers To box enter the following formula:

```
=INDIRECT("'Fig22.29'!$B$3:"&ADDRESS(3,COUNTA(Fig22.29!$B$3:$AA$3)+1))
```

3. Repeat the process defining a second name, Yvalues, as:

```
=INDIRECT("'fig22.29'!$B$"&Choice+3&":"&ADDRESS(Choice+3,COUNTA
➥(Fig22.29!$B$4:$AA$4)+1))
```

The first formula in the preceding instructions is designed to define the range where the X-axis titles are defined as XAxis. The first portion of the formula 'Fig22.29'!$B$3:" defines the first cell of the desired range. The second portion of the formula, ADDRESS(3,COUNTA(Fig22.29!$B$3:$AA$3)+1)), determines how far to the right titles extend. The choice of $AA$3 as the ending cell is arbitrary; you should enter the column letter of the last column you expect to ever contain data. The COUNTA function counts the number of columns containing data. One is added to this result because the first set of data is in column B. The address function returns an address based on row and column numbers. For example, if data extends to column I, the COUNTA function returns 8, and the ADDRESS function becomes ADDRESS(3,8+1). The titles are on row three. The result of this function is the address $I$3. In this example, the INDIRECT function is using the range $B$3:$I$3 in the sheet Fig22.29 to define XAxis.

The second formula works in a similar manner, but because it must reference different rows, the row argument also is calculated. The row argument is returned by the Choice+3 portions of the formula. Remember that Choice is the number of the product the user has chosen to display. Because the first set of data starts four lines below the top of the spreadsheet in figure 22.29, you must add 3 to return the correct row number.

Initially, you will plot the range A3:B9 as your chart area; however, the actual choice is unimportant, because you will redefine this range later. To create the chart shown in figure 22.28 follow these steps:

1. Select the range you wish to plot and then choose <u>I</u>nsert, <u>C</u>hart, <u>A</u>s New Sheet. In the ChartWizard, choose a 3-D Ar<u>e</u>a with a format of 6. At Step 5 of the ChartWizard, set Add a Legend? to <u>N</u>o.

2. To make the chart ranges dynamic you need to replace the current ranges in the Series function with the previously defined names. Select the series marker and on the edit line change the formula:

```
=SERIES(Fig22.29!$A$4,Fig22.29!$B$3:$I$3,Fig22.29!$B$4:$I$4,1)
```

to read:

```
=SERIES(CHAP22B.xls!Title, CHAP22B.xls!AXis, CHAP22B.xls!YValues,1)
```

3. To add the drop-down list, display the Forms toolbar and use the Drop-Down tool to create a drop-down list on your chart. You may need to resize your chart to place the drop-down list where you want it.

22

4. With the drop-down list selected, choose Format, Selected Object, and click the Control tab. In the Input Range box, enter the range where the list of items you want displayed is located. For the current example, enter **Items**, the name you gave to the range A4:B9 of figure 22.29, the list of products in your database.

5. In the Cell Link box enter the cell address where you want the user's response placed. In this example, enter the range name **Choice**.

6. Enter a number in the Drop Down Lines box to indicate how many items you want the list box to display before a scrollbar is displayed. For the present data, **5** would be a good choice. Turn on 3D Shading if you want.

7. To add drop lines choose Format, 3-D Area Group, and click the Options tab and check Drop Lines. You can format the drop lines by selecting any one of them and choosing Format, Selected Drop Lines, and then setting the desired Patterns options in the Format Drop Lines dialog box.

9. Link the title to the spreadsheet range Title by entering a formula on the edit bar while the title is selected. In figure 22.28 a button object was used for the title, so the button objects text is linked with the formula =CHAP22B.xls!Title.

10. By default, Excel displays a Y-axis title. To remove this, choose Insert, Axis, and deselect Series (Y) Axis.

You now have a chart that will automatically update to display just the number of months for which you have data. One warning: if you change the name of the sheets referenced by the defined names used by the SERIES formula, you will need to modify the defined names. Because of this, it's easiest to finalize the sheet names prior to defining the dynamic names.

Designing One Graph that Does it All

Quite often your charting needs may seem to exceed what Excel can accomplish with just one chart. For example, one user may want to view the sum of sales by city and year using a column chart. Another user may want to view a pie chart of the data broken out by sales region for a specific year. And yet another user may want a pie chart showing the sum of sales for a given year and sales category broken out by the consumer market that uses those products. With some work, a single chart can be designed to handle all of these needs. In fact, one chart can be designed to handle all of your charting needs.

Introducing the Mini-App Components

This final collection of graphing techniques will add even more flexibility to the graphing process. In this case, you will design a dynamic chart that can view the data views in any number of ways depending on the users' needs. Suppose you have a database that tracks yearly sales figures for you and your competitors. This particular database might be laid out as shown in figure 22.18. You want to allow your viewer to have the option to choose the chart type, and what data is displayed. In the following example your users will be able to cut the data by a particular year, segment, sector breakout, and market. Figure 22.30 is the end product that you will create.

 Note

In the business community the term *cut* is often used, as it is here, to mean you want to examine the data in different ways—that is, why you want to take different cuts of the data.

This chart will change its type depending on what the viewer asks to see. For example, when the user wants to display the breakout of data by market, the chart will automatically change to a 3D pie chart. When they choose to see the data by Sector, it will appear as a 3D column chart.

As has been typical with most of the dynamic graphing techniques presented in this chapter, a major component of this mini-app is the dynamic data collection area. In this example, the data collection area, shown in figure 22.31, is designed for possible printout, which makes the charting task somewhat more challenging. Because the data collection area is being printed, the charts are not plotted directly from this area. They use two other ranges, which are shown in figure 22.32. In addition, you will need to create criteria areas, design the control panel to the right of the chart, and add the VBA code that integrates the entire mini-application.

Fig 22.30

This is the dynamic graph we will design in this section. Notice the control panel on the right enables users to pick exactly what they want to see on the chart.

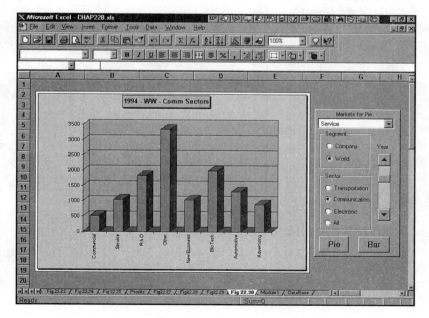

Fig. 22.31

This is the dynamic data collection area for the chart in figure 22.30. The formula in J6 is displayed on the edit bar.

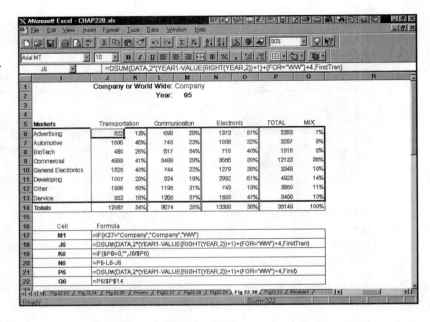

Fig. 22.32

These are the ranges that are plotted on the graph in figure 22.30. Both of these ranges get their data from the data collection range shown in figure 22.31.

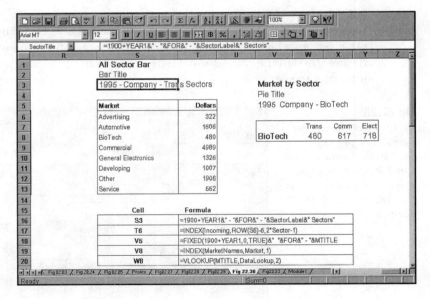

Reviewing the Database Layout

Figure 22.33 will remind you what the database looks like. The information you want to summarize is the sales figures, which are accumulated by year for your company and the entire world (Mrk). For any given row of sales figures you also know what market category the buyer falls into, what type of product you sold (electronic, transportation, or communication), and where the products were sold (region). The breakout of the data is sufficiently complicated to demonstrate techniques that will let you deal with almost any real-world situation.

Before leaving the database area keep in mind that cell F1, which contains the label FY93, is named YEAR. This range will be used to determine which column of data to display as the user request data for a given year. The database, including the first row of titles, has been named DATA.

Fig. 22.33

This is the sample database area you will be using in this section.

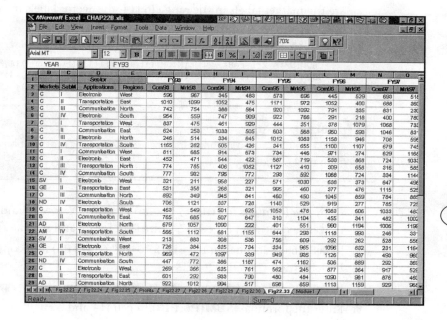

Designing a Data Collection Area

In this section you will design the data collection area shown in figure 22.31. Many of the formulas used in this area require criteria ranges, which will be discussed in the following section.

In addition to Excel's database functions, there are a number of techniques available for working with data in a database, including the Data, Filter, AutoFilter; Data, Filter, Advance Filter; Data, Subtotal; and Data, Pivot Table commands. Which technique you choose is often based on the way you need to display your data. The data collection area you need in this example dictates the use of the DSUM function.

To create a data collection area similar to the one shown in figure 22.31, follow these steps:

1. In cell M1, enter a formula that will show whether the user is viewing the sales results for your companies or for the entire world (the range named SegmentLabel will be discussed later):

   ```
   =IF(SegmentLabel="Company","Company","WW")
   ```

2. Name the cell M1 FOR, and cell M2 Year1. (Cell M2 can be left blank initially.) Also add labels, if you want, in cells L1 and L2.

3. Enter the row and column titles for the data collection area. In figure 22.31 these are the market labels in the range I6:I14, the Sector labels in cells J5, L5, N5, and P5.

4. In cells J6, L6, and P6 enter the following formulas:

   ```
   =DSUM(DATA,2*(YEAR1-VALUE(RIGHT(YEAR),2))+1)+(FOR="WW")+4,FirstTran)
   =DSUM(DATA,2*(YEAR1-VALUE(RIGHT(YEAR),2))+1)+(FOR="WW")+4,FirstComm)
   =DSUM(DATA,2*(YEAR1-VALUE(RIGHT(YEAR),2))+1)+(FOR="WW")+4,First)
   ```

 Note

FirstTran, FirstComm, and First are criteria ranges that will be set up and named in the next section.

---

5. Copy the formulas in cells J6, L6, and P6 down to row 13 and then edit the criteria to read SecondTran for cell J7, ThirdTran for J8, and so on.

6. In cell K6 enter the formula **=IF($P6=0,"",J6/$P6)** and copy it to the ranges K7:K14, M6:M14, and O6:O14.

7. In cell Q6 enter the formula **=P6/$P$14** and copy it to the range Q7:Q14.

8. Enter the formula **=SUM(P6:P13)** in cell J14 and copy it to cells L14, N14, and P14.

9. Name the range J6:P14 Incoming and the range I6:Q14 DataLookup. These two ranges are where the charting areas will get their data.

Add any formatting you want and your data collection area is ready. Of course, you still need to design the criteria areas.

What do these formulas do? First consider the formulas that are in columns J, L, and P. All the formulas are of the same basic form as the one in cell J6:

```
=DSUM(DATA,2*(YEAR1-VALUE(RIGHT(YEAR),2))+1)+(FOR="WW")+4,FirstTran)
```

This DSUM function sums all the data in the specific column of the range named DATA, which meets the conditions of the criteria FirstTran. The column calculation is the complicated portion of this formula. In this case, our users are only maintaining five years worth of data at any one time, so the formula must be flexible enough to determine what year's data is wanted.

The 2*(YEAR1-VALUE(RIGHT(YEAR,2))+1)+(FOR="WW")+4 portion of this formula calculates the column number of the database which must be summed. The cell named YEAR contains the label FY93, which represents the first year of data in the database. This figure will change every year since only five years of data are kept. The cell YEAR1 is the link cell for the scroll bar control on the control panel that allows the user to pick the year for which data is displayed. The link cell will be discussed in the section dealing with the design of the control panel.

The (FOR="WW") portion of the formula evaluates to TRUE if the user chooses to see figures for the entire world and FALSE if he requests the companies figures. The figures for the world are always one column to the right of the companies figures in the database, so when the user chooses to see world wide figures, the column count is increased by 1 because TRUE added to a value takes a value of 1 and FALSE a value of 0. If the user picks World 1994, then this portion of the formula evaluates to 2*(94-93+1)+(1)+4 or 2*2+5 = 9. Referring to figure 22.33, you will see that the ninth column of the database contains the world figures for 1994. Although you haven't set it up yet, the criteria FirstTran will find all the rows in the database for which the Markets column contains the abbreviation for Advertising, AD, and has a value in the Sector Applications column of Transportation. Thus, the criteria states that the Sector Applications field of the database contains Transportation, and the Markets field contains AD. Therefore, the entire formula sums the ninth column of the database, DATA, which meets the two criteria just listed.

The formulas in columns L and P work in a similar manner. But for column P you want all sectors (Transportation, Communication, and Electronic) so your criteria range will only need to specify which market you are interested in. On row six this would be Advertising.

Because there are only three Sectors and we know two plus the total, we can calculate the third one, Electronic, by subtracting the first two from the total. This is what the formula in cell N6, =P6-L6-J6, is doing. This rather unusual approach will make the criteria area simpler to design.

The formulas in columns K, M, and O calculate what percent of a given market the current sector represents. This is a row-wise percentage. For example, the formula in cell K6 calculates what percent the Transportation sector is of the total Advertising market. The formulas in column Q are column-wise percentages of the totals. For example, the formula in cell Q6 calculates what percent of all sales is the total Advertising market sales.

Creating a Criteria Area

For each DSUM function in the data collection area you will need to create a different criteria range. In this example that means twenty-four criteria ranges. Remember, the DSUM function needs to know for which items it should sum in a given range. Considering the data collection area that was shown in figure 22.31, the DSUM formulas need to know for which market (shown in column I) and which sector (shown on row 5) it should be getting data from the database. A portion of the criteria ranges are shown in figure 22.34.

Fig. 22.34

A portion of the criteria range is shown here.

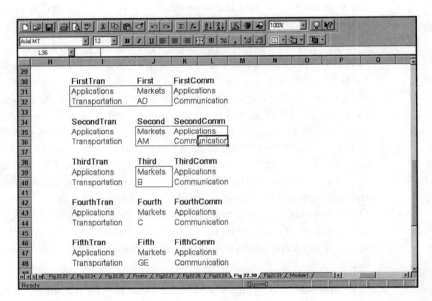

To create the criteria ranges for the Advertising market, follow these steps:

1. The criteria range for the DSUM function in cell J6 of figure 22.31 is shown in cells I31:J32. The labels on the first row above the data in the database are Applications and Market. The actual title of the Applications column is Sector Applications but you can only use the line immediately above the data as titles in the criteria range. So enter **Applications** in cell I31 and Markets in cell J32.

2. Enter the criteria **Transportation** in cell I32 and **AD**, the abbreviation used in the database for Advertising, in J32.

3. Name the range I31:J32 **FirstTran**.

4. The criteria for the DSUM function in cell L6 is the range J31:K32. Notice that the Markets portion of the two criteria overlap; this means you only need to enter the

Markets portion of the criteria once. Follow steps 1-3 above to create this criteria but enter **Communication** in cell K32. Then name the range **FirstComm**.

5. The criteria DSUM function in the TOTAL column, cell P6, for example, only needs to specify the market not the sector. For this reason you can use the Markets portion of the previous criteria. Just name the range J31:J32 **First** and you're with the first set of criteria; now you need to prepare the remaining seven sets.

The overlapping nature of the criteria ranges is illustrated in figure 22.34 where FirstTran is bordered for the first set of criteria, SecondComm is bordered in the second set, and Third is bordered in the third set. The names above the criteria ranges are not necessary but provide useful documentation.

Designing the Charting Ranges

Next turn to the two charting ranges shown in figure 22.32. The range S6:T13 is used to plot the bar chart of all the markets for a particular sector as shown in figure 22.30. The range V7:Y8 is used to plot the breakout of a particular market into its sectors as is shown in the pie chart in figure 22.35.

Fig. 22.35

This is another cut of the data using the same chart area to plot a breakout of the BioTech market into its three component sectors.

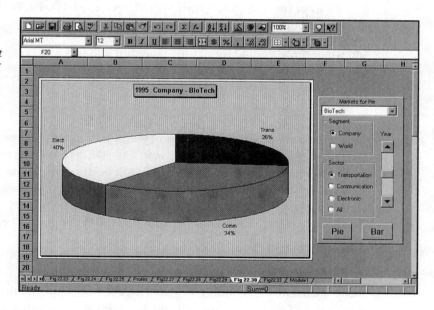

To set up these charting ranges, follow these steps:

1. In cell S3 enter the formula that used as the bar chart's title and name the cell **BarTitle**:

```
=1900+YEAR1&" - "&FOR&" - "&SectorLabel&" Sectors"
```

2. In cell T6 enter the following formula, which picks the appropriate column of data from the data collection area, and then copy it down to T13:

```
=INDEX(Incoming,ROW(S6)-5,2*Sector-1)
```

3. Name the range S6:S13 **MarketNames**.

4. In cell V5 enter the following formula for the title of the pie chart shown in figure 22.35, and then name the range **PieTitle**:

```
=1900+YEAR1&" "&FOR&" - "&MTITLE
```

5. In cell V8 enter the following formula, which determines which Market you are breaking out into sectors, and then name the cell **MTITLE** (the range Market will be discussed in the next section.):

```
=INDEX(MarketNames,Market,1)
```

6. In cell W8 enter the following formula, which returns the Sector figures for the market specified in cell MTITLE, and then copy this formula to X8:Y8 and change the last argument to 4 and 6, respectively:

```
=VLOOKUP(MTITLE,DataLookup,2)
```

7. Name the Range S5:T13 **Data2**. This range is used by a macro to create a column chart of the data. Name the range V7:Y8 **Graph1Data**. This range will be used by the VBA code to create a 3D pie chart.

Add whatever labels and formatting you want and this area is complete.

How do the formulas in this area work? The formula in cell S3 is used as a dynamic chart title:

```
=1900+YEAR1&" - "&FOR&" - "&SectorLabel&" Sectors"
```

This formula concatenates a number of items. First it adds the two-digit year in the cell YEAR1 to 1900 to create a four-digit year. The FOR cell contains either the label Company or WW. The SectorLabel cell, which will be discussed in the next section, contains the name of the sector the user has chosen to view. The formula in cell V5 works in a similar manner. It is the dynamic title for the pie chart. The only difference is its last argument, MTITLE, which concatenates the Market name to the end of the chart title.

Column T contains formulas of the form:

```
=INDEX(Incoming,ROW(S6)-5,2*Sector)
```

The range named Incoming is the data range J6:P14, shown in figure 22.31. The range named Sector is the link cell which records the user's choice of sector on the control panel in figure 22.30 and will be discussed in the next section. The INDEX(*range,row,column*) function returns the information at the intersection of *row* and *column* in *range*. For example, suppose the user has chosen to view the Electronic sector, column N in the data collection area, then the formula in cell T6 becomes =INDEX(J6:P14,6-5,2*3) or =INDEX(I6:P14,1,6). The first row and sixth column of the Incoming range is the cell containing the Advertising markets Electronic figures.

The second charting range contains two basic formulas: =INDEX(MarketNames,Market,1), which is in cell V8 and is named MTITLE, and VLOOKUP(MTITLE,DataLookup,2), which is in cell W8. Market is the link cell for the market drop-down list on the control panel, which will be discussed in the following section. The INDEX function determines the name of the market the user requested. For example, if the user picks the first Market on the list, the INDEX function becomes =INDEX(MarketNames,1,1), which evaluates to Advertising, the value in the first row and column of the range named MarketNames. The VLOOKUP functions in cells W8:Y8 look up the sector figures for the chosen market. For example, if the user has chosen the BioTech market then the formula in cell W8 looks up BioTech in the DataLookup range and returns the value from the second column of that range.

Designing a Control Panel

The control panel is the center of all the action. The user never needs to see anything but the graph and the control panel. The control panel controls every change you want to make to the chart.

To design the control panel, the form controls were put on top of a large button to which a macro is not assigned. Using the Forms toolbar, two group boxes are added for Segment and Sector. Option buttons, also from the Forms toolbar, are placed inside the groups. A scrollbar for scrolling through the available years is added, along with two buttons to modify the current chart to a pie or 2D bar. Finally a drop-down list is added for picking the market if the user wants to see a pie chart of one specific market. If you know how to set up these controls, skip this section. Otherwise, to set up the control panel, follow these steps:

1. Display the Forms toolbar by right-clicking any toolbar and choosing Forms.
2. Click the Create Button tool and drag to create a button of the size large enough to handle all the controls. When the Assign Macro dialog box appears, click Cancel. Then remove the button text by selecting it and pressing Delete.
3. To add a group box, click the Group Box tool and drag to create a box of the desired size. Highlight the group box text and replace it with any desired text. In the current example, the first group box text is Segment and the second one is Sector.
4. Because many of the form controls return values to the spreadsheet, you need to set up the link ranges for the control panel. Figure 22.36 shows this range. Currently, the only thing you need to do is name cells C23, C24, and C25 Market, Sector, and Segment, respectively, and if you want add the labels shown in cells B23:B25, you can.
5. Within the group boxes you need to add option buttons. To do this, click the Option Button tool and drag to create an option button inside one of the group boxes. Replace the option button text with the text you want. In this example, the first option button's text is Company.

22

Fig. 22.36

This is the link range for a number of controls on the control panel.

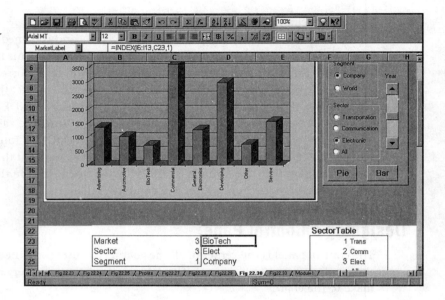

6. To format the option button, right-click it, choose Format Object, and select the Control tab. For the Company button you should enter Segment in the Cell Link box, and then turn on 3D Shading.

7. Add the five remaining option buttons (repeat steps 5 and 6 for each button). Place an additional option button in the Segment group box and change its text to World.

   Add four additional option buttons to the Sector group box, naming them Transportation, Communication, Electronic, and All. Using the method in step 6, link any one of the Sector option buttons to the cell named Sector. Notice that all option buttons in a single option box automatically link to the same cell, so you only need to link one to link them all.

8. Follow the procedure in step 2 to add two more buttons at the bottom of the control panel. For these two buttons change their text to read Pie and Bar.

9. Using the Label tool on the Forms toolbar add any labels you need. In this example, add a label at the top reading Markets for Pie and one to the right of the Segment option box reading Year.

10. Use the Scroll Bar tool on the Forms toolbar to add a scroll bar. In this example the scroll bar will allow users to pick the year they want to see. Right-click the scroll bar and select the Control tab and set the various options as desired. For the current example, set the Minimum Value to 93, the earliest year in the database. Set the Maximum Value to 97, the Incremental Change to 1, and the Page Change to 2. Enter the range named YEAR1 in the Cell Link box and turn on 3D Shading.

11. Add a drop-down list using the Drop-Down tool on the Forms toolbar. Then right-click the drop-down list, select the Control tab and set the desired options. In the current example, enter **MarketNames** in the Input Range box to tell Excel where the list to be displayed is located. Also, enter the range name **Market** in the Cell Link box to indicate where the user's response will be placed. Set the Drop Down Lines box to the number of items you want displayed without a scrollbar, in this case, enter **8**.

12. When the results of the controls are returned to the spreadsheet you may want to convert the numerical values into their text equivalent. To do this you should add a lookup table for the possible sectors. In cells F23:F26 enter the numbers **1** to **4**. In the cells G23:G26 enter the labels **Trans**, **Comm**, **Elect**, and **All**. Name the range G23:G26 **SectorTable**.

13. Enter the following formula in cells D23:D25 to convert the numeric responses to text, and then name the cells **MarketLabel**, **SectorLabel**, and **SegmentLabel**, repetively:

```
=INDEX(MarketNames,Market,1)
=VLOOKUP(Sector,SectorTable,2)
=IF(Segment=1,"Company","World Wide")
```

Creating the VBA Code

In this section you will create the code necessary to automate the entire charting process from the control panel. First, you should create any type of chart using one of the two charting ranges and place that chart near the control panel. With a basic chart created you can then record the process of modifying it to create the types of charts you want. Finally, you modify the code as necessary and link the code to various controls on the control panel. To assign a macro to a control, right-click the control and choose Assign Macro. Select the macro you want to assign to the control the Macro Name/Reference list. All of the following code is included on the Module1 sheet in the file Charting.xls on the included disk.

The following macro creates a 2D column chart based on the currently selected data. It is attached to the button labeled Bar on the control panel.

```
Sub Bar()
    Application.ScreenUpdating = False
```

The final line suppresses screen redrawing while the macro is running, which makes your code run faster. This line cannot be recorded.

The next eight lines select the chart, change it to a column chart, remove the data labels and legend, and position the plot area on the chart.

22

```
ActiveSheet.DrawingObjects("Chart 10").Select
ActiveChart.Type = xlColumn
ActiveChart.ApplyDataLabels Type:=xlNone, LegendKey:=False
ActiveChart.PlotArea.Select
Selection.Top = 37
Selection.Height = 178
Selection.Left = 3
Selection.Width = 278
```

The color and pattern for the chart and plot area are set with the next nine lines.

```
With Selection.Interior
    .ColorIndex = 38
    .Pattern = xlSolid
End With
ActiveChart.ChartArea.Select
With Selection.Interior
    .ColorIndex = 39
    .Pattern = xlSolid
End With
```

Next, the title is formatted, the chart deactivated, and the cursor placed in cell G6.

```
ActiveChart.ChartTitle.Select
With Selection.Border
    .Weight = xlHairline
    .LineStyle = xlAutomatic
End With
Selection.Shadow = True
Selection.Interior.ColorIndex = xlNone
ActiveWindow.Visible = False
Windows("Charting.xls").Activate
Range("G6").Select
End Sub
```

The following code is linked to the control panel button entitled Pie. This macro creates a 3D Pie chart based on the currently selected data.

The first lines of code work exactly as in the Sub Bar marco except that a pie chart is created.

```
Sub Pie()
    Application.ScreenUpdating = False
    ActiveSheet.DrawingObjects("Chart 10").Select
    ActiveSheet.ChartObjects("Chart 10").Activate
    ActiveChart.AutoFormat Gallery:=xl3DPie, Format:=7
    ActiveChart.SeriesCollection(1).Points(1).Select
```

The following lines set the color and patterns for a number of pie slices.

```
With Selection.Interior
    .ColorIndex = 28
    .Pattern = xlSolid
End With
ActiveChart.SeriesCollection(1).Points(2).Select
With Selection.Interior
    .ColorIndex = 5
    .Pattern = xlSolid
```

```
      End With
      ActiveChart.SeriesCollection(1).Points(3).Select
      With Selection.Interior
          .ColorIndex = 14
          .Pattern = xlSolid
      End With
```

The next lines format the chart area and the chart title.

```
      ActiveChart.ChartArea.Select
      With Selection.Border
          .Weight = xlHairline
          .LineStyle = xlAutomatic
      End With
      ActiveChart.ChartTitle.Select
      With Selection.Border
          .Weight = xlHairline
          .LineStyle = xlAutomatic
      End With
      Selection.Shadow = True
      With Selection.Interior
          .ColorIndex = 1
          .Pattern = xlSolid
      End With
```

The edit mode is deactived and the cursor moved to cell G6.

```
      ActiveWindow.Visible = False
      Windows("Charting.xls").Activate
      Range("G6").Select
  End Sub
```

The following macro is assigned to all four option buttons in the Sector option box. When you assign a macro to a control and use the linked cell, the linked cell is changed first and then the macro runs. The following code rebuilds the chart from scratch, creating a 3D column chart of all of the markets for the selected Sector. Whatever Segment and Year are currently being used are not changed during the macro. Those attributes are independent of the sector.

Again the screen redrawing is suppressed and then the chart selected.

```
  Sub SectorBreakout()
      Application.ScreenUpdating = False
      ActiveSheet.DrawingObjects("Chart 10").Select
      ActiveSheet.ChartObjects("Chart 10").Activate
```

The ChartWizard creates a 3D column chart using the data in range Data2.

```
      ActiveChart.ChartWizard source:=Workbooks("Charting.xls").Sheets("Fig 22.30" _)
          .Range("Data2"), PlotBy:=xlRows, CategoryLabels:=1, _
          SeriesLabels:=1
      ActiveChart.AutoFormat Gallery:=xl3DColumn, Format:=4
```

22

The chart title is linked to the range named SectorTitle and formatted.

```
ActiveChart.ChartTitle.Select
Selection.Text = "='[Charting.xls]Fig 22.30'!SectorTitle"
With Selection.Border
    .Weight = xlHairline
    .LineStyle = xlAutomatic
End With
  Selection.Shadow = True
With Selection.Interior
    .ColorIndex = 24
    .PatternColorIndex = 1
    .Pattern = xlSolid
End With
```

The chart area is formatted and the title positioned.

```
ActiveChart.ChartArea.Select
With Selection.Border
    .Weight = xlHairline
    .LineStyle = xlAutomatic
End With
ActiveChart.ChartTitle.Select
Selection.Left = 150
Selection.Top = 5
```

The category axis is formatted and the chart area formatted.

```
ActiveChart.ChartArea.Select
ActiveChart.Axes(xlCategory).Select
Selection.TickLabels.Font.Size = 7
Selection.TickLabels.Orientation = xlUpward
ActiveChart.ChartArea.Select
Selection.Shadow = True
Selection.Interior.ColorIndex = 34
ActiveChart.Walls.Select
With Selection.Border
    .ColorIndex = 1
    .Weight = xlThin
    .LineStyle = xlContinuous
End With
Selection.Interior.ColorIndex = 37
ActiveChart.Floor.Select
Selection.Interior.ColorIndex = 41
```

The chart is deactivated and the cursor placed at cell G6.

```
    ActiveWindow.Visible = False
    Windows("Charting.xls").Activate
    Range("G6").Select
End Sub
```

The fourth and final macro is assigned to the drop-down list on the control panel. This macro creates a pie chart of the chosen market. It displays market sales broken out by sector.

The macro begins as did the prior macros and then uses the ChartWizard to produce a 3D pie from the data in the range named GraphData.

```
Sub Markets()
    Application.ScreenUpdating = False
    ActiveSheet.DrawingObjects("Chart 10").Select
    ActiveSheet.ChartObjects("Chart 10").Activate
    ActiveChart.ChartWizard source:=Workbooks("Charting.xls").Sheets("Fig 22.30" _)
        .Range("Graph1Data"), PlotBy:=xlRows, CategoryLabels:=1, _
        SeriesLabels:=1
    ActiveChart.AutoFormat Gallery:=xl3DPie, Format:=7
```

Next the chart area is formatted and the title linked to the cell named PieTitle and then formatted.

```
    ActiveChart.ChartArea.Select
    Selection.Shadow = True
    With Selection.Interior
        .ColorIndex = 24
        .PatternColorIndex = 2
        .Pattern = xlGray25
    End With
    ActiveChart.ChartTitle.Select
    Selection.Text = "='[Charting.xls]Fig 22.30'!PieTitle"
    Selection.Shadow = True
    Selection.Interior.ColorIndex = 24
```

Some of the pie slices are formatted and then the cursor ends in cell G6.

```
    ActiveChart.ChartArea.Select
    ActiveChart.SeriesCollection(1).Points(1).Select
    With Selection.Interior
        .ColorIndex = 9
        .PatternColorIndex = 9
        .Pattern = 17
    End With
    ActiveChart.SeriesCollection(1).Points(2).Select
    With Selection.Interior
        .ColorIndex = 13
        .PatternColorIndex = 9
        .Pattern = 17
    End With
    ActiveWindow.Visible = False
    Windows("Charting.xls").Activate
    Range("G6").Select
End Sub
```

For the control panel created in this section, four VBA subroutines were created: one each for the Pie and Bar buttons, one for the Markets drop-down list, and one for the Sector option buttons. The same macro was assigned to each of the sector option buttons. Because you can run code from your control panel, you can automate anything you want Excel to do to your chart.

22

Summary

In this chapter you have seen how to create a number of "impossible" but useful charts. You have also designed a number of dynamic charts that adjust to display what the user wants by either clicking a control or by using dynamic names. You have discovered that form controls can be added onto the worksheet, onto chart pages, or even onto charts that are imbedded on worksheets. Of course, these controls are also designed for creating custom dialog boxes, something you did not do in this chapter. Finally, you put together a mini-application that used VBA code to control the charting process, which might be difficult to control with any other technique. When you have mastered all the techniques in this chapter, you should be well on your way to being an expert chart maker. Hopefully, the ideas introduced here also will suggest other possibilities, as yet unimagined.

Programming with VBA

chapter 23

Managing Dialogs in VBA

23

by Conrad Carlberg

In this chapter

◆ **What dialog boxes can do for you**
Why you should go to the trouble of creating and managing them.

◆ **Building dialog boxes**
The process of placing and naming controls, and assigning accelerator keys.

◆ **Using controls effectively**
How to arrange for a preliminary validation of the input, and how to set the tab order.

◆ **Setting and returning values**
How to initialize the controls in a dialog box.

◆ **Displaying dialog boxes**
The logical flow of initializing, showing, and validating a dialog box's elements.

◆ **Trapping errors**
How to check that the user entered valid information, and how to get the user to correct it.

◆ **Using dialog boxes as placeholders**
How to display information instead of entering it.

D ialog boxes are a critical part of many Excel activities. You see a different dialog box when you choose most of the possible items from Excel's main menu, such as File, Open or Tools, Scenarios. They are the principal means you use to communicate your intentions to Excel.

Many of the VBA macros that you write do not need dialog boxes. You don't need to enter information in a dialog box when you press F9 to calculate a worksheet, and you don't need to provide a dialog box if you write a macro that just puts random integers in worksheet cells. But many VBA applications do need a dialog box. You can't, for example, find even one tool in the Analysis ToolPak that doesn't require you to supply information in its own custom dialog box.

You have access to all of Excel's built-in dialog boxes within VBA. So, if part of your application calls for the user to navigate to a location on the hard disk and open a particular file, you can use VBA to automatically invoke the Open dialog box. Very often, however, none of the built-in dialog boxes do exactly what you need them to do. In these cases, you probably need to create a custom dialog box that contains the functionality you need and skips the functionality you don't.

You can find basic information about creating dialog boxes in Excel's Help files. This chapter focuses on slightly more sophisticated issues.

What Dialog Boxes Can Do for You

If you use VBA to speed up data management or to ease data analysis, dialog boxes are often the best way to get information from a user on what the VBA code should do. After you've written your VBA code, you often need a method of getting information from the user, such as:

▶ Where Excel will find the data that your macro needs

▶ Where your macro should write its results

▶ Any processing options that your macro can accommodate

▶ Any customizing, such as chart labels, that your user might want to supply

Although you could use a series of input boxes to obtain this information, that approach is inefficient. It requires the user to respond to a potentially lengthy set of questions and answers. By the time that the user has reached the tenth input box he might have forgotten what went into the first box. Further, the user might enter two or more responses that contradict one another. You would like to be in a position to evaluate all the user's responses, and request clarification if necessary, without having to start a long sequence of input boxes all over again.

Dialog boxes help you do that. From just one dialog box, you can usually get all the information that your macro needs. Your code can evaluate the information, request any needed corrections, and proceed with the processing in what appears to the user to be one step.

For example, figure 23.1 shows a dialog box that's used by the Analysis Toolpak. It's the dialog box that you see when you run the Regression tool.

Fig. 23.1

The Regression dialog box gets all the needed information from the user: where to find the data, what options to use, and where to write the output.

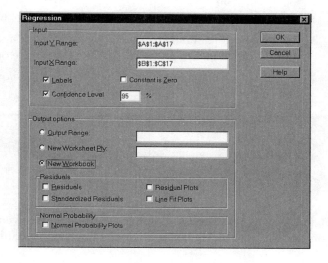

Once the user has finished entering information into the dialog box, the information is available to VBA to complete the processing as specified.

This chapter uses the dialog box in figure 23.1 to guide you through the steps involved in designing dialog boxes, retrieving and evaluating the information the user has supplied, and making the information available to your code for further processing. You need not know anything about regression to understand the information in this chapter. The Regression dialog box was chosen only because it uses most of the controls discussed in this chapter.

Building Dialog Boxes

A replica of the Regression dialog box has been created for you, and can be found on the companion CD in the file named Chap23.xls. All the controls found in the Regression dialog box are also on a dialog sheet named RegressionBox in Chap23.xls.

Placing Standard Dialog Box Controls

There are a few conventions, relating to the placement of the OK, Cancel, and Help buttons, that are used in most of Excel's built-in dialog boxes:

▶ The OK, Cancel, and Help buttons are placed in the upper-right corner of the dialog box. Use the Toggle Grid button on the Forms toolbar to display the grid. Place an OK button two grid rows below the bottom of the dialog box's title bar.

▶ Place a Cancel button one grid row below the OK button.

▶ Place a Help button two grid rows below the Cancel button.

▶ All three buttons should be ten grid columns wide and three grid rows tall. Each button should be two grid rows from the right edge of the dialog frame.

▶ No dialog box element should be placed directly below the OK, Cancel, and Help buttons.

 Note

You can find information on creating Help files for dialog boxes in Chapter 27, "Creating Custom Help for VBA Applications."

Figure 23.2 displays the dialog box after using these conventions. If you follow these conventions your dialog boxes will look more like standard Microsoft dialog boxes.

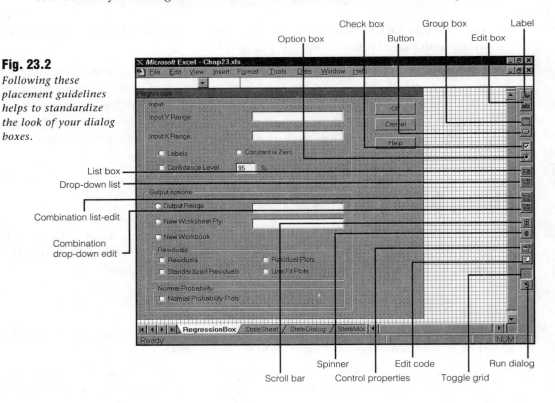

Fig. 23.2

Following these placement guidelines helps to standardize the look of your dialog boxes.

Placing the remaining controls of a dialog box within its frame is a matter of clicking the appropriate button on the Forms toolbar, and then dragging within the box's frame to position the control.

Naming Dialog Box Controls

Your VBA code needs to refer to the controls in a dialog box to obtain any references, values, and choices the user has supplied. Excel supplies a default name for each control in the dialog box, but these names are not useful for coding purposes. As you're writing, debugging, and revising your VBA code, you normally choose to refer to a control with a name such as *OutputRangeButton* instead of *Option Button 6*.

When you place a new control in a dialog box, Excel's default name for the control is a combination of the control type and a numeric increment. For example, when you create a new dialog box in a workbook, Excel automatically supplies three controls: the dialog box frame, an OK button, and a Cancel button. These controls are, by default, named Dialog Frame 1, Button 2, and Button 3. If you now add, say, an option button, its default name is Option Button 4.

Use the Name box in the dialog sheet to rename a dialog box control. Click the control to select it, then click in the Name box. Type a new name for the control, and press Enter. The process is nearly identical to naming a cell or range on a worksheet.

You can then refer to the dialog box controls in your VBA code by names that are meaningful to you, rather than having to remember that, say, Option Button 4 represents a choice to place output on the active worksheet.

Defining Accelerator Keys

Several dialog box controls have a label associated with them. For example, when you put a check box in a dialog box, its label automatically extends to the right of the check box itself. You can drag across the default label—which is the same as the control's default name—and type the label that you want to appear on the dialog sheet. A new button's label appears on the button itself, and a group box's label appears near the left of the group box's top border. Again, just drag across the default label and type the label that you prefer.

23

Note

A group box has a couple of useful functions. Cosmetically, it sets off different areas of a dialog box from one another. This can make it easier for the user to understand the different elements in the dialog box. A group box also establishes the relationship among option buttons. If four option buttons are on a dialog box, but there is no group box, only one of them can be chosen. But if a group box surrounds the first two option buttons, one of them can be chosen and one of the second two buttons can also be chosen.

After you have created a new label, you can define an accelerator key for the associated control. Suppose you place an option button in a dialog box, and give it the label Output Range. You want the accelerator key to be the letter "O." Follow these steps:

1. Select the option button.
2. Click the Control Properties button on the Forms toolbar, or choose Format, Object.
3. Click the Control tab in the Format Object dialog box.
4. Type the letter **O** in the Accelerator key text box, and choose OK.

The letter "O" in the label is underlined when the dialog box is run. The accelerator key is case-sensitive as to identifying the letter that is underlined. Suppose that you use the Worksheet Range label. If you specify "R" as the accelerator key, the label will appear as Worksheet Range. If you specify "r" as the accelerator key, the label will appear as Worksheet Range. The accelerator key is *not* case-sensitive when the user employs it. The same control is chosen whether the user types Alt+R or Alt+r.

The controls that have automatic labels include the dialog frame, group boxes, buttons, option buttons, and check boxes. The remaining controls—edit boxes, list boxes, drop-down boxes, combination list-edit boxes, combination drop-down edit boxes, scroll bars, and spinners—do not come with their own default labels. To associate an accelerator key with these controls, you must place a label on the dialog box, near the control itself, and specify an accelerator key for that label. When you do so, the next item in the dialog box's tab order gets the focus when the user selects the accelerator key.

To define the letter "Y" for the Input Y Range edit box on the Regression dialog box, follow these steps:

1. Create the edit box itself, and the Input Y Range label.
2. Select the label, and specify the letter "Y" as its accelerator key, as described.
3. Select Tools, Tab Order. The dialog box shown in figure 23.3 appears.

Fig. 23.3

The Tab Order dialog box enables you to place a label immediately above an element such as an edit box or a list box.

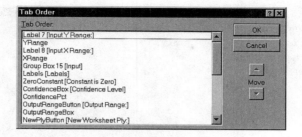

4. Using the scroll bar, locate the Input Y Range label. Click the label in the list box, and use the spinner to move the label up or down in the list.

5. Move the label to a position in the list box immediately above the control you want to associate with the label. In this example, you would move the Input Y Range label in the list box immediately above the InputYRange edit box.

Now, when the user presses Alt+Y, the edit box labeled Input Y Range becomes active. Making a particular dialog box control active, whether as a user and from the keyboard, or as a developer and by means of VBA code, is called *setting the focus*.

Using Controls Effectively

A dialog box's controls—edit boxes, option buttons, list boxes, and so on—are critical for the valid entry and retrieval of the user's specifications. Setting the controls' properties and initializing their values makes them much easier to manage.

Arranging a Preliminary Check for Valid Input

You can avoid much of the tedium of checking for valid input by use of the Control Properties dialog box. With a VBA dialog sheet active, place an edit box control on the dialog box, and click the Control Properties button on the Forms toolbar (or, double-click the edit box). The Format Object dialog box appears. If necessary, click the Control tab, which appears as in figure 23.4.

By selecting one of the option buttons, you can restrict user input in the edit box to the type that your VBA code expects. Particularly useful is the Reference edit validation. If you set an edit box's edit validation to Reference, Excel stops processing with a warning message when a user enters a value that Excel cannot interpret as a worksheet reference.

Similarly, setting an edit box's edit validation to Integer prevents the user from entering a text value, a cell reference, or a floating point number.

Fig. 23.4

The Format Object dialog box lets you define the type of input to allow for an edit box.

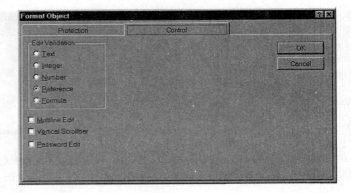

Managing the Tab Order

Once you have placed all the controls you want on the dialog box, choose <u>T</u>ools, Ta<u>b</u> Order. This invokes the Tab Order dialog box (refer to fig. 23.3).

To move a control higher or lower in the list box, select the control and then use the spinner. Moving a control higher in the list box means that the control is selected earlier; moving it down selects the control later. As the user presses the Tab key on the keyboard, the focus changes from the currently selected control to the next one down in the tab order for the dialog box.

 Note

When you move a control using the Tab Order dialog box, be sure to also move its label (if it has one) accordingly. This keeps the label's accelerator key associated with the right control.

It's considerate to establish a tab order for all the controls on your dialog box, so that the user can move from control to control in a logical order. Note, though, that you can override the default tab order that you establish by means of event handlers. You can associate a VBA subroutine that executes when a user manipulates one of the dialog box's controls. When the user attempts to move to the next control, the event handler executes, and can set the focus, if necessary, according to any information that was entered or choice that was made.

Associate an event handler with a control by clicking the control and choosing <u>T</u>ools, Assi<u>g</u>n Macro. Or, right-click the control and choose Assign Macro from the shortcut menu. Choose the macro that you want to execute when the control is used from the Macro Name/Reference list box.

Setting and Returning Values

It often happens that you want to supply default values for dialog box controls on your user's behalf. For example, in the Regression dialog box, the Confidence Level edit box contains the value 95. This is a conventional value that's used for many statistical tests. Although the user might well want to change it to some other value, it's still the confidence level that's used most frequently, and you can make things a little easier for the user by assigning it the default value of 95.

Alternatively, you usually want edit boxes, such as that for the Input Y Range and for the Input X Range, to be empty when the dialog box first appears. When a user clicks OK or Cancel in the dialog box, the values that have been entered into edit boxes (and the option buttons and check boxes that have been chosen) are saved in the dialog sheet. In most cases, you should arrange to clear those values before the user runs the dialog box again.

Therefore, it's useful to have code that sets or clears specific dialog box controls. This code should execute just prior to code that shows the dialog box.

The With...End With and the For Each...Next structures in VBA are helpful when you initialize the values of controls in a dialog box. If you're not familiar with these structures, here's a quick overview.

In VBA, when you want to refer to something that belongs to an object, you need to qualify that something by referring to the object it belongs to. For example, suppose that you want to set the value of the Confidence Level edit box in the Regression dialog box to 95. Your VBA code might look like this:

```
ThisWorkbook.DialogSheets("RegressionDialog").EditBoxes("ConfidencePct").Text = 95
```

In the statement, a period separates each object from the next object—the subsequent object belongs to the prior object. The Text property belongs to the edit box. The edit box belongs to the dialog sheet, and the dialog sheet belongs to ThisWorkbook.

23

> **Tip**
>
> ThisWorkbook specifically identifies the workbook that contains the VBA code that's executing. It's a useful way to refer to the workbook that contains the VBA code when another workbook is active.

Now suppose that you also want to clear the Input Y Range edit box. The two commands might look like this:

```
ThisWorkbook.DialogSheets("RegressionDialog").EditBoxes("ConfidencePct").Text = 95
ThisWorkbook.DialogSheets("RegressionDialog").EditBoxes("YRange").Text = ""
```

Because the Regression dialog box contains five edit boxes, you might think that you have to repeat this code five times. But the With structure provides a shortcut:

```
With ThisWorkbook.DialogSheets("RegressionDialog")
    .EditBoxes("Yrange").Text=""
    .EditBoxes("Xrange").Text=""
    .EditBoxes("ConfidencePct").Text=""
    .EditBoxes("OutputRangeBox").Text=""
    .EditBoxes("NewPlyBox").Text=""
End With
```

By surrounding the commands with the With…End With statements, you cause VBA to treat each object that's preceded by a period as belonging to the object you specify in the With. The With structure saves a lot of keystrokes and typographical errors.

But you can do even better by combining the With structure and the For Each structure. For Each is similar to a For…Next loop. Here's an example:

```
Dim Ctrl As Variant
For Each Ctrl in ThisWorkbook.DialogSheets("RegressionDialog").EditBoxes
    Ctrl.Text = ""
Next Ctrl
```

Ctrl is declared as a variant variable (you could, of course, name it something other than Ctrl if you wanted). When VBA encounters this For Each statement, it looks to the collection of all the edit boxes on the dialog sheet. It assigns each edit box in turn to the variant named Ctrl. So Ctrl stands, first, for the YRange edit box, then for the XRange edit box, then for the ConfidencePct edit box, and so on. As the loop executes, the text value in each edit box is set to a null value.

Notice that you don't have to know or to type the names of the edit boxes—using For Each causes VBA to identify them automatically.

In the case of the Regression dialog box, though, you want to initialize not only the edit boxes, but also the option buttons and the check boxes. The variant Ctrl variable can stand in for any of these. So, you can write your initialization code most efficiently by combining the With and the For Each structures, like this:

```
Sub InitializeControls()
Dim Ctrl As Variant
With ThisWorkbook.DialogSheets("RegressionBox")
    For Each Ctrl In .EditBoxes
        Ctrl.Text = ""
    Next Ctrl
    .EditBoxes("ConfidencePct").Text = 95
    For Each Ctrl In .OptionButtons
        Ctrl.Value = xlOff
    Next Ctrl
    For Each Ctrl In .CheckBoxes
        Ctrl.Value = xlOff
    Next Ctrl
End With
End Sub
```

(You can find this code, as well as the other examples used later in this chapter, in the module named RegressionMacros, in the file named CHAP23.XLS on the book's companion CD.)

The code shown here first establishes a With structure, so that subsequent objects that belong to the dialog sheet—preceded by periods, as in .EditBoxes—are treated as such. Within the With…End With block, the three For Each structures loop first through the dialog sheet's collection of edit boxes, then through its collection of option buttons, and finally through its collection of check boxes. Notice that the one edit box that you want set to the value 95 is handled with its own line of code (the seventh line, in the example), so that it is not left empty when the dialog box appears.

Displaying Dialog Boxes

Now that you've defined the main attributes of the dialog box—its edit boxes, list boxes, buttons, and so on—it's time to display the dialog box on the user's screen. The VBA command to display the dialog box is Show, and that's all you really have to do:

```
ThisWorkbook.DialogSheets("MyDialog").Show
```

Of course, there's more to it if you want to check any of the user's entries for errors. Or, if it's possible for an error to appear at a later point in the VBA code, you might want to return the user to the dialog box to make a change.

One good way to structure your code is so that it checks for user errors and returns to the dialog box if any are found. To do that, you can set a Boolean variable to False prior to showing the dialog box. If any input errors are found in your error-trapping routine, that routine sets the Boolean variable to True. And if the Boolean is True, your code displays the dialog box again so that the user can correct the error.

Although the VBA Help documentation states correctly that For loops are a more structured way to execute a loop than is a Do loop, you can assume that your user is *not* structured. There's no way to predict if or when a user will create a problem by entering data into the dialog box. A Do loop is more useful for this purpose. In pseudocode, a good overall structure might look like this:

```
FoundError = True
Do While FoundError = True
   FoundError = False
   ThisWorkbook.DialogBoxes("MyDialog").Show
   ErrorTrap FoundError
Loop
```

23

This structure results in the following sequence:

1. The Boolean variable named FoundError is set to True.

2. The Do loop begins execution because its logical condition is met: FoundError is True.

3. Once inside the loop, FoundError is set to False. In this way, any of the many error-checks in the error-trapping routine can set FoundError to True if an error is encountered.

4. VBA shows the dialog box on the screen.

5. When the user chooses the OK button, the dialog box is dismissed and the error-trapping routine is called, with FoundError as an argument.

6. If the error trapping routine finds an error in the user input, it sets FoundError to True and returns control to the Do loop.

7. The Loop statement passes control back to the Do statement, which again checks the logical condition. If the condition is met, the loop is repeated; so, if an error was found, the error-checking routine has set FoundError to True and the loop executes again. If no error was found, FoundError continues to be False and the loop terminates. In that case, VBA continues execution at the first statement following the Loop statement.

With this structure, you can repeatedly show and dismiss the dialog box until the user's entries have passed all of the checks that you place in the error-trapping routine.

Trapping Errors

One of your most important tasks when you front-end an application with a dialog box is to identify potential problems in advance. One mark of a well-developed application is its capability to determine that the user has failed to enter required information, information that will cause the application to crash, or conflicting information. It's considerate to check for problems like these in your code and return the user to the dialog box before they cause your application to fail. You should also display information about the error in an appropriate and meaningful error message, by way of a MsgBox statement.

The basic flow is

1. Initialize the controls and show the dialog box.

2. Dismiss the dialog box.

3. Check for possible errors in the dialog box's controls. If none are found, go to step 7.

4. Display an explanatory message, or ask the user to confirm the information.

5. Reset the dialog box's focus to the control that caused the error.

6. Go to step 1.

7. Continue with the application.

In the example Regression dialog box, there are several ways that the user could go wrong. For example, the user could:

▸ Fail to enter an Input Y Range, an Input X Range or both.

▸ Enter an Input Y Range that overlaps the Input X Range: for example, the user specifies A1:A20 as the Y Range, and A1:B20 as the X Range. (For Regression to work properly, the two ranges must contain different values.)

▸ Provide a different number of rows in the Y Range than in the X Range. (Again, for Regression to work properly, the two ranges must have the same number of data points.)

▸ Click the Confidence Level check box, but fail to enter a number greater than zero and less than 100 in the associated edit box.

▸ Specify an output range that could overwrite existing data. For example, the user could specify A1:A20 as the Y Range and A1 as the output range.

There are many other ways that the user's inputs could go wrong; you should generalize from these examples to your own application.

The steps—initializing the controls, showing the dialog box, and testing for valid input—are represented in the following code from the RegressionMacros module:

```
InitializeControls
ErrorsExist = True
Do While ErrorsExist
    ErrorsExist = False
    ThisWorkbook.DialogSheets("RegressionBox").Show
    TrapErrors ErrorsExist
Loop
```

The .Show statement displays the dialog box, and when the user has chosen OK, VBA dismisses the dialog box. The next line following the .Show statement is

```
TrapErrors ErrorsExist
```

This statement calls the VBA subroutine named TrapErrors, passing the Boolean variable named ErrorsExist as a parameter. At this point, the parameter's value is False. When TrapErrors has finished and returns control to the main subroutine, it might have changed the value of ErrorsExist to True. Then, the Loop statement passes control back to the Do statement, where the While clause tests to see if ErrorsExist is True. If it is, the loop is entered again. If it is False, the statement after Loop is executed.

23

The next three sections describe how the subroutine TrapErrors determines that a potential error situation exists, informs the user, and sets the stage for VBA to redisplay the dialog box.

Trapping Invalid Ranges

The code in TrapErrors (found in the RegressionMacros module) that is concerned with the input ranges is as follows:

```
With ThisWorkbook.DialogSheets("RegressionBox")
```

A With statement begins the code, so that the subsequent references to edit boxes and check boxes do not need to be qualified by referencing the workbook and the dialog sheet.

Then, the code sets three object variables to the worksheet ranges specified by the user. In each case, an If statement allows for the possibility that the user did not place an entry in the edit box. If the edit box were empty, the Set statement would fail.

```
If .EditBoxes("YRange").Text <> "" Then
    Set InputYRange = Range(.EditBoxes("YRange").Text)
End If
If .EditBoxes("XRange").Text <> "" Then
    Set InputXRange = Range(.EditBoxes("XRange").Text)
End If
If .EditBoxes("OutputRangeBox").Text <> "" Then
    Set StartOutputRange = Range(.EditBoxes("OutputRangeBox").Text)
End If
```

Next, the code checks that the user has made an entry in the Input Y Range edit box:

```
If .EditBoxes("YRange").Text = "" Then
    MsgBox "Please enter a range for the y-values"
    Set ErroredControl = .EditBoxes("YRange")
    FoundError = True
```

If the Input Y Range edit box is empty, the application will be unable to continue, so the code insists that the user enter a worksheet reference in the edit box. Because its control properties have been set to accept a worksheet reference, any other type of entry is automatically rejected (see "Arranging a Preliminary Check for Valid Input" earlier in the chapter). However, a null entry passes this initial check, and the code must take account of that situation.

A message box is displayed, describing the problem for the user. The global object variable named ErroredControl is set to the dialog box control that caused the problem—in this case, that control is the edit box named YRange. Finally, the Boolean variable FoundError is set equal to True.

When this TrapErrors subroutine terminates, FoundError (which is equivalent to ErrorExists: it is passed to TrapErrors by reference, and can be given any name) is True. So control passes to the Do While statement, and the dialog box is redisplayed.

The dialog box frame has an event handler—a subroutine—assigned to it. When the dialog box frame appears on the screen, its associated event handler executes. That event handler is the subroutine named SetTheFocus. It's just a one-line macro, and its single statement sets the dialog box's focus to the dialog box control that caused the error found by TrapErrors:

```
Sub SetTheFocus()
ThisWorkbook.DialogSheets("RegressionBox").Focus = ErroredControl.Name
End Sub
```

In this way, when the dialog box is redisplayed, the active control is the one that the user must change in order to correct the error.

This probably seems an involved way to set a dialog box's focus. Why not just set the dialog box's focus to the appropriate control within the TrapErrors subroutine? The reason is that when you want to set the focus to a particular control on the basis of a user action, you can get lost in a Catch-22. The problem is this apparent contradiction:

▶ You can set the focus of a dialog box only if the dialog box is active.

▶ When the dialog box is active, your VBA code does not have control of the dialog box's settings—therefore, once the dialog box is active, your code cannot set the focus.

The solution is to set the focus *as the dialog box appears*. Recall that the subroutine SetTheFocus is assigned to the dialog box's frame. When the frame appears on the screen, SetTheFocus executes, setting the dialog box's focus to the name of the control that caused the problem.

In this fashion, you can set the focus of the dialog box to any control you wish, on the basis of the tests you have set up in your error-trapping routine.

Note

This usage of an event handler that's attached to the dialog box frame means that the event handler shouldn't also initialize the dialog box's controls. If it did, it could wipe out all the information that the user has already entered.

Also, the InitializeControls procedure should set ErroredControl to the name of the first control in the dialog box's tab order. This way, when the dialog box frame *first* appears and SetTheFocus executes, the proper control will have the focus.

Continuing with the TrapErrors subroutine, the code checks to verify that the user has made an entry for the Input X Range. The logic is identical to that for the check of the Input Y Range. If the edit box is empty, a message is displayed, the object variable ErroredControl is set to the offending dialog box control. In this way, the control will have the focus. Then, the error status is set to True:

```
ElseIf .EditBoxes("XRange").Text = "" Then
    MsgBox "Please enter a range for the x-values"
    Set ErroredControl = .EditBoxes("XRange")
    FoundError = True
```

The code then checks to make sure that the user did not inadvertently use the same worksheet range for the Y Range and the X Range:

```
ElseIf InputYRange.Column >= InputXRange.Column And InputYRange.Column <=
InputXRange.Column _
        + InputXRange.Columns.Count Then
    MsgBox "Please make sure that the y-range does not overlap the x-range"
    Set ErroredControl = .EditBoxes("YRange")
    FoundError = True
```

The preceding segment makes use of the object variables InputXRange and InputYRange, which were set at the beginning of the subroutine. The key here is the comparison of the columns occupied by each range. Error processing (that is, the assignment of ErroredControl and of FoundError, and the redisplay of the dialog box) occurs if the Y Range's column is the same as the X Range's column. It also occurs if the X Range occupies multiple columns, and the Y Range occupies one of them. This could happen if the user specified, say, B1:D20 as the X Range, and C1:C20 as the Y Range.

The code then checks to make sure that the two worksheet ranges have the same number of rows. If not, error processing begins:

```
ElseIf InputYRange.Rows.Count <> InputXRange.Rows.Count Then
    MsgBox "Please make sure that the y-range has the same number of rows as the x-range."
    Set ErroredControl = .EditBoxes("YRange")
    FoundError = True
```

Again, there are other potential error situations pertaining to input ranges that you could check. In this case, you would probably want to test that the Input Y Range contains just one column (a requirement of the Regression application itself), that the input data are oriented as lists (variables occupy columns and observations occupy rows within the columns) and so on.

Checking for Unused Ranges

Your user might specify an output range that contains existing data. It's a good idea to check the range that the output will occupy to see whether it already contains information. If it does, you can display a warning message that gives the user an opportunity to decide whether to continue processing.

The sample code in the TrapErrors subroutine accomplishes this by checking the output worksheet's used range. UsedRange is an object that represents the range of a worksheet that is in use. The following code checks to see whether the output range specified by the user is within the used range of the output sheet. In this case, information of value to the user might be overwritten, and the user is given an opportunity to bail out.

The code begins by setting two object variables: one to represent the *range* where the output will start, and one to represent the *sheet* where the user has specified that the output is to appear.

```
Set StartOutputRange = Range(.EditBoxes("OutputRangeBox").Text)
Set OutputSheet = StartOutputRange.Parent
```

Notice the use of the Parent property of the range object. A range's parent is the worksheet that it occupies, so the object variable OutputSheet is set equal to the sheet the user has chosen for the output.

Then, the variable UsedColumns is set equal to the number of columns in the output sheet's used range, and UsedRows is set equal to the number of rows in the used range:

```
UsedColumns = OutputSheet.UsedRange.Columns.Count
UsedRows = OutputSheet.UsedRange.Rows.Count
```

The code then tests whether the starting point of the output would overlap the output sheet's used range:

```
If StartOutputRange.Column <= UsedColumns Or StartOutputRange.Row <= UsedRows Then
```

If the output begins inside the used range, the code displays a message box to warn the user that data might be overwritten:

```
Msg = "Your output range specification, starting at " &
➡.EditBoxes("OutputRangeBox").Text & _
    ", might overwrite existing values. OK to continue?"
Style = vbYesNo + vbQuestion + vbDefaultButton2
Title = "Possible overwrite"
Response = MsgBox(Msg, Style, Title)
```

If the user responds "No" to the message box—"No, it's not OK to continue"—error processing is initiated, just as occurs with errors found in the input ranges:

```
If Response = vbNo Then
    Set ErroredControl = .EditBoxes("OutputRangeBox")
    FoundError = True
End If
End If
```

23

Checking User-Supplied Values

When you want your user to supply a value to a dialog box, the usual way to obtain the information is with an edit box. The Regression dialog box has several edit boxes: two for the input ranges, one for an output range, one for the name of a new worksheet, and one for the value of the Confidence Level.

These edit boxes are expected to contain three different kinds of information: the addresses of worksheet ranges (references), the name of a new worksheet ply (a string), and a confidence level (a number). Their control properties are set so that Excel will prompt for a proper value if the user enters text instead of a number, or a number instead of a reference.

Nevertheless, when you want access to the edit boxes' values, it's necessary to treat them as text. For example, this statement is used in the section of the sample code that checks the input ranges:

```
If .EditBoxes("YRange").Text <> "" Then
    Set InputYRange = Range(.EditBoxes("YRange").Text)
End If
```

You are guaranteed that the contents of the YRange edit box conforms to a reference, because that's how you set its control property. At the point that this code executes, Excel has already checked the contents of the edit box and has found that it conforms to a worksheet reference—*conforms to* a reference, please note, not *is* a reference. Therefore, to set the object variable InputYRange to refer to the actual worksheet range, it's necessary to use the Range method on the text in the edit box, to return an actual reference.

You use a similar process to convert the contents of an edit box that is intended to capture a number. This code checks the contents of the confidence percent edit box, which must be greater than 0 and less than 100:

```
ElseIf .CheckBoxes("ConfidenceBox").Value = xlOn Then
    If Val(.EditBoxes("ConfidencePct").Text) <= 0 Or
➥Val(.EditBoxes("ConfidencePct").Text) > 100 Then
        MsgBox "Please enter a value larger than 0 and less than 100 for the Confidence Level"
        Set ErroredControl = .EditBoxes("ConfidencePct")
        FoundError = True
    End If
```

Notice the use of the Val function. This is not an Excel function, but a VBA function that converts a text value to a numeric value. By using the Val function on the edit box's text, the code can determine whether the number entered by the user is within the required limits. If it is not, error processing starts.

Checking Reference Edit Boxes

In most cases, you can directly use the information that the user has entered into a reference edit box. This statement, for example:

```
Set InputYRange = Range(.EditBoxes("YRange").Text)
```

uses the information in the edit box to define the location of the worksheet range. It works properly, regardless of whether the text in the edit box is an absolute reference or a relative reference. If the user employs the mouse pointer to identify the range, Excel inserts dollar signs to make the reference an absolute reference. If the user types the address directly into the edit box, the reference could be absolute or relative. But when the Range object is used as shown here, it converts a relative reference in the edit box to an absolute reference.

A name is not used in the Regression dialog box, but suppose that you want to assign a name to a worksheet on the basis of information in a reference edit box. For example:

```
ActiveWorkbook.Names.Add Name:="YRange", RefersTo:= _
    "=" & ThisWorkbook.DialogSheets("RegressionBox").EditBoxes("YRange").Text
```

Suppose that a name is added to a worksheet, whether by means of VBA or by means of Insert, Name, Define. Then, if the address supplied is a relative reference, the address is interpreted as *relative to the active cell*.

To convince yourself of this, take these steps:

1. Open a worksheet and select cell A1.

2. Choose Insert, Name, Define. In the Define Name dialog box, enter a name such as TestName in the Names in Workbook edit box.

3. In the Refers to edit box, type **=C3**, and choose OK.

4. With cell A1 still active, choose the Name box drop-down, and click TestName. Cell C3 becomes the active cell.

5. With cell C3 still active, choose the Name box drop-down list and click TestName again. Cell E5 becomes the active cell.

Because TestName's reference was defined using relative reference notation, it is always relative to the active cell. In the previous example, TestName is always two columns right and two rows below the active cell.

The same effect occurs when a user types a reference into an edit box and a name is defined in this fashion:

```
ActiveWorkbook.Names.Add Name:="YRange", RefersTo:= "=" & _
    ThisWorkbook.DialogSheets("RegressionBox").EditBoxes("YRange").Text
```

If the contents of the YRange edit box consist of a relative reference, the name will always be relative to the active cell. Depending on what cell is active when the statement is executed, this can cause problems for later processing: the name YRange might not refer to the range that your code expects.

It is by no means unusual for a user to type a range address rather than point to it with the mouse. If the range that the user wants to use is hidden by the dialog box, it might be more convenient to type letters and numbers than to move the dialog box around the screen. Or, if the range is a very large one, the user might well find it faster to type, say, A1:T100 than to highlight 100 rows and twenty columns.

The solution is to use the Address method of the Range object:

```
ActiveWorkbook.Names.Add Name:="YRange", RefersTo:= "=" & _
    Range(ThisWorkbook.DialogSheets("RegressionBox").EditBoxes("YRange").Text).Address
```

When used with no arguments, the Address method returns an A1-style, absolute reference. In this way, you can be sure that a range name that your code adds to a worksheet refers to the proper cells, and does not depend on the address of whatever cell happens to be active.

Although this section stresses the use of absolute addresses for range names, don't neglect the relative reference worksheet name. It can be a handy way to access a cell that is offset from the active cell by a constant number of rows and columns. The next section illustrates the technique in the context of dialog boxes.

Using Dialog Boxes as Placeholders

Dialog boxes can be thought of as a means of data entry, or of informing Excel where to find or to save a file. But they are also useful for *displaying* information.

Suppose that you want to view different data series in your worksheet on a chart. You might have a list that contains in its columns different financial results for different departments in your company. You would like to be able to choose a particular department and easily view a chart of its financials.

The straightforward way to do this is to create a multiple selection—the list's header row, which contains labels for each financial statistic, and the row containing the department in question. Then, you activate the Chart Wizard and create the chart.

To view a chart of another department, you could create it from scratch, or you could edit the original chart so that its data series refers to a different department.

There are problems with these approaches. One is that it takes time to create each new chart—not only the time it takes to go through the Chart Wizard's steps, but also the time that it takes Excel to set all the options that you might have chosen. Or, if you embed the charts in the worksheet, you quickly run out of real estate on the screen. Or, if you create charts on separate sheets, you're constantly switching back and forth between the charts and the source worksheet. Furthermore, if you have more departments than you can view on the screen, it's often necessary to scroll back and forth between different sets of source data.

Any one of these inconveniences is trivial by itself. But in combination, they're a hassle. Dialog boxes, though, have some characteristics that you can use to minimize the problems. If, for example, you put a chart on a dialog box, you could easily show the dialog box and its accompanying chart no matter where you are on the worksheet.

If, in addition, you had a way to easily change the data series reference, then the chart would update automatically. You wouldn't have to create a new chart every time you wanted to view a different data series.

The file named Chap23.xls on the companion disk contains an example of how this works, and figure 23.5 shows how the chart appears.

Fig. 23.5

The chart shown in the figure is actually found on a dialog sheet.

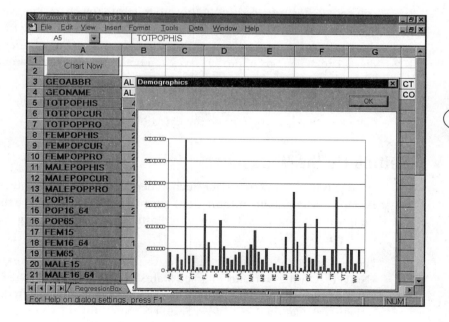

Figure 23.5 displays information taken from the file Mapstats.xls, provided with version 7 of Excel. Mapstats.xls contains, among other demographic information, data on different population segments in each of the 50 states. In the figure, and in Chap23.xls, the information has been transposed so that states occupy columns, and different population variables occupy rows.

To see what happens in real time, open Chap23.xls and choose the sheet tab named StateSheet. Select cell A6, and choose the Chart Now button. You will see the chart, on a dialog box, appear on your screen. Close the dialog box and select cell A7. Again, choose the Chart Now button and you will see the chart again, but with a different data series.

Notice that you can scroll up or down to any row in the worksheet's list, and the Chart Now button displays the chart in the active window.

How is this different from alternatives? Well, it's a lot faster than creating a new chart from scratch every time. But suppose that you created one chart whose data series' reference depended on the active cell, such that the chart is visible when row 1 is also visible. If you now scroll down a page and select, say, A25, you could recalculate the chart, but it wouldn't be visible. However, when you show a dialog box, it automatically appears on the visible part of the worksheet.

You could, of course, code a VBA macro to create the chart. But even using VBA, it takes Excel some time to establish the chart, and it takes some coding to make sure that the chart will appear where you want it to as you move among different areas of the worksheet. The dialog box approach saves you both execution time and coding time.

There are three sheets involved in setting up this capability: the worksheet with the data, the dialog sheet with the dialog box, and a VBA module sheet with four lines of code that execute when you choose the Chart Now button.

Setting Up the Worksheet

Once you have the source data (such as department financials or, as in the disk file's example, demographic information) on the worksheet, you have three easy tasks to accomplish: placing a volatile function on the worksheet, entering some range names, and setting up the chart itself.

The first task is very simple: just choose an empty cell on the worksheet and enter **=NOW()**. On the worksheet named StateSheet in Chap23.xls, the formula is found in cell B7, hidden behind the worksheet's chart. The reason for entering a volatile function is that recalculation does not occur unless something on a worksheet has changed since the last calculation. Using the NOW( ) function guarantees that something on the sheet will have changed between recalculations.

The second task is to create two range names. On StateSheet, the names are defined as StateLabels and StateData. StateLabels is defined as StateSheet!$B$3:$AZ$3. Notice that the reference is absolute. This range is used to define the x-axis labels on the chart. The chart labels do not vary as a function of which cell is active.

The range named StateData is defined as StateSheet!$B*r*:$AZ*r*, where *r* stands for some row number. The row number depends on the row of whatever is the active cell. Notice that this is a *mixed* reference: one whose rows or columns, but not both, are relative. In this case, the rows are relative. To define the name StateData, select the cells from column B through column AZ in any row. Then:

1. Choose Insert, Name, Define. The Define Name dialog box appears.
2. In the Names in Workbook edit box, enter **StateData**.
3. In the Refers to edit box, remove the dollar signs before the row number. If you began by selecting cells B5:AZ5, the entry in the Refers to edit box should be:

   =StateSheet!$B5:$AZ5

4. Choose OK.

You have now defined a name whose reference depends on the active cell. If cell A5 is active, StateData refers to $B5:$AZ5. If cell E19 is active, StateData refers to $B19:$AZ19.

The third task is to create the chart itself. On the StateSheet worksheet, the chart is found in cells BA5:BA26. To create the chart, select any range of numeric cells and start the Chart Wizard. Embed a new chart somewhere out of the way on the worksheet. Format it as you want, choosing a chart type, including or omitting a legend, and so on. When the Chart Wizard has finished creating the chart, take these steps:

1. Double-click the chart to open it for editing.
2. Click the data series so that you can see its formula in the formula bar.
3. Edit the series' formula in the formula bar so that it reads:

   =SERIES(,Chap23.xls!StateLabels,Chap23.xls!StateData,1)

   Of course, you would replace the name of the Chap23.xls file with the name of your workbook.

4. Press Enter, and deselect the chart.

You could stop at this point, if you wanted. The chart contains a data series that depends on the location of the active cell. If you now choose a cell in a different row and press F9, the sheet recalculates. When it does so, the series shown in the chart adjusts to display the values in the new reference of StateData.

If you had not placed a volatile function like NOW( ) in the worksheet, Excel would conclude that there is nothing to recalculate, and would not modify the chart. But because at least a few seconds have passed since the sheet's last calculation, the value of NOW( ) is different, so Excel recalculates the sheet, including the chart, when you press F9.

Stopping at this point, however, means that you need to have the chart visible on your screen to see the effect of choosing a new cell and recalculating the worksheet. But if you copy the chart to a dialog sheet, the chart appears in the dialog frame when you show the dialog box. The next section describes how to do this.

Setting Up the Dialog Sheet

You can make the dialog box as simple or as complicated as you want, placing different controls on it. It is wise to include a button, such as OK or Cancel, that dismisses the dialog box. But the only essential ingredient is the chart itself.

Begin by choosing Insert, Macro, Dialog. When you have a new dialog sheet in your workbook, switch back to the worksheet that contains the chart. Then:

1. Click the chart to select it.
2. Choose Edit, Copy.
3. Activate the dialog sheet.
4. Choose Edit, Paste Special.
5. In the Paste Special dialog box, click Picture in the As list box. Then, choose OK.
6. With the picture object still selected, click in the Formula Bar, and enter a reference to the sheet and cells where the chart exists. Press Enter.

 Tip
You might find it quicker and easier to place the chart on the dialog box when you first create it. When the Chart Wizard prompts you to drag to create the chart, switch to a dialog sheet and establish an embedded chart inside the dialog frame.

In CHAP23.XLS, the dialog sheet is named StateDialog. The entry in the formula bar is

```
=StateSheet!$BA$5:$BI$26
```

On StateSheet, the chart is embedded over cells $BA$5:$BI$26. See figure 23.6 for an example of how the dialog sheet might look after you have pasted the chart onto the sheet and entered a reference to the worksheet's chart.

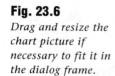

Fig. 23.6

Drag and resize the chart picture if necessary to fit it in the dialog frame.

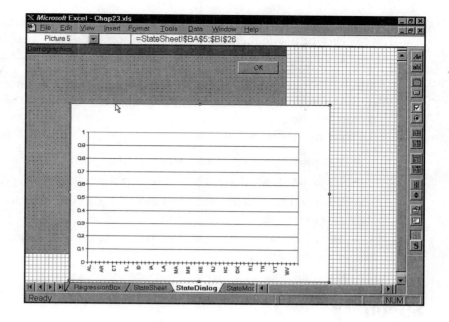

Setting Up the Module Sheet

The final job is to make it easy for the user to display the dialog sheet with its chart. This is easiest if, as with the StateDialog worksheet, there's a button that invokes a macro to show the dialog. It's a simple process:

1. Choose Insert, Macro, Module to place a new module sheet in your workbook.

2. Enter this code in the module:

```
Sub ShowTheDialog()
Calculate
ThisWorkbook.DialogSheets("StateDialog").Show
End Sub
```

You can, of course, name the dialog sheet and the macro whatever you want.

3. Switch to the worksheet with the source data. Choose View, Toolbars and click the Drawing toolbar in the Toolbars list box. Then, choose OK.

4. Click the Button toolbar button on the Drawing toolbar, and drag through some convenient area on the worksheet to establish the button.

5. Right-click the button, and choose Assign Macro from the shortcut menu. In the Assign Macro dialog box, choose ShowTheDialog in the Macro Name/Reference list box, and choose OK.

6. If you want, you can display a name such as Chart Now on the button by right-clicking it, and then dragging across its default name. Then, type a new name on it and click outside the button to deselect it.

After you have set up the worksheet, the dialog sheet, and the module sheet as described, all you need to do is choose a cell in a row that contains the data for some state, some department, or any other record identifier. Then, clicking the worksheet button displays the chart for you, with these advantages:

▶ You need not create a new chart every time you want to change its data.

▶ The charted data depend on whatever cell you select before choosing the button.

▶ You don't have to scroll to one area of the worksheet to select data and to another area to view the chart.

▶ You need not write complex VBA code to arrange for the chart to appear in the active window.

Summary

Very likely, you had more than a nodding acquaintance with custom dialog boxes when you began reading this chapter. By this point, you should know more about managing dialog box controls, trapping errors, and displaying information in a dialog box.

By using a control's properties, you can cause Excel to perform preliminary tests of the information your user enters in a dialog box. By writing an error-trapping routine that executes when your user dismisses a dialog box, you can extend those tests beyond the simple syntax of the information to ensure that your VBA code obtains the right data. You can set the focus of the dialog box programmatically, to make it more convenient for your user to correct erroneous information. And by placing a linked graphic on a dialog box, you can make it easier to summarize information that extends well beyond the boundaries of the active window.

The next chapter provides you with more advanced dialog box techniques, such as enabling and disabling controls, and checking user input on the fly.

chapter 24

Advanced Dialog Boxes

by Ron Person

In this chapter

◆ **Naming controls**
Dialog box controls that have English-like names are easier to read and manage.

◆ **Checking data**
Check data as you type it into an edit box for better data entry control.

◆ **Accept passwords**
Create password edit boxes that display asterisks (*) instead of text.

◆ **Enable and disable controls**
Enable and disable controls in a dialog box to prevent inappropriate selections.

◆ **Resize dialog boxes**
Expand or contract dialog boxes to show optional or advanced controls.

◆ **Fill scrolling lists with new contents**
Change scrolling list contents while the dialog box remains displayed to give users additional choices.

◆ **Change dialog boxes while they display**
Interactively redraw live charts in a dialog box.

◆ **Allow multiple selections**
Learn how to create multiple selection list boxes.

◆ **Control list selections**
Learn how to build and reorder lists in a dialog box.

Well-designed dialog boxes can make custom applications in Excel much easier to work with. Once you learn how to create the simple dialog boxes described in Chapter 23, "Managing Dialogs in VBA," you will be able to handle most of your dialog box needs. But, just when you're feeling smug about your new programming abilities you will probably face the need for an advanced dialog box.

While simple dialog boxes are easiest for people to understand and use, some programs require more extensive control. If you only know how to program simple dialog boxes, you may end up with a program that contains large, cluttered dialog boxes or multiple layers of dialog boxes. Through the use of a few advanced dialog boxes you can present a simple appearance and operation to the user and give yourself the advanced program control you need.

Note

All examples in this chapter are shown with Option Explicit as the first line of the module. This prevents you from incorrectly creating variables. Excel will automatically enter Option Explicit on new module sheets if you choose Tools, Options, select the Module General tab, and select the Requires Variable Declaration check box.

Tip

Most of this chapter can be programmed in Excel 5. With the exception of the Passwordedit property, the examples in this chapter can be created in Excel 5.

Naming Dialog Box Controls

Your VBA procedures will be easier to read and maintain if you assign names to the controls you draw in dialog boxes. For example, if you draw a list box, Excel will automatically assign it a name such as List Box 4. When you write your procedure you will need to enter statements such as ListBoxes("List Box 4") to specify that list box. Your code will be more manageable if you rename the list box control to an understandable name.

To rename a control in a dialog box, select the control by clicking it. To the left of the formula bar you will see the control's name assigned by Excel, such as Edit Box 6 or Button 5. Figure 24.1 shows the reference area where a control's name appears. Click this name to select it. Type a more descriptive name and press Enter. Notice that the name to the left of the formula bar changes to the name you typed.

Fig. 24.1

Rename controls by clicking in the reference area and typing a new name.

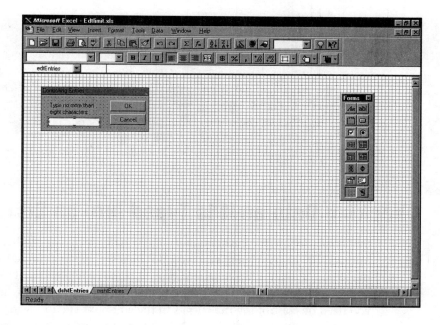

Although you can assign names to dialog box controls, the names will be much easier to understand if you use a system of prefixes that indicate the type of control. For example, for a list box containing the names of countries, you might want to use a name such as lstCountries. For option buttons of countries, you might use optCountries. Table 24.1 lists some commonly used prefixes.

Table 24.1 Prefixes for Control Names

Control Type	Prefix	Example
List box	lst	lstCountries
Option button	opt	optColors
Edit box	edt	edtName
Check box	chk	chkBold
Button	btn	btnNext

Tip

While the dialog sheet is displayed, you can choose the <u>T</u>ools, Ta<u>b</u> Order command to display the Tab Order dialog box. The order in which controls appear in the list is the order in which the Tab key selects them. To change a control's position in the order, select it, then click the up or down arrow. Select and move multiple adjacent controls by clicking the first control, then Shift+click on the last control, and then click the up or down arrow.

Checking Data as it Is Typed into an Edit Box

Edit boxes are used to gather typed data. Usually that data can be widely varying text or numbers. If the data being entered must be restricted to a limited set of entries, then you should use a list or drop-down list box. In some cases, you need a combination of the free-text entry afforded by an edit box and the limitations set by lists. You can get what you need by controlling the entries in the edit box. The following example creates the text edit box shown in figure 24.2 that accepts no more than eight characters.

Fig. 24.2

Your edit boxes can limit the type of text they accept.

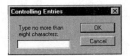

To control a user's entries in an edit box, you will need to assign a procedure to the edit box that checks the current contents of the edit box. This procedure runs each time the user types a letter or number in the edit box. Some of the ways you can use this are to:

▶ Limit edit boxes to a specific number of characters

▶ Limit edit boxes to only text or only numbers

▶ Limit edit boxes to a specific pattern or mask where certain numbers and letters must be in specific positions

▶ Use the initially entered characters to look up a completed part number, description, or allowable entry much like Excel 95's AutoComplete feature

Preparing the Data Entry Sheets

To build this example, begin by opening a new workbook. Insert a module sheet and a dialog sheet. Rename these sheets by double-clicking the sheet tab, typing a name into the Rename Sheet dialog box, and clicking OK. Rename with the names shown in the following table:

Inserting and Naming Sheets

Sheet Type	Sheet Name
Dialog sheet	dshtEntries
Module sheet	mshtEntries

A worksheet is not used with this example.

Drawing the Data Entry Dialog Box and Naming its Controls

This is the simplest of dialog boxes that you might create. To create the dialog box shown in figure 24.2, select the dialog sheet, and then drag across Dialog Caption in the title bar. Change the title bar name to Controlling Entries.

 Tip

Don't let the frame around a control (the dashed rectangle that shows when it is selected) overlap the frame of another control. If they do overlap, the results of clicking a control may be unpredictable.

Click the label button and drag across the area where you will enter a text label. Enter the label Type (no more than eight characters) as shown in figure 24.2.

Click the edit box button and drag across where the user will enter text. Size the edit box by dragging a corner so that it fits under the label and is wide enough to show the text being entered.

To make programming easier and more manageable you should name the edit box. Use the naming method described in the section "Naming Dialog Box Controls" at the beginning of this chapter. Name this edit box as shown in the following table.

Prefixes for Control Names

Control Type	Prefix	Example
Edit box	lst	edtEntries

Creating and Assigning the Show Dialog Procedure for Data Entry

After you have named the sheets and the edit box on the dialog sheet, you can enter the following code on the module sheet. The initial code you must type into the module is shown in listing 24.1.

Listing 24.1   EDTLIMIT.XLS

```
Option Explicit

Dim objedtEntries As EditBox

Sub EntriesShow()
    Set objedtEntries = DialogSheets("dshtEntries").EditBoxes("edtEntries")
    DialogSheets("dshtEntries").Show
End Sub
```

This code displays the dialog box. The Option Explicit is used to ensure that variables are entered correctly. The only variable declared, optedtEntries, is declared as a specific object variable EditBox. This saves memory and improves performance slightly over declaring it as a generic object variable using the statement Object.

Throughout the examples in this chapter, object variables are used to reduce the amount of typing required and to make code easier to read. In this example, there is only one object variable, objedtEntries. This object uses two prefixes to make it easier to understand. The prefix obj indicates that this is an object variable. The second prefix (edt) indicates that it represents an edit box. Object variables are not defined with an equals sign as other variables are. Instead you must use a Set statement. In this example the object variable is set with

```
Set objedtEntries = DialogSheets("dshtEntries").EditBoxes("edtEntries")
```

The object variable objedtEntries can be used throughout the rest of the module whenever you need to reference DialogSheets("dshtEntries").EditBoxes("edtEntries").

After you have entered the code shown in listing 24.1, you can display the dialog box by clicking within the EntriesShow() procedure and clicking the Run Macro button or pressing F5. If the dialog box does not display, check that the flashing insertion point is inside the EntriesShow procedure before you attempt to run. Also check the spellings of names you have used.

Setting the Default and Checking Results for Data Entry

One of the best ways to set the defaults in a dialog box is to assign a default procedure to the frame of the dialog box. When the dialog box shows on-screen, the procedure assigned to the frame runs before the dialog box displays. At the bottom of the module sheet, enter the procedures shown in listing 24.2 to learn how to set defaults and display the results of the dialog box.

Listing 24.2   EDTLIMIT.XLS

```
Sub Entries_OnFrame()
    objedtEntries.Text = ""
End Sub

Sub Entries_OnOK()
    MsgBox objedtEntries.Text
End Sub
```

Assign the Entries_OnFrame procedure to the frame of the dialog box by selecting the dialog box sheet. Right-click the frame, the edge of the dialog box, and choose the Assign to Macro command. Select the Entries_OnFrame procedure and choose OK. Repeat the same process to assign the Entries_OnOK procedure to the OK button in the dialog box.

The Entries_OnFrame procedure runs when the dialog box and its frame appear. Its single line of code specifies that the text property for the object variable objedtEntries, the edit box, should be set to no text. No matter what the user entered when the dialog box last appeared, this line of code clears the edit box when it next displays.

By assigning the Entries_OnOK procedure to the OK, you specify that it will run when the user clicks the OK button. The line in this procedure uses a message box to display the current text that is in the edit box.

Creating and Assigning the Editing Control Procedure for Data Entry

The code you have entered so far displays a simple dialog box containing an edit box that is set to blank contents. The code in listing 24.3 illustrates how to limit what is typed into an edit box. Enter this procedure as the last procedure in the module sheet.

Listing 24.3   EDTLIMIT.XLS

```
Sub Entries_OnEditBox()
    If Len(objedtEntries.Text) > 8 Then
        objedtEntries.Text = Left(objedtEntries.Text, 8)
        MsgBox "Please type no more than eight characters"
    End If
End Sub
```

After you enter the procedure, select the dialog sheet. Right-click the edit box and choose Assign to Macro. Select Entries_OnEditBox from the list, then choose OK.

This procedure now runs whenever the user types a character into the edit box. The procedure limits the number of characters in the edit box to eight. Its first line is an IF statement that examines the length of text in the edit box. If there are eight or fewer characters, then the procedure doesn't run. If there are more than eight characters, then the second line of the procedure runs. It sets the text in the edit box to the left eight characters that have been entered so far. The third line displays a message box telling users what they did wrong.

You can assign a procedure to buttons, edit boxes, lists, check boxes, and option buttons in your dialog boxes. When the user clicks or makes an entry in the object, then the assigned procedure runs.

Running the Limited Edit Box

To run this example, click inside the EntriesShow procedure and click the Run Macro button or press F5. When the dialog box appears, attempt to type more than eight characters into the edit box. When you type the ninth character a message will appear.

Reading the Entire Data Entry Procedure

Listing 24.4 shows all the procedures used to create an edit box that limits the data entries. The complete workbook containing this example is stored in the file EDTLIMIT.XLS on the CD-ROM that comes with this book.

Listing 24.4 EDTLIMIT.XLS.

```
Option Explicit

Dim objedtEntries As EditBox

Sub EntriesShow()
    Set objedtEntries = DialogSheets("dshtEntries").EditBoxes("edtEntries")
    DialogSheets("dshtEntries").Show
End Sub

Sub Entries_OnFrame()
    objedtEntries.Text = ""
End Sub

Sub Entries_OnOK()
    MsgBox objedtEntries.Text
End Sub

Sub Entries_OnEditBox()
    If Len(objedtEntries.Text) > 8 Then
        objedtEntries.Text = Left(objedtEntries.Text, 8)
        MsgBox "Please type no more than eight characters"
    End If
End Sub
```

Creating Password Dialog Boxes

If your custom Excel programs involve confidential data or their use needs to be restricted to authorized people, then you should probably learn how to create password edit boxes. Creating a password edit box is very simple to do.

Password edit boxes look the same as normal edit boxes, but the text that you type does not appear in the edit box. Instead, asterisks (*) appear in the edit box for each character typed as shown in figure 24.3. This prevents unauthorized users from seeing the password on-screen. The characters typed in the edit box can be stored in a VBA variable and used by your program to open protected files, log onto networks, or access restricted databases through MS-Query.

In the following example you will learn how easy it is to set the PasswordEdit property of an edit box so that it shows asterisks. The procedure then stores the entered password in a variable and uses that stored password to open a protected worksheet.

Fig. 24.3

Asterisks appear in place of characters in a password edit box.

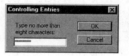

> ## α Note
>
> The PasswordEdit property is only available to Visual Basic for Applications in Excel 7. It is not available in Excel 5.

Preparing the Password Sheets

This example uses the previous example of a limited edit box as a base of code you will modify. If you have not built the previous example, please build it at this time or open the file EDTLIMIT.XLS from the CD-ROM that comes with this book.

In addition to the workbook containing the code, you will need a workbook on disk that has been file protected. To prepare this workbook file, follow these steps,

1. Choose File, New and double-click the Workbook icon to open a new blank workbook.

2. Select cell B2 and type **This file is protected with the password "TryMe."**

3. Choose File, Save As and change to the directory in which you created the EDTLIMIT.XLS file. Enter the file name CONFIDTL.XLS in the File Name box. Do not click OK yet.

4. Click the Options button to open the Save Options dialog box.

5. Type **TryMe** in the Protection Password edit box. Notice how it is capitalized. You must retype passwords using the same capitalization as when the password was created. Click OK.

6. Retype **TryMe** in the Confirm Password dialog box and click OK.

7. Click OK in the Save As dialog box, and then close the worksheet.

Test your protected workbook file by clicking File, Open and attempt to open the CONFIDTL.XLS file. You should be prompted for a password. You must type in TryMe in order to open the file.

Setting an Edit Box's PasswordEdit Property

One property of an edit box in Excel 95 is PasswordEdit. If you set this property to TRUE before the dialog box is shown, then all characters typed into the edit box will appear as asterisks in the dialog box. This prevents unauthorized users from reading the password from the screen. You can modify the EntriesShow procedure in EDTLIMIT.XLS to set this property. The modified procedure should appear as shown in listing 24.5. The added line is shown in bold. After you modify this procedure, save the EDTLIMIT.XLS workbook with the new name EDTPASSW.XLS.

Listing 24.5   EDTPASSW.XLS

```
Sub EntriesShow()
    Set objedtEntries = DialogSheets("dshtEntries").EditBoxes("edtEntries")
    objedtEntries.PasswordEdit = True
    DialogSheets("dshtEntries").Show
End Sub
```

An alternative method of creating a password edit box is to double-click the edit box and select the Password Edit check box from the Format Object dialog box. While this accomplishes the same result, it is a bad habit that can cause problems when you develop more complex dialog boxes and programs. First, setting the edit box's PasswordEdit property with code documents the setting for that property. Second, the use of code to set an object's property, in this case PasswordEdit, insures that the property is set as expected by the rest of the procedure. If you manually set a property with the Format object dialog box, another procedure in the module may change it, leaving it in an unexpected state.

Using the Password in Your Program

To use your password you must store the text in the edit box in a string variable and then use that string variable wherever a password is needed in your program. In the following simple example, the password typed into the edit box is used to open the protected workbook file CONFIDTL.XLS.

In more complex real-world situations you might use a password to open multiple files, to unprotect worksheets so that constants or formatting can be changed, or to pass to a protected SQL database that Excel queries for data.

To see how the password can be used to open the protected file, modify the Entries_OnOK procedure so that it appears as shown in listing 24.6.

Listing 24.6   EDTPASSW.XLS

```
Sub Entries_OnOK()
    Workbooks.Open Filename:="Confidtl.xls", password:=objedtEntries.Text
End Sub
```

To make sure that your code cannot be modified to reveal passwords or to give unauthorized access, you should save the modules containing password-related code as an add-in.

Resizing Dialog Boxes to Show Additional Options

One way of keeping dialog boxes simple and easy to use is to hide the advanced features that are used infrequently. The best way of making these features unobtrusive, but still making them easily accessible, is to add an Option button in the dialog box. Clicking the Option button expands the dialog box to show the additional features. To see a dialog box in Excel that uses resizing to show more features, choose Format, AutoFormat. When the AutoFormat dialog box appears, click the Options button to see the dialog box expand.

In this section you will learn how to create the dialog box shown in figure 24.4. When you click the Makes You Larger button, the dialog box expands to show the additional controls shown in figure 24.5. Clicking the Makes You Smaller button reduces the height of the dialog box so that only the upper buttons are shown.

Fig. 24.4

Clicking the Makes You Larger button resizes the dialog box to show additional dialog box controls.

24

Fig. 24.5
*Expanded dialog boxes
can show infrequently
used controls.*

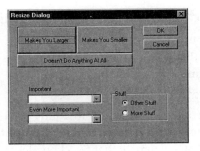

Preparing the Sheets for Resizing a Dialog Box

To build this example, begin by opening a new workbook. Insert a module sheet and a dialog sheet. Rename these sheets by double-clicking the Sheet tab, typing a name into the Rename Sheet dialog box and clicking OK. Use the names shown in the following table.

Inserting and Naming Sheets

Sheet Type	Sheet Name
Dialog sheet	dshtExpand
Module sheet	mshtExpand

The worksheet is not used in this example.

Drawing the Resized Dialog Box and Naming its Controls

To create the dialog box shown in figure 24.6, select the dialog sheet, then drag across Dialog Caption in the title bar. Change the title bar name to Resize Dialog.

Draw the controls as shown in figure 24.6. Resize the dialog box on the dialog sheet by dragging its corners so that only the upper controls are within the dialog box frame, as shown in figure 24.6.

To make programming easier and more manageable, you should name controls in the dialog box. Use the naming method described in the section "Naming Dialog Box Controls" at the beginning of this chapter. In this example the only controls that need to be named are the controls, that will be hidden when the dialog box is reduced. The following table shows the names used in this dialog box. These controls should be named so that code can refer to them to disable the controls when they are hidden and enable the controls when they show.

Fig. 24.6

Use the Height property of the dialog frame to increase the height of the dialog box and show the hidden controls.

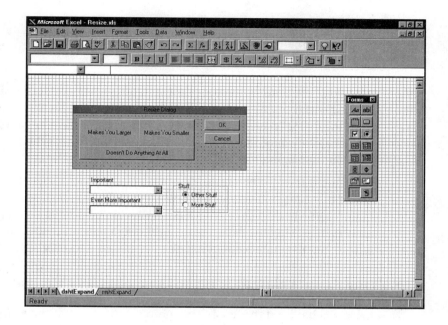

Define Control Names

Control Type	Prefix	Name
Drop-down list	ddn	ddnImportant
Drop-down list	ddn	ddnMore
Option button	opt	optOther
Option button	opt	optMore

Creating and Assigning the Show Dialog Procedure for Resizing a Dialog Box

After you have named the sheets and the controls on the dialog sheet, you can enter the following code on the module sheet. The initial code you must type into the module is shown in listing 24.7.

24

Listing 24.7   RESIZE.XLS

```
Option Explicit

Sub ResizeShow()
    'Set dialog box height to default in case it was previously enlarged
    DialogSheets("dshtExpand").DialogFrame.Height = 100
    DialogSheets("dshtExpand").Show
End Sub
```

After you have entered the code shown in listing 24.7, you can display the dialog box by clicking within the ResizeShow procedure and clicking the Run Macro button or pressing F5. If the dialog box does not display, check that the flashing insertion point is inside the ResizeShow procedure before you attempt to run. Also check the spellings of sheet and control names you have used.

Note that this dialog box does not use a separate procedure to set the starting or default size of the dialog frame. You must set the size of the dialog box before it displays. In this example, the DialogFrame.Height properties are used to set the height to 100 in the line prior to displaying the dialog box. Depending upon your video settings you may need to change 100 to a number appropriate to your screen resolution.

Creating and Assigning the Resizing Procedure

Once you have run the ResizeShow procedure to test that the dialog box displays, you can add the code that resizes the dialog box. In the module, type the code shown in listing 24.8.

Listing 24.8   RESIZE.XLS

```
Sub LargerButton_OnClick()
    'Change height of dialog box
    DialogSheets("dshtExpand").DialogFrame.Height = 200
End Sub

Sub SmallerButton_OnClick()
    'Change height of dialog box
    DialogSheets("dshtExpand").DialogFrame.Height = 100
End Sub

Sub GotMe()
    MsgBox "Got me"
End Sub
```

You will want these procedures to run when you click controls in the dialog box. To assign a procedure to a control in a dialog box, right-click the control in the dialog box and choose Assign Macro. In the Assign Macro dialog box, select the procedure you want assigned to the control you selected, then click OK. Assign the three procedures from listing 24.8 to the controls as shown in the following table.

Control	Procedure
btnLarger	LargerButton_OnClick
btnSmaller	SmallerButton_OnClick
ddnImportant	GotMe
ddnMore	GotMe
optOther	GotMe
optMore	GotMe

Running the Resizable Dialog Box

To run this example, click inside the ResizeShow procedure and click the Run Macro button or press F5. When the dialog box appears, click the Larger or Smaller buttons to make the dialog box expand or contract. Notice that when you click the drop-down lists or option buttons, Excel beeps.

The dialog box and code have a flaw as they currently exist. If the keyboard is used, a user can still select from the drop-down lists or option buttons even when the drop-down list and option buttons do not show. To see this happen, display the dialog box, then click the Makes You Smaller button so the lower controls are not visible. Press Tab to move between the controls on the box. Notice that sometimes pressing Tab doesn't seem to have any affect. This is because it is selecting one of the hidden controls. When you think a hidden control is selected, press the spacebar. If a hidden control is selected, pressing the spacebar activates the GotMe procedure, which displays the Got Me message box.

You probably don't want users selecting from controls outside the visible dialog box, so you should disable the controls when they are not visible and enable them when they are visible.

Enabling and Disabling Hidden Controls

Enabling and disabling controls is an effective way of preventing users from making incorrect selections. For example, if the user made previous selections in a dialog box that makes some options inappropriate, you should disable those inappropriate options. This prevents users from even having a chance to make the wrong selection.

Add the procedures in listing 24.9 to see how to enable and disable controls. The listing shows all procedures entered so far. Modifications to previous procedures and new procedures are shown in bold.

Listing 24.9   RESIZE.XLS

```
Option Explicit

Sub ResizeShow()
    'Disable options and lists that are not visible
    DisableOptions
    'Set dialog box height to default in case it was previously enlarged
    DialogSheets("dshtExpand").DialogFrame.Height = 100
    DialogSheets("dshtExpand").Show
End Sub

Sub LargerButton_OnClick()
    'Enable options and lists that are now visible
    EnableOptions
    'Change height of dialog box
    DialogSheets("dshtExpand").DialogFrame.Height = 200
End Sub

Sub SmallerButton_OnClick()
    'Disable options and lists that are not visible
    DisableOptions
    'Change height of dialog box
    DialogSheets("dshtExpand").DialogFrame.Height = 100
End Sub

Sub Beep()
    MsgBox "Got me"
End Sub

Sub EnableOptions()
    DialogSheets("dshtExpand").DropDowns("ddnImportant").Enabled = True
    DialogSheets("dshtExpand").DropDowns("ddnMore").Enabled = True
    DialogSheets("dshtExpand").OptionButtons("optOther").Enabled = True
    DialogSheets("dshtExpand").OptionButtons("optMore").Enabled = True
End Sub

Sub DisableOptions()
    DialogSheets("dshtExpand").DropDowns("ddnImportant").Enabled = False
    DialogSheets("dshtExpand").DropDowns("ddnMore").Enabled = False
    DialogSheets("dshtExpand").OptionButtons("optOther").Enabled = False
    DialogSheets("dshtExpand").OptionButtons("optMore").Enabled = False
End Sub
```

Notice that you will not assign the procedures EnableOptions and DisableOptions to controls. These procedures run as subroutines within the procedures that resize the dialog box. The first three procedures call the appropriate enabling or disabling procedure by entering the subroutine's name as a line of code.

When the dialog box first displays, it has a short height so the DisableOptions procedure is called. After that, clicking the Larger button shows the controls so the EnableOptions procedure runs. Conversely, clicking the Smaller button hides the controls and runs the DisableOptions procedure.

To enable or disable a control, specify the object then follow the object with the Enabled property. Setting that property equal to True enables a control; setting that property equal to False disables a control.

Running the Resizable Dialog Box with Hidden Controls Disabled

Now when you display the dialog box, you cannot move to or select dialog box controls that are not visible because they have been disabled by the DisableOptions dialog box. Pressing the Tab key only moves to the controls that show.

Switching Between List Contents

Lists are commonly used to make data entry easier. With a list you don't have to remember or type product codes or exact descriptions. Lists also reduce the number of typographical errors. However, one frequently requested modification that programmers hear is to make a list that shows two or three different types of contents in the same list box. For example, some people may want to look up a company's stock by the company name, such as Microsoft, while others want to look up the stock by its stock market symbol, MSFT. Switching the contents of a list is also very useful when you are dealing with inventory or product SKUs. Some people will want to enter or look up an item using the product code or SKU number, while others are more familiar with a product's text description. If you learn how to use the following technique you can create list boxes that switch their contents at the click of an option button.

The following example shows you how to create a list box that switches its contents between company names and stock market symbols. All the user has to do is click the appropriate option button. In figure 24.7 the Names option button has been selected so that company names show in the list. In figure 24.8 the Symbols option button has been selected so that stock symbols show in the list.

Fig. 24.7

Selecting the Names option button displays a list of company names in the list box.

24

Fig. 24.8
*Selecting the Symbols
option button displays
a list of company stock
symbols in the list box.*

Preparing the Sheets for Switchable Lists

Open a new workbook and save the workbook with the name Lists_sw.xls. This file name will later be used in the VBA code.

To build this example, begin by opening a new workbook. Insert a module sheet and a dialog sheet. Rename these sheets by double-clicking the sheet tab, typing a name into the Rename Sheet dialog box and clicking OK. Rename with the names shown in the following table

Sheet Type	Sheet Name
Worksheet	wshtSwitchList
Dialog sheet	dshtSwitchList
Module sheet	mshtSwitchList

On the worksheet you will need to create a list and three range names. Enter the list of computer company names and symbols as shown in figure 24.9. These lists will be used as the contents of the list box. Since the list box will be able to switch between the two lists, you should have the lists so that items in the rngNames lists match the corresponding item in the rngSymbols list.

Type the headings rngNames and rngSymbols at the top of the lists. Select the headings and the lists, cells F2:G9 and choose Insert, Name, Create. When the Create Names dialog box displays, select only the Top Row check box and click OK. This applies the name rngNames to F3:F9 and the name rngSymbols to G3:G9.

You will also need a named cell where the selection from the list box will be placed when the user clicks the OK button in the dialog box. Select a cell to receive the data (D6 was used in the figure), then click Insert, Name, Define and enter the name rngStock. Click OK.

Fig. 24.9

*The list in your
dialog box will switch
between the lists on
the worksheet.*

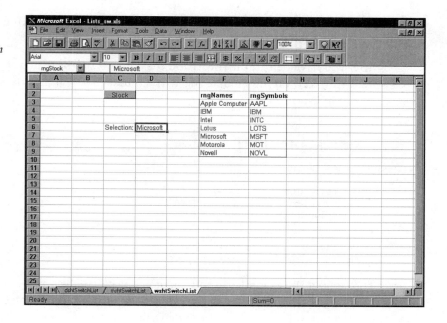

Drawing the Dialog Box and Naming its Controls for Switchable Lists

To create the dialog box shown in figures 24.7 and 24.8, select the dialog sheet, then drag across Dialog Caption in the title bar. Change the title bar name to Switch Lists.

Name the controls using the names shown in the following table so that the code will find controls with the correct names. Use the naming method described in the section "Naming Dialog Box Controls" at the beginning of this chapter.

Names for Controls in the Switch List Dialog Box

Control Type	Prefix	Example
Option button	opt	optNames
Option button	opt	optSymbols
List box	lst	lstStocks

Creating and Assigning the Show Dialog Procedure for Switchable Lists

After you have named the sheets and the controls on the dialog sheet, you can enter the following code on the module sheet. The initial code you must type into the module is shown in listing 24.10.

Listing 24.10   LISTS_SW.XLS

```
Option Explicit

Dim objlstStocks As ListBox
Dim objoptSymbols As OptionButton
Dim objoptNames As OptionButton

Sub SwitchList_Show()
    DialogSheets("dshtSwitchList").Show
End Sub
```

Throughout the examples in this chapter, object variables are used to reduce the amount of typing required and to make code easier to read. Object variables are described more fully in the earlier section "Checking Data as It Is Typed into an Edit Box."

In this example there are three objects variables, objlstStocks, objoptSymbols, and objoptNames. These objects use two prefixes to define them. The prefix obj indicates to the reader that this is an object variable. The second prefix indicates that it represents a list or option button.

Once you have entered the code shown in listing 24.10, you can display the dialog box by clicking within the SwitchList_Show procedure, then clicking the Run Macro button or pressing F5.

If you want to quickly run the SwitchList_Show procedure, assign the procedure to a macro button on the worksheet by following these steps:

1. Activate the worksheet.
2. Right-click a toolbar and select the Drawing toolbar. You will need the Drawing toolbar to draw a button that will run your procedure.
3. Click the Create Button button found at the mid-point of the Drawing toolbar, then drag across the location on the sheet where you want the button. Let go of the left mouse button when you have outlined the button.
4. Select the SwitchList_Show procedure from the Macro Name list, then choose OK.

Clicking this button runs the SwitchList_Show procedure that displays the dialog box. Because the contents of the list box have not yet been specified, the list appears blank when the dialog box displays.

Setting the Default and Checking Results for Switchable Lists

One of the best ways to set the defaults in a dialog box is to assign a default procedure to the frame of the dialog box. When the dialog box displays, the procedure assigned to the frame runs. At the bottom of the module sheet, enter the procedures shown in listing 24.11 to learn how to set defaults.

Listing 24.11   LISTS_SW.XLS

```
Sub SwitchList_OnFrame()
    'Set dialog box defaults
    'Name object variables
    Set objlstStocks = DialogSheets("dshtSwitchList").ListBoxes("lstStocks")
    Set objoptSymbols = DialogSheets("dshtSwitchList").OptionButtons("optSymbols")
    Set objoptNames = DialogSheets("dshtSwitchList").OptionButtons("optNames")
    'Set defaults
    objoptNames.Value = xlOn
    objoptSymbols.Value = xlOff
    objlstStocks.ListFillRange = "lists_sw.xls!rngNames"
End Sub

Sub SwitchList_OnOK()
    Dim snResult As String
    'Get text selection of stock list, then enter in range on sheet
    snResult = objlstStocks.List(objlstStocks.ListIndex)
    Range("rngStock").Value = snResult
End Sub
```

Assign the SwitchList_OnFrame procedure to the frame of the dialog box by selecting the dialog box sheet. Right-click the frame, the edge of the dialog box, and choose the Assign to Macro command. Select the SwitchList_OnFrame procedure and choose OK. Repeat the process to assign the SwitchList_OnOK procedure to the OK button in the dialog box. By assigning the SwitchList_OnOK procedure to the OK, you specify that it will run when the user clicks the OK button.

The SwitchList_OnFrame procedure sets three object variables that can be used to refer to the list and option buttons throughout the rest of the module. This reduces typing, saves memory, and reduces errors. The procedure then uses the Value property to set one option button on and the other off. Only one can be on at a time. The default contents for the list are specified with the line:

```
objlstStocks.ListFillRange = "lists_sw.xls!rngNames"
```

The ListFillRange property fills the contents of the list object specified by the variable objlstStocks. The contents of the list will be found in the workbook lists_sw.xls. You should have saved your workbook with this name. If you have not, do so. The cells that hold the contents are in the range rngNames.

After entering and assigning these procedures, your dialog box should display with a filled list. Selecting an item from the list and clicking OK will take the selected item from the list and enter it in the range named rngStock. The first line of the following list uses the ListIndex property to extract the item number of the currently selected item. Using this number as the index number for the List property returns the actual text item selected. The text is stored in the variable snResult. The second line sets the value of the rngStock range equal to the text stored in snResult.

```
snResult = objlstStocks.List(objlstStocks.ListIndex)
    Range("rngStock").Value = snResult
```

Creating and Assigning the List Switching Procedures

Now that your dialog box displays and the selected list item appears when you choose OK, you can write two additional lines of code that will switch the contents of the list in the dialog box. Go to the bottom of the module and enter the lines in listing 24.12.

Listing 24.12   LISTS_SW.XLS

```
Sub SwitchList_OnNames()
    'If Names option clicked, then refill list with rngNames
    objlstStocks.ListFillRange = "lists_sw.xls!rngNames"
End Sub

Sub SwitchList_OnSymbols()
    'If Stocks option clicked, then refill list with rngStocks
    objlstStocks.ListFillRange = "lists_sw.xls!rngSymbols"
End Sub
```

Activate the dialog sheet, then assign the SwitchList_OnNames procedure to the Names option button. Assign the SwitchList_OnSymbol procedure to the Symbols option button.

Running the Switch List Dialog Box

To run this example, click inside the SwitchList_Show procedure and click the Run Macro button or press F5. When the dialog box appears, you can select an item from the list. Click the unselected option button to switch the list to its alternate contents. Notice that the selected item remains valid. Both lists must be in corresponding order if you want to be able to switch back and forth and have the same selection refer to the same stock. Clicking the OK button puts the text of the selected item into the rngStock range on the worksheet.

Reading the Entire Switchable Lists Procedure

Listing 24.13 shows all the procedures used to create the Switch List dialog box. The complete workbook containing this example is stored in the file Lists_sw.xls on the CD-ROM that comes with this book.

Listing 24.13   LISTS_SW.XLS

```
Option Explicit

Dim objlstStocks As ListBox
Dim objoptSymbols As OptionButton
Dim objoptNames As OptionButton

Sub SwitchList_Show()
    DialogSheets("dshtSwitchList").Show
End Sub

Sub SwitchList_OnFrame()
    'Set dialog box defaults
    'Name object variables
    Set objlstStocks = DialogSheets("dshtSwitchList").ListBoxes("lstStocks")
    Set objoptSymbols = DialogSheets("dshtSwitchList").OptionButtons("optSymbols")
    Set objoptNames = DialogSheets("dshtSwitchList").OptionButtons("optNames")
    'Set defaults
    objoptNames.Value = xlOn
    objoptSymbols.Value = xlOff
    objlstStocks.ListFillRange = "lists_sw.xls!rngNames"
End Sub

Sub SwitchList_OnOK()
    Dim snResult As String
    'Get text selection of stock list, then enter in range on sheet
    snResult = objlstStocks.List(objlstStocks.ListIndex)
    Range("rngStock").Value = snResult
End Sub

Sub SwitchList_OnNames()
    'If Names option clicked, then refill list with rngNames
    objlstStocks.ListFillRange = "lists_sw.xls!rngNames"
End Sub

Sub SwitchList_OnSymbols()
    'If Stocks option clicked, then refill list with rngStocks
    objlstStocks.ListFillRange = "lists_sw.xls!rngSymbols"
End Sub
```

24

Interactively Changing Live Charts in a Dialog Box

Excel is one of the premiere software packages for creating Executive Information Systems. EISs, also known as Enterprise Information Systems, display strategic and tactical financial, sales, and marketing information in easily interpreted charts and tables. EISs usually display data that is kept very current through frequent downloads from mainframes to Excel directories or by making Excel directly access SQL databases. Well-designed EISs are known for being easy to use even though they present complex, frequently changing information.

Related to EISs are Decision Support Systems. DSSs are also strategic business tools that are frequently built on spreadsheets containing formulas, tables, and databases. DSSs attempt to emulate how a business reacts within its environment. Analysts and managers frequently use DSSs to understand or forecast the affect of changes in their business. Input to a DSS might be product pricing, discounts, commissions, regional buying patterns, and so forth. A DSS uses its mathematical or rule-based model to show the resulting affect on a company's finances, sales, or marketing.

In both EIS and DSS, users often enter data, check a result in a graph or worksheet, then reenter the data. They continue this iterative process of entering data and checking results until they find the combination of data that produces a realistic output. One way to make this iterative process easier is to display charts showing the affect of the input directly in the data entry dialog box. In the following example, shown in figure 24.10, as data are entered in the edit boxes, a chart in the dialog box immediately shows the results from the newly entered data. The chart immediately updates as the user types new numbers. The user doesn't need to close the dialog box to see the result he is looking for.

Fig. 24.10

Live charts in dialog boxes enable the user to enter data and immediately see the result in a chart.

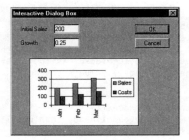

Preparing the Interactive Chart Sheets

To build this example, begin by opening a new workbook. Insert a module sheet and a dialog sheet. Rename these sheets by double-clicking the sheet tab, typing a name into the Rename Sheet dialog box, and clicking OK. Rename with the names shown in the following table.

Sheet Type	Sheet Name
Worksheet	wshtInteractive
Dialog sheet	dshtInteractive
Module sheet	mshtInteractive

The Interactive dialog box uses Sales and Cost forecast data that is on the worksheet. The worksheet and a set of data are shown in figure 24.11. The worksheet is designed so that numbers entered into the Initial and Growth cells generate new Sales and Costs figures. The chart that will be created on the dialog sheet will be based on the worksheet's Sales and Costs figures. When new Sales and Costs calculate, the chart updates.

Fig. 24.11

The worksheet data will be used to create a chart in the dialog box.

To create the worksheet, type the text labels as shown in table 24.2.

Table 24.2   Creating Labels on the Worksheet

Cells	Label
A2	Initial
A3	Growth
D2	Sales
D3	Costs
E1	Jan
F1	Feb
G1	Mar

Name the cells B2 and B3 with the labels in cells A2:A3, by selecting A2:B3, then choosing Insert, Name, Create. Select the Left Column check box, then click OK. This assigns the names Initial and Growth to cells A2 and A3.

To give the program some initial data, type 200 into cell B2 and type 1 into B3. These numbers will later be updated by entries into the edit boxes in the dialog box.

Enter the formulas in table 24.3 to create the Sales and Costs forecasts.

Table 24.3   Creating Formulas for Sales and Costs Forecasts

Cell	Formula
E2	=B2
E3	=0.5*E2
F2	=E2*(1+$B$3)
F3	=0.5*F2
G2	=F2*(1+$B$3)
G3	=0.5*G2

Drawing the Interactive Chart Dialog Box and Naming its Controls

To create the dialog box shown in figure 24.12 select the dialog sheet, then drag across Dialog Caption in the title bar. Change the title bar name to Interactive Dialog Box.

Fig. 24.12

Your dialog boxes can contain objects from a worksheet.

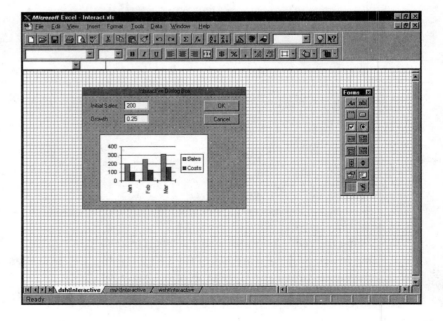

To make programming easier and more manageable, you should name the controls in the dialog box. In this case there are only two controls that need to be named, the two edit boxes. When you draw the edit boxes and labels, make sure you leave enough room for the chart.

Use the naming method described in the section "Naming Dialog Box Controls" earlier in this chapter. The names used by the example code that follows are shown in the following table.

Control Type	Prefix	Example
Edit box	edt	edtSales
Edit box	edt	edtGrowth

Creating the Interactive Chart in the Dialog Box

Now create the chart you see in figure 24.12 by selecting the worksheet data in cells D1:G3, then clicking the ChartWizard button in the Standard toolbar. Switch to the dialog sheet by clicking the tab for dshtInteractive. You will not loose the ChartWizard crosshairs when you do this.

When the dialog sheet appears, drag the crosshairs across the area of the dialog box where you want the chart. When you release the mouse button, make the necessary selections from the ChartWizard to create a chart of the type you want. Remember that a chart in a dialog box will be small so you will want to limit the use of legend, titles, and so forth.

Creating and Assigning the Show Dialog Procedure
for an Interactive Chart

After you have named the sheets and the dialog box, you can enter the following code on the module sheet. The initial code you must type into the module is shown in listing 24.13.

Listing 24.13   INTERACT.XLS

```
Option Explicit

Dim objedtSales As EditBox
Dim objedtGrowth As EditBox
```

continues

24

Listing 24.13   Continued

```
Sub ChartShow()
    'Set variable names for objects
    Set objedtSales = DialogSheets("dshtInteractive").EditBoxes("edtSales")
    Set objedtGrowth = DialogSheets("dshtInteractive").EditBoxes("edtGrowth")
    'Set edit box input type and default text
    objedtSales.InputType = xlNumber
    objedtSales.Text = Worksheets("wshtInteractive").Range("Initial").Value
    objedtGrowth.InputType = xlNumber
    objedtGrowth.Text = Worksheets("wshtInteractive").Range("Growth").Value
    'Display dialog box
    DialogSheets("dshtInteractive").Show
End Sub
```

Throughout the examples in this chapter, object variables are used to reduce the amount of typing required and to make code easier to read. Object variables are described more fully in the earlier section "Checking Data as It Is Typed into an Edit Box." The object variables in this procedure are objedtSales and objedtGrowth. They represent the Sales and Growth edit box objects, respectively.

The type of entry allowed in the edit boxes is set by specifying the InputType as xlNumber. The default values for the edit boxes are set by setting the Text property of the edit boxes equal to the Value property of the Initial or Growth ranges on the worksheet.

After you have entered the code shown in listing 24.13, you can display the dialog box by clicking within the ChartShow procedure and clicking the Run Macro button or pressing F5. You can also draw a macro button on the worksheet and assign the ChartShow procedure to that button. If the dialog box does not display, check that the flashing insertion point is inside the procedure before you attempt to run. Also, check the spellings of names you have used.

Updating the Worksheet and Interactive Chart

After you have the dialog box displaying with both the chart and the default edit box values, you can learn how to update the chart. In reality, there is nothing to updating the chart. All you need to do is make the edit boxes transfer their contents into the worksheet whenever a user types in the edit box. As soon as the worksheet updates, the chart in the worksheet will update.

To make the edit boxes transfer their contents to the worksheet ranges on each keystroke, you will need to enter listing 24.14 at the bottom of the module sheet.

Listing 24.14   INTERACT.XLS

```
Sub UpdateChart_OnKeystroke()
    'Transfer edit box numbers into ranges on worksheet
    Worksheets("wshtInteractive").Range("Initial").Value = objedtSales.Text
    Worksheets("wshtInteractive").Range("Growth").Value = objedtGrowth.Text
End Sub
```

This procedure sets the value of the Initial and Growth ranges on the worksheet equal to the values in the corresponding edit box. When the values in the worksheet change, then the chart changes. The trick is to get this procedure to run each time the user types a new number into an edit box.

To make this procedure run when someone types in an edit box, assign the procedure to each edit box. Select one of the edit boxes, choose Tools, Assign Macro, select UpdateChart_OnKeystroke from the list, then choose OK. Repeat the process for the other edit box. This procedure will now run each time a user types in an edit box.

Running the Interactive Chart Dialog Box

To run this example, click inside the ChartShow procedure and click the Run Macro button or press F5. You may want to draw a macro button on the worksheet and assign the ChartShow procedure to that button. Clicking the macro button runs the procedure.

When the dialog box appears, type new numbers. The chart updates.

Reading the Entire Procedure for an Interactive Chart

Listing 24.15 shows all the procedures used to create the Interactive Dialog Box. The complete workbook containing this example is stored in the file INTERACT.XLS on the CD-ROM that comes with this book.

24

Listing 24.15   INTERACT.XLS

```
'Interactive Dialog Box

Option Explicit

Dim objedtSales As EditBox
Dim objedtGrowth As EditBox

Sub ChartShow()
    'Set variable names for objects
    Set objedtSales = DialogSheets("dshtInteractive").EditBoxes("edtSales")
    Set objedtGrowth = DialogSheets("dshtInteractive").EditBoxes("edtGrowth")
    'Set edit box input type and default text
```

continues

Listing 24.15   Continued

```
        objedtSales.InputType = xlNumber
        objedtSales.Text = Worksheets("wshtInteractive").Range("Initial").Value
        objedtGrowth.InputType = xlNumber
        objedtGrowth.Text = Worksheets("wshtInteractive").Range("Growth").Value
        'Display dialog box
        DialogSheets("dshtInteractive").Show
End Sub

Sub UpdateChart_OnKeystroke()
        'Transfer edit box numbers into ranges on worksheet
        Worksheets("wshtInteractive").Range("Initial").Value = objedtSales.Text
        Worksheets("wshtInteractive").Range("Growth").Value = objedtGrowth.Text
End Sub
```

Creating Multiple Selection List Boxes

Multiple selection list boxes can save your program's users from displaying the same list multiple times. They enable a user to select one or more items in a single list box. VBA can then store all the selected items in an array variable. Your program can then work with each item in the array variable. For example, you may have a client who wants to select multiple reports from a list of all the reports available. With a multiple selection scrolling list they can select more than one report from within the same list. Figure 24.13 shows a multiselect list with three items selected.

Fig. 24.13

Multiselect lists make it easy for users to capture multiple items quickly.

 Note

Multiple selection list boxes don't store items in the same order in which they are selected.

If you need to know the order in which items are selected from a multiselect list box, then you should use the procedure described in the upcoming section "Building and Reordering Lists in a Dialog Box." This procedure enables a user to select items in a specific order. Users can even reorder their list of selections.

Preparing the Multiple Selection Sheets

To build this example, begin by opening a new workbook. Insert a module sheet and a dialog sheet. Rename these sheets by double-clicking the sheet tab, typing a name into the Rename Sheet dialog box, and clicking OK. Rename with the names shown in the following table

Sheet Type	Sheet Name
Worksheet	wshtMulti
Dialog sheet	dshtMulti
Module sheet	mshtMulti

The worksheet will contain the contents of the list and an array of TRUE and FALSE values that specify the default selections in the list. Figure 24.14 shows the worksheet. Enter the values as shown in the figure. Name the range A2:A6 with the name rngContents. Name the range B2:B6 with the name rngSelections.

The contents of A2:A6 will appear in the list box. The TRUE values in B2:B6 specify which items in the list box are selected when the list box displays.

Fig. 24.14

The worksheet contains two ranges, a list of contents and a TRUE/FALSE list specifying selected items.

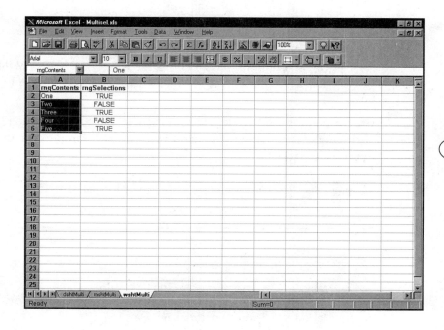

24

Drawing the Multiple Selection Dialog Box and its Controls

To create the dialog box shown in figure 24.15, select the dialog sheet, then drag across Dialog Caption in the title bar. Change the title bar name to Multiple Select List.

Fig. 24.15

Multiselect list boxes enable users to select more than one item.

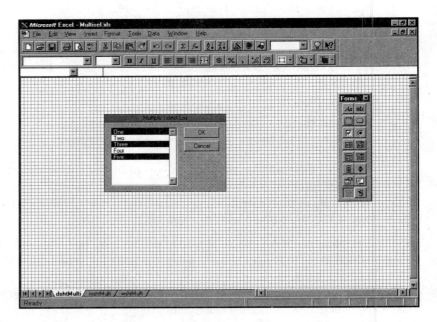

To make programming easier and more manageable, you should name the controls in the dialog box. In this case, there is only one control that needs to be named: the list box.

Use the naming method described in the section "Naming Dialog Box Controls" at the beginning of this chapter. The names used by the example code that follows are shown in the following table.

Control Type	Prefix	Example
List box	lst	lstMulti

 Tip

If you double-click an item in a list box, it is the same as selecting an item, and then clicking OK. If you do not want double-clicking to choose OK, then right-click the OK button in the dialog sheet, choose Format Object, and deselect the Default check box.

Note

Some users won't know how to use a multiselect list. Include text in your dialog box describing how to select multiple items.

Creating and Assigning the Show Dialog Procedure for Multiple Selection

After you have named the sheets and created the list box on the dialog sheet, you can enter the following code on the module sheet. The initial code you must type into the module is shown in listing 24.16.

Listing 24.16   MULTISEL.XLS

```
Option Explicit

Dim objlstMulti As ListBox
Dim aSelections
Dim aResults

Sub MultiListShow()
    Set objlstMulti = DialogSheets("dshtMulti").ListBoxes("lstMulti")
    'Set list property as xlNone, xlSimple, or xlExtended
    objlstMulti.MultiSelect = xlExtended
    DialogSheets("dshtMulti").Show
End Sub
```

Throughout the examples in this chapter, object variables are used to reduce the amount of typing required and to make code easier to read. In this example, the object variable objlstMulti represents the list box on the dialog sheet. Object variables are described more fully in the earlier section "Checking Data as It Is Typed into an Edit Box."

An important line in this code is where the MultiSelect property for the list box is set to xlExtended. This specifies that the list box will be a multiple selection list box. There are three selection types for a list box. Each of these types are set by setting the MultiSelect property equal to an xl constant as shown in listing 24.16. The different selection types available are shown in table 24.4.

Table 24.4   List Box Selection Types

Type	xlConstant	Description
Single Select	xlNone	Select only one item at a time.

continues

24

Table 24.4   Continued

Type	xlConstant	Description
Simple Multiselect	xlSimple	Select one or more items by clicking them. Items toggle on or off when clicked a second time.
Extended Multiselect	xlExtended	Click an item to select the item and deselect all others. Select multiple adjacent items by clicking the top item, then Shift+click the last. Select non-adjacent items with a Ctrl+click each item.

You can see how different types of multiselect list boxes work by changing the xlExtended constant in this example to xlNone or xlSimple.

 Note

Early versions of Excel 5 have a problem with multiselect lists. Versions of Excel 5 prior to Excel 5.0c were not coded correctly for the constants xlNone, xlSimple, and xlExtended. For these versions, use the numbers 1, 2, and 3, respectively.

After you have entered the code shown in listing 24.16, you can display the dialog box by clicking within the MultiListShow procedure and clicking the Run Macro button or pressing F5. If the dialog box does not display, check that the flashing insertion point is inside the procedure before you attempt to run. Also, check the spellings of names you have used.

Setting Multiple Selection Defaults and Checking Results

One of the best ways to set the defaults in a dialog box is to assign a default procedure to the frame of the dialog box. When the dialog box shows on-screen, the procedure assigned to the frame runs before the dialog box displays. At the bottom of the module enter the procedures shown in listing 24.17.

Listing 24.17   MULTISEL.XLS

```
Sub MultiList_OnFrame()
    'Define list contents
```

```
    objlstMulti.ListFillRange = "wshtMulti!rngContents"
    'Define default selection as array of True/False
    ReDim aSelections(5)
    aSelections = Worksheets("wshtMulti").Range("rngSelections").Value
    objlstMulti.Selected = aSelections
End Sub

Sub Multi_OnOK()
    Dim i As Integer

    'Store contents of multiple selection in array variable
    aResults = objlstMulti.Selected
    'Show contents of selection
    For i = LBound(aResults) To UBound(aResults)
        If aResults(i) Then MsgBox objlstMulti.List(i)
    Next
End Sub
```

Assign the MultiList_OnFrame procedure to the frame of the dialog box by first selecting the sheet containing the dialog box. Right-click the frame, the outside edge of the dialog box, and choose the Assign to Macro command. Select the MultiList_OnFrame procedure and choose OK. Repeat the same process to assign the Multi_OnOK procedure to the OK button in the dialog box.

The MultiList_OnFrame procedure fills the list with contents and selects which items in the list are selected. It runs when the dialog box and its frame appear. The first line of code specifies that the list box is filled with the cell contents in the range rngContents. In the second line of code, the array variable aSelections is used to store TRUE and FALSE values that are used to specify which list items are selected when the list displays. The aSelections variable is redimensioned to hold five elements. The array variable is then loaded with TRUE and FALSE values by setting it equal to the TRUE and FALSE values in the worksheet range rngSelections. The last line of code actually specifies which items in a multiselect list are selected. By setting the Selected property equal to the array of TRUE and FALSE in aSelections, you specify which items are selected when the dialog box displays. Items that correspond to a TRUE value are selected. You can change the default selections in the list by changing the TRUE and FALSE values in the range rngSelections.

By assigning the Multi_OnOK procedure to the OK, you specify that this procedure will run when the user clicks the OK button. The Multi_OnOK procedure extracts only selected items from the list and displays them in a message box. Multiple selections are pulled from a list box through the use of the Selected property and a loop. In the Multi_OnOK procedure, the variable aResults is used to store all selected items from the list. The variable aResults is set equal to the array returned by the Selected property of the list box object. A For...Next loop is then used to loop through each element in the aResults array and display each element in the message box. Notice that the Lbound and Ubound functions are used to calculate the upper and lower limits for the loop.

24

Note

To learn how to extract multiple selected items and put them into adjacent cells in a worksheet see "Transferring Multiple Selected Items to the Worksheet," near the end of this chapter.

Running the Multiple Selection Dialog Box

To run this example, click inside the MultiListShow procedure and click the Run Macro button or press F5. When the dialog box appears, notice that there are three items selected in the list box. Clicking any item deselects the previously selected items.

To select multiple adjacent items from the list, first click the topmost item in the list you want selected. Then, Shift+click on the last item you want selected.

To select non-adjacent items from the list, hold down Ctrl as you click items. Clicking a selected item deselects it.

Clicking the OK button displays a series of message boxes showing you which items were selected.

Reading the Entire Procedure for Multiple Selection

Listing 24.18 shows all the procedures used to create the multiple selection list box. The complete workbook containing this example is stored in the file MULTISEL.XLS on the CD-ROM that comes with this book.

Listing 24.18   The Complete Listing for Multisel.xls.

```
'Multiple Selection List Box

Option Explicit

Dim objlstMulti As ListBox
Dim aSelections
Dim aResults

Sub MultiListShow()
    Set objlstMulti = DialogSheets("dshtMulti").ListBoxes("lstMulti")
    'Set list property as xlNone, xlSimple, or xlExtended
    objlstMulti.MultiSelect = xlExtended
    DialogSheets("dshtMulti").Show
End Sub
```

```
Sub MultiList_OnFrame()
    'Define list contents
    objlstMulti.ListFillRange = "wshtMulti!rngContents"
    'Define default selection as array of True/False
    ReDim aSelections(5)
    aSelections = Worksheets("wshtMulti").Range("rngSelections").Value
    objlstMulti.Selected = aSelections
End Sub

Sub Multi_OnOK()
    Dim i As Integer

    'Store contents of multiple selection in array variable
    aResults = objlstMulti.Selected
    'Show contents of selection
    For i = LBound(aResults) To UBound(aResults)
        If aResults(i) Then MsgBox objlstMulti.List(i)
    Next
End Sub
```

Building and Reordering Lists in a Dialog Box

In some cases the user may want to build a list of items selected in a specific order from a list box. In that case you can't use a multiselect list box like the one described in the previous section. A normal multiselect list box does not tell you the order in which items were selected. The way around this dilemma is to create a dialog box containing two lists like the one shown in figure 24.16. In this dialog box, you can select an item in the left list and click the Add button to add the item to the right list. The list on the left keeps items in the order in which they were added. If you want to reorder the list on the left, then you can select an item in the list on the left and click the Move Up or Move Down buttons.

Fig. 24.16

With the list builder, users can build a new list and change the order of items.

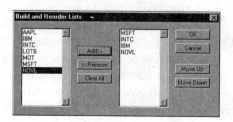

24

Note

For some procedures, such as selecting pages to be printed in a specific order, your procedure will need to know the order in which a user selects items from a list box. However, if your procedure doesn't need to know the order in which items are selected from a list box, then you should use the procedure described in the preceding section, "Creating Multiple Selection List Boxes." That procedure displays a single list from which users can select multiple items. It is easier and faster to program.

Preparing the Buildable List Sheets

To build this example, begin by opening a new workbook. Insert a module sheet and a dialog sheet. Rename these sheets by double-clicking the sheet tab, typing a name into the Rename Sheet dialog box, and clicking OK. Rename with the names shown in the following table.

Sheet Type	Sheet Name
Worksheet	wshtBuildList
Dialog sheet	dshtBuildList
Module sheet	mshtBuildList

You will need to create two ranges on the worksheet and populate one with names. Fill the range F4:F10 with text or numbers, then assign the name rngSource to that range. The contents of this range will be the contents of the source list box, the list box on the left in figure 24.16.

Select cell G4 and assign it the name rngTarget. When you click OK in the dialog box the list you build will be placed in the cell named rngTarget and those cells below it. The name rngTarget does not expand to include the items entered in the worksheet. The range rngTarget is only used as a reference point for the top of the list. The finished sheet is shown in figure 24.17.

Fig. 24.17

Create a worksheet with ranges for list contents and list results.

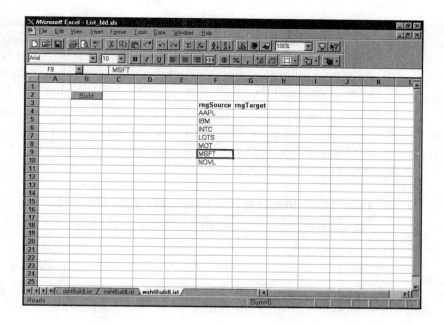

Drawing the Buildable List Dialog Box and Naming its Controls

To create the dialog box shown in figure 24.18, select the dialog sheet, then drag across Dialog Caption in the title bar. Change the title bar name to Build and Reorder Lists.

Fig. 24.18

The Build List dialog box uses macro buttons with procedures assigned.

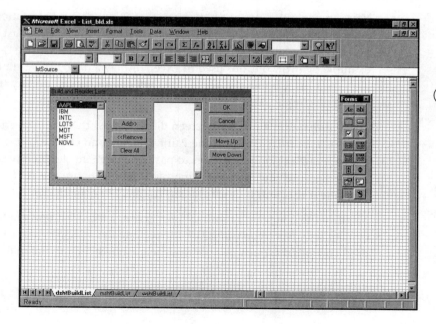

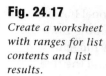

Draw the items in the dialog box using two list boxes and four additional buttons. Buttons are drawn with the Button tool found on the Macro toolbar or on the Drawing toolbar. You can put a new name on the button while it is selected by dragging across the button title and typing a new name. Click outside the button to end the title. Do not press Enter to end the title as that creates a second title line.

To make programming easier and more manageable you should name the controls referred to by your code. Use the naming method described in the section "Naming Dialog Box Controls" at the beginning of this chapter. The names used by the example code that follows are shown in table 24.5.

Table 24.5   Names for Controls in the Build List Dialog Box

Control Type	Prefix	Example
List box	lst	lstSource (left list)
List box	lst	lstTarget (right list)
Button	btn	btnAdd
Button	btn	btnRemove
Button	btn	btnClearAll
Button	btn	btnMoveUp
Button	btn	btnMoveDown

You can add noncopyright buttons or tool faces to your applications by copying them from the display of other applications. For example, the Build List dialog box could use up- and down-arrow buttons instead of the Move Up and Move Down buttons. To see an example of arrow buttons used in Excel, display a dialog sheet that contains a dialog box with controls. Choose the Tools, Tab Order command to display the Tab Order dialog box, then click an item in the list.

To capture buttons from any screen display, press the Print Screen key to copy the screen to the Clipboard. Now, start the Paint program and choose Edit, Paste to paste in the screen image. Respond with Yes to pasting a large image, then press Esc to deselect the image. Because you are using a graphic as a button, use the Text tool in Paint to type a new title if the button or graphic needs one. Drag the title into the appropriate location.

Magnify the image by choosing View, Zoom, Large Size. This enables you to see and copy exactly what you want. Use the rectangular selection tool to select the button, then choose Edit, Copy to copy your selection. Switch to the dialog box sheet and choose Edit, Paste to paste the button. Drag it into position. To assign a procedure to the pasted button, right-click the button and choose Assign Macro.

Creating and Assigning the Show Dialog Procedure for a Buildable List

Once you have named the sheets and the controls on the dialog sheet, you can enter the following code on the module sheet. The initial code you must type into the module is shown in listing 24.19.

Listing 24.19   LIST_BLD.XLS

```
Option Explicit

Dim objlstSource As ListBox
Dim objlstTarget As ListBox

Sub BuildList_Show()
    'Name variables
    Set objlstSource = DialogSheets("dshtBuildList").ListBoxes("lstSource")
    Set objlstTarget = DialogSheets("dshtBuildList").ListBoxes("lstTarget")
    DialogSheets("dshtBuildList").Show
End Sub
```

Throughout the examples in this chapter, object variables are used to reduce the amount of typing required and to make code easier to read. This procedure uses the object variable objlstSource to refer to the source list box. The object variable objlstTarget refers to the target list on the right. Object variables are described more fully in the earlier section "Checking Data as It Is Typed into an Edit Box."

After you have entered the code shown in listing 24.19, you can display the dialog box by clicking within the procedure and clicking the Run Macro button or pressing F5. If the dialog box does not appear, check that the flashing insertion point is inside the procedure before you attempt to run. Also, check the spellings of names you have used.

Filling the Buildable List Box

The procedure in listing 24.20 fills the source list box by specifying a range of filled cells on the worksheet. The ListIndex property then sets the default selected item in this list as the first item. Type this procedure in below the BuildList_Show procedure. Assign this procedure to the dialog box frame by selecting the edge of the dialog box, the frame, then right-clicking the edge and choosing Assign Macro. Select the procedure you want to run when the frame displays, in this case BuildList_OnFrame, then click OK.

24

Listing 24.20 LIST_BLD.XLS

```
Sub BuildList_OnFrame()
    'Set dialog box defaults
    'Fill source list from worksheet
    objlstSource.ListFillRange = "list_bld.xls!rngSource"
    'Set selected item in list
    objlstSource.ListIndex = 1
End Sub
```

If you run the BuildList_Show procedure at this time, the dialog box should display with the left list filled. The first item in the left list should be selected.

Adding Items to the Target List

You can add items to the target list on the right through the use of the procedure in listing 24.21. The BuildList_OnAdd procedure is designed to run when you click the Add button. After you enter this procedure, assign it to the add button by right-clicking the Add button, then choosing Assign Macro. Select the BuildList_OnAdd procedure and click OK.

The procedure begins by storing in the text variable snResult the currently selected item from the source list.

Listing 24.21 LIST_BLD.XLS

```
Sub BuildList_OnAdd()
    Dim snResult As String
    'Get text selection in source list
    snResult = objlstSource.List(objlstSource.ListIndex)
    'Prevent duplicate items from being added to target list
    'If target list is empty then add snResult item
    If objlstTarget.ListCount = 0 Then
        objlstTarget.AddItem Text:=snResult
    'If snResult does not match an item in target list, causing #N/A error,
    'then add snResult item
    ElseIf IsError(Application.Match(snResult, objlstTarget.List, 0)) Then
        objlstTarget.AddItem Text:=snResult
    End If
End Sub
```

In its simplest form the text in snResult could then be added to the bottom of the target list with the line:

```
objlstTarget.AddItem Text:=snResult
```

While this adds the item in snResult to the bottom of the target list, it has one practical drawback. It adds the item to the target list even if it already exists in the target list. This allows the user to build a target list containing duplicates. In most cases you won't want to allow duplicates in the target list.

Tip

Excel worksheet functions can be used within VBA, but they must be proceeded by the Application object. For example:

```
Application.Match()
```

To prevent duplicate items from being added to the target list, the procedure uses the Match() worksheet function to check whether the item stored in snResult is an exact match against any item in the target list, objlstTarget.List. The procedure accomplishes this with the code,

```
Application.Match(snResult, objlstTarget.List, 0)
```

The Match() function returns a #N/A error when there is no match. So if there is an error, the procedure should add the contents of snResult to the end of the target list. By enclosing the Application.Match function in an ISERROR function, a TRUE is produced whenever the #N/A error occurs. This TRUE result will be used by an ElseIf statement to run another line of code.

The use of the Match() function creates a new situation that must be accounted for if the procedure is to run smoothly. If you attempt to run the Match() function shown here against an empty target list, then the Match() function will fail with the error Match method of Application class failed. This error is not trapped by the ISERROR function and prevents a user from adding the first item to an empty target list.

A block IF statement controls the program flow to handle these two situations. The first IF statement uses the ListCount property to check if the target list is empty. If the list is empty, then a simple AddItem method adds the text in snResult to the bottom of the target list.

The ElseIf statement runs when the target list contains items. It runs the Match() function, which checks for duplicates. As just explained, the combination of ISERROR and Match produce a TRUE when there is no duplicate, so the AddItem method adds the text in snResult to the bottom of the target list. If there is a duplicate, then the item in snResult is not added to the target list.

If you display the dialog box at this point, you should be able to add items to the target list by selecting an item from the left list, then clicking the Add button.

Transferring Multiple Selected Items to the Worksheet

Thus far you can add selected items to the target list, but the procedures don't put the target list onto the worksheet. The BuildList_OnOK procedure shows you how to put multiple selected items stored in a list or array into a worksheet range. Enter listing 24.22 at the bottom of the module. Assign this procedure to the OK button.

24

Listing 24.22   LIST_BLD.XLS

```
Sub BuildList_OnOk()
Dim iCount As Integer
    'Clear range on sheet by as many cells as items in Source list
    Range("rngTarget").Resize(objlstSource.ListCount, 1).Clear
    'Copy items from target list to area below rngTarget
    For iCount = 1 To objlstTarget.ListCount
        Range("rngTarget").Offset(iCount - 1, 0) = objlstTarget.List(iCount)
    Next
End Sub
```

The first line of code clears a range starting at the rngTarget cell that is the same size as the source list. The Clear method clears the range specified by Range and Resize. The Range("rngTarget") specifies a starting cell. The Resize method resizes this starting point to be as many cells tall as there are items counted in the source list. The resized range is explicitly set as one column in width.

The For...Next loop loops through as many items as there are in the target list. During each loop the iCount variable is used to calculate the cell where data will be placed and which item from the target list should be put in that cell.

The Offset method calculates a new range object that is offset from the original rngTarget. For example, when iCount is 2, then Offset produces the cell one down from rngTarget.

The new calculated cell object is set equal to an item in the target list with the List property. The iCount variable specifies the item from the list that will be placed in the cell.

If you display the dialog box at this time, fill the target list with a few items and click OK. The items should be transferred to a column in the worksheet. If they are not, check that you assigned the BuildList_OnOK procedure to the OK button. Also check that the name rngTarget was defined on the worksheet.

Clearing All Items from the Target List

Clearing all items from the target list requires but a single line of code. Enter the procedure shown in listing 24.23 and assign that procedure to the Clear button. In this procedure the RemoveAllItems method removes all items from the target list.

Listing 24.23   LIST_BLD.XLS

```
Sub BuildList_OnClearAll()
    objlstTarget.RemoveAllItems
End Sub
```

Removing a Selected Item from the Target List

To remove a selected item from the target list, add listing 24.24 to the bottom of the module. Assign this procedure to the Remove button.

To run this procedure, add items to the target list. Select an item in the target list you want to remove, then click the Remove button.

Listing 24.24   LIST_BLD.XLS

```
Sub BuildList_OnRemove()
    On Error GoTo NoSelectionOnRemove
    If objlstTarget.ListCount < 1 Then GoTo EndOnRemove
    objlstTarget.RemoveItem Index:=objlstTarget.ListIndex
EndOnRemove:
Exit Sub
NoSelectionOnRemove:
End Sub
```

The On Error in the first line traps for the error that would occur if the user did not select an item in the target list, but then clicked the Remove button. The IF statement then checks to make sure there is at least one item in the target list. If there is, then the RemoveItem method removes the item that is currently selected in the target list. The item selected is specified by objlstTarget.ListIndex. The ListIndex property returns the number of the currently selected item in a list.

Moving an Item Up the Target List

Moving an item up or down in the target list can give your custom list a lot of flexibility. One way it can be used is within a list of reports that you are going to print. Reordering the reports in the list reorders the order in which the reports print. It can also be used to reorder the order in which information on multiple products might be queried by MS-Query.

Moving an item up or down in a list is an easy concept. Rather than having to move large amounts of data, you only need to switch the two items that are adjacent to each other. For example, if you want to move item C up into item B's location you only need to switch the two items. One of the items must be stored in a third location so it will not be replaced when the other item moves.

Type the procedure in listing 24.25 in the bottom of the module and assign it to the Move Up button. To run this procedure, select an item in the target list, then click the Move Up button. The selected item should move up and the item above should move down.

24

Listing 24.25   LIST_BLD.XLS

```
Sub BuildList_OnMoveUp()
Dim snSelectedItem As String
Dim snMovedItem As String
    On Error GoTo NoSelectionOnMoveUp
    If objlstTarget.ListCount < 1 Then GoTo EndOnMoveUp
    'Store item being replaced
    snMovedItem = objlstTarget.List(objlstTarget.ListIndex - 1)
    'Move selected item up
    objlstTarget.List(objlstTarget.ListIndex - 1) = _
        objlstTarget.List(objlstTarget.ListIndex)
    'Move replaced item down
    objlstTarget.List(objlstTarget.ListIndex) = snMovedItem
EndOnMoveUp:
Exit Sub
NoSelectionOnMoveUp:
End Sub
```

The On Error traps in case no item is selected in the target list when the Move Up button is clicked. The first If statement checks to make sure there are at least two items in the list.

Before moving an item up, the item above must be stored or it will be replaced by the item moving in. The text variable snMovedItem stores the text of the item that is one above the selected item in the target list. The List property returns the text of the specified by an index number. The index number used is ListIndex-1. Because ListIndex is the number of the current selection, ListIndex-1 is the number of the item above the current selection.

The line that follows replaces the item above with the item below:

```
objlstTarget.List(objlstTarget.ListIndex - 1) = _
        objlstTarget.List(objlstTarget.ListIndex)
```

Finally, the stored item is put into location of the item that was moved up by the line:

```
objlstTarget.List(objlstTarget.ListIndex) = snMovedItem
```

Moving an Item Down the Target List

Moving an item down in the target list requires almost exactly the same code as moving an item up. The difference is primarily the sign of the 1 added to the ListIndex.

Add the procedure in listing 24.26 to the bottom of the module and assign the procedure to the Move Down button. To run it, display the dialog box, select an item in the target list that has an item below it, and click the Move Down button.

Listing 24.26   LIST_BLD.XLS

```
Sub BuildList_OnMoveDown()
Dim snSelectedItem As String
Dim snMovedItem As String
    On Error GoTo NoSelectionOnMoveDown
    If objlstTarget.ListCount < 1 Then GoTo EndOnMoveDown
    'Store item being replaced
    snMovedItem = objlstTarget.List(objlstTarget.ListIndex + 1)
    'Move selected item Down
    objlstTarget.List(objlstTarget.ListIndex + 1) = _
        objlstTarget.List(objlstTarget.ListIndex)
    'Move replaced item up
    objlstTarget.List(objlstTarget.ListIndex) = snMovedItem
EndOnMoveDown:
Exit Sub
NoSelectionOnMoveDown:
End Sub
```

Reading the Entire Procedure for a Buildable List

Listing 24.27 shows all the procedures used to create the list builder. The complete workbook containing this example is stored in the file LIST_BLD.XLS on the CD-ROM that comes with this book.

Listing 24.27   LIST_BLD.XLS

```
Option Explicit

Dim objlstSource As ListBox
Dim objlstTarget As ListBox

Sub BuildList_Show()
    'Name variables
    Set objlstSource = DialogSheets("dshtBuildList").ListBoxes("lstSource")
    Set objlstTarget = DialogSheets("dshtBuildList").ListBoxes("lstTarget")
    DialogSheets("dshtBuildList").Show
End Sub

Sub BuildList_OnFrame()
    'Set dialog box defaults
    'Fill source list from worksheet
    objlstSource.ListFillRange = "list_bld.xls!rngSource"
    'Set selected item in list
    objlstSource.ListIndex = 1
End Sub

Sub BuildList_OnOk()
Dim iCount As Integer
    'Clear range on sheet by as many cells as items in Source list
    Range("rngTarget").Resize(objlstSource.ListCount, 1).Clear
    'Copy items from target list to area below rngTarget
    For iCount = 1 To objlstTarget.ListCount
```

24

continues

Listing 24.27   Continued

```
            Range("rngTarget").Offset(iCount - 1, 0) = objlstTarget.List(iCount)
    Next
End Sub

Sub BuildList_OnAdd()
    Dim snResult As String
    'Get text selection in source list
    snResult = objlstSource.List(objlstSource.ListIndex)
    'Prevent duplicate items from being added to target list
    'If target list is empty then add snResult item
    If objlstTarget.ListCount = 0 Then
        objlstTarget.AddItem Text:=snResult
    'If snResult does not match an item in target list, causing #N/A error,
    'then add snResult item
    ElseIf IsError(Application.Match(snResult, objlstTarget.List, 0)) Then
        objlstTarget.AddItem Text:=snResult
    End If
End Sub

Sub BuildList_OnRemove()
    On Error GoTo NoSelectionOnRemove
    If objlstTarget.ListCount < 1 Then GoTo EndOnRemove
    objlstTarget.RemoveItem Index:=objlstTarget.ListIndex
EndOnRemove:
Exit Sub
NoSelectionOnRemove:
End Sub

Sub BuildList_OnClearAll()
    objlstTarget.RemoveAllItems
End Sub

Sub BuildList_OnMoveUp()
Dim snSelectedItem As String
Dim snMovedItem As String
    On Error GoTo NoSelectionOnMoveUp
    If objlstTarget.ListCount < 1 Then GoTo EndOnMoveUp
    'Store item being replaced
    snMovedItem = objlstTarget.List(objlstTarget.ListIndex - 1)
    'Move selected item up
    objlstTarget.List(objlstTarget.ListIndex - 1) = _
        objlstTarget.List(objlstTarget.ListIndex)
    'Move replaced item down
    objlstTarget.List(objlstTarget.ListIndex) = snMovedItem
EndOnMoveUp:
Exit Sub
NoSelectionOnMoveUp:
End Sub
```

```
Sub BuildList_OnMoveDown()
Dim snSelectedItem As String
Dim snMovedItem As String
    On Error GoTo NoSelectionOnMoveDown
    If objlstTarget.ListCount < 1 Then GoTo EndOnMoveDown
    'Store item being replaced
    snMovedItem = objlstTarget.List(objlstTarget.ListIndex + 1)
    'Move selected item Down
    objlstTarget.List(objlstTarget.ListIndex + 1) = _
        objlstTarget.List(objlstTarget.ListIndex)
    'Move replaced item up
    objlstTarget.List(objlstTarget.ListIndex) = snMovedItem
EndOnMoveDown:
Exit Sub
NoSelectionOnMoveDown:
End Sub
```

Summary

Once you have seen example VBA code for simple dialog boxes, you may find them easy to create and understand. But simple dialog boxes won't always work as the best way for Excel users to enter data reliably and error free. By reviewing and plagarizing the examples in this chapter and on the CD you will be able to create complex dialog boxes that meet nearly all your dialog box needs.

Remember that Visual Basic for Applications gives you the ability to change or read nearly all the properties of controls in a dialog box. This gives you the ability to do such things as resize dialog boxes, enable or disable options, and create interactive charts in a dialog box. Once you understand array variables and FOR...NEXT loops, you can save your users' time and create professional looking programs through the use of multiple selection dialog boxes.

24

chapter 25

VBA Arrays

by Conrad Carlberg

25

In this chapter

◆ **Understanding VBA arrays**
An introduction to array concepts such as dimensions, dimension bounds, and single-dimension arrays.

◆ **Using variant arrays**
Learn special ways to use variant arrays that make your VBA code execute faster.

◆ **Creating arrays with a user-defined data type**
How to use a custom data type to create an array of multivariable records.

◆ **Writing custom functions that return arrays**
The structure of a function that puts values in more than one cell at once.

◆ **Sorting VBA arrays**
Learn efficient methods to sort VBA arrays.

Using arrays in VBA gives you a fast and powerful way to manipulate data without necessarily using a worksheet. If you've programmed in Fortran, Pascal, C, or some other array-oriented language, you are probably familiar with what arrays can do for you, and have favorite ways to accomplish your tasks by using arrays. Of course, different languages—including VBA—have slightly different syntaxes for array definition and manipulation, but the basic techniques are the same as the ones you're used to.

If you aren't an array wonk, consider becoming one. Arrays can make tasks like the following faster and easier:

▶ *Making intermediate calculations.* Suppose that, as part of a payroll calculation, you want to calculate each employee's current FICA payment. You can do this on a worksheet with a range that contains the total year-to-date salary, and another range that contains the current period's salary. (You need to check year-to-date salary against the maximum to which FICA applies.) After performing the check, you would probably want to clear the year-to-date range and, perhaps, move all the other data around to fill the empty worksheet space. Using VBA, you can read year-to-date salaries from another file into a VBA array, perform the check, and if the limit has not yet been met, continue with the current FICA calculation.

▶ *Working in three dimensions.* If you've ever sweated out the creation and manipulation of 3-D ranges in a workbook, you'll appreciate being able to use three-dimensional arrays in VBA. Of course, a three-dimensional array can quickly become extremely large—perhaps too large for VBA to handle—but if you exercise some restraint you'll find that it's a great technique. As a bonus, you can go to four or more dimensions in a VBA array. Try *that* in a workbook.

▶ *Manipulating objects automatically.* Suppose that each sheet in a workbook contains information on a different employee, and the sheet is given the employee's last name. You want the sheet tabs to appear in alphabetical order. You could do this manually, by dragging sheet tabs to the right and left. But if a VBA array named NameArray contains employee names, just sort NameArray into alphabetical order and then use a loop like this:

```
ThisWorkbook.Sheets(NameArray(1)).Move Before:=Sheets(2)
```

NameArray is in alphabetical order, and contains the names of all the employees. Start by making the sheet that corresponds to the first name in NameArray the first one in the workbook. Then, loop through the remaining names in NameArray:

```
For SheetCounter = 2 To EmployeeCount
    ThisWorkbook.Sheets(NameArray(SheetCounter)).Move
After:=Sheets(NameArray(SheetCounter - 1))
Next SheetCounter
```

As the loop proceeds through the rest of NameArray, the sheet that corresponds to each name is moved to the next position in the workbook.

This little loop puts the sheet tabs in the active workbook into the same order that their names are found in the VBA array NameArray. If you don't yet know how to sort a VBA array, you can find out in the section named "Sorting VBA Arrays," later in this chapter.

Understanding VBA Arrays

It's easiest to think of a VBA array as though it were a worksheet range, but one that doesn't have to appear on the worksheet. The array could have just one element, like a single worksheet cell or a named constant. It could have one "column" consisting of several "rows," just like the worksheet range A1:A10. Or it could have several columns and several rows, just like the worksheet range A1:C10.

One difference between an array and a range is that you can specify the *type* of data that an array can hold. You do this with the VBA Dim statement. For example:

```
Dim NameArray As String(10)
```

This statement makes it possible for NameArray to hold text values, such as *Jones Distributing*. In contrast, this statement:

```
Dim FactorArray As Single(15)
```

lets you store, in FactorArray, single precision floating point values such as *3.1416*.

Defining the Size of Arrays

When you dimension an array with a statement like this:

```
Dim SalaryArray(10)
```

you are not necessarily defining its maximum size as ten elements. Rather, the number 10 defines the index of SalaryArray's final element. The maximum number of elements that SalaryArray can contain depends on whether you use the Option Base 1 statement at the beginning of your module.

If you do use Option Base 1, the value of the first *index* in SalaryArray is 1. That is, using Option Base 1, this statement:

```
FICA = SalaryArray(1) * .5
```

is legal, if pessimistic. This statement:

```
FICA = SalaryArray(0) * .5
```

would not be legal. Option Base 1 specifies that the first index in any array dimensioned in the module must be 1: SalaryArray(0) is undefined.

By default, VBA assigns the value of an array's first index as 0. Thus, if you do *not* use Option Base 1, this statement:

```
FICA = SalaryArray(0) * .5
```

would be legal. However, when most of us count, we start with 1, not with 0. Therefore, it's usually best to use Option Base 1. Especially when you're tracing or debugging code, remembering that "The 19th value in SalaryArray is SalaryArray(18)" is just another headache you don't need. (Many programmers do favor the alternative, Option Base 0, because it lets them use some fancy coding tricks. But it's mainly a matter of personal preference.)

What about this one?

25

```
Dim SalaryArray(5 To 10)
```

The index of SalaryArray's first element is 5, and that of its last element is 10. This is true regardless of whether or not you use Option Base 1.

This type of Dim statement is often useful to help you keep indices straight. Suppose that you wanted to write the contents of SalaryArray to column A in a worksheet, beginning in row 5. If you had declared SalaryArray like this:

```
Dim SalaryArray(1 To 6)
```

or, assuming that you used Option Base 1, like this:

```
Dim SalaryArray(6)
```

then your code would have to be something like:

```
For RowCounter = 5 to 10
     Cells(RowCounter,1) = SalaryArray(RowCounter - 4)
Next RowCounter
```

or

```
For RowCounter = 1 to 6
     Cells(RowCounter + 4,1) = SalaryArray(Rowcounter)
Next RowCounter
```

That is, you would have to adjust the index for SalaryArray to conform to the index for RowCounter—or vice versa. For example, the first time through the loop, you want VBA to put the *first* value in SalaryArray in the *fifth* row of the worksheet. You must either subtract 4 from 5 to get the first element in SalaryArray, or add 4 to 1 to get the fifth worksheet row.

But if you dimension SalaryArray as

```
Dim SalaryArray(5 to 10)
```

then your code could be

```
For RowCounter = 5 to 10
     Cells(RowCounter,1) = SalaryArray(Rowcounter)
Next RowCounter
```

Again, this helps you stay clear with what's going on in your code. It's never fun to be mentally adding or subtracting a constant from an index to trace the logic in the code.

Another option that you can set in a VBA module is *Option Explicit*. Setting this option means that any variable used in your module must be explicitly declared, perhaps with a Dim statement, before you can use it. You can select Tools, Options, choose the Module General tab, and check the Require Variable Declaration check box to specify that all new modules begin with Option Explicit. This protects you against accidentally mistyping the name of a variable (thus, creating a new variable when you meant to refer to an existing one).

There is no similar option to require that Excel automatically put Option Base 1 at the beginning of a module. You can, however, create a module template that will insert this option on your behalf. To do so, follow these steps:

1. Open a new workbook.
2. Choose Insert, Macro and select Module from the cascading menu.
3. Switch to Sheet1, and choose Edit, Delete Sheet. Choose OK in response to the warning message. Your workbook should now have Module1 as its only sheet.
4. Enter Option Base 1 at the top of the module.
5. Choose File, Save As.
6. In the Save As Type drop-down box, choose Template(*.xlt). In the File Name edit box, enter **Module**. Ensure that Templates is the active folder in the Save In box. Then, choose OK.

When you want to insert a new module in a workbook, follow these steps:

1. Right-click a sheet tab that you want to *follow* the new module.
2. Choose Insert from the shortcut menu.
3. If necessary, click the General tab in the Insert dialog box.
4. Click Module.xlt, then choose OK.

A new module, containing whatever you keyed into the module template, appears in your workbook immediately before the tab that you right-clicked.

Note that you cannot insert a new module based on the template by choosing Insert, Macro, Module. You must use Insert in the sheet tab shortcut menu to have access to the template.

 Note

The example code in the remainder of this chapter assumes that Option Base 1 has been set.

Single Dimension Arrays

When you declare an array with only one dimension, VBA acts as though the dimension is a row that contains some number of columns. For example:

```
Dim Rates(5) As Double
```

The array named Rates has five elements, of course, but those five elements occupy five columns in one row. You could visualize it as follows:

Column: 1   2   3   4   5

Row:

1   .18   .05   .075   .034   .025

Contrast the layout shown here with an array that contains five rows and one column:

Column: 1

Row:

1   .18

2   .05

3   .075

4   .034

5   .025

In most cases, this orientation is of little interest to you, because you won't care whether Rates is oriented horizontally or vertically. However, if you use Rates as an argument to a function, or if you subsequently write the Rates array to a worksheet, then the orientation is important.

Suppose that you dimension Rates as follows:

```
Dim Rates(5) As Double
```

Rates has one row with five columns. After you populate Rates with five values, you use this statement to write Rates to a worksheet range:

```
ActiveSheet.Range(Cells(1,1), Cells(5,1)) = Rates
```

This statement calls for the range A1:A5 to be filled with the values in the array named Rates. VBA will execute the statement, but because A1:A5 has one column and five rows (the reverse of the orientation in the Rates array), cells A1:A5 will each contain the value in Rates' first column. Instead, you would want to use something such as:

```
ActiveSheet.Range(Cells(7,1), Cells(7,5)) = Rates
```

This distinction is shown in figure 25.1.

Fig. 25.1

The VBA array Rates is dimensioned by Dim Rates(5), which gives it one row and five columns.

ActiveSheet.Range(Cells(1,1), Cells(5,1)) = Rates

ActiveSheet.Range(Cells(7,1), Cells(7,5)) = Rates

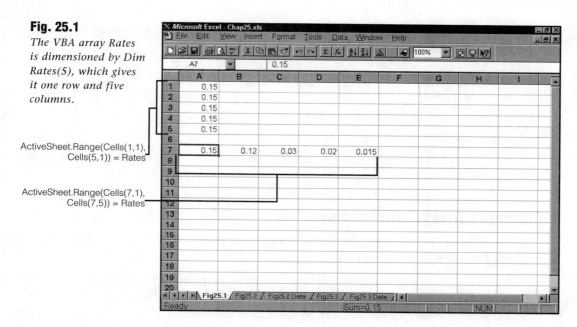

Or, consider the SumProduct function. This function multiplies two arrays together, and returns the sum of the products of their individual elements. You might use SumProduct with Rates to multiply employees' Federal tax rates, state tax rates, pre-tax savings rates, post-tax savings rates, and so on by different dollar amounts in the paychecks. After multiplying the corresponding amounts, SumProduct would return the sum of the deductions.

Again, if Rates is declared this way:

```
Dim Rates(5) As Double
```

it has one row and five columns. If DollarAmounts is declared in this way:

```
Dim DollarAmounts(1,5)
```

or

```
Dim DollarAmounts(5)
```

then this statement works fine:

```
TotalDeductions = Application.SumProduct(Rates, DollarAmounts)
```

because both DollarAmounts and Rates each have one row and five columns. But if Rates is declared in this way:

```
Dim Rates(5,1)
```

25

then the function SumProduct fails, because Rates has five rows and one column, and DollarAmounts has one row and five columns.

Therefore, it's helpful to define even single-dimension arrays explicitly:

```
Dim Rates(1,5)
```

(which has one row and five columns), or

```
Dim Rates(5,1)
```

(which has five rows and one column). So doing helps you keep straight as to the *orientation* of the array's dimension.

Changing Arrays' Dimensions

What if you don't know at the time that you write your code how large an array needs to be? That's where ReDim comes in.

Suppose that, as part of a larger inventory analysis application, you are preparing a VBA subroutine that determines the value of a company's inventory. Your macro will pick up the product code and the quantity on hand from a worksheet, do a table lookup to determine the unit cost of each product, multiply the cost times the quantity, and eventually sum the results to return a total inventory valuation.

The number of different products in the inventory changes from time to time, so you can't tell in advance how many product codes to allow for in your arrays. You do know, however, that you will have finished picking up product codes and quantities from the worksheet when you reach the final entry in worksheet column A. With the product codes in column A and their quantities in column B, your code might look something like this:

```
Option Base 1
Sub GetData()
Dim ProductCodes() As String, Quantity() As Long
Dim RowCount As Integer, RowCounter As Integer
RowCount = Columns(1).End(xlDown).RowReDim ProductCodes(RowCount, 1)
ReDim Quantity(RowCount, 1)
For RowCounter = 1 To RowCount
    ProductCodes(RowCounter, 1) = Cells(RowCounter, 1)
    Quantity(RowCounter, 1) = Cells(RowCounter, 2)
Next RowCounter
End Sub
```

Let's walk through this subroutine. Notice that in the first Dim statement:

```
Dim ProductCodes() As String, Quantity() As Long
```

the names of the two variables ProductCodes and Quantity are followed by a pair of empty parentheses. This indicates to VBA that both variables are arrays, but that their dimensions are as yet undefined.

Then, the variable RowCount is used to store the number of products that the macro is to deal with. This statement:

```
RowCount = Range("A1").End(xlDown).Row
```

assigns to the variable RowCount the number of the row that contains the last contiguous value in column 1. Perhaps a safer way to obtain the final product code in column A is

```
RowCount = Range("A16384").End(xlUp).Row
```

This returns the row that would be active if, on the worksheet, you activated cell A16384 and used Ctrl+up arrow. Suppose that cells A1:A5 contain data, A6 is empty, and A7:A100 contain data. In that case, going down from A1 would miss cells A7:A100, whereas going up from A16384 would find the lowermost cell that contains data.

It's now time to assign dimensions to the arrays. The two ReDim statements:

```
ReDim ProductCodes(RowCount, 1)
ReDim Quantity(RowCount, 1)
```

do this, assigning each array one column and a number of rows equal to the value of RowCount. By using ReDim, you can defer the decision of how large to make the array until your macro has had a chance to examine the data with which it will be working. The remainder of the subroutine picks up the values from the worksheet cells and puts them into the VBA arrays.

> ### ❊ Tip
>
> You cannot use a variable to dimension an array in a Dim statement. You must use the ReDim statement instead. For example, if RowCount is a variable, then:
>
> ```
> Dim Product(RowCount)
> ```
>
> is not legal, but both
>
> ```
> Dim Product (100)
> ```
>
> and
>
> ```
> ReDim Product (RowCount)
> ```
>
> are legal.

If you work with very large arrays, and want to recapture some memory after you have finished with an array, you can use this statement:

```
ReDim TemporaryArray(1)
```

to shrink the size of the array to a minimum, making the memory it used available for other purposes.

When you ReDim an array, you lose the values of all variables in the array. You can use ReDim Preserve instead of ReDim if, for some reason, you need to change the size of an array without loss of data. For example, suppose that TemporaryArray is originally defined as follows:

```
Dim TemporaryArray(10) As String
```

In your VBA code, you populate TemporaryArray with 10 string values. Subsequently, you need TemporaryArray to have 15 (or 5, or some other number) of elements. If you ReDim TemporaryArray using the Preserve keyword:

```
ReDim Preserve TemporaryArray(15)
```

then the original ten values are retained; you simply have an additional five elements available to you.

There is, however, a restriction on ReDim Preserve. If you use it on a multidimensional array, you may redimension only its *final* dimension, and then only the *upper bound* of its final dimension. Suppose that you originally declared TemporaryArray as follows:

```
Dim TemporaryArray(10,10) As Single
```

You could redimension it via:

```
ReDim Preserve TemporaryArray(10,15)
```

(which increases the number of elements in its final dimension) or by means of:

```
ReDim Preserve TemporaryArray(10,5)
```

(which decreases the number of elements in its final dimension). But you could *not* redimension it by:

```
ReDim Preserve TemporaryArray(5,10)
```

because you cannot successfully use ReDim Preserve to change the number of elements in other than its final dimension. Nor could you use:

```
ReDim Preserve TemporaryArray(10, 5 To 10)
```

because only the upper bound of its final dimension can be modified, and still maintain its existing values—this statement tries to modify the final dimension's *lower bound*.

These restrictions severely limit the usefulness of ReDim Preserve.

Using Variant Arrays

One special type of array is a variant array:

```
Dim TemporaryArray As Variant(10)
```

A *variant array* can contain different types of elements. For example, TemporaryArray(1) could contain 3.1416, TemporaryArray(2) could contain "Jones," and TemporaryArray(3) could contain FALSE.

Reading Data from Worksheets into Variant Arrays

A particularly handy use of a variant variable is to move data from a worksheet into a VBA array quickly. For example:

```
Dim ArrayFromSheet As Variant
ArrayFromSheet = ActiveSheet.Range(Cells(1,1),Cells(20,20))
```

When VBA executes this pair of statements, it brings the contents of the range A1:T20 into the variant array named ArrayFromSheet. Note in particular that ArrayFromSheet is *not* declared as an array: the Dim statement specifies neither dimensions nor dimension bounds. VBA assigns these when it populates the array, in effect turning what was originally a single-valued variable into a dimensioned array.

 Note

Be sure you understand the difference between a variant array and a variant variable. A variant array is one that can contain values that have different data types (for example, 3.1416 and "Jones") as its elements. A *variant variable* can contain a single value of any data type, *unless* you subsequently assign a worksheet range to it—then, it can contain many elements, each of which can be of any type.

This technique is much quicker than an alternative—for example, this loop:

```
For RowNumber = 1 to 20
   For ColumnNumber = 1 to 20
      ArrayFromWks = Cells(RowNumber,ColumnNumber)
   Next ColumnNumber
Next RowNumber
```

The relative speed of the two approaches is shown in figure 25.2.

25

Fig. 25.2
Comparing loop assignment speed with variant assignment speed.

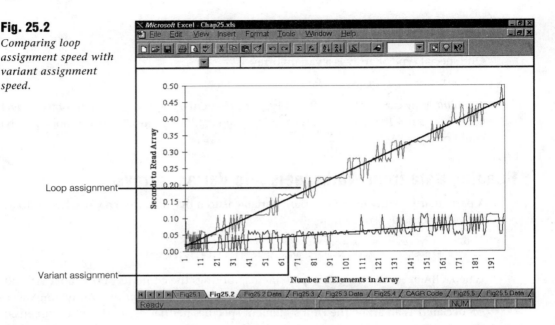

As convenient as the variant assignment method is, however, it has three drawbacks:

▶ The array must be dimensioned as Variant. As noted previously, a variant array takes up more memory than any other type.

▶ The array can have as many as 2,730 elements, and no more. This means that a square array can be as many as 52 rows by 52 columns. The limit is slightly smaller than it is in Excel version 5 (which allows 3,276 elements), due to the additional overhead required by Excel 7.0's 32-bit architecture.

▶ The precision of the data in the array can be affected by the format of the worksheet data. If the worksheet cells are formatted as Currency, for example, the value 2.3456789 could come into the VBA array as 2.35.

Writing Data from Arrays to Worksheets

There are three basic techniques for moving a VBA array to a worksheet:

▶ *Cell-by-cell*. This technique loops through the rows and columns of the VBA array and writes the value in each array cell to a worksheet cell.

▶ *Range assignment*. This technique sets the value of the worksheet range to the VBA array.

▶ *Array formula assignment*. This technique puts an array formula into the worksheet range, setting the range equal to a custom function that references the array. Then, the range array formula is copied and pasted back to the range as values.

The *cell-by-cell* approach is almost always the slowest. Benchmarked on a 486-DX33 computer, it takes 4.8 seconds to write a 50 row by 10 column array to a worksheet range.

The *range assignment* technique is significantly faster than the cell-by-cell approach. This technique uses code such as the following:

```
Set WorkSheetRange = Worksheets(1).Range(Cells(1,1),Cells(50,10))
For i = 1 to 50
   For j = 1 to 10
      DeductionArray(i,j) = Salary(i) * Rate(j)
   Next j
Next i
WorkSheetRange.Value = DeductionArray
```

The final statement shown here writes the VBA array directly to the worksheet range. On a 486-DX33, the benchmark took 2.1 seconds—less than half as long—to move the VBA array to the worksheet range.

In contrast to the cell-by-cell and the range assignment approaches, the *array formula* approach requires a user-defined VBA function. This function is set equal to the VBA array, and the worksheet range is then set equal to the function by means of the range's FormulaArray property. Finally, the range is copied to the Clipboard and pasted back to the worksheet as values. Here is some sample code:

```
Option Explicit
Option Base 1

Dim DeductionArray(50, 10) As Double
Sub WriteWithArrayFormula()
Dim WorkSheetRange As Range
Dim i As Integer, j As Integer
For i = 1 to 50
   For j = 1 to 10
      DeductionArray(i,j) = Salary(i) * Rate(j)
   Next j
Next i
Set SheetRange = Range(Cells(1, 1), Cells(50, 10))
SheetRange.FormulaArray = "=WriteToRange()"
SheetRange.Copy
SheetRange.PasteSpecial Paste:=xlValues
Application.CutCopyMode = False
End Sub


Function WriteToRange() As Variant
WriteToRange = DeductionArray
End Function
```

It might surprise you to learn that this array formula technique is usually the fastest method—it's definitely fastest with an array of any appreciable size. The DX33 benchmark took two-thirds of one second to complete, even taking into account the copy-and-paste operation that converts the worksheet array formula to values. That's more than seven times faster than the cell-by-cell approach.

Figure 25.3 shows the length of time needed to write a VBA array to a worksheet using both the range method and the array formula method, across different array sizes.

Fig. 25.3

Writing an array to a worksheet with an array formula is much faster than writing it by assignment to a range.

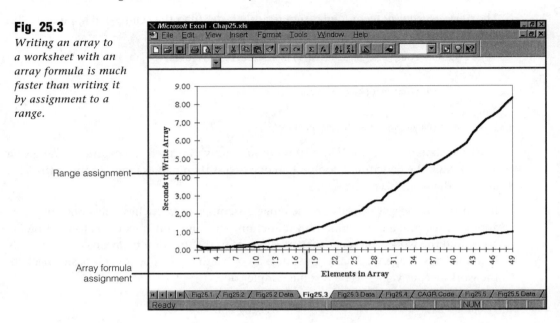

Again, there are drawbacks to the array formula technique. The most obvious is that it requires more VBA code than the range assignment method. Less obvious is the limit on the number of elements that can be written to the worksheet. The fact that the code returns the array via a user-defined function means that you must declare the function as a variant: this is a restriction that is built into VBA. It follows that the size of the array that is assigned to the function with

```
WriteToRange = VbaArray
```

is subject to the same restriction involved in reading a range into a VBA array: 2,730 elements is the maximum.

Creating Arrays with a User-Defined Data Type

This chapter has already mentioned variant arrays: arrays that can contain data of various types. These can be very useful tools for handling what Pascal terms "records," and what C terms "structs."

Suppose that you want to use VBA to manage employee records. There might be several employee variables of interest to you:

- Name
- Salary
- Title
- Social Security number
- Date hired

To process the employee records conveniently, define a new data type at the top of your module:

```
Type Employee
    Name As String
    Salary As Single
    Title As String
    SSN As String
    HireDate As Date
End Type
```

Each part of the Employee data type is termed an *element*: Name is an element, Salary is an element, and so on. You can now use the Employee data type just as you would use the String, Integer, Double, or any other data type. For example:

```
Dim EmployeeArray(100) As Employee
```

The array named EmployeeArray can now contain the five elements that you have defined as composing the Employee data type. As dimensioned, EmployeeArray can contain all five elements that describe each of 100 employees.

To assign values to each element of a record in the array, the With statement is both convenient and efficient. Suppose that you have these five elements in columns A through E, rows 1 through 100, on a worksheet. You could put them into the array by means of a With statement inside a For loop:

```
For RowCounter = 1 To 100
    With EmployeeArray(RowCounter)
        .Name = Cells(RowCounter, 1)
        .Salary = Cells(RowCounter, 2)
        .Title = Cells(RowCounter, 3)
        .SSN = Cells(RowCounter, 4)
        .HireDate = CDate(Cells(RowCounter, 5))
    End With
Next RowCounter
```

You can now use this array to analyze data on employees. For example, if you were interested in determining the average salary for all employees who have been hired since January 1, 1995, you could use code like this:

```
For EmployeeCounter = 1 To UBound(EmployeeArray)
    With EmployeeArray(EmployeeCounter)
        If .HireDate >= CDate(#1/1/95#) Then
            MeanSalary = MeanSalary + .Salary
            Qualifying = Qualifying + 1
        End If
    End With
Next EmployeeCounter
MeanSalary = MeanSalary / Qualifying
```

There is another use for arrays of a user-defined data type, discussed later in the section "Sorting VBA Arrays."

Writing Custom Functions that Return Arrays

Excel has various worksheet functions that *must* be array-entered to return the full range of their results. Examples include TRANSPOSE, MINVERSE, MMULT, TREND, and LINEST. Also, if you use an array constant as an argument to a function, it might be necessary to array-enter the formula. For example:

```
=FORECAST({0.99,0.11},A1:A5,B1:B5)
```

Here, because there are two values (0.99 and 0.11) in the first argument to the FORECAST function, the formula must occupy a 1-row, 2-column range, and it must be array-entered in that range to return both results correctly.

On occasion, you might find it necessary to write your own, user-defined function (UDF) to get a result that Excel's worksheet functions do not offer. And if you want your function to return an array of results, you will need to deal with VBA arrays.

Here is an example of how to do that. The UDF described below accepts as inputs the original price of several investments, their ending prices, and the length of time each investment was held. The UDF returns the cumulative annual growth rate (CAGR) of each investment. Unlike a simple growth rate formula such as:

```
Annual Growth Rate =((StopPrice - StartPrice)/StartPrice)/Term
```

the CAGR takes compounding into account:

```
CAGR = (StopPrice / StartPrice) ^ (1 / Term)
```

So, you can obtain the ending price of an investment by:

```
StopPrice = StartPrice * (CAGR ^ Term)
```

Although you can use this UDF to find the CAGR for a group of investments, its main point is to demonstrate the necessary components of a UDF that returns an array.

As discussed in the section "Defining the Size of Arrays," earlier in the chapter, the first two statements:

```
Option Explicit
Option Base 1
```

protect against misspelled names (Option Explicit) and force the first element in any dimension in any array to be element number 1 instead of element number 0 (Option Base 1).

The next statement:

```
Function CAGR(StartDollars, StopDollars, Term) As Variant
```

names the function as CAGR. It also specifies that the function takes three arguments, named StartDollars, StopDollars, and Term. These arguments are range objects: the intention of the function is to calculate the CAGR using the information in three worksheet ranges, and a worksheet range is an object.

Suppose that the range of terms is in B2:B5, beginning prices in C2:C5, and ending prices in D2:D5. When the function is entered on a worksheet so as to calculate the CAGR, it would be array-entered as

```
=CAGR(C2:C5,D2:D5,B2:B5)
```

A function that returns an array, whether to a worksheet or to another VBA function or procedure, must be declared as a Variant. The function CAGR is intended to return an array, and is therefore declared as Variant at the end of the argument list.

Notice that this requirement places a limit on the number of elements that can be returned as an array from a UDF: 2,730 elements and no more—the maximum number of elements in a VBA variant array.

Next, these declarations:

```
Dim Temp() As Double
Dim StockCount As Integer, i As Integer
```

establish the names and the types of the variables that the function uses to calculate its results. Their purposes are

- ▶ StockCount is used to hold the number of stocks for which the function returns a CAGR.
- ▶ i is a counter variable that controls a For...Next loop in the function.
- ▶ Temp is declared as an array variable whose dimensions will be defined later in the code. Notice the empty parentheses in the Dim statement. They are there to indicate that it *is* an array, and therefore capable of taking on specific dimensions later on. At the end of the function's code, the CAGR function itself will be set equal to Temp.

25

A count of the number of stocks to process is needed. This statement:

```
StockCount = StartDollars.Rows.Count
```

looks to the range that contains the stock starting prices, and counts the number of rows in the range. Recall that this range was defined by the use of the name StartDollars as the first argument in the UDF's argument list. The name corresponds to the range identified in, say:

```
=CAGR(A1:A5,B1:B5,C1:C5)
```

as entered on the worksheet. StartDollars corresponds to A1:A5, so StockCount is set equal to the number of rows in A1:A5, or 5.

Because CAGR will return as many result rows as there are rows in the input ranges, the array variable Temp is re-dimensioned to contain the proper number of rows and one column:

```
ReDim Temp(StockCount, 1)
```

The only function that ReDim performs is to re-dimension an existing array. Therefore, Temp must already have been declared as an array, even one with no dimensions. The ReDim statement would fail if Temp had originally been declared without the pair of empty parentheses, which establish that it is an array variable.

Then, the main loop is entered. The loop repeats as many times as there are stocks to analyze:

```
For i = 1 To StockCount
    Temp(i, 1) = (StopDollars(i, 1) / StartDollars(i, 1)) ^ (1 / Term(i, 1))
Next i
```

The CAGR for each stock is calculated by the second statement in the loop. The CAGR is placed in the appropriate row of the array named Temp.

After the loop has finished—when the value of the counter variable named i exceeds the value of StockCount—the Temp array has been fully populated. Recall that it has been re-dimensioned to contain as many rows as there are rows in the first input range. It's now time to set the function itself equal to the Temp array, and terminate the function:

```
CAGR = Temp
End Function
```

Because the function itself was declared as a Variant, you can set the function equal to the array Temp with the simple assignment statement CAGR = Temp.

Because the function CAGR now contains an array, the user must know its dimensions beforehand, to highlight the proper range of cells before array-entering the formula. In this case, if the range of arguments has five rows, the user must highlight a range consisting of five rows and one column before array-entering the formula. This is generally true of array formulas. To use, for example, the TRANSPOSE function, you have to know that it returns an array of values whose dimensions are the opposite of those of its argument.

The inputs to function CAGR and its results are shown in figure 25.4.

Fig. 25.4

A user-defined function returns an array of values if, in the code, the values are assigned to the function's name.

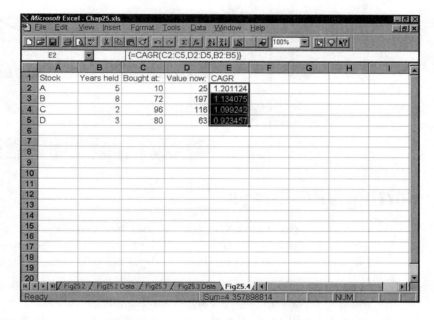

When should you write a custom function instead of using a built-in function? Probably under one of two conditions:

▶ If the built-in function does not operate precisely as you want it to.

▶ If the built-in function has limits that you cannot live with.

Otherwise, you should try to stay with the built-in functions. A built-in function usually operates much faster—particularly on arrays—than does a custom function. For example, figure 25.5 shows the length of time it takes to execute a UDF that emulates Excel's MMULT function versus MMULT itself, as the arguments increase in size from 2 to 12 rows.

25

Fig. 25.5

Built-in functions complete much faster than UDFs as input arrays grow in size.

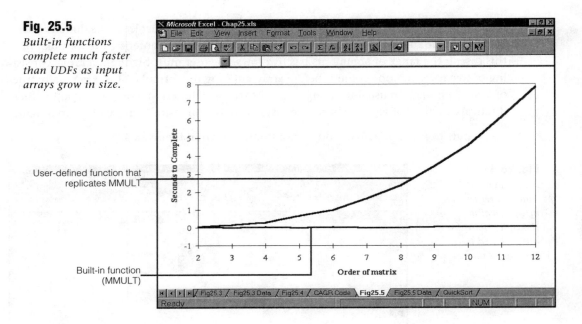

User-defined function that replicates MMULT

Built-in function (MMULT)

Sorting VBA Arrays

Once you have data in a VBA array, it often happens that you need to sort it. It might be, for example, that you want to output the array to a worksheet in sorted order, or that subsequent work in VBA on the array depends on the array being sorted.

One way to do this would be to write the data to a worksheet, use the Data, Sort command to sort the data on the sheet, and then (if necessary) read the data back in to the array. The difficulty is that if your array is at all large, all this output and input can take a long time. It often makes more sense to sort the array directly in memory, by means of a subroutine.

Using Exchange Sorts

You could, for example, use a simple exchange sort. Suppose that you have an array of one dimension named UnSorted. Here is standard code used to sort UnSorted in ascending order:

```
For I = 1 To UBound(UnSorted, 1) - 1
   For J = I + 1 To UBound(UnSorted, 1)
      If UnSorted(I, 1) > UnSorted(J, 1) Then
         Temp = UnSorted(I, 1)
         UnSorted(I, 1) = UnSorted(J, 1)
         UnSorted(J, 1) = Temp
      End If
   Next J
Next I
```

The logic of this code is as follows. There are two For loops: the outer loop is driven by the control variable named I, and the inner loop is driven by the control variable J. The outer loop executes one time fewer than there are elements in the array, starting with 1. Each time that the outer loop executes, the inner loop executes I–1 times.

At the outset, the first item in the array is compared to the second item. If the value of the first item is greater than that of the second item, their positions in the array are swapped by the code within the If...End If block. Then, the first item in the array is compared to its third item. Again, if the first item's value is greater than that of the third item, their order is swapped. When the outer loop completes the first time, the smallest value in the array is at the top. The next iteration of the outer loop places the second lowest value in the second position, and so on.

The process of swapping the positions of two values is accomplished by the If...End If block, and the logic in that block is typical of most sorting algorithms. A placeholder variable is needed; this code names it Temp. Suppose that the values 10 and 9 need to be swapped. Here's what happens, both in the code and in terms of values:

Code	Values
Temp = UnSorted(I, 1)	Temp = 10
UnSorted(I, 1) = UnSorted(J, 1)	UnSorted(I,1) = 9
UnSorted(J, 1) = Temp	UnSorted(J,1) = 10

Of course, you cannot merely use code like this:

```
UnSorted(I,1) = UnSorted(J,1)
UnSorted(J,1) = UnSorted(I,1)
```

because that would set both array elements to the same value. The placeholder variable, Temp, is needed to preserve the first value while the second value is moved into the position originally occupied by the first value.

The inner loop, driven by the control variable named J, continues until its value is greater than that of UnSorted's upper bound. At that point, due to the swapping of the order of the array's elements that has occurred, the first value in UnSorted will be the smallest value in UnSorted.

Then, the outer loop, driven by the control variable I, executes again. This time, though, it begins with the second element in UnSorted. The second element is compared to the third, fourth,...last element and swapped if necessary. When the outer loop has completed for the second time, the second element in UnSorted must be its second-smallest value.

25

The outer and inner For loops continue until I, which controls the outer For loop, equals UnSorted's upper bound, –1. At that point, UnSorted is fully sorted in ascending order.

Using a More Efficient Sort: QuickSort

It turns out that the method just described is an inefficient way to sort the array. Suppose UnSorted has ten elements. Regardless of the initial order of the array—ascending, descending, or random—there must be 45 comparisons (9 the first time the outer loop executes, 8 the second time, and so on). Furthermore, when an element must be moved to another location, it is not necessarily moved to its eventual destination: it might be moved only part way there.

For example, what if the first element in the array were 9 and the second element 8? When these two elements are compared, 9 is moved to the second position and 8 is moved to the first position. It would be much more efficient to continue comparing 9 with the remaining elements in the array, and not to move it until either the value 10 is found, or the end of the array is reached. If things were managed that way, 9 would be moved—if not necessarily to its final destination, at least further down the array than just to the second position.

VBA code that manages the array in that fashion appears here:

```
Sub QuickSort(SortArray, OriginalLowerBound, OriginalUpperBound, Direction)
    Dim CurrentLowerBound As Integer, CurrentUpperBound As Integer, HalfWayThruObs As
    ➥Variant, TempVal As Variant
    CurrentLowerBound = OriginalLowerBound
    CurrentUpperBound = OriginalUpperBound
    HalfWayThruObs = SortArray((OriginalLowerBound + OriginalUpperBound) / 2)
    While (CurrentLowerBound <= CurrentUpperBound)
    If UCase(Direction) = "UP" Then
        While (SortArray(CurrentLowerBound) < HalfWayThruObs And CurrentLowerBound <
        ➥OriginalUpperBound)
            CurrentLowerBound = CurrentLowerBound + 1
        Wend
        While (HalfWayThruObs < SortArray(CurrentUpperBound) And CurrentUpperBound >
        ➥OriginalLowerBound)
            CurrentUpperBound = CurrentUpperBound - 1
        Wend
    Else
        While (SortArray(CurrentLowerBound) > HalfWayThruObs And CurrentLowerBound <
        ➥OriginalUpperBound)
            CurrentLowerBound = CurrentLowerBound + 1
        Wend
        While (HalfWayThruObs > SortArray(CurrentUpperBound) And CurrentUpperBound >
        ➥OriginalLowerBound)
            CurrentUpperBound = CurrentUpperBound - 1
        Wend
    End If
    If (CurrentLowerBound <= CurrentUpperBound) Then
        TempVal = SortArray(CurrentLowerBound)
        SortArray(CurrentLowerBound) = SortArray(CurrentUpperBound)
        SortArray(CurrentUpperBound) = TempVal
```

```
        CurrentLowerBound = CurrentLowerBound + 1
        CurrentUpperBound = CurrentUpperBound - 1
    End If
Wend
If (OriginalLowerBound < CurrentUpperBound) Then Call QuickSort(SortArray,
OriginalLowerBound, CurrentUpperBound, Direction)
If (CurrentLowerBound < OriginalUpperBound) Then Call QuickSort(SortArray,
CurrentLowerBound, OriginalUpperBound, Direction)
End Sub
```

You can also find the code in a module sheet named QuickSort on the companion CD. This code was shown in an article in the May 1995 *Visual Basic Programmer's Journal* and modified by Jim Rech. The current author has made some additional modifications. It is slightly faster than the simple exchange sort shown previously for small arrays, and it becomes more advantageous as the size of the array increases. It is ten times faster than the simple exchange sort for an array with 500 elements.

You would call this sub by means of a command such as:

```
Call QuickSort(UnSorted,1,10,"up")
```

where the second argument is always 1, the third argument is the number of elements in the array, and the fourth argument is "Up" to sort ascending, or anything else, such as "Down," to sort descending. You can make this a more general call by using:

```
Elements = UBound(UnSorted)
Call QuickSort(UnSorted,1,Elements,"Down")
```

for a descending sort or, most generally:

```
Elements = Ubound(ArrayName)
Direction = "up"
Call QuickSort(ArrayName,1,Elements,Direction)
```

The subroutine calls itself (see its final two If statements) under certain conditions. The process that occurs when a function or subroutine calls itself is termed *recursion*. When the recursion occurs in QuickSort, it redefines either the upper bound of the array or the lower bound of the array. In this way, the subroutine constantly sorts subsets of the original array—either the elements at the start of the array or the elements at the end of the array.

α Note

It is because of recursion that it is necessary to use the second and third arguments in the call to QuickSort. When you first call it, you normally want the sort to begin with array element number 1 (the second argument) and to end with the number of elements in the array (the third argument). But when QuickSort calls itself, it needs to pass new values as the second and third arguments. Therefore, these arguments are explicit in the argument list.

These sub-arrays are usually smaller than the original array. The net effect is to reduce the number of element-to-element comparisons that QuickSort must make.

You can pass any type of array (for example, Integer, Double, String, Variant, and so on.) to QuickSort. Simply declare the array that you intend to pass according to the type of data that it will contain.

Note, though, that QuickSort can handle arrays of only one dimension. If you want to sort a two-dimension array, consider changing it to a one-dimension array with a user-defined data type. Earlier in this chapter, in the section titled "User-Defined Data Type Arrays," the data type Employee was defined:

```
Type Employee
    Name As String
    Salary As Single
    Title As String
    SSN As String
    HireDate As Date
End Type
```

and EmployeeArray was dimensioned as type Employee:

```
Dim EmployeeArray(100) As Employee
```

EmployeeArray was populated by reading into it, from a worksheet, the values in A1:E100, where each column contained a different element of the Employee data type. This range is effectively a two-dimensional array: one dimension is its rows, the other dimension is its columns. But putting the data into EmployeeArray makes it a one-dimensional array with five elements.

To use QuickSort to sort this array on any element, a few changes are required. It's necessary to inform QuickSort which element it should use as a sort key.

Suppose that you wanted to sort EmployeeArray on Name. The changes to QuickSort are summarized here. The required changes are shown in boldface:

```
Sub QuickSort(SortArray() As Employee, OriginalLowerBound, OriginalUpperBound,
➥Direction)
```

The first change is in the procedure definition. If the first argument—the array itself—in the calling statement uses a built-in data type such as Integer, this type is automatically passed to QuickSort itself. If the array is untyped, as in the earlier version of QuickSort, SortArray is assumed to be of type Variant.

But VBA cannot assign an array of a user-defined data type to a Variant array: therefore, in this case it's necessary to explicitly define SortArray() as type Employee. Furthermore, it's necessary to indicate in the procedure definition that SortArray *is* an array, so the argument includes the empty pair of parentheses after SortArray.

Then, the placeholder variable must be assigned a custom type:

```
    Dim CurrentLowerBound As Integer, CurrentUpperBound As Integer,
➥HalfWayThruObs As Variant, Temp As Employee
```

The variable named Temp, which is the placeholder variable, is now typed as Employee. This means that Temp has all the elements of the Employee data type. Therefore, when the swap of positions occurs further down in QuickSort, a record in EmployeeArray can be assigned, *including all its elements*, to Temp.

```
    CurrentLowerBound = OriginalLowerBound
    CurrentUpperBound = OriginalUpperBound
    HalfWayThruObs = SortArray((OriginalLowerBound + OriginalUpperBound) / 2).Name
```

Here, HalfWayThruObs is assigned the value of the Name element of the record that is halfway through EmployeeArray. Because HalfWayThruObs takes on only the value of the Name element—rather than all the elements of the Employee data type—it can be dimensioned as a Variant instead of as Employee.

```
    While (CurrentLowerBound <= CurrentUpperBound)
    If UCase(Direction) = "UP" Then
        While (SortArray(CurrentLowerBound).Name < HalfWayThruObs And
        ➥CurrentLowerBound < OriginalUpperBound)
```

The second While statement compares HalfWayThruObs to the Name element of the record identified by CurrentLowerBound. The While loop increments CurrentLowerBound by 1 as long as the Name element in the current lower bound's record is less than that of the Name element in HalfWayThruObs.

```
            CurrentLowerBound = CurrentLowerBound + 1
        Wend
        While (HalfWayThruObs < SortArray(CurrentUpperBound).
        ➥Name And CurrentUpperBound > OriginalLowerBound)
```

Again, the Name element is compared to HalfWayThruObs, and the CurrentUpperBound is decremented by 1 as long as HalfWayThruObs' Name is less than that in the array's CurrentUpperBound.

```
            CurrentUpperBound = CurrentUpperBound - 1
        Wend
    Else
    While (SortArray(CurrentLowerBound).Name > HalfWayThruObs And CurrentLowerBound <
    ➥OriginalUpperBound)
```

The Else statement initiates the same comparison processing structure in case the Direction specified in the argument list is some value other than "UP." The only difference is that the direction of the comparison operators is reversed.

```
            CurrentLowerBound = CurrentLowerBound + 1
        Wend
        While (HalfWayThruObs > SortArray(CurrentUpperBound)
        ➥.Name And CurrentUpperBound > OriginalLowerBound)
```

25

This While statement constitutes the final comparison of Name to HalfWayThruObs. The remainder of the subroutine is unchanged. And you call QuickSort, as modified to sort on a user-defined data type array, exactly as you call the unmodified version. For example:

```
Elements = UBound(EmployeeArray)
QuickSort EmployeeArray, 1, Elements, "up"
```

You will find a subroutine, TestQuickSort, in the module named QuickSort on the companion CD. You can use TestQuickSort to pass a worksheet range to QuickSort and return it in sorted order. Normally, of course, if you had to sort a worksheet range, you would use Data, Sort. The subroutine named TestQuickSort is included simply to enable you to test QuickSort in a worksheet context.

Summary

Arrays in VBA are enormously useful structures. You can use them to speed up your VBA code, by storing temporary values in the arrays rather than writing them to worksheets. They are absolutely necessary if you want to create a user-defined function that is array-entered by the user. They enable you to work in three or more dimensions, as when you want to analyze, say, product line by year by region by financial indicator. And you can define arrays to contain custom data types that represent full records instead of single values.

There are special techniques available to read worksheet values into VBA arrays, and to write VBA arrays to worksheets, that speed the transfer processes.

Arrays also enable you to perform tasks in worksheets, such as sorting sheet tabs, that you would otherwise have to do by hand. By becoming familiar with the uses of VBA arrays, you can eventually save yourself a considerable amount of time.

chapter 26

Custom Menus

26

by John Green

In this chapter

◆ **Excel's menu structure**
Excel has a hierarchical menu structure providing both menus and submenus.

◆ **Manually editing Excel's menus**
You can use the Menu Editor to manually update Excel menus and create your own menus.

◆ **Using VBA to dynamically manage Excel's menus**
You can change the structure of Excel's built-in menus to respond to user actions.

◆ **Using VBA to create and manage custom menus**
You can create entirely new custom menus using VBA.

◆ **Avoiding potential traps and bugs associated with menus**
There are a number of unexpected features and bugs you should know about when managing Excel's menus in VBA.

What is it that really gives an application that professional touch? What makes it really easy for users to find their way around? To really draw an application together you need a well-designed set of menus. Toolbars and buttons have their place in accessing single, often used commands, but a menu is the way to find your way through the most complex system.

With menus, you can arrange your interface in a logical, structured manner. You can take inexperienced users by the hand and guide them through the myriad of choices you have to offer.

Imagine what it would be like to find your way around Excel itself without the menu structure. With experience you start to use shortcut keys and toolbars, but when you need to find that command you know must be there, you search through the menus.

Excel provides great flexibility in allowing you to tailor your own menu structure. At one extreme, you might choose to make simple adjustments to Excel's built-in menus. At the other, you might decide to remove the normal menu structure completely and devise your own menus from scratch.

Excel enables you to design menus either manually, using the Menu Editor, or with VBA-coded procedures. The Menu Editor is the easiest way to set up your own menus, but VBA is more powerful as it allows you to make changes that you cannot make manually. For example, you can disable and enable menus with VBA and change the menu structure as the application runs to provide feedback to the user and to interact with the user.

If you want to have the best possible interface for the applications you develop in Excel, read on.

Menu Structure

Before making modifications to the menu structure, you need to understand the terminology used by Excel. Figure 26.1 shows the major elements involved.

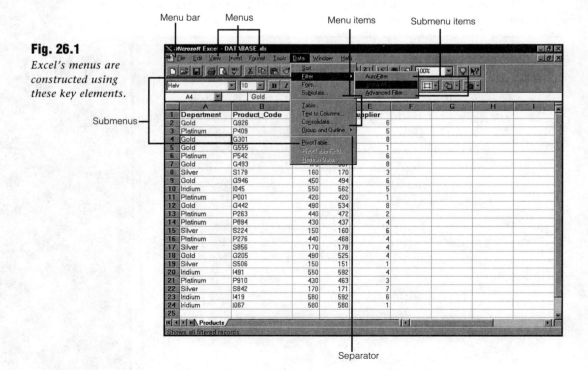

Fig. 26.1
Excel's menus are constructed using these key elements.

Menu Bars

Excel's active *menu bar* lies immediately below the title bar at the top of the Excel window. There are a number of permanent menu bars defined in Excel that are referred to as the built-in menu bars. As you change from one type of sheet to another, the menu bar changes to the one that is appropriate for your working environment.

The shortcut menus that appear when you right-click are also considered to be grouped on menu bars. All of the built-in menu bars are shown in table 26.1

Table 26.1   Excel's Built-In Menu Bars

Menu Bar	Description
No Documents Open	The menu bar when all workbooks are closed.
Worksheet	The menu bar in a worksheet or Excel 4 macro sheet.
Module	The menu bar in a VBA module.
Chart	The menu bar in a chart window.
Short Cut Menus 1	The shortcut menus for toolbars, toolbar buttons, worksheet cells, columns, rows, workbook tabs, macrosheet cells, window title bars, desktop, modules, watch pane, immediate pane, and debug pane.
Short Cut Menus 2	The shortcut menus for drawing objects, buttons, text boxes, and dialog sheets.
Short Cut Menus 3	The shortcut menus for chart series, chart text, chart plot area, entire chart, chart axis, chart gridlines, chart floor, and chart legend.

You can create completely different menu bars if you do not want to use the standard ones. In addition to the built-in menu bars, you can have as many as fifteen new ones at any one time. This is an excessive number for most applications, but in the unusual situation where you need more, you can use VBA code to modify the menu bars dynamically.

Menu bars have numeric codes associated with them. For example, the normal Worksheet menu bar in Excel 5 and Excel 7 is number 7. The optional Excel 4 worksheet menu is menu bar 1. However, using numbers can be confusing and you do not need to use them as Excel gives you methods for referring to menu bars by names or constants.

26

Note

> If you use the Excel 4 XLM macro functions to manage menus in Excel 5 or Excel 7, the menu bar numeric codes can be different from those used in VBA. For example, the standard worksheet menu bar has a numeric code of 10.

Menus

A menu can be referred to by its numeric position on the menu bar, starting with menu one on the left. It can also be referred to by its caption or, in other words, the name of the menu that appears on the menu bar. Many menu bars start with the File and Edit menus and end with the Help menu, for example.

You can add your own menus to any of the built-in menu bars or to your own menu bars. Under Windows, if there are too many menus to fit across the menu bar, they will display over multiple lines. As the limit on the total number of menus is 255, you can actually fill a VGA screen with your menus, should you ever want to do so. On the Macintosh, the menus must fit across the one line menu bar or they disappear off the screen.

You can modify the built-in menu bars, or your own menu bars, by deleting any of the existing menus. You can even delete them all and leave the menu bar empty.

 Note

> The Control menu allows you to restore, move, size, minimize, maximize, and close windows. The Control menu for Excel is located at the top-left corner of the Excel window. The Control menu for each workbook window is located in the top-left corner of the window if the workbook window is restored. The Control menu for a workbook window moves to the left of the File menu when the window is maximized and unprotected.
>
> You can remove the workbook Control menu by protecting the workbook. Choose Tools, Protection, Protect Workbook and click the Windows check box in the Protect Workbook dialog box.
>
> You can't delete the Control menu in the top-left corner of the Excel window using Excel's menus or standard VBA commands. However, it can be removed in a VBA procedure by making calls to the Windows API (Application Programming Interface). The procedure is different for Excel 5, which is a 16-bit application, and Excel 7, which is a 32-bit application. See the section "Removing the Excel System Menu," later in the chapter, for the VBA code required to do this.

Using VBA, you can disable the built-in menus or your own menus. Disabled menus appear gray and can't be selected. You can disable any number of menus on a menu bar at the same time, even all of them.

Menu Items

Each menu has one or more *menu items* that drop down when the menu is clicked. The menu items can be grouped by placing horizontal separator bars across the menu. These separators are considered to be menu items themselves, although they can't be selected and never perform any actions. They are included in the count of the number of menu items and have a numeric position in the menu.

Like menus, menu items can be referred to by either their position or name. Separators are an exception and can only be referred to by position.

The File menu in Excel starts with the three menu items New, Open, and Close followed by a separator bar. The separator bar has position number 4 on the menu.

Menu items, except for submenus, are normally associated with actions. In the case of custom menus, each menu item is associated with a macro that runs when the menu item is selected.

As with menus, you can delete menu items from the built-in menus and from your own menus. You can also add new menu items to both the built-in menus and your own menus.

Using VBA, you can enable and disable your own custom menu items, but not the built-in menu items. You can also place a check mark against your own custom menu items, but not the built-in menu items.

Submenus

A *submenu* is a special type of menu item. You can tell the difference between a submenu and a menu item by the arrowhead that appears to the right of a submenu. If you click a submenu, Excel displays the *submenu items* attached to it. An example is the Filter submenu on the Data menu shown in figure 26.1. Its submenu items, such as AutoFilter, appear to the right of the submenu in this figure.

As you might expect, you can add your own submenus to the built-in menus or your custom menus. You can also delete built-in submenus and custom submenus.

However, it is not possible to disable built-in submenus or custom submenus.

26

Submenu Items

Submenu items behave in much the same way as menu items. You attach macros to them that are executed when the submenu items are selected. You can add and delete submenu items for both the built-in menus and custom menus.

As you would expect, you cannot disable submenu items in the built-in menus. However, you would expect that you could disable your custom submenu items, but this does not always work. Under some circumstances you must have the worksheet restored to successfully disable submenu items. When the worksheet is maximized, the effect is not apparent.

Shortcut Menus

The *shortcut menus* are what you see when you right-click objects such as worksheet cells and toolbars. The shortcut menus are stored in Excel as if they were menus belonging to the three dummy menu bars shown in table 26.1.

You can't create new shortcut menus but you can modify the existing ones. You can delete menu items and add new menu items and attach macros to them.

Manually Editing Menus

Excel's built-in menus are a part of Excel itself. The easiest way you can change Excel's menus is to use the Menu Editor. Any changes you make to these menus are stored in the workbook where you make the changes as a list of edits.

When you open a workbook that has a menu edit list, those edits are immediately applied to the Excel menus. As you switch from one type of sheet to another, such as from a worksheet to a module, the edited menus are automatically displayed. When you close the workbook, the edits are removed. This means that it is very easy for you to customize the built-in menus for a particular workbook.

 Note

If you open more than one workbook with stored menu edits at the same time, the effect is cumulative. When you set up an application involving multiple workbooks, it is a good idea to confine the menu edits to a single master workbook. If you decide to have menu edits in more than one workbook, you need to coordinate the interaction between the workbooks.

As well as editing the built-in menus, you can create new menu bars using the Menu Editor. However, you need to use VBA to activate these menu bars. They will not be automatically shown.

The Menu Editor

You can access the Menu Editor by clicking the Menu Editor toolbar button on the VBA toolbar, which is shown in figure 26.2. You can do this while you are in a worksheet or a VBA module.

Alternatively, you can activate a VBA module and choose Tools, Menu Editor. Menu Editor is not available in the worksheet Tools menu.

Fig. 26.2

You can open the Menu Editor dialog box by clicking the Menu Editor button on the VBA toolbar.

Menu Editor button

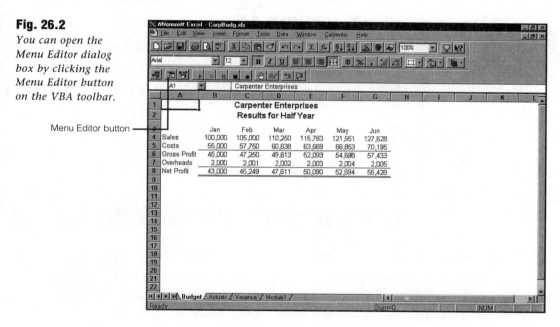

The Menu Editor dialog box is shown in figure 26.3.

Fig. 26.3

You can use the Menu Editor to change the structure of the built-in menu bars or to construct entirely new menu bars.

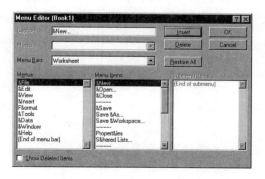

26

Adding New Menus

You can see a custom menu added to the worksheet menu bar in figure 26.4. Note that the new Carpenter menu has the C underlined. This means that you can activate this menu from the keyboard by holding down the Alt key and pressing the underlined letter, just like the regular Excel menus. When you define the caption for the menu in the Menu Editor dialog box, you precede the letter to be underlined with an &.

Fig. 26.4

Carpenter is a custom menu that has been added to the worksheet menu bar using the Menu Editor.

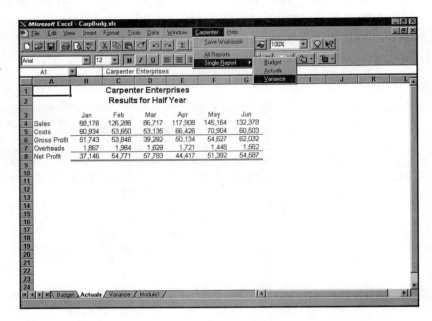

To add a new menu such as the Carpenter menu shown in figure 26.4, follow these steps:

1. Start the Menu Editor by clicking the Menu Editor toolbar button on the VBA toolbar, or by activating a VBA module and choosing Tools, Menu Editor.

2. From the Menu Bars drop-down list, select the menu bar required.

3. In the Menus list box, click the menu name that you want to come after your new menu. Click [End of menu bar] if you want it to be the last menu.

4. Click the Insert button to open up a new menu position.

5. In the Caption edit box, enter the caption for the new menu. Precede the character to be underlined by an &.

Caution

Don't be tempted to press the Enter key before you have finished editing in the Menu Editor dialog box. As Enter is equivalent to clicking OK, you will dismiss the dialog box and have to open it again to continue. Only click OK or press Enter when you have finished editing menus.

Adding New Menu Items

When you add a new menu item, you define the text to appear in the menu by entering it in the Caption edit box of the Menu Editor. You can use an & in the caption to indicate the character to be underlined, in the same way as with menus. If you want, you can make the menu item a separator line by entering its caption as a dash or minus sign.

To add new menu items to a menu, such as the Save Workbook menu item in the Carpenter menu (refer to fig. 26.4), follow these steps:

1. In the Menus list box of the Menu Editor, select the menu to which you want to add menu items.

2. In the Menu Items list box, click the menu item you want to follow the new menu item. Click [End of menu] if you want it to be the bottom menu item.

3. Click the Insert button to open up a new menu item position.

4. In the Caption edit box, enter the caption for the new menu item. Precede the character to be underlined by an &. If you want the new menu item to be a separator line, enter in a single dash or minus sign as the caption.

Adding Submenu Items

When you add new submenu items, such as the Budget submenu item shown in figures 26.4 and 26.5, Excel converts the selected menu item, which is shown as highlighted in figure 26.5, to a submenu. You do not have to do anything else. The process is automatic. As with menu items, you can underline a character. You can also make the submenu item a separator line.

To enter a new submenu item, follow these steps:

1. In the Menu Items list box, select the menu item that you want to make a submenu and to which you want to add menu items.

2. In the Submenu Items list box, click the submenu item you want to follow the new submenu item. Click [End of submenu] if you want it to be the bottom submenu item.

26

3. Click the Insert button to open up a new submenu item position.

4. In the Caption edit box, enter the caption for the new submenu item. Precede the character to be underlined by an &. If you want the new submenu item to be a separator line, enter in a single dash or minus sign as the caption.

You can see the structure of the Carpenter menu as it has been set up in the Menu Editor in figure 26.5.

Fig. 26.5

You create new menus, such as the Carpenter menu, by inserting the menu elements into the Menu Editor dialog box.

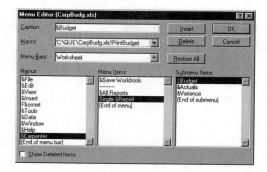

Assigning Macros to Menu Items

When you have defined your menu structure, you can start attaching macros to the menu items and submenu items. When you click one of these items in your application, the attached macro runs. Listing 26.1 shows the macros in Module1 that are attached to the corresponding menu items and submenu items.

 Note

As with all our examples, you will find the file CARPBUDG.XLS on the CD that accompanies this book.

Listing 26.1   26LISO1.TXT: VBA Macros that Are Attatched to Carpenter Menu

```
'Macros attached to Carpenter menu on Worksheet menu bar
' in CarpBudg.xls

'Reports, Save Workbook
Sub SaveWorkbook()
    ActiveWorkbook.Save
End Sub

'Reports, Single Report, Budget
Sub PrintBudget()
```

```
        Sheets("Budget").Select
        ActiveWindow.SelectedSheets.PrintOut Copies:=1
    End Sub

    'Reports, Single Report, Actuals
    Sub PrintActuals()
        Sheets("Actuals").Select
        ActiveWindow.SelectedSheets.PrintOut Copies:=1
    End Sub

    'Reports, Single Report, Variance
    Sub PrintVariance()
        Sheets("Variance").Select
        ActiveWindow.SelectedSheets.PrintOut Copies:=1
    End Sub

    'Reports, All Reports
    Sub PrintAll()
        Call PrintBudget
        Call PrintActuals
        Call PrintVariance
    End Sub
```

To attach a macro to a menu item or submenu item, follow these steps:

1. Activate the Menu Editor and, in the Menus list box, select the menu containing the item to which you want to attach a macro.

2. In the Menu Items list box, click the menu item or submenu containing the item to which you want to attach a macro.

3. If the item is a submenu item, in the Submenu Items list box, click the submenu item to which you want to attach a macro.

4. From the Macro drop-down menu, select the name of the macro you want to attach to the selected menu item or submenu item.

5. Click OK or press Enter to dismiss the Menu Editor dialog box.

Changing Macros Assigned to Menus

If you want to change the macro attached to a menu item or submenu item, use the same steps as just shown and select a new macro. If you want to remove the macro, delete the text from the Macro drop-down edit box.

Displaying Status Bar Help for a Menu Item

You can have a help message appear on the Status Bar at the bottom of the screen when a menu item is selected. To do this, you enter the status bar message in the Macro Options dialog box for the attached macro. You can access the Macro Options dialog box from the Object Browser which is shown in figure 26.6. The Macro Options dialog box is shown in figure 26.7.

26

Fig. 26.6
In the Object Browser you can see the macros you have created in your modules.

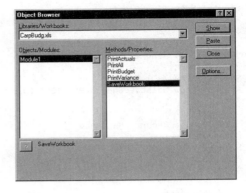

Fig. 26.7
In the Macro Options dialog box you can define the status bar text for your macro.

To associate status bar text with a menu item or submenu item, follow these steps:

1. In the VBA module, either choose View, Object Browser or press F2.

2. In the Libraries/Workbooks drop-down menu, select the name of the workbook containing the macro.

3. In the Objects/Modules list box, select the name of the module containing the macro.

4. In the Methods/Properties list box, select the name of the macro.

5. Click the Options button to open the Macro Options dialog box.

6. In the Status Bar Text edit box, enter the required message text.

7. Click OK to dismiss the Macro Options dialog box and click Close to dismiss the Object Browser.

Activating Custom Menus

So far you have modified the built-in menus. What about creating a new menu bar and showing it? You might want to restrict users to just the necessary operations for your application so that they are not confused with the myriad of choices in the normal worksheet menu bar.

You could decide to have just the menu items for opening and closing your standard file for printing reports. Figure 26.8 shows how this menu bar looks.

Fig. 26.8

The worksheet menu bar has been replaced by a custom menu bar containing two menus, File and Reports. The File menu has menu items Close Report, Save Report, a separator, and Exit.

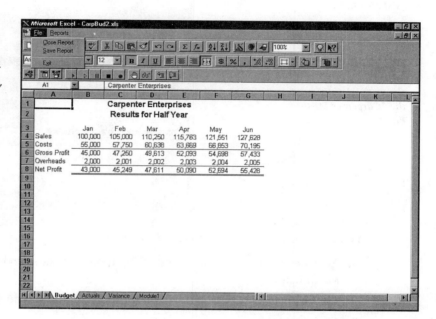

Creating a Custom Menu Bar

There is a trick to creating a new menu bar in the menu editor. You must make sure that no menus, menu items, or submenu items are selected when you click the Insert button. You do this by selecting any menu bar from the Menu Bars drop-down list. Even if you re-select the current menu bar, the trick works. Figure 26.9 shows what the Menu Editor dialog box looks like before you click Insert.

You can now click the Insert button, which creates a new menu bar. The default caption is "New Menu Bar1," which you can change to something more meaningful by editing the contents of the Caption edit box. You can then proceed to add your menus, menu items, submenus, and submenu items as already described. Figure 26.10 shows how a menu bar with two menus might appear.

26

Fig. 26.9

There is a trick to creating a new menu bar. Select any existing menu bar from the Menu Bars drop-down list. This ensures that nothing is selected in the list boxes below, as shown here.

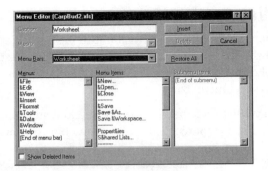

Fig. 26.10

The Menu Editor shows the definition of the "Carpenter Menu Bar."

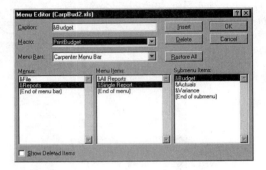

To create a custom menu bar, follow these steps:

1. Activate the Menu Editor from the VBA toolbar or, in a module, by choosing Tools, Menu Editor.

2. Click the Menu Bars drop-down menu and select any menu bar.

3. Click Insert.

4. In the Caption edit box, type in a name for the new menu bar.

5. Create the menus, menu items, submenus, and submenu items for the new menu bar as described previously.

6. Click OK to dismiss the Menu Editor.

Showing the Custom Menu Bar

When you edit the built-in menu bars using the Menu Editor, the changes are automatically applied and removed as you open and close the worksheet. This is not the case with custom menu bars.

Your custom menu bar does not appear automatically. You have to write a macro to activate it. You can give that macro the name of Auto_Open as shown in listing 26.2. This means that it will be executed automatically when you open the worksheet.

The Auto_Open macro uses the Activate method of the MenuBar object. The menu bar required is referenced by its caption property, "Carpenter Menu Bar," which was defined in the Menu Editor.

The custom menu remains active until it is changed by another macro, or you exit from Excel. Even if you close the worksheet, the menu bar remains on the screen. Therefore, it is a good idea to activate the built-in worksheet menu bar when the worksheet is closed. You can do this in an Auto_Close macro as shown in listing 26.2. However, you can only activate the worksheet menu bar if you are in a worksheet. For that reason a test has been included so that if any other type of sheet, such as a module, is active, the Budget sheet is activated. The macro then uses the Reset method to remove any Menu Editor changes to the worksheet menu bar and then activates it. You can refer to the built-in menu bars using Excel VBA constants such as xlWorksheet.

 Note

The Auto_Close macro runs if you close the worksheet using standard Excel methods such as clicking Close in the worksheet Control menu. It doesn't run automatically if you close the worksheet using another macro. The same principle applies to the Auto_Open macro if you open the worksheet using another macro.

If you want an Auto macro to run when you open or close a workbook using a macro, you use the RunAutoMacros method of the workbook. This is shown in the CloseWorkbook macro in listing 26.2. This macro ensures that the Auto_Close macro runs, using the Excel VBA constant xlAutoClose, before it closes the workbook.

Listing 26.2   26LIS02.TXT: The VBA Macro Code Attached to the Carpenter Menu Bar

```
'Macros attached to Carpenter menu bar
' in CarpBud2.xls

'File, Save Report
Sub SaveWorkbook()
    ActiveWorkbook.Save
End Sub

'Reports, Single Report, Budget
Sub PrintBudget()
    Sheets("Budget").Select
    ActiveWindow.SelectedSheets.PrintOut Copies:=1
End Sub
```

26

continues

Listing 26.2 Continued

```
'Reports, Single Report, Actuals
Sub PrintActuals()
    Sheets("Actuals").Select
    ActiveWindow.SelectedSheets.PrintOut Copies:=1
End Sub

'Reports, Single Report, Variance
Sub PrintVariance()
    Sheets("Variance").Select
    ActiveWindow.SelectedSheets.PrintOut Copies:=1
End Sub

'Reports, All Reports
Sub PrintAll()
    Call PrintBudget
    Call PrintActuals
    Call PrintVariance
End Sub

'Activate Menu Bar
Sub Auto_Open()
    MenuBars("Carpenter Menu Bar").Activate
End Sub

'Activate Normal Worksheet Menu Bar
Sub Auto_Close()
    If TypeName(ActiveSheet) <> "Worksheet" Then Sheets("Budget").Activate
    MenuBars(xlWorksheet).Reset
    MenuBars(xlWorksheet).Activate
End Sub

'File, Close Report
Sub CloseWorkbook()
    ActiveWorkbook.RunAutoMacros xlAutoClose
    ActiveWorkbook.Close
End Sub

'File, Exit
Sub ExitExcel()
    Application.Quit
End Sub
```

Managing Menus with VBA

The Menu Editor is a relatively easy way to customize menus, but it is not as powerful as VBA code. This section discusses how to write VBA procedures that perform all the operations shown earlier in this chapter and lots more. It also discusses some bugs in both the Menu Editor and VBA menu operations.

Creating Menus

To work with Excel's menus in VBA code, you need to be aware of the hierarchical relationship of the menu elements in the Excel Object Model. This is illustrated in figure 26.11, which has been taken directly from the Excel Help screens. The Application object, which is Excel, contains the collection of menu bars. Each menu bar contains a collection of menus and each menu contains a collection of menu items.

Excel's documentation is lacking when it comes to submenus. The following information should bridge the gap.

The menu items collection is a bit unusual. It can also contain submenus. Although submenus are members of the menu items collection, they have different characteristics from menu items. You need to take a little care in dealing with submenus, as shown here.

Each submenu contains a collection of menu items. This leads to further conceptual problems, from a VBA coding point of view, a collection of menu items that belong to a higher level menu item. The coding examples that follow show you how you deal with this situation.

Fig. 26.11

This figure, taken from Excel's Help screens, shows the hierarchical relationship of the menu objects.

Creating Menu Bars

You create new menu bars by applying the Add method to the MenuBars collection. The method has only one argument, which defines the Caption for the menu bar. You can add as many as fifteen extra menu bars this way at any one time. As you have already seen, you display a menu bar using the Activate method.

You can also use the Delete method to remove custom menu bars, but you can't delete the built-in menu bars.

After you activate a custom menu bar, Excel no longer automatically changes the menu bar as you move from one type of sheet to another. You have control of the menus until you activate a built-in menu bar.

Creating Menus

You use the Add method of the Menus collection to create new menus for your custom menu bars or for the built-in menu bars. Used with Menus, the Add method has three arguments. The first defines the Caption for the menu and is required. The second argument defines the position of the menu by referencing the name or numeric position of the menu item before which the new one will be placed. If it is not specified, the new menu goes at the end of the menu bar or to the left of the Help menu on a built-in menu bar. The third argument restores built-in menus that you have changed.

Listing 26.3 shows the statements used to add a new menu bar and populate it with menus, then activate it. The resulting menu bar is shown in figure 26.12. Note that the code is rather cumbersome with the repetition of the menu bar reference. You can make the code easier to write and read using either of the two techniques shown in listing 26.4 and listing 26.5. These techniques also speed up the execution of the code.

Listing 26.3   26LIS03.TXT: Creating a Menu Bar and Adding Menus

```
Sub NewMenuBar()
    MenuBars.Add "Carpenter VBA Menu Bar"
    MenuBars("Carpenter VBA Menu Bar").Menus.Add "&File"
    MenuBars("Carpenter VBA Menu Bar").Menus.Add "&Edit"
    MenuBars("Carpenter VBA Menu Bar").Menus.Add "&Select"
    MenuBars("Carpenter VBA Menu Bar").Menus.Add "&Reports"
    MenuBars("Carpenter VBA Menu Bar").Menus.Add "&Help"

    MenuBars("Carpenter VBA Menu Bar").Activate
End Sub
```

Fig. 26.12

To create this new menu bar in VBA code, you use the Add method of the MenuBars collection. To create menus, you use the Add method of the Menus collection.

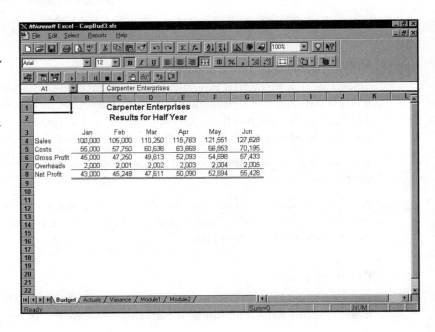

The Set statement in listing 26.4 creates an object variable. You can use the object variable rather than the full object reference in subsequent code. The With...End With construction used in listing 26.5 is another method for reducing the repetition of references. These techniques are used frequently in the examples that follow.

Listing 26.4   26LIS04.TXT: Using the Set Statement

```
Sub NewMenuBar()
    Dim mbCarpenter As MenuBar

    Set mbCarpenter = MenuBars.Add("Carpenter VBA Menu Bar")
    mbCarpenter.Menus.Add "&File"
    mbCarpenter.Menus.Add "&Edit"
    mbCarpenter.Menus.Add "&Select"
    mbCarpenter.Menus.Add "&Reports"
    mbCarpenter.Menus.Add "&Help"

    mbCarpenter.Activate
End Sub
```

 Note

In listing 26.3, when using the Add method for the MenuBars collection, the caption for the new menu bar is not enclosed in parentheses. In listing 26.4, the caption is enclosed in parentheses. In VBA, when you want to assign the return value of a procedure to a variable, or use it in an expression, you must enclose the procedure's arguments in parentheses.

Listing 26.5   26LIS05.TXT: Using the With Statement

```
Sub NewMenuBar()
Dim mbCarpenter As MenuBar

    With mbCarpenter.Menus
        .Add "&File"
        .Add "&Edit"
        .Add "&Select"
        .Add "&Reports"
        .Add "&Help"
    End With

    mbCarpenter.Activate
End Sub
```

26

When you are developing menus, you might want to include code that ensures that you do not try to add the same menu bar twice. If you do try to add the same menu bar a second time, the macro will halt with an error message. However, if you try to delete a custom menu bar that does not exist, you will also get an error.

 Note

You can execute code that tries to delete the built-in menu bars without causing an error, even though you can't delete them. Excel just ignores the attempt. This is handy when you want to delete all the custom menus because you can loop through the entire MenuBar collection with a For Each…Next loop trying to delete all menu bars but, in fact, only deleting the custom menu bars.

Listing 26.6 shows how to delete a custom menu bar without causing an error. Because you can't delete a menu bar while it is active, you must first ensure that another menu bar is active. Here you activate the built-in worksheet menu bar, making sure that you do that while in a worksheet. Because you would not be sure whether the custom menu bar exists at this point, you use the On Error statement to say that if an error occurs, ignore it and go on to the next statement (Resume Next). You can then safely try to delete the menu bar. If the custom menu bar exists, it will be deleted. If it does not exist, VBA will ignore the error.

It is a good idea to resume normal error checking after getting past the problem area. This is accomplished by using On Error GoTo 0.

Listing 26.6   26LIS06.TXT: Ensuring That the Menu Bar Is Deleted

```
Sub NewMenuBar()
    Dim mbCarpenter As MenuBar

    If TypeName(ActiveSheet) <> "Worksheet" Then Sheets("Budget").Activate
    MenuBars(xlWorksheet).Activate
    On Error Resume Next
    MenuBars("Carpenter VBA Menu Bar").Delete
    On Error GoTo 0

    Set mbCarpenter = MenuBars.Add("Carpenter VBA Menu Bar")
    With mbCarpenter.Menus
        .Add "&File"
        .Add "&Edit"
        .Add "&Select"
        .Add "&Reports"
        .Add "&Help"
    End With

    mbCarpenter.Activate
End Sub
```

Creating Menu Items

You create new menu items by using the Add method of the MenuItems collection. Listing 26.7 shows how this is done. You can see the resulting menu items in figure 26.13.

For MenuItems, the Add method has only one required argument. This is the first argument that defines the Caption for the menu item. However, Add has seven optional arguments. There is a list of all its arguments in table 26.2.

Unless the menu item is a separator or submenu, you would normally specify the second argument that is the name of the macro you want to associate with the menu item. The Before argument defines the menu item you want the new menu item to go before. It can be either the caption of the existing menu item, or its numeric position in the menu. If you omit this argument, the menu item will be placed after the last one.

Table 26.2   Arguments for the Menuitems.Add Method

Argument	Description
Caption	The menu item text that appears in the menu. A single hyphen (-) creates a separator bar.
OnAction	The name of the macro you want to run when the new menu item is selected.
ShortcutKey	Used only on the Apple Macintosh. Specifies the shortcut key for the menu item as text.
Before	The menu item before which the new item will be added.
Restore	Excel will restore the previously deleted built-in menu item named in the caption if this is set to TRUE.
StatusBar	Help text that will display in the status bar when the menu item is highlighted by the user. Otherwise the default status bar text assigned to the macro is used.
HelpContextID	The context ID for the custom Help topic of the menu item. This is discussed in Chapter 27, "Creating Custom Help for VBA Applications."
HelpFile	The Help file name containing the custom help topic of the menu item. This is discussed in Chapter 27.

26

Fig. 26.13

These new menu items on the Custom menu were created using the Add method of the MenuItems collection as shown in listing 26.7.

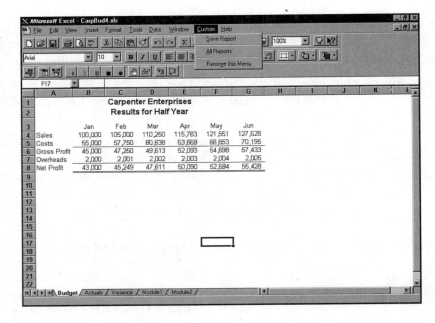

Listing 26.7   26LIS06.PCX: Creating New Menu Items

```
'Add Custom menu to Worksheet menu bar
Sub NewMenu()
    Dim mnCustom As Menu

    MenuBars(xlWorksheet).Reset
    Set mnCustom = MenuBars(xlWorksheet).Menus.Add("&Custom")
    With mnCustom.MenuItems
        .Add "&Save Report", "SaveWorkbook"
        .Add "-"
        .Add "&All Reports", "PrintAll"
        .Add "-"
        .Add "Remo&ve this Menu", "Restore"
    End With
End Sub

'Reset the built-in Worksheet menu bar
Sub Restore()
    MenuBars(xlWorksheet).Reset
End Sub
```

Creating Submenus

You create submenus by using the MenuItems.AddMenu method. This method has a required Caption argument and optional Before and Restore arguments that are shown in table 26.3.

Table 26.3   Arguments for the MenuItems.AddMenu Method

Argument	Description
Caption	The caption to use for the new submenu.
Before	If this argument is present, it specifies the menu item before which this submenu should be inserted.
Restore	If this argument is TRUE, Microsoft Excel will restore the previously deleted built-in submenu named by the caption argument.

Submenus are regarded as members of the MenuItems collection. For example, to find the numeric position, or index, of the submenu, you use the following code:

```
MenuBars(xlWorksheet).Menus("Custom").MenuItems("Single Report").Index
```

This code returns a value of 4 when applied to the menu in figure 26.14. The separator bar counts as a member of the collection as well.

Submenus have some peculiar characteristics. For example, you can access the caption of the submenu with:

```
MenuBars(xlWorksheet).Menus("Custom").MenuItems(4).Caption
```

However, you can't change the caption using this construction. You can use the following rather odd technique:

```
MenuBars(xlWorksheet).Menus("Custom").MenuItems(4).Parent.Caption = "One Report"
```

Another example of the strangeness of submenus is that you can't disable them. You can disable menus and submenu items, but not submenus.

Listing 26.8   26LIS08.PCX: Creating New Submenus and Submenu Items

```
'Add Custom menu to Worksheet menu bar
Sub NewMenu()
    Dim mnCustom As Menu

    MenuBars(xlWorksheet).Reset
    Set mnCustom = MenuBars(xlWorksheet).Menus.Add("&Custom")
    With mnCustom.MenuItems
        .Add "&Save Report", "SaveWorkbook"
        .Add "-"
        .Add "&All Reports", "PrintAll"
        .AddMenu "&Single Report"
        With .Item("Single Report").MenuItems
            .Add "&Budget", "PrintBudget"
            .Add "&Actuals", "PrintActuals"
```

continues

26

> **Listing 26.8   Continued**
>
> ```
>                 .Add "&Variance", "PrintVariance"
>           End With
>           .Add "-"
>           .Add "Remo&ve this Menu", "Restore"
>       End With
> End Sub
>
> 'Reset the built-in Worksheet menu bar
> Sub Restore()
>     MenuBars(xlWorksheet).Reset
> End Sub
> ```

Fig. 26.14
You can add new submenus to a menu using the MenuItems.AddMenu method.

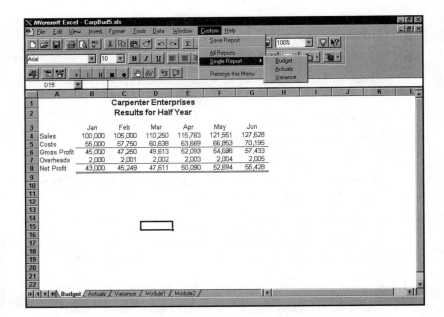

Creating Submenu Items

You add submenu items to submenus using the MenuItems.Add method. You treat the submenu as a member of the menu's MenuItems collection. For example, the following code adds a new submenu item, "Budget," to the "Single Report" submenu and attaches a macro called "PrintBudget":

```
MenuBars(xlWorksheet).Menus("Custom").MenuItems("Single Report").MenuItems.Add
   "&Budget" , "PrintBudget"
```

When you see the length of this type of expression, you can appreciate the more compact code used in listing 26.8. It uses a nested With...End With construction to avoid repeating the same object specifications.

The available arguments for this form of MenuItems.Add is identical to the form used to add menu items. Refer to table 26.2 for the complete list.

Overriding Excel's Menu Item Procedures

There are occasions when it is handy to replace Excel's built-in menu procedures with customized procedures. For example, you might perform many extracts of data from a list to a new location using the <u>D</u>ata, <u>F</u>ilter, <u>A</u>dvanced Filter submenu item. You might find it annoying that each time you use the dialog box associated with this operation, you have to click the option to <u>C</u>opy to Another Location, as the default is <u>F</u>ilter the List. Also, you have to enter the same cell locations each time to get the input you can see in figure 26.15.

Fig. 26.15

This is the way you would like to see the Advanced Filter dialog box appear each time you use it.

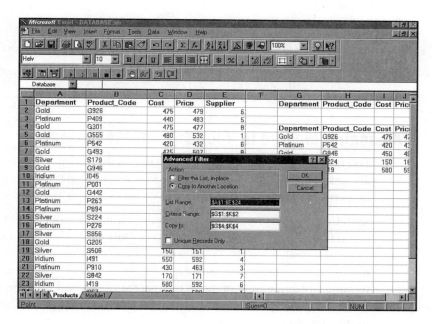

You can write your own macro to display the built-in dialog box and change the default values as shown in listing 26.9. The NewAdvancedFilter macro sets the option buttons to the second option with the value 2 as the first argument. The macro also ensures that the names Database, Criteria, and Extract will be used in the edit boxes of the dialog box.

You could run this macro instead of the <u>A</u>dvanced Filter submenu item. However, it would be better to change the way the submenu item works. The Auto_Open macro in listing 26.9 does that job.

26

You can't assign a macro to a built-in menu item or submenu item. What you can do is delete the built-in item and replace it with one that looks identical by giving it the same caption. Naturally, you can attach whatever macro you want to your own custom item.

Listing 26.9   26LIS09.TXT: Customized Advanced Filter Macro

```
'Data, Advanced Filter
'Set Action to Copy to New Location
Sub NewAdvancedFilter()
    Application.Dialogs(xlDialogFilterAdvanced).Show _
        2, _
        Range("Database"), _
        Range("Criteria"), _
        Range("Extract")
End Sub

Sub Auto_Open()
    Dim smFilter As Object
    Set smFilter = MenuBars(xlWorksheet).Menus("Data").MenuItems("Filter")
    smFilter.MenuItems("Advanced Filter...").Delete
    smFilter.MenuItems.Add "&Advanced Filter...", "NewAdvancedFilter"
End Sub
```

Assigning Macros to Your Custom Menu Items

You have already seen how to assign a macro to a menu item when creating it. You can also assign a new macro at any time to your custom menu items by setting the OnAction property of the menu item. You can't do this with the built-in menu items.

Sometimes, when creating your own menu structure, you would like to have a group of menu items carry out the same basic procedure but with one or two variations for each item. In this situation, you can take two different approaches. The first is to use the same macro on each menu item and use the Application.Caller property in that macro to determine which menu item called the macro. The second is to specify one or more arguments for the one macro and have each menu item call the macro with different values for the arguments.

Using Application.Caller

The Application.Caller property returns different results depending on the context in which it is used. In the case of a menu or submenu item, it returns a four-element array with the information shown in table 26.4.

Table 26.4   Values Returned by Application.Caller When a Macro Is Called from a Menu

Value	Description
Element 1	The index of the menu item in the menu or the submenu item in the submenu.
Element 2	The index of the menu in the menu bar.
Element 3	The index number of the menu bar. (This result is not reliable. Instead of using MenuBars(Application.Caller(3)), use the ActiveMenuBar property.)
Element 4	The index number of the submenu in the menu. It has a value of zero if the caller was a menu item. This element is not documented in Excel. It is not generated in Excel 5.0 or 5.0a. It was introduced in Excel 5.0c.

 Note

The undocumented Element 4 in table 26.4 cannot be accessed by a reference such as Application.Caller(4). You must first assign the value of Application.Caller to an array variable as shown in listing 26.10. You can then reference the fourth element in the array.

Prior to Excel 5.0c, the fourth element was not available and it was not possible to determine which submenu called the macro using this technique. It was not even possible to tell whether the macro was called by a menu item or a submenu item. Even in Excel 5.0c and Excel 7, the fourth element is not documented.

The first element of Application.Caller can also return incorrect results from a menu created using the Menu Editor. It performs properly with VBA-generated menus. The problem arises if you create a submenu using the Menu Editor. The menu items that follow the submenu generate index numbers lower than they should be.

The third element of Application.Caller does not return an index number that you can rely on. For the Worksheet menu bar, it returns a value of 10, which corresponds to the index used by XLM macros, instead of 7. If your macro were attached to the Worksheet menu bar, the following attempt to display the Caption property of the calling menubar would fail.

```
MsgBox MenuBars(Application.Caller(3)).Caption
```

26

Instead, you can use the following simpler construction which does work.

```
MsgBox ActiveMenuBar.Caption
```

Figure 26.16 shows how you can use Application.Caller to good effect. You need to extract data from your list for each supplier, so you want a menu with each supplier appearing as a menu item. The code in listing 26.10, AlterWorksheetMenu, creates that menu and attaches the same macro, ExtractSupplier, to each menu item. This macro determines which menu item has called it by placing the elements of Application.Caller into a variable named Called and taking the first element of the resulting array. It is a good idea to feed Application.Caller into an array. Otherwise, Excel does not let you use the fourth element.

ExtractSupplier places the menu item index, which is the same as the supplier number, into the criteria range under the Supplier heading. It then uses the AdvancedFilter method to copy the supplier data to the output range.

Fig. 26.16

*You can attach the
same macro to each
of the Supplier menu
items and detect
which one executed
the macro using
Application.Caller.*

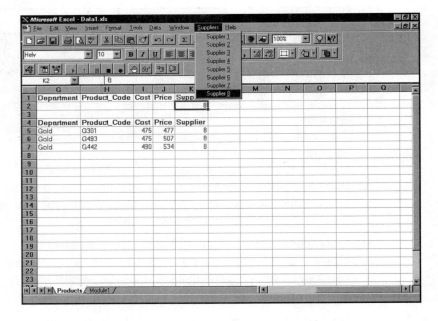

Listing 26.10   26LIS10.TXT: Detecting the Calling Menu Item with Application.Caller

```
'Add Suppliers menu to worksheet menu bar
Sub AlterWorksheetMenu()
    Dim mSuppliers As Menu
    Dim i As Integer

    MenuBars(xlWorksheet).Reset
    Set mSuppliers = MenuBars(xlWorksheet).Menus.Add("&Suppliers")
```

```
        With mSuppliers.MenuItems
            For i = 1 To 8
                .Add "Supplier &" & i, "ExtractSupplier"
            Next i
        End With
End Sub

'Extract specified Supplier data
Sub ExtractSupplier()
    Dim Called As Variant
    Dim SupplierNo As Integer

    Called = Application.Caller
    SupplierNo = Called(1)
    Range("Criteria").Offset(1, 4).Resize(1, 1).Value = SupplierNo
    Range("Database").AdvancedFilter _
        Action:=xlFilterCopy, _
        CriteriaRange:=Range("Criteria"), _
        CopyToRange:=Range("Extract"), _
        Unique:=False
End Sub
```

Macros with Arguments

Another way you can distinguish which menu item or submenu item called a macro is to use a macro that accepts one or more arguments. When you attach the macro to a menu item, you also attach different argument values as shown in listing 26.11. Note that the ExtractSupplier macro now expects SupplierNo as an input argument value.

Listing 26.11   26LIS11.TXT: Detecting the Calling Menu Item with a Macro Argument

```
'Add Suppliers menu to worksheet menu bar
Sub AlterWorksheetMenu()
    Dim mSuppliers As Menu
    Dim i As Integer

    MenuBars(xlWorksheet).Reset
    Set mSuppliers = MenuBars(xlWorksheet).Menus.Add("&Suppliers")
    With mSuppliers.MenuItems
        For i = 1 To 8
            .Add "Supplier &" & i, "'ExtractSupplier """ & i & """'"
        Next i
    End With
End Sub

'Extract specified Supplier data
Sub ExtractSupplier(SupplierNo)

    Range("Criteria").Offset(1, 4).Resize(1, 1).Value = SupplierNo
    Range("Database").AdvancedFilter _
```

26

continues

Listing 26.11   Continued

```
            Action:=xlFilterCopy, _
            CriteriaRange:=Range("Criteria"), _
            CopyToRange:=Range("Extract"), _
            Unique:=False
    End Sub
```

The action macros attached to the menu items now have to specify a supplier number. The way this has to be coded is a bit complex. You need to end up with a macro attached to the menu item that looks like the following:

```
'ExtractSupplier "1"'
```

The whole macro reference is enclosed in single quotation marks. The argument value is enclosed in double quotation marks. If you were making all the action macro arguments the same, you could specify this in your code as

```
.Add "Supplier &" & i, "'ExtractSupplier ""1""'"
```

The quoted text has to contain double quotation marks. You follow the convention of providing two double quotation marks to represent a single double quotation within the quoted text. This is complex enough, but you also want to insert the argument value using the value of the i variable. To do this you need:

```
.Add "Supplier &" & i, "'ExtractSupplier """ & i & """'"
```

It gets even more challenging if you want to use more than one argument. Say you wanted to call a macro named ActionMacro and define three arguments with values of One, Two, and Three respectively. You need to end up with the following macro specification:

```
'ActionMacro "One","Two","Three"'
```

If you were holding the parameter values in variables called First, Second, and Third, the code to do this looks like:

```
.Add "Supplier &" & i, "'ActionMacro """ & First & """,""" & Second & """,""" &
Third & """'"
```

As you can see, there are trade-offs between Application.Caller and parameter values. You need to decide which you prefer to use.

Enabling and Disabling Menus and Menu Items

It can be handy, as in Excel, to make certain menu elements temporarily unavailable without removing them from the menu structure. Users can see that the elements exist but know that they are not appropriate for the current activity.

You can gray out, or disable, the built-in menus as well as your custom menus. However, although you can disable your own menu items, you can't disable the built-in menu items. In fact, Excel automatically updates many menu items periodically and even if, for example, you change the captions of these items, they quickly revert to their standard captions.

Figure 26.17 shows the effect of the code in listing 26.12. You can enable these elements again by setting their enabled property equal to TRUE.

Fig. 26.17

You can gray out Excel's built-in menus, such as the File and Edit menus, by setting the Enabled property of the menu to FALSE as shown in listing 26.12.

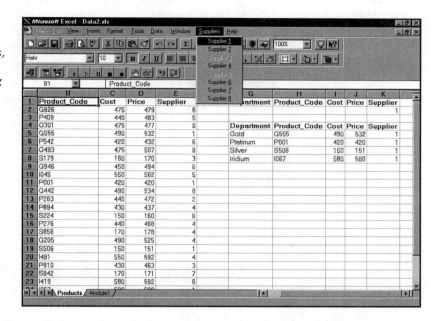

Listing 26.12   26LIS12.TXT: Macro to Disable Menus and Menu Items

```
Sub DisableMenus()
With MenuBars(xlWorksheet)
        .Menus("File").Enabled = False
        .Menus("Edit").Enabled = False
        With .Menus("Suppliers")
            .MenuItems("Supplier 3").Enabled = False
            .MenuItems("Supplier 5").Enabled = False
        End With
    End With
End Sub
```

26

Deleting Menus and Menu Items

If you want to make it very plain to users that they are not supposed to carry out certain actions such as file operations or copy and paste, you can remove the menu or the menu items. You can do this with both built-in and custom menus.

The code in listing 26.13 produces the effect you can see in figure 26.18. The File and Format menus have been deleted and the copy, cut, and paste items have been removed from the Edit menu. This code refers to the menu items by their index numbers. You could also refer to them by name, which gives longer but arguably more readable code.

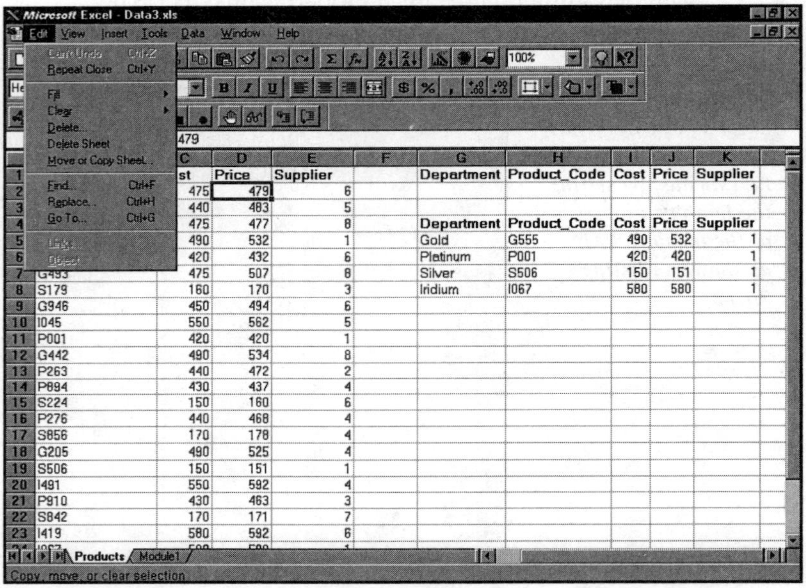

Fig. 26.18

You can delete menus and menu items from your custom menus and the built-in menus.

Listing 26.13   26LIS13.TXT: Macro To Delete Menus and Menu Items

```
Sub RemoveMenus()
    Dim i As Integer

    With MenuBars(xlWorksheet)
        .Menus("File").Delete
        .Menus("Format").Delete
        With .Menus("Edit")
            For i = 8 To 4 Step -1
                .MenuItems(i).Delete
            Next i
        End With
    End With
End Sub
```

Restoring Menus and Menu Items

The easiest way to return an edited built-in menu bar to its standard form is to use the Reset method on the menu bar. However, you will lose all editing changes this way.

If you want to retain some changes, but restore deleted menus and menu items, you use the Add method together with the Restore argument. You also need to specify the correct location for the restored element or it will go at the end of the other elements.

The code in listing 26.14 restores the File and Format menus and the Edit menu items that were deleted by the code in listing 26.13. The Supplier menu is left intact.

Listing 26.14   26LIS14.TXT: Macro to Restore Deleted Menus and Menu Items

```
Sub RestoreMenus()
    With MenuBars(xlWorksheet)
        .Menus.Add Caption:="File", Before:="Edit", Restore:=True
        .Menus.Add Caption:="Format", Before:="Tools", Restore:=True
        With .Menus("Edit")
            .MenuItems.Add Caption:="Cut", Before:="Fill", Restore:=True
            .MenuItems.Add Caption:="Copy", Before:="Fill", Restore:=True
            .MenuItems.Add Caption:="Paste", Before:="Fill", Restore:=True
            .MenuItems.Add Caption:="Paste Special...", Before:="Fill", Restore:=True
            .MenuItems.Add Caption:="-", Before:="Fill"
        End With
    End With
End Sub
```

Placing Check Marks on Menu Items

You can place a check mark against your custom menu items to indicate that an option is active or to indicate that the option has already been processed. You do this by setting the Checked property of the menu item equal to TRUE (see fig. 26.19). You can remove the check marks by setting the Checked property equal to FALSE.

Check marks can also be placed against submenu items (listing 26.15). They behave in the same way as menu items in this regard.

Listing 26.15   26LIS15.TXT: Macro to Place Check Marks Against Menu Items

```
Sub CheckMenuItems()
    With MenuBars(xlWorksheet).Menus("Suppliers")
        .MenuItems("Supplier 1").Checked = True
        .MenuItems("Supplier 2").Checked = True
    End With
End Sub
```

26

Fig. 26.19

You can set the Checked property of your custom menu items equal to TRUE to place a check mark against the item.

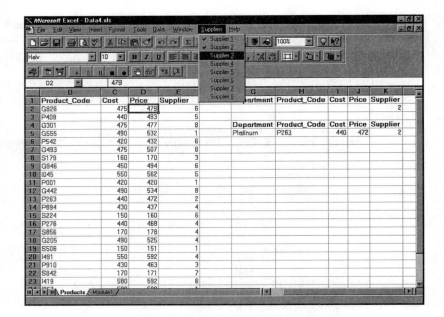

Special Considerations for Submenus

You have seen a number of references in this chapter to the differences between menus and submenus. This section summarizes the peculiarities of submenus and submenu items.

It seems that custom submenus must have been added a little hastily to Excel because there are illogical differences when they are compared with menus. There are also a number of what could only be called bugs in submenus.

Submenus

If you create a submenu using the Menu Editor, remember that this can cause problems in using Application.Caller. The first element of this property, which indicates the index number of the menu item or submenu item that called the macro, can return erroneous results for items below the submenu. This problem does not occur when submenus are created using VBA code.

You create submenus using the AddMenu method of the MenuItems collection. Although submenus and menu items are quite different, you reference a submenu as a member of the menu items collection. Some of the properties of submenus, such as the Caption property, do not behave as they do for menu items.

You can't disable custom submenus. This seems illogical when you can disable both built-in and custom menus.

Prior to Excel 5.0c, you could not determine, using Application.Caller, which submenu called the macro. Although the feature is undocumented, Excel 5.0c added a fourth element to the values returned by Application.Caller that gives the index of the calling submenu. To access this value, you must first assign Application.Caller to a variable, then use an index value of four in the resulting array.

Submenu Items

In general, submenu items behave in the same way as menu items, and their properties and methods are the same. You can assign macros, change the caption, and place check marks in the same way with both.

One exception is that although you can disable submenu items, they behave in an odd way. If the workbook window is maximized, so it takes up all the available space in the Excel application window, the disabled submenu items appear enabled and can be selected. If the workbook window is in a restored state, so that it takes up only part of the Excel window, the disabled items behave as expected.

Removing the Excel System Menu

The Excel system menu can be removed and restored by making calls to the Windows API (Application Programming Interface). Different functions are used in Excel 5 and Excel 7 because Excel 5 is a 16-bit application and Excel 7 is a 32-bit application. Listing 26.16 contains the code for Excel 5 and listing 26.17 contains the code for Excel 7.

When setting up API calls, you must declare the names of the API functions at the top of the module containing the code. You must be very careful to get the declarations exactly right and to use the correct variable types in your macros. These functions delve deep into the heart of Windows and can cause it to crash if there is the slightest error. Make sure you have saved every open file in every application before you test this code.

Listing 26.16   26LIS16.TXT: The API Code to Remove and Restore the Excel 5 System Menu

```
Declare Function GetWindowLong Lib "USER" ( _
    ByVal hWnd As Integer, _
    ByVal nIndex As Integer) As Long
Declare Function SetWindowLong Lib "USER" ( _
    ByVal hWnd As Integer, _
    ByVal nIndex As Integer, _
    ByVal dwNewLong As Long) As Long
```

continues

Listing 26.16   Continued

```
Declare Function FindWindow Lib "USER" ( _
    ByVal lpClassName As Any, _
    ByVal lpWindowName As Any) As Integer

Global Const GWL_STYLE = (-16)
Global Const WS_SYSMENU = &h80000

Sub RemoveConMenuExcel5()
    Dim WinName As String
    Dim WinStyle As Long
    Dim hWnd As Integer
    Dim x

    WinName = Application.Caption
    hWnd = FindWindow(0&, ByVal WinName)
    WinStyle = GetWindowLong(hWnd, GWL_STYLE)
    WinStyle = WinStyle And (Not WS_SYSMENU)
    x = SetWindowLong(hWnd, GWL_STYLE, WinStyle)
End Sub

Sub RestoreConMenuExcel5()
    Dim WinName As String
    Dim WinStyle As Long
    Dim hWnd As Integer
    Dim x

    WinName = Application.Caption
    hWnd = FindWindow(0&, ByVal WinName)
    WinStyle = GetWindowLong(hWnd, GWL_STYLE)
    WinStyle = WinStyle Or WS_SYSMENU
    x = SetWindowLong(hWnd, GWL_STYLE, WinStyle)
End Sub
```

Even if you are running Excel 5 under Windows 95, you need to use the listing 26.16 code. Windows 95 supports both the 16-bit and 32-bit APIs and Excel 5 uses the 16-bit version.

Listing 26.17   26LIS17.TXT: The API Code to Remove and Restore the Excel 7 System Menu

```
Declare Function GetWindowLongA Lib "USER32" ( _
    ByVal hWnd As Integer, _
    ByVal nIndex As Integer) As Long
Declare Function SetWindowLongA Lib "USER32" ( _
    ByVal hWnd As Integer, _
    ByVal nIndex As Integer, _
    ByVal dwNewLong As Long) As Long
Declare Function FindWindowA Lib "USER32" ( _
    ByVal lpClassName As Any, _
    ByVal lpWindowName As Any) As Long
```

```
Global Const GWL_STYLE = (-16)
Global Const WS_SYSMENU = &h80000

Sub RemoveContMenuExcel7()
    Dim WinName As String
    Dim WinStyle As Long
    Dim hWnd As Long
    Dim x

    WinName = Application.Caption
    hWnd = FindWindowA(0&, ByVal WinName)
    WinStyle = GetWindowLongA(hWnd, GWL_STYLE)
    WinStyle = WinStyle And (Not WS_SYSMENU)
    x = SetWindowLongA(hWnd, GWL_STYLE, WinStyle)
End Sub

Sub RestoreContMenuExcel7()
    Dim WinName As String
    Dim WinStyle As Long
    Dim hWnd As Long
    Dim x

    WinName = Application.Caption
    hWnd = FindWindowA(0&, ByVal WinName)
    WinStyle = GetWindowLongA(hWnd, GWL_STYLE)
    WinStyle = WinStyle Or WS_SYSMENU
    x = SetWindowLongA(hWnd, GWL_STYLE, WinStyle)
End Sub
```

Summary

Excel provides you with almost unlimited control over its menu structures. You can change the menus manually using the Menu Editor or you can control the menus dynamically using VBA procedures. However, you do need to be aware of some idiosyncrasies and poorly documented features, particularly in regard to submenus.

Despite the pitfalls, you can generate very effective menu structures from simple additions to the standard menus to a complete reconstruction of the user interface. With custom menus, you can achieve that professional touch that makes your Excel application stand out from the rest.

26

chapter 27

Creating Custom Help for VBA Applications

27

by Willis Howard

In this chapter

◆ **Value of custom Help**
Learn how to improve your applications by writing custom Help.

◆ **Writing Help in Excel**
Create custom Help systems in Excel through VBA programming, including dialog boxes, hot keys, and the drop-down menu.

◆ **Writing Help files**
Write basic Windows Help files using Word for Windows and the Microsoft Help Compiler.

Your application is already written. You know how to use it, and what any potential problem areas may be. The users need your expert knowledge to help them learn and implement your application. Excel can provide access to any Topic page of a standard Windows Help file through the Windows Help Application. Providing custom Help is the best way of sharing what you know.

Custom Help is more than just a file with a few hints and tips. It can:

▶ Provide a general reference guide to your application, accessed through a table of contents.

▶ Allow the user to jump from one topic to another through hyperlinks.

▶ Provide more detailed instructions than you can place in a simple message box.

▶ Give a detailed explanation of input fields and controls.

▶ Give immediate feedback to complicated error conditions.

Improving Your Applications with Custom Help

Many software vendors are providing the majority of their documentation through on-line help. There are many reasons for this. The product is easy to distribute. On-line help is easy to use. Vendors have also discovered that users generally prefer custom, context-sensitive help more than searching through printed pages. You will find that custom Help can also improve your application.

The new user wants to find out how to get started. More experienced users want clarification of how things are organized. Some users need assistance in understanding input fields and controls. Others need to be reminded or learn how to perform a specific task. Everybody is interested in learning shortcuts.

In your application, you provide messages for warnings, errors, or information. Your application will be improved if you can also provide extended assistance to the user through context-sensitive help on the message, input, and dialog screens. These are often good spots to place help because the user gets additional help on demand.

If you use a drop-down menu, your application will be improved if you include a Help item. This item should cause the Contents page of your Help file to be displayed. If you do not have a drop-down menu, your application will be improved if you include a custom Help hotkey that provides instant access to the Contents page of your Help file.

The user can resize the Help window. By providing short instructions for specific tasks, your help can be viewed while the user continues with his or her work. Users really appreciate this kind of assistance.

Creating Custom Help Systems in Excel

In this section you learn various techniques for VBA programming in Excel to access standard Windows Help files. When making your own custom Help system within Excel, you will always need to know two things:

▶ The name of the Help file
▶ The Context ID of the Topic page

Tip
Look at files HelpDemo.* on the companion CD for all of the examples in this chapter. The CD also contains the I'm No Accountant and Objectives Management workbooks for Excel. They both provide examples of how to give context-sensitive help on dialog boxes and drop-down menus.

The Help file is separate from the Excel workbook. You will need to write and compile your custom Help file. An introduction to creating Help files is given at the end of this chapter. Your workbook is an XLS file. The Help file is an HLP file. In the examples used here, I refer to demo help file HELPDEMO.HLP and workbook file HELPDEMO.XLS. You will probably want to give your Help file the same simple name as your Excel file.

Caution

For your custom Help to work, Windows must be able to find your Help file. Be sure that the Help file is located on the system path, and that the users know where to copy it. The best place to put the file is probably the WINDOWS root directory. For Windows 3.1 and Windows 95, this is usually C:\WINDOWS. But, it could be different on your system.

Your Help file should have a Contents page that serves as an index or table of contents. The Help file should also have a Topic page that covers each topic that you want to give help on. Excel identifies the Contents page and each Topic page by a number. That number is called the Context ID. It is a number that you get to assign when the Help file is compiled.

Tip

In your Excel VBA module, use the Const statement to define names for all Context ID numbers. It is easier to remember topics by name than by number.

In this section you learn to

- ▶ Provide access to help in a message box
- ▶ Include help with an input box
- ▶ Include help on a dialog sheet
- ▶ Provide help as an item on a drop-down menu
- ▶ Give help directly on a worksheet
- ▶ Define a special hotkey for custom Help
- ▶ Respond with help to specific events

Providing Access to Help in a Message Box

The message box is one of the most common methods of providing information to the user. You use it for a variety of reasons. It is quick and easy to code. It provides error, sign-on, and status messages. Information in a message box is usually kept brief. To provide extended, detailed information you can add a Help button to the message box.

You add custom Help to a message box just by appending the Help file name and Context ID as the fourth and fifth arguments in the call to the VBA MsgBox() function.

For example, if a numeric string was expected as an input, but the user typed in an alphabetic string, you can give an error message by running the subroutine shown in listing 27.1.

Listing 27.1   HELPDEMO.XLS: Message Box Without Help

```
Sub HelpDemoMessageWithoutHelp()
    MsgBox "You did not enter a number.". _
        vbOKOnly, _
        "Message Without a Help Button"
End Sub
```

When this section of your VBA code runs, a message box is displayed with the text You did not enter a number., an OK button, and your custom message box title. This is shown in figure 27.1.

Fig. 27.1

A message box without a Help button. On a simple message box, there is no Help button.

Sometimes a simple message is enough to tell the user everything. Other situations can call for extended help, especially for a new user.

To provide access to custom Help, append the Help file name and the Context ID to the MsgBox command. The updated subroutine looks like listing 27.2. In the Visual Basic module, the Help file name and Context ID were globally defined with Const statements.

Listing 27.2   HELPDEMO.XLS: Message Box with Custom Help Button

```
Sub HelpDemoMessageWithHelp
    MsgBox "You did not enter a number.". _
        vbOKOnly, _
        "Message With a Help Button", _
        HelpFileName, _
        NOT_NUMBER
End Sub
```

When this section of your VBA code runs, the same message will be displayed, but now there will also be a Help button in the message box. Clicking the Help button displays your Topic page with the Context ID defined by NOT_NUMBER in the Help file given by HelpFileName. The new message box is shown in figure 27.2.

Fig. 27.2

A message box with a Help button. By adding the Help file name and Context ID to the call to the MsgBox function, a Help button is automatically added to the displayed message box.

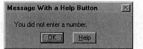

The help button in a message box works properly with both Excel 5.0 for Windows 3.1 and Excel 7.0 for Windows 95. However, if the user presses the Contents button in the Help application window while the help topic is displayed, Excel 7.0 will display Help for Excel and not the custom Help Contents page. There is no workaround for this situation.

Using context-sensitive help in a message box like this gives the user help at the time that help is needed. The user does not need to go to printed documentation, or to the Contents page of your Help file and search for answers. The Help file is automatically open at the proper page.

Adding help to a message box is good for both the novice and experienced user. For both of them, the message provides information about the current situation. The novice has the benefit of requesting additional information from the Help file. The experienced user has the benefit of not seeing a detailed explanation that is already understood.

27

Including Help with an Input Box

You use the input box to allow the user to provide a single piece of information to your application. The text that you use to prompt the user can get as long as 1,000 characters. This lets you tell the user a lot about what the input should be.

In general, you should not add custom Help to the input box function. If the 1,000 character string is not enough to tell the user everything that is required, use a dialog box with a Help button instead. Adding custom Help to the dialog box is described next.

You add custom Help to an input box by appending the Help file name and Context ID as the sixth and seventh arguments in the call to the VBA InputBox function. However, this only works with Excel 5.0 for Windows 3.1. If you are using Excel 7.0 for Windows 95, a Help button will not be displayed on any input box. There is no workaround for this situation.

 Tip

Do not try to include a Help button with the input box function. Use the dialog box instead.

Including Help on a Dialog Sheet

You use dialog boxes to get all kinds of input from the user. You can get numbers and strings. You can allow the user to make a selection from a variety of control options. The dialog box is one of your most powerful tools for getting information from the user into the program.

Dialog sheets can often appear very imposing to a new user. The numerous edit boxes, drop-down boxes, check boxes, and buttons can be tersely labeled. The first-time user of a dialog box can become very confused. To help the users, all of the control options and the meanings of the empty boxes can be described in detail in your custom Help. You can also explain how everything fits together. To provide direct access to the Topic page explaining a dialog sheet, you can add a Help button to the dialog box.

If you have complicated dialog boxes, you should always try to include custom Help in your application. The many combinations of input allow the user to easily make mistakes. Custom Help makes it easier for the user to learn how to use your workbook.

You add custom Help to a dialog box in two steps. First, write the VBA subroutine that calls the custom Help. Then, add a button to the dialog box, label it "Help," and assign the macro to it.

An example of a dialog box with no Help button is shown in figure 27.3. This is a simple dialog box. There is a short prompt, an edit box, and an OK button.

Fig. 27.3

Only the most simple dialog boxes should be without a Help button. The complex inputs required in the dialog box need the most explanation.

To add help, you first have to write the VBA subroutine that calls up the Help Application with the appropriate Help file name and Context ID. It was mentioned in the section on the message box that if the user presses the Contents button in the Help application window while a help topic is displayed, Excel 7.0 will display Help for Excel and not the custom Help Contents page. Although there is no workaround for the message box, there is a way to fix this problem when the Windows Help application is called directly with VBA code. This is done by a direct API call.

To cause the Help Application to act properly, first define the API call by including the one line of code given in listing 27.3 in your VBA module, but outside of any subroutine.

Listing 27.3   HELPDEMO.XLS: Define the API Call for Windows Help

```
Declare Function WinHelp Lib "USER32" Alias "WinHelpA" (ByVal hwnd As Long,
ByVal lpHelpFile As String, ByVal wCommand As Long, ByVal dwData As Long)
As Long
```

When you are ready to call the Help Application, use the API call for Excel 7.0, but Application.Help for other versions of Excel. Listing 27.4 shows a VBA subroutine that calls up the Help Application. The Help file name and Context ID are globally defined in Const statements. The listing below illustrates the syntax for the two calls.

Listing 27.4   HELPDEMO.XLS: VBA Code to Call the Help Application

```
Sub HelpDemoDialogHelp()
    If Application.Version = "7.0" Then
        WinHelp 0&, HelpFileName, &h1, NEED_NUMBER
    Else
        Application.Help HelpFileName, NEED_NUMBER
    End If
End Sub
```

27

Each time that HelpDemoDialogHelp is run, the Help file defined by HelpFileName is opened to the Topic page given by Context ID NEED_NUMBER. With the exception of functions like MsgBox( ) that have built-in methods for calling up the Help Application, this is the way that you have to set up your calls to the Help Application. The Help file name is common to the calls in your application. The Context ID is different for each different Help file page that you want to display.

To add a custom Help button to your dialog box, follow these steps:

1. Select the dialog sheet.

2. Use the Forms toolbar to add a new button to your dialog box. Just click the Create Button button, move the mouse to one corner of the new button location, and drag the mouse to the diagonal corner of the button.

3. Select the "Button n" text string on the button using the mouse and then type **Help**. At this point you have created a Help button. However, it does not yet have an action associated with it. As an example, the updated screen from figure 27.3 now looks like figure 27.4.

Fig. 27.4

A dialog box with a Help button. After a Help button has been added to the dialog box, it is still necessary to assign the action of the button to a subroutine.

4. Right-click the Help button, and then click Assign Macro from the new menu.

5. From the list, select the name of your VBA subroutine that will provide help when the Help button is clicked. Then click OK. This completes assignment of an action to the Help button.

6. Right-click the Help button, and then click Format Object from the new menu.

7. Click the Control tab, and make sure that only the Help check box is checked. Then click OK. This ensures that using the Help button does not cause the dialog to exit. It also ensures that pressing the F1 key while this dialog box is displayed provides your context-sensitive help.

When your dialog box is shown, clicking the Help button will display your context-sensitive help information.

A Help button on a dialog box is especially important. If you have no other custom Help, think about adding a Help button here. The most complex user inputs are generally made with the dialog box. To minimize the chance of an improper response, the user needs to know what the different fields and controls mean. Custom Help access in dialog boxes significantly helps users to enjoy using your application.

Providing Help as an Item on a Drop-Down Menu

If your application has a custom drop-down menu, you can add a menu item to provide instant access to your custom Help file. For more information about adding custom menus to your application, see Chapter 26, "Custom Menus."

Usually, you will want to go directly to the Contents page of the Help file from the Help menu item. Users seeking help at this point could be after anything. Make sure that your Contents page allows them to quickly locate anything that you have provided in the Help file.

Providing help as an item on a drop-down menu is a two-step process. First, code the subroutine that will run to provide help. Second, add a new menu item to your drop-down menu that calls up the subroutine to provide help.

If you want to explicitly identify the Contents page or to identify another Topic page as the Help page to show from the drop-down menu, use a subroutine like that in listing 27.4. You may want to define a new subroutine just for showing the Contents page. An example is given in listing 27.5.

> **Listing 27.5   HELPDEMO.XLS: Routine to Display the Contents Page of the Help File**
>
> ```
> Sub HelpDemoHelpContents()
>     If Application.Version = "7.0" Then
>         WinHelp 0&, HelpFileName, &h1, CONTENTS
>     Else
>         Application.Help HelpFileName, CONTENTS
>     End If
> End Sub
> ```

You will typically set up your drop-down menu in the Auto_Open function. This is explained in Chapter 26, "Custom Menus." This function automatically runs whenever the workbook is opened with the File Open command from Excel. It will not run if opened from the File, Find File command under Excel 5.0. If you use the Auto_Open function, caution your Excel 5.0 users not to open your workbook through the File, Find File command.

27

To call up help from an item on a drop-down menu, set the OnAction property to the name of the VBA subroutine that will call the Help Application in the ...MenuItems.Add line. Also set the Caption to Help.

A sample Auto_Open function is shown on listing 27.6. A HelpDemo item is added as the ninth item, just in front of the Excel Help item. When clicked, the only item in the drop-down list is Help. Clicking the Help item displays the Contents page of the Help file.

Listing 27.6   HELPDEMO.XLS: Auto_Open Function That Sets Up a Drop-Down Menu with a Help Item

```
Sub Auto_Open()
    MenuBars(xlWorksheet).Menus.Add Caption:="&HelpDemo", Before:=9
    MenuBars(xlWorksheet).Menus("&HelpDemo").MenuItems.Add _
    Caption:="&Help", Before:=1, OnAction:="HelpDemoHelpContents"
End Sub
```

When it is time to exit your application, you should remove the drop-down menu that the Auto_Open subroutine created. You can do this in the Auto_Close subroutine. Listing 27.7 shows how the HelpDemo menu is removed when the workbook is closed.

Listing 27.7   HELPDEMO.XLS: Removing a Drop-Down Menu with Auto_Close

```
Sub Auto_Close()
    Dim MenuName As Object
    For Each MenuName In MenuBars(xlWorksheet).Menus
        If MenuName.Caption = "&HelpDemo" Then
            MenuName.Delete
        End If
    Next MenuName
End Sub
```

A drop-down menu is a very powerful tool for your application. It allows the user to immediately select the function to be performed without too much thought. If you use a drop-down menu, your application is probably complex enough to really benefit by a Help file. Seriously consider adding a Help item to your drop-down menu.

Including a Help Button Directly on a Worksheet

There may be occasions when you want to add a Help button directly to a worksheet. In general, you may want to avoid excessive use of buttons on worksheets. Buttons can cover up data. Resizing cells can move a button off the screen, hiding available functions. For some applications, though, a button on a worksheet is exactly what is needed.

To add a Help button to a worksheet, do the following:

1. Create the VBA subroutine that you want to run when the button is clicked. This is a subroutine like that shown in listing 27.4.

2. Select the worksheet on which you want to have the Help button.

3. Choose View, Toolbars, check the Forms check box, and click OK. The Forms toolbar is shown.

4. Click the Create Button button. Place the mouse at the location on the worksheet where one corner of the button will be. Drag the mouse to the diagonal corner and release.

5. The available VBA subroutines are automatically displayed. Select the one you want, and click OK.

6. Select the "Button n" string and then type **Help**.

7. The Forms Toolbar can be closed at this point if no longer needed.

Clicking the newly created Help button displays context-sensitive help when the user needs it. A worksheet with a Help button is shown of figure 27.5. The advantage of this kind of Help button is that it is immediately visible to the user whenever the worksheet is selected. There is no searching around for how to get started or get help.

Fig. 27.5

A button can be added at any location on a Worksheet using the Forms toolbar. After the button is created, you will need to assign the action of the button to a VBA procedure.

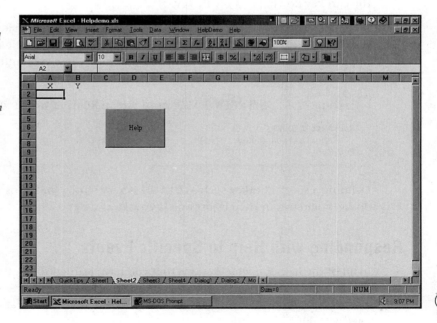

Defining a Special Key for Custom Help

You can assign a specific key to bring up your custom Help. In Excel, pressing the F1 key provides help on Excel. You can, for example, setup the Ctrl+F1 key as a hotkey to provide your custom Help to the user.

To define a hotkey to give help, you associate the keystroke with a VBA subroutine name by using the Application.OnKey statement. It is probably best to do this in the Auto_Open subroutine. Listing 27.8 shows how to use this function. After this routine runs, pressing the Ctrl+F1 keystroke automatically runs the HelpDemoHelpContents routine. To find out how to set up other keys, see the Excel Help covering the OnKey property.

Listing 27.8   HELPDEMO.XLS: Auto_Open Routine to Assign Ctrl+F1 to Give Help

```
Sub Auto_Open()
    Application.OnKey "^{F1}", "HelpDemoHelpContents"
End Sub
```

In listing 27.8, the caret (^) indicates the Ctrl key. Placing F1 in braces as {F1}, indicates the F1 function key. Together, they indicate Ctrl+F1, or while pressing and holding the Ctrl key down, press the F1 key.

Before the workbook is closed, it is important to restore the previous meaning to the Ctrl+F1 key. You restore the key by leaving off the subroutine name from the Application.OnKey call. This is shown in the Auto_Close subroutine in listing 27.9.

Listing 27.9   HELPDEMO.XLS: Auto_Close Routine to Restore Ctrl+F1

```
Sub Auto_Close()
    Application.OnKey "^{F1}"
End Sub
```

Defining a special hotkey such as Ctrl+F1 is very handy for the user. Whatever the user is doing, your custom Help is just one keystroke away.

Responding with Help to Specific Events

In all of the help implementations that you have learned so far, the user has always been required to click a button or menu item to get help. Sometimes a user can make a serious mistake and you will want to immediately display the Help file at the appropriate Topic page without a user request.

Several events can activate custom Help when that event occurs. In most cases, you will first want to find out what actually happened, and only then provide custom Help if there is an error or other significant event.

The list of items that fit in this category is quite large. It includes the OnAction property of many objects, and several On... properties of worksheets.

To give custom help to specific events, do the following:

1. Write a VBA subroutine that first checks for specific errors or harmful conditions. If help is needed, call Help Application with the appropriate Help file name and Context ID.

2. Assign the VBA routine to run when the event occurs. This is done by setting the On... property to the name of the VBA subroutine somewhere in your code.

The OnAction subroutine runs whenever the associated object is clicked. The OnCalculate subroutine runs when a worksheet is recalculated. The OnSheetActivate subroutine runs when a specific worksheet is activated. You can find other On... properties and methods by searching the Excel VBA online reference for words starting with "On."

For example, a line of code in the Auto_Open subroutine can setup the application to provide help when Sheet3 is activated. Listing 27.10 shows how this is done.

Listing 27.10   HELPDEMO.XLS: Auto_Open Routine to Show Help on Sheet3 Activation

```
Sub Auto_Open()
    Sheets("Sheet3").OnSheetActivate = "HelpDemoSheetNoFillHelp"
End Sub
```

Although this is a powerful way of letting the user know about something that needs attention, be careful about using it. If your user has not properly installed the Help file to the proper directory, then your custom Help will not be available at all. It may be safer to provide a short message box with a Help button.

Giving Help Anywhere

Of course, you can really give access to help at any point of your VBA code. The call to the Help application as illustrated in listing 27.4 has arguments of the Help file name and Context ID. This does not need to be coded as a stand-alone function. It can appear anywhere in your code that you feel is appropriate for displaying your help file.

27

The best places to provide custom Help are as buttons on message boxes and dialog boxes, as an item on a drop-down menu, and as a special hotkey such as Ctrl+F1.

Timesaving Tricks

Your custom Help files already provide a great time savings to your users. You can further help them by providing a QuickTips worksheet with important information for novice users. There are also numerous ways that you can save your own time while writing your application. These methods, discussed in the following sections, include:

▶ Provide a QuickTips worksheet

▶ Organize your application

▶ Define Context IDs with Const statements

▶ Make separate Help subroutines with informative names

▶ Get the Windows Help Authoring Guide and other software tools

Provide a QuickTips Worksheet

Get the new user up to speed with a QuickTips Worksheet. Name the first WorkSheet in your application "QuickTips." Program the Auto_Open() function to Activate the QuickTips Worksheet when the program loads. An example of how to do this is given in listing 27.11.

Listing 27.11   HELPDEMO.XLS: Activate the QuickTips Sheet at Open

```
Sub Auto_Open()
    WorkSheets("QuickTips").Activate
End Sub
```

On the QuickTips worksheet, give the user instructions about getting the application started. Also give the user instructions on how to get help. If you have programmed a custom Help hotkey, tell the user how to activate it. If you have a drop-down menu with a Help item, tell the user how to get to it.

By including brief startup and help information on the first worksheet that the user sees, you save the user time in getting started. The user also knows how to access your custom Help from the minute that the worksheet is loaded.

Organize Your Application

To give really good help, your application should be well-planned and organized. Develop your application around separate tasks that can be explained with separate Topic pages. If the tasks can be easily explained, you will be able to quickly write the custom Help file for the user.

In general, I start by defining the functions that will appear on the drop-down menu. If there are any sub-menus, I also try to define them. This clearly identifies the major functions of the application. Each of these drop-down items will generally need a Topic page in the Help file.

Then, I try to identify how the information will be organized. I lay out the worksheets as accurately as possible, defining titles and labels of the columns.

Next, I create the major dialog sheets for information input. Finally, I start coding the VBA module to perform startup actions, process input, perform requested processing, output reports, and provide help.

Define Context IDs with Const Statements

Try to be consistent in naming the Context IDs that are used in both the Visual Basic module and Help RTF file. In the MAP section of the HPJ file (described in the Help Project File [MAP] section), you associate Context ID strings with numbers using the #define statement. This is because the Topic pages are referenced inside the HLP file only by the Context ID text string and outside the HLP file only by Context ID number.

In your Visual Basic module, you can use Const statements to define constant expressions that associate text strings with numeric Context IDs. For example, if the MAP section contains the line `#define CONTENTS 100`, then you can have a corresponding VBA statement `Const CONTENTS = 100`.

This technique allows you to reference the same Context ID by the same name in the RTF file and in the XLS file. This simplifies your programming and reduces the chance of giving help on the wrong topic.

Make Separate Help Subroutines with Informative Names

Write a separate subroutine like that shown in listing 27.4 for each different Context ID that you give help on. The routine can then be called from other routines, or assigned to buttons or other objects. Separately test each subroutine to verify that the proper Help Topic page is displayed.

27

Use long subroutine names that readily identify the function of the routine. This makes it easier to call the right subroutine and give help on the right topic.

Get the Windows Help Authoring Guide and Other Tools

To get information and tools relevant to creating Help files, a good place to look next is the Microsoft *Help Authoring Guide*. Also use the references at the end of this chapter to identify sources of tools that can help you to easily and quickly produce your custom Help.

Writing Windows Help Files

Although this is a book about Excel, you need to make Windows Help files for your custom Help in Excel. The method described here gives you the basics needed to create a functional Windows Help file. In addition to Excel, you will need Word for Windows and the Microsoft Help Compiler.

If you are using Windows 3.1, you should use Word for Windows 6.0. If you are using Windows 95, you should use Word for Windows 6.0 or 7.0. Both of these versions of Word for Windows will produce proper RTF files. WordPerfect can also be used to produce RTF files. The techniques described in this section only apply to Word for Windows.

There are four versions of the Windows Help compiler that need to be considered. If you are writing only for Windows 3.0, then Help compiler HC30.EXE is the compiler to use. If you are writing only for Windows 3.1, then Help compiler HC31.EXE is the compiler to use.

Microsoft has recently published the Windows 95 Help Authoring Kit that includes help compiler HCW.EXE, now renamed the Help Workshop. The Help Workshop compiles Help files that will not run directly under Windows 3.1 unless you also distribute a copy of Microsoft Win32s with your application. This is explained in more detail in the product documentation.

If you are writing for Windows 3.1 and Windows 95 users, and you do not want to distribute Win32s with your application, the Help compiler to use is HCP.EXE. Although it does not have all of the features of the Help Workshop, files appear to be compatible with both systems. The following discussion is based on the use of the HCP.EXE Help compiler. If you are using the Help Workshop, see the documentation on that product.

This section describes how to create a custom Windows Help file that works with your Excel custom Help. You learn to

▶ Use Word for Windows to create a Help RTF file

▶ Use Word for Windows to create an HPJ file

▶ Use the Windows Help Compiler HCP.EXE to make the Help file

Using Word for Windows to Create a Help RTF File

Although many tools are available for helping you create Help files, you can use Word for Windows to create very usable Help files. The Help file is made of one Contents page and several Topic pages. The Contents page provides links that allow the user to find help on several topics. The individual Topic pages contain help information on specific topics. The file that is created with Word for Windows will be saved as a Rich Text Format (RTF) file that can be processed by the Windows Help compiler.

Creating a New Help File and the Contents Page

To create a new Help file, first open Word for Windows. On the top line of the new file, enter a title for the Contents page. Skip one line, and start the text. In general, all of your Help file pages will have a title line, a blank line, and then the descriptive text.

You may want to have a one paragraph introduction to your application as the start of the text on the Contents page, followed by a table of contents in list or descriptive format.

You will need to create hyperlinks to your main Topic pages. This can be done later. For now, just enter the text that refers to the Topic pages. This is normally done as a list of items. When the user sees this list, it is only necessary to click any of the items to get detailed help on that topic.

The title should be in a larger font size than the other text. Microsoft recommends 12-point MS Sans Serif for headings and 10-point MS Sans Serif for text. Slightly larger point sizes can be used if you like. Fonts that are generally available on most Windows systems include Helvetica, Courier, Times New Roman, Arial, and Symbol.

Creating Topic Pages

At the end of the text of any page, press Ctrl+Enter to create a new Topic page. Enter the new topic title and text on the newly created page. Repeat this process for each new Topic Page. You will be able to see more text if you keep Word for Windows in Normal mode. To do this, select View, Normal from the menubar. You will get a better idea of what the user will see in page layout view. To do this, select View, Page Layout from the menubar.

The top line of each Topic page should contain a title. Skip one line, and then start your text. Use the same fonts and sizes as the Contents page. By the time you have finished writing the Topic Pages, all of the information that you need to provide to the user is entered. The next step is to create the Context IDs and hyperlinks between the pages.

Creating Context IDs for All Pages

You need to create a Context ID for the Contents page and for each of the Topic pages. The Context ID is used to tell the Help Application which page in a Help file to display. Although you can alternately get to a Topic page in a Browse sequence or by keyword, using the Context ID is the way to reference a page with the Help Application.

A *Context ID* is a word or series of words separated by underscores or dollar symbols. Each Context ID must be unique and should be in all uppercase letters. Although uppercase letters are not absolutely required, the Help Compiler can tell the difference between upper- and lowercase. You can reduce the chance of making a mistake if you always use uppercase letters for Context IDs.

To define a Context ID for a page, place the cursor in front of the title on the top line of that page. Choose Insert, Footnote. Click Custom mark, enter the pound symbol (#) as the mark, and click on OK. Enter the Context ID as the footnote. You can select footnote Close at any time.

Creating Hyperlinks to Topic Pages

A *hyperlink* allows the user to click on one part of the text in a Help file and automatically be taken to another page of the Help file. The hyperlink is the most common way of moving around within a Help file.

On the Contents page, you should create a hyperlink to each of your main Topics pages.

To create a hyperlink, first type in the text that the user must click. This may be just an item in a list. Select the text, choose Format, Font, and set the underline selection to double underline. The text that is double underlined is visible to the user, and is the hot spot for a jump. Immediately following that text, type in the Context ID of the page to which the jump should take the user. Do not separate the text from the Context ID with any spaces. Select the Context ID, choose Format, Font, and check the hidden attribute, but without any underline. The hyperlink is complete.

Be sure to include a hyperlink to the Contents page on each Topic page. You cannot depend on the Contents button in the Help Application to display your Contents page. In Excel 7.0 for Windows 95, the Contents button in the Help Application may show the Contents page for Excel Help, not for your custom Help. This is especially important for pages that are displayed as a result of pressing a Help button on a Message box.

 Tip

Include a hyperlink to your custom Help Contents page on each of your Topic pages for topics displayed by pressing a Help button on a Message box.

Including Graphics in Your Help File

Graphics in your Help file can be very helpful to the user when it is difficult to describe some things with words. However, graphics should be used sparingly and only when necessary. Most of the information that you want convey can be done with text.

The Help Application can display a graphics file in the BMP or SHG format. To include the graphics in the Help file use the bmc instruction followed by the file name, all within braces. For example, using the command {bmc FILENAME.BMP} will place the graphics file FILENAME.BMP at the left of the window without any wrapped text.

Saving Your Work

After you have finished, choose File, Save As, and then under Save as Type, Rich Text Format (RTF). The RTF file type is required by the Help Compiler. Provide any name for your file that you like. You may want to use the same simple name as your Excel file.

An RTF Example

An example of a complete though very small RTF file with a Contents page and one Topic page is shown on figure 27.6. Each page has Context ID as a # footnote. Each page has a hyperlink to the other. The hot spots are double underlined. The context IDs of the hyperlinks are normally hidden, but are shown here as dotted underlined. The source for this RTF file along with the HPJ file is provided on the CD-ROM that accompanies this book. This example is named MinRTF.RTF, and is about as small a Help file as you can make. It does demonstrate the principles of Context ID and hyperlinks.

27

Fig. 27.6

Example of an RTF file MinRTF during a Word for Windows editing session with one Contents page and one Topic page.

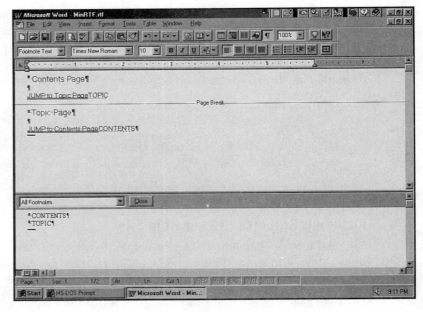

Creating an HPJ File with Word for Windows

A help project file (HPJ) contains instructions to the Help compiler about how to create a Help file, including the names of the files that need to be processed. The HPJ file defines all of the parts of the Help file so that the Help Compiler can put them together. Listing 27.12 shows a sample HPJ file. It contains all of the elements that you need to get started.

Listing 27.12   HELPDEMO.HPJ: HelpDemo Help Project File

```
[OPTIONS]
COMPRESS=HIGH
CONTENTS=CONTENTS
REPORT=ON
TITLE=Help for HelpDemo
WARNING=3

[FILES]
HELPDEMO.RTF

[BITMAPS]
HELPDEMO.BMP
```

```
[MAP]
#define CONTENTS       100
#define NOT_NUMBER     200
#define NEED_NUMBER    210
#define FILL_SHEET     220
#define NO_FILL_SHEET  230
```

There are four sections in the sample file: [OPTIONS], [FILES], [BITMAPS], and [MAP]. Sometimes you may also include a [CONFIG] section. You will need a [CONFIG] section if you have any Browse sequences or Help Macros (not described here).

You can use Word for Windows to create, edit, and save the HPJ file. To create a new HPJ file, first open Word for Windows. Then enter the contents of the file. After the editing session is over, select File, Save As, and then under Save as Type, select Text only. The simple name of the file can be the same as the Rich Text Format file. Be sure to give HPJ as the file extension.

Help Project File [OPTIONS] Section

The first item in listing 27.12 is COMPRESS=HIGH. It tells the Help Compiler to use the highest degree of compression. I always use this option, and have never found a reason to use anything else.

The CONTENTS= item identifies the default Topic page. In the [OPTIONS] section, be sure to include a CONTENTS= statement. It tells the Help Application which page to display if no Context ID is given.

The REPORT=ON line asks the Help Compiler to tell you what it is doing during the compilation. This keeps the screen busy while it is working.

The TITLE= statement defines what will be shown at the top of the screen in the caption bar while the Help Application shows your Topic pages.

The WARNING=3 asks the Help Compiler to show you all messages.

Help Project File [FILES] Section

For small Help Applications, there will only be one RTF file. However, you can have several different RTF files that can be combined by the Help compiler to generate one Help file. Whether you have one or more, include the file names in this section.

27

Help Project File [BITMAPS] Section

If you include any BMP or SHG bitmap graphics in your Help file, name them all in the BITMAP section. Otherwise, leave out this section. If the graphics files are not in the default subdirectory with the other files, you will need to consult the documentation on the Help compiler to find out how to access them.

Help Project File [MAP] Section

Any Context IDs that you want to reference from Excel must be defined in the MAP section. With the #define statements in the MAP section, each Context ID string is associated with a number. These numbers are very important. When you use Excel VBA calls to get help, these numbers must be given as the Context ID.

Using the Help Compiler to Compile the RTF and HPJ Files into a Help File

You will find it helpful to make a separate subdirectory for all the Help BMP, DOC, RTF, PH, HPJ, and HLP files. Change to your working subdirectory, and make sure that all the needed files are there.

If you use any compression, a phrase file will be automatically created by the Help compiler. To maximize compression, any old phrase files should be deleted. To do this from MS-DOS, type **DEL *.PH**.

If you are using the Help compiler HCP.EXE, then type **HCP MYAPP** where MYAPP.HPJ is the name of your Help project file. The Help file will be created.

If there were no errors, copy the HLP file to the Windows root directory. Otherwise, first identify and correct the cause of the error.

Finding Tools and Sources of Help for Writing Help Files

The procedure described here is a starting point. It allows you to quickly get important custom Help to the users of your application. As a next step, you may want to learn how to include keywords for searches and Browse sequences in your Help files.

A lot of information is available to help you write Windows Help files easier, faster, and fancier. The list of reference information provides access to books, other sites, vendors, shareware authors, and users. You can use the information to help you locate the files and software for your specific application.

Tip

You can find additional World Wide Web sites by using Webcrawler to search on the topic WINDOWS HELP AUTHORING.

▶ World Wide Web site: **http://www2.primenet.com/~wai/universe.html**

▶ World Wide Web site: **http://sky.net/~parnote/welcome.html**

▶ Internet Newsgroup: **comp.os.ms-windows.programmer.winhelp**

▶ CompuServe library on Windows Help: go **CIS:WINDSK**, WinHelp section #16

▶ FTP site: **gmutant.wrlc.org/pub/winhelp**

▶ FTP site: **oak.oakland.edu/SimTel/win3/winhelp**

▶ FTP site: **ftp.microsoft.com** file softlib/mslfiles/HC505.EXE as a source for Microsoft Help Compiler HCP.EXE.

▶ CD-ROM: Microsoft Developer Network Development Level 1 includes the *Windows (3.1) Help Authoring Guide*, Windows Authoring Tools, Microsoft Help Compiler HCP.EXE, and full Help Compiler documentation. This is available for $195.00 plus shipping from Microsoft Developer Network at 800-759-5474.

Summary

Custom help will make your application easier and more enjoyable to use. It is a readily acceptable form of documentation, replacing lengthy printed manuals that often take a long time to produce.

Your Excel dialog screens and VBA modules can include context-sensitive help using very simple calls to the help application. Custom Help shows specific topic pages in your custom Help file. Help can also be provided with hotkeys or on a drop-down menu.

Writing custom Help files involves using Word for Windows to produce an RTF file containing text and graphics. MS-DOS based Help compiler HCP.EXE can be used to make Help files for Windows 3.1 and Windows 95. The Windows 95-based Help Workshop can be used to make Help files for Windows 95.

Coding Gems

Everyone knows what a gem is, so you might expect that a section entitled "Coding Gems" is simply a collection of small pieces of Excel code that shine brightly. Our gems, however, are quite a bit more than just simple little tricks. In this section you'll not only find expert tricks and techniques you can use in your own Excel applications, but you'll also find several complete, ready-to-use applications, each of which is included on the CD-ROM.

You'll notice that we've included contact information for the "Coding Gems" authors. If you or your business needs the services of a real Excel expert, this information will make your task a little easier. Oh, and don't forget to register any shareware you find useful—remember, shareware registration is important to all of us.

Excel VBA Tips and Tricks by Liam Scanlan

Liam Scanlan
Reportech, Inc.
13720 SE 58 Place
Bellevue, WA 98006
1-206-644-9646
1-800-662-4317
liams@reportech.com
http://www.halcyon.com/patricks/informer.html

When you develop Excel applications, there are a number of important tips and tricks that will make your task easier. In this section, you'll learn some of the insider information discovered at Reportech during the development of the Informer add-in.

Creating Large Applications with VBA

By large application, I am referring to any Excel add-in that contains more than several hundred thousand bytes of XLA compiled file, when you add the sizes of all the XLAs in the application.

Understanding Size and Capacity Issues

Several issues relating to the size of your modules can have profound effects on the success of your applications. These include:

▶ Excel versions 5.0 and 5.0c are more sensitive to capacity issues that Excel 7. See "A Difference in Resource Limits" later in this appendix.

▶ When a source code module size goes above a certain threshold, things stop working. For example, sometimes error-trapping fails to catch errors, xlodbc functions stop working, and so on. Keep each module below about 10K (exact threshold uncertain) in size. One way of checking size is by pasting the contents of a module into a text file and saving it.

▶ Keep each procedure (function or macro) within a few thousand bytes long (ideally, no more than 2K apiece).

Improving the Start-Up Time of an Excel Add-In

You have probably noticed by now that an add-in's start-up time tends to increase, sometimes intolerably, as the add-in gets larger. There is a way to fix this. Let's look at a typical example. You have 6 XLAs. One of them is a library of functions that is referenced by the other 5 XLAs, and one of those is the "lead in" XLA (that is, the XLA that you included as an add-in under the Excel Tools, Add-Ins menu). You notice that when the user first calls the first macro in your add-in, it seems to take forever to respond.

It is indeed a mystery to all but the people who wrote Excel what exactly happens during this waiting period. Fortunately, there is an excellent workaround that allows you to reduce this start-up time dramatically. The following two scenarios demonstrate a typical situation *before* you apply the workaround, and the improvement that occurs *after* you apply the workaround.

Before: ProjectA.xla is the "lead-in" add-in. It references ProjectB.xla, ProjectC.xla, ProjectD.xla, and ProjectE.xla. ProjectE.xla is a function library that is also referenced by

ProjectB, C, and D.xla. The user clicks a menu item created by ProjectA.xla and waits...and waits...

After: ProjectX.xla is a small, let's call it "boot-strap," XLA with just one menu item and one purpose. It is the "lead-in" XLA (the job once held by ProjectA.xla). The macro behind its solitary menu item captioned "Start Sarah's program..." opens the XLAs in *reverse referenced order*. That is, it opens the XLAs at the end of the referencing food chain, in this case ProjectE.xla, then the next level up, and so on. This loads directly into memory all referenced XLAs *before* they are called.

```
Workbooks.Open Filename:=ThisWorkbook.Path + "\ProjectE.xla"
Workbooks.Open Filename:=ThisWorkbook.Path + "\ProjectC.xla"
Workbooks.Open Filename:=ThisWorkbook.Path + "\ProjectB.xla"Workbooks.Open Fil...
↪etc., etc.."
```

This workaround assumes that all XLAs are in the same directory.

If your application runs in Excel 7, there is a case-sensitivity issue. It tries to re-load them, and consequently ends up with a confusing duplication of macros that will give you errors from `Object variable not set` to `Compile error in hidden module`.

This can sometimes be fixed by making sure that the projects were opened with the same case, letter-by-letter, that they had when they were first referenced, regardless of whether they are now the same case. This error seems only to occur in Excel 7, when long filenames become an issue and case-sensitivity appears to rear its ugly head. In other words, in Excel 7:

```
Workbooks.Open Filename:=ThisWorkbook.Path + "\projectb.xla"
```

is not the same as

```
Workbooks.Open Filename:=ThisWorkbook.Path + "\PROJECTB.xla"
```

It is the case you use to open the XLA that Excel 7 thinks the file actually is, regardless of how it looks on disk. This is important. When you decompress XLAs, they will have lowercase names. When you open them with uppercase, Excel 7 thinks they are uppercase names. Sound confusing? It is. Hopefully Microsoft will fix this whole area with the next version of Excel or in a patch to the current version.

Creating an Application that Works in Both Excel 5 and Excel 7

Many large corporations take years to embrace a new version of a software package. The larger they are, generally, the more cautious they are, and the longer they take. There will be Excel 5 users out there into the next century. Many corporations have invested heavily in 16-bit environments and in applications that work in Excel 5. These applications usually don't work in Excel 7, so there is a collateral cost with upgrading to Excel 7.

If you develop your application to work both in Excel 5 and Excel 7, you not only reach both markets, but you may also empower your customer to upgrade to Excel 7 without ramification to your application. This has immediate marketing advantage.

As any programmer knows, it is also advantageous to have just one set of source code. Fix a bug and you fix it everywhere, if you've written your program correctly.

A Difference in Resource Limits

Excel 5 will generally not allow you to overlay one dialog sheet on top of another dialog sheet. Without going into great technical detail about why, it often results in an Out of stack space error when you try to do it. Excel 7, on the other hand, has a little more "elbow room" and will allow you to overlay one atop another, but usually not a third. So if you are designing your application mostly in Excel 7, be aware of this issue that may arise when someone executes it in Excel 5.

Watch Out for Different Versions of Excel 5

When Microsoft initially shipped Excel 5.0, there were a couple of bugs present that were subsequently fixed with Excel 5.0c, which came out a few months later. Some of the bugs in 5.0 are

▶ Several ODBC functions called from xlodbc.xla will not work. Getting a list of table names will sometimes give an error. Alphanumeric fields containing a number, for example "000," will get returned as "0." Thus, inappropriate leading-zero-blanking, which can make some report/queries unusable because Excel doesn't differentiate between an alpha code of "042" and "42," which may represent two totally different data elements in your database. These ODBC problems can be worked around by replacing xlodbc.xla and xlodbc.dll with those from a PC that has the 5.0c version. Check first, though, any Excel licensing restrictions that may apply to performing such a copy.

▶ In Excel 5.0, you will get an error if you try to set the status bar property of an Excel menu item that you have created.

▶ "Caller" returns from the menu a different sized array when used in Excel 5.0 and Excel 5.0c. So, be aware that your application must cater to both if it is being used in both releases.

There are other bugs here and there. You should be aware that your application needs to be fully tested in both 5.0 and 5.0c, so your user can have either version.

You can easily check to see which version you are running in by looking at Application.Version. It will return `5.0` or `5.0c` or `7.0`.

As if this weren't enough to keep you busy, there is also a version of Excel 5 that is 32-bit. It will return `5.0` if you call Application.Version, and there may be a `5.0c` version of that out there too. We know that there are relatively few 32-bit versions of Excel 5, but it is best that you make a decision about whether or not your application will support that version.

"Wrapping" a Function

For many 16-bit API functions, some of which you may have already used in the 16-bit Excel 5 environment, there is an equivalent in the 32-bit environment. For example:

In Excel 5, you may have used the following function to retrieve a value from an INI file:

```
Declare Function GetPrivateProfileString Lib "KERNEL" (ByVal lpApplicationName As
String, ByVal lpKeyName As Any, ByVal lpDefault As String, ByVal lpReturnedString As
String, ByVal nSize As Integer, ByVal lpFileName As String) As Integer
```

However, in the 32-bit environment, in Excel 7, you need to use a slightly different one:

```
Declare Function GetPrivateProfileStringA Lib "KERNEL32" (ByVal SectionStr As String,
ByVal ItemName As String, ByVal ItemDefault As String, ByVal ResultBuffer As String,
ByVal MaxResult As Integer, ByVal IniFileName As String) As Integer
```

Note the differences. For the most part, both of these functions perform the same task, but if you try to call the 16-bit one (the first one) when running in Excel 7, you will get an error and/or a crash.

In terms of using such API functions as these, to make your application run in both Excel 5 and Excel 7 is not very difficult. What I suggest is the following:

▶ *Wood-for-the-trees*: Change your underlying Windows API function declarations to "Private Declare Function...". Then, in the same module create, let's call it a general equivalent function (GEF) for each such pair. In this GEF, check which version you are working with and call the correct function accordingly. This means that later, when you are using the GEF, you no longer have to check which version you are in and you don't get confused by seeing the underlying *Declare Function*s when you are browsing.

▶ *Simplify*: This method gives you an opportunity to greatly simplify how you use such functions. Usually, API functions need extra VBA code to go with them to make them really work. If you spend some time "wrapping" these functions early on, it will save you lots of time later.

For example:

```
Function GetFromDisk(file As String, Paragraph As String, LineItem As String) As
String
Dim vINIReturn As String
vINIReturn = Space(255)
  Select Case lfn16or32bit
    Case "16"
      ires = GetPrivateProfileString(Paragraph, LineItem, "", vINIReturn,
        ➥Len(vINIReturn), file)
    Case Else
      IL& = GetPrivateProfileStringA(Paragraph, LineItem, "", vINIReturn,
        ➥Len(vINIReturn), file)
  End Select
A$ = Trim(vINIReturn)
GetFromDisk = lfnRemoveCharacter(A$, Chr$(0))
End Function
```

Notice that I have also used another function *lfnRemoveCharacter()*, which I will also
provide:

```
Function lfnRemoveCharacter(StringToRemoveFrom As String, CharacterToRemove As String)
As String
A$ = StringToRemoveFrom
For J% = 1 To Len(CharacterToRemove)
  B$ = ""
  For I% = 1 To Len(A$)
    C$ = Mid(A$, I%, 1)
    If C$ <> Mid(CharacterToRemove, J%, 1) Then
      B$ = B$ + C$
    End If
  Next I%
  A$ = B$
Next J%
lfnRemoveCharacter = B$
End Function
```

Creating an Application that Is Easy to "Internationalize"

I use the term *internationalize* rather than *localize* because you should consider
removing all hard-coded text from your program and placing it in a text file or other
resource file outside of the program itself. In the evaluation copy of Informer 1.5 on
the accompanying CD, you can see that *iminimum.txt* and *imessage.txt* contain every
piece of English-language text that the program uses. To create a French version, for
example, it is necessary to only translate the two text files and the Help file. It is not
necessary to recompile the program or have more than one version of it.

Here are the steps to follow:

1. Create a routine that handles all MsgBox executions. The first time it is called, it
   needs to read the text file and store the messages or pieces of text. This function
   returns the value that the MsgBox function within it returns.

2. Call the message box routine and supply the message number you wish to use.

3. Before each dialog is shown for the first time per Excel session, load its objects containing text with text from the text file.

This might sound a little tedious, but in fact it's easy to do.

You can also change text in the program during testing without having to recompile your program. You can re-use messages and captions that are used in different places in your program. For example, suppose you want to change the text "Update" that appears on many buttons in your application to "Save," if you have that stored in your text file, you need only change it once. Basic stuff, really, but it can give your software product a longer life.

Internationalizing your application is a long-term bet. Do you expect to have customers in non-English-speaking countries? If you do, and there is a mushrooming market of Excel users out there in non-English-speaking countries, consider internationalizing.

Creating a Setup Program for Your VBA Application

You can, if you have the energy and the time, write a setup program using VBA, which we have done. You can also write your setup program using one of a number of applications that will take the drudgery out if it for you. Some examples follow.

Product	Est. Price	Manufacturer	Phone	Comments
InstallShield3	$580	Stirling Technologies	708-240-9120	Very comprehensive, but tough to use if you're not a C programmer. Tough to get the Excel add-in registration entries to work.
Wise Installation 4.0	$199	Great Lakes Business Solutions	1-800-554-8565	Easy to use. Fairly easy to make registration entries for Excel Add-ins.
PC Install 4.0	up to $250 depending on platform	20/20 Software	1-800-735-2020	We didn't fully evaluate this one, but it looked very easy to use from what we saw. Be aware that you need to buy a different copy for a 16-bit versus 32-bit platform.

All three will do the full Uninstall program for you, which is what you need if you are planning to get your product through Windows 95 compatibility testing. (E-mail **winlogo@microsoft.com** for details on that program). We ultimately went with Wise Installation 4.0 because it compiles one all-contained setup executable that works in all Windows environments, and only adds about 80K to the overall size of your compressed files. If you are using Wise Installation, e-mail me for the script you will need to make the registration entries. They're only a few lines but this might save you an hour or two.

Excel Examples by John Lacher

John Lacher
73447.2431@compuserve.com
johnlacher@aol.com
jlacher@msn.com

You can learn more about Excel's features in the example Excel workbook files described in this section. Use the Keywords listed below each file name to locate an example of interest to you.

Using a List Box to Display Values in a Table

File: LACHER01.XLS

Keywords: Listbox, OFFSET, Learn, Tutorial

Learn to use a List Box to update values displayed on your worksheet. Use the OFFSET function to return values from a table. Select an item in the List Box and see values for that item appear on a worksheet.

 Tip

Use Excel's list box feature to look up values and change the worksheet display. You can use a list box to change the display of data without using any VBA. With the OFFSET function, you can display data based on the value returned by the ListBox.

Note

When you select a field in the ListBox, the column "Description" is updated with information from "Custn" depending on which field was selected in the ListBox. See example on Sheet1 and Sheet2 for more details.

Importing Text Files

File: LACHER02.XLS

Keywords: Text, Import, OpenText, Visual Basic, Text Import Wizard, Learn

Use either the OpenText or Dialogs methods to import text into an open workbook. Select the file to import from a built-in dialog box.

 Tip

You can use either of two VBA methods to automate the process of importing text into a workbook. The OpenText method controls all of the text import parameters from the Visual Basic Code. To give the user complete control over Text Import Wizard parameters, use the Dialogs (xlDialogsOpen).Show method.

 Note

Click the Import Using the OpenText button or Import Using Dialogs button to demonstrate these methods.

Creating Running Totals

File: LACHER03.XLS

Keywords: Running Total, Cumulative Total, Note

You can add a running total to a single cell or a column of data. Includes a Visual Basic macro and example formulas.

Tip

Excel provides several methods for creating running totals. You can use a work-sheet function like =SUM($A$1:A1) where the values to total are in column A and the formula is copied down column B. You can also use a Visual Basic macro to store a running total in the note field of a cell. When a new value is entered to the cell, the value in the note field is added to the value in the cell.

 Note

The example on Sheet1 shows two methods of storing cumulative totals—read the notes in the macro on the module sheet (Module1) to understand how to store a cumulative total in the note value of a field.

Linking a PivotTable to a Chart

File: LACHER04.XLS

Keywords: PivotTable, Chart, Data Form

Learn how to use a PivotTable as a source for a chart—link a range of source data to the chart so that additions are automatically added to the chart.

 Tip

If you use a range of data as input to a PivotTable—and name that range "Data-base," the Data Form will add new records and include them in the named range. They will be included in the PivotTable (after it is refreshed). You can link a chart to a PivotTable so that changes in the PivotTable automatically change the chart.

 Note

Worksheet "Pivot Table Data" contains a data range named "Database," which is also PivotTable source range.

The chart on "Pivot Table and Chart" worksheet uses PivotTable as data source.

To demonstrate the advantages of this arrangement, follow these steps:

1. Use <u>D</u>ata, F<u>o</u>rm menu option to add a new record to worksheet "Pivot Table Data." Excel automatically expands "Database" range to include new data. Press the Refresh button on PivotTable worksheet and new data is automatically included in table.

2. Change PivotTable by grouping data fields into quarters. Use the Group button to automatically change monthly data into quarterly data. Then hide the monthly data and the chart will automatically reflect new arrangement of data.

3. Move product PivotTable field from its column position to be a page field. The chart automatically adjusts and can be used to chart each product.

Creating a PivotTable from Multiple Ranges of Data

File: LACHER05.XLS

Keywords: PivotTable, Multiple Consolidation, Accounting, Tutorial

Use the multiple consolidation range feature of PivotTables to summarize accounting data arranged in columns by month. Summarize the PivotTable by quarter using the built-in PivotTable grouping feature.

 Tip

Use the multiple consolidation range feature of PivotTables to summarize accounting data arranged in columns by month. The PivotTable data can be summarized by quarter using the built-in PivotTable grouping feature. Each page of data included in the PivotTable can be assigned a unique identifier in a new page field that is created when you define the PivotTable.

 Note

Use the PivotTable Wizard button on the Query and Pivot toolbar to look "inside" the definition of the PivotTable. Select a cell in the PivotTable, click the Wizard button and use the Prior and Next buttons to move through all screens of the definition.

Simplifying Data Input and Analysis

File: LACHER06.XLS

Learn how to link named ranges, the Data Form, PivotTables, and charts to produce an information system. Use a button to add data to the worksheet and a Vlookup formula to link Excel lists.

 Tip

You can link charts, PivotTables, and ranges of data to produce a basic information system. With a Command button, you can use the built-in Data Form to add data to the range. If you name the range "Database," you can link the PivotTable to the named range. When you add new data, the range will expand and the new data will be included in the PivotTable. You can link a chart to the data range of the PivotTable and the chart will automatically change to show new values in the PivotTable.

 Note

Use the Home buttons on the worksheet to activate Excel's built-in data input form and add data to the BonusCalculation and CandleMaster worksheets. You can view a summary of the BonusCalculation worksheet in the worksheet named "PivotTableSheet."

Creating a Custom Dialog and List Box

File: LACHER07.XLS

Keywords: List Box, VLOOKUP, Command Button, Dialog Sheet

Create a custom dialog box to select items from a master list and enter a value in a worksheet cell.

 Tip

You can use a simple VBA procedure to display a custom dialog and list box. If you use worksheet ranges to control the list box, it is easy to return the selected value to a location on your worksheet. With only twelve lines of VBA code, you can build a useful lookup feature.

Note

Select a blank cell in column A of the "Demonstration" worksheet. Click the Insert Sales Value button and pick an item from the sales catalog. The name of the item will be returned to the cell you selected and its price to the cell in Column B.

Performing a List Box Lookup

File: LACHER08.XLS

Keywords: List Box, Lookup, Dialog Sheet, Edit Box

Select items from a list box by entering the first few characters of the item's name. The first matching item in the list box is automatically highlighted.

 Tip

You can look up entries in a list box by entering the first few letters of the entry in an edit box. With a VBA procedure, the matching entry in the list box will be highlighted. When you change the text in the edit box, the list box will scroll and change its selection value.

 Note

Click the Demonstration button on the List Box Lookup Demonstration sheet.

The dialog, control, and module sheets are hidden. To view them, choose Format, Sheets, Unhide. Try adding your own entries to the list box contents range on the control sheet.

Calculating the Number of Days, Months, and Years Between Two Dates

File: LACHER09.XLS

Keywords: Dates, User Defined Function

Create a user-defined function that uses the DateSerial function to calculate the time elapsed between two dates.

Tip
You can create a VBA user-defined function to return the number of years, months, and days from a start date to an end date. Use the function in formulas or to create a text string:

"As of yy/yy/yy, nn Years, mm Months, and pp Days have elapsed from the start date xx/xx/xx."

Note
The following user-defined function,

```
Elapsed(StartDate As Date, EndDate As Date, ReturnType As Integer)
```

will return the number of whole years, months, and days depending on value of return type. See examples on Sheet1.

Changing Cell Formatting

File: LACHER10.XLS

Keywords: Formatting, Macro Recorder, Do Loop, With

Use a VBA subroutine to shade selected cells on the worksheet. This example shows how to add a Do Loop and With statement to a recorded macro.

Tip
You can modify recorded macros with Do Loop and With, End With to create VBA procedures that perform an operation on a block of cells. Use the macro recorder to record the action of changing one cell, then modify the macro to loop through a selected range. With these VBA tools, you will be able to add power to your recorded macros.

Note
A copy of the recorded macro and step-by-step instructions for modifiying it are shown on the sheet "Visual Basic Example." Sheet1 and Module2 demonstrate the macro in use.

Using a Dialog Box to Filter Data

File: LACHER11.XLS

Keywords: AutoFilter, VBA, Criteria Range, InputBox

Use a button, dialog box, and simple VBA macro to filter data on a worksheet. When you click the button and enter values for year and month, the list is automatically filtered.

Tip
You can create an AdvancedFilter with a criteria range on a hidden worksheet. If you control the values in the hidden criteria range with a simple VBA procedure, you can click a button, enter criteria values with the InputBox method, and change the filter. This technique is useful when you need to protect the criteria range and make the process of selection simple for the worksheet user.

Note
The CriteriaValues worksheet and Module1 are hidden. To make them visible, choose Format, Sheets, Unhide. Click the button on the DataValues sheet and enter year and month to demonstrate the process.

Using an Animated Line Chart

File: LACHER12.XLS

Keywords: Chart, Wait Method, Chart Series

This example uses a VBA procedure to update and display different values for a line chart. Each value is displayed for one second.

Tip

You can use the Wait method in VBA to animate the display of a chart. If you use the Wait method and change the properties of the Series object, the chart will appear to be animated. Each value will show on the chart in sequence. The user of the chart can see the shape of the line change over time.

 Note

Scroll the worksheet Sheet1 so that the line chart is visible. Click the Animate Graph button and view changes in the line chart. The data series used to animate the graph are shown at the top of Sheet1. Module1 contains the Animate and ReplaceSeries procedures.

Using a PivotTable to Calculate Budget Variances

File: LACHER13.XLS

Keywords: PivotTable, % of PivotTable field calculation, hiding columns

A VBA procedure useful in displaying Budget variances. The procedure hides columns in a PivotTable based on the values in the PivotTable data fields.

 Tip

When you create a PivotTable field to show Budget Variance with the "% of" calculation option, the PivotTable will show Actual as a percent of Budget and Budget as a percent of Budget. You can create a VBA procedure that will hide the Budget as a percent of Budget columns.

 Note

Source data for the PivotTable is in the worksheet "PivotTable Database." Buttons above the PivotTable on the "PivotTable" worksheet hide and unhide the columns in the table that contain all 100% values. By hiding these columns, you can use the % of calculation option and eliminate the "Budget as a percent of Budget" columns.

Creating a Chart Controlled with Buttons

File: LACHER14.XLS

Keywords: Chart, Dialogs method

Example of control buttons on a chart used to change the 3-D view and trend line settings.

 Tip

You can use a very simple VBA procedure to call any one of Excel's hundreds of built-in dialogs. This example shows the Dialogs method used to call the 3-D view and trend line dialogs.

 Note

Data for the charts is contained in worksheet "Chart Data." Buttons on sheets "Chart1" and "Chart2" call procedures in Module1.

Linking a Chart to a Worksheet Range

File: LACHER15.XLS

Keywords: Chart, PivotTable, Named Range, Link

Demonstration of two methods of linking a chart to a worksheet range. When data in the range changes, the chart updates automatically.

 Tip

When you create a chart, the source range for the chart will not change as new data is entered into the worksheet. If you specify a named range as the source for the chart, the ChartWizard will convert the named range to cell addresses. If later, the size of the named range changes, the chart will not reflect the changes.

You can link a chart to a named range using VBA or with a PivotTable.

Note
The sheet "Chart" uses the sheet "Data" as its input range. If you click the Update Chart button on the sheet "Data," the ChartWizard method resets the Chart's input range. The sheet "Chart2" obtains its data from the PivotTable sheet. See the details on the worksheet "Demonstration."

Clicking a Chart to Select a New Source Range

File: LACHER16.XLS

Keywords: Chart, InputBox, Hidden Rectangle

In this example, you can click a chart and enter a new source range. The chart will redraw to show the data in the range you select.

  Tip
You can create a VBA procedure to prompt for a chart's input range. When you click the chart, the prompt allows you to enter or select a new input range with the mouse. For a chart sheet, you can use a hidden rectangle to initiate the procedure. For an embedded chart, you can assign the procedure directly to the chart object.

  Note
A hidden rectangle is drawn over the chart on the chart sheet "Chart1." When you click inside the rectangle, a VBA procedure prompts you for the source range. Another procedure is assigned to the embedded chart on "Sheet1." Module 1 contains the code for both procedures.

Comparing Three Different Sort Methods

File: LACHER17.XLS

Keywords: Sort, Timer, Random Number

Comparison of the time required to sort a VBA Array using three methods.

Tip

You can sort an array by transferring it to the worksheet and using Excel's built-in sort. Another sorting method is the VBA "Bubble Sort." Quick Sort, adapted from the *Visual Basic Developer's Guide* by D.F. Scott, is a third method. You can create a test array with random values and use the Timer method to compare the time required to perform the sort using each of the three methods.

 Note

Click the Sort an Array Using Three Different Techniques button on Sheet1. Enter the size of the array you want to test. A message box will display the three times.

Converting Feet and Inches to Decimal Values

File: LACHER18.XLS

Keywords: Inches, Feet, Measurement, User Defined Function

One VBA user-defined function converts from decimal inches to feet, inches and fractions. The second function converts from feet and inches to decimal inches.

 Tip

You can create these user-defined functions:

CFeet converts from decimal inches to feet, inches and fractions of inch. The second parameter of CFeet specifies the smallest fraction of an inch for rounding. If omitted, fractions are rounded to 9999th's of an inch. CInches converts from feet, inches and fractions of an inch to decimal inches.

 Note

To use these functions, insert a module page in your workbook and copy the functions from Module 1 to your module page. Functions will then appear in the function Wizard under "user-defined functions." Even if you are not a Visual Basic Coder, you can read comments in Module 1 to understand the logic of each function. See examples on Sheet1.

Creating a Custom Dialog

File: LACHER19.XLS

Keywords: Database, Custom Dialog, Update, Scroll

This is an example of a simple VBA procedure that displays a custom dialog box and updates a database.

 Tip

You can create a custom dialog box that updates a database with a VBA procedure. The dialog box can add new records, and edit or delete existing records. If you want to find a record, you can use a scroll bar to page through the database. The Module page in this example includes comments designed for novice users of VBA.

 Note

Press the Show Dialog and Update Database button on Demonstration sheet. Examine controls on DBUpdate dialog sheet. Read comments and code in Module 1. Database is contained in range named "Database" on worksheet named "Datasheet."

Selecting a Custom Header

File: LACHER20.XLS

Keywords: Custom Dialog, Header, Option Buttons

A custom dialog box and VBA procedure provides a choice of three custom headers that can be assigned to a worksheet.

 Tip

You can have Excel store frequently used custom headers and choose them from a menu option in a worksheet. A VBA procedure and custom dialog box can be used to store header information, select a header using options buttons, and copy the header information to the three header areas of the PageSetup object.

Note

To use the macro, select Custom Header from the Tools menu option. Change one of the three custom headers, select the header, and print the worksheet. To make this file into an add-in, choose menu option Tools, Make Add In. Excel will create an add-in file that you can add to any open workbook with the Tools, Add Ins menu option. See the Excel manual for instructions on "Installing Add-Ins."

Data Validation

File: LACHER21.XLS

Keywords: Custom Dialog, Validation, Dialog Frame, Focus

Demonstration of custom dialog box procedure that checks for errors and prompts user for correct input.

 Tip

A VBA procedure and a custom dialog box can be used to prompt user to correct input errors. If you assign a VBA procedure to the frame of the dialog box, you can set the focus of the dialog box to highlight the first field with errors.

 Note

Click the Run Dialog button on the sheet named "Notes." Enter incorrect values and test the operation of the VBA procedures contained in the module "Module1."

Using IRR, XIRR, NPV, XNPV Functions

File: LACHER22.XLS

Keywords: IRR, XIRR, NPV, XNPV, Worksheet Function, Auditing Features, Precedents

Demonstration of financial functions used to calculate internal rate of return and net present value.

Tip

You can use IRR and NPV to calculate internal rate of return and net present value for even cash flows. For uneven cash flows, use the XIRR and XNPV functions found in the Analysis Pak add-in.

Note

Formulas on the worksheet "Financial Functions" demonstrate Net Present Value and Internal Rate of Return for both regular and irregular cash flows. The arrows provided by the Audit feature show where each formula obtains its input values.

Highlighting Exception Values

File: LACHER23.XLS

Keywords: OnEntry, Font, ColorIndex, If, Exception

This example displays a date less than the current date in red. It uses a VBA procedure to set the color of the text.

Tip

You can use the OnEntry property to run an exception check. The procedure can change the font color of the cell and can perform an operation on the ActiveCell if you want to validate or change color cell where data is entered. There is a "hole" in the logic of OnEntry: when the user copies a cell and pastes the value on the worksheet, the OnEntry property does not run.

Note

Enter a date in cell A10 on Sheet1. If the date is less than the current date, the text color will show as red. If the date is equal to or greater than the current date, the text will show as black.

Creating a GANTT Chart for Scheduling Resources

File: LACHER24.XLS

Keywords: GANTT, Resources, Time, Bar Chart

Create a GANTT chart showing when resource is scheduled using a bar chart and VBA procedure.

Tip
You can create a VBA procedure that uses a list of start and stop times on a worksheet to build a table of durations for a bar chart. The bar chart can display the date in a resource using GANTT format.

Note
The raw time data is contained in sheet "TimeData." Click the button on the TimeData worksheet to call the procedure "CreateTimeChartData" and update the ChartData and TimeChart sheets.

Forcing Uppercase Entry

File: LACHER25.XLS

Keywords: OnEntry, Convert, Uppercase

Example VBA procedure converts lowercase text entered in a column to uppercase.

Tip
You can use an OnEntry procedure to run a VBA procedure each time that data is entered into the worksheet. The procedure can convert lowercase text to uppercase if the active cell is in a specified range. The example converts entries in the second (B) column to uppercase.

Note

Enter values in the first and second columns of Sheet1. Entries in the second column will be converted to uppercase upon entry.

Using a Maximum Sustainable Growth Model

File: LACHER26.XLS

Keywords: Iteration, Circular Reference, Accounting, Growth, Auditing

Excel's iteration feature solves circular references in the maximum sustainable growth model.

Tip

You can use Excel's iteration feature to solve a circular reference. In a maximum sustainable growth model, Excel can iterate to solve the circular formulas where maximum sales growth depends on profit generated and profit depends on sales. If you set the iteration parameters when the workbook opens with a Visual Basic macro, Excel will iterate to find the maximum sustainable growth. You can use the Tools, Auditing features to trace the circular references.

Note

The Auto_Open macro sets the iteration parameters so that Excel can solve circular references on the worksheet "Growth Model."

Using PivotTables with Accounting Data

File: LACHER27.XLS

Keywords: PivotTable, Multiple Consolidation Range

This workbook demonstrates three PivotTables built using the multiple consolidation range option with source data in standard accounting format. The PivotTables take advantage of Excel's capability to group dates in PivotTables.

Tip

The powerful grouping capability of PivotTables can be used to bring flexibility to the manipulation of financial totals by month, quarter, and so on. If the source data is arrayed as columns of monthly accounting data, you can use the PivotTable Multiple Consolidation Range option to create a date field you can group by month, quarter, or year.

 Note

The source data table on the "Source Data" worksheet is shown in three PivotTables by quarter, month, and by month with quarterly totals. Use the PivotTable Wizard to review the setting of the PivotTables.

Creating a Pop-Up List Box

File: LACHER28.XLS

Keywords: ListBox, Data Entry

VBA procedure draws a list box aligned with the active cell and inserts the value selected from a list box into an active cell.

 Tip

You can create a VBA procedure that creates a new list box "on the fly" when a command button is clicked. The list box can be positioned near the active cell and the value selected copied to the active cell. When the copy is complete, the list box can be deleted from the worksheet.

 Note

Select a cell and click the Pick from List button. Choose an item from the list and it will be copied to the active cell. The "Control" sheet contains the list values used by the ShowList and ListClick procedures in Module1.

Adding Percent Labels to a Bar Chart

File: LACHER29.XLS

Keywords: Stacked Bar Chart, Data Labels

Example of special data labels on stacked bar chart. The data labels show values from the source data range of the chart, but the series associated with the labels is hidden so only the labels are visible on the chart.

 Tip

You can add special data labels to a stacked bar chart and have the labels display percentage values. If you create the percentage values in a column in the chart's source data, you can display the series of percentages on the chart as a hidden data series. Even though the data series is hidden, you can have it display its values in data labels. The result is a chart showing actual values with data labels showing percentages.

 Note

The chart is created with columns B - E on Sheet1. The data series containing the percentage (column E) is hidden on the chart by setting its pattern to none and border to none. Even though the series is hidden, it still displays values as data labels.

Applying Styles to PivotTables

File: LACHER30.XLS

Keywords: PivotTables, Format

This example worksheet demonstrates how to apply special styles to parts of a PivotTable.

 Tip

When you change a PivotTable it will lose its formatting. You can create a VBA procedure that will apply styles to each portion of a PivotTable. If you use the Format, Style option to create special styles, the VBA procedure can apply those named styles to the areas of the PivotTable.

Note
Change the PivotTable on the PivotTable and Data sheet by moving a row field to a page field or selecting a new page field value. These changes will redraw the table and all special formatting will be lost. Click the Apply Styles to Pivot Table button and the VBA procedure will restore special formatting to each area of the PivotTable.

Controlling a Chart with a List Box

File: LACHER31.XLS

Keywords: Indirect, List Box, Chart

This example uses a list box and worksheet formulas to change a chart's source range using a list box.

Tip
You can use a list box to change the values in a chart by using the list box control ranges and the Indirect function. When the list box selection changes, the value of the reference used by the Indirect function points to a different location in the workbook. If you use the indirect formulas as the source range for the chart, when the Indirect functions return new values, the chart will reflect the change.

Note
Select the sheet named Chart1. Click list box value and the chart will change to reflect data on worksheet. See notes on the Control sheet to understand how list box and formulas work.

Creating a User-Defined Function for Week Numbers

File: LACHER32.XLS

Keywords: Format, UserDefined Function, Week, Date

Example of user-defined function that returns the week number of any date.

Tip

You can use the "ww" value of the Format function to return week number. This value is not available in the user interface. If you include it in a user-defined function, you can use it to calculate week number in worksheet formulas.

Note

Column C in Sheet 1 contains the formula: =WeekNumber(B3).

Using the PivotTable Tutorial

File: LACHER33.XLS

Keywords: PivotTable, Excel List, Tutorial, Vlookup

PivotTable, Vlookup, and Excel List Tutorial based on "Building Profits with Excellent Tools" by John F. Lacher, *Maximize* Magazine, Special #1, November, 1995.

Tip

You can link named ranges and PivotTables. If you name the range "Database," you can add new records to the range with the built-in Data Form and the named range will be extended to include the new records. If you use named ranges, Excel lists, PivotTables, and Vlookup formulas, you can create a simple but powerful database system in an Excel workbook.

Note

Review the database stored in the worksheet "DataTable." Understand the look-up tables: "Problem Table" and "CauseTable." Use the PivotTable Wizard to explore values in "PivotTable."

3-D Special by David C. Hager

David C. Hager
CompuServe: **73512,1133**

Filename: FSPHAGER.XLS

With the introduction of version 5, Excel workbooks featured some very useful 3-D functionality. However, the ability to fill formulas in the 3-D environment remained limited in that the familiar relative filling of formulas on a single worksheet could not be extended in the "z" direction, or down through the worksheets in the workbook. A related problem was discovered by users who attempted to break down a large worksheet into multiple pages in a workbook. They found that unless the sheetname was an implicit part of each reference in every formula, error values would result when they cut/pasted those formulas to another worksheet.

The VBA code contained in FSPHAGER.XLS was constructed to circumvent these problems. The Sub procedure

```
Add_Sheet_Name_to_Formulas()
```

adds the sheetname to all formula references in the current selection. If you intend to use this on an entire worksheet, insert the following code before With Selection, which will select all of the formulas on the active sheet.

```
Selection.SpecialCells(xlFormulas, 23).Select
```

The Sub procedure FillSpecial( ) performs the relative filling process. Its success depends to some extent on the length of the formulas to be filled and the worksheet grouping pattern selected. Thus, it is recommended that small selection areas, simple formulas, and contiguous workbook groups be used for optimum results.

The menu command 3-D Special is available in the Edit Fill submenu when FSPHAGER.XLS is placed in your XLSTART directory. Its use is similar to the Across Worksheets command, which is also located in the Edit, Fill submenu, in that a selection of cells to be filled is made on the active worksheet and additional sheets to be filled to are selected in a group. Grouping worksheets is done by holding down the Ctrl key while clicking the tabs of the worksheets to be included in a group. When the Across Worksheets command is used, the entries in the filled cells are identical to those in the source worksheet. Thus, if a formula such as =SUM(Sheet2: Sheet5!A1:B5) was filled from a cell in Sheet1 to Sheet2, it would remain as =SUM(Sheet2: Sheet5!A1: B5). If the 3-D Special command is used, the filled formula in the cell on Sheet2 will be returned as the sheet-relative form =SUM(Sheet3:Sheet6!A1:B5).

It is important to note here that the sheet position in the workbook determines the relative sheetnames and not an arbitrarily assigned user order based on worksheet names. Also, there may be sheetnames in your workbook that contain spaces. In order for this command to construct formulas that can undergo 3-D filling, you will be asked if the sheetname in question can be modified. You must answer YES for the filling process to operate correctly.

Additional functionality is available in 3-D Special in its ability to add the sheetnames to all formula cell references. As an example, the highlighted range in Sheet1 is B1:B100 and B1 contains the formula =A1+A2. When this formula is filled to B100, B2 contains =A2+A3, B3 contains =A3+A4, and so on. If this entire range is filled through Sheet3 using the Across Worksheets command, all of the filled cells contain formulas identical to those in Sheet1. When the add sheetname option is used with 3-D Special, the formula in B2 of Sheet2, for example, will now appear as =Sheet2!A2+Sheet2!A3.

If adding the sheetnames to formula references is the only operation that you want to perform, use 3-D Special by making a selection on the active worksheet without selecting any other worksheets to group together. After all of the formulas have been converted, they can be cut/pasted to other worksheets while retaining their original reference links. If an error message stating `Illegal formula reference` appears, it is likely that a 4.0 macro sheet or a module sheet is either part of your worksheet grouping, or you are trying to create a formula that refers to cells on those sheets, which Excel does not allow. Also, like the Across Worksheets command, 3-D Special cannot be used with multiple selections. If a problem occurs during the sheetname to reference conversion process, the following error message will appear: `Not all references may have converted correctly.` The filling process will not occur in this case, and you will need to examine your formulas before a retry. This should be a rare event.

It is hoped that you will find these to be very useful tools in 3-D workbook construction. Success is not 100% guaranteed, since the procedures presented here are only workarounds for a true 3-D workbook environment.

Excel Examples by John Green

Linking a Spinner, Edit Box, and Worksheet Cell

File: SPINLINK.XLS

The idea is to let the user choose from among the three methods to enter a value. It can be typed into an edit box in a dialog box or a cell in a spreadsheet. In the dialog box, the value can also be increased or decreased by using a spinner. No matter how it is entered or changed, the values of all three objects remain synchronized.

Using a Spinner to Increment a Value in an Edit Box, Cell, or Number in a Text Box

File: SPININC.XLS

Rather than set the object equal to the value of the spinner, this technique increases or decreases the value of the other object by a set amount (say +1 or -1). This means that values outside the normal range of a spinner (0 to 30,000) can be obtained, including negative values.

Browsing ToolBar Buttons and Editing Tooltips

File: TOOLTIPS.XLS

A dialog box contains a list box of all the user's toolbars. When a particular toolbar is selected, a second list box shows all the toolbar buttons on it. When a particular toolbar button is selected, its image is displayed in the dialog box and its tooltip is displayed in an edit box. The tooltip can be edited and applied to the toolbar button.

Subtotal Bug Fix by Bob Umlas

Bob Umlas
424 White Oak Road
Palisades, NY 10964
CompuServe: **70302,3432**
E-mail: **r_umlas@j51.com**

File: SUBTOTAL.XLA

Microsoft Excel versions 5 and 7 have a great feature: Data, Subtotal. This enables you to quickly summarize data arranged in a particular sort sequence and take subtotals at key breaks in the data.

Unfortunately, there's a bug in it! To see this bug, we'll work through an example, then show how the enclosed VBA procedure fixes that bug by replacing the Data, Subtotal command in Excel.

Look at the worksheet in figure A.1. Notice that there are two divisions—East and West—and within the East division there are two departments, Finance and Personnel. Notice also that the Personnel department "flows into" the West division because the West division doesn't contain a Finance department. This is when the bug occurs—when the *minor* break spans the *major* break. You'll see the problem in a moment.

Fig. A.1

A worksheet with data that doesn't work correctly when using nested subtotals.

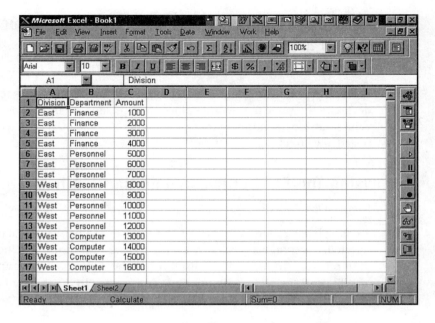

When you issue the <u>D</u>ata, Su<u>b</u>total command, you get the dialog box shown in figure A.2.

Fig. A.2

Excel's Subtotal dialog box.

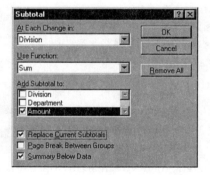

This requests that at every change in Division, place the subtotal under the Amount column. This works fine, and you get the worksheet shown in figure A.3.

Fig. A.3

Subtotals on the major break, Division.

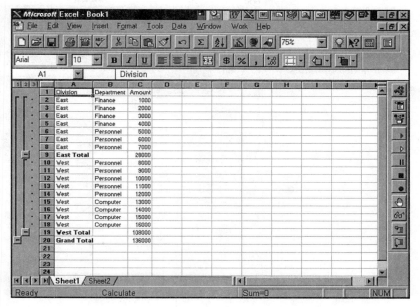

Now you need to request the nested subtotal by invoking the Data, Subtotal command again, this time changing the request from Division to Department, as shown in figure A.4.

Fig. A.4

Excel's Subtotal dialog box, requesting a second-level break (notice the Replace Current Subtotals check box is not selected).

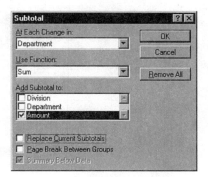

This produces the bug (horror show, actually!) as shown in figure A.5. Notice that there is *no subtotal for Personnel in the East Division!* Where did it go? Excel thinks the Personnel total is in row 16, when the department changes to Computer, but look at the total in C16:, 68000, is simply wrong, because it spans East and West divisions.

Fig. A.5

An erroneous result of using the Data, Subtotal command with nested subtotals.

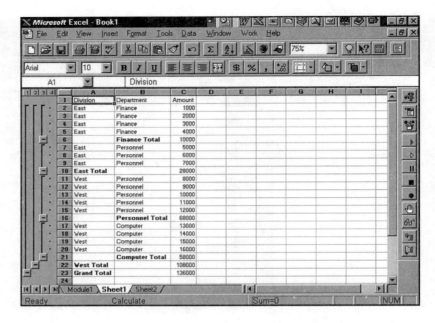

Further, if you click the outline level 2, you see the worksheet shown in figure A.6. Where is the East total? Gone? That makes no sense!

Fig. A.6

Misaligned outlining due to Excel's Subtotal bug.

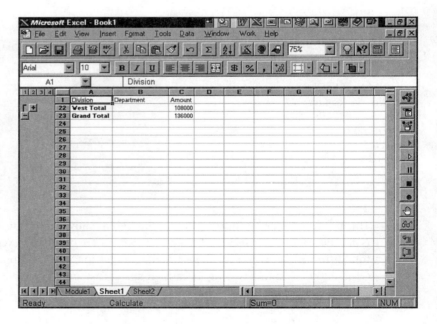

Shown in figure A.7 is level 3 outline. This also makes no sense. Shouldn't the intermediate totals reflect the subtotal from rows above? That is, shouldn't cell C22 be made up of cells C16 and C21? Where is it getting the 108000 from?

Fig. A.7

More misaligned outlining due to Excel's Subtotal bug.

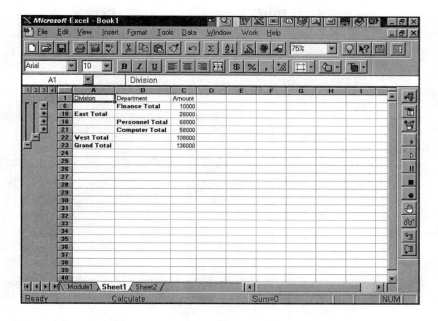

The solution to this mess is the file SUBTOTAL.XLA on the CD, which you should install into your XLSTART directory. This will replace the Data, Subtotal command. You will not notice a difference in the menu, but when you issue the command, the dialog box you see will be slightly different (see fig. A.8).

Fig. A.8

The revised SubTotal dialog box.

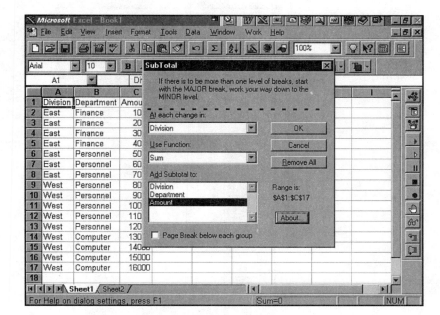

When you issue the command for the second time, to get the Department subtotal, the result is shown below in figure A.9. Notice that the East total, 28000, is C6+C10. This makes sense. Finally, look at the last two screen shots, figures A.10 and A.11, showing level 2 outline and level 3 outline, both of which now make sense. You will want to use the replacement workbook.

Fig. A.9

The correct subtotals from using the SUBTOTAL.XLA add-in.

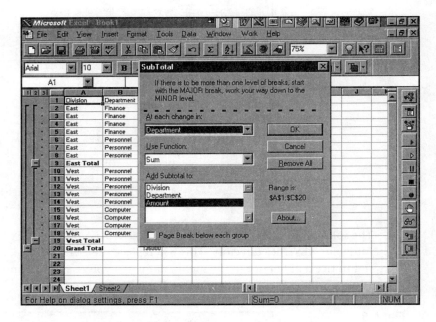

Fig. A.10

The correct level 2 outline.

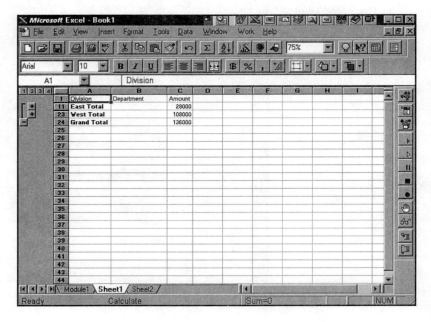

Fig. A.11

The correct level 3 outline.

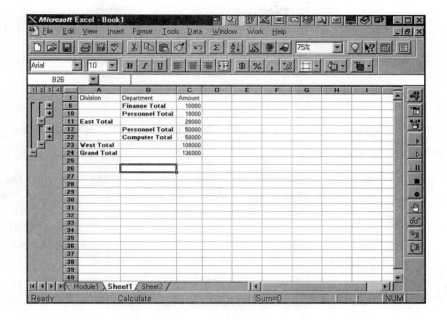

Backup Calendar Generator by Wassim Nassif

For information, send e-mail to **74164.3611@compuserve.com**.

File: BKUPCLDR.XLS

This is an Excel workbook that is made into a perpetual (as long as Excel can detect the dates and their formats) calendar. The intent of this workbook is to provide a visual reminder for a 15 tape backup schedule.

It prints a month's calendar with the days Monday-Friday colored to match with the color-coded tapes.

To activate this calendar generator all you need to do is open the file in Excel version 5.0c or later and follow the prompts on the screen.

System requirements include the following:

▶ Any system capable of running MS Excel version 5.0c or later.

▶ A printer (a color printer if you would like to print the calendar in color).

 Note

To see how this application works, click the View Application button in the opening dialog box. Ignore any error messages, and use the Format, Sheet, Unhide command to display Main Module.

Using the I'm No Accountant™ Workbook for Excel

by Willis E. Howard, III
2716 E. Jackson Blvd.
Elkhart, IN 46516
WEHoward@aol.com

http://members.aol.com/WWWEHoward/software.htm

File: INA185.ZIP

Electronic spreadsheets have been around for many years now. They were originally modeled on printed spreadsheets that have been used in accounting for an untold number of years. A remarkable thing about electronic spreadsheets is that very few people use them for accounting. Integrated packages like Quicken have taken hold of the accounting market for PCs. But, there is still a place for the electronic spreadsheet in accounting, especially when direct access to the data is required.

When I needed to start doing accounting tasks, I looked at a lot of the available commercial accounting packages. I'm no accountant, but I wanted to easily enter my checkbook transactions, keep track of transactions by account and business, reconcile my expenses and income with the bank statement, generate a small number of reports at the end of the year for my taxes, and have immediate access to all the data.

I found that the commercial packages were too complex for my needs. I also found that many of them did not give me direct access to all of the transaction information in my accounts. I looked at the way that many small businesses with single entry, cash flow, non-computerized accounting methods kept their books. I then transferred those methods to a dialog-oriented Excel workbook.

The I'm No Accountant workbook for Excel is organized around these components:

▶ A worksheet that gives the user information at startup on getting help

▶ The Transactions worksheet that keeps all income and expense transactions

▶ The Accounts worksheet that associates account names with account numbers

▶ For the multiple business version, pivot worksheets summarize expenses and income by business and by account

▶ The Balance worksheet that verifies account and checkbook balances

▶ The Extract worksheet that displays filtered transactions, showing transactions of a specific category within a specific date range

▶ A worksheet that keeps data on user name and next check number

▶ Several dialog sheets for obtaining user input

▶ The VBA module that coordinates all data entry, validation, storage, and printing

▶ A drop-down menu for the various tasks, including entering new transactions, entering new account names and numbers, entering new businesses, extracting transactions for display, printing transactions and accounts, and help

▶ A custom Help file for providing information to the user on software organization and usage

▶ A hot key for immediate access to help

Major advantages of the I'm No Accountant workbook for Excel are ease of data entry and availability of the source code in Visual Basic for Applications (VBA) for inspection and modification. The information is stored in worksheets that are completely accessible to the user. This open access allows experienced users to add custom functions for data transfer, analysis, and graphing.

The I'm No Accountant workbook for Excel that is included with the CD-ROM companion to this book is version 1.85. It has been specifically updated for Windows 95, although it still completely works with Windows 3.1.

The main changes that are needed in going from a workbook in Windows 3.1 to Windows 95 relate to custom Help. Help files need to be compiled with the protected mode help compiler HCP.EXE or the help compiler soon to be released for Windows 95. Earlier help compilers such as HC31.EXE or HC30.EXE do not give proper printouts under Windows 95. For Excel 7, the Application.Help routine must by worked around due to Excel implementation errors.

Printed in landscape mode, the I'm No Accountant workbook for Excel VBA source code is over 40 pages long. The code provides examples of these functions:

▶ Global definition of variables

▶ Setup of a menubar that includes custom Help from the Auto_Open function

▶ Definition of a hot key for custom Help in the Auto_Open function

▶ Proper removal of the menubar and hot key from Auto_Close

▶ A workaround to using Application.Help to provide help to the user

▶ Using MsgBox to provide an About function to the user

▶ Functions that setup and process data from dialog boxes

▶ Code that keeps the screen from blinking during data processing

▶ Code to dynamically show or hide specific fields on dialog boxes

▶ Code to define special printouts

Whether you want to use Excel to help you with your accounting or just learn more about VBA programming in Excel, the I'm No Accountant workbook for Excel may be worth looking at.

Using the Objectives Manager Workbook for Excel

by Willis E. Howard, III
2716 E. Jackson Blvd.
Elkhart, IN 46516
WEHoward@aol.com

http://members.aol.com/WWWEHoward/software.htm

File: OBMAN109.ZIP

An objective is something specific that you want to achieve by a specific date. It is a goal with a deadline that is specific, measurable, achievable, and realistic. Objectives are typically achieved by identifying and achieving specific action items within an overall plan. Defined in this way, objectives are goals that you really can achieve.

The Objectives Manager workbook for Excel is an aid in the definition and ranking of objectives. It allows action items to be identified and then later categorized as achieved, deleted, or deferred. Objectives are classified as active or achieved. They can be printed out in summary form or in detail with all action items. The printout in landscape mode makes an impressive record of your achievements.

The Objectives Manager workbook for Excel was primarily developed with business or professional objectives in mind. However, it can also be used for personal objectives.

When a new objective is defined, the goal and the deadline must be given. The qualities of being specific, measurable, achievable, and realistic are not evaluated within the software. The Help file that goes along with the workbook gives additional information on the qualities that your objectives should have.

Not all objectives are equal. Some are more important than others. As you add new objectives, they are automatically assigned a ranking, with the first one entered as #1 or most important. The ranking function allows you to redefine the priorities of your objectives. Two techniques are allowed. You can rank them one at a time by just assigning a number to each one. Or, you can use the pairwise ranking method. With this procedure, all objectives are compared to all others but just two at a time. Using the Saaty pairwise comparison method, all pairs of rankings are processed by solving for the principle eigenvector of the pairwise comparison matrix. This also allows a computation of the quality of the ranking as good, fair, or poor.

Action items may be defined for each objective. This is a kind of "to do" list, where the individual action items act as milestones towards your objectives. An action item can be added, removed, marked as achieved, or marked as deferred.

The workbook is organized around these components:

- A worksheet that gives the user information at startup on getting help
- The Objectives worksheet that gives a ranked summary of all objectives
- Individual worksheets for the individual objectives, containing all information together with the action items
- A blank individual worksheet that is copied when adding a new objective
- A worksheet to store deleted objectives
- A worksheet to save the user name and some variables
- Several dialog sheets for obtaining user input
- The VBA module that coordinates all data entry, storage, and printing
- A drop-down menu for various tasks, including adding, deleting, ranking, printing, and selecting objectives, as well as adding or moving action items; and for help
- A custom Help file for providing information to the user on software organization and usage
- A hot key for immediate access to help

The main advantages of using the Objectives Manager for Excel are the ease of entering objectives, versatile methods of ranking, detailed tracking of action items, and impressive printouts. Because all of the information is in a worksheet, it can be easily manipulated or transferred to other applications.

Like the I'm No Accountant workbook for Excel, the Help files have been compiled with the protected mode help compiler for this new release of the software, making the Help files more compatible with Windows 95. The Application.Help command has also been replaced by an API call to reduce the errors in the Windows 95 Help Application when running under Excel 7.

The code provides examples of these functions:

- Global definition of variables
- Setup of a menubar that includes custom Help from the Auto_Open function
- Definition of a hot key for custom Help in the Auto_Open function
- Proper removal of the menubar and hot key from Auto_Close
- A workaround to using Application.Help to provide help to the user
- Functions that setup and process data from dialog boxes
- Code that works with spinners on dialog sheets
- Code to perform matrix computations, including eigenvectors and eigenvalues

Whether you want to use Excel to help you with your objectives or just learn more about VBA programming in Excel, the Objectives Manager workbook for Excel may be useful for you.

Reportech Informer Software Overview

by Patrick Steele, Executive Vice President
Reportech, Inc.
patricks@reportech.com

Liam Scanlan, President and CEO
Reportech, Inc.
liams@reportech.com

Reportech, Inc.
13720 SE 58 Place
Bellevue, WA 98006
1-206-644-9646
1-800-662-4317
http://www.halcyon.com/patricks/informer.html

File: SETUP.EXE

To install, copy SETUP.EXE into a new directory on your hard disk and then run SETUP.EXE. In Excel, make INFORMER.XLA an add-in using the Tools, Add-Ins command.

Using Reportech Informer

Founded in 1995, Reportech, Inc., specializes in providing reporting solution applications and consulting services for the emerging client/server environment. The principals of the company have been developing software solutions since 1977 for companies including Nixdorf Computer AG, SeaFirst Bank, Boeing Advanced Technology Center, and Microsoft Corporation.

Informer Enterprise Edition (1.5) PivotTable Client/Server reporting software for Windows 3.*x*, Windows 95, and Windows NT operating environments brings system continuity and new ease of use to Client/Server multi-dimensional reporting.

Unlike other, stand-alone reporting applications, Informer integrates completely into the MS Excel environment so that users never leave MS Excel to define, execute, enhance, format, publish, or administratively control dynamic pivot reports throughout their enterprise. Informer is compatible with both 16- and 32-bit versions of MS Excel and Office so that users can sanely transition from one operating system and MS Excel application to another—whenever they are ready—without losing reporting continuity.

We've added new capabilities to our QuickReport features so that those who *use* reports—in addition to those primarily responsible for generating them—can access their information with simple menu selections. With this step, Informer becomes part of a complete reporting solution for *all* users—even those with very limited computing expertise.

We think PivotTables are the best way for people to work with their enterprise reporting, so we merged the power of pivots—multi-dimensionality, live data, ODBC connectivity to many databases—with powerful new features like Custom PivotFields, Informatter report styler, administrative controls, and Quick Report distribution and refreshing to add the features corporate users need for complete data analysis and reporting.

Power and Flexibility

Informer adds new power and flexibility to enterprise-wide reporting:

▶ *Use drag-and-drop to see your data in new ways.* PivotTables provide a great way to organize, summarize, and analyze data because you can instantly create different sorts and views of data by dragging and dropping column and row headings, and select different summary levels from drop-down list boxes. Informer offers expanded capacity, speed, data selection, analysis, and formatting features so that you *never* leave MS Excel to produce dynamic, finished reports with unparalleled ease.

▶ *Add custom PivotFields within the pivot.* Create and embed MS Excel formulas and calculations directly into an MS Excel PivotTable. You can use virtually any other MS Excel formula or function to define Custom PivotFields, and you can select the data fields included in calculations with point-and-click ease. Custom PivotFields become an integrated part of the pivot report, and you can drag and drop Custom PivotFields anywhere in the PivotTable—the same as fields in the datasource. Base your calculations on any available field in the datasource—even if that field is not displayed in the report results.

▶ *Save and share report definitions anywhere.* Store report definition files on a local workstation, a shared network device, or on a designated SQL server to structure report management at individual, workgroup, or enterprise-wide levels.

▶ *Modify data selections as you execute.* Use the Filter-on-the-Fly feature to modify existing reports to include filters that were not part of the original report definition.

▶ *Access a wide array of databases.* Retrieve data via ODBC drivers from Microsoft Access 1.0, 1.1, 2.0, and 7.0; MS SQL Server; ORACLE; WATCOM SQL; SyBase; Borland Paradox; and the X-Base Family (Borland dBase, MS FoxBase, and so on), among others.

▶ *Report directly from an Access query or Access external attachment.* Under MS Excel 7, users can now base a QuickQuery on a query or table attachment that has been created and saved in an Access database. Without launching MS Access, Informer executes the query and retrieves the data as if the query were a regular table. The query can be based on Access tables, other queries, or attachments to tables in other types and sizes of databases. Because of this, organizations can better preserve their existing investment in Access query design.

▶ *Custom PivotField browse.* Under Excel 7 you can browse and pick from Custom PivotFields/formulas that have been previously created and saved in other Informer report definitions.

Speed and Simplicity

Informer brings speed and simplicity to client/server reporting:

▶ *Create new reports without a separate query builder.* Use Informer's Quick Query feature to select datasource, table, and data filters all in one step, in one screen...within Excel.

▶ *Use your existing SQL queries or MS Excel worksheets to create reports.* Without ever leaving MS Excel, you can select the databases, tables, and views against which you want to report—*and* select data filters for your reporting in a matter of minutes. Use any existing PivotTable worksheet as the basis for the report. Or use Informer's Full Query feature to use existing SQL Statements—and add the power of PivotTables and Custom PivotFields to your existing definitions.

▶ *Use QuickLoad to speed data retrieval.* Informer's QuickLoad cached data lists optionally populate the report definition selection criteria to dramatically reduce server processing, and speed report production.

▶ *Access more data faster.* You can create PivotTable reports *nine times* the size of the default MS Excel 5 standard, and retrieve data for report generation in less than *half the time* as MS Query.

▶ *Informatter single-click report layouts.* Select from ten predefined report layout styles to format your report with a single-click, or create your own custom report style with total format and style control over all report elements.

▶ *Flexible QuickReports.* Now users or administrators can easily create lists of workbooks, and make them available as menu items for single-click viewing. Users simply set their Informer preferences to the location of a QuickReport list, and those workbooks are displayed on their individual QuickReports menu in Informer. Without using other Informer screens or selections, users can select a QuickReport from the menu and view it immediately. Because they are fully compatible with MS Excel, these QuickReports can include any formulas, pivots, or embedded charts and graphs for distribution throughout the enterprise— and they can be viewed and manipulated without any connections to the datasources.

▶ *Report Refresh.* With a single menu choice Informer enables users to refresh any displayed report—even QuickReport workbooks. Informer automatically queries the associated datasource(s), imports the revised data, updates any calculations and embedded charts or graphs, and reapplies any previously set Informatter styles. When combined with QuickReports, this Refresh feature lets users select a distributed report, automatically connect to the datasource, refresh the displayed pivot and report data for any changes since publication, and apply any format settings with just two mouse clicks.

Conserves Resources

Informer conserves network and human resources:

▶ *Structural Preview.* Unlike MS Excel's Print Preview, Informer's Structural Preview presents the data layout of any defined report *before* executing it—*before* committing server, network, or local PC resources to actual execution.

▶ *Automatic server disconnect.* Informer reduces network traffic by maintaining a live connection to a network server, datasource, or local database only when it is required.

▶ *Datasource performance-tuning.* Use the Informer Administrator to define Turbo Table relationships that can dramatically reduce server and network loads by more intelligently retrieving data filters from designated datasources.

▶ *Manage and control user and report access in groups within MS Excel.* You can set complete user and report access attributes (local databases like MS Access), or, if your datasources are SQL and network-based, you can use all the access and security protocols you've already established without conflict.

▶ *Workbook decompression.* Informer now supports the automatic decompression of any file that has been compressed using the Microsoft DOS program *compress.exe*. Since compressed MS Excel workbooks are one-half to one-seventh the original size, organizations can electronically share workbooks without hitting network resource ceilings.

Offers Continuity

Informer offers continuity as you migrate to Windows 95 and MS Excel 7:

▶ *Works where you are, adapts to where you're going.* Informer is already compatible with MS Excel 5 and 7, MS Office, Office 95, Windows 3.*x*, Windows NT, and Windows 95. When you do migrate to Office 95/Excel 7, you're ready.

▶ *Reduces hidden hardware upgrade costs.* Informer is "lighter" than MS Excel. If you can run the full product of MS Excel, you can run Informer.

▶ *Leverages your training and investment.* Stay in the environment you (and your employees) know—MS Excel. You'll need very little time to "ramp-up" to Informer.

▶ *Builds on your MS Excel expertise.* You can use all of MS Excel's formulas and functions to define Custom PivotFields, and add additional Formulas to your reporting. Calculations you've used in Excel are immediately transferable.

Availability, Pricing, and Upgrade Offers

Informer 1.5 is now shipping. Price at publication remains $295 (US) for a single license. Volume and site licensing options are available. Users of Informer full-product versions 1.1 and 1.2 can download a free upgrade to version 1.5 from the Reportech Web site at **http://www.halcyon.com/patricks/informer.html**.

A free 30-day evaluation copy of Informer 1.5 can be downloaded from the Web site.

Index

Check out Que® Books on the World Wide Web
http://www.mcp.com/que

As the biggest software release in computer history, Windows 95 continues to redefine the computer industry. Click here for the latest info on our Windows 95 books

Make computing quick and easy with these products designed exclusively for new and casual users

Examine the latest releases in word processing, spreadsheets, operating systems, and suites

The Internet, The World Wide Web, CompuServe®, America Online®, Prodigy® —it's a world of ever-changing information. Don't get left behind!

Find out about new additions to our site, new bestsellers and hot topics

In-depth information on high-end topics: find the best reference books for databases, programming, networking, and client/server technologies

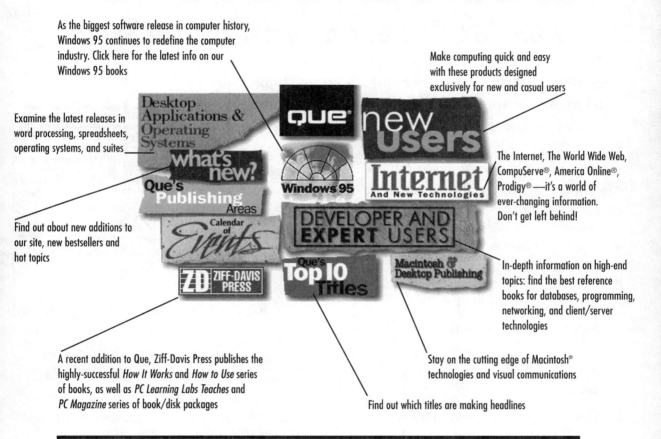

A recent addition to Que, Ziff-Davis Press publishes the highly-successful *How It Works* and *How to Use* series of books, as well as *PC Learning Labs Teaches* and *PC Magazine* series of book/disk packages

Stay on the cutting edge of Macintosh® technologies and visual communications

Find out which titles are making headlines

With 6 separate publishing groups, Que develops products for many specific market segments and areas of computer technology. Explore our Web Site and you'll find information on best-selling titles, newly published titles, upcoming products, authors, and much more.

- Stay informed on the latest industry trends and products available
- Visit our online bookstore for the latest information and editions
- Download software from Que's library of the best shareware and freeware

Complete and Return this Card
for a *FREE* Computer Book Catalog

Thank you for purchasing this book! You have purchased a superior computer book written expressly for your needs. To continue to provide the kind of up-to-date, pertinent coverage you've come to expect from us, we need to hear from you. Please take a minute to complete and return this self-addressed, postage-paid form. In return, we'll send you a free catalog of all our computer books on topics ranging from word processing to programming and the internet.

Mr. ☐   Mrs. ☐   Ms. ☐   Dr. ☐

Name (first) [_____]   (M.I.) [_]   (last) [_____]

Address [_____]

[_____]

City [_____]   State [__]   Zip [_____] [____]

Phone [___] [___] [____]   Fax [___] [____]

Company Name [_____]

E-mail address [_____]

Please check at least (3) influencing factors for purchasing this book.

Front or back cover information on book .... ☐
Special approach to the content .... ☐
Completeness of content .... ☐
Author's reputation .... ☐
Publisher's reputation .... ☐
Book cover design or layout .... ☐
Index or table of contents of book .... ☐
Price of book .... ☐
Special effects, graphics, illustrations .... ☐
Other (Please specify): _____ ☐

How did you first learn about this book?

Saw in Macmillan Computer Publishing catalog .... ☐
Recommended by store personnel .... ☐
Saw the book on bookshelf at store .... ☐
Recommended by a friend .... ☐
Received advertisement in the mail .... ☐
Saw an advertisement in: _____ ☐
Read book review in: _____ ☐
Other (Please specify): _____ ☐

How many computer books have you purchased in the last six months?

This book only .... ☐   3 to 5 books .... ☐
2 books .... ☐   More than 5 .... ☐

4. Where did you purchase this book?

Bookstore .... ☐
Computer Store .... ☐
Consumer Electronics Store .... ☐
Department Store .... ☐
Office Club .... ☐
Warehouse Club .... ☐
Mail Order .... ☐
Direct from Publisher .... ☐
Internet site .... ☐
Other (Please specify): _____ ☐

5. How long have you been using a computer?

☐ Less than 6 months   ☐ 6 months to a year
☐ 1 to 3 years   ☐ More than 3 years

6. What is your level of experience with personal computers and with the subject of this book?

	With PCs	With subject of book
New	☐	☐
Casual	☐	☐
Accomplished	☐	☐
Expert	☐	☐

Source Code ISBN: 1-7897-0386-6

7. Which of the following best describes your job title?

Administrative Assistant .... ☐
Coordinator .... ☐
Manager/Supervisor .... ☐
Director .... ☐
Vice President .... ☐
President/CEO/COO .... ☐
Lawyer/Doctor/Medical Professional .... ☐
Teacher/Educator/Trainer .... ☐
Engineer/Technician .... ☐
Consultant .... ☐
Not employed/Student/Retired .... ☐
Other (Please specify): _____ ☐

8. Which of the following best describes the area of the company your job title falls under?

Accounting .... ☐
Engineering .... ☐
Manufacturing .... ☐
Operations .... ☐
Marketing .... ☐
Sales .... ☐
Other (Please specify): _____ ☐

Comments: _____
_____
_____

9. What is your age?

Under 20 ....
21-29 ....
30-39 ....
40-49 ....
50-59 ....
60-over ....

10. Are you:

Male ....
Female ....

11. Which computer publications do you read regularly? (Please list)

_____
_____
_____
_____
_____
_____
_____
_____
_____

Fold here and scotch-tape to r

Using the Companion CD-ROM

The CD-ROM included with this book is packed with shareware and freeware software for your use. Also included on the CD-ROM are the source code examples and applications found in this book.

In addition, you'll find an installer to help you install the specific programs you want. The installer is easy to use; just follow these steps:

1. Insert the CD-ROM in the drive. The Setup program automatically starts, copies the installer files onto your hard drive, and runs the installer.

2. A window appears with four tabs—Cursors, Screen Savers, Shareware, and Internet Shortcuts. Select one of these tabs.

 Note

You can restart the installer anytime you like. From the Start menu, choose Programs, Que, Excel Expert Solutions.

 Tip

To see the program's README file, click View Application.

License Agreement

This package contains one CD-ROM that contains software described in this book. See applicable chapters for descriptions of these programs and instructions for their use.

By opening this package you are agreeing to be bound by the following:

This software is copyrighted and all rights are reserved by the publisher and its licensers. You are licensed to use this software on a single computer. You may copy the software for backup or archival purposes only. Making copies of the software for any other purpose is a violation of United States copyright laws. THIS SOFTWARE IS SOLD AS IS, WITHOUT WARRANTY OF ANY KIND, EITHER EXPRESS OR IMPLIED, INCLUDING BUT NOT LIMITED TO THE IMPLIED WARRANTIES OF MERCHANTABILITY AND FITNESS FOR A PARTICULAR PURPOSE. Neither the publisher nor its licensers, dealers, or distributors assumes any liability for any alleged or actual damages arising from the use of this software. (Some states do not allow exclusion of implied warranties, so the exclusion may not apply to you.)